AGAINST THE LAW

AGAINST THE LAW

The Nixon Court and Criminal Justice

LEONARD W. LEVY

HARPER & ROW, PUBLISHERS

NEW YORK, EVANSTON, SAN FRANCISCO, LONDON

FIRST EDITION

Designed by Sidney Feinberg

Library of Congress Cataloging in Publication Data

Levy, Leonard Williams, 1923–
    Against the law; the Nixon Court and criminal justice.
    1. Criminal procedure—United States. 2. United States. Supreme Court.
I. Title.
KF9619.L48   347'.73'265   74-1831
ISBN 0-06-012594-2

To Elyse with deepest love

Contents

vii

Preface

To disagree with the decisions of the Nixon Court merely because they are conservative instead of liberal is like preferring chocolate to vanilla. More than taste is at issue, however, when evaluating Court opinions. Appellate courts, especially the Supreme Court, are unique because they are the only branch of our government obligated to explain what they are doing and why. An opinion representing the views of the highest court must be persuasive in order to merit respect. The quality of reasoning in an opinion measures its result. That is why one must meet the Court on its own terms, disinterestedly evaluating its opinions in order to validate approval or criticism of its results. A microanalysis best does the job. Although a book on only four years of criminal-justice cases may seem narrow, the method of execution, if successful, can teach more than a short summary of many cases over a far longer period of time.

I have always found fascination in the quality of judicial reasoning. The life of the law is not merely logic, because experience counts as well. The two must be blended with a spice of insight if the conclusion is to be convincing. My favorite story, which I owe to my friend Professor Saul Benison of the University of Cincinnati, concerns the blend of logic, experience, and insight that produces reasoned judgment. Regrettably, the story loses much of its flavor when not told in Yiddish dialect, but even printed in English its lesson remains. It is a story about Jews who lived outside the ghetto communities of nineteenth-century Russia. Such Jews could not travel without official permission. After months of negotiation, an old Jewish scholar who lived in Odessa got permission to travel from Odessa to Moscow. He boarded the train, and after one stop a young man got on and sat down opposite him. The old scholar looked at the young man and said to himself:

> He doesn't look like a peasant, and if he isn't a peasant, he prob-ably comes from this district. If he comes from this district, he must be Jewish because this is a Jewish district. But, if he's Jewish, so where could he be going? I'm the only one in the district who has permission to travel to Moscow. To what village would he not need permission to travel? Oh, just outside Moscow there's the little village of Mozhaisk, and to Mozhaisk you don't need permission. But who could he be visiting in Mozhaisk? There are only two Jewish families in the whole of Mozhaisk, the Linskys and the Greenbaums. I know the Linskys are a terrible family, so he must be visiting the Green-baums. But who would undertake a trip at this time of year unless he were a close personal relative? The Greenbaums have only daugh-ters, so perhaps he's a son-in-law. But, if he's a son-in-law, which daughter did he marry? Esther married that nice young lawyer from Budapest. What was his name? Alexander Cohen. Who did Sarah marry? Sarah married that no-goodnik, that salesman from Zhado-mir. It must be Esther. So, if he married Esther, his name is Alex-ander Cohen and he comes from Budapest. Oh, the terrible anti-Semitism they have there now! He probably changed his name from Cohen. So what's the Hungarian equivalent of Cohen? Kovacs. But, if he's a man who changed his name from Cohen to Kovacs, he's a man who shows a basic insecurity in life. However, to change his name because of anti-Semitism, a man would need status. So what kind of status could he have? A doctor's degree from the university.

At this point the old scholar got up, tapped the young man on the shoulder, and said, "Dr. Alexander Kovacs?" "Why, yes," said the young man, "but how did you know?" "Oh," replied the old scholar, "it stands to reason."

A preface is the appropriate place for an author to expose his own values. I am a liberal, although I have not been a card-carrying member of the ACLU for a dozen years. I do not like judicial activism, but forced to choose between liberal activism on the part of the Court or conservative activism, I much prefer the former. I believe that the intellectual integrity and professional expertise of the Court, the validity of the route that it takes to reach a result, rank in importance with the result itself.

Felix Frankfurter was probably the foremost influence on my thinking about the Court. As a young instructor, I had written a series of journalistic articles severely criticizing decisions that sustained Jim Crow laws. Justice Frankfurter wrote a letter reproving me for my choice of language. My reply led to a correspondence and then to an invitation to come to Washington to meet him and hear the arguments on the constitutionality of compulsory racial segregation in the public schools. The moment I entered his chambers, Frankfurter exclaimed, "There's that damn Jeffersonian liberal!" He constantly baited me and finally succeeded in provoking an argument in which I sought to defend liberal activism on the part of the Court against judicial self-restraint. In the heat of the argument, I began criticizing several of his opinions on grounds of inconsistency. While talking and pacing before his long desk, I suddenly noticed that his face reddened. Then the slight, distinguished, scholarly jurist rose from his high-backed chair and approached me with a clenched fist. I froze and thought, "My God, I'm going to be struck by a Justice of the Supreme Court of the United States." He came right up to me, poked a finger under my nose, and declared, "Good point, young man!" Then he returned to his chair and beamed at me, delighted that I had supported my argument even at his expense. Eventually he taught me to criticize even my most cherished beliefs by demanding valid evidence for any proposition. I have tried to apply the lesson in this book.

It is not a book that is favorable to the Nixon Court. But I do not apply a double standard. In an anthology, *The Supreme Court Under Earl Warren* (1972), I censured result-oriented jurisprudence, calling it a political and judicial monstrosity that gains nothing when the Court reaches a just result merely because of its identification with underdog litigants like radicals, aliens, Negroes, the poor, and criminal defendants who have been victimized by suppression. I am on record as declaring that the liberal activists on the Warren Court did not offer adequately reasoned justifications or intellectually coherent explanations for their results. My bias is in favor of well-wrought opinions that demand respect even from doubters who prefer different results. Regrettably, the judicial crusaders exert a greater influence than the judicial craftsmen. The public cares about results and has little patience for reasons.

The swift and striking changes in the Court's criminal-justice opinions since the resignations of Justice Abe Fortas and Chief Justice Earl Warren in the spring of 1969 justify a seemingly premature book on the Nixon Court and criminal justice. In Justice William O. Douglas's phrase, "a 'law and order' judicial mood" now dominates the bench. After Justice Harry A. Blackmun joined Chief Justice Warren E. Burger, the Court reached a watershed in constitutional law. Its criminal-justice opinions sharply accentuated that shift in course. As early as 1971, an eminent scholar, Professor Philip B. Kurland, used the phrase "the Nixon Court" in the closing passage of his book on *Politics, the Constitution, and the Warren Court*. When President Nixon appointed justices Lewis F. Powell and William H. Rehnquist later that same year, the phrase "the Nixon Court" received the imprimatur of a White House speechwriter, as well as of the national press. In the sense that the President has not yet appointed a majority of the members of the Court, there is no "Nixon Court." The phrase is, in part, a shorthand convenience for referring to the Court after Warren's time. In the field of criminal justice, which is my subject, to speak of "the Burger Court" makes as much sense as reference to "the Nixon Court," but the President's choice of four men who suited his law-and-order philosophy is the decisive factor that warrants the more popular usage.

I have few acknowledgments to make. Justice Hugo Black once rebuked me because I had not submitted the manuscript of *Legacy of Suppression* for criticism by people who agreed with his absolutist interpretation of the First Amendment. He also refused to read my *Jefferson and Civil Liberties: The Darker Side*, because the subtitle indicated that he would disagree with my viewpoint. This book has a neutral title, unless readers choose to see a pun in it, and owes nothing to scholars of my persuasion or any other. I write this book alone, contracting no debts.

Two close friends, the late Harold Weisberg of Brandeis University and John P. Roche, now of the Fletcher School of Diplomacy at Tufts, urged me to try a change of pace from my usual antiquarian subjects. David Brudnoy and Stephen Whitfield were in no position to help; John Niven did not try. William Buckley has not seen fit to remove from his desk the signed photographs of the last four appointees to the Court. The names of my children, Wendy and Leslie, have appeared in my former prefaces; this time there is no reason for including them.

I am pleased to acknowledge that small sections of this book originated in my Gaspar Bacon Lectures in Constitutional Law at Boston University and my Shelden Elliott Memorial Lectures at the University of Southern California School of Law. Mrs. Catherine H. Tramz, the secretary of the Graduate Faculty of History at the Claremont Graduate School, found time to type the manuscript in addition to her many other duties and has my thanks for her indispensable cooperation. The President of the Claremont Graduate School, Barnaby Keeney, offered encouragement in subtle ways, approved a full year's leave of absence for me to do the writing, and allowed me to have a research assistant during my year off. President Keeney is, however, a much better fisherman than a critic of constitutional law. Barry F. Helfand, a doctoral candidate at the Claremont Graduate School, was an excellent research assistant. He expedited the completion of this book by doing much of the leg-work, leaving me free to read and write. I relied on my set of the *Supreme Court Reporter;* Mr. Helfand converted all citations to the *United States Reports* and checked all quotations. He also kept me supplied with books and journals, did most of my Xerox copying, read the whole manuscript, offered some useful suggestions, and assisted with the index.

Jeannette Hopkins, my editor at Harper & Row, proved to my amazement that the Maxwell Perkins art of editing still flourishes. I had been used to editors who unobtrusively corrected my punctuation and spelling. Jeannette had the *chutzpah* to scrawl her "queries" and "suggestions" in blue ink over scores of pages of my "finished" typescript, challenging my viewpoint, the sequence of arguments, and fine points of law. I found her editing exasperating, provocative, and enormously constructive, proving the old adage that one need not be a chicken to know a good egg from a bad one.

The dedication to my wife, Elyse, does not remotely suggest my appreciation for her very real inspiration, her sacrifices, and her improvements in my style. I wrote this book for her, and without her I do not believe I could have done it. On the other hand, she is to blame for the passages where I appear blunt and personal. She thinks that objectivity in a book of this kind is a scholar's pretense.

LEONARD W. LEVY

Claremont Graduate School
February, 1974

AGAINST THE LAW

CHAPTER ONE

The Supreme Court

THE WARREN COURT'S CRIMINAL JUSTICE "REVOLUTION," LTD.

When Earl Warren became Chief Justice of the United States in 1953, American constitutional law, like the nation it served, teetered between two worlds. One, which nothing short of lethal could move or remove, deserved a speedy, contemptible death; it was the world of racism, political rotten boroughs, McCarthyism, discriminations against the poor, puritanism in sexual matters, denial of the suffrage, and egregious infringements on the rights of the criminally accused. The other was a world struggling to be born, eager to remedy injustices and make the fundamental law of the land have a liberating and egalitarian impact. The Supreme Court under Warren was a sometime midwife to the newer world. Freedom of expression and association, and, even more important, racial justice, criminal justice, and political justice became the Court's obsession. Never since the early nineteenth century, when the great John Marshall presided, had the Court made our constitutional law so generative, even transforming—indeed there were friends and foes alike who spoke of a "revolution" presided over by judges; and not since Marshall's time had the Court, which periodically suffered withering criticism, been so vilified by its critics and so rapturously acclaimed by its supporters.

1

The Court operates in the main as a judicial team, every man playing a vital part, rather than as individual stars. The principle of majority rule, based on "one man, one vote," has always prevailed within the Court. It is a collective institution with a perpetual corporate life. The Chief Justice, however, was its symbol, literally its head, figuratively its heart. Like a lightning rod, he drew the kudos as well as the aspersions, even the psychotic hatreds epitomized by the scream "Impeach Earl Warren!" Nervous nellies, who cautiously approved of the law's new direction but worried about the swiftness and extent of change, blamed him for the Court's having overreached itself. Distinguished law-school professors parsed his opinions; their concern for legal *petit point* caused them to lose sight of his grand enterprise and the functional nature of law, and they clucked disapprovingly of Warren when they detected a missing or botched stitch.[1] * President Dwight Eisenhower, who had appointed him, grew to regret his choice and is supposed to have said it was the "biggest damnfool mistake I ever made." President Lyndon Johnson handed Warren the accolade "the greatest Chief Justice of them all."[2]

Warren served with able associates—sixteen altogether during the length of his tenure—and they, as much as he, shaped the Court's controversial opinions, even when bickering and dissenting. Still, the public identified the Court with its Chief Justice, and he did in fact associate himself with its trailblazing decisions in every area of constitutional law except on the subject of obscenity. Although Warren was not responsible for the constitutional "revolution," he was responsive to it, and in the crucial areas of civil rights and electoral representation he led it. That revolution might not have taken place without him. He certainly lent it respectability, the public influence of his high position, and above all, perhaps, his universally recognized attributes of "humanity . . . fairness, integrity, dignity," to quote the words of President Nixon, one of the most vociferous critics of the "Warren Court."[3]

Nixon made the Warren Court a major political issue in his 1968 presidential campaign. The politics of law and order, capitalizing on genuine fears about crime in America and deeper racial anxi-

* Notes begin on page 443.

eties, paid off handsomely. In one speech Nixon would allege that the courts should be respected and in the next breath denigrate them. When he accepted the nomination of his party, he expressed a theme that persisted throughout the fall campaign: Judicial decisions, he said, "have gone too far in weakening the peace forces as against the criminal forces in this country. . . . If we are to have respect for law in America we must have laws that deserve respect."[4] In his first campaign speech on crime Nixon left the impression that the courts were to blame for the frightening increase in the crime rate. "Today," he concluded, "all across the land guilty men walk free from hundreds of courtrooms. Something has gone terribly wrong in America."[5] The message was clear: Permissive judges enforced the Warren Court's strained interpretations of the Constitution in favor of the criminal forces. Nixon popularized and gave respectability to that charge that had originated with right-wing groups and many law-enforcement officials. The charge damaged the Supreme Court's moral authority by diminishing public confidence in it. A Gallup Poll revealed that the majority believed that the Court was "too soft" on criminals, protected their rights at the expense of society, and was "making" rather than "interpreting" the laws.[6]

If Nixon had been able to dictate the decisions of the Court in every case dealing with criminal justice during the years when Warren was Chief Justice, the crime rate in America in 1968 would have varied little if at all. Decisions of appellate courts have approximately the same effect upon the causes of crime as gamma rays. The courts rarely set the guilty free. Four years after Warren retired, the Supreme Court unanimously held that when there has been a denial of speedy trial in violation of the Sixth Amendment, the case against the defendant must be altogether dismissed.[7] That decision was unique. If there has been a denial of any other constitutional right of the criminally accused, the reversal of a conviction does not liberate the criminal (assuming that the defendant is guilty); reversal returns his case to the trial court, which can try him again, on the prosecution's initiative, according to the law as determined by the appellate court.

The Supreme Court is not a supreme jury. It does not decide guilt or innocence. It concerns itself with means, not ends. It decides whether proper procedures have been followed and whether proper evidence has been admitted, not whether the verdict was proper. A lawful end cannot be achieved by means dishonoring the Constitution or by using illegally obtained evidence. To make the law an instrumentality for securing convictions by violating individual rights would in the long run corrupt the integrity of the law and of the courts, brutalize the police and impair methods of detection, and turn the criminal law into a tool of tyranny. Justice Felix Frankfurter once pointed out, "The history of liberty has largely been the history of the observance of procedural safeguards."[8] Justice Robert Jackson declared that he would rather live under Soviet law enforced by American procedures than under American law enforced by Soviet procedures. "Procedural fairness and regularity," said Jackson, "are of the indispensable essence of liberty."[9] That is the reason why most of the provisions of the Bill of Rights are procedural in character. They protect society, as well as the accused, against law-enforcement excesses that taint the government.

The criminal-justice system in this country has been grinding to a halt and is in danger of massive breakdown, but not because of the Bill of Rights or its interpretation by the Warren Court. The fundamental cause is the staggering rise in the number of crimes and the resultant congestion of prosecutorial case loads and court dockets. The Warren Court unquestionably contributed to that congestion by revitalizing old rights and recognizing new ones that prolonged the criminal process from arrest to final appeal. Swift and certain punishment has always been about as effective a deterrent to crime as any our criminal-justice system can provide. The Warren Court, on balance, made a negative contribution in that direction. Its decisions tended to make convictions more difficult to get, verdicts of guilty were difficult to stick, and sentences more difficult to execute. Nevertheless, even punishment that is swift and certain cannot alter the conditions that breed crime, nor can the toughest law-and-order policies like third-degree tactics, the use of evidence that is not subject to suppression, more convictions, severer sentences, and harsher prisons. When the criminal process was summary in form, when pickpocketing was a capital crime, and when executions were public spectacles, pickpockets fleeced the crowds that turned out to watch other pickpockets being hanged after a swift trial. Swift and harsh punishment was not a deterrent to the other criminals: In the 1920s, when the police used rubber truncheons to beat confessions out of suspects and searched and seized virtually at will, they did not reduce the crime rate. Law-and-order advocates always contend that if accused persons receive some right or other, the crime rate will burgeon, the guilty will go free, and the law-abiding will be unsafe. Four years of law-and-order policies of the Nixon Administration and of pro-prosecutorial decisions by the appellate courts did not stem the tide. Crimes of violence are still on the increase.[10]

If the courts did not restrain the police or reverse the convictions of the guilty, and if prosecutors gained convictions of all who are guilty, crime in America would not significantly decrease. The number of people imprisoned would increase. We might be a safer society, but not by much, and we would probably be a less free society. Society is hurt when the criminal escapes punishment because of a "legal technicality," but in the long run a democratic society is hurt still more when lawless conduct by law-enforcement agencies goes unchecked. Further, the men behind bars eventually come out. Our prisons not only fail to rehabilitate but seem to serve as training schools for the production of more criminals and more dangerous ones. Ex-convicts return for the most part to lives in circumstances like those that led them to crime. Rejuvenating our cities, our schools, and our economy would deter crime far more effectively than swift and certain justice, or turning the Supreme Court around, or watering down the Bill of Rights.

The Warren Court did "handcuff the cops," in some respects; its job was to do just that by keeping the police within the law they enforced. The Constitution deliberately provided for this conflict between the courts and the law-enforcement agencies. When a defendant has the benefit of legal counsel or demands trial by jury or invokes any other constitutional right, police power is circumscribed. The Warren Court enlarged the rights of the criminally accused, evoking strenuous protests from responsible as well as hysterical opponents. Every expansion of the rights of the criminally accused in American history has confronted the warning that handicapping the state makes conviction of the guilty more difficult.

More than six decades ago, an essay by a prosecutor on "Coddling the Criminal" attributed the failures of law enforcement to judicial observance of the constitutional protections against double jeopardy and compulsory self-incrimination.[11] The presumption of innocence, trial by jury, writ of habeas corpus, and every other procedural safeguard has been blamed at one time or another for causing crime or hampering the police.

The courts would have little reason to reverse convictions if the police did not break the law in order to enforce it. The argument against the Warren Court's strict observance of the Bill of Rights was essentially an argument that the police should be above the law in order to protect society from those who violate it. Our constitutional law is intended to secure all of us from improper, even criminal, police conduct and from prosecutorial shortcuts with the law. The object of the criminal law is to assess guilt or innocence according to canons of fairness and see that justice is done; the object is not simply to convict the guilty by whatever means. "If the exercise of constitutional rights will thwart the effectiveness of a system of law enforcement," as the Warren Court said, "then there is something very wrong with that system."[12] We should not fear if an accused person receives the assistance of a lawyer, if he learns what his rights are and exercises them.

In *Miranda*, his most controversial criminal-justice opinion, Chief Justice Warren quoted these words:

> Law enforcement, however, in defeating the criminal, must maintain inviolate the historic liberties of the individual. To turn back the criminal, yet, by so doing, destroy the dignity of the individual, would be a hollow victory. . . .
>
> We can have the Constitution, the best laws in the land, and the most honest reviews by courts—but unless the law enforcement profession is steeped in the democratic tradition, maintains the highest in ethics, and makes its work a career of honor, civil liberties will continually—and without end—be violated. . . . The best protection of civil liberties is an alert, intelligent and honest law enforcement agency.[13]

The author of that statement, made before Warren joined the Court, was no permissive judge or soft-headed social theorist; he was the director of the FBI, J. Edgar Hoover.

Hoover's statement suggests that Supreme Court decisions are not self-enforcing. The Court has no way of effectively monitoring compliance with its mandates. The opposition of law-enforcement agencies can obstruct change commanded by the Court. The Court cannot even ensure that state trial courts, let alone lower appellate courts, will adhere faithfully to its decisions. The Court has other incapacities. It cannot, by its adjudicatory process, overhaul the criminal-justice system. It can decide only individual cases. It cannot initiate cases; it must wait for a case or controversy to come before it. Thus, the Court is not able to revolutionize the rules of criminal procedure and evidence. It cannot bring about sudden, drastic, or wholesale change. The Warren Court allegedly revolutionized the constitutional law of criminal procedure and evidence, yet the trial courts of the nation still operate substantially as they did before the revolution. Criminal prosecutions still shame the constitutional principles of due process of law and equal justice under the law. In the main, the Warren Court only marginally affected practices, though it changed our idealized picture of the criminal prosecution. Whether the Court was responsible for a "revolution" at any level is, perhaps, a subjective judgment that depends on one's tolerance for the pace and character of change.[14]

Essentially, the revolution took the form of a case-by-case abolition of an old double standard that had prevailed in state and federal criminal cases. The Court simply applied the Bill of Rights to the states, commanding them to follow the same Fourth, Fifth, and Sixth Amendment procedures that previously had applied only to cases arising in the federal courts. The states have always had the responsibility for prosecuting the overwhelming bulk of criminal cases, and in the execution of that responsibility they had an obligation under the United States Constitution to honor only the Fourteenth Amendment. That amendment, which was adopted in 1868, provides that no state—and that includes the local police officer, prosecutor, and trial court—shall deny to any person life, liberty, or property without due process of law, nor deny to any person the equal protection of the laws. Before Warren's time, the Court had kept the federal law-enforcement agencies and federal courts to a fairly strict observance of the Bill of Rights, but had left the states pretty much alone, allowing them to define due process of law, for all practical purposes, as they pleased in matters of criminal justice.[15]

The Court superintended the state administration of criminal justice only enough to ensure that due process of law meant a respect for the "decencies of civilized conduct" and an avoidance of "conduct that shocks the conscience" or offends the "sense of justice" or of "fair play."[16] The only particular procedural right that the Court regarded as "fundamental," in the sense that to deny it denied due process, was the right to counsel in capital cases.[17] Otherwise, due process was so nebulous a standard that it varied in meaning from case to case and depended on the idiosyncracies of a majority of the Court at any given moment. For example, in a case decided in 1952 the Court ruled that forcing incriminating evidence from a person by means of a stomach pump was equivalent to compelling him to testify against himself criminally and therefore denied due process.[18] A year later the Court had the case of an illiterate black man whom North Carolina sentenced to death on the basis of a confession that he made after having been held on suspicion for five days without being charged with a crime and for eighteen days thereafter without being brought before a magistrate for a preliminary hearing. Nor did he have counsel until the day of his trial. The Court held that because these facts did not prove that he had confessed his guilt involuntarily, the state had not denied due process.[19] Justices Hugo L. Black and William O. Douglas believed that state criminal cases should be decided like federal ones according to the specific requirements of the Bill of Rights. In their view, the Fourteenth Amendment "incorporated" or embodied the Fourth Amendment's protection against unreasonable searches and seizures, the Fifth's safeguard against double jeopardy and compulsory self-incrimination, and the Sixth's battery of rights applicable to "all criminal prosecutions."

Beginning in 1961 the Supreme Court under Warren finally began to accept the views that Black and Douglas had advocated, on the theory that the rights in question, contrary to earlier rulings, were fundamental to the American system of justice. In 1961 the Court incorporated the Fourth Amendment within the Fourteenth, making the fruits of an illegal search and seizure excludable as evidence in a state trial; thereafter, the federal rules on the exclusion of evidence governed state cases.[20] A year later the Court incorporated the Eighth Amendment's ban against cruel and unusual punishments.[21] In 1963 the right to be represented by counsel in all felony cases joined the list of due-process rights, as applicable against the states as against the United States. Thus, the states had to provide counsel for all felony defendants too poor to hire their own.[22] A year later the Court ruled that state denial of the Fifth Amendment's right not to be a witness against oneself in a criminal case was a denial of due process.[23] In 1965 the Court incorporated the right of the defendant to confront the witnesses against him and two years later incorporated other Sixth Amendment safeguards— the right to a speedy trial and the right to compulsory process in securing witnesses in one's behalf.[24] In 1968 the Court added trial by jury to the incorporated rights and in the following year, on the last day of Warren's tenure, the right against double jeopardy.[25] Thus, by a piecemeal process of selective incorporation, the Court extended to the states most of the criminal-justice provisions of the Bill of Rights—indeed, all the essential ones except the right to bail. The Warren Court's criminal-law revolution, then, consisted in nationalizing the Bill of Rights.

The Warren Court was not equally innovative in expanding the meanings of old rights to new situations. A 1956 opinion expressed the truly radical principle that there cannot be equal justice under the law "where the kind of trial a man gets depends on the amount of money he has."[26] However, when Warren retired thirteen years later, the Court had done no more than require that indigent defendants must receive at public expense necessary transcripts, filing costs, and legal services on appeals or postconviction proceedings.[27] In 1963 the Court substantially expanded postconviction remedies by allowing federal courts, on a writ of habeas corpus, to review state convictions allegedly in violation of constitutional rights.[28] That did not expand the scope of the rights at issue. Nor did the Court's extension of various procedural rights to juvenile-delinquency proceedings.[29] Of all constitutional rights, the Court most expanded the least controversial, the right to the assistance of counsel. The Court extended it to indigents wherever it was applicable and applied it to pretrial judicial proceedings, to pretrial custodial police proceedings, to juvenile proceedings, and to appellate proceedings.[30] The Court also expanded the most controversial of all rights, not to be a witness against oneself criminally, by ruling that it applied to custodial interrogations in the police station, where it was most needed.[31]

Consistency, however, has rarely been a virtue of the Supreme Court, and under Warren its record was par for the course. The question of consistency, or rather, the lack of it, does point to a fact about the Warren Court that stressing its affirmations of Bill of Rights freedoms often obscures. On balance, it was liberal activist, but many of its decisions were deplored by libertarians as encroachments on the rights of the criminally accused. Such decisions do not square with the Court's reputation for hostility to the police or with Warren's professed dedication to passing on to future generations a better Bill of Rights, burnished by growing use and imaginatively applied to new situations.[32] The controversial Fifth Amendment right, which the Court kept tightly reined in many cases, is a good example.

Rejecting claims based on the right against self-incrimination, the Court sustained the constitutionality of a congressional immunity act that forced witnesses to testify against themselves concerning subversive activities.[33] In three cases the Court upheld the dismissals from public service of persons who refused to answer concerning their alleged Communist affiliations.[34] In still other Fifth Amendment cases not dealing with internal security, the Court denied that the right against self-incrimination protected against blood tests to determine drunkenness. In one case the police had taken blood from an unconscious driver whose vehicle killed others, and in another case from a suspected drunk who protested against the test.[35] The rationale of these decisions narrowly limited the Fifth Amendment to a safeguard against testimonial compulsion and excluded real or physical evidence that was nontestimonial in character. In related cases, which prosecutorial forces usually depicted as showing that the Warren Court released criminals on constitutional technicalities at the expense of society, the Fifth Amendment also fared badly.[36] The Court broadened the Sixth Amendment right to counsel in these cases, by extending it to police lineups conducted for purposes of identifying suspects; but, the Court rejected the claims that lineups, fingerprinting, photographs, and physical measurements violated the Fifth Amendment. In view of the previous distinction between testimonial and nontestimonial evidence, there was nothing surprising in the lineup cases to this point. However, the Court went beyond the rationale of its precedents when it ruled that the Fifth Amendment does not prevent suspects from being compelled to speak at a lineup or to give samples of handwriting. Speaking and writing seem to be inherently testimonial in character.

In another case the Court rejected the contention that the admission in evidence of criminal revelations unwittingly made to a paid government informer, who posed as a close associate, violated the Fifth Amendment.[37] The Court reasoned that the incriminating statements were not the product of compulsion, and they were not. The significance of the decision is that by construing compulsion so literally, the Court denied the protection of the amendment to confessions obtained by deceit rather than by force. Consequently, the Court legitimated police tactics of considerable value to law enforcement.

The police and prosecutors also received substantial aid from several important search-and-seizure cases that limited the protection of the Fourth Amendment. In one the Court sustained a conviction based on the testimony of an undercover narcotics officer who entered the accused's home under false pretenses to buy marijuana from him.[38] In a related case the Court sustained a conviction in which the evidence consisted of an informer's tape recording of an attempted bribery.[39] The Court sided with the police when it rejected a challenge to a warrantless arrest by a defendant who claimed that unless the officer was compelled to disclose the name of an anonymous informer on whose tip the police acted, there was no way to determine whether probable cause for the arrest existed or whether the informer actually existed.[40] In another case the Court overruled the doctrine that since 1921 had restricted the introduction in evidence of any property seized by the police if it was "mere evidence."[41] They could seize contraband such as narcotics, which a citizen may not lawfully possess; they could seize the fruits of a crime, such as stolen goods, or the instrumentalities of a crime, such as a getaway car or weapons; but, they could not seize private property, such as clothing that identified the criminal, because it was "mere evidence." Overruling that doctrine opened the door to convictions that otherwise might not be possible.

The same result flowed from a decision that civil libertarians applauded. Although the Court overruled a 1927 precedent that excluded wiretapping from the Fourth Amendment's protection, and reversed a conviction obtained by warrantless electronic eavesdropping, it rejected the claims that all wiretapping and eavesdropping necessarily violated the amendment.[42] The Court refused to endorse the argument that there is no way to frame a sufficiently specific search warrant because of the inherently dragnet character of surveillance by tapping and bugging. Thus, the Court opened the door to evidence seized on the authority of valid warrants issued to sanction the use of secret eavesdropping. In another unprecedented decision the Court ruled that even if the police have no probable cause for making an arrest or a search, they may stop a suspicious person and frisk him for a weapon.[43]

The Warren Court did decide many other Fourth Amendment cases against the police; however, the Warren Court had a genuine concern for the needs of law enforcement. Its decisions did not at all show a single pattern of upholding the claims of the criminally accused. Its "revolution" in criminal procedures and evidence was distinctly limited. It often, and in important cases, did not handcuff the cops when civil libertarians thought that it should have.

CHIEF JUSTICE BURGER

In June of 1968, as the Court neared the close of its term, Earl Warren informed President Johnson that for reasons of age, he intended to retire as soon as his successor as Chief Justice was appointed and confirmed. Warren thus offered Johnson the opportunity of replacing him. Johnson himself had already astonished the nation by an announcement that he would not seek or accept his party's nomination for re-election. He was a lame-duck President with only about six months left to serve, a discredited President, who was a political casualty of his disastrous military campaigns in Indochina. Even before Johnson declared his choice for Warren's successor, half the Republican contingent in the Senate announced that the next President should nominate a new Chief Justice. Richard M. Nixon, the most likely Republican candidate, agreed. Johnson, underestimating the strength of the opposition, nominated his good friend and adviser Abe Fortas, who had been a member of the Supreme Court since October 1965. In only a few years on the Court, Fortas had earned a reputation for dazzling brilliance and consummate legal craftsmanship that he devoted, on the whole, to positions favored by Warren and those members of the Court whom the press described as liberals. By choosing Fortas for the chief justiceship, Johnson created a vacancy that he sought to fill by nominating Homer Thornberry of Texas, a judge on the United States Court of Appeals for the Fifth Circuit.

Fortas, however, proved to be a vulnerable nominee and fell victim to the Dixiecrat opposition. Although the Senate Judiciary Committee had unanimously endorsed Fortas in 1965 to be an Associate Justice and the full Senate had confirmed him by voice vote, Fortas in 1968 had to defend his judicial record against the attacks of political conservatives, his friendship with Johnson against cries of "cronyism," and his ethics in the face of a charge of impropriety for accepting a large lecture fee while a member of the Court. The judiciary committee voted 11-to-6 in his favor, but a successful filibuster on the Senate floor prevented a vote on his nomination. At Fortas's request, Johnson regretfully withdrew the nomination, decided not to make another, and asked Warren to remain at his post. About a month later, Nixon won the presidential election. In May of 1969, when Nixon was deliberating on Warren's successor, the press revealed that Fortas had received a $20,000 fee from the family foundation of a man in legal troubles with the government for having sold unregistered stock. Attorney General John Mitchell conferred with Warren, advising him that unless Fortas resigned, more damaging information would surface. Fortas was undoubtedly guilty of an impropriety unbecoming a member of the Supreme Court. Public opinion forced him to resign, thereby giving Nixon the opportunity of making two nominations to the Court.[44]

One week later, on May 21, 1969, President Nixon announced his choice of Warren Earl Burger to be Earl Warren's successor as the fifteenth Chief Justice of the United States. Those interested in symbolism may have noted that Burger's first two names reversed

Warren's. Nixon chose his man with care, aware that the most important nomination a President can make is that of a Chief Justice. He declared that "history tells us that our Chief Justices have probably had more profound and lasting influences on their times and on the direction of the Nation than most Presidents have had."[45] Burger was "superbly qualified" by integrity and experience; he had the necessary intellectual and administrative qualities for the position. Since 1956 he had served on the United States Court of Appeals for the District of Columbia. Burger lacked the brilliance and objectivity of a Frankfurter or a Harlan but this was not a handicap. Besides, Burger was at least as well qualified as Warren had been at the time of his own appointment.

Burger's performance as a federal circuit judge bolstered Nixon's confidence in him. Nixon described him as a "strict constructionist" who brought Frankfurter to mind. Frankfurter, said Nixon, though personally a liberal, demonstrated an unquestionable capability of supporting the constitutionality of "conservative" legislation; Nixon neglected to add that Frankfurter also demonstrated a capability of supporting criminal procedures that he found to be personally abhorrent or unwise. "That is the kind of judge I was looking for here," a Frankfurter, Nixon told a press conference. "I am not concerned about whether the man is a liberal or conservative in his economic or social philosophy. My interest is how does he regard his role with regard to the Constitution. I happen to believe that the Constitution should be strictly interpreted. . . ." In fact, of course, Nixon selected Burger, as was his right, precisely because he found his brand of conservatism appealing. Burger had proved himself on the "firing line," said Nixon; he was a judge whose "track record" was known.

Indeed, it was extremely well known because Burger was a highly articulate and aggressive hard-liner who freely spoke his mind both on and off the bench. On a Court of Appeals that during the 1960s differed little from the Warren Court in its criminal-justice opinions, Burger became a flamboyant dissenter. Nixon had studied his opinions, read some of his speeches and articles, and concluded that his legal philosophy "is close to mine." His appointment as Chief Justice, Nixon predicted, would affect "the direction of the Court," with the result that some of the 5-to-4 Warren

Court decisions might in the future go 5-to-4 the other way. Nixon felt that Burger's criminal-justice opinions represented a minority view on the Supreme Court, "which happens to be my own view," but he hoped that Burger's accession would make it the majority view.[46] Nixon's praise for Burger's legal philosophy and judicial temperament made sense to tough law-and-order advocates. Burger was Nixon's kind of judge, and he had every justification for choosing a man whose opinions he admired.

Burger's opinions on the Court of Appeals had demonstrated a harshness and stridency not ordinarily associated with the passive virtues of strict constructionism. Even his style of expression could be vinegary and pugnacious, or, more charitably, heartily plainspoken. In the 1960s, his differences with some of his associates were sharp enough to cause "mutual disrespect," according to a press report.[47] In one of his earliest dissenting opinions, he construed the Fourth Amendment's protection against unreasonable searches and seizures to exclude illegally possessed narcotics. He found that a "presently confessed, previously convicted narcotics violator" is not entitled to the privacy rights that ordinarily render warrantless searches illegal. "But I refuse to join in what I consider an unfortunate trend of judicial decisions in this field which strain and stretch to give the guilty, not the same, but vastly more protection than the law-abiding citizen."[48] In a case where the defendant had pleaded guilty on the advice of his lawyer and later claimed that he had not had the effective assistance of counsel, Burger argued that such a claim could arise only when a trial as a whole showed a "mockery of justice." Mere mistakes, carelessness, and bad strategy or tactics did not constitute ineffective assistance of counsel.[49] In another case a convicted robber claimed that he had a constitutional right to have had counsel present at a police lineup conducted for purposes of identifying him as the criminal; he alleged, too, that his court-appointed counsel proved incompetent. Burger dismissed such contentions by lampooning them as "Disneyland" in character.[50]

In 1960 he wrote an opinion that found an exception to the rule excluding the admission in evidence of confessions obtained during a period of illegal detention.[51] Burger made a specialty of finding exceptions to exclusionary rules that suppressed illegally obtained evidence. His 1960 exception turned on the fact that after the period of illegal detention, the prisoner had the assistance of counsel and received a preliminary hearing before a magistrate who notified him of his right to remain silent. Despite judicial notice of his rights and against the advice of counsel, the prisoner reaffirmed his confession. Burger's opinion upholding his conviction was sound. Two years later, though, when his court reversed a conviction based on a reaffirmed confession, he erupted with an extravagantly acerbic and unsound opinion.[52] The majority of the court regarded the use of the second confession as a stark violation of the prisoner's rights because the police had obtained it before he received the assistance of counsel and before the completion of his preliminary hearing. The presiding magistrate had adjourned the hearing for a couple of weeks to allow the prisoner to get a lawyer, yet the police persuaded him to reaffirm his guilt the very next day. The Court of Appeals held the second confession to be as illegally procured and inadmissible in evidence as the first one. The majority opinion was strongly reasoned, carefully limited to the facts of the case, and made a point-by-point rebuttal of "Judge Burger's unusual dissenting opinion."[53] Burger's opinion was unusual because his disagreement took the form of outrage—and outrageous distortion of the case. He found difficulty, he said, in overstating the enormity of the majority's incredible interpretation, but he managed to overcome that difficulty. The majority, he claimed, had engaged in gossamer assumptions, gone to ridiculous lengths, offended common sense, boldly invaded legislative authority, abused judicial power, and made a mockery of the precedents—all for the purpose of hampering effective law enforcement by turning a rule of evidence into a "weapon of special advantage exclusively for the guilty."[54] The court decided the case by a 5-to-4 vote; none of the other dissenters joined Burger's opinion.

Burger also dissented when his court reversed a conviction on the ground that the prosecution did not reveal evidence, unknown to the defense, that could have raised a reasonable doubt of guilt.[55] In another case on evidence, Burger accused his associates of usurping the jury's function, and he added: "I suggest that the kind of nit-picking appellate review exhibited by reversal of this conviction may help explain why the public is losing confidence in the administration of justice."[56]

He dissented too from a ruling that extended *Miranda* v. *Arizona*, the Warren Court's most controversial criminal-justice decision. For the purposes of his opinion he accepted the principle of *Miranda* when interpreted merely to exclude testimonial compulsion; but, of its extension, he declared:

> The seeming anxiety of judges to protect every accused person from every consequence of his voluntary utterances is giving rise to myriad rules, sub-rules, variations and exceptions which even the most alert and sophisticated lawyers and judges are taxed to follow. Each time judges add nuances to these "rules" we make it less likely that any police officer will be able to follow the guidelines we lay down. . . . We are well on our way to forbidding *any* utterance of an accused to be used against him unless it is made in open court. Guilt or innocence becomes irrelevant in the criminal trial as we flounder in a morass of artificial rules poorly conceived and often impossible of application.[57]

When his associates voted to return a case to the trial court for an explanation of why it denied bail, Burger made them sound as if they were mindless or ignorant as he curtly observed, "The reasons for the District Court's denial of bail are so obvious as to require no explanation."[58]

If strict constructionism meant minimizing the rights of the criminally accused and maximizing the prosecutorial position, Burger was a powerful, if intemperate, strict constructionist on the Court of Appeals. Strict construction greased his path toward upholding convictions. The innocent do not appeal verdicts in their favor. When those who have been found guilty appeal, the judge who is acutely concerned with the obligation of courts to determine guilt or innocence fairly, in consonance with the Bill of Rights, has the burden of explaining the reasons for favoring a reversal of convictions. He appears to be the activist who "makes" the law, while the judge, like Burger, who reads rights out of the law appears to be the passivist, merely deferring to the judgment of the trial court, or the prosecution, or the legislature.

In his off-court statements Burger had championed a variety of proposals to alter American law. He advanced constructive ways to expedite trials by better management on the part of courts.[59] He harshly criticized the generally low level of professional competence on the part of American trial lawyers, and he suggested specific programs for improvement.[60] On numerous occasions he blasted all exclusionary rules of evidence.[61] In a commencement speech, he urged the adoption of better psychiatric, vocational, and educational programs to rehabilitate convicts. In the same speech he condemned procedural technicians on the courts who impeded the conviction of the guilty, and he drew into question the value of trial by jury, the right against compulsory self-incrimination, and the elaborate system of appeals and hearings after conviction. He found nothing sacrosanct about our system of criminal justice.

> The People have a right and the ultimate power to change it. Neither the laws nor the Constitution are too sacred to change—we have changed the Constitution many times—and the decisions of judges are not Holy Writ. These things are a means to an end, not an end in themselves. They are tools to serve us, not masters to enslave us. And we should not hesitate to change or discard mechanisms which do not work to the benefit of Society.[62]

Within the walls of one of the nation's self-appointed bastions of liberalism, the Center for the Study of Democratic Institutions, Burger overstated his position to provoke discussion. He believed that our "adversary system is not the best system of criminal justice, and that there is a better way." He did not hesitate to attack the presumption of the innocence of the accused, the right to remain silent, the use of juries, the exclusion of evidence, placing upon the prosecution the burden of proving guilt, and specific decisions of the Supreme Court. He reported that one Supreme Court Justice had said in a seminar that the presumption of innocence is "rooted in the Constitution." If strict constructionism means literalism, Burger was correct in his rejoinder: "Well, it may be rooted there, but you cannot find it there." Civilized countries in Europe required criminal defendants to answer incriminating questions and drew unfavorable inferences in cases of refusal, "So I am no longer sure that the Fifth Amendment concept, in its present form and as presently applied and interpreted, has all the validity attributed to it."[63] Burger obviously was not a run-of-the-mill conservative. He questioned first principles, including some whose constitutional status was explicit.

In a provocative address to the Ohio Judicial Conference in 1968, Burger assaulted the overall approach of the Warren Court in the field of criminal justice. Its decisions created a "revolution" that produced the world's most complicated system of criminal justice and the most difficult one to administer. "To a large extent this is a result," he declared, "of judicial decisions which in effect made drastic revisions of the code of criminal procedure and evidence and to a substantial extent imposed these new procedures on the states." Whatever the merit of those decisions, the Court had achieved its results the wrong way. It should have used an administrative mechanism—its power, conferred by Congress, to make rules of criminal procedure systematically and on a wholesale basis in the form of a code, "rather than changing the criminal procedure and rules of evidence on a case-by-case basis."[64]

In performing its basic function of deciding cases, Burger argued, "the court of last resort must, as we all know"—he was talking to judges, not politicians—"construe and interpret constitutions, statutes, rules . . . and in so doing it will frequently 'make' law. This is inherent in the evolution of the common law." Making codes of procedure or evidence was, he thought, "essentially a legislative function," although by no means beyond the competence of the Supreme Court. It should proceed, however, by exercising the broad powers vested in it by Congress; that is, it should promulgate an entire code after carefully studying the recommendations of an advisory committee. The Federal Rules of Criminal Procedure of 1954 had been adopted that way and constituted a model that the Court ought not amend on a case-by-case basis. The Court's ad hoc adjudications had substantially revised the 1954 rules without the participation of Congress, "whose acquiescence made them law." Legislating piecemeal by closely divided decisions rather than wholesale, with the support of Congress and the legal profession generally, posed the threat of impermanence. The "advent of one or two new Justices," Burger prophesied, might produce different results.[65]

He castigated the Court's "almost undignified haste to clothe detailed rules of evidence and police station procedures in the garb of constitutional doctrine." In particular, he ridiculed the decision that required the assistance of counsel at police lineups. The "whole area of criminal procedure and all problems touched upon in the holdings on interrogation, preliminary hearings, police line-ups, eyewitness identification, for example [should] be committed to reexamination and re-appraisal." There should be new rules to protect "an ordered liberty" as well as the rights of accused persons.[66] In effect, Burger advocated the repeal of the Warren Court's criminal-justice "revolution" and the formulation of a revised code. After he became Chief Justice, he adopted his wholesale approach. Drawing on the recommendations of a broad-based advisory committee, the Court utilized its rule-making powers by promulgating a fresh set of the Federal Rules of Evidence. Ironically, Congress resented this judicial legislation as an infringement of congressional prerogatives. The new rules died in committee.[67]

Burger's speeches, articles, and judicial opinions as a member of the Court of Appeals showed vigorous convictions that boldly challenged conventional wisdom. In his willingness to reassess and even root out much that the judiciary took for granted, he was a "radical" in the literal sense of that word. In the context of the usual terminology employed to characterize judges, "conservative activist" may be a better term, but like the inappropriate label of "strict constructionist," it probably obscures as much as it reveals. Whatever the appropriate characterization of Burger's record on criminal justice, Nixon understandably found the handsome and aggressive sixty-two-year-old Minnesotan eminently suitable as Warren's successor.

Through no fault of Burger, the hearings on his nomination by the Senate Committee on the Judiciary were fatuous, adulatory, and perfunctory. Senate liberals on the committee, like Edward Kennedy of Massachusetts and Birch Bayh of Indiana, chose not to interrogate him. The recent Fortas fiasco had compromised and stunned the liberals. Nixon's election gave him the right to nominate any person with the requisite qualifications, and Burger's qualifications made him invulnerable. Committee members who had been so hostile to Fortas could not restrain their pleasure with Burger.

Senator James Eastland of Mississippi, the chairman of the committee, set the tone of the hearings:

The Chairman. Do you think the Supreme Court has the power to amend the Constitution of the United States by judicial interpretation?

Judge Burger. No; clearly no. It has no power to amend the Constitution.

The Chairman. Does the Supreme Court have the power to legislate judicial interpretations?

Judge Burger. I think as you put the question, clearly it has no such power. No court has that power.[68]

Senator Sam Ervin of North Carolina, passing up the opportunity to interrogate Burger, praised him because in criminal cases he had evinced a belief that society and the victims of crime "are just as much entitled to justice as the accused."[69] Senator Robert C. Byrd of West Virginia stated his approval of Burger's many opinions against hampering the police "by hypertechnical guidelines laid down by the Federal courts." He happily quoted from a 1967 speech in which Burger had questioned the value of a system of criminal justice that assured protection from the excesses of the police at the expense of exposing law-abiding citizens to the attacks of criminals. "I suspect," Burger had said, "that most people would rather have more protection from the criminal element and a little less protection from police errors."[70] Other Senators also entered Burger's opinions on the record.

Receipt by the full Senate of its committee's fulsome endorsement of Burger was the signal for an orgy of condemnation of the Warren Court by conservatives. There were only three votes against Burger; they were eccentric protests against the excessive speed of the confirmation proceedings. Senator Everett Dirksen of Illinois reflected the attitude of the upper house when declaring that Burger "looks like a Chief Justice, he speaks like a Chief Justice, and he acts like a Chief Justice."[71]

When Warren retired on June 23, 1969, President Nixon stood before the Court, a representative of the American bar, to give a muted tribute to Warren, a price worth his paying to witness the unique event in the Court's history of the retiring Chief Justice swearing in his successor, Warren E. Burger, Nixon's appointee. The President declared that the sixteen years during which Warren had presided "without doubt, will be described by historians as

years of greater change in America than any in our history. . . .
Change with continuity," he ventured, "can mean progress," and
quite remarkably he added that of the three great branches of the
government, none had been more responsible "for that continuity
with change than the Supreme Court of the United States."[72] The
nation already knew what the President belatedly, if only cere-
monially recognized, that the Constitution had triumphantly survived the change and still stood, despite all vicissitudes, but that it
most definitely had not stood still: Under Warren it had progressed.

In his extemporaneous response, the retiring Chief Justice
stressed the theme of continuity with change. Observing that the
Court is a continuing body, he pointed out the stunning fact that
the judicial careers of just seven men, including the still-sitting
Hugo L. Black, connected without break the 180-year history of
the Court. Then Warren added, "We, of course, venerate the past,
but our focus is on the problems of the day and of the future as far
as we can foresee it." In one sense at least, he declared, the Court's
position was similar to that of the President, for it had the awesome
responsibility quite often of speaking the last word "in great governmental affairs" and of speaking for the whole American public.
"It is a responsibility that is made more difficult in this Court because we have no constituency. We serve no majority. We serve no
minority. We serve only the public interest as we see it, guided only
by the Constitution and our own consciences. . . ." The Court,
he concluded, had applied constitutional principles, so broadly
stated in the document, in a manner consistent with the public
interest and with the future "so far as it can be discerned."[73]

Warren's candid and simple valedictory in effect endorsed the
view, stated by both the Court's admirers and critics, that the Justices seemed to consider themselves as movers and shakers of the
country's destiny rather than as impersonal spokesmen of "the
law." Warren would surely have agreed with Woodrow Wilson,
who declared that the country looked for "statesmanship" in its
judges, because the Constitution was not "a mere lawyers' document" but, rather, the "vehicle of a nation's life."[74] Chief Justice
Burger quite as clearly professed a far more restrictive view of the
Court's role, one more in keeping with the "strict construction" of
the Constitution that President Nixon avowed to be the proper

standard for members of the high tribunal in the exercise of constitutional adjudication.

By coincidence, both Earl Warren and Warren E. Burger expressed themselves in off-Court, public statements two years after their respective appointments as Chief Justice, and the contrast was both startling and revealing. Warren, in an article on "The Law and the Future" published in *Fortune* magazine in 1955, was characteristically expansive, warm, and idealistic. His prime concern for the law was that it must adapt to changing circumstances by keeping its rules in harmony with the enlightened common sense of the nation. That meant to him that the Supreme Court faced "a single continuous problem: how to apply to ever changing conditions the never changing principles of freedom." The Constitution, existing for the individual as well as the nation, best fulfilled its mission, he asserted, by serving the unchanging cause of human justice. Significantly, he fastened upon "the 462 words of our Bill of Rights" as "the most precious part of our legal heritage," yet he presided over the Court at a time, he said, when the Bill of Rights confronted subtle and pervasive attack. Turning to needed reforms of our constitutional system, he noted that the proud inscription above the portals of the Supreme Court Building—"Equal Justice Under Law"—described a goal by no means secured for all citizens. The rights due to them, particularly to oppressed minorities and the poor, had been infringed, neglected, or unperfected. Focusing on the fact that our system of criminal justice was "pockmarked with . . . procedural flaws and anachronisms," making for unequal access to justice, he observed: "Suspects are sometimes arrested, tried, and convicted without being adequately informed of their right to counsel. Even when he knows of this right, many a citizen cannot afford to exercise it." The remark foreshadowed some of the most disputed reforms inaugurated by the Warren Court.

Freedom, like justice, Warren continued, required constant vigilance. Making no allowance for exceptions, he declared that when the rights of any individual or group were "chipped away, the freedom of all erodes." Warren's statement recognized implicitly that the Supreme Court had a crucial responsibility, one that could not be evaded, for helping to regenerate and fulfill the noblest aspirations for which this nation stood. In effect, he was saying that the law, though remaining constantly rooted in the great ideals of the past, must change in order to realize them. Thus, when posterity receives the Bill of Rights from the present generation, the document will not have the same meaning as it had when we received it from past generations. "We will pass on a better Bill of Rights," Warren asserted, "or a worse one, tarnished by neglect or burnished by growing use. If these rights are real, they need constant and imaginative applications to new situations." Such "constant and imaginative applications" earned for the Warren Court its reputation for "activism."[75]

On July 4, 1971, *The New York Times* published excerpts from an exclusive interview with Chief Justice Warren E. Burger, headlining the front-page story that accompanied the interview, "Burger Asserts Reform Is Not Role of Courts." Unlike the interventionism that permeated Warren's philosophy, Burger embraced the philosophy of judicial self-restraint. Moreover, he was surprisingly unimaginative, conservative, and even a bit crabbed. Immediately he de-emphasized the influence that the Supreme Court might have for changes in the law. "And changes in the law made by judicial decisions," he added, "ought to be approached with considerable caution. It was never contemplated in our system that judges would make drastic changes by judicial decision. That is what the legislative function and the rule-making function is all about." The Court sat, he declared, merely to decide cases. From its decisions, he acknowledged, "some changes develop, but to try to create or substantially change civil or criminal procedure, for example, by judicial decision is the worst possible way to do it." When asked whether youthful hopes might be justified by "the prospects of accomplishing a change in the system through law," Burger replied: "I sincerely trust that some of their hopes may be justified, but I am beginning to have an uneasy feeling that this may be another one of the situations in this era that we are living in of creating expectations that are beyond fulfillment." He added that young people entering the legal profession "on the theory that they can change the world by litigation in the courts" were bound to be disappointed. They were entering the profession for the wrong reason, because the law "is not the route by which basic changes in a country like ours should be made. That is a legislative and policy process, part of the political process. And there is a very limited role for the courts in this respect."

When asked what he saw as the greatest challenge to the Supreme Court in the next few years, he did not discourse on the Bill of Rights or on reform of any sort; he replied, "I would say the greatest challenge is to try to keep up with the volume of work and maintain the kind of quality that ought to come from this Court." At the conclusion of the interview, Burger summed up his judicial philosophy as follows: "Inherently, the Supreme Court function is one in which nothing ought to happen very rapidly except the disposition of specific cases. In the evolution of legal doctrine, legal principle can't be sound if its growth is too fast."[76] He might have added, though he did not, that legal principle cannot be sound if its growth is too quickly stunted or if the Court overruled, blunted, or distinguished away recent decisions merely because new members of the Court disliked them.

STRICT CONSTRUCTION CONSTRUED

From the beginning of its history the Supreme Court displayed an audacious capacity to manipulate precedents, to reveal its own values and policy choices, and to read the Constitution to mean whatever it wanted. Despite pretenses to the contrary, the Court could do no other, for as beauty exists in the eye of the beholder, so American constitutional law exists in the collective eye of those who happen at any moment in time to dominate the Court. What counts is not what the Constitution says, because it says so very little; what counts, rather, is what the Court has said about the Constitution—in more than four hundred volumes thus far. The Constitution itself necessarily plays a secondary role in American constitutional law. It is too concise and ambiguous to be any more than a point of departure in judicial decisions. As Justice Jackson once observed, when the Court had to construe the First Amendment's injunction against establishments of religion, it was "idle to pretend that this task is one for which we can find in the Constitution one word to help us as judges to decide where the secular ends and the sectarian begins in education."[77] That principle of realism applies with equal force to any case within the field of criminal justice.

Justices who look to the Constitution, its Bill of Rights, or the Fourteenth Amendment for more than a Delphic phrase delude themselves. They might just as well turn to the newest fiction list for all the guidance they will find on how to decide most of the great cases that involve national public policy, whether the question relates to regulation of the economy, racial segregation, reapportionment, abortion, subversive activities, public-school prayers, or pornography. In the field of criminal justice, the Court must decide questions on the presumption of innocence, the death penalty, proof of guilt beyond reasonable doubt, nonunanimous jury verdicts, juries of less than twelve, exclusionary rules, cross-examination, warrantless searches and seizures, electronic eavesdropping, juvenile courts, stop and frisk, police lineups, custodial interrogation, and use immunity, to mention a few. There is surely no clear word in the Constitution on these or most of the subjects of great import with which the Court must deal. The framers of the Constitution had a genius for studied imprecision and calculated ambiguity. Their Constitution, which they expressed in very generalized terms, resembled Martin Chuzzlewit's grandnephew who, Dickens said, had no more than "the first idea and sketchy notion of a face." It thereby permitted, even encouraged—nay, necessitated—continuous reinterpretation and adaptation to changing circumstances and needs. Thus, the commerce clause today applies to Telstar communication, racial discrimination in motels, stolen cars, stock-exchange transactions, and the wages of window washers.

The document itself, with all its amendments, clearly delineates the structure of the American national government but only roughly maps the contours of power and the rights that it guarantees. We know unmistakably that there is to be a President whose term of office is four years; but what is "the executive power" with which he is vested? Chief Justice John Marshall once happily noted that the Constitution has none of the prolixity of a legal code. It has, rather, the virtue of muddy brevity. Very few of its several thousand words have any significance in constitutional law or criminal procedure and evidence. Almost without exception these significant words are the purposely protean or undefined words like general welfare, due process of law, commerce among the states, equal protection, privileges and immunities of citizenship, direct taxes, and necessary and proper. Other words of crucial importance in constitutional law are not even in the Constitution, including clear and present danger, fair trial, equal justice, self-incrimination, presumption of innocence, cross-examination, separate but equal, separation of church and state, the police power, community standards, exigent circumstances, privacy, hearsay, and the war powers. They are all judicial glosses.

Even the seemingly specific injunctions of the Bill of Rights do not always exclude exceptions to their rules, nor are they self-defining. What is an "establishment of religion"? Freedom of speech and press may not be "abridged," but what is an abridgment and what, indeed, is the freedom of speech that is protected? Libels, obscenity, and pornography (whatever they may mean), as well as direct and successful verbal incitements to crime, were not intended to be within the constitutional protection. The guarantee of freedom of religion is that it may not be "prohibited." May freedom of religion be abridged or regulated in some way short of a prohibition? There shall be no laws "respecting" an establishment of religion; can there be laws respecting freedom of speech or press without abridging them? What is an "unreasonable" search or seizure? No warrants shall issue "but on probable cause." What is "probable cause," and may there be searches without warrants? What is an "infamous" crime? What is the meaning of compulsion in the safeguard that no person shall be compelled in any criminal case to be a witness against himself? What is the process of law that is "due" to anyone who might be denied life, liberty, or property? What is "public use" or "just" compensation? Do the many rights of the Sixth Amendment really extend to "all" criminal prosecutions? What, indeed, is a "criminal prosecution"? What is a "speedy" trial or an "impartial" jury, and what does the "assistance of counsel" mean? What is "excessive" bail or a punishment that is "cruel and unusual"?

There are no constitutional absolutes; the words on the parchment do not speak precisely and clearly; and, there is no constitutional question, at least none that has come before the Court, that can be sliced so thin that it has only one side. During Burger's first term as Chief Justice, the Court decided the Alabama preliminary-hearings case.[78] The question was whether there is a right to the assistance of counsel at a preliminary hearing, prior to indictment, even if the state in which the case arose did not require that hearing in every prosecution. Long before, the Court had held that a person accused of crime "requires the guiding hand of counsel at every step in the proceedings against him."[79] In this case, Justice Brennan, for a majority of the Court, enumerated the various reasons that counsel must be furnished at a preliminary hearing, when there is one, in order to protect "the indigent accused against an erroneous or improper prosecution."[80] Justice Black, who was from the state in which the case arose, explained in a concurring opinion why the preliminary hearing was a critical step in that state's prosecution, and he observed that the "plain language" of the Sixth Amendment requires that in "all criminal prosecutions, the accused shall enjoy the right . . . to have the assistance of counsel for his defence."[81] Justice Douglas, also concurring, made Black's point explicit when he declared, rather amazingly, that "a strict construction of the Constitution requires the result reached."[82] Justices White and Harlan agreed that recent decisions of the Court furnished ample ground for holding that the preliminary hearing was a critical event in the progress of a criminal prosecution, warranting the right to counsel. Harlan asserted that had he been free to consider the case "upon a clean slate," he would have voted to affirm the convictions, but that was not a course open to him given his "due regard for the way in which the adjudicatory process of this Court, as I conceive it, should work."[83] Justice Stewart dissented because the trial record did not show that evidence from the preliminary hearing was used against the accused at their trial.

Given this posture of the Court, Burger's dissenting opinion was excessively distempered. He accused the majority of making new law on the basis of their views of "sound policy." He also displayed an egregious contempt for precedents and for the facts of constitutional life, when he declared:

. . . I do not acquiesce in prior holdings that purportedly, but nonetheless erroneously, are based on the Constitution. That approach simply is an acknowledgment that the Court having previously amended the Sixth Amendment now feels bound by its action. . . . I am bound to reject categorically Mr. Justice Harlan's and Mr. Justice White's thesis that what the Court said lately controls over the Constitution. While our holdings are entitled to deference I will not join in employing recent cases rather than the Constitution, to bootstrap ourselves into a result, even though I agree with the objective of having counsel at preliminary hearings. By placing a premium on "recent cases" rather than the language of the Constitution, the Court makes it dangerously simple for future Courts, using the technique of interpretation, to operate as a "continuing Constitutional convention."[84]

Reading the Sixth Amendment literally, Burger found that it did not stipulate the right to counsel at a preliminary hearing. He then accused the majority of seeking to "reshape the Constitution in accordance with predilections of what is deemed desirable."[85]

Burger's dissenting opinion had a Lockean quality in at least one sense. The great John Locke, a dreadfully inept constitution maker, believed that written statements of fundamental law must, like the laws of the universe, be immutable in order to be eternal. He once framed for Carolina a constitution expressly providing that "every part thereof, shall be and remain the sacred and unalterable form and rule of government for Carolina forever." As insurance, he added that "all manner of comments and expositions on any part of these fundamental constitutions, or on any part of the common or statute laws of Carolina, are absolutely prohibited."[86] By contrast the framers of the United States Constitution recognized the inevitability of change and the need for plasticity. They therefore provided for an orderly amendment procedure and for a "judicial power of the United States" that "shall extend to all cases, in law and equity, arising under this Constitution, the Laws of the United States, and Treaties made, or which shall be made. . . ." That required courts to engage in what Locke called "all manner of comments and expositions." Burger's literalism or strict construction, had it prevailed, would have enshrined Locke's approach, wiped the slate clean of precedents, and put the Constitution into an eighteenth-century deep-freeze.

Burger to the contrary, the Supreme Court is and must be for

all practical purposes a "continuous constitutional convention" in
the sense that it must keep updating the original charter by reinterpretation—and in the sense that it simply cannot decide cases
on the basis of what the Constitution says. One who used the
phrase so repugnant to Burger was a very conservative Solicitor
General of the United States who accurately described the duties of
the Court as "political in the highest sense of the word as well as
judicial."[87] Many scholars and even members of the Supreme
Court who had an appreciation of the realities of the situation have
used the phrase too. In very much the same sense, many Justices,
including such distinguished ones as Brandeis, Frankfurter, and
Black, have described the Court, sometimes despairingly, as a
superlegislature. It is that in some respects and cannot help but
be so. The reason is simply that the Constitution, as Jefferson said
in exasperation, is "merely a thing of wax" which the Court "may
twist and shape into any form they please."[88] Judge Learned Hand
observed that when a judge must pass on a question of constitutional law, "The words he must construe are empty vessels into
which he can pour nearly anything he will."[89] Frankfurter, whom
Nixon held up as the model of the strict-constructionist judge, explained that the words of the Constitution are so unrestricted by
their intrinsic meanings, or by history, or by tradition, or by prior
decisions, "that they leave the individual justice free, if indeed they
do not compel him, to gather meaning not from reading the Constitution but from reading life. . . . The process of constitutional
interpretation compels the translation of policy into judgment, and
the controlling conceptions of the justices are their 'idealized political picture' of the existing social order."[90] Nixon's search for conservative strict constructionists was more than a candid attempt to
alter the trend of decision; it was an acknowledgment that at the
very apex of our system of government of laws and not of men, the
men who interpret the laws, rather than the laws themselves, are
the decisive factors. Warren showed his understanding of that fact
when, on the occasion of his retirement, he noted that the Court
consisted of nine independent men "who have no one to be responsible to except their own consciences." Strict constructionism
can be a balm for the judicial conscience, but not much more.

The imprecision of the constitutional text makes strict constructionism a faintly ridiculous usage; indeed, our national experience makes it slightly sinister in its implications. The term originated in the pre-Civil War era as an argument in the armory of state's rightists who opposed the development of a strong Union detrimental to the proslavery interests. If words have symbolic value, strict constructionism means reversing the decision of Appomattox, crippling government regulation of the economy, a return to the legal order of Jim Crow, and letting the police have their way with suspects in the basement of the station house.

Notwithstanding Nixon's professed admiration for strict constructionism, his presidency stood for a promiscuous expansion of national powers, especially of the executive powers of the United States. Strict construction in the mouth of President Nixon was like the word love in the mouth of a whore, except that Nixon deceived only the public, not himself. As a lawyer and politician, he knew that inherently vague words cannot be strictly construed. He acknowledged that constitutional lawyers honestly disagree "as to where and how" to maintain "that delicate balance between the rights of society and the rights of defendants accused of crimes against society." [91] Nixon knew too that strict constructionism can be an instrumentalist tactic for reaching desired results under a judicial guise of objectivity. It is a form of judicial laissez-faireism by which the judge acquiesces, as if in humility, to the status quo and defers to the other branches of the government, or to the states, or to law-enforcement agencies, as the case may be.

In the Alabama preliminary-hearing case, Douglas and Burger were on opposite sides, yet both purported to pursue a strict construction of the Sixth Amendment's right-to-counsel clause. That Douglas, a liberal activist, should have taken a strict-constructionist stance, was not really a surprise; after all, the law-and-order critics of the Warren Court bitterly complained that it enforced the Bill of Rights too strictly against law-enforcement officials. Nevertheless, both Douglas and Burger were pursuing an elusive will-o'-the-wisp when seeking a strict-constructionist interpretation. Each reasoned from unquestioned premises to a foregone conclusion that had some logical form, yet represented, at bottom, a choice of competing values. Each relied on the rhetoric of strict constructionism to bolster the pretense that he was being impersonal in his judgment. Either would scrap that rhetoric if it stood in his way. Burger's rhetorical stance in effect proclaimed: "Whatever my personal wishes may be, I find nothing in the language of the Constitution that actually says that the accused must have counsel at a preliminary hearing." Nevertheless, in voting to deny trial by jury to accused persons if they are juveniles[92] or if they face imprisonment for not more than six months,[93] Burger abandoned strict constructionism because it did not ease the way to the desired result. The Sixth Amendment, which requires a trial by jury in "all" criminal prosecutions, makes no exception for juveniles or petty offenders. But even words like "all" are malleable.

Burger is no more a strict constructionist than Douglas. The Chief Justice is, rather, a "judicial conservative" in Nixon's usage of that term. He meant a judge who sides with law-enforcement officials. When nominating Lewis F. Powell Jr. and William H. Rehnquist, Nixon both clarified and obscured his objective. His nominees, he conceded, "are conservatives . . . but only in a judicial, not a political sense." He wanted men on the Supreme Court who would share "my judicial philosophy, which is basically a conservative philosophy." To explain his meaning, he declared:

> As a judicial conservative, I believe some court decisions have gone too far in the past in weakening the peace forces as against the criminal forces in our society. In maintaining, as it must be maintained, the delicate balance between the rights of society and defendants accused of crimes, I believe the peace forces must not be denied the legal tools they need to protect the innocent from criminal elements.

There was no doubt about which way Nixon wanted his nominees to vote in criminal-justice cases, but he used a political standard, not a judicial one, just as he confounded the meanings of "judicial philosophy" and "judicial conservative." He said, quite properly, that a judge "should not twist or bend the Constitution in order to perpetuate his personal political and social views," but he knowingly chose men who, he hoped, would do exactly that in criminal-justice cases.[94] The term "judicial philosophy" refers to a concept of the judicial function and of the role of the Court in a political democracy. Frankfurter, for example, was a judicial passivist because he believed that the Court was inherently oligarchic in character. By the exercise of its power it could frustrate the representative institutions that are the product of the electoral process. The Court may be responsive to the people, but it need not be, and it is not responsible in a political sense. Majorities make mistakes, but the Court is also liable to err, and when it checks the majority Frankfurter believed that it has sapped the capacity of the people to learn from experience and correct their own mistakes. Frankfurter also worked out sophisticated theories about the judicial craft of interpreting statutes, the role of precedents in constitutional decisions, the jurisdiction of the Court, and the constitutional relationship between the nation and the states. He did not speak of supporting one side to a controversy over another, nor did he endorse a "conservative" judicial philosophy. Like Harlan, to whom he was close, Frankfurter had a due regard for the adjudicatory process of the Court. He did not express contempt for precedents, as Burger does. Frankfurter emulated Brandeis in adhering to a series of rules by which the Court avoids passing on constitutional questions when it can, avoids doctrines broader than required to settle a case, and avoids nullifying an act of government that can be given a constitutional construction.

A member of the Court who has a judicial philosophy of self-restraint is not one who will vote in an easily predictable way in a given case. He will differ from the liberal activist who sees the Court as one of democracy's institutions and the Constitution as a hedge against the excesses of majorities and of law-enforcement officials, clads himself in the armor of the Bill of Rights, and sets out to intervene as much as his judicial position will permit. The liberal activist is St. George or Don Quixote who tries to use his position to make the nation a better place or a fairer one by righting wrongs against the poor, the unpopular, and the disadvantaged. His votes are fairly predictable. So are the votes of the conservative activist or alleged strict constructionist of the Nixon sort. But a judge with a judicial philosophy like Holmes, Brandeis, Hughes, Frankfurter, or Harlan regularly defies the crystal ball of professional Court-watchers because he has abandoned his role as an advocate and does not sit on the bench to represent any particular interests or causes.

The members of the Court should, to the extent humanly possible, be aware of their own predilections and attempt to decide cases without consciously yielding to their own sympathies or deliberately reading the Constitution in the light of their own policy preferences. Yet even the best and most impartial of judges, those in whom the judicial temperament is most finely cultivated, cannot escape the currents that have tugged at them throughout their lives and inescapably color their judgment. Personality, the beliefs that make the man, has always made the difference in the Supreme Court's constitutional adjudication. There has never been a constitutional case before the Court in which room was lacking for personal discretion to express itself. In constitutional law there simply are no legal rules that are objective or neutral or value-free, enabling every judge, regardless of his identity and without regard to the litigants, to apply those rules in the same way with the same results. The rules themselves reflect considerations of policy and social advantage.

Legal erudition, legal rules, legal logic, legal research, and legal precedents do not decide cases involving the ambiguous clauses of the Constitution, the very clauses usually involved in those cases whose outcome helps to determine justice, the shape of public policy, and the degree of liberty or equality that exists in this country. Although some judges can intoxicate themselves with the belief that precedents control their decisions, decisions by the post-Warren Court, like decisions by its predecessors, prove that the Justices are intellectually supple enough to find their way around encumbering precedents. Moreover, the Court always has available to it alternative principles of constitutional construction—broad or narrow—as well as alternative lines of precedent, with the result that the Court has "a freedom," in the words of Edward S. Corwin, "virtually legislative in scope in choosing the values which it shall promote through its reading of the Constitution."[95] The Lord High Chancellor in *Iolanthe* might have characterized the Constitution and the Supreme Court when he humorously asserted, "The Law is the embodiment of everything that's excellent. . . . And I, my Lords, embody the Law."

The most gifted judge who has a deep understanding of himself and a deeper strain of self-skepticism cannot avoid the fact that every case presents a choice of competing considerations that are necessarily value-laden. His idealized picture of the social order, or his conception of the public interest, or his vision of the future, swerve his judgment one way or the other. "We may try to see things as objectively as we please," Justice Cardozo wrote. "Nonetheless, we can never see them with any eyes except our own."[96] Inevitably, then, our constitutional law is subjective in character and to a great degree result-oriented. We may not want judges who start with the answer rather than with the problem. We may not want such judges, but as long as mere mortals sit on the Court and must construe that majestic but muddy Constitution, we will rarely get any other kind. Not that the Justices knowingly or deliberately read their prejudices into law. There has probably never been a member of the Supreme Court who consciously decided against the Constitution or was unable, in his own mind, to square his opinions with it. Most judges convince themselves, or at least profess to believe the fiction, that they respond in the main to the clarity of words on parchment, illuminated, of course, by historical or social imperatives. The illusion may be good for their psyches or for the public's need to believe that the men who sit on the nation's highest tribunal really are Olympians, untainted by the considerations that move lesser beings. Even those Justices who start with the problem rather than with the result cannot transcend themselves nor transmogrify the obscure and inexact into simon-pure truth or impersonal principle. Even they cannot avoid the fact that constitutional law, more than any other branch of law, is a reflection of great public policies enshrined in the form of supreme and fundamental commands. It is truer of constitutional law than of any other branch that "what the courts declare to have always been the law," as Holmes put it, "is in fact new. It is legislative in its grounds. The very considerations which judges most rarely mention, and always with an apology, are the secret root from which the law draws all the juices of life. I mean, of course, consideration of what is expedient for the community concerned."[97] That applies as well to the realm of criminal justice. Judicial self-restraint and strict constructionism are at best factors that merely temper the ineluctible activism requisite for constitutional adjudication. Self-restraint and strict constructionism can also enable a member of the Court to achieve a pose which permits him to reach a preferred end in an apparently impersonal way. The judicial process is overwhelmingly a means of rationalizing preferred ends.

THE COURT THAT BURGER JOINED

When he succeeded Warren as Chief Justice, Burger joined a Court of uncommon talent. As a result of the resignations of Warren and Fortas, the Court had just lost a "great" Chief Justice and a "near great" Justice, according to scholars who rated all the men who had served from the beginning.[98] Nevertheless, Hugo L. Black, a "great" Justice, remained on the Court, and its other six members included William O. Douglas, John Marshall Harlan, and William J. Brennan, who rated "near great." Potter Stewart, Byron R. White, and Thurgood Marshall ranked in the "average" category. There was not a man on the Court whom the scholars classified as a "failure" or even "below average."

Black, the senior member of the Court when Burger became its Chief, was one of the titans in our judicial history. Only two or three others before him had a greater impact on our constitutional law than Black. His influence derived from a combination of aggressive advocacy, a coherent judicial philosophy, consistency, and longevity. He was a New Deal Senator when Roosevelt chose him for the Court in 1937, and he remained a New Dealer throughout his career on the high bench. His opinions had scrappy fervor, ennobling eloquence, and oversimplism. He represented the paradox of the overpowering advocate who saw himself as the constitutional literalist or strict constructionist. In Black the judicial temperament flickered unevenly; his deepest convictions could not be bridled. Unshakably he believed not only that he was right but had a mission to impose his convictions on the nation. Such men most lastingly leave their marks on the Constitution. They are the judicial activists in whom the capacity for self-doubt has atrophied. They do not understand Holmes's dictum that the civilized jurist must be skeptical of his own first principles. Black had a nearly limitless ability to persuade himself that truth, history, wisdom, and the exact words of the Constitution were on his side and governed his opinions, which did little more than declare what the fundamental law is. For Black, the Supreme Court was a platform from which to preach to the nation, secure in the knowledge that what was best was what he believed and that what he believed derived straight from the Constitution, above all from the Bill of Rights.

On balance, Black was a liberal activist. He was the principal architect of the criminal-law "revolution"—and much else—that was a hallmark of the Warren Court. He saw himself as the strict constructionist obligated by the First, Fifth, and Sixth Amendments to take an absolutist's position, and he read the Fourteenth Amendment as extending to the states the same restraints and standards that the Bill of Rights imposed on the United States government. On the other hand, he could not see in the Eighth Amendment's ban on cruel and unusual punishments any restriction on the death penalty, nor could he see in the Fourth Amendment's search-and-seizure provisions any restrictions on wiretapping, electronic eavesdropping, or warrantless searches that he regarded as reasonable. When Frankfurter or Harlan applied the same flexible standard of reasonableness to the Fourteenth Amendment's due-process clause, Black censured them as activists who indulged in discretionary personal judgments. As a result of his peculiar brand of strict constructionism, Black in his later years did not fulfill the expectations of libertarians; they thought he had gone over to the conservative side on poll taxes, birth control laws, warrantless searches, and civil-rights demonstrations. Black's sympathies remained pretty much with underdog litigants, but he was more the advocate of a particular and systematic judicial philosophy than of social causes. He consecrated himself to keeping the constitutional faith and text as he understood them.[99]

Douglas, whose length of service on the Court finally exceeded Black's and everyone else's, was for much of his career a worthy successor to Brandeis, whose seat he took. Douglas's appointment in 1939 capped a teaching career at Yale Law School and service as a New Deal administrator. Except for Fourth Amendment cases, Douglas was Black's closest associate. He was even more of a St. George intent on slaying the dragon that threatened racial, religious, and political minorities, the poor, the oppressed, and the despised. To say that his crusading zeal exceeded his judicial craftsmanship is a way of remarking on the ferocity of the former without detracting too much from the quality of the latter. In his declining years, however, Douglas's undiminished torrential energies and remarkably facile pen have produced opinions that lacked rigor. The brilliance and versatility of his legal intellect have lost little luster but much power of close analysis. His opinions have become increasingly predictable, shrill, and marked by signs of haste to reach subjective results. Brandeis's seat was no longer the model of intellectual rectitude and professorial proficiency. Douglas's opinions provoked some of his liberal admirers to take the cynical position that if constitutional adjudication is basically result-oriented, Douglas voting for the "right" side was better than any Nixon appointee voting the other way. Even with a diminished patience for trying to convince his opponents on the Court, Douglas could outmatch, though not outvote, them by the force and pith of his arguments.[100]

Harlan, a Wall Street lawyer whom Eisenhower appointed to the Court in 1955, was a judicial conservative of intellectual eminence. He became Frankfurter's closest associate and like him was a model of austere integrity and craftsmanship. Harlan's finely wrought opinions rested on painstaking analysis, relatively neutral principles of law, and a fair evaluation of opposing arguments. He could be relied upon for an accurate statement of the facts, a lucid definition of the issues, and a reasoned judgment. As a proponent of judicial self-restraint and one who possessed a rather exaggerated regard for the values of the federal system, he had his share of beliefs that influenced his judgment. But the rationale of an opinion, not the result that it reached, was most important to him. He commanded respect even from those who most disagreed with him. He listened, considered, evaluated, explained, and answered, and he was judicious. His opinions, like the man, had character in the common meaning of that word. He usually fashioned his principles from the facts of a case, reasoning from the particular to the general, rather than from some overarching philosophy as Black and Douglas did. There was an ascetic quality to a Harlan opinion: tight control, cool elegance, and searching honesty. He confounded behavioralist observers of the Court who liked to predict judicial results on the basis of voting patterns. Although he rejected Black's theory that the Fourteenth Amendment incorporated Bill of Rights freedoms, requiring of the states the same standards as for the

United States government, he had exacting standards for the reasonableness of searches and seizures. Like Cardozo and Frankfurter he saw in the due-process clause principles of ordered liberty, civilized decency, and fundamental fairness. Such views, despite his commitment to judicial self-restraint, vested him with considerable discretion in reaching a judgment, but he exercised his powers responsibly, always mindful of the need to persuade others. If the life of the law is logic, and it is not, Harlan was a master of the law. He was certainly the conscience of the Court. During the 1960s, when the liberal activists were in control, Harlan offered temperate, disciplined criticism. After 1969, as the conservative activists increasingly controlled the Court, he remained as independent and critical as ever. He was the judge's judge, severely impartial, technically proficient, and impatient with opinions that revealed convictions but did not convince.[101]

Brennan's appointment to the Court by Eisenhower in 1956 was surprising. The new Justice was a liberal Democrat, and though he possessed many of Harlan's qualities—a judicial temperament, thoroughness, and rigor—they could not suppress the outcropping of his personal values. When he was a member of the New Jersey Supreme Court, he made off-the-bench speeches against McCarthyism; McCarthy was the only Senator who voted against Brennan's confirmation. He became a cautious supporter of the Warren-Black-Douglas wing of the Court on most civil-liberties issues, writing a disproportionate number of liberal-activist opinions. Though he shared an instinct for the just result, he was more methodical than other members of that wing of the Court in rationalizing his decisions. He gave the impression of being more temperate and less inclined to dogmatism, more balanced and under a greater obligation to explain himself fully with all the respect that he could muster for positions unacceptable to him. His opinions tended to be detailed treatises that explored every aspect of an issue and sought laboriously to demonstrate that he had given the fullest consideration to it. Brennan seemed to require the most diligent and systematic proofs. Though he lacked the fire and brilliance of some of his libertarian colleagues, he was sounder, fairer, and weightier. With each passing year he has grown in stature and attainments.

In the area of criminal justice he identified with the major rulings that comprised the "revolution" of the 1960s, but Brennan was no absolutist. He could see distinctions and matters of degree in disputes involving the rights of the criminally accused. Some of the leading opinions of the Warren Court on self-incrimination were Brennan's, including opinions that drew lines favorable to prosecutorial claims. On the whole his attachment to the Bill of Rights countervailed against such claims, but predicting which way Brennan might vote in a particular case could be difficult. He always had to find reasons that satisfied him and would not disagree with a position without first troubling to understand it. Frankfurter, who was one of Brennan's teachers at Harvard Law School, is supposed to have said that he always wanted his students to think for themselves, "but Brennan goes too far." As the Court became more splintered and political in the 1970s, Brennan emerged as the most respected of the decreasing number of Justices who represented the heirs of the Warren Court's legacy in criminal-justice cases.[102]

Stewart came to the Court in 1958, after four years of seasoning on the United States Court of Appeals for the Sixth Circuit. He had a finely honed judicial temperament and a constipated understanding of the judicial function in the realm of constitutional law. The qualities of judicial modesty, deference, and self-restraint were most attractive to him. Warren's capacity for bold generalizations, Douglas's eagerness to settle the constitutional issues, and Black's righteousness were traits that Stewart found unbecoming in a judge. The Court was not for him the keeper of the nation's conscience nor the instrument of social change. He was deeply mistrustful of judicially imposed limitations that cut into government powers and was even reluctant to read the Bill of Rights as a set of restraints on government except in the clearest cases. The conservative judicial philosophy of Frankfurter and Harlan appealed to him, but that philosophy requires an exceptionally sophisticated intellect and a capacity for elaborate explanation in order for its devotee to be noticed. Lacking those qualities, he is likely to lack impact. The activist, whether liberal or conservative, who indulges his preferences for public policy in constitutional adjudication has a far easier task in creating a clearly defined image for himself and an influence. Stewart could not be less interested in his image or in directing public policy from the bench. He was a moderate man who attached great importance to jurisdictional and procedural matters. He wrote opinions that were clear, dispassionate, and to the point—to as narrow a point as he could find. His concern for procedure and respect for precedent might lead him to agree with the need to reverse a conviction of guilty in a particular case, but he would rarely agree with the sweeping grounds of decision so characteristic of the Court's liberal activists. Stewart was the competent technician for whom the technical aspects of a case dominated the greater issues from which he shied. His thinking, like his concept of the judicial function, was taut. The formidably complex and massive analysis of an issue that characterized an opinion by Harlan or Brennan was not beyond Stewart's powers; it was simply uncongenial to his temper and contrary to his notion of what an opinion should be like. Precision, conciseness, and directness were Stewart's strengths. He wrote not for posterity but only to settle the issue at hand in as constricted a way as he could find. He was a fair-minded, able judge, but neither an imaginative nor influential one.[103]

White owed his appointment to the Kennedys. He served with vigor and loyalty as the second in command of the Department of Justice. His elevation to the Court in 1962 seemed natural. He had been a Rhodes scholar like Harlan, an honor graduate of Yale Law School, and a law clerk to Chief Justice Fred Vinson for the 1946–47 term of the Court. White was the first law clerk who became a member of the Court. After he had served for a decade, scholars rated him as merely "average," doubtless a reflection of White's having disappointed the high expectations that he generated. If he had a judicial temperament, he managed to keep it well smothered. He wrote opinions that tended to be superficial in analysis, one-sided, hostile to opposing views, given to misstating them, and much too cocksure. In the area of criminal justice he sounded like a local prosecutor running for political office on a law-and-order platform.[104]

Some of the shrillest and most unfair censure of the Warren Court can be found in dissenting opinions by White, stoking the coals of public apprehensiveness that the liberal majority of the

1960s was turning the country over to criminals and sacrificing the rights of law-abiding citizens. When, for example, the Court reversed a conviction because the police illegally prevented a killer from talking to his lawyer, White alleged that law enforcement "will be crippled and its task made a great deal more difficult, all in my opinion, for unsound, unstated reasons."[105] When the Court required the police to provide counsel and notification of the right of silence to prisoners, White claimed that "the Court's rule will return a killer, rapist or some other criminal to the streets," and he called upon "good common sense"—he could find nothing in the Constitution supporting the majority—to support his view that the deterrent force of the criminal law dissipated when the Court let criminals "get away with rape and murder. . . ."[106] White reluctantly accepted the incorporation theory of the Fourteenth Amendment, preferring to keep the states unrestrained by specific provisions of the Bill of Rights. Harlan had the same preference, but he acted out of a coherent philosophy of judicial self-restraint, while White became more and more a conservative activist. No member of the Court is completely consistent, of course. There were opinions by White that supported and even spoke for the Warren wing, but usually on narrow grounds. As the Court changed during the early 1970s on criminal-justice matters, White found the judicial environment more to his liking. The press depicted him as a "swing" man on the Court, in the sense that he often provided the fifth and determinative vote. In the sense of being mediators between the Brennan wing on the one hand and the Burger wing on the other, the real swing men were Harlan and Stewart.

When appointing Marshall to the Court in 1967, President Johnson observed that Marshall had already earned his place in history. Indeed, he had. As chief counsel and director of the NAACP's Legal Defense Fund, Marshall masterminded the litigation of the civil-rights movement for almost a quarter of a century. He won twenty-nine out of thirty-two cases before the Supreme Court and numerous victories in the lower courts. He convinced the Supreme Court to declare unconstitutional the white primary, the racially restricted covenant in private housing, and, above all, compulsory racial segregation in public facilities and schools. As a lawyer defending the criminally accused, he also won notable victories on behalf of due process and equal justice. In 1961, Kennedy appointed Marshall to the United States Court of Appeals for the Second Circuit, where he earned a distinguished record especially in civil-rights and criminal-law cases. Four years later, Johnson persuaded Marshall to leave his judicial career to become Solicitor General of the United States, the officer in charge of all federal litigation before the Supreme Court. The position added a new dimension to Marshall's experience; for the first time he had to argue constitutional issues from a prosecutor's standpoint. After two years, he became a member of the Court that he knew so well. Surrounded by a galaxy of liberal luminaries—Warren, Black, Douglas, Brennan, and Fortas—Marshall played a subordinate role on the Court during his first two years, which were Warren's last two. Voting most often with Warren and Brennan, Marshall seemed to favor liberal activism, but there was not enough evidence to characterize him definitely before Burger became Chief Justice. In each of his two years of service, Marshall had written the fewest number of opinions of the Court and rarely wrote dissenting or concurring opinions of his own. He wrote no opinion of significance in the criminal-justice field. As the composition of the Court changed, however, Marshall changed. He became increasingly outspoken and liberal. By 1972, Brennan, Douglas, and he constituted a clearly defined voting bloc. Marshall still wrote the fewest number of opinions of the Court, but the number of his concurring and dissenting opinions multiplied and grew in length, aggressiveness, and incisiveness.[107]

NIXON'S ASSOCIATE JUSTICES

Harry A. Blackmun

After Burger's appointment, Nixon's efforts to fill other vacancies on the Court encountered difficulties, because he inclined to favor men whose ethical probity or competence was questionable. In midsummer of 1969, he nominated Clement F. Haynsworth Jr. to fill the Fortas seat. The nomination touched off a political donnybrook. Those who had blocked Fortas's nomination as Chief Justice had already politicized the confirmation process, and

Nixon himself had politicized the appointment process. He sought to repay a political debt to the South by choosing a very conservative Southerner. Haynsworth, a member of the United States Court of Appeals for the Fourth Circuit, was a judge of modest talents whose civil-rights opinions seemed tinged with racism. His confirmation looked definite until investigation revealed improprieties in conflict-of-interest cases. Despite the President's undiminished support, the Senate rejected Haynsworth by a ten-vote margin; seventeen of forty-five Republicans voted against him.[108]

Nixon attributed the rebuff to the opposition of liberal organizations like the NAACP, the ACLU, the ADA, and the AFL-CIO. Determined to restore "balance" to the Court by choosing a Southerner with judicial experience who was conservative, a strict constructionist, and who shared his philosophy of the Constitution, Nixon next nominated G. Harrold Carswell of Florida. Less than a year earlier, Nixon had elevated him from his federal district judgeship to the United States Court of Appeals for the Fifth Circuit. But Carswell looked like an incompetent Haynsworth. When opposition to him mounted, Nixon behaved as if the Senate should rubber-stamp anyone whom he nominated for the Court unless there was proof that the nominee was a criminal or so stupid that he did not know a tort from a tart. The evidence of Carswell's racism was irrefutable. If that and his lack of candor before the Senate Judiciary Committee were not enough, his judicial record raised serious questions about his fitness. The Ripon Society, a liberal Republican organization, charged that Carswell's performance as a federal judge was "significantly below the average level of competence"; higher courts overruled him in 58 percent of the cases appealed from his decisions.[109] Senator Roman Hruska (Rep., Neb.), a Carswell supporter, inadvertently damaged his chances of confirmation. In a widely publicized remark that embarrassed the President, who kept insisting that Carswell was eminently qualified, Hruska said of him, "Even if he were mediocre, there are a lot of mediocre judges and people and lawyers and they are entitled to a little representation, aren't they? We can't have all Brandeises, Frankfurters, and Cardozos."[110] The Senate defeated the nomination by a vote of 51-to-45; the majority included thirteen Republicans. More would have voted against Carswell had the White House not made support of him a matter of personal loyalty to Nixon. The Republican leader in the Senate, Hugh Scott of Pennsylvania, later conceded that he supported Carswell against his better judgment. Scott admitted to a "sense of guilt" for "making a damn-fool vote" for that "racist." Yes, he told newsmen, he meant Carswell and was speaking for the record.[111] Nixon speciously claimed that the Senate would not vote for any conservative Southerner. The "real reason" for the rejection of Haynsworth and Carswell, he told the press, "was their legal philosophy, a philosophy that I share, of strict construction of the Constitution . . . and the fact that they were born in the South." He would choose a Northern judge of the same philosophy.[112]

Nixon's next nominee was Harry A. Blackmun, a Northern judge, who easily won confirmation because his integrity and credentials withstood scrutiny. Blackmun had majored in math at Harvard College, graduated *summa cum laude,* earned his law degree from Harvard Law School, and won a law clerkship to a federal judge. When that judge a quarter of a century later retired from the United States Court of Appeals for the Eighth Circuit, he swore in his former clerk as his successor. In the years between Blackmun's clerkship and his appointment by Eisenhower as a federal judge in 1959, he practiced law in his home state of Minnesota. Burger, also a Minnesotan, was a good friend of Blackmun and may have had something to do with his appointment to the Court. The two had known each other from boyhood; they went through grade school together and maintained a close relationship even after their paths separated. Blackmun had been best man at Burger's wedding.

On the day that news of Blackmun's nomination became public, a reporter asked him whether he was a strict constructionist. He replied deftly, "I've been called a liberal and a conservative. Labels are deceiving."[113] The Department of Justice avoided labels when preparing a memorandum for the Senate Judiciary Committee summarizing Blackmun's representative opinions as a circuit judge.[114] He ordered racial desegregation in public schools and supported Negro faculty members who alleged discrimination against them. On the other hand, Blackmun wrote an opinion denying that a civil-rights act of 1866 was, in effect, a nationwide open-housing law applicable to private housing; the Supreme Court reversed him.[115] His criminal-law decisions tended to reject defendants' claims. In three cases Blackmun wrote opinions sustaining the death penalty against various attacks—that it violated due process because juries had standardless discretion, that it violated the equal protection of the laws because Negroes bore the brunt of the penalty, and that it violated the Eighth Amendment because it was a cruel and unusual punishment. In one of those cases Blackmun reversed the conviction because of an error based on the admission of the defendant's confession.[116] In another the black defendant convicted for the rape of a white woman said that a white man would not have received the death penalty for the same crime. Blackmun replied, "We are not yet ready to condemn and upset the result reached in every case of a Negro rape defendant in the State of Arkansas on the basis of broad theories of social and statistical injustice."[117] As he said before the Senate Judiciary Committee, upholding the death penalty was "excruciating for one who is not convinced of the rightness of capital punishment as a deterrent in crime." That was his "personal philosophy"; he would not allow it to influence his decision as a judge. He felt bound, he told the Senators, to follow the judgment of the legislature that fixed death as a penalty, unless, of course, a legislature were to impose death upon pedestrians crossing against a red light.[118] No Senator explored this revelation that Blackmun exercised discretion in deciding what constituted cruel and unusual punishment for one crime but not another. In other decisions Blackmun had held that beating a convict with a strap was cruel and unusual punishment,[119] and he had rejected a double-jeopardy claim.[120] In the latter case a man who had committed a single robbery with several victims was tried and acquitted of robbing one and then was tried and convicted for robbing another on the same occasion. When the Supreme Court reversed Blackmun's judgment in this case, only Burger dissented.[121]

During the Senate Judiciary Committee hearings on his nomination, Blackmun was candid enough to be intriguing. Eastland asked him whether a judge, when interpreting the Constitution, should take into account his own enlightened ideas on public policy. Blackmun began by saying, "Of course, this is a changing world," and then, more cautiously, acknowledged that the Constitution is a written document that a judge ought not construe in the light of his own philosophy. He would, he promised, interpret the document according to its determined meaning. "Of course," he added, "many times this is obscure."[122] Eastland, deciding not to rock the boat, yielded the microphone to the next Senator. Eventually, Senator Philip A. Hart of Michigan, a liberal Democrat, got a chance to ask Blackmun to explain his remark about the obscurity of the Constitution. Blackmun replied that the framers of the Constitution could not have anticipated our problems. "That is, I suppose, what we have . . . Federal courts for, to construe the Constitution in the light of current problems."[123] Hart, unfortunately, did not pin Blackmun down.

Senator Birch Bayh, who led the fight against Haynsworth and Carswell, asked him whether he would feel bound by past Supreme Court precedents. Blackmun gave a properly ambiguous answer. Precedents were very valuable but not absolute. The members of the Court, he added, "are humans and I suppose attitudes change as we go along." Bayh did not take advantage of the opening that reply gave for questioning Blackmun about his attitudes toward specific precedents of the Warren Court. When asked for his comments about the Bill of Rights, Blackmun thought that saying anything beyond "very precious to me" would be improper.[124] It was all very decorous, an expression of the relief felt by Senators that Nixon had finally chosen someone acceptable. The committee recommended Blackmun by unanimous vote and by the same vote the Senate confirmed him. He took his oath of office too late to participate in the spring decisions of 1970.

Lewis F. Powell Jr.

Sixteen months later, within the same week during the summer of 1971, Black and Harlan retired. Black, who died a few days later at the age of eighty-five, had served over thirty-four years on the Court. The loss of the Court's greatest member could be borne because of his age and the fact that he had already made his contribution. The loss of Harlan, who died before the year was over, was mourned by civil libertarians as much as by others. Harlan had been on the Court for sixteen years; at the age of seventy-two, he was at the pinnacle of his intellectual powers. He was so principled, so respectful of the Court's traditions, and so respected, that he alone could have a restraining influence on his conservative brethren.[125]

Nixon had two more appointments to make. "This is a historic opportunity," one White House official told the press. "The next Court will be known as the Nixon Court, not as the Burger Court. . . ."[126] After Nixon made his two appointments, *Time* magazine carried a feature story on "Nixon's Court,"[127] and a cartoonist depicted the Court remade in Nixon's image with all the Justices looking like the President himself. Finding the right men to fill the Black and Harlan seats would under any circumstances have been difficult. Nixon made the process aggravating for the nation. First, the White House leaked the news that the President meant to nominate Congressman Richard Poff of Virginia. The same labor and civil-rights groups that opposed Haynsworth and Carswell began to mobilize against Poff. He withdrew his name from consideration to avoid a controversial and protracted confirmation process. Then the name of Senator Robert Byrd of West Virginia surfaced. The press revealed that Byrd had been an organizer of the Ku Klux Klan, had a night-school law degree, and had never passed a bar examination. *The New York Times* apoplectically editorialized: "If President Nixon and Attorney General Mitchell deliberately set out to destroy the prestige and authority of the Supreme Court of the United States, they could hardly pick a more likely course than that which they now seem to be following." For Byrd to succeed "such giants as a Harlan or a Black, would be nothing less than a travesty . . . an insult to the American people and a mockery of the Court itself."[128]

Two days later, on October 14, Nixon requested the fitness committee of the American Bar Association to determine the qualifications of six persons being considered for appointment to the Court. Byrd was one of the six, but the two who had priority were Herschel Friday, a Little Rock lawyer who specialized in municipal bonds and represented Arkansas school districts against desegregation suits, and Mildred Lillie, a member of a lower appellate court in California whose previous experience was on a domestic relations court.[129] Nixon demanded that the ABA committee make its fitness report on the candidates in time for him to announce his selections on October 22. On October 21, *The New York Times* reported that on the next day the President would probably nominate Friday and Lillie. On the same day, the *Los Angeles Times,* using front-page headlines, announced "Justice Lillie Not Fit, Bar Unit Says. ABA Panel Also Calls Friday Unqualified for High Court." The ABA, which had been rating prospective members of the Court since Eisenhower's time, had never before found a nominee unqualified. Senator Edward Kennedy remarked that as a group the six prospects reflected Nixon's "utter contempt for the Court."[130] Although the public reaction persuaded the President to change his mind, the dismay and consternation which he had generated worked in his favor to soften the response to his final choices. Hours before his scheduled TV address on October 22, he had not yet conclusively made up his mind. His final choices came as a surprise even to one of the nominees, as well as to the ABA, which he failed to consult. He nominated Lewis F. Powell Jr. and William H. Rehnquist.[131] Their credentials left the Senate and the nation with an enormous sense of relief and disarmed most critics, however much they deplored the conservatism of both men.

At sixty-four, Lewis Powell of Virginia, one of the nation's most respected lawyers, was older than most appointees. "Ten years of Powell," explained Nixon, "is worth thirty years of anyone else."[132] The nominee was an alumnus of Washington and Lee University; he remained there for his law degree, graduating first in his class, and then earned a Master of Laws degree from Harvard, where he came under the influence of Professor Felix Frankfurter. Powell had no previous judicial experience. He spent his entire professional career in private practice, a director of eleven corporations and a senior partner in Virginia's largest law firm. Powell won the highest recognition that the bar can bestow; he had been president of the American Bar Association, of the American Bar Foundation, and of the American College of Trial Lawyers. He had served on several presidential commissions, most notably the National Commission on Law Enforcement and the Administration of Justice, and on the state commission that proposed a new constitution for Virginia.[133]

As a prominent attorney Powell had made several speeches and statements on criminal justice, none of which would make a lawyer for the ACLU dance for joy. On the other hand, only one was immoderate in either tone or substance. Powell was a deliberative, temperate man with an enormous respect for the law, even when he disagreed with it, and he inclined to see both sides of a question even if, on balance, he cautiously emerged on the conservative side. He lacked a strong ideological orientation; injudicious rhetoric about coddling criminals and handcuffing the cops was temperamentally alien to him. His conservatism was not that of the pro-prosecutorial activist; it seemed, rather, reminiscent of Frankfurter or Harlan.

In 1964, when speaking in favor of equal justice for the poor, Powell said that "wealth, social position, and race of clients may affect the standards of justice available."[134] In 1965, when he was head of the American Bar Association, he declared:

> Historic decisions of the Supreme Court in recent years have strengthened significantly the rights of accused persons. Most notably, these decisions have extended standards from the Bill of Rights Amendments to the state courts. . . . There is, of course, room for considerable difference of opinion with respect to some of these decisions—and lawyers differ widely as do members of the Court on occasions. Yet, it must be remembered that in all of these cases the Court was confronted with the difficult question of protecting the constitutional rights of the individual against alleged unlawful acts of government. Unfortunately, the Court itself has been unfairly criticized for some of these decisions. . . .
>
> Many of the decisions of the Supreme Court which are criticized today are likely, in the perspective of history, to be viewed as important milestones in the ageless struggle to protect the individual from oppressive government.[135]

In a speech of 1966 he warned that statements by overzealous or publicity-seeking law-enforcement officials about alleged confessions or incriminatory evidence jeopardized the rights of the accused.[136] In the following year, when the National Commission on Law Enforcement and the Administration of Justice made its monumental report, praising the criminal-justice decisions of the Warren Court, Powell was one of four members who filed an independent statement criticizing the controversial *Escobedo* and *Miranda* opinions.[137] The statement was far more temperate than some of the dissents in those cases. Powell and his colleagues expressed concern that the effect of those opinions might be to eliminate all pretrial interrogation and the use of confessions. They advocated the continued use of interrogation "with appropriate safeguards to prevent abuse" and of confessions that met "due process standards of voluntariness." They also endorsed comment on the failure of an accused to take the stand, which the Warren Court had banned as violative of the Fifth Amendment.[138]

A statement typical of Powell's inclination to balance his judgment was the one in 1968 when he declared, "We have witnessed in recent years an unprecedented concern for the rights of accused persons. In many areas this was overdue but the net effect of court decisions over the decade has been adverse to law enforcement."[139] He had earlier remarked on the unfortunate tendency of some to see the problem as a conflict between a "law enforcement view" and an "individual rights view"; he thought that was a false conflict which obstructed sensible solutions.[140] As time passed, however, he seemed more sympathetic to the law-enforcement view. In 1971, he observed in passing that there ought to be a relaxation of "some of the artificial rules engrafted upon the Fourth, Fifth and Sixth Amendments by divided votes of the Court in cases like *Miranda* and *Escobedo*."[141]

In the same year, just a couple of months before his nomination, he wrote a widely publicized article for the *Richmond Times-Dispatch* under the title "Civil Liberties Repression: Fact or Fiction? Law-Abiding Citizens Have Nothing to Fear."[142] At the hearings on his nomination, several liberal Senators questioned him in detail about this article. Kennedy noted "a certain hardness creeping into some of your writings" compared to an earlier style that was "extremely balanced and measured."[143] The article used phrases like "standard leftist propaganda," "sheer nonsense," "predictable voices cried repression and brutality," and suggested that persons concerned with civil liberties had promoted or accepted "the propaganda of the radical left." Powell had seemed to justify wiretapping in national-security cases without prior court authorization. "The outcry against wiretapping," he wrote, "is a tempest in a teapot." Defending the Administration's mass arrests of the May Day demonstrators in Washington earlier that year, he declared that the alternative "was to surrender the government to insurrectionaries." He vigorously defended the American system of criminal justice against charges of repression and concluded, ". . . our system subordinates the safety of society to the rights of persons accused of crime. The need is for greater protection—not of criminals but of law-abiding persons."[144] The article was a routine right-wing effusion that was out of character with anything in Powell's record; more likely than not, it tipped the balance in his favor when Nixon had to cast about at the last minute to find replacements for Friday and Lillie, his preferred candidates for the Court.

When members of the judiciary committee quizzed Powell about the article, he seemed to regret his ill-considered journalistic statement. He candidly answered all questions. There was nothing evasive about him, although to some questions he replied tentatively because, he explained, he had not studied the matter as thoroughly as he would like to. He appeared to be anything but doctrinaire and showed not a hardness, but a tendency to equivocate.

When questioned about the Fifth Amendment, he indicated his continued opposition to the *Miranda* decision, but acknowledged that experience had proved his fears that it would end confessions might not have been warranted. He still favored the admission of voluntary confessions made without prior notification of the suspect's rights.[145] On the other hand, he respected precedents—"all precedents," he said, though a recent precedent decided by a 5-to-4 vote did not have the same presumption in its favor as an older precedent decided unanimously.[146] He would not have joined the dissenters in *Escobedo* because he agreed with the decision of the majority; yet, he thought its opinion was unnecessarily overbroad.[147] He was no longer sure of his own opinion about the desirability of commenting on the accused's failure to take the stand; in any case, the decision of the Court on that matter was seven years old and should be respected as a precedent.[148] When asked whether protection for law-abiding citizens must be at the expense of the criminally accused, he replied:

No, not necessarily, and I would like to make perfectly clear that I don't think I have ever criticized the Court for deciding those historic cases. . . . I emphasized the fact that probably most of the decisions of the so-called Warren Court in the criminal justice area will be regarded as landmarks in the law. The two you mentioned [*Escobedo* and *Miranda*] were two that were exceptions from the broad sweep of my judgment on that line of decisions.[149]

Senator Hart asked the most direct and challenging question. Nixon, he observed, wanted the direction of the Court in the field of criminal justice to be reversed and had said that he selected men whose philosophy indicated to him that they shared his feeling. "As one who has felt that the Warren Court was good medicine for the country, I find myself sort of presented with a miserable dilemma." Powell seemed to him to have all the marks of excellence and no hostility to the Warren Court. "How would you counsel me on this: if, indeed, I thought the Warren Court made sense and that you were nominated, in order to reverse that, shouldn't I vote against you?" Powell replied that though he doubted the wisdom of some of the decisions, he favored most. "As a lawyer, I never had any trouble with the Warren Court." He then quoted from his 1965 speech saying the decisions that were being criticized today would likely be viewed by history as milestones in the struggle to protect the individual from oppressive government. Senator Hart answered, "All right."[150]

Senator Bayh put the inevitable question about the meanings of "strict construction and a judicial conservative." Powell read a prepared answer, expressing his belief in the separation of powers, the federal system, judicial restraint in the sense of avoiding a decision on constitutional grounds where others are available, a strong presumption in favor of precedent, a determined effort on the part of a judge to put aside his own predilections, and, finally, the responsibility of the Court to "uphold the rule of law and to protect and safeguard the liberties guaranteed all of our people by the Bill of Rights and the 14th Amendment."[151] Questioning revealed that Powell could support his general principles.

In the end, the Senate Judiciary Committee unanimously recommended his confirmation. Senators Bayh, Hart, Kennedy, and Tunney joined in a separate statement commending Powell for his "outstanding legal ability, unimpeachable personal integrity, and a demonstrated commitment to the protection of human rights and individual liberty." They noted that his *Richmond Times-Dispatch* article defended positions of the Nixon Administration that they considered "dangerous and potentially destructive of our constitutionally guaranteed right of privacy." Powell's testimony as well as his record as a whole showed that the problems "we originally had with this article are much less serious than we had thought at first." It was a journalistic piece that did not spell out matters he would consider as a lawyer or as a judge in deciding on the constitutionality of a specific course of action.[152] The Senators were right. When the Court had to rule on the inherent power of the President to wiretap in domestic national-security cases without a court-approved warrant, Powell wrote the opinion repudiating the Administration's claims.[153] The Senate liberals concluded that Powell possessed a strong dedication to preserving the civil liberties and civil rights of all citizens. When the whole Senate voted on him, only one member, Fred Harris (Dem., Okla.), opposed confirmation because of populistic prejudices against any corporation lawyer. The vote on Powell belied Nixon's statement that the Senate would not confirm a Southern conservative of his choice.

William H. Rehnquist

When someone asked Assistant Attorney General William H. Rehnquist whether he had a chance of being appointed to the Supreme Court, he replied, no, "because I'm not from the South, I'm not a woman, and I'm not mediocre."[154] All of those were true. Rehnquist was certainly not mediocre. Even his enemies credited him with superior intellect and formidable legal skills. At Stanford he won a Phi Beta Kappa key, earned a Master of Arts degree in Government in one year, and graduated first in his class at the law school. He served as law clerk to Justice Robert H. Jackson for the 1952–53 term of the Supreme Court. In 1953 he moved to Phoenix to establish himself in private practice. By 1964 he was a locally prominent Goldwater Republican. When Nixon became President, Rehnquist moved to Washington as head of the Office of Legal Counsel in the Department of Justice. In effect, he was Attorney

General Mitchell's lawyer, and in that capacity was an architect and advocate of the Administration's stern law-and-order policies. Rehnquist championed no-knock warrants, preventive detention, the end of habeas-corpus proceedings after trial, executive authority to wiretap alleged subversives without court approval, unrestricted government surveillance of dissident citizens, and the abolition of exclusionary rules of evidence. He endorsed the massive police roundups of the 1971 May Day demonstrators, whose leaders threatened to shut down the operations of the federal government in Washington. The police arrested about 12,000 people, illegally detained them until the demonstration was broken, and finally released all but the handful against whom there were charges. Rehnquist left the impression that he favored the imposition of a "qualified martial law" on the authority of the police. Emergency situations, he believed, justified extraordinary procedures.[155]

Rehnquist was only forty-seven at the time of his appointment. If he served as long as Black, he would still be on the Court in the year 2006 at the age of eighty-one. As Nixon said to the public, when announcing his choices of Powell and Rehnquist, the decisions of the Court "will affect your lives, and the lives of your children for generations to come. . . ." The question for the Senate was whether a man of exceptional ability who lacked compassion for civil rights and fidelity to the Bill of Rights should be confirmed for a seat on the Court.

Opinion on Rehnquist sharply divided. *The New York Times,* which worried about his potential for sinister influence, called him a "radical rightist,"[156] and Joseph L. Rauh, Jr., representing Americans for Democratic Action, vehemently opposed his confirmation on the ground that he was "probably farther to the right than any appointee to the Supreme Court this century."[157] Yet, Paul A. Freund of Harvard Law School, the most respected constitutional lawyer in the academic profession, commended Rehnquist for having a "powerful mind," and while noting that he was "very conservative," predicted that "the net result is that he will contribute to the deliberations of the Court because of his intellect."[158] Phil C. Neal, the Dean of the University of Chicago Law School, who also knew Rehnquist at Stanford, recommended him too and added that he was a "fair minded and objective man" who would "add great strength to the Court."[159] The ABA's fitness committee, after canvassing a great many law school deans, as well as judges and lawyers, found no one who cast doubt on Rehnquist's "brilliant intellectual qualifications" but conceded that a "significant minority" opposed his confirmation because of the undesirability of "so conservative an addition to the court."[160] Apparently, most academic lawyers could accept someone with Carswell's ideas if he had *summa cum laude* credentials. An "A" record outweighed reactionary opinions.

Rehnquist himself believed that the Senate had a duty to scrutinize a nominee's beliefs. In an article of 1959 he approvingly quoted an old editorial upholding the Senate's right to block a nominee who would add to the top-heavy conservative bias of the Court.[161] The provisions of the Constitution that most produce judicial lawmaking were, by no coincidence, Rehnquist observed, the vague ones like the due-process and equal-protection clauses. The Senate ought to recognize that the Constitution is what the judges say it is. If the Senate wanted members of the Court committed to judicial self-restraint, Rehnquist declared, it should restore the practice of "thoroughly informing itself on the judicial philosophy of a Supreme Court nominee before voting to confirm him. . . ."[162]

At the hearings on his own nomination, however, Rehnquist time and again refused to state his personal views on controversial policies of the Administration. He invoked the privilege deriving from the attorney-client relationship as the basis for his refusal to answer, reasoning that as Assistant Attorney General he had served as an advocate for the President and the Attorney General. He conceded that no previous nominee for the Court, many of whom went to the Court from the Department of Justice, had ever invoked the privilege on which he relied. On the very issues of due process of law and the equal protection of the laws, as to which he had declared in 1959 that the Senate should learn of the "sympathies" of the nominee, he declined answer.

Notwithstanding the praise of so many for Rehnquist's capacity for objectivity, some of his own criticisms of the Warren Court were of a character that cast doubt on whether he was fair-minded and reached judgments by constitutional standards. He declared in 1957 that the liberal viewpoint consisted of an "extreme solicitude for the claims of Communists and other criminal defendants, expansion of the federal power at the expense of State power, great sympathy toward any government regulation of business—in short, the political philosophy now espoused by the Court under Chief Justice Earl Warren."[163] In a 1958 article he began by saying that "Communists, former Communists, and others of like political philosophy scored significant victories during the October, 1956, term of the Supreme Court of the United States, culminating in the historic decisions of June 17, 1957."[164] There were four decisions of that date, and in every one Justices Frankfurter and Harlan, the apostles of judicial self-restraint, voted with the Court majority. Indeed, Harlan wrote the opinion of the Court in two of the four cases. One held that the Smith Act was aimed at the teaching and advocacy of concrete action for the forcible overthrow of the government, not at abstract principles divorced from action. Only Justice Clark dissented.[165] Harlan's other opinion spoke for a unanimous Court which ruled that the discharge of a State Department employee on loyalty-security grounds in violation of the department's own procedural regulations was illegal.[166] Warren was the spokesman in the other two cases of June 17, 1957. In one the Court, with only Clark dissenting, reversed the contempt conviction of a witness before the House Un-American Activities Committee who refused to answer a question whose pertinency to the investigation had not been explained.[167] In the last case, the Court held, 7-to-2, with Clark and Burton dissenting, that a state investigative inquiry into the contents of a professor's lectures and of his knowledge of the Progressive Party of New Hampshire violated his liberties in the areas of academic freedom and political expression.[168]

Contrary to Rehnquist, the victories of June 17, 1957, did not belong to Communists; the Court, by lopsided majorities, had sustained Bill of Rights freedoms. Rehnquist's language and grounds for criticizing the Court reflected an ideology, not a legal analysis. His tactics were closer to those of McCarthyism than to passive virtues of strict constructionism. He gave every indication of being a zealot who favored construing the Constitution as an activist devoted to achieving the supremacy of political conservatism. His approach was that of an ideologue advocating the embodiment of his policy choices in constitutional law. He was at the polar extreme from passivism, judicial self-restraint, or strict constructionism. When the *Washington Post* exulted over the Senate's rejection of Carswell, Rehnquist wrote a letter to the editor commending Carswell for a "judicial philosophy which consistently applied would reach a conservative result both in civil rights cases and in other areas of the law."[169] No philosophy that always reaches a conservative (or a liberal) result is a judicial philosophy. Rehnquist sought the "conservative result," not the impartial judging of cases. He was sufficiently realistic and cynical to understand that judges to some degree make policy and decide on the basis of personal predilections. That, for him, was not the problem with the Warren Court. The problem, rather, was that the Court's results were liberal rather than conservative in matters of First Amendment freedoms, civil rights, and the rights of the criminally accused. In short, Rehnquist promised to be a mirror image of the later Douglas.

There are a lot of right-wingers, and one might argue that they are entitled to one member of the Court to represent them. The difficulty, however, is that a member of the Court should be sensitive to claims that derive from the Bill of Rights, not interpret away its provisions. The Bill of Rights is really a bill of restraints, filled with thou-shalt-not injunctions against government. Rehnquist showed an enormous insensitivity to the Bill of Rights, especially when government had to cope with the enemies of society—criminals, Communists, and civil disobedients.

At the hearings on his nomination, Rehnquist showed ceremonial respect for the Bill of Rights and the principle of judicial impartiality. He told the Senate Judiciary Committee that if confirmed he would not feel free to implement his personal views in matters involving criminal justice. As a judge he might not reach positions that he advocated as a lawyer. He would, of course, "take to the Court what I am at the present time. There is no escaping it. I have lived for 47 years, and that goes with me." But he would not allow his prior positions to influence his judgment. Senator Hart asked Rehnquist how a man could be nominated to tip the balance toward government in criminal-justice cases and still decide without regard to a personal philosophy of law and order. Rehnquist replied that the pendulum had swung too far toward accused persons because of the personal philosophy of some Justices. When Hart inquired whether Rehnquist would not also have a personal philosophy as a member of the Court, the answer was, "Well, my personal philosophy I would hope to dissociate to the greatest possible extent from my role as a judge." Implicitly, Rehnquist was saying that to decide for the accused is personal, for the prosecution impersonal. On the other hand, he assured Hart that he would have no hesitancy in protecting the constitutional rights of any individual or group. Hart pointed out that some of the Court's decisions had handcuffed the police, and he asked, "But what is the purpose of the Bill of Rights? Is that not exactly what it is supposed to do?" Rehnquist obligingly acquiesced.[170]

The majority of the Judiciary Committee finally decided that all charges brought against Rehnquist by civil-rights leaders and civil libertarians were "totally unfounded."[171] In its report recommending confirmation, the committee looked at the nominee's record on desegregation, minority voting, civil-rights demonstrations, wiretapping, government surveillance, pretrial detention, and no-knock searches. The conclusion: Rehnquist was a man of balanced judgment with an unvarying commitment to the Constitution.

Four of the sixteen members of the committee—Bayh, Hart, Kennedy, and Tunney—dissented on every point. The record, as they saw it, showed a man who "gives short shrift to individual liberty when it hinders the pursuit of order and authority," and they could find no explanation in "strict construction":

> On the contrary, his approach to Constitutional interpretation seems strangely elastic. The Bill of Rights, and decisions upholding them against competing interests, are read as narrowly as possible, with little heed to their underlying concerns. But provisions and precedents conferring Executive power and declaring the general purposes of government are read loosely and expansively, to justify the most intensive kinds of interference with those rights.[172]

The four Senators went over the same issues as the majority of the committee and found a consistent hostility toward efforts to secure rights for victims of discrimination; a position on search warrants that, if accepted, "would reverse the whole course of Fourth Amendment law in this country"; a refusal to recognize that unrestrained government surveillance has a chilling effect on the exercise of First Amendment freedoms; "the same insensitivity to Bill of Rights guarantees in the criminal process" and an appetite for misconstruing the Supreme Court's decisions in favor of the criminally accused; and, an "astounding" position on the bail clause of the Eighth Amendment that makes it mean "what Mr. Rehnquist wants it to mean: viz., preventive detention. . . ."[173] The dissenting Senators concluded that in place of a balanced approach, the nominee employed a double standard: broad construction of government powers that militated against civil-liberties interests and a narrow construction of the provisions of the Bill of Rights. His record demonstrated a "dangerous hostility to the great principles of individual freedom . . . and equal justice for all people." His promise to dissociate himself from his personal views, if confirmed, was inadequate, "given the nature of the judicial process." The four therefore recommended rejection of the nomination.[174]

The full Senate supported Rehnquist by a vote of 68-to-26. Whether he had the temperament for being a member of the Court or a devotion to the Bill of Rights seemed unimportant compared to his integrity and brains. Some liberals who held their noses and voted for him did so because to vote him down would, they thought, establish a precedent that one day might be used against a liberal nominee. They forgot that the impropriety issue was only a pretext to prevent Fortas from becoming Chief Justice.

Powell and Rehnquist took their oaths of office on January 7, 1972. The four Nixon appointees immediately demonstrated a remarkable cohesiveness, voting together as a conservative bloc in almost every criminal-justice case. The vote of one other Justice, usually White or Stewart or both, put them in a position to control the Court. On a case-by-case basis they began changing the constitutional law of criminal justice.

CHAPTER TWO

The Fourth Amendment:
Search and Seizure

VIOLATIONS AND REMEDIES

Under the heading of "Terror in the Night—In the U.S.," the nation's leading newspaper recently reported the following story:

> Doors crumbling under the weight of policemen. Unkempt officers, some fresh from stops at local bars, ransacking homes, breaking furniture and shouting obscenities while holding terrified families at gunpoint.
>
> Germany in the 1930's?
>
> No, the United States in the 1970's as the "the Narks," the street term for Federal, state, and local narcotics agents, go about their routine business of fighting what President Nixon has called "the most despicable crime"—drug dealing.
>
> Last week the results of a two-month investigation by the New York Times were published and revealed that scores of agents, in their zeal to crush illicit drug trafficking, have mistakenly broken into the homes and apartments of dozens of innocent families, terrorizing the occupants and heavily damaging property.[1]

Incidents of this kind have occurred across the country, from Winthrop, Maine, to Whittier, California, sometimes resulting in the deaths of innocent people. The police shot one man through the head as he sat in his living room cradling his infant son. The police had a search warrant, but they were at the wrong address. In another case where the police and federal agents had the right address and a warrant, they swooped down in a helicopter to conduct an armed assault on a mountain cabin that was the supposed site of a "giant lab" for producing drugs. When the unarmed frightened occupant of the cabin fled, an agent shot him fatally in the back. The raid turned up no incriminating evidence. In another case, a woman awoke in the middle of the night to sounds in her house. Hearing someone begin to batter down her locked bedroom door, the terror-stricken woman, who had been a burglary victim, grabbed her revolver and shot through the door, killing a policeman. In another incident, fifteen officers broke down the front and back doors of a residence, herded a woman and her child into the living room, and aroused a man out of his sleep to face several gun barrels. It was another case of a mistaken address. "I didn't know police operated like that in America," said one innocent victim afterward.[2] The tragic mistake is, of course, exceptional. The police usually turn up at the right place, but they too often act on the uncorroborated tips of informants and do not have probable cause or a warrant either to search or to seize.

Although narcotics raids are hardly typical of all searches and seizures, with or without warrants, *The New York Times* exposé served as a vivid reminder that police discretion must be kept under restraints. The Fourth Amendment is not merely a relic recalling that the British on the eve of the American Revolution violated the common-law right of people to be secure in the privacy of their homes against the arbitrary invasion of law-enforcement officials. Unlike the Third Amendment's protection against the quartering of troops, which is a relic, the Fourth is a vital and continually necessary guarantee that imposes a strait jacket on the police in order to maintain freedom. Judicial enforcement of the Fourth undoubtedly hampers even competent, trained officers and benefits criminals; but the same may be said with equal validity about the Bill of Rights generally. There is no way to maintain freedom and the right to privacy without hamstringing the police. If they are not answerable to constitutional limitations, we would lose far more than we would gain. Those who favor broader police powers in the war against crime, in order to protect society, employ the rhetoric of ridicule to undermine the Fourth Amendment. Its judicial enforcement, they say, rests on "technicalities," although they are quite adept at inventing their own technicalities to find ways around the dictates of the Fourth Amendment. Their technicalities, which they invariably think of as reasonable exceptions, are blind to the policies underlying the amendment and jeopardize the security of the society which zealous police action frequently assaults.

The Fourth Amendment states:

> The right of the people to be secure in their persons, houses, papers, and effects, against unreasonable searches and seizures, shall not be violated, and no warrants shall issue, but upon probable cause, supported by Oath or affirmation, and particularly describing the place to be searched, and the persons or things to be seized.

The amendment lays down no absolute rule. It does not ban all searches and seizures, only "unreasonable" ones. The standard of reasonableness obviously allows for considerable latitude of discretionary judgment, initially on the part of the police and later on the part of judges who must evaluate whether the state lawfully got evidence it seeks to use to prove criminality. "What is a reasonable search," the Supreme Court has said, "is not determined by any fixed formula. The Constitution does not define what are 'unreasonable' searches and, regrettably, in our discipline we have no ready litmus-paper test."[3]

The standard of reasonableness is not the only issue in a Fourth Amendment case. The textual omissions of the amendment are significant. It declares only two broad principles—no unreasonable searches and seizures and no warrants except specific ones issued on "probable cause"—which is definable with the same opacity as "unreasonable."[4] The amendment does not include sanctions for its violation, leaving the issue in doubt. It does not state that a court must suppress illegally obtained evidence, or allow a suit for damages against the offending police officers, or permit their prosecution, or provide some other remedy. The amendment does not even say that only a court may determine probable cause for the issuance of a search warrant. According to the Supreme Court, "the point of the Fourth Amendment, which often is not grasped by zealous officers, is not that it denies law enforcement the support of the usual inferences which reasonable men draw from evidence. Its protection consists in requiring that those inferences be drawn by a neutral and detached magistrate instead of being judged by the officer engaged in the often competitive enterprise of ferreting out crime." If the police have the authority to decide that the evidence is adequate to establish probable cause, thereby justifying their search without a warrant, their authority "would reduce the Amendment to a nullity and leave the people's homes secure only in the discretion of police officers."[5]

There are, nevertheless, circumstances that justify warrantless searches. As a matter of fact, "the search warrant is rarely used."[6] An overwhelming majority of police searches, at least 90 percent of those that come to the attention of courts, are warrantless.[7] That is a staggering fact. A police officer may engage in a search without prior approval of a magistrate if the search is incident to a lawful arrest, or is conducted under emergency conditions, or has the voluntary consent of the party searched. When making an arrest, an officer may search suspects and the immediately surrounding vicinity for weapons and evidence of crime. He may also seize evidence and weapons in plain view. If the opportunity for a seizure will be lost unless the police act swiftly, they need not apply for a warrant. An officer may always conduct a search to protect himself and others, or to prevent the loss or destruction of evidence of a crime. Obviously, an officer in "hot pursuit" or faced with some exigency cannot be expected to call time out while he obtains a warrant. Searches of vehicles that can drive off with the fruits of a crime also fall within the list of exceptions to the constitutional requirement of a warrant. However, warrantless searches are usually invalid unless conducted at the same time as an arrest; a delayed search made at leisure, well after an arrest or a seizure, is generally unlawful.[8]

When the police violate the Fourth Amendment, their victim has no effective legal redress. The law on the books seems to promise both criminal and civil remedies, but the law in practice belies the promise. Complaining to the police that they have acted illegally is not likely to result in a criminal prosecution. A police captain or a district attorney will not take criminal action against a subordinate. Prosecutors do not prosecute the police. Even if a prosecutor is not himself involved in the criminal behavior of the police, he cannot survive in his job by damaging the intimate relationship he must maintain with other law-enforcement agencies. Nor would a prosecutor relish the thought of going before a jury in a public trial to obtain a verdict of guilty against an officer who has criminally trespassed against a citizen of unsavory reputation or record. A jury will condone the mistake of an overzealous officer if the prosecutor cannot prove that he acted wantonly or maliciously. Most states do not even have criminal sanctions that relate to unreasonable searches and seizures. Those that do, require either proof of malicious procurement of a search warrant or proof of willful excess of authority in the execution of a warrant. Very few states impose criminal liability for a warrantless search or a search with an invalid warrant, and their laws repose quietly on their books.[9]

The federal criminal law is not much more than a sham either. There are three criminal statutes of relevance. Since 1921 a federal agent who conducts a warrantless search of a residence, or "maliciously and without reasonable cause" conducts a warrantless search of any other place, may be fined $1,000 for a first offense and for a second may be fined and imprisoned for not more than one year.[10] That law is practically a dead letter. The Department of Justice did not even enforce it during the prohibition era when warrantless searches by federal agents were common. Another federal law imposes the same misdemeanor penalty against a local, state, or federal officer who executes a search warrant with willful excess of authority or unnecessary severity.[11] That law, too, remains unenforced. A federal civil-rights act that dates back to 1866 is scarcely more effective in vindicating the right of privacy against unreasonable searches and seizures. One reason is that the prosecution has the burden of proving willfulness.[12]

In 1973 the Department of Justice obtained from a federal grand jury indictments against eight federal agents and three local policemen in connection with sensationally notorious drug raids in Collinsville, Illinois. The prosecution was as extraordinary as the raids themselves. The officers, who had neither warrants nor the permission of their superiors, broke into private homes in the middle of the night, smashing down doors, ransacking the houses, destroying furniture, and brutalizing the families with guns, handcuffs, obscenities, and threats of death. Moreover, the victims were innocent and the officers had the wrong addresses. In the face of adverse national publicity, the United States had no choice except to prosecute.[13] But, short of an unreasonable search that is so violent, publicized, and mistaken, criminal sanctions do not deter violations of the Fourth Amendment.

Nor do civil suits for money damages. Unless the police misbehave as egregiously as during the Collinsville raids, no jury, state or federal, will likely award compensation to the victim of policemen who act in the line of duty. Police infractions of the Fourth Amendment almost always strike suspected criminals whom juries compare unfavorably with an officer of the law defending himself against a suit for trespass, assault, or battery. His victim will probably not even bring the suit. He may fear police reprisals; the police can trump up charges of disorderly conduct or resisting arrest, or engage in various forms of intimidation. A plaintiff with the means and foolhardiness to sue is not likely to find a lawyer because damage suits against policemen do no build reputations, nor are they financially rewarding. The law limits damages to pecuniary loss of property unless the plaintiff can prove malice or actual physical harm. Further, the policeman's salary is too little to justify much more than psychic compensation in the form of a nominal award. All in all, as the author of an authoritative study said, the civil suit is a "completely impotent" remedy for violations of the Fourth Amendment as far as state laws are concerned.[14]

Federal law presents only a slightly more promising situation and possesses all the traps and complexities of a civil suit in a state court. No federal statute authorizes a damage suit against federal officers for unreasonable searches, although the laws of the states, in theory, permit suits against federal officers, and there is, ironically, a federal statute that allows suits against state officers in federal courts.[15] In 1961 the Supreme Court held that although a policeman is liable for damages to a victim of an illegal search, the policeman's employer—the state or municipality—is not liable, thus making the suit not worth pursuing.[16] Ten years later, the Court estimated that if the number of cases under this federal statute increased by 900 percent, "every federal district judge could expect to try one such case every 13 years."[17] The occasion for making that estimate was a path-breaking case in which the Court held that despite the absence of a federal statute making federal officers liable for damages caused by violations of the Fourth Amendment, the amendment itself permits damage suits for injuries sustained in an illegal federal search. That decision may eventually alter the constitutional law of search and seizure by providing an effective remedy for lawless police conduct, but for the time being the decision does no more than make federal officers personally liable for money damages in the same way that state and local officers have been—without effect—under a federal statute.[18]

The Court's unprecedented decision came in the case of an ex-convict, Webster Bivens, who tried to sue six agents of the Federal Bureau of Narcotics. The legal troubles of Bivens, who in this instance was innocent, illustrate the plight of the victim of an illegal federal search. In 1965 the agents entered his apartment without probable cause or a warrant for arrest or search. They arrested him for an alleged narcotics violation, manacled him in front of his wife and children, and searched his entire apartment. Although they found nothing to confirm their suspicions, they took him to a federal courthouse where they interrogated, booked, and strip-searched him. Eventually they dropped the charges against him. Bivens sued them in a federal district court; he sought $15,000 in damages from each for inflicting mental anguish. There was no way for him to sue the United States government because of its sovereign immunity.

The district court dismissed the suit on the ground that Bivens had no basis for a cause of action. If the search was lawful, the suit was without foundation. If it was unlawful, the agents did not act on behalf of the government. Since the Fourth Amendment prohibits unreasonable searches only by the government, not by private persons, the agents were not liable. The prestigious Court of Appeals for the Second Circuit sustained that judgment. In 1971 the Supreme Court handed down its surprising decision reversing both lower federal courts. The case went back to the district court, which again dismissed the suit, this time on the theory that the federal agents had official immunity that barred such suits against them. In 1972 the Second Circuit ruled that the agents possessed no official immunity. Thus, after seven years of litigation, Bivens won the right to sue the agents, but he had not won his case against them. If the agents can prove that they believed in good faith that their conduct was lawful, they will not be liable for damages. Even if they are liable, the law prevents damages for mental anguish unless Bivens can prove that the agents harmed him or acted out of malice against him personally, rather than out of a sense of public duty. Until such time as the Supreme Court rules, or Congress provides, that the government is liable for substantial damages whenever a plaintiff can prove an illegal search, there will be no deterrent effect on official misconduct under the Fourth Amendment and no effective remedy to redress a violation of it. Accordingly, *Bivens* v. *Six Unknown Named Agents of the Federal Bureau of Narcotics* remains merely a gesture in the right direction.[19]

THE EXCLUSIONARY RULE

The other direction that the law takes for ordinary violations of the Fourth Amendment is the exclusionary rule. The Court inferred that rule from the amendment fifty-seven years before *Bivens*. In *Weeks* v. *United States,* decided in 1914, the Court unanimously held that evidence of criminality obtained in violation of the amendment must be excluded from trials in federal courts.[20] In 1961 the Court for the first time held that the exclusionary rule applies to all courts, state as well as federal.[21] Suppressing evidence that is real, reliable, and relevant seriously weakens the truth-finding purpose of a trial, cripples the prosecution, and can result in acquittals of the guilty. Yet, admitting unconstitutional evidence as proof of guilt sullies the judicial process and allows the police to act as if they are above the law that they are supposed to enforce. The Fourth Amendment, like much of the Bill of Rights, deliberately built tensions into the constitutional system in the belief that restraints upon government might inhibit its abridgments of freedom and privacy.[22] The courts alone must police the police, because no other agency of government can or will. To deter lawless police action by making the police observe the law, the Court devised the exclusionary rule of the Fourth Amendment that has dominated the constitutional law of search and seizure since 1961. "Its purpose," the Court has said, "is to deter—to compel respect for the consti-

Elkins vs. U.S.

tutional guaranty in the only effectively available way—by removing the incentive to disregard it."[23] There is another consideration. If courts permit the government to profit from the fruits of unconstitutional searches and seizures, the courts themselves become accomplices to the criminal conduct of the police and make a mockery of the Fourth Amendment. The admission of illegally obtained evidence would sanction violations of constitutionally protected rights, rendering those rights "an empty promise."[24] Finally, the Court has claimed that there is little if any justification for the assumption that the exclusionary rule fetters law enforcement. Noting that the rule had long been the law of the federal courts, the Supreme Court cited J. Edgar Hoover as its authority for the view that the rule has not made the Federal Bureau of Investigation ineffective and has not disrupted the administration of criminal justice in the federal courts.[25]

There are exclusionary rules with respect to Fifth and Sixth Amendment rights, too. Coerced confessions that violate the constitutional command that no person shall be compelled to be a witness against himself in a criminal case are inadmissible as evidence. Evidence obtained in violation of the right to the effective assistance of counsel at any critical stage of a prosecution is also inadmissible. If the police fail to inform a suspect of his right to remain silent and his right to counsel, any incriminating statements that he makes during a custodial interrogation are excluded from the consideration of a jury.[26] If the police exhibit an accused person at a lineup for the purpose of obtaining an eyewitness identification against him, his counsel must be present to monitor the proceeding in order to inhibit undue police suggestiveness and to preserve the right to a meaningful cross-examination at his trial.[27] Excluding defense counsel from a critical stage of the prosecution means excluding the evidence obtained at that stage. The right to confront and cross-examine prosecution witnesses also makes inadmissible in evidence any hearsay testimony that is untrustworthy.[28] Exclusionary rules envelop large areas of criminal justice, but with the possible exception of a coerced confession that is true, the evidence excluded is, in legal theory, of doubtful probative value.

When the police conduct an illegal search, the evidence that they seize—a bloody knife, a packet of heroin, or counterfeit plates—is as trustworthy and material as if the search had been legal. Excluding it from a trial may turn a guilty person loose on the ground that the police have intruded upon his right to privacy. The more rational course would be to use the evidence and then punish the errant policeman either civilly or criminally or both; but, as the Court said, the exclusionary rule is "the only effectively available way" to compel respect for the constitutional right against unreasonable searches and seizures, and it is the way that preserves the integrity of the trial process.[29] When the Court first applied the rule to state courts, it said:

> There are those who say, as did Justice (then Judge) Cardozo, that under our constitutional exclusionary doctrine "[t]he criminal is to go free because the constable has blundered." . . . In some cases this will undoubtedly be the result. But, . . . "there is another consideration—the imperative of judicial integrity." . . . The criminal goes free, if he must, but it is the law that sets him free. Nothing can destroy a government more quickly than its failure to observe its own laws, or worse, its disregard of the charter of its own existence. As Mr. Justice Brandeis, dissenting, said . . . "Our government is the potent, the omnipresent teacher. For good or for ill, it teaches the whole people by its example. . . . If the government becomes a lawbreaker, it breeds contempt for law. . . ."[30]

The purpose of the paradoxical rule is to deter lawless police practice, but the impact of the rule misses the police and falls upon prosecutors. The purpose is to compel respect for the judicial process, but respect does not come easily when the courts suppress evidence of value and, as a result, have to turn the guilty free. The exclusionary rule cannot inspire respect for the amendment or the courts if, as Burger has said, "Suppressing unchallenged truth has set guilty criminals free. . . ."[31] Burger is the Court's most persistent and vehement critic of the rule. In *Bivens* he traveled far from the issue of the case to incorporate in his dissent an extended denunciation of the rule in an effort to prove that it exacts too high a price from society even as it fails to deter the police. If the rule does not in fact deter the police and is a failure, hard-liners on law and order, like Burger, would let sleeping dogmas lie. The rule deters not the police but the conviction of the guilty. That is the real reason that the rule is under heavy fire. It works effectively, but against the wrong target. The police can and do flout the Fourth Amendment with impunity, notwithstanding the exclusionary rule, but the public does not understand that fact.

Moreover, the rule does not significantly cut down on illegal searches. It works only in the striking minority of criminal prosecutions that go all the way to trial. Most cases, perhaps 90 percent, end not in trial but in pleas of guilty.[32] The exact figure varies with the nature of the crime charged and with the varying practices of the many jurisdictions in the country, but by any reckoning the exclusionary rule applies to a trivial fraction of all prosecutions. There is also a huge discrepancy between the total number of arrests and prosecutions. Also, many persons whom the police arrest are not charged with crime, and prosecutors dismiss the charges against many who are charged.

The exclusionary rule does not apply in the very cases that most cry out for a remedy. A number of these involve illegal searches against innocent persons. Dismissing their cases because of innocence means that the exclusionary rule never comes into play. Others involve illegal searches that the police make for a purpose other than collecting evidence for a prosecution. If the goal of an illegal search and seizure is unrelated to trial and punishment, police behavior cannot become a Fourth Amendment issue. Warren once admitted, "Regardless how effective the rule may be where obtaining conviction is an important objective of the police, it is powerless to deter invasions of constitutionally guaranteed rights where the police either have no interest in prosecuting or are willing to forgo successful prosecution in the interest of serving some other goal."[33] To the police and their victims, arrest followed by an illegal search and seizure is a punitive end in itself. The police utilize that tactic to control victimless crimes, such as gambling and prostitution, or to confiscate weapons, contraband, and stolen property, or to maintain a highly visible profile for the purpose of deterring crime or satisfying a public clamor for aggressive police action.[34] The public tends to worry more about the impotence of the police than about their abuse of powers. Without getting into the seamy side of the matter, Burger pointed out, in his *Bivens* dissent, that the deterrent value of the exclusionary rule "is diluted by the fact that there are large areas of police activity that do not result in criminal prosecutions—hence the rule has virtually no application and no effect in such situations."[35]

The rule does not personally affect the officer whose misconduct leads to the suppression of evidence. His superiors do not discipline him; prosecutors do not prosecute him; and he is practically judgment-proof against a civil suit for damages. Neither the trial judge who suppresses the evidence, nor the appellate court which may do so in the event that the trial judge has not, nor the prosecutor who cannot introduce the evidence, explains to the policeman the error of his ways so that he may reform his behavior in the future. Burger has pointed out that the "presumed educational effect of judicial opinions is also reduced by the long time lapse—often several years —between the original police action and its final judicial evaluation."[36] If a guilty policeman should hear that a court has excluded evidence that was the fruit of his infringement on the Fourth Amendment, he will probably have forgotten the details of the event. If the message does get through to him and his fellow officers, there are no incentives or sanctions that will alter his future conduct.

The police officer responds not to judicial decisions, which he regards as unrealistic if they thwart him, but to the policies of his department, the approval of his fellow officers and superiors, and to the situation on his beat. When he deals with people who, from his perspective, are criminals, he sees the reasonableness of his search and seizure in a way that a court is not likely to appreciate. He has a low tolerance for procedural niceties. Confident that he is doing his job by protecting society against criminals, he will, if necessary —and with the approval or advice of his superiors and of prosecutors—lie about his conduct when making out his report of a search and seizure or when testifying in court. In a swearing contest between an officer of the law and a criminal defendant whose respectability is not beyond dispute, a judge and jury will tend to believe the testimony of the officer. He will report that he made a warrantless search and seizure because emergency circumstances gave him no choice, or because the search was incident to an arrest on probable cause, or because the evidence that he seized was in plain view or within reach or about to be destroyed or thrown away. When prosecution and conviction is the object of a search and seizure, deliberately perjured police testimony, tempered by a disposition to rationalize conduct that others may not understand, is common.[37] So, too, is evasion or circumvention of the exclusionary rule by tactics of search and seizure that will pass a reviewing court. The police may, for example, arrange to make a legitimate arrest at a place where they can plausibly conduct a warrantless search incident to that arrest. They construct cases in advance and reconstruct them after the event to avoid the impact of the rule.

When from the standpoint of a court the police miscalculate, the impact of the exclusionary rule hits the prosecutor, who is seeking a conviction. Dissenting in *Bivens,* Burger observed that appellate courts sometimes assume that the prosecutor's office is responsible for illegal searches and seizures by the police:

> But the prosecutor who loses his case because of police misconduct is not an official in the police department; he can rarely set in motion any corrective action or administrative penalties. Moreover, he does not have control or direction over police procedures or police actions that lead to the exclusion of evidence. It is the rare exception when a prosecutor takes part in arrests, searches, or seizures so that he can guide police action.[38]

Thus, the prosecutor, who is not responsible for the police, bears the punishment for their misconduct.

In the most systematic and objective study of the exclusionary rule, which Burger cited with approval, Dallin H. Oaks, the author, summarized his findings as follows:

> As a device for directly deterring illegal searches and seizures by the police, the exclusionary rule is a failure. There is no reason to expect the rule to have any direct effect on the overwhelming majority of police conduct that is not meant to result in prosecutions, and there is hardly any evidence that the rule exerts any deterrent effect on the small fraction of law enforcement activity that is aimed at prosecution. What is known about the deterrent effect of sanctions suggests that the exclusionary rule operates under conditions that are extremely unfavorable for deterring the police. The harshest criticism of the rule is that it is ineffective. It is the sole means of enforcing the essential guarantees of freedom from unreasonable arrests and searches and seizures by law enforcement officers, and it is a failure in that vital task.

The use of the exclusionary rule imposes excessive costs on the criminal justice system. It provides no recompense for the innocent and it frees the guilty. It creates the occasion and incentive for large-scale lying by law enforcement officers. It diverts the focus of the criminal prosecution from the guilt or innocence of the defendant to a trial of the police. Only a system with limitless patience with irrationality could tolerate the fact that where there has been one wrong, the defendant's, he will be punished, but where there have been two wrongs, the defendant's and the officer's, both will go free. This would not be an excessive cost for an effective remedy against police misconduct, but it is a prohibitive price to pay for an illusory one.[39]

Significantly, neither Oaks nor Burger advocates the abolition of the exclusionary rule—at least, not until an effective substitute remedy can replace it as a means of enforcing the commands of the Fourth Amendment.

Burger dissented in *Bivens* because he believed that the Court, by inferring from the amendment a right to bring a civil suit for damages against federal officers who violated it, was improperly engaging in judicial legislation. Black and Blackmun, who also dissented, agreed with that charge. Burger proposed that Congress should enact a statute establishing "an administrative or quasi-judicial remedy against the government itself to afford compensation and restitution for persons whose Fourth Amendment rights have been violated."[40] Congress has not responded. If it did enact such a statute, its effectiveness as a deterrent to lawless search and seizure by federal officers would depend upon the plaintiff's burden of proof and the yardstick for determining compensation. If the plaintiff had to establish willfulness, malice, or physical injury in order to make out his case, or if the statute allowed compensation only for actual damage to property or required a nearly impossible showing of mental anguish, the statute would neither deter federal officers nor protect Fourth Amendment rights. At best it would provide a remedy only against federal violations. There is no reason to assume, as Burger did, that all the states will follow the federal model. Infractions by federal officers are few in number compared to those of state and local officers.

Whatever the future brings in the form of changed remedies, for the present as in the past, the Court has, for all practical purposes, only its exclusionary rule with all its faults. In the more than half century of the history of the rule, there may have been, as Burger alleged, "thousands of cases in which the criminal was set free because the constable blundered" and no benefits to the innocent.[41] But the Court has no choice; it is stuck with the rule for lack of a better alternative. In the absence of meaningful, substitute remedies, the exclusionary rule has great symbolic value at the same time that it has the qualities of a legal fiction that requires of society a heavy expense for attaching some credibility to the Fourth Amendment.

WARRANTLESS SEARCHES AND PROBABLE CAUSE

The Difference Between Houses and Cars

Vale v. *Louisiana* was the first search-and-seizure case decided by the Court under Burger.[42] He joined Black in a dissent from an opinion that continued a course, plotted by the Warren Court, for restricting the area of permissible search.[43] Louisiana had convicted Vale for felonious possession of heroin. The police, who had a warrant for his arrest but none for a search of his house, kept Vale's house under surveillance. After observing him make what they believed to have been a sale of narcotics to a known drug addict while the addict was in his car, which was parked near the house, the police closed in. They arrested Vale and the addict, who quickly swallowed something, and immediately conducted a warrantless search of Vale's house for drugs. In a rear bedroom they found a cache of narcotics.

The Court, voting 6-to-2, ruled that Louisiana had committed constitutional error in admitting into evidence the fruits of an illegal search. Stewart, for the majority, declared that no precedent could sustain the validity of a search in this case. For a search of a dwelling to be valid as an incident of arrest, the arrest must take place inside the dwelling. The probable cause for the search, according to Stewart, did not justify a warrantless search of the house because the police made the arrest outside. The majority of the Court saw no exigent circumstance that would bring the case within the few exceptions to the general rule requiring a search warrant. The police were not responding to an emergency, nor in hot pursuit of a fleeing suspect; nor was there any danger that a confederate within the empty house would destroy the illegal drugs. The officers, who had obtained the arrest warrant in advance, should have also obtained a search warrant.

The dissenters disagreed on the facts. They found the warrantless search to be reasonable. Black claimed that the police could not have known that no one else was home when they entered the house to search and seize evidence that someone within, observing the arrest from a window, might attempt to destroy. More likely, however, the police knew that Vale was alone at the time. Having had the house under surveillance, they must have seen his mother and brother leave earlier. But both returned just a few minutes after the police entered the house. If the police had then left to get a search warrant, Vale's relatives might have destroyed the evidence. So Black reasoned, but there is nothing in the record that indicates whether they knew that Vale had heroin hidden in the house or where it was. According to Black, no probable cause for a search had existed before the alleged street sale, so the officers could not have obtained a search warrant in advance. The reasonable belief of the police that Vale's confederates might destroy vital evidence was the exigent circumstance that justified the search, whether or not it was incident to the arrest.

Black concluded his dissent bluntly:

> This case raises most graphically the question how does a policeman protect evidence necessary to the State if he must leave the premises to get a warrant, allowing the evidence he seeks to be destroyed. The Court's answer to that question makes unnecessarily difficult the conviction of those who prey upon society.[44]

Given the state's failure to prove the warrantless search of a home reasonable, Black's law-and-order question-and-answer was both misleading and unnecessarily alarming. The Court decided the case properly, though a contrary decision would hardly have jeopardized the sanctity of the home. There is no certainty that the police knew the house was empty when they entered it, and the sudden return of Vale's relatives might have made the police reasonably apprehensive that the evidence they were sure they would find might be destroyed. *Vale* is significant because it undercut the authority of an important line of lower federal court and state court cases that had upheld warrantless searches of houses or rooms apart from the place of arrest.[45]

The Court announced its decision in *Vale* on the same day as it settled *Chambers v. Maroney*, this time on the side of the police.[46] The opinions in the two cases read as if different courts had sat in judgment, but one case involved a house, the other a car, and the Court has always allowed greater latitude for warrantless searches of cars.[47] The problem in *Chambers* was that the police did not search the car on the spot. After the arrest, they drove it to a police station and searched it there, finding the evidence that they expected without troubling to get a warrant first. Thus, there was no way to justify the search as incident to the arrest. Undeniably, probable cause for the search existed, but as White, for the Court, conceded, "Only in exigent circumstances"—which the facts did not show in this case—"will the judgment of the police as to probable cause serve as a sufficient authorization for a search."[48] Generally, a magistrate must determine probable cause and authorize a warrant. Here, the police seized the car without a warrant and searched it later, at their convenience, without a warrant. White declared, however, that there was "no difference between on the one hand seizing and holding a car before presenting the probable cause issue to a magistrate and on the other hand carrying out an immediate search without a warrant." Either course was "reasonable under the Fourth Amendment."[49]

But the police had followed neither course in this case. White fudged the issue. He simply asserted, without support, that probable cause still existed when the car was at the police station. By then, however, the felons were in custody. By the Court's own standard of reasonableness, warrantless search is impermissible unless conducted under exigent circumstances at the time and place of arrest. In the absence of such circumstances, or a search validly incident to arrest, or consent, the police may not conduct a warrantless search of a house. The case of a car may be different if there is a danger that the robbers may drive it away with the fruits of their crime. But the "constitutional difference between houses and cars," to which White referred, did not matter in this case. If the Fourth Amendment permitted the seizure of the car, "there is little," he said, "to choose in terms of practical consequences between an immediate search without a warrant and the car's immobilization until a warrant is obtained."[50]

White's logic was irrefutable—and irrelevant. The police did not obtain that warrant, although they might have. Harlan, who was, surprisingly, the only dissenter, declared that the majority approved the search "without even an inquiry into the officers' ability promptly to take their case before a magistrate."[51] The Court, as Harlan believed, needlessly sacrificed the interest in privacy that the Fourth Amendment protects. And yet, if the police could have seized the car without a warrant, as Harlan conceded, and if they could have searched it on the spot, the requirement of a warrant seems like a *pro forma* technicality of slight cause for Harlan's concern that the Court had created "a special rule for automobile searches that is seriously at odds with generally applied Fourth Amendment principles."[52] Harlan's most likely allies in this case—Douglas, Brennan, and Marshall—sided with the majority. Yet, his lone viewpoint is more persuasive than the evasive majority's. Until this case, mere probable cause for a search as judged by a police officer did not by itself justify a warrantless search. The case is important for its implied rule that exigent circumstances need not any longer justify the warrantless search of a car.

Taken together, *Vale* and *Chambers* spread the breach between the warrantless search of a residence, which the Court will severely scrutinize, and the warrantless search of a car, which the Court will almost presume valid unless there is no connection between the arrest and the search. *Chambers* emasculated recent decisions of three federal circuit courts and half a dozen state courts that voided the warrantless search of cars at the police station after the arrest of the occupants.[53] *Vale* and *Chambers* added to the confusion that the Court's search-and-seizure decisions have often provoked. *Chambers* does not help the police to understand when they cannot search a car. If there is no violation of the Fourth Amendment by a warrantless search of a car in police custody, when its occupants are in jail and there is no possible loss of the evidence, what limits are there on automobile searches?

After *Whitely* v. *Warden,* however, the question was whether any warrantless search of a car would meet the Court's approval.[54] The police must have been bewildered. Whitely was a burglar who, with a partner, robbed a hardware store. They committed the crime in a rural area where most people knew each other and the local sheriff was an old hand at his job. Acting on a tip, the sheriff got an arrest warrant from a justice of the peace and broadcast a police radio bulletin calling for the arrest of the suspects. The bulletin gave their names and described them, the car they were probably driving, and the items stolen, including old coins. An officer relying on the bulletin, but having no warrant, arrested the men, searched their car, and found irrefutable proof of their crime—burglars' tools, a loaded gun, and the stolen items. The state convicted Whitely on that evidence and on the testimony of his partner, who turned prosecution's witness. Whitely objected that the trial court should have suppressed the evidence, because the search and seizure depended on an arrest warrant issued without probable cause. The Court, voting 6-to-3, reversed the conviction. There are few better examples of the exclusionary rule defeating justice or of the Court making itself look ridiculous by arid judicial logic. Doubtlessly, the Court intended its opinion to defend the integrity of the process by which officers obtain arrest warrants. But the Court exacted a steep price for the formalities that it demanded.

Harlan, for the majority, reasoned that the uncorroborated tip of an informant is an insufficient basis for the arrest warrant. The justice of the peace had issued it on nothing more than the sheriff's complaint, without sufficient information to support his own independent and disinterested judgment. That the information proved accurate enough to identify the burglars and their car, and led to the recovery of the stolen property, seemed to be of no importance. Harlan declared that "the discoveries of an illegal search cannot be used to validate the probable-cause judgment upon which the legality of the search depends."[55] The state argued futilely that the police officer who had made the arrest had sufficient information to support a finding of probable cause without a warrant. That argument stood on the proposition that a court's review of the arresting officer's assessment of probable cause for a warrantless arrest—and for a search incident to that arrest—should not be as stringent as review of a magistrate's assessment of probable cause. Harlan correctly answered that the Court had consistently rejected that argument, but his reason confounded reality: "Less stringent standards for reviewing the officer's discretion in effecting a warrantless arrest and search would discourage resort to the procedures for obtaining a warrant."[56] The fact that the justice of the peace had issued the warrant without probable cause, in the opinion of the Court, decided the case. The arrest having been illegal, the evidence seized incident to that arrest had to be excluded from the trial.

Black, supported by Burger and Blackmun, dissented. He scorched the feeble opinion of the Court which resulted, he said, in "a gross and wholly indefensible miscarriage of justice" of the sort that made "many good people believe our Court actually enjoys frustrating justice by unnecessarily turning professional criminals loose to prey upon society with impunity."[57] Black's view was that the original arrest warrant was based on probable cause; but, even if it was not, the police on mere suspicion had probable cause to stop the car and, after identifying the occupants as those described in the police radio bulletin, then had probable cause to arrest them and conduct the search. Black viewed the search as justifiable either as incident to the arrest or on the ground that moving vehicles are an exception to the usual requirement for a search warrant. "I consider it a travesty of justice to turn this man out of jail or give him a new trial," Black remarked with indignation.[58]

There should be little objection to the principle that a magistrate who must decide probable cause for issuing an arrest warrant ought to have enough information on which to make a judgment independent of the police complainant. Black, however, believed the Court applied that principle in a way that required too much—a "little trial" to determine probable cause. Curiously, he did not challenge the underlying reason advanced by Harlan for the Court's opinion—that relaxing judicial review of the officer's discretion in conducting a warrantless arrest and search "would discourage resort to the procedures for obtaining a warrant." The opposite is true. The more stringent the standards for review and the more formal the procedures, the more likely the police will find ways to circumvent the need for a warrant.

The Court's opinion hampered law-enforcement authorities.

The sheriff here acted in good faith and got a warrant. The arresting officer, wholly apart from that warrant, had probable cause for the arrest and search, and he did his job well. To dismiss his conduct as lawless and to condemn the work of the police in this case verged on the ritualistically doctrinaire. "A contrary rule," said Harlan of the Court's finding on probable cause, "would, of course, render the warrant requirements of the Fourth Amendment meaningless."[59] That judgment seems exaggerated. A contrary rule would make the amendment less effective, not meaningless, and the problem was whether its diminished effectiveness was tolerable in the face of an individual's constitutional right for protection against baseless police intrusions. Harlan was not a judge who made a practice of overstatement. He founded his apprehension about the meaninglessness of the amendment on the reasonable ground that a probable-cause hearing before a magistrate must not be a *pro forma* one in which the magistrate rubber-stamps an officer's judgment. By examining the affidavit submitted by an officer, an appellate court can determine whether the facts permitted a magistrate to conclude that probable cause for a warrant existed. But to penalize the police by holding that a magistrate had not scrutinized the facts with enough independence is comparable to penalizing a prosecutor by holding that the police obtained the evidence illegally. The sanction of the law strikes the wrong party when the police have obtained a warrant.

Warrants Based on an Informer's Tip

Whitely represents the climax of a line of cases dealing with the issue of probable cause which elusively defines the amount of evidence required for an arrest warrant or a search warrant. Traditionally the Court has pretended that there is nothing technical about the meaning of probable cause, but whether finding such a cause to be present or absent, the Court has been far more technical than its mythically "reasonable" or "prudent" man would be. Moreover, the Warren Court brought probable cause to a degree of technicality that requires rather "precise analysis" of evidence.[60] Theoretically, probable cause is sufficient cause for the belief, as determined by an independent magistrate, that the person who is the target of a warrant has committed a crime. For a reasonable man to possess such a belief, he must have more than mere suspicion but less than proof of guilt beyond a reasonable doubt. "In dealing with probable cause," the Court has unilluminatingly said, ". . . we deal with probabilities. These are not technical; they are the factual and practical considerations of everyday life on which reasonable and prudent men, not legal technicians, act." Since probable cause is "a reasonable ground for belief of guilt," it exists when an officer has personal knowledge or trustworthy information to justify the belief of a reasonable man that the party has committed a crime.[61]

The Warren Court sought inconsistently to encourage more frequent use of warrants by the police and, at the same time, to tighten the requirements for warrants. To a Court which took invasions of privacy and security more seriously than its predecessors, the circular reasoning and vague terminology of past decisions no longer seemed commendable. The Court continued to claim that magistrates must judge affidavits for search warrants in a common-sense, realistic, nontechnical fashion,[62] but in opinions of 1964 and 1969 went a long way, from the standpoint of dissenters, toward elevating the magistrate's probable-cause hearing into a mini-trial governed by strict rules of evidence. In *Aguilar* v. *Texas* (1964), the Court developed a two-pronged test for measuring the amount of evidence needed to establish probable cause.[63] The Court ruled that although hearsay information—the tip of an informer not reflecting the personal knowledge of the police—may provide the basis of an officer's affidavit for a search warrant, he must additionally state the reasons underpinning his belief that his informant is trustworthy or that his information is reliable. The *Aguilar* test sought to insure that a magistrate would have enough detail to know that he was issuing a warrant based on more than underworld rumors or the suspect's bad reputation. In *Spinelli* v. *United States* (1969), a closely divided Court expanded the *Aguilar* test, in the words of Black, dissenting, "to almost unbelievable proportions."[64] Although a meticulously detailed FBI affidavit in *Spinelli* provided corroboration of an anonymous tip, the Court insisted on a degree of corroboration that proved the truthfulness of the tip apart from the evidence that subsequently verified it. In effect, the Court escalated the constitutional requirement of probable cause to reasonably certain cause, in order to insure that a magistrate, standing between the police and the citizenry, can evaluate the facts for himself.

Whitely, under the Nixon Court, made consistent law, in the light of *Aguilar* and *Spinelli,* but those cases made the law only for the small fraction of cases in which police seek to clinch an arrest and search by securing a warrant in advance. The Court's desire to hold high the standards of the Fourth Amendment motivated this line of decisions, but its effect could spur the police to perjure themselves and to seek pretexts for avoiding search warrants before acting. There must be compelling reasons for the police making most of their searches without a warrant—reasons that relate to the law rather than just exigent circumstances or consent. There is little point in getting a warrant when an appellate court is liable to hold it unconstitutional.

The judicial logic that stuns the police and turns them against courts is present in *Whitely,* wholly apart from the fact that the decision reversed the conviction of a guilty person. Harlan reasoned that finding evidence of crime does not validate the probable cause upon which the legality of a search depends. But, obviously there was probable cause for a search that successfully uncovered incriminating evidence. In *Aguilar, Spinelli,* and *Whitely* the police were not charging into the homes of innocent persons, nor conducting fishing raids to run down rumors or suspicions. The problem is not that probable cause did not exist, as Harlan reasoned in *Whitely,* but that the legal foundation for it was too sparse or that the officer's paperwork was faulty.

If the evidence was too sparse, a court must reverse the conviction because the probable cause that exists in reality does not exist as a matter of law. However, if the law corresponded with reality or possessed the practicality or nontechnicality that the Court insistently alleges, the law would validate a fruitful search based on a warrant. If, however, the officer's paperwork was faulty, the reason is that his affidavit did not provide enough hard facts to convince a magistrate that he had creditable information based on a credible source. In that event, the magistrate's interrogation can establish whether the officer has sufficient evidence to justify a warrant and, if so, can help the officer swear out a valid affidavit—one that states the probable cause to the satisfaction of a reviewing court. There is something wrong with the system if the magistrate from whom he seeks a warrant cannot explain the law to him, so that his affidavit will withstand subsequent judicial scrutiny. In any case, to state that finding incriminating evidence bears no relation to the legality of a search conducted with a warrant is to oversimplify.

When an appellate court excludes evidence long after an illegal search, the officer who made it may never know or understand his error. If probable cause exists in fact but not in law, or if the magistrate cannot help correct the officer's administrative error, or if error is a constitutional one for which the magistrate is to blame (though the police, the prosecutor, and the public suffer the consequences), then courts of law are in trouble.

In *United States* v. *Harris,* decided only a few months after *Whitely,* the Court veered sharply and suddenly away from an old trail to a new one for finding probable cause in cases where warrants rested on tips from anonymous informers.[65] The case fragmented the Court even more than its 5-to-4 vote suggested. Douglas, Brennan, and Marshall united behind Harlan's dissent, championing the principles of *Aguilar-Spinelli-Whitely.* To the dissenters, not even the precedents that predated the Warren Court justified the reinstatement of a conviction which the lower court had reversed. The majority members of the Court agreed only in the result—reinstating the conviction. Each of the five recorded a different view. Burger represented a plurality that changed with each part of his opinion. Blackmun, who joined Burger, would have gone farther by overruling *Spinelli;* Black agreed with both, but would have overruled *Aguilar,* too. White and Stewart concurred in different sections of the Chief Justice's opinion. The resulting chaos left the law inconclusive, but the Court had clearly shifted. Burger's opinion, though vigorously claiming to rely on a common-sense, practical approach, makes technical distinctions that would glaze the mind of a medieval scholastic. To the extent that Burger sought to reconcile his views with the precedents, he wrote constitutional humbug, as Harlan exquisitely proved in his point-by-point rebuttal. If the question one asks is not whether Burger integrated *Harris* with previous law, but whether the Court reached the right result, regardless of its reasoning, the answer calls for restrained but apprehensive applause.

It calls for applause because the Court validated the seizure and use of physical evidence that proved the defendant's criminality after a search based on a warrant. Restraint is called for because Burger botched the opinion. Apprehensiveness is called for because the Court went too far in deferring to the police assessment of probable cause and too far in authorizing magistrates to credit unverified hearsay. Had the Chief Justice massed a majority for his constitutional views, as well as for the final judgment, *Harris* would have had a transforming effect that endangered a scrupulously enforced warrant system. *Harris* stood for eliminating the requirement that the police must demonstrate the truthfulness of an anonymous informant's tip or his personal credibility. It stood for the implication that a person with a bad reputation does not have Fourth Amendment rights worthy of respect. It stood for the power of the police to search on the basis of a suspicion reinforced by information whose probative value a magistrate cannot test. It stood for the proposition that magistrates may accept the word of the police without conducting an independent evaluation of the worth of their determination that probable cause exists. In place of the amount and kind of corroboration demanded by *Aguilar-Spinelli-Whitely,* the Court permitted the police to rely on an informant's tip when it matched their suspicion and revealed the informant himself to be a criminal suspect.

To epitomize *Harris* so baldly ignores Burger's make-believe that he rooted his opinion in past cases. He even passed *Aguilar* off as a case that "in no way departed from . . . sound principles" of "realistic" and "commonsense" precedents in which the Court had condemned the issuance of warrants based on nothing more than a "mere affirmation of suspicion and belief" on the part of the police.[66] If *Aguilar* had done no more than that, it had unnecessarily excited angry dissent. If the warrant here, in *Harris,* had issued on something more than suspicion and belief, the *Harris* dissenters were also alarmed unnecessarily. They did not, of course, share Burger's contempt for *Spinelli.* Despite its teachings, the Chief Justice regarded as "probative information" an officer's assertions that (1) the defendant "had a reputation with me for over 4 years as being a trafficker of nontaxpaid distilled spirits"; (2) "over this period I have received numerous information [*sic*] from all types of persons as to his activities"; (3) another officer once found "illicit whiskey in a building under Harris' control"; and (4) an unnamed informant claimed to have bought such whiskey from Harris and knew others who had done the same.[67] The affidavit provided no proof for any of these claims. "To the extent that *Spinelli* prohibits the use of such probative information," Burger extravagantly declared, "it has no support in our prior cases, logic, or experience and we decline to apply it to preclude a magistrate from relying on a law enforcement officer's knowledge of a suspect's reputation."[68] Harlan parsed that sentence word by word in connection with prior cases, found it groundless, and exposed the absence of the "probative information" on which Burger relied. Only two members of the Court joined Burger's treatment of *Spinelli*.

Burger found an additional reason for crediting the informant's tip: Because his confession was against his penal interest, it justified a finding of probable cause. From the magistrate's standpoint, of course, the tip was uncorroborated hearsay that could have no evidentiary value at a trial and could have been bought by a police promise not to prosecute. Such objections did not faze Burger. Harlan replied that the prosecution had not even suggested that the informant's assertions deserved credit merely because they constituted a confession of crime. To credit unsubstantiated hearsay by an anonymous informer had no support in precedent, particularly when the informant stood to gain police absolution for his crime and, therefore, stood in no jeopardy. Thus, the fact that his tip seemed to be against his penal interest was not in itself significant. The crux of the controversy, according to Harlan, was whether the tip, or the tipster himself, was believable. If so, the warrant was valid. On the basis of the affidavit, however, as Harlan proved beyond doubt, the magistrate had no evidence whatever to make his own assessment. Logic and prior cases supported Harlan. Experience, though, was on Burger's side: The tip proved to be reliable.

In effect, *Harris,* like its predecessors in *Aguilar, Spinelli,* and *Whitely,* raised the question whether a search is illegal on ground that the affidavit of the officer does not establish probable cause as a matter of fact or experience. The dissenters claimed that a contrary finding would not hamper "fair and vigorous" law enforcement. The one theme that ricocheted throughout the dissent was that the affidavit was "barren of anything that enabled the magistrate to judge for himself of the credibility of the informant."[69] Harlan insisted that the magistrate must make his own judgment on more than the say-so of the police and that they could comply with the Fourth Amendment without compromising their effectiveness. They could bring the informant before the magistrate, allowing him the opportunity of assessing his probable veracity, or, if the informant's identity must be kept secret, the police should corroborate his tip. Presumably they might have done so by any of the usual techniques—surveillance, infiltration, or entrapment. The dissenters in *Harris* would have accepted corroboration that fell far short of proof. The police had only to state their reasons for believing that the informant was trustworthy and that he had no motivation to lie. To Harlan, police testimony to the effect that the informant had no inducement to cooperate would also have been persuasive.

In sum, *Harris* encouraged the police to take the word of informants rather than find substantiating evidence, and it diminished the obligation of a magistrate to determine probable cause for himself. *Harris* tended to allow a magistrate to rubber-stamp assessments of probable cause by the police when they backed up their suspicions of a disreputable person with a tip from someone criminally involved with him.

Limitations on Warrantless Searches

The Court decided *Harris* and *Coolidge* v. *New Hampshire*[70] just a week apart, but Stewart's plurality opinion in *Coolidge* was a light-year away from Burger's in *Harris*. The Court careened from one end of the spectrum of Fourth Amendment law to the other, as it had on the day a year earlier when deciding *Vale* and *Maroney*. *Coolidge* was a major triumph for those who would hold the police to a strict accounting under a generous interpretation of the right to be free from unreasonable searches and seizures. The dissenters' preference for a more permissive attitude toward the police prompted a stricter reading of the Constitution. Significantly, the controlling opinion reflected the mood of the Court's first important Fourth Amendment case eighty-five years earlier, from which Stewart quoted a famous passage:

It may be that it is the obnoxious thing in its mildest and least repulsive form; but illegitimate and unconstitutional practices get their first footing in that way, namely, by silent approaches and slight deviations from legal modes of procedure. This can only be obviated by adhering to the rule that constitutional provisions for the security of person and property should be liberally construed. A close and literal construction deprives them of half their efficacy, and leads to gradual depreciation of the right, as if it consisted more in sound than in substance. It is the duty of courts to be watchful for the constitutional rights of the citizen, and against any stealthy encroachments thereon.[71]

The mood of the Court seemed so different in *Coolidge,* as compared to *Harris,* because the *Harris* dissenters controlled the Court when Stewart added his voice and vote to theirs. Stewart himself did not switch his constitutional views; the two cases involved different Fourth Amendment issues, allowing the members of the Court to realign with no loss of personal consistency. Nevertheless, the Court as an institution surely looked inconsistent and was aware of that. White, who dissented in *Coolidge,* claimed that the Court made the law "confused and confusing" as to when there must be a search warrant to validate a seizure. Harlan, who concurred in the result reached by the Stewart-Douglas-Brennan-Marshall plurality, observed that the several opinions filed in this case—there were five of them covering eighty-four pages—made apparent

that the law of search and seizure is due for an overhauling. State and federal law enforcement officers and prosecutorial authorities must find quite intolerable the present state of uncertainty, which extends even to such an everyday question as the circumstances under which police may enter a man's property to arrest him and seize a vehicle believed to have been used during the commission of a crime.[72]

Stewart acknowledged that the Court's decisions over the years "point in differing directions and differ in emphasis," but he thought that neither a "trick of logic" nor a "single coherent analytical framework" would make for "perfect" consistency. As long as courts and law-enforcement officers can easily understand and apply the principle of the case—"that the police must obtain a warrant when

they intend to seize an object outside the scope of a valid search incident to arrest"—consistency was unnecessary.[73]

Of the Fourth Amendment cases decided in the post-Warren era,
Coolidge was the most important, excepting, perhaps, those that
involved wiretapping and electronic surveillance. The Warren Court
would have decided *Coolidge* the same way, but by a clear majority.
Only two of Nixon's four appointees sat on the *Coolidge* bench, but
there is no certainty that the subsequent addition of Rehnquist and
Powell has altered the voting strength of the positions reflected in
Coolidge. Black's literalist approach to Fourth Amendment questions led him to a rejection of the exclusionary rule and to an acceptance of police and prosecutorial views; he dissented in *Coolidge*,
"with vehemence," as Stewart said. Rehnquist has been no different.
Nor has Powell significantly diverged from the independent concurrence expressed by Harlan in *Coolidge*. Harlan thought that "the
case is a close one" to be resolved by following the precedents,
though he did not personally approve of them. The precedents required a uniform standard for state and federal searches and seizures. A contrary result in *Coolidge* would, therefore, dilute the federal standard, a consequence not acceptable to Harlan, for whom the
federal warrant requirement was clear and vitally important. On the
basis of Powell's performance, thus far, in search-and-seizure cases,
one can imagine him writing a similar opinion. In any event, there
has been no case since the appointments of Powell and Rehnquist
in which *Coolidge's* meaning has been an issue. Its validity thus
remains unimpaired. Should the occasion arise for following or
distinguishing it, Powell's vote will be decisive.

Except for *Chimel* v. *California,* decided during Warren's last
term,[74] *Coolidge* is the leading exposition of the constitutional limitations on warrantless searches and seizures. *Chimel* drastically
altered the law of search and seizure by revitalizing Fourth Amendment protections. For a generation, the warrant requirement of the
amendment had remained in uncertain limbo. The Court had permitted an extraordinary latitude for warrantless police searches incidental to a valid arrest. When the police arrested someone, they
could seize evidence of his suspected crime anywhere within the area
under his "control" or "possession."[75] In *Chimel,* they entered the
home of a suspected burglar, lawfully arrested him, and then ran-

sacked his entire house, including attic, garage, and workshop. Deciding that the evidence so seized could not be admitted against him, the Court held that a warrantless search made incident to arrest extends only to the person of the suspect and to the area "within his immediate control," which the Court defined as the area within which he might reach a weapon or destroy evidence.[76] *Chimel* left several issues unresolved, among them the effect of the holding on automobile searches and on the rule that the police may seize evidence in plain view but beyond the immediate control of the suspect. *Coolidge* resolved those issues.

New Hampshire convicted Coolidge for the brutal murder of a young girl. The state's case depended on evidence consisting of vacuum sweepings from his car, showing the high probability of a connection between the defendant and the victim. The police had searched the car on the basis of a warrant that proved to be defective, leaving the question whether an emergency existed that could justify a warrantless search. Finding none, the Court held that the search of the car had been unconstitutional, making inadmissible the evidence obtained by the search. Burger, who concurred in the dissenting opinion of White, could not resist a brief solo dissent in which he claimed to find "not the slightest basis" for reversing the conviction and ordering a new trial at which relevant and reliable evidence would be withheld from the jury's consideration. "This case," he expostulated, "illustrates graphically the monstrous price we pay for the Exclusionary Rule in which we have imprisoned ourselves."[77] Stewart's answer, which he elaborately supported, was the mild reminder that the Court's duty was to decide the issues according to the Constitution. A jury, not the Court, decided guilt or innocence on the basis of evidence properly admitted.

The police seized the car, which Coolidge had parked in his driveway, on the basis of a warrant issued by the chief law-enforcement officer of the state, its attorney general, who acted in his capacity as a justice of the peace at the same time that he personally directed the police investigation of the murder; later, he acted as the chief prosecutor at the trial. Such a confusion of roles had been common in New Hampshire, where, until recently, police captains, serving as justices of the peace, issued search and arrest warrants. The Court condemned the warrant for the search of Coolidge's car on ground that it patently violated a long-standing rule that only a neutral and detached magistrate can issue a warrant. Neither the police nor prosecutors can maintain the independence of judgment required to evaluate their own assessments of probable cause. The warrant being void, the issue became whether there were any special circumstances that made a warrantless search and seizure imperative. New Hampshire advanced three separate arguments to justify such a search and seizure as a reasonable exception to the normal requirement of a warrant: (1) search incident to a valid arrest, (2) search of a vehicle, and (3) seizure of evidence in plain view of the arresting officers. The Court systematically rejected each.

Stewart observed that after *Chimel* a lawful arrest made within a residence could not justify, as incident to the arrest, the seizure of a car parked outside, far from the immediate control of the person arrested. There was no way for Coolidge to gain possession of a weapon in the car or destroy evidence in it. But because the search of the car had occurred long before the decision in *Chimel,* the Court assessed the state's first argument on the basis of the law as it existed before *Chimel*. Relying on a strained view of previously governing precedents, which *Chimel* had overruled, Stewart declared that a search incident to arrest had to occur at the time of the arrest and within an area controlled by the person arrested. In this case, the police did not touch the car until several hours after removing Coolidge from the scene. Then they seized it and towed it to the station house, where they searched it, for the first time, a day or two later, and twice again over a year later. Stewart reasoned that even if, for the sake of an argument that he could not accept, the police might have searched the car in the driveway when they arrested Coolidge in his house, "they could not legally seize the car, remove it, and search it at their leisure without a warrant" on the theory that they acted incident to arrest.[78]

In its second argument, the state sought to rationalize the warrantless seizure and subsequent searches of the car on the basis of the old distinction between movable vehicles and other property. Only a year before *Coolidge,* in *Chambers* v. *Maroney* the Court had held that when exigent circumstances established a probable cause for a warrantless search of a car, the police may seize it, take it to their station, and search it later.[79] Harlan was the only dissenter from that amazing decision, which Stewart now distinguished. Stewart conceded that the search in *Chambers* had occurred after the emergency had passed. The facts in *Coolidge* showed no emergency either. If the police in *Chambers* had acted reasonably by searching a car without a warrant, after they had it in their station and had its occupants in jail, what was unreasonable about the seizure and search in *Coolidge?*

Even White, dissenting in *Coolidge*, did not press *Chambers* to justify the searches made more than a year later. But Stewart found a different distinction. He reasoned that *Chambers* purported to deal only with vehicular situations in which the police may lawfully act without a warrant. The rationale of that case, he said, was that *after* the justification for a search arises, there is little difference between a search on the street at the time of the arrest and a later search at the station. "Here," claimed Stewart, "we deal with the prior question of *whether* the initial intrusion is justified."[80] His distinction between the cases was accurate if Talmudical. There had indeed been a point in time when circumstances undeniably gave the *Chambers* police probable cause for a warrantless search in connection with a highway arrest. The *Coolidge* police, however, could not remotely rest on exigent circumstances at any point in time as an explanation for their inability to secure a valid warrant.

The rule requiring warrants permits an exception for cars only because they are quickly movable. But that rationale did not apply in Coolidge's case. Although he had known for some time that he was a suspect and had had ample opportunity to get rid of the car or destroy incriminating evidence in it, he had cooperated with the police in every way, according to Stewart. But Stewart could not know whether Coolidge had removed incriminating evidence. The police had to vacuum-sweep the car and make a microscopic analysis of the particles to find evidence in it. Still, the police had long suspected the criminal involvement of the car, and they knew its exact location. They had time to get a warrant for its search—and of course they did, though that warrant proved to be invalid. Stewart found no justification for a warrantless search. The objects that the police sought in the car were neither dangerous, stolen, nor contraband. The chance to search the car was not a fleeting one, as when the police stop a car on a street. Coolidge, on being arrested, offered no resistance and could not reach his car, nor could his wife, the only other adult in his house. "In short," Stewart concluded, "by no possible stretch of the legal imagination"[81] was this a case where securing a warrant was impracticable or where exigent circumstances justified a warrantless search. The conclusion made good sense if the constitutional requirement of a warrant is deserving of respect.

In its final argument in defense of the search, the state rested on the "plain view" exception to the warrant requirement. Stewart conceded that the precedents authorized the police to seize evidence in plain view without a warrant "under certain circumstances," which he sought to identify. Any of the recognized exceptions to the warrant requirement that would justify an initial police intrusion would also justify their seizure of evidence in plain view. Thus, they might chance upon the evidence while in hot pursuit of a fleeing suspect, or they might chance upon it when making a valid search incident to an arrest. That led Stewart to the not wholly convincing formulation which he used to reject the application of the plain-view exception in this case. He found that all the plain-view cases had in common "a prior justification for an intrusion in the course of which he [the officer] came inadvertently across a piece of evidence incriminating the accused."[82]

Thus, Stewart limited the plain-view rule by reading into it two qualifications: There must be probable cause for the search—"the prior justification for an intrusion"—plus inadvertent discovery, before a warrantless seizure can receive constitutional coloration. Plain-view seizure was "a major gain in effective law enforcement," but under no circumstances could plain view justify "a general, exploratory rummaging." "No amount of probable cause," Stewart said, "can justify a warrantless search or seizure absent 'exigent circumstances.' "[83] When the police anticipate the discovery of evidence, they must get a warrant. Only when they come across the evidence inadvertently is there support for seizure without a warrant. In this case the police had time to get a warrant, had a description of the car, knew it was always in the driveway, and intended to seize it all along. There was nothing inadvertent in their discovery of the car in the driveway where it was always in plain view. The car's seizure was, therefore, unconstitutional, as were the later searches at the station.

The weakness of Stewart's rejection of the plain-view exception was that it conflicted with the rule of *Chimel,* as White punishingly observed. *Chimel* confined warrantless searches and seizures to the physical area within the immediate control or reach of the person arrested. If the police in the course of making a valid arrest, without a search warrant, plainly see incriminating evidence in the next room, to deny them a right to seize it because it is beyond the spatial limits of *Chimel* is to deprive the state of valuable evidence. There is also something anomalous in expecting the police to pass up the chance to seize evidence in plain view when they are lawfully present for an arrest without a search warrant. In this case they knew all about the car being parked outside. But if the evidence was in the house and they came across it in a place well distant from the point of arrest as they swept through the house to protect themselves from someone who might attack them, they would have to perjure themselves to justify its plain-view seizure. A quick tour through the premises for purposes of self-defense, without an exploratory search in mind, might inadvertently bring within view unexpected evidence far from the arrested person's grasp and well beyond plain view of the point of arrest. Moreover, if the police do expect to uncover evidence but lack probable cause for a search beyond plain view, even though they have an arrest warrant, *Coolidge* requires them to forgo a search or lie about it.

White, who dissented in *Chimel,* went to an extreme in his *Coolidge* dissent. He believed that a police determination of probable cause allowed warrantless entry and search as well as seizure and search of the car. To the plurality, the logic of his position could validate any warrantless search or seizure and read the Fourth Amendment right out of the Constitution. Black, in his dissent, would have sustained the warrant; even if it was unconstitutional, he thought that the seizure and searches of the car were constitutional under each and every argument advanced by the state. Not bothering to evaluate Stewart's opinion critically, Black simply denied it. He convinced only Blackmun. In sum, the Court rightly decided *Coolidge,* even if Stewart's long opinion is not airtight at every point.

Recent Warrantless Searches

In more recent decisions on warrantless automobile searches, the Court neither clarified nor departed from settled law. The precedents are sufficiently numerous, ambiguous, and inconsistent to permit any result that is the choice of a majority. Two 1973 cases, both decided by 5-to-4 votes on the same day, are illustrative. Powell's views controlled the disposition of both cases. In one, *Cady* v. *Dombrowski,* the Court sustained as not unreasonable a warrantless automobile search that an officer made for a purpose other than finding evidence of crime which his search inadvertently disclosed.[84] In the other, *Almeida-Sanchez* v. *United States,* the Court reversed a conviction obtained by the use of evidence that was the fruit of an unjustifiable warrantless search made by a roving patrol of the federal border police.[85]

Cady v. *Dombrowski* involved a one-in-a-million situation. The police in a small Wisconsin town arrested Dombrowski for drunken driving following an accident that disabled his car. He identified himself as an off-duty Chicago police officer. In the belief that he had to carry his revolver at all times, the local police followed a standard procedure that required them to find missing police weapons. One of the oddities of the case is that no one asked Dombrowski whether he had his service revolver. It was not on his person or in the front of the car. Before the search was completed, a wrecker came and towed the car to a private garage. Because the garage was far from the police station and was unguarded, the police feared that vandals might loot the car and find the missing revolver, or so an officer later testified. He drove to the garage several hours later and without a warrant broke into the trunk of the car to search for the gun. He found, instead, evidence that led to the conviction of Dombrowski for murder.

If the officer had reasonable cause for his warrantless search, he could seize the inadvertently discovered evidence that was in plain view when he opened the trunk. Rehnquist, for the Court, analyzed the analogous precedents, which he admitted, in an understatement, were "not on all fours with the instant case," but he concluded that the search of the trunk at the garage was not unreasonable. In the course of his opinion, Rehnquist did not even refer to

Coolidge, nor did he explain or even state what principle of law justified the warrantless search. He made much of the fact that there was a constitutional difference between searches of cars and of homes, and he referred several times to *Chambers* v. *Maroney,* yet he did not draw from it, or any other case, a legal principle applicable to this case. He did not claim that this was a search incident to arrest, or a search of a movable vehicle, or a search made under emergency conditions, or a consent search. Rehnquist simply observed that the officer made the search, "wholly ignorant that a murder, or any other crime, had been committed," to retrieve a service revolver pursuant to standard procedures of his department and to prevent vandals from getting the weapon. Rehnquist did not explain why local police procedures should supersede the warrant requirement of the Fourth Amendment. Nor did he claim that the retrieval of the gun, which the officer reasonably believed to be in the trunk, was justified because of the alleged danger from vandals.

Brennan, for the dissenters, called the search "a serious departure," and a "totally unjustified" one, "from established Fourth Amendment principles."[86] In view of the unusual facts of the case that seems an exaggeration, but Brennan did demolish Rehnquist's loose discussion of supposed precedents. The decision, as Brennan demonstrated, "finds no support in any established exception" to the requirement of a warrant. The fact that the officer purportedly made the search to protect the public safety rather than to seek evidence of crime did not eliminate the need to get a warrant: "Although a valid public interest may establish probable cause to search," Brennan said, "absent exigent circumstances, the search must be conducted pursuant to a 'suitably restricted search warrant.' "[87]

That was indeed the settled law until this case and after it, but not during it. *Dombrowski* was unique, decided on its peculiar facts. It proved that there are some cases that the Court cannot pigeonhole, notwithstanding Rehnquist's solemn effort. All rules relating to warrantless searches supported the dissent. Since there is no likelihood that *Dombrowski* will diminish those rules in future cases because it cannot transcend the facts on which it is based, one must conclude that the Court majority operated on the unspoken belief that it had found a rare case in which to circumvent the exclusionary rule by refusing to reverse the conviction of a murderer.

Almeida-Sanchez, decided the same day, was a case of broader import because it dealt with the warrantless searches of cars by the federal border police.[88] Because they cannot possibly maintain inspection stations at every point along our international boundaries, they engage in roving patrols under authority of an act of Congress that authorizes warrantless searches of vehicles, within reasonable distance from our borders, to detect illegal aliens. In 1972 the border police found about 30,000 aliens who had entered the United States by illegally crossing the border at a point other than a port of entry. A roving patrol stopped Almeida-Sanchez's car about fifty road miles north of the Mexican border on the only north-south highway in California coming from the Mexican border that did not have an established checkpoint. Although Almeida-Sanchez was a Mexican citizen, he held an American work permit, entitling him to be in the country, and he was alone at the time. Nevertheless, the police searched his car for hidden aliens and inadvertently discovered a cache of marijuana. It became evidence to convict him of a federal crime.

Powell separately agreed with the four *Dombrowski* dissenters— Stewart, Douglas, Brennan, and Marshall—that the seizure of the marijuana was unconstitutional. Brennan, for the plurality of four, claimed that there was no probable cause of any kind even for stopping Almeida-Sanchez, let alone for searching his car. Powell declined to express an opinion on the lack of probable cause, but he concurred in the view that persons lawfully in the country and entitled to use its highways cannot arbitrarily be stopped and searched. Powell believed that the use of a general-area warrant would not frustrate the legitimate government purpose of searching for illegal aliens. The plurality did not require a warrant; a showing of probable cause would have satisfied them. They did not comment on the proposal for a general-area warrant. Given Powell's willingness to accept such a warrant, which would be easy to obtain from a federal magistrate on a showing of less than probable cause, there are not likely to be any further reversals of convictions in subsequent cases. A general-area warrant hardly comports with the specific constitutional requirement of a particular warrant issued on probable cause. Since the dissenters in *Almeida-Sanchez* regarded the search for aliens by a roving border patrol as reasonable, even in the absence of probable cause or any sort of a warrant, they would support Powell in a future case where the border police back their search with an area warrant, however vague. Such a warrant would also establish prior justification for an intrusion that inadvertently uncovers narcotics, contraband like undutied goods, or evidence of any crime. *Almeida-Sanchez* was no victory for the Fourth Amendment because it opened the way to general warrants for border searches.

Other cases decided in 1973 show more clearly the tendency of the reconstituted Court to choose the prosecutorial viewpoint. Stewart's opinion for a seven-member majority in *Cupp* v. *Murphy* is an illustration.[89] The case was not as open-and-shut as Stewart made it seem. Oregon convicted Murphy for the strangulation murder of his wife. The conviction rested on scrapings from his fingernails as evidence. The scrapings contained traces of the skin and blood of the victim and of the fabric from her nightgown. The police took the scrapings under protest from Murphy and without a warrant when he voluntarily went to the station house for questioning. If there was probable cause to believe that he had committed the murder, the taking of the scrapings from his fingernails, which constituted a search and seizure, possessed no constitutional taint. But at no point did Stewart explain why, in the absence of an arrest or a search warrant, probable cause existed. He simply relied on the fact, not confirmed by the United States Court of Appeals for the Ninth Circuit, that there was unanimity among the lower courts that probable cause existed. Additionally, Stewart offered the preposterous assertion that the search was constitutionally permissible under *Chimel* v. *California* as a search incident to arrest,[90] although Stewart himself admitted that Murphy was not under arrest at the time. Indeed, the police did not arrest him until a month later, suggesting, as Douglas and Brennan pointed out in their separate dissents, that probable cause might not have existed.

The record provided no basis for determining whether it had existed, and the Ninth Circuit had not considered the question. Given the absence of an initial determination of probable cause by a magistrate and the silence of the Ninth Circuit, the dissenters would have remanded the case to the Ninth Circuit for a ruling on probable cause. They objected to the majority's haste in deciding the issue on an insufficient record. The jury's finding of guilt "based on the illegally obtained evidence," said Douglas, was the only consideration that turned suspicion into probable cause, "making the end justify the means."[91]

Douglas's harsh conclusion did not meet the one point in Stewart's opinion that deserved respectful consideration. Almost as a throwaway, in his closing sentences, Stewart, though still faultily relying on *Chimel,* observed that the police made a very limited search to preserve "the highly evanescent evidence" under Murphy's fingernails. The fact that a fingernail file might quickly destroy the evidence created an exigent circumstance—though Stewart did not say so—justifying the limited search and seizure. In his concurring opinion, Marshall noted that detaining Murphy under close surveillance while the police went for a warrant could not have guaranteed the preservation of the evidence and would have constituted as much of a seizure, of his person, as taking the scrapings. If so, the Court may have decided the case correctly but on the wrong grounds. Stewart's opinion looked too much like an ill-considered determination to save the jury's verdict by saving the admissibility of the incriminating evidence.

Searching with Consent

The Court's decision in *Schneckloth* v. *Bustamonte* was extremely important because it governs the law of search and seizure on the issue of consent.[92] A search and seizure that would otherwise be unconstitutional is lawful if the police have the consent of the person whose privacy they seek to invade. One who consents to a search waives or relinquishes his Fourth Amendment rights. Ordinarily, courts indulge every reasonable presumption against a waiver of constitutional rights, especially when the waiver, as in a consent search, is an extrajudicial one not made under the protection of a court. Such a waiver is suspect, or should be, because the police can be intimidating. Only a voluntary waiver of Fourth Amendment rights establishes lawful consent. The presence of duress or coercion, even if only by implication, invalidates the consent to search. Mere submission or acquiescence to the authority of police officers does not create a lawful waiver of Fourth Amendment rights. Clearly, consent is unquestionable if the party knows his constitutional rights and knows that he may withhold consent, thus requiring the police to obtain a warrant. In *Schneckloth* v. *Bustamonte* the question was whether the police must inform the party that he has a constitutional right to deny consent. Until that case there was, in the words of one authority, "a noticeable trend to restrict the circumstances under which a valid consent must be given."[93] *Bustamonte* reversed the trend.

By a 6-to-3 vote, the Court, speaking through Stewart again, overruled a decision of the United States Court of Appeals for the Ninth Circuit that consent to a search is not voluntary unless given with the knowledge that it can be withheld. Douglas, Brennan, and Marshall, in separate dissents, would have accepted the decision of the Ninth Circuit. Stewart acknowledged that consent must be voluntary and that the burden of proving its voluntariness rests on the prosecution. But he did not regard knowledge of the right to deny consent as necessary to prove its voluntariness. Proof that the consent was given and was not the product of coercion, however subtle, was sufficient. The reason was that to impose on consent searches the requirement of an effective police warning was "thoroughly impractical."[94] Therefore, the police do not have to tell a person that he has a right to refuse consent.

Even if Stewart was right in saying that it is impractical for the police to advise that consent may be withheld—and the impracticality is not at all clear—then practicality, the chance of losing evidence, outweighed the values protected by the Fourth Amendment. Until this case the Court had required a showing of an "intentional relinquishment or abandonment of a known right or privilege."[95] One cannot give up a right that he does not know that he possesses. But the Court now stated that that standard for waiver did not apply in Fourth Amendment cases; the standard applied only in the context of safeguards for a fair criminal trial. The protections of the Fourth Amendment "are of a wholly different order, and have nothing whatever to do with promoting the fair ascertainment of truth at a criminal trial."[96] The amendment protected the security of one's privacy against arbitrary police intrusions.

Stewart was doubly wrong. In the first place, the standard of waiver does not apply only to the rights stated by the Court; the right not to be a witness against himself in a criminal case is not a right that advances the cause of truth, yet it cannot be waived except knowingly and intelligently. In the second place, Stewart provided his own rebuttal to the point that the Fourth Amendment is unrelated to the determination of truth at a trial. He argued that encouraging consent to a search serves society by yielding "necessary evidence for the solution and prosecution of crime, evidence that may insure that a wholly innocent person is not wrongly charged with a criminal offense."[97] That assertion hinged, of course, on the value of consent searches, but it applied equally to reasonable searches conducted without consent. They invade privacy, to be sure, but for the object of securing evidence for a fair trial. What Stewart was saying, in effect, was that unreasonable or unconstitutional searches yield evidence as reliable as constitutional searches. He was, therefore, circumventing the exclusionary rule.

Wholly apart from that issue, Stewart did not give a reasoned explanation why trial rights cannot be waived except knowingly, while privacy rights can be waived unknowingly. Nor did he explain his insistent claim that "it would be next to impossible to apply to a consent search the standard of 'an intentional relinquishment or abandonment of a known right or privilege.' " He simply asserted that it would be "unrealistic" to expect an officer, "upon pain of tainting the evidence obtained," to tell a person that he has a right to deny consent.[98]

Marshall, dissenting, confessed that he was "at a loss to understand" why consent cannot be taken to mean a knowing choice. Calling "unrealistic" or "impractical" a requirement that the police apprise a person of his right to refuse consent was, Marshall implied, unworthy of reply. He put the issue realistically when he said:

> I must conclude, with some reluctance, that when the Court speaks of practicality, what it really is talking of is the continued ability of the police to capitalize on the ignorance of citizens so as to accomplish by subterfuge what they could not achieve by relying

only on the knowing relinquishment of constitutional rights. Of course it would be "practical" for the police to ignore the commands of the Fourth Amendment, if by practicality we mean that more criminals will be apprehended, even though the constitutional rights of innocent people also go by the board.[99]

Brennan had much the same viewpoint:

> The Court holds today that an individual can effectively waive this right even though he is totally ignorant of the fact that, in the absence of his consent, such invasions of his privacy would be constitutionally prohibited. It wholly escapes me how our citizens can meaningfully be said to have waived something as precious as a constitutional guarantee without ever being aware of its existence.[100]

Bustamonte was a major search-and-seizure case that the Warren Court surely would have decided differently. One characteristic of the Nixon Court is its willingness to sacrifice Fourth Amendment rights, under the guise of preserving them, in order to escape the consequences of the exclusionary rule. Consent searches must remain voluntary, but voluntariness has become a luxury for those who already know their rights and are not overawed by the police.

THE STOP AND FRISK

On an occasion of major significance the Warren Court once played hopscotch with the exclusionary rule and jumped over it. That was in 1968 when the Court for the first time sustained the constitutionality of the everyday police practice of stopping and frisking suspicious persons without a warrant or probable cause.[101] Four years later the Nixon Court substantially relaxed constitutional restraints retained by the Warren Court.[102] The stop and frisk and the exclusionary rule are a pair of necessary but contradictory evils that bedevil the law of search and seizure. A "stop" is a temporary "seizure" of a person short of arrest. As Warren said, the Fourth Amendment controls the seizure of a person whether or not resulting in a trip to the police station, and "whenever a police officer accosts an individual and restrains his freedom to walk away, he has 'seized' that person."[103] Similarly, a "frisk" is a search in the constitutional sense, though technically limited in purpose to the detection of concealed weapons.[104]

The constitutional problem created by the stop and frisk is that it is a seizure followed by a search conducted without a warrant and on less than probable cause for an arrest. In a street situation, which allows for no time to get a warrant, a police officer may conclude that he has probable cause for an arrest, and incident to that arrest he may make a search. But if he lacks probable cause for an arrest, he cannot lawfully search. Nevertheless, the Warren Court sustained the admissibility of evidence discovered in a stop and frisk. Because the Fourth Amendment permits a search and seizure or a seizure and search—the sequence does not matter—only when probable cause exists, and because a stop and frisk, by definition, occurs before there is probable cause, a stop and frisk must, as a matter of logical necessity, be unconstitutional. It is not, nor should it be.

From the standpoint of the Fourth Amendment, only one kind of stop and frisk is constitutional: when the frisk is a precautionary measure incident to a stop. But the legitimate frisk may give rise to an illegitimate search, and the distinction between the two in real-life situations is elusive. The stop must be investigative in character. The officer has reasonable grounds for suspecting that a person has committed a crime or may be about to do so. Various considerations may arouse the officer's suspicion, though fall short of establishing probable cause for an arrest. The person's demeanor, age, sex, race, and dress, when taken in the context of the neighborhood, its crime rate, and the time of day or night, are all relevant factors that determine whether the officer should check on that person by a forcible stop and interrogation. The officer must have "reasonable" suspicion, not just "mere" suspicion or a hunch, though the officer himself may not be able to articulate the difference between the two. The purpose of his making a stop is to ascertain who the person is, what he is doing, where he is going, what he is carrying—in short, whether he is on the right side of the law. Depending on the person's response to the stop and the interrogation, the officer may decide to frisk him. The frisk should be no more than a quick "pat-down" outside the person's clothing to feel for bulges that betray a weapon. If the officer thinks he feels a weapon, he may reach into the clothing to grab it.

The frisk insures that the answer to a question is not a bullet. The officer has an undeniable right to protect himself. Armed violence against the police has become an appalling phenomenon in recent years. When the Warren Court sustained a stop and frisk in 1968, it referred to official statistics for 1966 revealing that assaults on the police injured more than 9,000 and that gunshot wounds, mostly from easily concealed handguns, killed 57.[105] When the Nixon Court expanded the scope of stop and frisk in 1972, it referred to figures showing that in 1971, 125 policemen were murdered, almost all by guns and nearly one-third when approaching a suspect in a car.[106] The officer about to make a street arrest in a high-crime area must be alert to the danger that he is a prospective victim of sudden violence. He must be equally apprehensive when, lacking probable cause for an arrest, the necessity of the situation requires a precautionary frisk. Realistically, no court can prevent his trying to insure his own safety, and no court should attempt to. His judgment that the person whom he has stopped may be armed and dangerous must be sovereign.

The sole justification for the constitutional frisk, then, is self-defense. The frisk is unconstitutional when, as commonly occurs, the officer takes advantage of the situation to conduct a general search or even a casual search for evidence of crime other than a weapon. The constitutional frisk is a swift and limited search for a weapon, unrelated to a search for evidence of a crime. Thus, the Warren Court ruled that when an officer frisked not for a weapon but for narcotics, the evidence that he seized was not admissible.[107] Often, however, an officer, having reassured himself about his safety by having frisked for a weapon, will feel uncertain about the results of his interrogation. He lacks probable cause for an arrest yet remains reasonably suspicious. If he resolves his doubt by making a thorough search of the person—a common practice— the search is clearly illegal. Should that search produce evidence of crime, the officer will likely claim that he made an arrest first and then conducted the search incident to the arrest. If he can, retrospectively, manufacture plausible reasons for alleging that he had probable cause, the courts will probably sustain the search.[108]

If his frisk produces a weapon, and the person cannot show a permit for it, the officer has grounds for an arrest and a thorough search. Too frequently the officer has no basis for reasonable suspicion, let alone probable cause, and conducts a stop and frisk to intimidate, harass, and deter possible crime. Such police conduct is illegal, but the courts cannot prevent it. The police, on aggressive-preventive patrols, may also seek to detect crime, as well as deter it, and they use the stop and frisk to conduct illegal searches. When they find nothing, the victim has no practical remedy. When they find something incriminating, they claim that they made an arrest on probable cause.

When ruling that a stop and frisk does not necessarily violate the Fourth Amendment, the Warren Court conceded that the exclusionary rule is ineffective as a deterrent to lawless police action in many kinds of street encounters between citizens and the police. If the police have no interest in getting evidence of crime for purposes of a prosecution, or if they have any nonprosecutorial goal in mind, like harassment, the exclusionary rule is irrelevant as a deterrent to the police. "The wholesale harassment by certain elements of the police community, of which minority groups, particularly Negroes, frequently complain," Warren declared, "will not be stopped by the exclusion of any evidence from any criminal trial."[109] On the other hand, Fourth Amendment standards become operative when the police mean to get a conviction and when courts weigh its constitutionality. To recognize the constitutionality of evidence legitimizes the conduct that procured it. To admit evidence procured by a stop and frisk sanctions the stop and frisk. The difficulty is that the stop and frisk is so protean in character.

Validating a limited and legitimate stop and frisk does not open the door to grave abuses of police authority. The abuse is real enough, but it is not the result of judicial decisions that sanction the entry of the camel's nose. As a general rule, only when the police produce evidence for a prosecution does their conduct become reviewable by courts. When a stop and frisk produces evidence of guilt in the absence of probable cause, judges can finesse the problem as well as police. Douglas, who dissented in *Terry* v. *Ohio,* the case in which the Court first upheld a stop and frisk, claimed that the decision took "a long step down the totalitarian path."[110]

He was alone with his irresponsible convictions in that case. In a companion case, however, even Douglas joined a decision sustaining a conviction for possession of burglar's tools that an officer seized when he frisked for a weapon after collaring a furtive suspect who tried to flee from him.[111] The case showed how evanescent is the difference between a stop and frisk, on the one hand, and a seizure and search on the other. At some indeterminable moment during his brief chase after the suspect, the officer's reasonable suspicion became probable cause, making the frisk for a weapon a search incident to arrest. To validate the conviction, the Court was obligated by the Fourth Amendment to find probable cause for a frisk that produced incriminating evidence other than a weapon. To have found otherwise would have interfered with the officer's performance of his duty.

Acting on an Informer's Tip

Adams v. *Williams,* the stop-and-frisk case of 1972, also showed how swiftly a frisk assumes the stature of a constitutional search. The case arose when an informant known to an officer told him that a person seated in a nearby vehicle had narcotics and kept a gun in his waistband. The time was 2:15 AM and the place a city street in a high-crime area. After calling for assistance on his car radio, the officer approached the suspect's vehicle to check out the tip. The motor was not running; the suspect sat quietly in his car, and there was no indication that he was about to drive off. But the situation was a potentially dangerous one. The officer intended to make a frisk as soon as he could. Without preliminary questioning, he tapped on the car window and requested the suspect to open the door and get out. That is a common police practice preliminary to a frisk, enabling the officer to watch his suspect more carefully. Getting him out of the car also prevents him from destroying evidence in it or driving it away. In this case, the suspect did not comply, but he rolled down the driver's window. The officer might have said something like, "I'm told you have a gun; do you have a permit for it?" And he might have been shot. When the suspect rolled down the window, the officer, though not able to see a gun, reached in and grabbed a fully loaded revolver from the suspect's waistband—exactly where the informant said it would be.

The officer should have secured his own safety and then should have interrogated the suspect. But he did not even determine whether the suspect had a permit for the weapon. Rather, he immediately arrested him for its unlawful possession, a charge which the facts later justified, and held him until fellow officers arrived in reply to the radio call for assistance. In a search incident to the arrest, they found heroin on his person and in the car, plus additional weapons—a machete and a second revolver. On these facts, the Court divided 6-to-3 in favor of sustaining the conviction based on evidence found by the frisk and the subsequent search.

Rehnquist, for the majority, delivered a surprisingly brief opinion that ignored or summarily disposed of the dissenters' objections. The frisk produced a weapon whose possession provoked an arrest, though at the time of the arrest the officer had no basis for believing that the suspect possessed the gun unlawfully. Rehnquist simply asserted that the discovery of the gun established probable cause for an arrest. Unlike *Terry,* where an officer made a stop and frisk when his own observation had created a reasonable suspicion of criminal activity, the officer in *Adams* relied wholly on a tip from an informer. That tip had no value for establishing probable cause. Did it establish reasonable suspicion for the stop and frisk?

The officer knew the informant only from a single previous tip that proved to be unreliable. Rehnquist did not mention that fact. One must read Marshall's dissent to learn that the informant never before had supplied information concerning the possession of narcotics or illegal weapons, and had previously misled the officer with an unfounded tip about homosexual behavior. The factual basis for his tip in this case remained unknown. Rehnquist, nevertheless, found that it had "enough indicia of reliability to justify the officer's forcible stop."[112] The informant had voluntarily come forward to give information that the officer could immediately verify. Moreover, if the tip proved to be incorrect the officer could have arrested the informant for making a false complaint. Such were Rehnquist's "indicia of reliability." The informant's previously unreliable tip had not resulted in his arrest. Moreover, state law required proof that the informant "knowingly" made a false complaint, a difficult standard of proof. The informant probably felt safe from arrest; though tips are often misleading, the police find them indispensable to their work. The fact that the officer could immediately verify the tip did not, of course, add anything to its reliability. Rehnquist's "indicia of reliability" were not very reliable; but, reasonable suspicion, not probable cause, was all that the officer needed for a stop and frisk.

Terry, as the dissenters stressed, commanded that reasonable suspicion be based on the officer's own observations or on "well authenticated information." There was no such information in this case. But the frisk authenticated the reliability of one part of the tip and led to the Court's reinstatement of the conviction that the lower federal court had set aside. Although the tip here proved to be reliable, *Adams* stands for the proposition that an unauthenticated tip from an informer of questionable reliability justifies a stop and frisk. Accordingly, Douglas, Brennan, and Marshall, in separate dissents, criticized Rehnquist's casual assertions in support of that proposition, and they correctly read *Adams* as going far beyond *Terry.* As Marshall said, *"Terry* never meant to approve the kind of knee-jerk police reaction that we have before us in this case." But he also said, "Today's decision invokes the spectre of a society in which innocent citizens may be stopped, searched, and arrested at the whim of police officers who have only the slightest suspicion of improper conduct."[113] The second remark lacked the accuracy of the first. An officer who approaches a car at 2:15 AM in a high-crime area of a city to check out a tip that the occupant has a gun and illegal heroin may be excessively dedicated to his duty and aggressive in carrying it out, but he does not act on whim. A contrary ruling would have invoked the specter of a society in which armed men can go about their business of crime without fear that a police officer can accost them on the basis of unsubstantiated tips. Either way, judges who demand reliable and authenticated information should not be frightened of specters.

There are enough real violations of the Fourth Amendment to occupy the Court's energies without its worrying about hypothetical violations based on an officer's whim. The police can manufacture their own "tips" and invent informants whose identity, as *Adams* showed, they need not reveal. They can and do frisk or search unconstitutionally, for evidence of crime, especially for illegal possession of narcotics. Yet, the Court is powerless to reform such police conduct especially when, as in most instances, it produces no evidence of crime or has no prosecutorial purpose. The Court has conceded that its exclusionary rule cannot deter such lawless police conduct. When the Court is powerless, criticism of it is misdirected.

Searches Incident to Arrest

When, however, there is a prosecution, the Court should justify an important exception to the Fourth Amendment's requirement of a warrant. There is cause for real alarm now that the Court has shown itself to be unwilling to deter the police when it can and should; it surely is unwilling to pronounce as lawless a search conducted for evidence unconnected with an arrest or the finding of a concealed weapon. That was the result of the late 1973 decision in *United States* v. *Robinson*.[114] As a result of *Robinson,* an officer may arrest a person for a traffic violation as an excuse to search him for evidence of other crime.

Arrest on some pretext or other is a common police practice to justify a search incident to arrest. But the motor-vehicle laws are so numerous and complex that an alert officer can almost always find probable cause to arrest a driver. Officers have stated:

> You can always get a guy legitimately on a traffic violation if you tail him for a while, and then a search can be made.

> You don't have to follow a driver very long before he will move to the other side of the yellow line and then you can arrest and search him for driving on the wrong side of the highway.

> In the event that we see a suspicious automobile or occupant and wish to search the person or the car, or both, we will usually follow the vehicle until the driver makes a technical violation of a traffic law. Then we have a means of making a legitimate search.[115]

Until *United States* v. *Robinson* most courts held such searches to be violations of the Fourth Amendment, contrary to police notions.[116]

In *Robinson* the Supreme Court did not, from a technical standpoint, hold that an arrest for a traffic violation can serve as a pretext for a search for narcotics. The Court held, rather, that an arrest for a traffic violation, or any lawful arrest for any offense, justifies a full, though warrantless, search of the person arrested and that the Fourth Amendment does not prevent the use as evidence of heroin, or any other illegal possession, discovered by the officer during a search of the person at the time of a lawful arrest. By ruling that a lawful arrest validates an unlimited search of the arrestee and his personal effects, the Court finessed the question whether the officer's motive for the arrest was to make the search. In this case, the legitimacy of the arrest was beyond dispute; only the legitimacy of the search's thoroughness was at issue. The Court refused to place any limits on the officer's search of the person and of the effects on his person.

The case arose in the District of Columbia where an officer, knowing that Robinson's driver's license had been revoked, spotted him driving and signaled him to the curb. Robinson complied and quietly surrendered a temporary driver's permit that he had obtained fraudulently. The officer immediately arrested him and before taking him to the police station for booking conducted a full search. The officer was doing his duty to the letter of his departmental regulations when he examined everything found on Robinson. The officer did not search his car, because his departmental regulations provided that "there is no probable cause to believe that the vehicle contains fruits, instrumentalities, contraband or evidence of the offense of driving after revocation."[117] The difficulty was that the search of Robinson's personal effects could not possibly have had any relation to the offense either. Nothing found on him, other than his driver's permit, was relevant to the offense of driving after its revocation. There was no dispute about the officer's right to frisk; everyone agreed on the validity of a pat-down for a weapon. The facts incontrovertibly showed, however, that the search went far beyond a frisk to secure the officer's safety; indeed, he admitted that he did not even fear for his safety and was not searching for a weapon. He even conducted the search face-to-face rather than from the rear; he did not spread-eagle his suspect with arms outstretched on the car. Feeling something in Robinson's breast pocket that he knew was not a weapon, the officer pulled out a crumpled cigarette package. If it contained anything dangerous, like a razor blade, confiscating the package deprived Robinson of its use. The officer had no need to examine the contents of the package to insure his safety or prevent an escape, but the officer made that examination. He found gelatinous capsules of white powder that proved to be heroin. The officer probably knew Robinson's police record for previous narcotics convictions and was looking for such evidence. Could the police use it to obtain another conviction for narcotics?

The Court divided 6-to-3 in favor of the admissibility of the evidence. Rehnquist, delivering the Court's opinion, took the position that a warrantless search of a person incident to his arrest for custodial purposes has no limits. Rehnquist's opinion was unprecedented in the view of Marshall, Douglas, and Brennan, who dissented. But the majority saw *Robinson* as a spin-off from *Adams.* There, a warrantless frisk, made on suspicion that the defendant possessed a weapon and narcotics, produced the gun that legitimated an arrest; the arrest, in turn, led to a search for heroin and legitimated a prosecution for a crime unrelated to the cause of arrest. *Adams* thus pointed toward *Robinson:* A valid arrest justifies a search for evidence of any crime, however unrelated to the arrest. But the *Adams* officer acted on a tip, while the *Robinson* officer was on a fishing expedition, leaving the question whether the arrest that he made justified his search.

Rehnquist's opinion showed a consummate disregard for the obligations of his craft. He did not attempt to justify the search other than to assert that any search of the person incident to his arrest is a recognized exception to the Fourth Amendment's requirement of a warrant issued on probable cause. He cut the anchor to the traditional need for examining the facts of the case to assess the legitimacy of the search. Explicitly, Rehnquist repudiated the long-standing rule of the Court that a case-by-case consideration of the facts must determine the lawfulness of a search, a seizure, and the admissibility of evidence. When the Court of Appeals for the District of Columbia had reversed Robinson's narcotics conviction, it ruled that in every case there must be a judicial examination of the facts to determine the presence of a reason supporting the authority of the search incident to the arrest.

Thus, if an officer makes an arrest for a burglary, he may search for evidence of that crime. Any arrest, of course, justifies a search for weapons. But the Court of Appeals found groundless a search that could not possibly reveal further evidence of the particular offense for which the officer arrested Robinson. Rehnquist responded by admonishing lower courts for inquiring whether there was a reason for a warrantless search incident to an arrest on probable cause. He declared:

> But quite apart from these distinctions, our more fundamental disagreement with the Court of Appeals arises from its suggestion that there must be litigated in each case the issue of whether or not there was present one of the reasons supporting the authority for a search of the person incident to a lawful arrest. We do not think the long line of authorities of this Court . . . requires such a case by case adjudication. A police officer's determination as to how and where to search the person of a suspect whom he has arrested is necessarily a quick *ad hoc* judgment which the Fourth Amendment does not require to be broken down in each instance into an analysis of each step in the search. . . . A custodial arrest of a suspect based on probable cause is a reasonable intrusion under the Fourth Amendment; that intrusion being lawful, a search incident to the arrest requires no additional justification. It is the fact of the lawful arrest which establishes the authority to search, and we hold that in the case of a lawful custodial arrest a full search of the person is not only an exception to the warrant requirement of the Fourth Amendment, but is also a "reasonable" search under that Amendment.[118]

Rehnquist's opinion was grossly overbroad. Worse still, it was unconvincing because it was unreasoned; he offered no pertinent arguments to prove his thesis and arrogantly ignored the counterarguments of the dissenters who supported the finding of the Court of Appeals. But for *Adams,* Rehnquist's opinion was unprecedented, yet even *Adams* did not give him the support that he pretended. The search there did uncover heroin, which was good evidence of a crime not connected with the arrest on a weapons charge. Nevertheless, *Adams* turned on the fact that a tip, supposedly surrounded by indicia of reliability, led to finding a loaded gun. Robinson had no weapon, a fact of distinguishing importance. Rehnquist discoursed in *Robinson* at considerable length and irrelevantly on the uncontested right of an officer to frisk for a weapon and the significance of its presence in justifying a thorough search. But the officer in *Robinson* believed and acted as if he were in no danger. The tip in *Adams,* corroborated by the finding of the gun, also indicated illegal possession of narcotics. The officer in *Robinson* had no tip, no illegal weapon, no fear for his safety, and no cause to examine the crumpled cigarette package. Rehnquist ignored the differences between the cases. Throughout, he displayed contempt for reasoned judgment. He simply did not consider the reasons for assessing whether there should be any limits on the scope of a search incident to arrest. As an intellectual feat, his opinion was a travesty on judicial review. With the votes of a majority on his side, he behaved heedless to the need either for rational persuasion. or for demonstrating a modicum of respect toward his dissenting brethren and the careful judgment of the Court of Appeals. His opinion reads like an edict backed up by *force majeure.*

Consider, for example, Rehnquist's abuse of the precedents. Excepting *Adams,* not one quoted by him supported his opinion that the police may seize evidence absolutely unrelated to the cause of arrest. On behalf of his contention that no search of a person incident to an arrest violates the Fourth Amendment, he quoted a 1914 case on the point that the police may "seize the fruits or evidences of crime," but the "evidences" seized in that case related to the crime charged on the arrest.[119] He quoted a 1925 opinion in which the Court explicitly sustained a seizure of "things *connected with the crime* as well as weapons and other things to effect an escape from custody. . . ."[120] Wrongly, Rehnquist concluded that "no doubt has been expressed as to the *unqualified* authority of the arresting authority to search the person of the arrestee."[121] The dissenters disproved that. Rehnquist even relied on a passage in *Chimel* where the Court approved of the reasonableness of a search for weapons, which no one in *Robinson* doubted.[122] He included a long quotation from *Terry* v. *Ohio,* the first stop-and-frisk case, which in no way supported his proposition that any search incident to arrest is lawful.[123] In *Terry* the Court painstakingly decided on a close analysis of the facts presented—the very approach that the Court here repudiated as unnecessary. Rehnquist quoted Harlan's concurrence in a companion case to *Terry*, in which Harlan declared that an officer arresting on probable cause "is entitled to make a very full incident search," but Rehnquist ignored the facts of that case; Harlan did not. The officer there arrested and searched a person suspected of burglary and found burglar's tools. That is scarcely analogous to a search of a cigarette package in connection with an arrest for driving after revocation of a driver's license.[124] Rehnquist even quoted a couple of nineteenth-century state decisions that did not prove his point. One upheld the right of an officer to search for weapons and means by which to effect an escape; the other held that there is "no right to take any property from the person of the prisoner except such as may afford evidence *of the crime charged,* or means of identifying the criminal, or may be helpful in making an escape."[125] Finally Rehnquist quoted from an opinion of the pre-eminently distinguished Chief Judge Benjamin Cardozo of New York on the right of an officer to be able to search to disarm; Cardozo concluded, "The search being lawful, he retains what he finds *if connected with the crime.*"[126]

Rehnquist admitted that he could find only dicta to support "an unqualified authority to search incident to a lawful arrest," though he did not admit, as he should have, that his precedents supported a qualified authority to search for evidence related to the arrest. Rehnquist cited no authority supporting a search for evidence unrelated to the cause of arrest. He did not even attempt to explain why a traffic arrest validated a search not touching the arrest, or a weapon, or a means of escape. His opinion was more than unsound; it simply lacked merit. A teacher confronting such a mess of irrelevancies, illogic, and improper use of precedents would chastise his student for incompetence. When the culprit is the Supreme Court, one must conclude that the majority Justices are displaying arbitrary power and have reached a predetermined result without caring whether they can justify it. In so doing they mocked the judicial process and its values, as well as the Fourth Amendment. Rehnquist had to travel far beyond the facts of the case, to which he was supremely indifferent, in order to subvert a crucial protection of the amendment by legislating a general rule: A search incident to a custodial arrest requires no justification beyond the fact of the search itself, however unrelated may be the cause of the arrest and the evidence found. That doctrine and approach conflicted with anything remotely resembling a strict construction of the Constitution. *Robinson* was, rather, the product of a law-and-order activism founded on a propensity to rewrite, or red pencil, the constitutional requirements of reasonable search and probable cause.

That Burger, Blackmun, and White joined Rehnquist's opinion is no surprise. That Stewart and Powell also did so is dismaying and perplexing. They should have written separate concurrences dissociating themselves from Rehnquist's distortions of the precedents and refusal to reason. They damaged their reputations for judiciousness by endorsing an oversight of the dissenting opinion, an overbreadth of doctrine, and an overbearing attitude. At the very least, they might have explained that when an officer conducts a lawful search, the law cannot expect him to ignore evidence of crime that he comes across inadvertently, but it can expect that the Fourth Amendment's standard of reasonableness confines his search to evidence of the crime charged, to weapons, and to instrumentalities of escape.

Marshall spoke for the dissenters. His opinion was everything that Rehnquist's was not—a triumph of cogency, rigor, and incisiveness. He carefully analyzed the facts in consonance with an honored tradition of restricting the rule of the case to its question: What is the "permissible scope of a search of the person incident to a lawful arrest for violation of a motor vehicle regulation"? Marshall believed that the conventional approach of making an "intensive, at times painstaking, case by case analysis" represented the only way of maintaining the integrity of constitutional rights of the judicial process. Without scrutinizing the reasonableness of a particular search and seizure, the Court, Marshall believed, conflicted with "fundamental principles"; moreover, the objective of freeing the "quick *ad hoc* judgment of police officers," he declared, was "inconsistent with the very function of the Amendment"—to subject police judgments to "review and control by the judiciary."[127]

"Nothing," thought Marshall, "could be further from the truth" than Rehnquist's suggestion that qualifications on searches incident to arrest were novel to the law. "The fact is," Marshall declared, "that this question has been considered by several state and federal courts, the vast majority of which have held that absent special circumstances a police officer has no right to conduct a full search of the person incident to a lawful arrest for violation of a motor vehicle regulation."[128] Marshall gave ample recent examples, each of which overturned narcotics convictions based on drug seizures in the course of traffic arrests. He also quoted the Court of Appeals for the Tenth Circuit, which summed up the precedents when stating in 1969 that it was "in complete agreement with the prevailing federal and state authority which condemns the search of persons and automobiles following routine traffic violations."[129] Following his presentation of the precedents-in-point, all of which the majority ignored, Marshall concluded that the opinion of the Court was "disingenuous." Rehnquist, he noted, had admitted that only dicta supported his unqualified rule and that an examination of judicial practice would be helpful, but had then made an examination "which is not only wholly superficial," said Marshall, "but totally inaccurate and misleading."[130]

The dissenters would have confined the search in this case to a weapons search. They agreed that an officer should always disarm the arrestee and seize all evidence of crime "for which the arrest is made," but in this case there could be no evidence beyond the driver's permit, which Robinson had surrendered on order. The removal of anything else from his pockets, known by the officer not to be dangerous, was unreasonable. Above all, a separate search of his effects could have had no protective purpose. The risk of danger disappeared once the officer made his frisk and took from the arrestee's pocket an article whose identity a pat-down could not discern.

The government claimed that the police had a right to make a full search of the offender at the time of the arrest because they could search him later at the station house when booking him and making an inventory of his personal effects. The majority did not discuss that government claim, but the dissenters did and they rejected it. Marshall observed that the offense, being a petty one, was bailable. Normally, the offender would not be jailed and therefore would not be searched later. If he could not make bail, there was still no need to examine the contents of the things in his pockets. The police could inventory them without opening them, stuff them into a package in the prisoner's presence, and seal it for safekeeping. In that way they prevent him from introducing contraband into the jail and minimize the intrusion on his privacy. Marshall should have added to an otherwise flawless opinion that if such a search and inventory necessarily bring evidence of crime into plain view, the Fourth Amendment does not exclude its use in a prosecution. There is no doubt, however, that the search at issue in this case went "far beyond what was reasonably necessary," as Marshall said. A warrantless search incident to arrest is an exception to the Fourth Amendment. The dissenters would have restricted that exception to the necessity of the case.

The Court founded its opinion to the contrary on humbug and promulgated a sinister expansion of the powers of the police. The rule of *Robinson* had one restriction only: It applied to the person of the arrestee and to his effects, but said nothing about a search of his vehicle or the immediate premises. Thus, the Court left intact, for the time being, the rulings in *Chimel* and *Coolidge*.[131] *Robinson* means that the police, on finding probable cause for a warrantless arrest, whether for a traffic violation or any other petty crime, may lawfully snoop at will in wallets, handbags, sealed envelopes, and whatever else the suspect carries. If the arrest is lawful, even though a mere pretense for the search, the exclusionary rule is no bar to the admissibility of whatever evidence may be found of prosecutorial value. If nothing of such value is found, the invasion of privacy has no redress. Search warrants long ago became exceptional, though the rule of the Fourth Amendment requires a "particular description" of the places to be searched and of "the things to be seized." Now the exceptions to the rule swell in dimension as the Court, forgetting the reasons that legitimate the exceptions, diminishes the scope of privacy.

THE THIRD EAR: ELECTRONIC EAVESDROPPING

The stop and frisk is a trivial annoyance to Fourth Amendment rights compared with massive electronic snooping that "seizes" the spoken word. The person who has never been on the wrong side of the law except for minor traffic violations is indifferent when some shady character runs up against a search without probable cause. In his own home or place of business the ordinary citizen, who tends not to understand that his own rights are worth no more than those of the criminally suspect, feels secure in his privacy. But privacy has become the illusion of contemporary life. The tap on a telephone wire and the miniature "bug," an electronic device, transmit private conversations to a third ear—the law-enforcement officer's tape recorder.

Electronic bugs, like the bacterial types, are democratically impartial: They respect no one, and no one is immune to them. However, while the victim of infection knows that he has been exposed, the victim of surveillance via a tap or bug does not know, and may never know, that there has been an invasion of his privacy. The bug catches every sound within its range; the tap overhears every conversation, however innocent and private. Surreptitious bugging can reach into any inner sanctum, even, a member of the Supreme Court has alleged, into the private conference room of the Court itself.[132]

Anyone seems to be a potential victim—college students, businessmen, housewives, civil-rights leaders, radicals, and Congressmen, as well as Mafia dons and foreign spies. Proof of the commonplaceness of the government's third ear is exceptionally difficult to come by because of its surreptitious nature. Law-enforcement agencies, in accordance with a 1968 act of Congress, must report only intercepts authorized by courts. That congressional statute, according to Senator Hiram Fong of Hawaii, began as the "Right to Privacy Act" and in completed form became the "End to Privacy Act."[133] It punishes illegal intercepts of oral and wire communications; it also prohibits the use in evidence of illegal intercepts. But it makes tapping and bugging lawful in a vast variety of cases, and the fruit of a lawful intercept is lawful evidence in a criminal prosecution. The federal government can tap and bug in any case involving a threat to national security, a major crime, or a matter relating to racketeering. Congress also authorized state and local authorities to tap and bug in any case involving a crime punishable by imprisonment for more than one year. Ordinarily, law-enforcement officers must get a warrant first—except for emergency situations, during which they are free to tap and bug first and get a warrant later; after forty-eight hours they must disconnect a warrantless intercept. Other crucial exceptions to the warrant requirement are cases involving executive protection of national security and those in which one party to the intercept consents, without the knowledge, of course, of the other. Thus, if an undercover police officer or an informer becomes a human walkie-talkie, the third ear may listen and transcribe lawfully and without the need of a warrant issued on probable cause.[134] Experts estimate that this technique is used "tens of thousands of times each year" by just the local police.[135]

There is no way of estimating the amount or extent of official eavesdropping. The most important limitations on secret eavesdropping seem simply to be its enormous drain on the time of law-enforcement officers and the fact that there are only so many of them. Only a minority of states have statutes that supposedly limit tapping and bugging except when approved in advance by a court, and these do not include some of the most populous states, among them, California, Texas, Pennsylvania, Illinois, and Ohio. Anyone who believes that tapping and bugging do not exist in those states has the happy fate of being divorced from reality.[136] Anyone who thinks that the reported instances of eavesdropping reveal its extent is similarly situated in never-never land. Federal law does not compel reporting of an interception of a communication in any case exempted from the requirement of a warrant. We know only the reported number of applications for warrants and the number granted; moreover, the figures cover only the federal government and those states whose laws command prior judicial approval. Published figures are always two years old. The report published in 1973 tells us that for the year 1971, when nineteen states in addition to the federal government required warrants, no court, state or federal, denied any application for a warrant to intercept. There were 816 applications to the courts, and the courts granted 816.[137] Of these, 531 were for intercepts by state and local law-enforcement agencies, 83 percent of which were in New York and New Jersey. The 531 were probably no more than the tip of the iceberg. As of the mid-1960s, Alan F. Westin, whose *Privacy and Freedom* is the most authoritative book on the subject, offered the "conservative estimate . . . that more than 10,000 wiretaps and bugs are installed annually by local law-enforcement agencies throughout the country."[138] Approval of all 285 federal requests for warrants in 1971 resulted in 281 installations that enabled federal agents to overhear more than 256,000 conversations involving almost 15,000 people. The state and federal figures combined show that more than 31,000 people had been overheard in 509,000 conversations in 1971.[139] For the three full years from 1969 through 1971, more than a million conversations by about 73,000 people were overheard, of whom about 72,000 were innocent, or, rather, were not guilty of any offense.[140] To say that the innocent have nothing to fear from tapping and bugging is quite true, if all that is meant is that they will not be convicted; but that puts a pretty cheap price on their privacy. It also ignores the possibility that they will be harassed and even blackmailed for overheard indiscretions.

The reported figures tell only part of the story. Senator Edward Kennedy obtained from a very reluctant Department of Justice some raw data that purportedly shows the extent of taps and bugs installed on the authority of the President of the United States during 1970. In that year, when there were 180 court-approved installations, a hundred fewer than the following year, the executive ordered only 113; but, the court-approved installations lasted an average of only thirteen days, while those ordered on executive authority lasted from 71 to 200 days each, eavesdropping on anywhere from 31,000 to 84,000 people that year.[141] Douglas, who appended some of this data to one of his opinions, declared, with reference to dissidents, "Their homes are bugged and their telephones are wiretapped. They are befriended by secret government informers. Their patriotism and loyalty are questioned. Senator Sam Ervin, who chaired hearings on military surveillance of civilian dissidents, warns that 'it is not an exaggeration to talk in terms of hundreds of thousands of . . . dossiers.' Senator Kennedy . . . found 'the frightening possibility that the conversations of untold thousands are being monitored on secret devices.' "[142]

That monitoring, known, unknown, and unknowable, whether lawful or unlawful, is like a dormant time bomb that may be triggered at any time for some disclosure or use, official or covert. The courts cannot deter the storage of intercepted information in government data banks. Most of the information has no prosecutorial value. It serves in mysterious ways to persecute. People lose jobs, security clearances, bank loans, and credit ratings; they have trouble getting a passport; their tax returns get audited. None of the information obtained by the third ear against political dissidents has proved to be of prosecutorial value in the various conspiracy trials of the 1960s and early 1970s; the juries, at least, did not convict, or, where convictions were obtained, they did not survive appellate scrutiny.

The value of bugging and tapping as a means of securing evidence of other crime is limited to only a few categories of offenses, not including major ones like arson, homicide, kidnaping, or others for which death used to be the penalty. The record of convictions based on evidence obtained by eavesdropping is, in the words of one expert, "at best poor."[143] Former Attorney General Ramsey Clark, who was in a position to know, claimed that the uninhibited use of wiretaps in some cities where organized crime is most severe proved to be ineffective and inefficient, and that "hundreds of man-years of agent time were wasted" when the FBI, from the late 1950s until mid-1965, used electronic surveillance against organized crime. "So far as is known," said Clark, "not one conviction resulted from any bugs."[144] If Clark used words with precision, his statement does not exclude the possibility that the government obtained convictions on the basis of evidence from wiretapping. Certainly, the record of convictions has improved since Clark's time. For the three years from 1969 through 1971, court-approved installations yielded over 6,000 arrests and 1,190 convictions.[145] There has been almost one conviction, on the average, for each installation. In 1969, when there were 270 installations, both state and federal, there were 294 convictions, and in the next year, when the number of installations increased to 582, the number of convictions, many from cases initiated earlier, jumped to 538. Inexplicably, the number of convictions fell to 322 in 1971 when there were 792 installations, though the record number of arrests in that year, 2,818, undoubtedly generated additional convictions for 1972 and 1973, years for which the government has not yet reported the figures. On the other hand, the 2,348 arrests in 1970, far from producing a bumper harvest of convictions in 1971, resulted in a 40 percent fall-off.[146]

Law-enforcement agencies tacitly admit that bugging and tapping are of little value in securing evidence of most offenses; they eavesdrop mainly in gambling and narcotics cases. In 1971, of the 281 federal installations, 251 involved gambling and 22 involved narcotics. The pattern is substantially the same for state and local installations. Of these, a total of 531 for 1971, 319 were for gambling and 104 for narcotics. The next highest category was homicide with 18.[147] Convictions follow in about the same proportion for the same offenses.[148] Probable cause existed in all these cases, although the incredible record of 100 percent court approval of applications to tap and bug raises doubts. There is no evidence that gambling and narcotics offenses have diminished as a result of these convictions, which amount to an infinitesimal percentage of the total number of police intercepts of suspects. Moreover, we simply do not know whether the convictions in these cases *depended* on evidence from intercepts, or whether, given the thousands and thousands of hours of surreptitious monitoring by the police, they could have obtained evidence to convict by other means of detection not requiring the secret rape of privacy. Detection by more traditional and orthodox means might have yielded comparable results. In any event the public has not yet learned that tapping and bugging have broken the Mafia's hold over gambling and narcotics, or that the big shots have landed in the penitentiary thanks to the effectiveness of the third ear. Ramsey Clark may not have exaggerated when he declared, "Joseph Valachi told the FBI as much as one agent could have learned if he spent fifty years listening to bugs."[149]

If intercepts were effective, efficient, and even indispensable to the prosecution of crimes involving gambling and narcotics, the case for the third ear would still be unproved to anyone who weighs the conviction record against the values of a free society that cherishes privacy. The electronic bug or wiretap may be a friend to the police, but it creates something more tangible than merely a specter of Big Brother's police state. The United States is not remotely a police state, but the secret third ear in an open society is a grave anomaly.

Bugging with Consent

Unlike the physical search of one's person or premises, the seizure of one's conversation occurs without his being aware of the loss: A search and seizure by means of tapping or bugging always entails an unknown loss of privacy. Electronic eavesdropping is even more deceptive than wiretapping. Anyone using a phone knows that it can be tapped, but when a person engages in a private conversation on a face-to-face basis, he does not expect to be overheard by a secret third ear. However, the right to engage in a private conversation on a face-to-face basis is denied if the police have the consent of one participant to listen in without the knowledge of the other. Although there is a right to engage in a telephone conversation free from warrantless wiretapping by the police,[150] if one party to a conversation permits the police to listen in, his consent destroys the other party's privacy. The consent of one voids the necessity of a warrant to seize the words of the other.

The Fourth Amendment has never protected against an informer's betrayal of another's incriminating secrets. But the testimony of an informer whose own reputation or conduct is not unimpeachable does not convict as effectively as the self-incriminatory remarks of the defendant when reproduced in his own voice or when confirmed by the testimony of the police who overheard him. To the defendant, the police who monitor his conversation is an unknown third party. Thus, the law refers to "third party bugging." A congressional act of 1968 authorized third-party bugging or eavesdropping with the consent of one party to a conversation.[151] Three years later the Supreme Court legitimated the practice when deciding *United States* v. *White*.[152] That case choked off the promise implied in the opinions of the Warren Court that warrantless electronic eavesdropping on "private" conversations abridged Fourth Amendment rights.[153] The replacement of Warren and Fortas by Burger and Blackmun enabled the reconstituted Court to mold the Fourth Amendment so that warrantless bugging would be as snugly constitutional as it had been back in 1952 when the Court decided *On Lee* v. *United States.*[154]

On Lee reflected an old principle that there must be a physical trespass or intrusion before the Fourth Amendment comes into play.[155] The bugged informer in *On Lee* entered the defendant's premises with his consent. The defendant did not, of course, consent to the sacrifice of his conversational privacy; but the Court refused to look beyond the law of trespass, thus declining to decide whether the Fourth Amendment prohibited the seizure of mere words when a trespass existed. Beginning in 1961 the Warren Court initiated a trend away from *On Lee*. In that year, when the facts of a case showed that an electronic device constituted a trespass, the Court for the first time implied that conversation can be the object of an unlawful search and seizure, even though not falling within the literal terms of the Fourth Amendment's references to "persons, houses, papers, and effects" or to "things to be seized."[156] In 1963 the Court for the first time held that when a physical trespass exists, "the Fourth Amendment may protect against the overhearing of verbal statements as well as against the more traditional seizure of 'papers and effects.' "[157] In 1967, when condemning "a roving commission" to overhear all of the suspect's conversations, the Court ruled that a warrant for electronic eavesdropping must particularly describe the conversations subject to seizure; the Court added that "a showing of exigency" is more important in eavesdropping cases than in those involving conventional searches and seizures.[158] But until the landmark *Katz* case, the Court had not abandoned its requirement that there must be a trespass or "an unlawful physical invasion of a constitutionally protected area" before the exclusionary rule comes into play against the fruits of electronic eavesdropping.[159]

Katz "swept away doctrines that electronic eavesdropping is permissible under the Fourth Amendment unless physical invasion of a constitutionally protected area produced the challenged evidence." So said the Court in *White* as it nearly swept away *Katz*.[160] In *Katz*, FBI agents who had no warrant attached an electronic listening and recording device to the top of a phone booth from which the defendant made calls that revealed violations of federal gambling laws. Because the device did not penetrate the booth, there was no trespass. The Court replied by repudiating the trespass doctrine and overruling the cases based upon it. To the government's contention that a phone booth is a public place rather than a constitutionally protected area, the Court responded that the Fourth

Amendment "protects people, not places. What a person knowingly exposes to the public, even in his own home or office, is not a subject of Fourth Amendment protection. . . . But what he seeks to preserve as private, even in an area accessible to the public, may be constitutionally protected."[161] The significant fact to the Court was that the government's warrantless seizure "violated the privacy upon which he justifiably relied" when making his calls. Therefore, the absence of a trespass "can have no constitutional significance."[162] *Katz* seemed to mean that a warrantless electronic intrusion on a conversation that a participant reasonably expects to be private infringes on the Fourth Amendment. Consent by one of the bugged parties was not an issue in *Katz,* but the Court's reliance on the rationale of a justifiable expectation of privacy conflicted with the view that the consent of one party legalizes a warrantless seizure of the other's conversation. That was the state of the law when *White* came before the Court in 1971.

The facts in *On Lee* and *White,* which a score of years separated, were almost identical. In both the government won narcotics convictions by using evidence that consisted of incriminating conversations overheard by federal agents who monitored bugs concealed on government informers whom the defendants made the mistake of trusting. The informers were decoys wired for sound to trap the defendants by transmitting their remarks to the ears of distant agents. A ruling in either case that warrantless electronic eavesdropping was unconstitutional would have put the government to the trouble of getting a warrant in advance.

From the time of the congressional act of 1968, the state and federal courts, through 1971, granted 1,887 requests for warrants out of 1,889 applications.[163] Showing probable cause does not, therefore, seem to pose too much of an obstacle to the will of the police when they seek a warrant to search and seize by tapping or bugging. In 1971, as a result of a decision handed down two months after *United States* v. *White,* the Nixon Court relaxed the standards of probable cause far beyond those imposed by the Warren Court in cases where the police rely on an informer's tip.[164] Even though getting a warrant has become easier than it was when the courts were complying with police requests almost 100 percent of the time, there are cases where probable cause simply does not exist even by the loosest of standards. *White* was such a case.

Federal agents had only unverified suspicions that White dealt in narcotics and were unsure of where he cached his supplies. Third-party bugging without a warrant held out the best promise of securing evidence for a conviction. Even so, the decoy had to meet White eight times before the government could clinch its case against him. The trial court sentenced him to twenty-five years as a second offender. The Court of Appeals for the Seventh Circuit reversed his conviction because the surreptitious monitoring and seizure of his conversations clearly violated his Fourth Amendment rights as construed by the Supreme Court in the 1967 *Katz* case;[165] the Seventh Circuit held that *Katz* in effect had overruled *On Lee.* On appeal before the Supreme Court, the government sought a reinstatement of White's conviction on ground that the Seventh Circuit had misread both *On Lee* and *Katz.* The government argued that the requirement of a warrant would definitely handicap police investigations and that the police needed warrantless bugging to verify a tip that did not meet the standard of probable cause.[166] *White* thus involved a re-evaluation of the continuing validity of *On Lee* in the face of *Katz,* when a cooperative informer gave consent to electronic surveillance of conversations between him and the defendant, who believed those conversations to have been private.

Justice White spoke in *White* for a four-member plurality of the Court that included Burger, Stewart, and Blackmun. Black joined the result for the reason stated in his *Katz* dissent: He believed that words are too intangible to be protected by an amendment that refers to "effects" and "things." Brennan agreed with the dissenters on the constitutional issues, but joined the plurality's result on a technicality: The events in *White* occurred before *Katz,* which had no retroactive application.[167] Thus, the disposition of the case turned on a 6-to-3 vote, though the Court split 5-to-4 on the meaning of *Katz* and its effect upon *On Lee.*

For Justice White, the decisive fact was that *Katz* did not control *White,* because the third ear did not listen in on the conversations in *Katz* at the invitation of one of the parties. Moreover, the Court in *Katz* had not stated that the defendant had a justifiable and constitutionally protected expectation that one to whom he spoke would not reveal his conversation to the police. Having distinguished *Katz* as a case not involving the consent of a bugged conversationalist, White sought support from other cases. His manipulation of the precedents drew protests from the dissenters. In one such precedent an IRS agent carrying a pocket tape recorder secretly transcribed his conversation with a suspect to have an unimpeachable record proving an attempted bribe. No third ear listened in.[168] In another precedent relied on by Justice White, a government informer betrayed to federal agents incriminating confidences that an unwary defendant had revealed to him. The case did not even involve electronic eavesdropping.[169] In White's final precedent, an undercover agent testified to the fact that he purchased narcotics from the accused. This case, too, did not involve electronic eavesdropping.[170] To the plurality there was no constitutional difference between these cases and *White*: "If the conduct and revelations of an agent operating without electronic equipment do not invade the defendant's constitutionally justifiable expectations of privacy, neither does a simultaneous recording of the same conversations made by an agent or by others from transmissions received from the agent [or informer] to whom the defendant is talking and whose trustworthiness the defendant necessarily risks."[171]

The problem in *White,* the plurality declared, was to determine what expectations the Fourth Amendment protects in the absence of a warrant. "If the law gives no protection to the wrongdoer whose trusted accomplice is or becomes a police agent, neither should it protect him when that same agent has recorded or transmitted the conversations which are later offered in evidence to prove the State's case."[172] The plurality saw no difference between a case involving a conventional betrayal of confidence and one involving an informer or agent "wired for sound" for the benefit of clandestine listeners. If there is no requirement of a warrant in the former case, there is none in the latter, despite the fact that it involves a live transmission to agents out of earshot. So reasoned Justice White by logic that enfeebled *Katz.* Of all the cases discussed by White, only *Katz* and *On Lee* showed electronic eavesdropping by the uninvited third ear. The absence of consent made *Katz* inapposite; its presence gave relevance to *On Lee. Katz,* White reasoned, undermined *On Lee* only on the point concerning physical trespass. But *On Lee* possessed continuing vitality because the Court in that precedent offered a second consideration: The informer participated in the bugging of his conversation with the defendant.

There were serious infirmities with this whole line of reasoning. The consent of the bugged informant in *On Lee* was merely the subject of an incidental dictum which the Court passed off without considering the absurdity of permitting the informer's secret consent to become the means of sapping the defendant's expectation of privacy. Moreover, in the other cases relied upon by the plurality, where the consent of an informer or agent had the same effect, there was no electronic eavesdropping by third parties. *White* was a case in which a bugged informer surreptitiously broadcast live "private" conversations to agents monitoring his frequency. *Katz* did not apply because, according to the plurality, the facts showed no informer or agent transmitting to the third ear, yet the plurality's precedents, except for *On Lee,* did not show instantaneous transmissions either. The extraordinary feature of White's logic was that in a case dealing with the constitutionality of warrantless electronic eavesdropping, the fact of electronic eavesdropping by third parties became irrelevant. There is no way to reconcile the plurality's explanation why the victim of bugging in *White* had no constitutionally recognizable expectation of privacy while the victim in *Katz* had that expectation. *White* held that if a party to a conversation could anticipate a risk of betrayal, the Fourth Amendment deserted him. That logic emasculated *Katz.* Yet the rule of *Katz* is that warrantless bugging violates a justifiable expectation of privacy. The plurality in *White* reached into Houdini's bag of tricks to make the expectation of privacy vanish without a trace simply because the bugged informer agreed to the other party's unknowing sacrifice of privacy.[173]

In *Katz* the Court said that when a person steps into the privacy of a phone booth, he does not consent to have his words "broadcast to the world."[174] The meaning of *White* is that if the same person talks to someone else when the two are alone together under circumstances of privacy, he is consenting to have his words broadcast to the world—or at least to the police, whose reproduction of his words becomes evidence to convict him.

The four dissenters, each in his own opinion, argued that *Katz* repudiated *On Lee*. Douglas and Brennan, more significantly, focused on the "qualitative difference" between electronic surveillance and conventional eavesdropping when the police are within earshot. The risk of being overheard or betrayed, Douglas argued, is normal. "But as soon as electronic surveillance comes into play, the risk changes crucially. There is no security from that kind of eavesdropping, no way of mitigating the risk, and so not even a residuum of true privacy."[175] The plurality's opinion, Douglas predicted, would have a "chilling effect on people speaking their minds. . . ." That possibility exists, to be sure, but it ignores the fact that the defendant in *White* was not debating with the bugged informer on the merits of using narcotics; he was engaged in illegal narcotics sales. Harlan also saw broad social implications in the plurality's endorsement of judicially uncontrolled electronic surveillance. Referring to the fact that "the Orwellian Big Brother" is technologically feasible, Harlan expressed concern about the extent of third-party bugging which, he said, is "used tens of thousands of times each year throughout the country, particularly in cases involving extortion, conspiracy, narcotics, gambling, prostitution, corruption by police officials . . . and similar crimes."[176] Suspects, even criminals, are, indeed, entitled to the same rights as the innocent, but the image of Big Brother is more relevant to cases of political and social dissent. Nevertheless, the danger of warrantless third-party bugging even in cases of conventional felonies is that it casts a net that inevitably captures every word of its victims, innocent or otherwise, on every subject. Harlan believed that third-party bugging might smother the spontaneity of discourse that "liberates daily life." He was strongest when he reminded that the issue before the Court was whether "to interpose a search warrant procedure between law enforcement agencies engaging in electronic eavesdropping and the public generally." He insisted that the warrant requirement is designed not to protect criminals but "to secure a measure of privacy and a sense of personal security throughout our society. . . . I think it must be held that third-party electronic monitoring, subject only to the self-restraint of law enforcement officials, has no place in our society."[177] Marshall agreed that the

Fourth Amendment requires a warrant in all cases of electronic surveillance.

Presidential Powers and Domestic Security

That Orwellian Big Brother has become a libertarian cliché whose reflexive invocation at almost every sign of government surveillance thrusts us beyond the capacity to recognize the real menace. *White,* however assailable its reasoning and its manipulation of precedents, did not show the face of Big Brother. *United States* v. *United States District Court* did.[178] It was the face of President Nixon. The Supreme Court, voting 8-to-0, severely rebuked him in 1972. In this instance he got exactly what he said he wanted from the Court: a "strict construction" of the Constitution. The President and his Department of Justice wanted the broadest possible construction; they argued that there is an implied inherent power in the Chief Executive to tap and bug subversives without court orders in cases involving "domestic national security interests."

United States District Court was one of those rare cases reassuring the nation that when a man becomes a Justice of the Supreme Court of the United States, he can on occasion subdue his own policy preferences, strain to achieve relative objectivity, and render judgment according to the law of the land when it is fairly clear. Powell, who spoke for the Court, had defended the Administration's electronic-surveillance policies before his appointment.[179] Blackmun joined his opinion; the Chief Justice simply noted that he concurred in the result. Rehnquist removed himself from participation in the case, because as an Assistant Attorney General he had helped formulate the Administration's practices that were at issue before the Court.

The Court held that "Fourth Amendment freedoms cannot properly be guaranteed if domestic security surveillances may be conducted solely within the discretion of the executive branch." In such cases the Fourth Amendment "contemplates a prior judicial judgment," that is, a warrant issued by a neutral and detached magistrate.[180] The Court announced this opinion two days after the police caught a secret White House criminal squad in an illegal entry into the headquarters of the Democratic Party. One objective of the Watergate conspirators was to install electronic listening devices. Rampant lawlessness honeycombed the Administration, which identified the domestic national-security interest with its own personal and political interests. Illegal eavesdropping on domestic subversives and on the opposition party was merely part of a pervasive pattern of deceit, perjury, extortion, graft, burglary, obstruction of justice, destruction of evidence, and corruption of the political process. The Administration embraced the doctrine that the ends justified the means, even if criminal. *United States District Court* involved just one facet of that doctrine.

In this case the government charged the defendants with conspiracy to destroy government property and accused one of them of the dynamite bombing of a CIA office. The defendants made a pretrial motion to compel the government to disclose any records of electronic surveillance over them; they also sought to obtain a pretrial hearing to determine whether the disclosures tainted either the evidence on which the federal grand jury had based its indictment or the evidence that the government intended to offer at the trial in a federal district court. The Warren Court in 1969 had put the government to a choice of dismissing its case or disclosing information secured by illegal eavesdropping so that the defendant may determine the extent to which the government based its case on that eavesdropping. He may then argue for suppression of the tainted evidence.[181] In *United States District Court,* the defendants sought the benefits of that precedent. Attorney General Mitchell filed an affidavit with the district court stating that he had authorized the wiretaps without a warrant under the authority of the President to safeguard domestic security. The district court granted the defendants' motions for disclosure and ordered a hearing to suppress evidence secured by warrantless wiretapping. The government turned to the United States Court of Appeals for an order vacating the command of the district court, but lost again. The case came before the Supreme Court on a request by the government for a writ commanding the district court to quash its orders in favor of the defendants—hence, the curious name of the case: *United States* v. *United States District Court.* The Solicitor General of the United States, Erwin Griswold, formerly Dean of the Harvard Law School, refused to argue the government's case before the Supreme Court. That *beau geste* cost Griswold his job.[182] Assistant Attorney General Robert Mardian, who had defended warrantless wiretapping on the authority of the President, presented the case and lost.

Had the Administration obtained its evidence in *United States District Court* by monitoring either a bugged informer or an undercover agent, *White* would have legitimated the use of that evidence in a criminal trial. In this case, however, there was no "consent." Government agents monitored wiretaps "which," in the words of Attorney General John N. Mitchell, "were being employed to gather intelligence information deemed necessary to protect the nation from attempts of domestic organizations to attack and subvert the existing structure of the Government."[183] Had the government first obtained a valid warrant, the constitutionality of its conduct would have been beyond reproach. If the activities of the domestic subversives had had a significant connection with a foreign power or its agents, the Court would have sustained the warrantless wiretapping. But this was not a case in which there existed any difficulty in distinguishing "domestic" and "foreign" subversion. Every President since Truman had employed electronic surveillance in domestic-security cases, but this was the first to come before the Court.[184] "The issue before us," Powell declared in his opening words, "is an important one for the people of our country and their Government. It involves the delicate question of the President's power, acting through the Attorney General, to authorize electronic surveillance in internal security matters *without prior judicial approval.*"[185]

This was not a case in which the government had outrageously eavesdropped on harmless radicals, but that fact did not affect the constitutional issue. If the executive branch can eavesdrop without a warrant on the conversations of any citizen whom it believes to be a subversive, there are no practical limits on its powers to violate the Fourth Amendment and none on its discretion to define who is subversive. The President believed that his own re-election in 1972 was essential to national security. As a result, the headquarters of the most legitimate dissenting organization in the country became a target for clandestine surveillance, search, and seizure. Similarly, the office of a psychiatrist was criminally entered and searched in order to serve the Administration's desire for data to construct a psychiatric profile of a suspected subversive, Daniel Ellsberg, whose complicity with a foreign power the Department of Justice never sought to prove in court, despite the opportunity. As Powell observed:

> History abundantly documents the tendency of Government—however benevolent and benign its motives—to view with suspicion those who most fervently dispute its policies. Fourth Amendment protections become the more necessary when the targets of official surveillance may be those suspected of unorthodoxy in their political beliefs. The danger to political dissent is acute where the Government attempts to act under so vague a concept as the power to protect "domestic security."[186]

The principle at stake in *United States District Court,* therefore, was whether the Chief Executive can secretly suspend the Fourth Amendment at his discretion in cases of domestic security.

Powell based his opinion for the Court on both statutory and constitutional grounds. First, he examined the government's argument that the eavesdropping provisions of the Omnibus Crime Control and Safe Streets Act of 1968 excepted domestic-security surveillances from the requirement of a warrant. Taken out of context one provision of the act did give the government an arguable case. That provision states:

> Nor shall anything contained in this chapter be deemed to limit the constitutional power of the President to take such measures as he deems necessary to protect the United States against the overthrow of the Government by force or other unlawful means, or against any other clear and present danger to the structure or existence of the Government.[187]

Taken literally, that loose language seems to empower draconian executive measures against an attempt to abolish the Electoral College or otherwise alter the structure of the government. The Court looked only at the overwhelming evidence that the legislative history of the statute clearly refuted the argument that the President could wiretap without a warrant in domestic-security cases. Congress simply meant that the statute did not affect the President's powers, whatever they are; there was no intention to add or detract from those powers as defined by the Constitution. Powell examined the President's constitutional powers and concluded that the warrant clause of the Fourth Amendment "is not dead language"—a proposition that he buttressed with reference to *Coolidge* v. *New Hampshire* as an authority for the point that warrants issued on probable cause by a magistrate should operate "as a matter of course to check the 'well-intentioned but mistakenly overzealous executive officers'. . . ."[188] Powell did not refer to *United States* v. *White,* which seemed to render the warrant clause obsolete in the presence of a bugged informer. Instead, *Katz* v. *United States,* like *Coolidge,* enjoyed a renaissance for its implicit recognition that "the broad and unsuspected governmental incursions into conversational privacy which electronic surveillance entails necessitate the application of Fourth Amendment safeguards."[189] Having carefully excluded from consideration cases involving subversion by foreign powers, Powell eloquently called on history to illuminate his finding that the constitutional requirement of a warrant best serves the needs of citizens for privacy and free discussion.

The government contended that the "special circumstances applicable to domestic security surveillances" required an exception to the usual requirement of a warrant. That requirement, the government claimed, "would obstruct the President in the discharge of his constitutional duty to protect domestic security."[190] The government also argued that the purpose of such surveillance, generally, was to keep tabs on subversives rather than to gather evidence for specific criminal prosecutions. That was a hollow contention in the face of a specific criminal prosecution. Nevertheless, the force of the government's position rested on the claim that when intelligence is the objective of official eavesdropping, the warrant requirement applicable to investigations of criminal activity should be suspended. Finally, the government urged, with astounding arrogance, that "as a practical matter" courts do not have the competence, knowledge, and techniques to determine whether probable cause exists to justify electronic surveillance "necessary to protect national security."[191]

The Court effectively repudiated this entire line of argument. Powell observed that even when the objective of official eavesdropping is merely to gather intelligence on alleged subversives, it "risks infringement of constitutionally protected privacy of speech." The inherent vagueness of the concept of domestic security and the "temptation to utilize such surveillances to oversee political dissent" led the Court to decide that although the President has a constitutional authority to authorize eavesdropping as a protection of domestic security, his power "must be exercised in a manner compatible with the Fourth Amendment. In this case we hold that this requires an appropriate prior warrant procedure."[192] To the claim that domestic-security cases involved considerations "too subtle and complex for judicial evaluation" of probable cause, Powell answered that "Courts regularly deal with the most difficult issues of our society." When senior law-enforcement officials of the government cannot explain to a court the significance of a domestic-security threat, "one may question whether there is probable cause for surveillance."[193] Given the fact that the congressional act of 1968 imposed on the judiciary the responsibility for deciding whether warrants should issue in cases involving treason and espionage, there was no reason to exempt from the warrant requirement cases involving "domestic security" threats. Although Powell conceded that the necessity of securing a warrant inconvenienced the government, that was a justifiable inconvenience to protect the constitutional values of a free society. No argument of the government convinced him that the traditional requirement of a warrant would impair its surveillance powers in domestic-security cases. That requirement, Powell believed, reassured the nation that "indiscriminate wiretapping and bugging of law-abiding citizens cannot occur."[194]

As a result of this decision, Mitchell's successor, Attorney General Richard G. Kleindienst, ordered the disconnection of fewer than ten warrantless domestic-security taps.[195] In view of the Administration's notorious lack of integrity, there is no reason to believe that there were so few warrantless taps at the time. The decision really meant that although the Court cannot prevent the government from engaging in covert and illegal tapping on any scale for "intelligence" purposes, the exclusionary rule bars the prosecutorial use of evidence thus obtained without a warrant.

One week after *United States District Court,* there were decisions in two related cases. In one, *Laird* v. *Tatum*, the Court split 5-to-4 against a request for a judgment that the Army's surveillance of lawful civilian activity should be enjoined as unconstitutional because of its chilling effect on First Amendment freedoms.[196] The Nixon appointees plus White constituted a majority. Speaking through Burger, they found that the complainants had not proved either that they had personally suffered some injury as a result of the Army's surveillance or that the Army had used some illegal means, such as warrantless eavesdropping. The Army supposedly maintained political dossiers on some 25 million Americans, including the members and supporters of "virtually every activist political group in the country," but despite tactics of infiltration, observation, tape recording at public meetings, photographing, clipping news stories, and other forms of intelligence gathering by the military, there was no Fourth Amendment issue present in this case.[197] The dissenters, on the other hand, saw the case as "a cancer in our body politic."[198] They believed that the majority of the Court was insensitive to the paralyzing effect on First Amendment freedoms when military intelligence officers, following a "Russian" model, checked the reading and associations of nonconformists.

On the same day, however, the Court protected federal-grand-jury witnesses from contempt citations based on a refusal to answer questions derived from illegal wiretapping by the government.[199] This time, in *Gelbard* v. *United States*, the four Nixon appointees dissented. Douglas, the only member of the Court to confront the broadest constitutional issue presented by the facts of the case, believed that any government employment of electronic surveillance violates the Fourth Amendment. He, therefore, argued the unconstitutionality of the provisions of the Omnibus Crime Control Act of 1968, which authorized electronic eavesdropping subject to prior judicial approval. The other members of the Court did not question the validity of the statute; nor did they reach the question whether the Fourth Amendment prevents findings of contempt against grand-jury witnesses who balk at interrogation founded on warrantless eavesdropping on their phone conversations. Except for Douglas, the Court saw only a narrow statutory issue: Did the act of 1968 protect recalcitrant grand-jury witnesses against contempt citations when the witnesses were victims of lawless wiretapping? One provision of the statute excludes evidence at any proceeding, including grand-jury hearings, derived from any illegally intercepted conversations. The majority, with Douglas's support, held for the witnesses. The dissenters, led by Rehnquist, executed petty pirouettes around the apparent implications of the statute. Rehnquist proved that a legal technician can bend words to mean whatever he pleases. Brennan, for the majority, played a similar game, but at least his opinion stayed closer to the text of the act.

Excepting its decision restraining warrantless electronic surveillance on authority of the President in domestic-security cases, the Nixon Court has steadily moved away from the disposition of the Warren Court to stress the need for particular warrants issued on probable cause by an independent magistrate. The recent decisions vividly show a propensity to extend exceptions to the warrant requirement in cases dealing with stop and frisk, automobiles, exigent circumstances, searches incident to arrest, and constructive consent. The Court has moved like a sidewinder, wriggling steadily in the direction of removing Fourth Amendment constraints on the police. Even in cases where the police have acted with warrants, the Court, after some vacillation, relaxed warrant requirements by finding probable cause based on informers' tips that definitely lacked the credibility and proof demanded by the Warren Court. By removing established constraints on the police, the Nixon Court has given its imprimatur to a variety of evidence secured by means that would have been suppressed under the exclusionary rule. Though not repudiating that rule, the new Court has shown its hostility to it and has circumvented it by findings that the evidence in dispute resulted from reasonable searches or searches conducted on probable cause.

The cases decided when Burger and Blackmun were the only Nixon appointees reflected a zigzag course, though when the Court applied the exclusionary rule, Burger and Blackmun always sided with the police. When Powell and Rehnquist became Justices, they clearly tilted the Court in favor of the prosecutorial position. When all four Nixon appointees joined together, they represented a minority only in the case supporting the right of grand-jury witnesses to refuse answer to questions based on information derived from illegal wiretapping. The Nixon Justices were on the victorious side in *United States District Court,* but that was a freak Fourth Amendment case, because it was the only one in which the participating members reached a unanimous judgment. Before Powell and Rehnquist joined the Court, Burger and Blackmun needed the support of Black, White, and Stewart to prevail. Stewart in those earlier cases was the swing man. After Powell and Rehnquist became members, the situation changed. Except for *Almeida-Sanchez,* the border-search case, where Powell in an independent opinion pointed the way to a position that can reunite the Nixon appointees, the four voted as a bloc in search-and-seizure cases, and White's became the decisive fifth vote. The four found him an eager partner. As often as not, Stewart joined the same bloc, leaving the libertarian remnants of the Warren Court—Douglas, Brennan, and Marshall—a dissenting minority. From their standpoint the trend of decision shows a distinct and ominous pattern. Beginning with the decisions of 1972, the Nixon Justices have not been on the losing side except in *Almeida-Sanchez,* when Powell deserted them, and in *Gelbard.* The only pre-1972 decision of continuing significance that rejected the prosecutorial position was *Coolidge v. New Hampshire.* It is still intact, but its demise by the current process of distinguishing away, rather than by overruling, governing precedents seems to be merely a matter of time and opportunity.

CHAPTER THREE

The Fifth Amendment:
The Right Against Self-Incrimination

In no area of criminal justice was the Nixon Court's new departure so swift and veering as in cases arising under the Fifth Amendment's self-incrimination clause. The Court decided fourteen such cases during just the first two years of Burger's incumbency. Taken together those cases call to mind the brief review by the music critic who wrote, "The orchestra played Beethoven; Beethoven lost." In all but one of the fourteen cases the right claimed under the Fifth Amendment lost. In the one exception, a shift in position by Harlan, who voted against the Fifth Amendment right in the other thirteen cases, made the margin of victory in a 5-to-4 decision. Not the constitutional issues but the presuppositions of the members of the Court, their attitudes toward the right against self-incrimination, influenced the outcome of the cases. Some members of the Court have reflected, if not an overt hostility to the constitutional right, a conviction that it must be kept tightly encircled with chickenwires of constraint.

In all fourteen cases Burger, joined by Blackmun in the 1970–71 term, and by Stewart and White, voted against the Fifth Amendment claim. Harlan added his vote in most cases. The three holdover Justices, Harlan, Stewart, and White, had been on the Warren Court in the mid-1960s when numerous decisions expanded the

139

protections of the self-incrimination clause, one of the Warren Court's foremost accomplishments in the field of criminal justice. They had dissented in several of those significant cases.

In *Malloy* (1964) when the Court took the monumental step of holding that the Fourteenth Amendment incorporated the self-incrimination clause, thus making it apply against state violation in the same way that it applies against federal violation,[1] Harlan, Stewart, and White dissented. In *Griffin* (1965) when the Court held that comment by the prosecutor or trial judge on the fact that a criminal defendant failed to testify penalized his right to silence by encouraging an inference of his guilt, thus adversely influencing the jury against him, they dissented again.[2] The three dissented also in the sensational *Miranda* case (1966) when the Court widened the perimeters of the right against self-incrimination beyond all precedent, yet not beyond its historical spirit and purpose.[3] To overcome the inherently coercive and inquisitorial atmosphere of the interrogation room and to insure that incriminating admissions are the product of free choice, the *Miranda* majority ruled in part that the police must apprise a suspect of his constitutional rights and make him understand that he has a right to remain silent, that his answers may be used against him, and that he is entitled to counsel in the police station in order to protect his rights under the Fifth Amendment. The public sees the evidence of this most forcefully on television shows. In *Garrity* (1967) Harlan, Stewart, and White dissented again when the Court held that the amendment prohibited the introduction at a criminal trial of incriminating testimony previously exacted from police officers under a threat of loss of employment; the majority ruled that public employees must not be forced to choose between testifying against themselves or forfeiting their jobs.[4] The three also disagreed with the majority in *Spevack* (1967) when an attorney who had been disbarred for invoking the Fifth Amendment received the Court's protection of his right to remain silent without suffering penalties.[5] They dissented, too, in *Gault* (1967) when the Court ruled that juveniles are entitled to the right against self-incrimination in delinquency hearings that may result in their imprisonment.[6]

The voting pattern of the Warren Court in Fifth Amendment cases was by no means uniform, however. Harlan, Stewart, and

White did not always vote against a right claimed under that amendment, nor did the majority, led by Black and Douglas, always vote for such a right. In several of the Warren Court's most important Fifth Amendment decisions, most notably those involving federal statutes whose registration provisions entailed a substantial risk of criminal prosecution for failure to comply, Harlan, Stewart, and White voted with the Black-Douglas majority.[7] The three also concurred with that majority, though separately and on constrictive grounds, in the judgment in *Murphy* (1964) broadening the reach of the Fifth Amendment: A state may not, under a grant of immunity from state prosecution, compel testimony or evidence that may be incriminating under federal law unless the compelled testimony cannot in any way be used by federal officials in a criminal prosecution.[8] In several cases during the mid-1960s that did not extend the amendment the three were with the majority of the Warren Court when it held that compulsion of an allegedly nontestimonial character, such as forcing a suspect to give a blood sample or a specimen of his handwriting, or making him speak at a police lineup, did not violate his right not to be a witness against himself.[9] The three also joined the majority in two cases in which the Warren Court decided against the retroactivity of recent decisions expanding Fifth Amendment rights.[10] Harlan, Stewart, and White never supported a Fifth Amendment claim that the Black-Douglas wing rejected. Thus, the cases of the 1960s reflected a discernible voting pattern among the Justices who remained on the Court after the resignations of Warren and Fortas. Black and Douglas, usually supported by Brennan and Marshall, voted for Fifth Amendment claims in most cases, while Harlan, Stewart, and White opposed such claims in most cases. In the Nixon Court, Burger and Blackmun converted the positions of the Warren dissidents into majority doctrine.

DEFENSE DISCLOSURES

On the most important self-incrimination issue decided in the 1969–70 term, when there were just eight Justices sitting for most of the year (Blackmun took his seat on June 9, 1970, as the term drew to a close), the Court divided 6-to-2 in *Williams* v. *Florida,* the "notice-of-alibi" case.[11] It involved what the legal profession calls "criminal discovery," the required disclosure, usually before trial, of essential aspects of the proposed case to be presented at the trial by the prosecution or defense or both. In civil cases, pretrial discovery is a common and uncontroversial phenomenon, but it is still unusual in criminal cases.

Prior to the notice-of-alibi case there were Supreme Court discovery precedents benefitting criminal defendants. In 1957 in *Jencks* v. *United States* the Court ruled that pretrial statements by government witnesses to the FBI must be produced on the request of defense counsel, whose purpose is to discredit those witnesses on cross-examination.[12] Congress reacted by passing a statute providing that the accused could not get access to any government documents until the witness has testified—that is, there could be no pretrial discovery.[13] In *Brady* v. *Maryland* (1963) the Court established a constitutional right for the defendant to discovery of evidence favorable to him in possession of the prosecution; the latter's suppression of such evidence violates due process of law.[14] In 1966 Congress amended the Federal Rules of Criminal Procedure by providing that should a federal court grant to a defendant discovery of anything but his own confession or grand-jury testimony, he must disclose to the government, on its motion, any papers or objects that he intends to introduce at his trial. This new rule made pretrial discovery in federal criminal cases reciprocal, though conditioning the government's right to disclosure by the defense on the latter's decision to use discovery. Douglas and Black futilely objected to the rule because in effect it forced the defendant to waive his right against self-incrimination by making him reveal his own evidence.[15] So matters stood until the notice-of-alibi case of 1970, when the Court for the first time ruled in favor of pretrial discovery by the prosecution in state cases.

Florida was one of sixteen states whose rules of criminal procedure provided for a notice-of-alibi rule. The Florida rule, unlike the federal one, gave the initial advantage to the prosecution by requiring the defendant, on the demand of the state, to give notice in advance of his trial whether he intended to use an alibi as part of his defense and if so to reveal that alibi together with the names and addresses of his alibi witnesses. In return, the prosecution must disclose the names and addresses of witnesses that the state proposed to call for the purpose of discrediting the alibi. If the defendant refused to comply, the trial judge might exclude the testimony of alibi witnesses.

In the case that came before the Supreme Court, the defendant under protest had complied with the rule, disclosing the name of an alibi witness whom the state questioned under oath before trial. At the trial that witness gave evidence that conflicted with her deposition; moreover, a police officer testified that he saw her alone on the street at a time when she claimed to be at home in the company of the defendant. The jury convicted. The defendant appealed on the ground that forced disclosure of his alibi witness had compelled him to be a witness against himself.

White, for the Court, explained that the state founded the notice-of-alibi rule on a legitimate interest in preventing the fabrication of alibis as an eleventh-hour defense. The adversary system of trial, White quipped, was not "a poker game in which players enjoy an absolute right to conceal their cards until played."[16] The rule violated neither due process of law nor fair trial because it was designed to "enhance the search for the truth" by guaranteeing both sides time enough, before trial, to investigate facts important to the jury's determination of guilt or innocence. White found no basis for the defendant's "major contention" that he was compelled to be a witness against himself. The "privilege against self-incrimination," White declared, "is not violated by a requirement that the defendant give notice of an alibi defense and disclose his alibi witnesses."[17]

In an irrelevant and mischievous passage, White pointed out that a criminal defendant is often forced by the nature of the prosecution's evidence to call witnesses on his behalf and invariably submit them to cross-examination which may be damaging to his defense. He might even be forced to take the stand himself to offer testimony. In either situation his attempted alibi defense might end in catastrophe; however testimonial or incriminating it proves to be, it cannot be considered compelled simply because he abandoned his right to complete silence and offered such a defense. White's analogy was misleading in the case of a defendant whom state law compelled to give pretrial notice of alibi and alibi witnesses, though

White insisted that the pressures bearing on the defendant's pretrial "decision" were of the same nature as those that might induce him to invoke an alibi defense at his trial. Contrary to White, the only "decision" that the notice-of-alibi rule allowed the defendant was whether to present alibi witnesses. But according to White, "At most, the rule only compelled him to accelerate the timing of his disclosure. . . ."[18] In the absence of such a rule, there was no constitutional bar to the trial judge's granting of a continuance to the state should it be surprised at the trial by a sudden alibi defense. Consequently, there should be no bar to a rule that, through pretrial discovery, avoided disruption of the trial. "We decline to hold," White concluded, "that the privilege against compulsory self-incrimination guarantees the defendant the right to surprise the State with an alibi defense."[19]

In his concurring opinion, Burger saw in the rule a means of disposing expeditiously of cases without trial, "a matter of considerable importance" when courts, prosecutors, and defender agencies are overburdened. The prosecutor, on receiving notice of the alibi before trial, might find that it is unimpeachable and, as a result, might dismiss the charges. On the other hand, the defense, if submitting an alibi that could be attacked as unreliable, might be willing to plead guilty to a lesser charge. "In either case," said Burger, "the ends of justice will have been served and the processes expedited."[20]

The ends of justice are unquestionably served by an expeditious revelation of the truth, assuming that the means used to reveal the truth do not encroach on the fundamental law. The difficulty with the majority viewpoint was that it diminished the meaning of the constitutional provision that no person should be compelled to be a witness against himself in any criminal case. The Fifth Amendment does not refer to any privileges; it refers to rights, though White repeatedly spoke of the "privilege against self-incrimination." A privilege is a revocable concession tolerantly granted by the government to its subjects. But in American constitutional theory, the rights of the people do not derive from the government; the Constitution, which secures those rights, is paramount to the government that it creates. To speak of the "privilege" against self-incrimination degrades it, inadvertently or otherwise, in comparison

to other constitutional rights, and opens the door to easy infringements.[21] Even to speak of the *right* against self-incrimination, for it
is a right equal in status to other constitutionally protected rights,
is crippling. The phrase, whether referring to a right or privilege
"against self-incrimination," is merely a shorthand, judicial gloss of
modern origin that implies a restriction not in the constitutional
clause itself. That is, the right of a person not to be "a witness
against himself" signifies a principle of much wider reach than
merely a right against self-incrimination; the constitutional right is
a guarantee against the involuntary self-production of any adverse
evidence that connects one to a crime.

Thus, the clause, by its own terms, extends to all of the injurious
as well as incriminating consequences of disclosure by the party.
White, for the Court, began with a stunted version of the constitutional right, enabling him to rationalize a new encroachment
upon it as if none at all had been made. The history of the right
proves conclusively that it was intended to protect the defendant
against any compulsion to assist the government in its prosecution
against him. The Bill of Rights, including the disputed clause of
the Fifth Amendment, was certainly not intended to serve prosecutorial efficiency, speed, or convenience, with which Burger too
casually identified the ends of justice. Nor was the clause intended
to serve the revelation of truth. Like the guarantees of a fair trial
and representation by counsel, the clause reflected the judgment of
its framers that in a free society, based on respect for the individual, the determination of guilt or innocence must be made in
accordance with just procedures by which the accused made no
unwilling contribution to his own conviction.[22] The one unanswerable objection to the Court's opinion is that at the very least the
state's pretrial discovery of the alibi defense forces the defendant
to abandon his right to silence until a case has been presented
against him. To use White's metaphor, the decision made the accused "show his hand" not at the eleventh hour but before the first
hour. He becomes a reluctant accomplice to the state's effort to
prove his guilt.

Black, joined by Douglas, dissented in an opinion that was filled
with exaggeration. Although the majority carefully limited its decision to the validity of Florida's notice-of-alibi rule, the dissenters

insisted that sustaining it opened the way for "a profound change in one of the most important traditional safeguards of a criminal defendant. The rationale of today's decision is in no way limited to alibi defenses, or any other type or classification of evidence."[23] According to Black, White's opinion inevitably would permit the state to obtain complete disclosure in advance of trial of "any and all" of the case that he intended to present in his defense. For that reason, Black spoke of the decision as a "radical and dangerous departure" from the historical and constitutionally guaranteed right of a criminal defendant "to remain completely silent, requiring the State to prove its case without any assistance of any kind from the defendant himself."[24] Compelling him to be a witness against himself, as in the use of pretrial discovery of his alibi defense, was, declared Black, unknown in English law "except for the unlamented proceedings in the Star Chamber courts—the type of proceedings the Fifth Amendment was designed to prevent."[25] Suggesting that the decision presaged a return to Star Chamber proceedings was unwarranted by White's explicit refusal to pass upon any question unpresented by the facts of the case. Black used the Star Chamber as a bogey-man. During its final period of control by Archbishop Laud, the Star Chamber operated for a century and a half as fairly as the common-law courts of the time, and its proceedings were similar to those of other English courts, those of chancery and admiralty among them.[26] But Black was not wrong in his main point: The decision was an unprecedented limitation by the Supreme Court on the applicability of the Fifth Amendment's clause in cases of criminal discovery.

Black revealed weaknesses in the majority opinion. He repudiated the notion that, at most, the notice-of-alibi rule forced the accused to accelerate a disclosure of his alibi. For Black the matter of timing made all the difference to the defense. Waiting until the prosecution showed its case at the trial before having to decide whether to present an alibi defense was wholly different from being compelled to decide whether to show that defense before the trial. Before trial, the defendant knows only what the prosecution's case might be; but the case looks quite different when actually tried, minimizing the guesswork and gamble that accompany a pretrial decision to reveal the alibi defense. The pretrial pressures on a defendant to reveal his alibi defense are not only different in nature from the trial pressures but significantly greater, as Black contended. If there were no qualitative difference between disclosure of the alibi defense before or during trial, as White alleged, then the discovery rule merely accelerated the decision to make that disclosure. That was the rationale that Black found to be overbroad, potentially justifying pretrial disclosure of all evidence, testimony, and tactics intended to be used by the defense. Thus, the prosecution could fix the defense in point of time and require its wholesale discovery.

Black went too far. For example, the sanctions for noncompliance with discovery were not, in this case, applied. As White indicated, whether and to what extent a state can enforce discovery rules against a recalcitrant defendant, by excluding his relevant, probative evidence, was a question not raised by the facts; if raised, it would pose a Sixth Amendment or fair-trial issue "which we have no occasion to explore." Additionally, a compliant defendant might reveal a proposed defense yet subsequently abandon it. The facts did not confront the Court with the question whether a defendant can be compelled in advance of trial to select a defense from which he could not deviate. Black countered that if an alibi defense was contemplated, a pretrial disclosure was obligatory to preserve the possibility of raising it later. White did not bother to point out that a genuine eleventh-hour alibi defense was possible under the Florida rule. A man might be innocent yet unable to prove an alibi until a witness belatedly turned up to testify that the accused was elsewhere at the time of the crime. "For good cause shown," the Florida rule provided, "the court may waive the requirements of this rule."[27] The rule was part of broader discovery provisions benefitting defendants and which the accused in this case invoked on his behalf.

The forced discovery of a faked alibi defense can, of course, be incriminating. A specious alibi exposed at a trial is the worst of all possible defenses. But the rule did not force the accused to fabricate an alibi, thus incriminating himself. Conversely, the best defense is an unshakable alibi; it is exculpatory, not incriminating. If the alibi is true, yet based on the word of witnesses of questionable character, their character and previous criminal records would ultimately be exposed at the trial even if there were no pre-trial discovery. In any case, a defendant who proposes to present an alibi that is reliable would inevitably present it without misgivings, rather than rest on his right to remain mute and force the prosecution to prove his guilt if it can. Revealing his defense does not involuntarily cooperate with the state in his self-destruction if his alibi can withstand critical scrutiny.

Although the rationale of the decision was overbroad, the reason for that overbreadth was not, as Black alleged, that the accused was forced before trial to provide incriminating information. The reason, rather, was that the majority insisted that a criminal trial is a search for the truth, not "a poker game" or sporting event. Yet, even poker games and sporting events are conducted in accordance with rules, as are criminal trials. The search for truth must be conducted within similar circumscribed bounds. Evidence and testimony may be true yet obtained in ways that taint them and make them properly excludable at the trial. Truthful evidence might be obtained by an unlawful search or by beating the accused. A guilty man is entitled to have his conviction reversed if his indictment contains an error or the trial judge improperly charges the jury. Due process in such a case demands a reversal. Similarly, the burden of proof is on the prosecution. No man, however guilty—and the purpose of the trial is to determine guilt or innocence fairly—should have to assist the prosecution in convicting him. Even if his alibi proves that he is innocent, he should not have to be a witness for the prosecution. "Rather," as Black stated, "he has an absolute, unqualified right to compel the State to investigate its own case, find its own witnesses, prove its own facts, and convince the jury through its own resources."[28] The fact remains, however, that an alibi that survives pretrial discovery and that proves innocence cannot be a device for making a defendant be a witness against himself. Black's anguished dissent was an expression of apprehension about what might happen if criminal discovery were expanded. Brennan and Marshall, no apostles of law and order without fairness and justice, concurred in White's opinion for the Court, one-sided as it was. In 1973 the Court ruled that in the absence of reciprocal discovery, a state may not force a defendant to give notice of his alibi.[29]

SUBVERSION OF *Miranda*

Brennan and Marshall rejoined forces with Black and Douglas in *Harris* v. *New York,* the "illegal confessions" case, decided in 1971.[30] That they had to speak in dissent and without the support of Harlan, Stewart, and White passes belief, because the opinion of the Court, given by Burger, was surely one of the most scandalous, extraordinary, and inexplicable in the history of the Court. Compared to most constitutional cases, this one was rather simple and noncontroversial. The police, suspecting that Harris was a pusher as well as a dope addict, arranged for an undercover agent to buy heroin from him. The officer later testified that he made the purchase from Harris and that on a subsequent day made another. (If Harris sold him heroin on the first occasion, why should the agent have made the second purchase?) The police arrested Harris and took him into custody for interrogation. They did not tell him his rights to silence and counsel. Though he asked for counsel, they ignored him and continued the interrogation until he incriminated himself.

The arrest took place before the *Miranda* decision,[31] though after the decision in *Escobedo* (1964), which required the presence of counsel, if requested, during a custodial interrogation in order to protect the suspect's right not to be a witness against himself.[32] Moreover, a New York statute required cautioning a suspect before an admissible confession could be taken. Harris made a statement admitting not that he sold heroin to the officer but that he had bought some; he claimed that he had acted as an intermediary for the police, who paid him for his services. His trial took place after the *Miranda* decision, which applied to all subsequent trials. At his trial, Harris took the stand to testify in his own defense and contradicted his earlier statement. Although he denied selling anything to the officer on the first occasion, he claimed that on the second he sold harmless baking powder that appeared to be heroin. On cross-examination the prosecutor used Harris's earlier statement against him for the purpose of discrediting his testimony. Defense counsel, overruled by the trial judge, objected that Harris's statement could not be used against him for any purpose because he had made it involuntarily and contrary to the requirements of

Miranda. The trial judge ruled that an illegally obtained statement, while inadmissible as proof of defendant's guilt, could be used to impeach his credibility as a witness. After the cross-examination, Harris's counsel restated for the record his objections to using the statement for impeachment purposes. The jury convicted Harris for having sold heroin on the second occasion only.

After New York's highest court sustained the conviction, Harris appealed to the Supreme Court. In the briefs and oral argument, as well as in the appellate proceedings in the state, the defendant through counsel persistently sought a reversal on ground that his involuntary statement should not have been used against him. During the oral argument, the following colloquy took place:[33]

> Q. Well, then, as to coercion, the involuntariness of this statement, do I understand it to be your submission that because of the attitude the prosecutor took, the ruling of the court was that even assuming it was coerced it could still be used?
> A. Exactly, but I also say—
> Q. We should decide this case therefore on the hypothesis, whatever the facts may be, that this was coerced?
> A. Exactly . . .

Counsel, in response to questions, also asserted that the statement was involuntary even in the pre-*Miranda* sense; in other words, that the statement had been coerced by the police and did not represent Harris's free will, even in the absence of any requirement that he be notified prior to interrogation that he had a right to counsel and to silence and that he could waive his rights only knowingly, voluntarily, and intelligently.[34]

Counsel for New York, acknowledging that defendant claimed the contrary, argued that Harris's statement had been voluntarily made. When asked whether a coerced confession could be used to impeach the defendant's testimony, counsel for the state also acknowledged that if the confession had been coerced it could not be used "for any purpose."[35] The question was further explored in this exchange between Stewart and counsel for the state:[36]

> Q. I didn't mean an untrue confession, I meant simply an involuntary confession, could you use that to impeach him?
> A. No. Mr. Justice Stewart, I don't think we could, for this reason:

The point I am trying to make is a voluntary confession, if it is voluntary in the traditional sense [i.e., pre-*Miranda*], can be relied upon to express the truth, whereas an involuntary confession is subject, to take the obvious example, a man will say anything to keep from being beaten and all we have to do is go to some of the countries beyond the Iron Curtain to demonstrate that. There is a point beyond which human endurance can't continue. . . .

Q. . . . And let's assume further that it is wholly true. Could you have used that to impeach him?

A. I don't think so, Mr. Justice Stewart, because the thought is that we must define a class of confessions which may be used for these purposes, and I think once you define the class as being a true confession rather than a voluntary confession, then you're getting into extraneous matters that perhaps aren't properly explored in the context of this.

Q. What you are saying then is that it can't be given any use because it is inherently unreliable as being involuntary?

A. As being involuntary, yes . . .

Despite his claim that Harris's statement was voluntary, counsel for the state admitted that the confession Harris had made about selling heroin on the second occasion—the only sale for which the jury convicted—was a "false account."[37]

When stating the facts of the case in his opinion for the Court, Burger, in a shocking distortion, declared flatly, "Petitioner makes no claim that the statements made to the police were coerced or involuntary."[38] The trial record, the appellate proceedings in the state, and the briefs and oral arguments before the Supreme Court show that Harris made exactly that claim from start to finish.[39] No one lacking powers of divination or access to candid statements from the members of the Court can explain Burger's misstatement of the record, nor the failure of those joining in the disposition of the case to correct that record in a separate, concurring opinion, nor the failure of even the dissenters to take issue with the Chief Justice's remark. The Court's failure on all sides shakes confidence in its integrity or its craftsmanship. Surely the route traveled by the Court, especially in a majority opinion, must be along the straightest path of intellectual rectitude and professional expertness in stating the facts, not to mention the controlling precedents.

Given the facts of this case, the Court might simply have found that, as the state acknowledged, a statement involuntarily made, whether in the pre- or post-*Miranda* sense, cannot be used in any way against the defendant, not even to discredit his testimony. In this case, given the dispute whether the statement had been voluntarily made, the Court might have ruled on the question of voluntariness, the record permitting, or might have remanded the case to the state courts for a determination whether Harris's statement was voluntary and, if so, whether usable to impeach him in light of *Miranda*. At no point in the state proceedings had there been a hearing to determine whether Harris had made his statement voluntarily, because the trial court had ruled that even an illegally obtained confession could be used to impeach the witness's credibility, and the high court of New York agreed, in a 3-to-2 decision.[40]

By alleging that Harris made no claim that his statement was coerced or involuntary, Burger altered the posture of the question before the Court and put himself into a position to ridicule contentions contrary to those which he asserted. Conceivably, the dissenters did not correct Burger's misstatement because they wanted to settle the question he in effect raised: whether the prosecution may use for the purpose of discrediting the defendant a statement made by him that was not coerced in any physical or psychological sense but was admittedly obtained in violation of the *Miranda* prescription that certain warnings must be made prior to in-custody interrogation. Was *Miranda* controlling? Burger acknowledged that there were "some comments" in Warren's opinion in the *Miranda* case that could be read as a bar against the use of any uncounseled statement for any purpose, but Burger dismissed such comments as mere dicta—a discussion of the issue "not at all necessary to the Court's holding and cannot be regarded as controlling."[41] Contrary to Burger, *Miranda* did not bar the use of uncounseled statements for any purpose, because the Court permitted a knowing, intelligent, and voluntary waiver of the right to counsel. More important, Warren in *Miranda* had made much more than merely "some comments" that might be read to decide the question before the Court as defined by Burger in *Harris*. There was nothing remotely equivocal about what Warren had declared.

Early in his opinion he announced that the Court's "holding" would be spelled out with specificity, "but briefly stated it is this: The prosecution may not use statements, whether exculpatory or inculpatory, stemming from custodial interrogation of the defendant unless it demonstrates the use of procedural safeguards effective to secure the privilege against self-incrimination." More than thirty pages later, Warren summed up as follows:[42]

> The warnings required and the waiver necessary in accordance with our opinion today are, in the absence of a fully effective equivalent, prerequisites to the admissibility of *any* statement made by a defendant. No distinction can be drawn between statements which are direct confessions and statements which amount to "admissions" of part or all of an offense. The privilege against self-incrimination protects the individual from being compelled to incriminate himself in any manner; it does not distinguish degrees of incrimination. Similarly, for precisely the same reason, no distinction may be drawn between inculpatory statements and statements alleged to be merely "exculpatory." If a statement made were in fact truly exculpatory it would, of course, never be used by the prosecution. In fact, statements merely intended to be exculpatory by the defendant are often used to impeach his testimony at trial or to demonstrate untruths in the statement given under interrogation and thus to prove guilt by implication. These statements are incriminating in any meaningful sense of the word and may not be used without the full warnings and effective waiver required for any other statement. . . . The principles announced today deal with the protection which must be given to the privilege against self-incrimination when the individual is first subjected to police interrogation while in custody at the station or otherwise deprived of his freedom of action in any significant way.

When Harris, after police defiance of the *Escobedo* decision, made an uncounseled statement denying the first sale and alleging that the second was merely of baking soda, he intended, of course, an exculpatory statement of *exactly* the sort described in *Miranda*. Warren's opinion for the Court laid down a general constitutional principle, not just a passing dictum. Six United States Courts of Appeals and the highest courts of fourteen states followed the *Miranda* holding on impeaching the credibility of the defendant; New York was one of four states whose appellate court found to the contrary. With good reason, Brennan, in his dissenting opinion

in *Harris,* quoted Warren to support an assertion that, "We settled
this proposition in *Miranda.* . . ."[43]

Burger, nevertheless, declared that *Miranda* did not establish
that evidence clearly inadmissible against the defendant to prove
the offense charged is barred for all purposes, "provided of course
that the trustworthiness of the evidence satisfies legal standards."[44]
If Warren had gone out of his way to decide too much, Burger did
not even bother to explain himself. The only legal standard that he
mentioned anywhere in his opinion was voluntariness. But if
Miranda had any meaning at all it was that in the absence of notice
and waiver of one's constitutional rights, custodial interrogation is
so inherently coercive that no statement can be voluntary. Moreover, a statement may be voluntarily given and still be untrustworthy. Men under police examination, even innocent men, have
been known to volunteer outright lies, false information, and, indeed, fabricated confessions. Some speak freely yet unreliably out
of fear, others out of a desire for notoriety. Motivation is complex,
but voluntariness is not alone a sure standard of the trustworthiness
of evidence. In the *Harris* case even the state admitted that the
confession that had been illegally obtained was false.

Burger himself made much of the point that men might give untrustworthy evidence even under oath, but he did so with verbal
trickery that was calculated to disparage the right against self-
incrimination. Every defendant, he pointed out, is "privileged to
testify in his own defense, or to refuse to do so. But that privilege
cannot be construed to include the right to commit perjury."[45] Nor
can it be construed to include the right to be Chief Justice of the
United States, to rocket to the moon, or to play the violin. No one
claimed that the Fifth Amendment vested a right to perjure, but
Burger went on to declare, redundantly, that *Miranda*'s shield "cannot be perverted into a license to use perjury by way of a defense,
free from the risk of confrontation with prior inconsistent utterances."[46]

In a footnote he gave as an example the hypothetical case of a
man who, under circumstances making his confession inadmissible
as evidence, admitted to a homicide and led the police to the body.
Harris's argument, Burger continued, would have the Court believe
that the murderer could take the stand, deny every fact disclosed

to the police or discovered from his confession, and be "free from confrontation with his prior statements and acts. The voluntariness of the confession would, on this thesis, be totally irrelevant. We reject such an extravagant extension of the Constitution."[47] In this example Burger once again took for granted that an illegally obtained confession could be voluntary. It would surely be trustworthy if leading to the discovery of the body, but if involuntary its use would as surely compel the man to be a witness against himself, as was the case, even more surely, in *Harris*. But there is a crucial distinction between the cases. In the hypothetical one posed by Burger the evidence was hard and irrefutable—the fact that the man led the police to the grave and the body itself. In Harris's case the evidence was soft, consisting of utterances made under an illegal interrogation. Burger failed to distinguish between "statements and acts." In the hypothetical case the police could testify as eyewitnesses to the man's taking them to the body, and there would be no need to impeach the defendant by using his otherwise inadmissible confession. In either case, once the defendant took the stand he in effect waived his right under the Fifth Amendment not to be a witness against himself; he could be cross-examined. But in neither, because the prior confession had been made under circumstances that rendered it inadmissible, could the defendant justly be said to have waived his right to let it speak against him, not even for impeachment purposes. The cases are otherwise dissimilar.

Burger's failure to distinguish between hard and soft evidence led him to a flagrant misuse of a roughly analogous 1954 decision that he treated as if it were controlling. He rode booted and spurred over *Miranda,* but in *Walder* v. *United States* he found a convincing precedent.[48] *Walder* was a sideshoot of the exclusionary rule developed by the Court in the *Weeks* case of 1914.[49] Evidence seized in violation of the Fourth Amendment's injunction against unreasonable searches and seizures may not be introduced as evidence at the trial. The purpose of the exclusionary rule is to deter the government and the police from engaging in unconstitutional searches and seizures. Presumably, if they cannot use the fruits of their unconstitutional behavior they will be deterred from continuing it. In *Walder* the Court permitted physical evidence, otherwise inadmissible to prove guilt, to be introduced to discredit the defendant. The Court distinguished between excluding the evidence to prove the crime charged and the defendant's use for his own advantage of the fact that the seizure was illegal; he sought to make its illegality a shield against contradiction of his own lies. Burger, having quoted the Court's exact words in making this point in *Walder,* continued the quotation without ellipsis marks as follows, giving the impression that the next words of the *Walder* opinion were:

> [T]here is hardly justification for letting the defendant affirmatively resort to perjurious testimony in reliance on the Government's disability to challenge his credibility.[50]

But for the bracketed capital letter that begins the quote, one would not know that Burger had emasculated the *Walder* opinion, omitting from it language that altered the impression left by his bowdlerized version.

Walder's case was wholly unlike Harris's. Tainted evidence was not used on cross-examination to impeach Walder's testimony on matters directly relating to the crime charged. In *Walder* the evidence was used to discredit the defendant's testimony on a different and unrelated matter. Indicted for purchasing heroin, he successfully moved to suppress the use of the physical evidence on ground that it had been illegally seized. The government dismissed the prosecution because it could not employ the fruits of an unconstitutional seizure. Two years later Walder was indicted for another narcotics violation unrelated to the earlier one. He took the stand and on direct examination denied that he had ever in his life possessed narcotics. That denial flatly contradicted the affidavit filed by him in the earlier proceeding. Over his objection the prosecution then questioned him about the heroin unlawfully seized on that occasion. When he persisted in his denial, the government did not introduce his affidavit against him. Government agents who had been involved in the illegal search took the stand to impeach his credibility. They could not and did not testify as to the crime for which he then stood indicted. The only issue in *Walder,* said Frankfurter, for the Court, was "whether the defendant's assertion on direct examination that he had never possessed any narcotics opened the door, solely for the purpose of attacking the defendant's credibility, to evidence of the heroin unlawfully seized in connection with the earlier proceeding."[51] By way of answer, Frankfurter declared, in words Burger ignored:

> Of his own accord, the defendant went beyond a mere denial of complicity in the crimes of which he was charged and made the sweeping claim that he had never dealt in or possessed any narcotics. Of course, the Constitution guarantees a defendant the fullest opportunity to meet the accusation against him. *He must be free to deny all the elements of the case against him* without thereby giving leave to the Government to introduce by way of rebuttal evidence illegally secured by it, and therefore not available for its case in chief. Beyond that, however . . .[52]

And at that point Burger continued his quotation from the case with the words quoted above that begin with the bracketed capital letter.

Brennan, dissenting in *Harris,* quoted from the omitted language in Frankfurter's opinion and drew from those words the lesson they taught. In *Walder* the Court distinguished the case of an accused whose testimony, as in *Harris,* was a denial of complicity in the crime charged. *Harris* was a case involving the use of illegally obtained evidence to impeach the accused's direct testimony on matters directly related to the case against him. He was free to deny "all the elements of the case against him" without the government's being able to use by way of rebuttal the forbidden evidence. Yet the evidence permitted by Burger for impeachment was a statement concerning the details of the very crime alleged in the indictment against Harris.

Brennan failed to add that *Walder* did not establish a new principle of law, as Burger seemed to suggest; rather, *Walder* was an exception to a principle established in a 1925 case, when the government, having been rebuffed in its effort to introduce tainted evidence to prove the crime charged, sought to smuggle it in by way of cross-examination—precisely the situation in the *Harris* case.[53] *Walder* was a special exception to the principle established by the 1925 precedent, namely that "the contention that the evidence of the search and seizure was admissible in rebuttal is without merit." The reason given for that principle was that the defendant, like Harris, "had done nothing to waive his constitutional protection or to justify cross-examination" in respect to that evidence.[54]

Burger in *Harris* admitted that there was a distinction between that case and *Walder*. "It is true," he said, "that Walder was impeached as to collateral matters included in his direct examination, whereas petitioner here was impeached as to testimony bearing more directly on the crimes charged." He immediately added, however, "We are not persuaded that there is a difference in principle that warrants a result different from that reached by the Court in *Walder*."[55]

The difference in principle that Burger failed to see did in fact exist. It was substantial and vital, the difference once again between hard evidence and soft as well as between a judicially made constitutional rule and the language of the Constitution itself. The difference, in short, is between the Fourth Amendment and the Fifth's self-incrimination clause. The Fourth, by judicial interpretation, prohibits the admission in evidence of illegal searches and seizures, while the Fifth, which by the force of its own terms is a constitutionally mandated exclusionary rule, prohibits the admission in evidence of statements unwillingly made by a witness against himself.

Judicial exceptions to the Fifth are not as warranted as in cases involving the Fourth. *Miranda* established a judicially made constitutional rule that applied the Fifth's exclusionary principle to custodial interrogation and to pretrial statements made in the absence of the *Miranda* notices of constitutional rights and waiver. *Miranda* was parallel to and had the same force of law as the Fourth Amendment interpretation in *Weeks* that created the exclusion of illegally obtained evidence. But the evidence excluded by *Miranda,* as well as by the Fifth Amendment itself, was testimonial in character and therefore not as trustworthy as the evidence that was the butt of the *Weeks* exclusionary rule. That rule addressed itself to evidence that is real, tangible, and physical, such as bags of heroin. The evidence excludable by the Fifth Amendment is inherently suspect and not on its face reliable, as bags of heroin are. The Fifth applies mainly to the words of the accused—his confession or statements in any degree or manner incriminating, even if they are intended as exculpatory but lend themselves to prosecutorial use as incriminatory. The statements of human beings, human nature being what it is, do not have the evidentiary value of their acts nor of things.

Contraband like bags of heroin are mute proof of fact that hardly need the same degree of corroboration as an outright confession, let alone a statement subject to contradiction. The trustworthiness of physical evidence is such that without it a case may not be supported. When the exclusionary rule forced the government to abandon its effort to admit in evidence the heroin illegally seized from Walder, the government was obliged to dismiss its prosecution. An illegally obtained statement, even if necessarily excludable as a violation of the Fifth Amendment, is not as crippling to the prosecution if it has other evidence such as physical proof and the statements of eyewitnesses. Consequently, the government can press its case in the face of violation of the self-incrimination clause without the jeopardy to itself as when it has violated the search-and-seizure clause.

Impeachment on testimony bearing directly on the crime charged is different in principle from impeachment on collateral matters, Burger's statement to the contrary notwithstanding. The differences between Harris's case and Walder's need not again be stated. The point is that the introduction of the evidence in question against Walder did not at all relate to the crime he was indicted for two years later. The jury, if believing that evidence, could only conclude that he was a liar. It could not convict on the basis of that evidence relating to a different crime at an earlier date. Harris's pretrial statement that was used against him concerned the very crime for which he was then being prosecuted. The trial judge warned the jury that the statement could be used only to attack Harris's credibility as a witness, not as proof of the crime itself. But juries, as fallible as the rest of humanity, are likely to conclude that if the defendant lies on the stand, he is probably guilty of the crime.

The use of Harris's pretrial statement to impeach his testimony necessarily influenced the jurors, perhaps prejudiced them against him. Why else would the prosecution wish to use an otherwise inadmissible statement that had been illegally obtained? Since it had been illegally obtained, its use against him forced him to be an unwilling witness against himself in violation of the Fifth Amendment. Jurors are not notably sympathetic to a defendant who openly invokes that amendment at his trial. Even if he does not take the stand, they tend to wonder whether he has something to hide, raising suspicions of his guilt. If he should risk taking the stand to tell his story, thereby exposing himself to cross-examination and impeachment, the trial judge's instruction to the jury to disregard his pretrial statement is unlikely to alter what they have heard. One authority has written that such an instruction,

> as seems to be generally agreed, is a mere verbal ritual. The distinction is not one that most jurors would understand. If they could understand it, it seems doubtful that they would attempt to follow it. Trial judges seem to consider the instruction a futile gesture. If the prior statement and the present testimony are to be considered and compared, what is the purpose? The intuitive good sense of laymen and lawyers seems to agree that the only rational purpose is not merely to weigh the credibility of the testimony, but to decide *which of the two stories is true*. To do this is ordinarily to decide the substantive issue.[56]

Thus, permitting the use of the defendant's illegally obtained statement intolerably burdens the constitutional right of a person not to be a witness against himself. He has not been a witness against himself of his own free will, least of all in the sense of *Miranda*. And he has been placed between hammer and anvil: If he fails to testify, thereby excluding any use of his pretrial statement, he exposes himself to the jury's suspicions; if he testifies, he exposes that illegal statement and his credibility too, and he stands in jeopardy of conviction. The right protected by the Fifth Amendment is inherently fragile; it cannot withstand the attenuation or the disparagement explicit in Burger's opinion. Nor can the jury in criminal cases be expected to withstand the tension placed upon it by the even more fragile instruction of a trial judge to ignore the evidence obtained in violation of the Fifth Amendment except to test the credibility of the defendant. As the Court said in a 1968 opinion, ". . . there are some contexts in which the risk that the jury will not, or cannot, follow instructions is so great, and the consequences of failure so vital to the defendant, that the practical and human limitations of the jury system cannot be ignored."[57] *Harris* was such a case. Burger cannot be believed when he said that the impeachment process in Harris's case "undoubtedly provided valuable aid to the jury in assessing petitioner's credibility, and," Burger added, "the benefits of the process should not be lost, in our view, because of the speculative possibility that impermissible police conduct will be encouraged thereby."[58]

Burger intended the reference to a "speculative possibility" as a rejoinder to Brennan's dissent. Brennan's outrage flared like a flame fed by a bellows. Deterring improper police conduct, he noted, was only part of the greater objective of protecting the integrity of our adversary system. Its basic mainstay is the right against self-incrimination whose values are jeopardized by the Court's exception to the principle against admitting "tainted" statements. "Moreover," Brennan declared,[59]

> it is monstrous that courts should aid or abet the lawbreaking police officer. It is abiding truth that "nothing can destroy a government more quickly than its failure to observe its own laws, or worse, to disregard the charter of its own existence." Thus even to the extent that *Miranda* was aimed at deterring police practices in disregard of the Constitution, I fear that today's holding will seriously undermine the achievement of that objective. The Court today tells the police that they may freely interrogate an accused incommunicado and without counsel and know that although any statement they obtain in violation of *Miranda* can't be used on the State's direct case, it may be introduced if the defendant has the temerity to testify in his own defense. This goes far toward undoing much of the progress made in conforming police methods to the Constitution.

"Monstrous" was the right word to describe the fundamentally immoral opinion by Burger. It was based on deceit and distortion. It denigrated the Fifth Amendment by allowing in evidence a statement violating the right not to be a witness against oneself, and it ridiculed the same constitutional provision by declaring that it did not extend to a right to commit perjury. It disparaged the Fourth Amendment's exclusionary rule as well as the Fifth's. It was an opinion rendered on the heels of political and police charges that the Warren Court, by decisions like that in *Mapp* and *Miranda,* had coddled criminals, contributed to the crime wave, and handcuffed the cops. In that context the opinion in *Harris* was an apostolic message to the police and prosecutors throughout the land that the courts would cooperate in condoning deliberate misconduct and excesses.

Miranda can have slight deterrent effect in ending illegal police behavior given the incentive provided by *Harris:* The courts will look the other way if the police disregard the *Miranda* requirements of notice of silence, of counsel, and of waiver rights. If the police, in violation of *Miranda,* can get a statement from the accused, they may not be able to use it to prove guilt but they will have something that might contribute to a jury's verdict of guilty if the victim of police misconduct dares to take the stand. The incentive to get the statement, despite *Miranda,* is increased because of the fact that the suspect may unwittingly provide leads to evidence otherwise not obtainable, and that evidence may be introduced at the trial to prove guilt. No exclusionary rule can operate with effective deterrence if it is riddled with loopholes sanctioned by the highest court and that court reveals its hostility to the rationale of such a rule. Justice Brandeis once pointed out that the government is the omnipresent teacher of the people it serves. "For good or for ill, it teaches the whole people by its example. Crime is contagious. If the government becomes a lawbreaker, it breeds contempt for law. . . ."[60] The opinion in *Harris* taught that government may commit crimes in order to secure the conviction of criminals. It taught the odious doctrine that in the administration of the criminal law, the end justifies the means and the Constitution can be circumvented.[61]

Harris did not overrule *Miranda*. *Harris* throttled *Miranda,* circumvented it, excepted it, and invited law-enforcement agencies to do the same; more, it provided them with advantages for doing the same. *Miranda* intended to create more respect for the law and, thus, in the long run, make the job of the police easier. In the short run, *Harris* and opinions like it will make their job easier, but the question is whether the welfare of our nation is secured by judicial opinions that say, in effect, that our legal system is stacked in such a way as to condone, conceal, and encourage criminal conduct on the part of our law-enforcement agencies. Never to be forgotten is that *Harris* plainly denied the truth, that the defendant did claim that his statement was involuntary, and that the Court did permit the use of a statement which it conceded had been illegally obtained. The Court's elephantine misrepresentations and mangling of precedents could not have been deliberately calculated. Incompetence may have some claim to an explanation of *Harris*. But the truth about it, which cannot be known, probably derives from the same sort of zeal that drives the police to become lawless in the act of apprehending and interrogating suspects. "The greatest dangers to liberty," Brandeis once warned, "lurk in insidious encroachment by men of zeal, well-meaning but without understanding."[62]

In sapping *Miranda*'s vitality, the Court followed the lead of Congress, whose Omnibus Act of 1968 purported to "repeal" *Miranda* at least in cases involving federal prosecutions.[63] The act of Congress instructed federal courts to accept as evidence for a jury's consideration any confession deemed by a trial judge to be voluntary under all the circumstances of a case. In determining whether a confession is voluntary—the product of a free and knowing mind —the judge may ignore the *Miranda* rules in whole or part; he may also require their observance, but the statute clearly invites him not to do so.

Miranda, like the act of 1968, was founded on the standard of voluntariness, but the Court in that case had prescribed specific warnings to help insure that confessions would in fact be voluntary. The *Miranda* Court believed that those warnings, if faithfully complied with, might remove the element of coercion inherent in custodial interrogation. The act of 1968, making those warnings discretionary, aimed at a restoration of the pre-*Miranda* test of voluntariness; it was an indefinable, subjective, and unworkable test devoid of standards for the guidance of trial or appellate judges. No court, least of all the Supreme Court, had ever applied that old test with evenhandedness or consistency.[64] Congress thus provided an alternative to the *Miranda* warnings for the purpose of emasculating them.

If *Miranda* meant anything it meant that the police had to show at least a *pro forma* respect for a suspect's constitutional rights before interrogating him. The effort to obtain his confession must be abandoned if he chose to remain silent. He had to know that he had a right to silence and to the assistance of counsel and that if he waived his rights, his statements could be used in evidence against him. The act of 1968 encouraged the police to risk ignoring the *Miranda* warnings in the hope that a court of review would find a confession to be voluntary even if the suspect was wholly ignorant of his constitutional rights and had no assistance of counsel.

Since the statute applied only to criminal prosecutions brought by the United States or by the District of Columbia, it left *Miranda* still operational for state prosecutions. Congress cannot regulate state criminal proceedings. But if the constitutionality of the act of 1968 should be sustained, the Supreme Court could not rationally impose upon the states a stiffer standard when judging voluntariness than is imposed on the United States. *Miranda* was a constitutional rule based on the Court's reading of the Fifth Amendment which is enforceable on the states only because the Fourteenth Amendment incorporates that rule—according to a 1964 opinion.[65] If the rule does not apply federally because of a congressional exemption, its application to the states would create an anomalous double standard, the standard for the states being higher than the federal one. Thus, Congress seems to have doomed *Miranda,* should the Court find the act of 1968 to be constitutional.

A hint that the Court will find that act constitutional and apply its standard to the states is lodged in a footnote to a 1972 opinion in *Lego* v. *Twomey*.[66] The question in that case was whether a state court should have found a confession to be voluntary on the basis of proof beyond reasonable doubt before admitting it in evidence against the accused. The standard of proof used in most states and in federal courts is substantially less severe: The confession may be introduced for the jury's consideration if found by the trial judge to be voluntary on the basis of a preponderance of the evidence. Does the Fifth Amendment demand proof beyond reasonable doubt that a confession is voluntary? White, speaking for a plurality of four (Powell and Rehnquist did not participate), declared, "Without good cause, we are unwilling to expand currently applicable exclusionary rules by erecting additional barriers to placing truthful and probative evidence before state juries and by revising the standards applicable in collateral [federal] proceedings."[67] Thus, the Court did not relax standards for admissibility or for conviction; it simply refused to tighten them or to escalate the prosecution's burden of proof under the Fifth Amendment.

Brennan, Douglas, and Marshall, dissenting, believed that because guilt must be established by proof beyond a reasonable doubt, the same standard must apply to the question whether an allegedly involuntary confession is admissible. By no other standard, they reasoned, could the command of the Fifth Amendment be met. They were appalled by the fact that a confession may be introduced in evidence even if there is a reasonable doubt whether it was voluntary. But, as White observed, experience has not shown that federal rights have suffered from the practice of determining admissibility by a preponderance of evidence. That degree of evidence should be sufficient to allow the introduction of a confession for a jury's consideration if the vitality of the *Miranda* rules remain unimpaired. But the Court's opinion in *Harris* together with Congress's act of 1968 hamstrung *Miranda,* leaving doubt whether the rule of *Lego* permits convictions that are based in part on coerced confessions. In *Lego,* White quoted approvingly as "relevant," if not applicable, the paragraph of the act of 1968 that allows a trial judge in a federal prosecution to determine voluntariness. When the full Court gets the opportunity to pass upon that act's constitutionality, there is little doubt that it will be upheld; the next step will be to apply its standard to the states.[68]

"HIT-AND-RUN" REPORTS

California v. *Byers* posed the question whether "hit-and-run" laws, which exist in every state and the District of Columbia, unconstitutionally compel automobile drivers to incriminate themselves if they get involved in an accident.[69] That question provided the Court with the opportunity of reconciling a variety of important contradictory decisions. Those decisions had been given in cases involving government measures, essentially noncriminal in character, that required self-reporting for regulatory or revenue purposes. Government today has become so complex, huge, and supervisory that it has developed an omnivorous appetite for information it regards as indispensable to the effective conduct of public policy and law enforcement. "Virtually every major public law enactment—to say nothing of state and local legislation—has record-keeping provisions," as Frankfurter once observed.[70] Failure to keep and report records, as required, almost invariably carries criminal penalties. Everyone must file income tax and census returns; merchants must maintain records to report excise taxes, sales, and prices; dealers in securities report to the SEC as well as

IRS, while common carriers report to the ICC or the CAB, druggists to the FDA, corporations to the FTC, landlords to rent-control agencies, and farmers to agencies regulating agriculture; all employers report on social security, wages, hours, and working conditions—the list could be extended almost indefinitely. As a result of such legislation, the constitutional right not to be an involuntary witness against oneself, like the so-called right to be let alone or the right to privacy, could be paralyzed if Big Brother's all-seeing eye can scrutinize even disclosures that might reveal violations of any of thousands of laws.

The "hit-and-run" case, decided in 1971, could have been the occasion for a ruling by the Court that would define the limits of government invasion of the Fifth Amendment. Instead, the Court let the occasion pass by evading the issue. It found, contrary to the courts of California, that there was not even a Fifth Amendment issue before it. That, at least, was the finding of a plurality opinion; Harlan, the fifth Justice, appreciated, at least rhetorically, the jeopardy of self-incrimination but concurred in the result of the plurality. His opinion, which proved to be decisive, was a mass of ambivalence buried in a seemingly sophisticated balancing of the public interest in disclosure and the private interest in noncompliance with disclosure requirements. At one point he grasped the broad issue of the case when he said, in guarded language, "If the technique of self-reporting as a means of achieving regulatory goals unrelated to deterrence of antisocial behavior through criminal sanctions is carried to an extreme, the 'accusatorial' system which the Fifth Amendment is supposed to secure can be reduced to mere ritual."[71] At another point he expressed a similar theme when he equivocally warned, "The sweep of modern governmental regulation—and the dynamic growth of techniques for gathering and using information culled from individuals by force of criminal sanctions—could of course be thought to present a significant threat to the values considered to underpin the Fifth Amendment. . . ."[72] Black did not express his dissent with comparable subtlety. In a foreboding that verged on hysteria he announced that the plurality opinion, if supported by a majority, "would practically wipe out the Fifth Amendment's protection against compelled self-incrimination."[73]

The incredible aspect of *Byers* is that Burger, who spoke for the plurality, could see no validity whatever in the Fifth Amendment claim. He settled the issue by resorting to one of his characteristic verbal stunts of denying the existence of a right that no one claimed. "There is no constitutional right," he said, ". . . to flee the scene of an accident in order to avoid the possibility of legal involvement."[74] The facts of the case show that Byers, who had been indicted for violations of the California Vehicle Code, had illegally passed another car thereby causing an accident; and, charged with failure to stop for the purpose of reporting the accident and identifying himself as the driver who was at fault, he demurred on ground that compliance exposed him to substantial hazards of compulsory self-incrimination. From the trial level to the supreme appellate level, the California courts sustained Byers's demurrer. Morever, a majority of the Supreme Court, unlike the four-man plurality, also recognized that the state "hit-and-run law" compelled self-incrimination.

The state supreme court solved the dilemma which the statute posed by ruling that no prosecutorial use could be made of its required disclosures. By immunizing Byers against prosecution, the statute forced him to comply free of any criminal jeopardy that flowed from his own statements. If the state could produce independent evidence of his guilt, not the fruit of his compelled admissions, the authorities could still prosecute. Meanwhile, the grant of "use immunity," as it is called, allowed the state to maintain the public interest in a system of personal financial responsibility for automobile accidents. Thus the state court accommodated the statute's self-reporting requirements to the values protected by the Fifth Amendment; the court achieved that result by reading into the statute the restriction on prosecutorial use of the information disclosed and its fruits.

Burger, joined by Stewart, White, and Blackmun, rejected the use-immunity principle of the state court by ruling that "there is no conflict" between the statute and the Fifth Amendment right. In 1964 the Court, when restating the appropriate test for determining the validity of an invocation of the Fifth Amendment right, placed upon the suspect the primary responsibility of deciding whether his disclosure would form an essential link in a chain of evidence that could be used to convict him. If he were required to prove that his disclosure constituted a criminal hazard, "he would be compelled to surrender the very protection which the privilege [of the Fifth Amendment] is designed to guarantee." To sustain that "privilege" the contextual implications of the disclosure or an explanation of why it cannot be made must be evidently dangerous. "We also said," the Court had declared, "that, in applying the test, the judge must be *'perfectly clear,* from a careful consideration of all the circumstances in the case, that the witness is mistaken, and that the answers *cannot possibly* have such a tendency' to incriminate."[75] In the hit-and-run case, Burger claimed that under the Court's holdings, "the mere possibility of incrimination is insufficient to defeat the strong policies in favor of a disclosure called for by statutes like the one challenged here. . . . In order to invoke the privilege it is necessary to show that the compelled disclosures will themselves confront the claimant with 'substantial hazards of self-incrimination.' "[76] To show that would, as the Court had said in 1964, compel a surrender of the very protection that the Fifth Amendment was designed to protect.

Burger's position was not altogether unsupported by precedents, though he troubled to mention only a 1927 one.[77] The Court had then held that the failure to file an income-tax return could not be constitutionally justified on ground that the completed return would reveal the amount of criminally obtained income. In the same case, however, the Court conceded that if the return required answers that were privileged on Fifth Amendment grounds, the defendant could have raised the objection in his return. In 1948 the Court had sustained a conviction based on the compulsory production of records that a businessman kept in conformance with price-control regulations.[78] That 5-to-4 decision was based on the dubious supposition that the right against self-incrimination could not be maintained with respect to allegedly public records required by law to be kept for valid regulatory purposes. In the 1960s, however, there was a batch of cases in which the purported regulatory purposes of the government were essentially a guise for criminal sanctions. The Court ruled in those cases that the Fifth Amendment protected Communists, gamblers, and possessors of illegal firearms in their noncompliance with compulsory registration provisions.[79]

Burger distinguished the cases of the 1960s on the ground that the required disclosures zeroed in on highly selective groups inherently suspect of criminal activities. The Fifth Amendment applied to areas permeated with criminal statutes, but not to an essentially noncriminal and regulatory area of inquiry, as in the case before the Court. The California Vehicle Code was primarily intended to promote the satisfaction of civil liabilities arising from automobile accidents rather than to facilitate criminal convictions. Like the income-tax laws, the statute was directed to the public at large—that is, to all persons driving cars in California—not to a highly suspect group. Unlike gambling, driving is a lawful activity; nor is it necessarily a crime to be the driver of a car involved in an accident, for accidents could be the fault of others or of no one, and most occur without creating criminal liability even if the drivers are negligent.

The answer to Burger, given by the four dissenters in opinions by Black and Brennan, was that the right to invoke the Fifth Amendment is personal and does not depend on affiliation with some inherently suspect group. It is a right that can be claimed in any situation posing a substantial hazard of self-incrimination, even in a civil case. The Court had sustained the invocation of the right as to bankrupt persons, businessmen, policemen, lawyers, and others not belonging to inherently suspect groups. Moreover, driving an automobile in California, while no crime in itself, is an activity controlled by hundreds of criminal statutes that comprise the bulk of the two-volume California Vehicle Code. The statute in the case before the Court applies not to the public at large but only to drivers involved in an accident causing property damage, a highly selective and inherently suspect group.

Burger asserted that to extend the Fifth Amendment right in the case before the Court would be extravagant because the conduct required of a driver involved in an accident is not "testimonial" in character and does not necessarily incriminate him. Making him stop to identify himself is no different from requiring a person in custody to stand in a police lineup or to give samples of his handwriting, fingerprints, or blood, all of which constitute nontestimonial conduct that the Court has exempted from the protection of the Fifth Amendment. Burger acknowledged, however, that after identifying himself, the driver involved in an accident reserves the right not to answer any further inquiries that may incriminate him. But simply identifying himself does not implicate him in criminal conduct. Accordingly, there is no need for a judicially created use restriction on the disclosures required by the statute.

Harlan, though concurring in the result, agreed with the four dissenters that within the context of the case before the Court identifying oneself as the driver of a car involved in an accident is both testimonial and incriminating. The purpose of the statute might be essentially nonprosecutorial, but the effect of the required disclosure rather than its regulatory purpose determine whether the Fifth Amendment comes into play. In Byers's case, compelling him to stop and identify himself not only focused official attention on him, but did so under circumstances that were particularly incriminating in view of the fact that he was charged not with being a driver who caused an accident, but with having criminally caused it by passing illegally. And "what evidence," as Black asked, "can possibly be more 'testimonial' than a man's own statement that he is a person who has just been involved in an automobile accident inflicting property damage?"[80] The point of the rhetorical question was that the evidence, if admitted at a criminal trial, would, as Harlan agreed, undoubtedly be testimonial—and incriminating. Moreover, in the cases relied upon by the plurality, those who had unsuccessfully invoked the Fifth Amendment were already in custody; forcing them to stand in a lineup or give blood or fingerprints did not focus official attention on an unknown suspect or compel them to communicate information by verbal means. Brennan sarcastically remarked, "Apparently the plurality believes that a statute requiring all robbers to stop and leave their names and addresses with their victims would not involve the compulsion of 'communicative or testimonial' evidence."[81]

The plurality opinion by Burger was wrong and discreditable. At the least it should have recognized the personal risk to Byers, rather than "indulging," as Harlan with unaccustomed acerbity said, "in a collecting of artificial, if not disingenuous judgments that the risks of incrimination are not there when they really are there. . . ."[82] Worse still, the plurality deferred uncritically to the government's assertion that the required disclosures were nonprosecutorial in character, thus vitiating the constitutional right not to be an unwilling witness against oneself in any situation in which the government exacts a self-reporting scheme that is ostensibly regulatory or whose purpose is not obviously criminal.

The last criticism also applies to Harlan's concurring opinion, notwithstanding his elaborate balancing test. His opinion was a model of intellectual rectitude compared to Burger's, but he sacrificed a constitutional right for the sake of government "efficiency." Despite his candor and insight about the dangers of compulsory self-reporting schemes as effective devices of criminal-law enforcement, Harlan believed that the regulatory objectives of the statute outweighed in importance the constitutional right. He felt constrained, he admitted, to hold that the presence of a real risk of self-incrimination "is not a sufficient predicate for extending the privilege . . . to regulatory schemes of the character involved in this case."[83] The scheme in this case aimed at "assuring personal financial responsibility for automobile accidents."[84] That was scarcely as crucial an objective as protecting national security or punishing crime, yet those objectives do not outweigh the constitutional right. To be more important than the values connected with that right a public interest should be so urgent that there is a need, without an alternative, to override it; constitutional rights are supposed to operate as limits on government power,[85] however salutary the regulatory purpose. If it is not compelling and the means adopted are not the only ones suited to achieve its ends, the regulation should be thwarted by giving effect to the constitutional right.

In this case the solution to the conflict between the regulation and the right was the one advanced by the California courts: a use immunity for the required disclosures. Yet Harlan unwarrantedly concluded, contrary to the express assertion of the California Supreme Court, that "the imposition of a use-restriction would *significantly* impair the State's capacity to prosecute drivers whose illegal behavior caused accidents."[86] But the state court, in an opinion which Harlan quoted at length, insisted that there would merely be "some burden" on prosecuting authorities who would "not be unduly hampered" by a use-immunity test. Drivers who had complied with the statute protected by such immunity might still be prosecuted if the state could establish that its evidence was not the fruit of disclosure. Imposition of "use-restrictions as described above," the state court concluded, "will neither frustrate any apparent legislative purpose behind the enactment . . . nor unduly hamper criminal prosecutions of drivers involved in accidents. . . ."[87] Harlan offered no explanation for his disputing that conclusion.

Conceding that self-reporting serves criminal-law objectives as well as regulatory ones, Harlan thought the "fair response" might be that the Fifth Amendment requires the state to choose the less efficient methods of an accusatorial system. That, however, was not his conclusion, for "it would not follow," he asserted as a subjective judgment, "that the constitutional values protected by the 'accusatorial' system . . . are of such overriding significance that they compel substantial sacrifices in the efficient pursuit of other governmental objectives"—that is, regulatory ones—"in all situations where the pursuit of those objectives requires the disclosure of information which will undoubtedly significantly aid in criminal law enforcement."[88]

Thus, Harlan operated within the same universe of discourse as the plurality for whom a constitutional right was of distinctly secondary importance when compared to the state interest in an efficient system of financial responsibility for automobile accidents. That the Fifth Amendment is the linchpin to the accusatorial system seemed to be of as little interest to Harlan as to the plurality. Among the values protected by it, which he did not find to be of overriding significance, is an "unwillingness," as the Court said in a 1964 opinion in which Harlan joined, "to subject those suspected of crime to the cruel trilemma of self-accusation, perjury or contempt."[89] Indeed, the right against self-incrimination originated not as a right to refuse answer to incriminating interrogatories but as a right to refuse to provide any information that could be used as the basis of a criminal accusation.[90] The hit-and-run statute, especially in the context of the criminal statutes of the California Vehicle Code, placed Byers within the "cruel trilemma." At no point did Harlan or the plurality explain why the right to resist self-accusation should yield to a government purpose that is primarily nonprosecutorial. Nor did the majority that rejected the use-immunity test of the California court give any satisfactory reason, or for that matter, any reason, for repudiating that test, or for claiming that it frustrated the legislative purpose or unduly hampered criminal prosecutions. The upshot of the case was that it downgraded the Fifth Amendment by giving a preferential position to regulatory schemes even if they incriminate.

USE V. TRANSACTIONAL IMMUNITY

California's use-immunity test was actually a moderate means of accommodating the regulation to the constitutional right. Brennan, dissenting with the support of Douglas and Marshall, would have gone farther by demanding transactional immunity. The chasm between use immunity and transactional immunity is vast and deep. Use immunity guarantees only that the compelled evidence and its fruits, evidence derived directly or indirectly from it, cannot be used in a subsequent criminal prosecution. But there can be such a prosecution based upon evidence that is independent from or unrelated to the compelled evidence. Under a grant of use immunity, for example, a man might confess to a crime secure in the knowledge that his confession could not be introduced against him. However, should the prosecution discover proof of his guilt without having used any leads drawn from his confession, he can be tried. By contrast, transactional immunity is a guarantee that in return for his evidence, he will under no circumstances be prosecuted for the transaction or crime concerning which he testifies.[91] Thus, transactional immunity insures absolute protection against prosecution. In its most important Fifth Amendment decision since Burger became Chief Justice, the Court held that use immunity rather than transactional immunity satisfies the constitutional assurance that no person shall be compelled to be a witness against himself criminally.

The case is *Kastigar* v. *United States,* decided in 1972.[92] *Kastigar* was born with a long, snowy beard of precedents, going back to the colonial period, which the Court cropped with ficticious distinctions. In 1698 Connecticut enacted what was probably the first immunity statute in Anglo-American jurisprudence. The act specified that witnesses in criminal cases must give sworn evidence, on pain of imprisonment for refusal, "always provided that no person required to give testimonie as aforesaid shall be punished for what he doth confesse against himself when under oath." Similarly, an act that Parliament passed against gambling in 1710, which New York copied in 1774, guaranteed transactional rather than the narrower use immunity. Those acts provided that gamblers who confessed their crime and returned their winnings "shall be acquitted, indemnified [immunized] and discharged from any further or other Punishment, Forfeiture, or Penalty which he or they may have incurred by the playing for or winning such Money. . . ." Confession, in other words, purged the offense; it did not trap or incriminate because the statute provided for complete immunity. Then, as now, self-incrimination meant to expose oneself to "punishment, forfeiture, or penalty," in the absence of which one cannot incriminate himself. Immunity was equivalent to a pardon, exempting the person whose evidence has been compelled "from all Prosecutions in virtue of this Act," to quote another colonial law.[93] Except for the Connecticut act of 1698, the Supreme Court in *Kastigar* cited these and other colonial examples of immunity in its references to my book *Origins of the Fifth Amendment,* but neglected to observe that all, in today's language, exemplified transactional immunity. Powell's history, in his opinion for the Court, served only as a purposeless grace note. In the early years of our republic, the right not to be a witness against oneself was considerably broader in certain respects than it is today. Some judicial opinions took literally the principle that no man need answer "against himself," thus extending the right to questions that could not incriminate but might injure one's civil interests or expose him to public disgrace.[94] When the right was so broadly construed, absolute immunity was the price that the law had to pay for exacting information that would otherwise be criminally actionable. From the law's perspective, the immunized witness stands to the offense as if he had never committed it: He is beyond the peril of penal sanctions. That was the state of constitutional law until 1972's *Kastigar* decision.

Congress enacted its first immunity statute in 1857 to assist it in an investigation, granting freedom from prosecution for any acts or transactions to which a witness offered testimony. Those who would otherwise have rested on their constitutional right to silence purged themselves of their crimes with impunity. Recoiling from the immunity "baths" that enabled corrupt rascals to escape from criminal liability, Congress in 1862 repealed the act of 1857, supplanting it with limited use immunity by a provision that no testimony given by a witness before a legislative committee shall be used as evidence against him criminally. Four years later Congress passed a similar act as to testimony that would be compelled before any federal judicial proceeding. In 1887 Congress included the same provision in the statute establishing the Interstate Commerce Commission, authorizing it to compel testimony, despite invocation of the Fifth Amendment, after a guarantee of limited use immunity.[95] In *Counselman* v. *Hitchcock,* decided in 1892, the Supreme Court, ruling for the first time on the question whether a grant of immunity could supplant the constitutional right of a person not to be a witness against himself, unanimously held the limited-use-immunity act unconstitutional.[96]

The Court pointed out that the act did not even do what it purported to do; it did not bar use of the compelled testimony, for its fruits could be used against the witness by searching out any leads he had provided to other evidence that could convict him. Evidence deriving from the compelled testimony must also be immunized. But the Court went even farther, indeed, about as far as it could go in determining whether a grant of immunity is commensurate with the constitutional protection. "We are clearly of opinion," the Court declared in what was technically a dictum, "that no statute which leaves the party or witness subject to prosecution after he answers the criminating question put to him can have the effect of supplanting the privilege conferred by the constitution. . . . In view of the constitutional provision, a statutory enactment, to be valid, *must afford absolute immunity against future prosecution* for the offense to which the question relates."[97] Congress responded with an act of 1893 that provided such immunity: "No person shall be prosecuted or subjected to any penalty or forfeiture for or on account of any transaction, matter or thing, concerning which he may testify, or produce evidence, documentary or otherwise" as compelled. In *Brown* v. *Walker,* decided in 1896, the Court held, 5-to-4, that the statute provided an immunity that was commensurate with the scope of the constitutional right.[98] The four dissenters believed that transactional immunity was not absolute or broad enough, because it did not immunize against self-infamation as well as self-incrimination. That is, the dissenters would have made the right not to be an unwilling witness against oneself a protection even against being forced to give evidence that exposed one to public disgrace. The majority thought that if the compulsory disclosure did not place one in criminal jeopardy, the demand of the Fifth Amendment had been satisfied.

If the Court in *Counselman* went farther than necessary when ruling that a grant of limited use immunity was unconstitutional, *Brown* v. *Walker* squarely decided that the Fifth Amendment required at least transactional immunity to displace a claim of the right against compulsory self-incrimination. *Counselman's* dictum became *Brown's* settled doctrine. *Brown* clarified the meaning of "absolute" immunity, the standard of *Counselman* that the Court quoted and reaffirmed in *Brown;* the Court held that "if his testimony operates as a complete pardon for the offense to which it relates,—a statute absolutely securing to him such immunity from prosecution would satisfy the demands of the clause in question."[99] As the Court succinctly restated the point ten years later, "if the criminality has already been taken away, the amendment ceases to apply."[100]

The transactional-immunity standard established by *Counselman-Brown* was consistently followed by the Court ever since, or until *Kastigar,* with but a single technical exception.[101] Until 1970 there were over fifty federal immunity statutes guaranteeing transactional immunity in conformance with the *Counselman-Brown* standard. In 1956, when deciding *Ullmann* v. *United States,*[102] the court replayed *Brown* v. *Walker.* Black and Douglas, dissenting, took the position that the transactional immunity guaranteed by the Immunity Act of 1954 did not meet the constitutional test of absolute immunity demanded by the Fifth Amendment. The majority quoted and re-endorsed the *Brown* standard of transactional immunity. Frankfurter, for the Court, declared that "the Court's holding in Brown v. Walker has never been challenged; the case and the doctrine it announced have consistently and without question been treated as definitive by this Court, in opinions written, among others, by Holmes and Brandeis. . . . The 1893 statute has become part of our constitutional fabric. . . ."[103]

The single technical exception in which the pre-*Kastigar* Court did not follow the *Counselman-Brown* standard was *Murphy* v. *Waterfront Commission*,[104] decided in 1964 on the same day that the Court took the giant step of ruling that the Fourteenth Amendment extended the guarantee of the Fifth Amendment to the states.[105] *Murphy*, though an exception to the *Counselman-Brown* standard, was nevertheless meant to be an extension of the Fifth Amendment. In 1931 the Court had introduced the so-called two-sovereignties rule—namely, that a person could not refuse to testify on ground that his disclosures would subject him to prosetion by another sovereignty or jurisdiction. Thus, he could be convicted of a federal crime on the basis of testimony that he was required to give in a state proceeding, or vice versa. In matters involving national supremacy Congress at its discretion could grant immunity against state prosecution, but not vice versa, nor could one state immunize against a prosecution in another. The Court mistakenly alleged in 1931 that the two-sovereignties rule had the support of historical precedents.[106] History clearly contradicted that rule, as the Court belatedly confessed when wholly scrapping it in *Murphy* in 1964.[107]

Justice Goldberg, the spokesman for the *Murphy* Court, declared, "Since a grant of immunity is valid only if it is coextensive with the scope of the privilege against self-incrimination [citing *Counselman*], we must now decide the fundamental constitutional question of whether, *absent* an immunity provision, one jurisdiction in our federal structure may compel a witness to give testimony which might incriminate him under the laws of another jurisdiction."[108] The Court held that in such a case, "absent an immunity provision," a state witness could not be compelled to testify "unless the compelled testimony and its fruits cannot be used in any manner" by the federal government.[109] Thus, *Murphy* was an exception to the transactional standard for it provided only use and derivative-use immunity in a two-sovereignties case when the second sovereignty had no appropriate immunity provision. *Murphy* could therefore stand for the proposition that where no immunity statute governs, the Fifth Amendment requires only full use immunity; or, taken literally, *Murphy* could stand for that proposition only in a two-sovereignties case. On the one hand, *Murphy* widened the scope of the amendment by junking the two-sovereignties rule, and on the other it restricted the amendment by departing from the *Counselman-Brown* standard.

That the Court intended *Murphy* as only a technical exception was apparent from its opinion in *Albertson* v. *Subversive Activities Control Board,* decided only a year later.[110] *Albertson* was a replay of *Counselman,* for the congressional act before the Court sought to supersede the Fifth Amendment right by offering only limited use immunity. The Court, unanimously holding the statute void, quoted from its opinion in *Counselman,* including the passage in which it laid down the rule that a valid immunity statute must supply "a complete protection from all the perils against which the constitutional prohibition was designed to guard" by affording "absolute immunity against future prosecutions for the offence to which the question relates." The Court explicitly declared that an immunity statute must be "measured by these standards" to be valid.[111] There was no reference to *Murphy,* indicating that it was indeed a very technical exception of no relevance when the threat of prosecution came from the jurisdiction seeking to compel the incriminating testimony. If *Murphy* had established new standards, they would have governed in *Albertson.*

By the Organized Crime Control Act of 1970, Congress abruptly altered the law governing immunity grants by a massive switch from transactional to use immunity.[112] The long and complex act was like a salvo of fragmentation grenades that missed their target and exploded against the Bill of Rights. The Bar Association of the City of New York condemned the act as a carelessly drafted, hasty effort to clear a path through the criminal law to get at organized crime by means that showed a disturbing impatience with constitutional safeguards. Some aspects of the act

> are almost Kafkaesque: a public official could be publicly condemned on the basis of accusations of the grand jury which he has had no opportunity to rebut at a trial; a grand jury witness could be imprisoned for three years for civil contempt without trial and without bail; a defendant could be prevented from raising constitutional objections to evidence introduced against him—even after having established conclusively that an unconstitutional search and seizure had taken place; and one convicted of any federal felony

could be sentenced to 30 years imprisonment on the basis of "information" which could never be used against him at a trial.[113]

Part of that statute, but in no way limited to matters relating to organized crime, was Title II, a new immunity law that replaced some fifty scattered federal acts with a single, comprehensive provision applicable to grants of immunity in all federal judicial, grand-jury, administrative, and legislative proceedings. The new law, which many states quickly copied, provided that when a witness is required to testify over his claim of the Fifth Amendment right, "no testimony or other information compelled under the order (or any information directly or indirectly derived from such testimony or other information) may be used against the witness in any criminal cases" except in a prosecution for perjury or failure to comply.

The new immunity act obliquely reflected a widespread malaise within the legal and police professions, as well as among the public, concerning the broad scope given to the Fifth Amendment by Supreme Court decisions of the 1960s. On the immunity issue itself the Court had not been divided, although other Fifth Amendment issues, as showcases of controversy and dissension among the Justices, fanned the old suspicion that one who invoked the "privilege" of silence on ground that his answer might tend to incriminate him was very likely guilty. Even lawyers and judges who should have known better fed the popular belief that only a person with some crime to hide would claim the Fifth Amendment. All lawyers and judges knew that the amendment, like *any* right of the criminally suspect, had benefitted the guilty as well as the innocent. In its sensational and unpopular *Escobedo* opinion, the Court observed, "If the exercise of constitutional rights will thwart the effectiveness of a system of law enforcement, then there is something wrong with that system."[114] Nevertheless, the Organized Crime Control Act of 1970 passed both houses of Congress by staggering majorities; few politicians were willing to take the risk of being considered soft on organized crime. Most politicians, like the press, the police, the prosecutors, and probably a great majority of the public, believed that if testimony could be more easily compelled, the war against crime might make more headway and fewer of the guilty would get away.

Title II, the new immunity act, was a product of the law-and-order mentality of the late 1960s, as were the increased use of wiretaps and conspiracy prosecutions, preventive detention and no-knock warrants, checks on exclusionary rules, limitations on the *Miranda* rules, and the judicial junking of the requirement of unanimous jury verdicts in criminal cases. Senator John McClellan, Democrat of Arkansas, who cosponsored the new immunity law, declared it to be "a victory for law and order in the country, for the safety of the American people."[115] The immunity act of 1970 mirrored the public mood of trusting those in authority, of giving the prosecution greater leeway in the war against crime, and of finding a way to get at the guilty who cloaked themselves in their constitutional privilege. But the act mirrored more than that. Reasonable men, professing allegiance to constitutional guarantees, genuinely believed that the Supreme Court had read more into the Fifth Amendment than it literally required.

The immunity act was the product of "strict constructionists" who had the support of some distinguished lawyers and a few legal scholars, as well as of the White House and its Department of Justice. President Nixon's National Commission on Reform of Federal Criminal Laws recommended the model for the new immunity act. "We are satisfied that our substitution of immunity from use for immunity from prosecution meets constitutional requirements for overcoming the claim of privilege," said the commission in its report to the President.[116] Nixon in turn commended to Congress the proposal, under which a witness, he said, "could not be prosecuted on the basis of anything he said while testifying, but he would not be immune from prosecution based on other evidence of his offense."[117] Congressman Richard Poff, Republican of Virginia, whom Nixon seriously considered for appointment to the Supreme Court, was the chief spokesman for the bill in the House. He boasted about the bill's pedigree and its efficiency in supplanting all previous immunity laws on the books with one uniform code. Relying on the judiciary committee hearings and reports of both houses, he also observed that the bill marked a "notable departure" from existing legislation on immunity, which "has gone beyond the breadth of the fifth amendment privilege by granting transactional immunity—by barring prosecution completely in respect to incriminating testimony. . . ." The new bill, he pointed out, created a restriction on the direct or indirect use of compelled testimony, so that no witness would be forced to be a witness against himself, "but prosecution itself will not absolutely be barred." Use immunity permits a prosecution based on evidence not derived from the testimony given under immunity.[118] Precisely for that reason the American Trial Lawyers Association and the Criminal Law Section of the American Bar Association opposed the new immunity act. They believed that only transactional immunity was coextensive with the Fifth Amendment rights.[119]

A few months after the new law became effective, Charles J. Kastigar was subpoenaed to appear before a federal grand jury to answer questions not about organized crime but about a dentist who was suspected of aiding him and others to evade the draft by providing them with unnecessary dental services that affected their military classification. Despite a grant of immunity under the act of 1970, Kastigar persisted in his refusal to answer the grand jury's questions and was committed for contempt. The Supreme Court agreed to settle the constitutional question raised by his refusal: Was an immunity grant protecting against only the use of the compelled testimony and its fruits sufficient to displace the Fifth Amendment right, or must transactional immunity be granted?

Rehnquist disqualified himself, probably because he had been a key member of the Department of Justice which recommended enactment of the new immunity law. Brennan also disqualified himself from judging the case, probably because of his son's involvement as counsel in a similar case. Also, Brennan's position on the issue was a matter of public record. The same question posed by *Kastigar* had come before the Court in an earlier case arising under New York law. Before the Supreme Court could render its decision, the state's highest court in another case ruled that transactional immunity must be granted before a witness could be compelled to testify over his Fifth Amendment claim. Accordingly, the Supreme Court, by a 5-to-4 vote, decided in early 1971 that the case before it was inappropriate for resolving the issue of whether use immunity would suffice. Brennan, one of the dissenters who thought that the case before the Court was ripe for decision, wrote a splendid opinion explaining why the constitutional right cannot be supplanted except by a grant of transactional immunity.[120] His failure to participate in *Kastigar* deprived that position of its most profound supporter. Black's death still further diminished the ranks of those who resisted dilution of the Fifth Amendment right. The Court sustained the constitutionality of the use-immunity act of 1970 by a vote of 5-to-2, in an opinion by Powell, Black's successor. Douglas and Marshall wrote separate dissenting opinions.

Powell's opinion was restrained; it had an air of sophistication— "judicious" would be the right word for its tone. Unlike a Burger opinion, there was no sarcasm or disparagement about alleged abuse of constitutional rights, nor was there any denigration of liberal precedents. Rather, Powell spoke about the Fifth Amendment "privilege" as reflecting "a complex of our fundamental values and aspirations"; he declared that it "marks an important advance in the development of our liberty."[121] The Court in past decisions had been zealous in safeguarding the values underlying the privilege, a proposition that Powell buttressed by a citation to *Miranda*. At that point he inserted some learned historical lore that immunity statutes are deeply rooted in our law and compatible with those values. Having struck the proper judicial ambiance with his introductory remarks, Powell summarily rejected as meritless the contention that any immunity statute, however broadly phrased, must violate the right to silence vested by the provision that no person shall be compelled to be a witness against himself criminally. That was the position advanced by the four dissenters in *Brown* in 1896, and in *Ullmann* in 1956 by Black and Douglas. Powell then reached the question whether the act of 1970 was commensurate with the scope of the Fifth Amendment right. At that point his argument became quite underwhelming, and the precedents, from *Counselman* to *Albertson,* like drops of quicksilver, spilled everywhere and disappeared, mostly in footnotes—all the precedents, that is, except *Murphy* v. *Waterfront Commission.* Ironically, that was the one irrelevant or, at best, tangential precedent, for *Murphy* was the case dealing with the two-sovereignties rule. It was the case in which the Court did not consider the standard of immunity necessary when prosecution loomed from the government compelling the reluctant testimony.

"We hold," Powell declared, "that such immunity from use and derivative use is coextensive with the scope of the privilege against self-incrimination, and therefore is sufficient to compel testimony over a claim of the privilege. . . . Transactional immunity, which accords full immunity from prosecution for the offense to which the compelled testimony relates, affords the witness considerably broader protection than does the Fifth Amendment privilege. The privilege has never been construed to mean that one who invokes it cannot subsequently be prosecuted."[122] That passage contradicted history and garbled the precedents.

Powell claimed that the holding was consistent with the conceptual basis of *Counselman* and with what Congress had deemed to be its conceptual basis. Congress, unlike the Court majority, had engaged in no chicanery. The avowed purpose of the immunity act of 1970 was to adopt the use-immunity concept "rather than the transactional-immunity concept of *Counselman* v. *Hitchcock,*" according to committee reports and floor debates. Congress explicitly relied on *Murphy* as a pretext for elevating expediency to the level of constitutional legitimacy. The sponsors of the immunity act of 1970 reiterated that *Murphy,* not *Counselman,* made use of immunity coextensive with the Fifth Amendment right.[123] As Powell read *Counselman,* it provided only full use immunity. He dismissed its much broader language that established the transactional immunity standard as mere dicta, "unnecessary to the Court's decision, and cannot be considered binding authority."[124] The footnote at that point disingenuously disposed of five precedents to the contrary, from *Brown* to *Albertson,* the cases before and after *Murphy* sustaining the transactional-immunity standard as the test to determine the validity of immunity statutes. In an equally stupefying tactic, Powell elevated *Ullmann* to the body of his opinion as an authority supporting the view that the actual holding in *Counselman* was narrow. He neglected to refer to Frankfurter's heavy reliance in *Ullmann* on *Brown* or to his declaration that the doctrine of *Brown,* never challenged, had been consistently sustained and was definitive.

Powell focused instead, and at length, on *Murphy,* though he acknowledged that it did not present "the precise question presented by this case."[125] He finally contended that the Court had never directly faced that question, because post-*Counselman* immunity acts had either followed the transactional-immunity standard or deficiently failed to prohibit all use of compelled testimony. Nevertheless, Powell announced, the reasoning and result of *Murphy* led inevitably to the conclusion that the statute before the Court was constitutional.

His prestidigitory manipulation of the precedents left them twisted like pretzels. He also enlisted on his side a point derived from *Murphy:* A witness who is immunized against use and derivative use of his forced testimony is in substantially the same position as if he had invoked the Fifth Amendment in the absence of a grant of immunity. "That," as Brennan had said in an earlier dissent, "is simply not true." One who relies on his constitutional right to silence forces the state to rely wholly on its own evidence to convict him. By remaining silent he gives the state no possible way to use his testimony, however indirectly, against him, and he has not remotely, from a legal standpoint, indicated any criminal implication. If, however, he is compelled to testify under a grant of use immunity, he incriminates himself on a matter for which he may still be prosecuted if the state can find independent evidence of its own. His admissions, though technically not incriminating under the grant of use immunity, are an open invitation for the state to conduct its own investigation against him, secure in the knowledge that he is implicated, if not guilty, by his own admission. As Brennan said, "use immunity literally misses half the point of the privilege, for it permits the compulsion without removing the criminality."[126]

The Court in *Murphy*, no less, provided a catalogue of the policies and values implicit in the right not to be an unwilling witness against oneself criminally. The Fifth Amendment, Goldberg had declared in *Murphy*, reflects:

> our unwillingness to subject those suspected of crime to the cruel trilemma of self-accusation, perjury or contempt; our preference for an accusatorial rather than an inquisitorial system of criminal justice; our fear that self-incriminating statements will be elicited by inhumane treatment and abuses; our sense of fair play which dictates "a

fair state-individual balance by requiring the government to leave the individual alone until good cause is shown for disturbing him and by requiring the government in its contest with the individual to shoulder the entire load"; our respect for the inviolability of the human personality and of the right of each individual "to a private enclave where he may lead a private life"; our distrust of self-depreciatory statements; and our realization that the privilege, while sometimes "a shelter to the guilty" is often "a protection to the innocent."[127]

Compelling testimony infringes most if not all of these values underlying the constitutional right. The reply is that its values are not infringed at all if the state prosecutes on evidence not related even indirectly to the compelled testimony. The burden of proving that its evidence derives from legitimate sources wholly independent of the compelled testimony lies upon the prosecution. Powell, imposing that burden of proof, claimed that it is "a very substantial protection" to the accused, commensurate with the protection arising from invocation of the privilege itself. But its invocation did not operate like the protective shield of a pardon because it did not bar prosecution. It does bar use of a coerced confession. Granting use immunity and requiring the government to prove that its evidence does not derive from the compelled testimony is, Powell reasoned, like barring use of a coerced confession. He concluded that prosecution for the criminal transaction is still constitutionally permissible.

Douglas, dissenting, rested mainly on an impressive array of the precedents and reference to his opinion in *Ullmann*. Marshall, borrowing from Brennan's position, answered Powell's analogy drawn from the exclusion of coerced confessions and his allegation that witnesses were protected because the burden of proof lay on the government. Marshall did not believe that the ban on derivative evidence could be effective if merely use immunity was granted. He thought, contrary to Powell's assertion, that the preservation of the witness's right was left dependent upon the integrity and good faith of the prosecuting authorities. The evidence would be controlled by those conducting the investigation who coerced the individual to testify against himself. They alone would or could know the chains of information by which evidence was gathered to produce a case against him supposedly independent of his testimony. The government would have little difficulty in meeting the burden of proof when there is no practical way for a witness to prove that the evidence against him did not derive in some way from something he said under compulsion.

With good reason, Marshall, like Brennan, did not trust the good faith of the government. Yet even those of good faith could not be sure that the sources of the information emerging from the labyrinth of their investigative apparatus were untainted by some prohibited use of the coerced testimony. Men working in the same department and exchanging information could not necessarily remember in retrospect the leads from which they constructed their case. "The Court today," Marshall declared, "sets out a loose net to trap tainted evidence and prevent its use against the witness, but it accepts an intolerably great risk that tainted evidence will in fact slip through that net."[128]

Marshall also believed that the Court "turns reason on its head" when comparing a statutory grant of immunity to the exclusionary rule governing coerced confessions. An immunity statute did not provide a remedy for police misconduct in the past; it was, rather, prospective in its operation, for it authorized an interrogation that would otherwise be illegal. It put the government under an obligation to remove completely the jeopardy of incrimination. An exclusionary rule adequately shielded the witness from the fruits of an illegal interrogation or search; but the only way to shield him from the fruits of testimony compelled by a grant of immunity would be to immunize him from prosecution for the crimes to which his testimony relates. An exclusionary rule becomes operative after an illegal interrogation or search has been made often hastily by an officer who is not a lawyer. To dismiss the entire prosecution, rather than exclude just the illegal evidence, would be exacting too high a price for police misconduct. The case of an immunity statute is different, Marshall reasoned. It should offer the prosecuting attorney the calm and reasoned opportunity of choosing between a compulsion of otherwise unattainable evidence at the cost of barring prosecution or forgoing the evidence. Marshall, like Douglas, believed that the Fifth Amendment required a greater margin of protection for the individual than use immunity provided. "That margin can be provided only by immunity from prosecution for the offense to which the testimony relates, *i.e.,* transactional immunity." The statute approved by the Court, he concluded, "fails miserably" to meet the constitutional standard.[129]

Powell did not even consider Marshall's rejection of the analogy based on the exclusionary rule. Something more than a strict construction of the Fifth Amendment right explains his opinion for the Court, because a strict construction would lead to the literal conclusion that any immunity statute was unconstitutional: It *compelled* a person to be a witness against himself criminally. Something more than judicial conservatism explains the decision, for conservatism is respectful of *stare decisis* as well as historical tradition. Powell's concocted analogy, his unveracious abuse of the precedents, and his allegation that the Court had never before faced the question stretch his credit to the breaking point. His placing the burden of proof on the prosecution was the proper move rhetorically, while leaving the Fifth Amendment right, from a practical standpoint, in the hands of its destroyers, like leaving the wolf in sheep's clothing to guard the flock of lambs. At bottom, the *Kastigar* majority are men who are prone to trust the good faith of the prosecuting authorities. If those who enforced the law could be trusted, there would be no need for the Bill of Rights, let alone the Fifth Amendment.

TAX RECORDS AND VOICE SAMPLES

The 1973 decisions in the tax-records and voice-sample cases exhibit the recent judicial animus against the amendment. In one the Court held that the right against self-incrimination does not protect a person from the compulsory production of business and tax records in the possession of an accountant, even though the Internal Revenue Service was investigating the possibility of a prosecution for income-tax fraud and had given the *Miranda* warnings.[130] In the other case the Court held that the right against self-incrimination does not protect a person from a court order to make a voice recording to be played before a federal grand jury seeking to identify a criminal by the sound of a voice on a legally intercepted phone conversation.[131]

In the first of these cases the decision turned on the fact that the owner of the records had given them to her accountant, who prepared tax returns from them and kept them indefinitely in his custody. The Court, speaking through Powell, acknowledged that, ever since a leading precedent of 1886, the Fifth Amendment bars the compulsory production of one's private papers if they can be used as evidence to convict a person of crime.[132] But Powell distinguished that precedent on the ground that the owner of the records in the case before the Court no longer had possession of them. She was unable to invoke her right not to be a witness against herself because her accountant, who retained the records, had been ordered to produce them against her. The right was a personal one. The accountant might have invoked it if he had reason to fear that the records might implicate him criminally. The owner might have invoked the right if she had kept possession of the records, but she could not invoke it to prevent his compliance with the order to produce them for use against her.

Brennan concurred on the narrowest of grounds, essentially that the accountant's possession of the records made all the difference. But Brennan insisted that the Fifth Amendment should be available to one who turns records over to another for custodial safekeeping. He dissociated himself from the Court's seemingly overbroad position that the right not to be a witness against himself depends on whether the owner is compelled personally to give the records to the government. If, for example, the government against an owner's will ordered a bank to surrender his private papers kept in a safety deposit box, Brennan believed that the owner could prevent their introduction as evidence on ground that he had been forced to incriminate himself. The government cannot nullify the Fifth Amendment by finding some way to obtain private papers without requiring their owner personally to hand them over.

Douglas and Marshall dissented in separate opinions. Marshall's was an irresolute analysis of the reasons that mere possession should not define the limits of the protection that the Constitution affords to private papers. Douglas began grandiloquently with the proposition that the majority's opinion "sanctions yet another tool of the ever-widening governmental invasion and oversight of our private lives," and concluded with the assertion that, "The constitutional fences of law are broken down by an ever-increasingly powerful government that seeks to reduce every person to a digit."[133] In between, he wrote an eloquent little essay on the right of privacy that for the most part transcended the facts of the case before the Court. Two of his points deserve passing notice. Douglas believed that the nature of an accountant-client relationship is a confidential one, roughly comparable to the privileged relationship between attorney and client, giving the client a right to expect privacy. The accountant's responsibility foreclosed his using the records for any purpose other than making tax returns. The majority's answer was simply that no confidential accountant-client privilege exists under federal law. Marshall rejoined that "privileged or not, a disclosure to an accountant is rather close to disclosure to an attorney."[134] Obviously, it is not close enough.

Douglas's other point turned on the allegedly doleful impact of the decision. He observed that few taxpayers can complete their tax returns without professional assistance because of the extraordinary complexity of our tax laws. From that fact he concluded that if a taxpayer wants to insure the confidentiality of his records, he must forgo such assistance or risk a penalty on the exercise of his right against self-incrimination. "It calls for little more discussion than to note," Douglas declared, "that we have not tolerated such penalties in the past."[135] Yet, the remedy for avoiding such a penalty and still securing professional assistance seems clear: The taxpayer need only demand the return of his records on the completion of his tax return.

Douglas rightly objected to the majority's attitude when construing the Fifth Amendment. Powell concluded his opinion with a revealing statement. Respect for the constitutional principles of personal liberty, he declared, "is eroded when they leap their proper bounds to interfere with the legitimate interest of society in enforcement of its laws and collection of the revenues."[136] The majority almost always finds that the interests of society outweigh the claims of personal liberty; it finds that such claims are the ones that overleap their bounds, rather than that the government is overleaping constitutional barriers by encroaching on the private enclave. One might have thought that the Court's respect for constitutional principles of personal liberty is eroded when a venerable Fifth Amendment precedent has to be distinguished and narrowed to establish the legitimacy of law enforcement. Although Powell's opinion made no momentous law, it did continue the recent trend of providing shortcuts to satisfy the appetite of prosecutors.

Although anyone might dodge the tax-records decision by recovering his records from his accountant, the voice-sample decision left no escape route. It derived from a trilogy of cases of the mid-1960s. Brennan, whose defection in these cases from the libertarian wing of the Warren Court reduced it to a minority, wrote the three opinions. The majority held that there was no violation of the self-incrimination clause if the police compelled the driver of an accident vehicle to give a sample of his blood for analysis of its alcoholic content,[137] or compelled a suspect in a lineup to utter before witnesses to a bank holdup the words used by the robber,[138] or compelled another suspected bank robber to submit a sample of his handwriting for comparison with a note given during the robbery to a bank teller.[139] These were the precedents governing the 1973 voice-sample case in which Stewart, for a seven-man majority, rejected the Fifth Amendment claim of a suspected gambler who refused to read into a recording machine the transcript of a court-ordered wiretap which revealed the voice of a man in the act of violating criminal laws against gambling.

The 1973 case and its precedents posed a thorny question for decision: When is a person who is compelled to hand to the state the evidence to incriminate him not a witness against himself in the Fifth Amendment sense? That was not the way the Court put the question. It was, rather, does nontestimonial compulsion force a person to be a witness against himself? The Court's consistent answer has been "no." Its reasoning is based on a supposed distinction between forcing either a suspect or an accused person to give evidence against himself of a testimonial or communicative nature and forcing him to be the source of physical evidence against himself derived from his own body. Although the Court did not say so, the distinction is presumably based upon the word "witness" in the clause protecting anyone from being an unwilling witness against himself. The word "witness" implies giving testimony based on one's knowledge, not on one's person. Compulsion to reveal knowledge or information other than one's physical characteristics is unconstitutional; compulsion to reveal one's physical characteristics is constitutional. John H. Wigmore in his great treatise on the law of evidence advocated the distinction to keep the "privilege" of the Fifth Amendment "within limits the strictest possible."[140] But the Court probably based its acceptance of the distinction on a common-sensical need to prevent the Fifth Amendment from disabling the police and witnesses when making simple identifications. Brennan in the trilogy of 1966–67 cases and Stewart in the 1973 one traced the distinction to a passing remark by Justice Holmes in 1910, when he dismissed as "an extravagant extension of the 5th Amendment" the claim that requiring a defendant to model a shirt for identification purposes breached his right to be free from compulsory self-incrimination. The prohibition against compelling a person to be a witness against himself, Holmes said, was a prohibition against "the use of physical or moral compulsion to extort communication from him, not an exclusion of his body as evidence when it would be material."[141]

The trouble with the distinction, between the compulsion of testimonial evidence, which is protected, and physical or identifying evidence, which is not, is that it collapses on analysis. Physical evidence can be communicative in character, as when a lab report, the necessary result of the drunken driver's blood sample, is introduced against him, or when a grand jury indicts a man because his voice, based on his speaking the words of an intercepted phone call, identifies him as the criminal gambler. He has not been forced to say, "I was drunk" or "I made the call," but the practical effect has been the same. There can be no doubt that the individuals in these cases, whether by writing, speaking, or giving blood, have been compelled to furnish evidence against themselves; to say that they have not been forced to "testify" against themselves is little more than a legal fiction.

If the "privilege . . . is as broad as the mischief against which it seeks to guard," as the Court said in 1892,[142] and if constitutional provisions for the security of the person "should be liberally construed," as the Court said in an even earlier Fifth Amendment case,[143] its literal interpretation based on the word "witness" diminishes the amendment. Yet, if its most fundamental meaning is that no person need be the unwilling instrument of his own undoing and that the state must find its own evidence against him without his involuntary cooperation, the police would not be able to fingerprint a suspect to see if his prints matched those left at the scene of a crime, nor could they make him stand in a lineup for identification by witnesses.

Any answer to the question presented by these cases is complicated by nagging anxieties, proving once again the old adage that there is scarcely a constitutional issue that can be sliced so thin that it has only one side. In these cases it is not the letter but the spirit that killeth by projecting absurd and impossible consequences that would really handcuff the police and render the Fifth Amendment ridiculous in the court of public opinion. The self-incrimination clause, like every other controversial part of the Constitution, lays down only a general rule. Marshall, vigorously dissenting in the voice-sample case, asserted that to draw from its language support for the testimonial limitation is difficult. "No person . . . ," according to the Fifth, "shall be compelled in any criminal case to be a witness against himself." "Nowhere," said Marshall, as had Black, Fortas, and Douglas before him, "is the privilege explicitly restricted to testimonial evidence." To read into it that limitation was a "crabbed construction" of the clause.[144] But to read into it the extension wished for by Marshall and Douglas, dissenting, might well have been "extravagant," as Holmes, whom the majority was fond of quoting on this point, had declared.

Little illumination is available from the face of the Fifth Amendment to support either position with confidence. In some respects its phrasing is quite broad because it protects against more than just compulsory self-incrimination or even disclosures merely tending to provide a link in a chain of circumstantial evidence that might be the basis of a prosecution. A person can also be a witness against himself in ways that do not incriminate him. He may, in a criminal case, injure his civil interests or disgrace himself in the public mind. Thus, the Fifth Amendment could be construed on its face to protect against disclosures that expose one to either civil liability or infamy, though the Court has not so held. The Court has construed the amendment to apply to ordinary witnesses as well as to the defendant himself. Unlike the Sixth Amendment, which explicitly refers to the accused, protecting him alone, the reference in the Fifth to "no person" makes it applicable to suspects and witnesses as well as to accused persons.

On the other hand, the self-incrimination clause has a distinctively limiting factor: It is restricted on its face to criminal cases. The phrase "criminal case" seems to exclude more than the invocation of the right in civil and equity cases. In the minds of some judges and legal scholars, no criminal case exists until a formal charge has been made against the accused by indictment, information, or complaint before a magistrate. Under such an interpretation the right would have no existence until the accused is put on trial; before that, when he is taken into custody, interrogated by the police, or examined by a grand jury, he would not have the benefit of the right. Nor would he have its benefit in a nonjudicial proceeding like a legislative investigation or an administrative hearing. But the Supreme Court has balked at taking the clause literally. Of no other provision of the Constitution has the Court declared that it cannot mean what it seems to say. Thus, in *Counselman* v. *Hitchcock,* a major Fifth Amendment case decided in 1892, the Court held that the clause did protect ordinary witnesses even in grand-jury proceedings. Unanimously the Court declared, "It is impossible that the meaning of the constitutional provision can only be that a person shall not be compelled to be a witness against himself in a criminal prosecution against himself."[145] Similarly, there was no disagreement from dissenters when the Court in 1956 declared that the clause "is not to be interpreted literally."[146] Had the framers of the amendment intended the literal or restrictive meaning, then their constitutional provision was a meaningless gesture because there was no need to protect the criminal defendant at his trial: He was not permitted to give sworn testimony until the later nineteenth century.

Over the long haul the Court has interpreted the clause as if its framers neither meant what they said nor said what they meant. Generally, the Court has acted as if the letter killeth. Seeking the spirit and policy of the Fifth Amendment, the Court has on the whole given it an ever-widening, liberal interpretation, on the principle that it embodies cherished objectives of a fair and free society. The guilty may benefit from it, as they do from every procedure of the Bill of Rights, but it benefits all, the innocent as well as the guilty, by keeping the government morally honest in producing its case and by respecting the sovereignty of the individual.

Restricting the operation of the Fifth Amendment to protect only testimonial compulsion, therefore, represented a departure from the general trend of decisions to widen its scope. Stewart's opinion for the Court in the voice-sample case merits respect for its practical consequences, but not for its intellectual rigor. Calling "nontestimonial" the evidence coerced from a suspect is semantically catchy but divorced from reality. Calling evidence "testimonial" and thus warranting protection gives it a talismanic character as if it were truly different from physical evidence derived involuntarily from the body. The distinction sounds as if it separates hard from soft evidence. An involuntary statement is not to be trusted (soft), but one's voice, like his handwriting or his appearance, has nothing to do with witnessing and may be trusted (hard). In fact, however, identifications are too often and notoriously mistaken. More to the point, the wiretapped gambler who records his voice for a grand jury is virtually indicting himself. There is substantial historical justification for the maxim that the Fifth Amendment guarantees the right to stand mute or remain silent. Stewart steered the Court around that incontrovertible maxim by noting that the voice recordings were to be used only to measure the physical properties of the witness's voice rather than the testimonial content of what he said. The rejoinder to that proposition is unanswerable: If the right against self-incrimination protects a man at his trial from having to speak up for the benefit of witnesses who may identify him from the sound of his voice, why does it not protect him in the grand-jury room, or in the interrogation room of the police station, or in the lineup?

Douglas, the only holdover from the dissenters in the cases of the mid-1960s, dissented again in the voice-sample case; he rested, he said, on his earlier dissents to the effect that the Fifth Amendment is not restricted to testimonial compulsion. Marshall, who came to the Court soon after the decisions of 1967, also dissented, expressing his agreement with Douglas. "I fear," he said, "the Court's decisions today are further illustrations of the extent to which the Court has gone astray in defining the reach of the Fifth Amendment privilege and has lost touch with the Constitution's concern for the 'inviolability of the human personality.' In both these cases, the Government seeks to secure possibly incriminating evidence which can be acquired only with respondents' affirmative cooperation."[147]

The element of "affirmative cooperation" was for Marshall the great divide between permissible and impermissible compulsion. Although the dissenters in the 1966 blood-sample case thought that drawing blood from a man against his will was akin to an act of violence on the human body, contrary to the injunction of the Fifth Amendment, Marshall thought that a distinction could be made between that and the subsequent cases. Forcing a man to submit to a blood test required from him only passive resistance. Presumably, the same point applies to fingerprinting and photographing him. By contrast, making him provide samples of his handwriting or of his voice, whether by uttering at the police lineup the words of a robber or by speaking for identification the words of a wiretapped gambler, enabled the government to secure from him incriminating evidence that could be obtained only by enlisting the active cooperation of his will. If he chose to deny that cooperation, by refusing to engage in a volitional act that might betray his guilt, the Fifth Amendment, Marshall believed, should protect him.

Marshall's distinction between affirmative cooperation and passive resistance was as tenuous as the majority's distinction between testimonial and physical evidence. A man who refuses to give a blood sample, or his fingerprints, may be overpowered in his body and subverted in his will. Marshall thought that the intrusion on his dignity was neither the same nor as severe as when he is forced to speak or write. No one strapped to a hospital table for the benefit of a doctor's needle or forced physically to yield his fingerprints would be likely to agree. For Marshall, and Douglas, the Constitution "protects at all costs the integrity of individual volition against subordinating state power."[148] The sentiment commands sympathy, respect, and probably the concurrence of the entire Supreme Court; but it was not a sentiment that satisfactorily settled the voice-sample case.

That case, significantly, was decided against the Fifth Amendment claim. The Marshall opinion could, theoretically, have been the opinion of the Court, for it was no worse if no better reasoned than Stewart's and did provide a way around some of the encumbering precedents. The Court, if it is so minded, can adeptly split legal hairs and reach any conclusion that it wishes. The practical decision was the one reached, and it was the decision that fit the pattern that emerged from the various Fifth Amendment cases decided by the Nixon Court. The notice-of-alibi, the illegal-confessions, the hit-and-run, the immunity, the tax-records, and the voice-sample cases, when taken together, revealed that the new Court majority had an abiding faith in the fundamental need to straitjacket the constitutional guarantee that no person shall be compelled to be a witness against himself criminally. Age cannot wither nor custom stale the monotony with which the Fifth Amendment claim is now rejected.

CHAPTER FOUR

The Sixth Amendment:
The Right to Counsel

The Sixth Amendment states in part, "In all criminal prosecutions the accused . . . shall have the assistance of counsel." That guarantee, like so many others in the Bill of Rights, has swollen in reach and meaning because of the latitudinarian interpretation given to it by the Supreme Court. At the time of its adoption the counsel clause of the Sixth Amendment meant no more than the right to retain counsel of one's choice at one's own expense. In the state courts, only New Jersey and Connecticut offered the accused an opportunity to have counsel assigned to him if he was unable to pay for the cost. In compliance with an act of Congress the federal courts assigned counsel on request only in capital cases, but gradually the practice developed of assigning counsel on request to indigents in most felony cases. There was no constitutional right to counsel except for those who could afford the price.[1] Not until 1938 did the Supreme Court rule, in *Johnson* v. *Zerbst,* that, "The Sixth Amendment withholds from federal courts, in all criminal proceedings, the power and authority to deprive an accused of his life or liberty unless he has or waives the assistance of counsel."[2] A conviction without representation by counsel or proper waiver would be void.

That rule was not extended to state criminal proceedings until 1963.[3] Yet the initial breakthrough on the right to counsel had come in a landmark decision by the Court in *Powell* v. *Alabama,* a 1932 case originating in a state trial.[4] The Court held that when a defendant is unable to employ counsel, his right to due process of law requires that counsel be assigned to him, whether requested or not, if the charge against him is a capital one and he is incapable of making his own defense because of special circumstances such as ignorance, feeble-mindedness, or illiteracy. In the course of his opinion, Justice Sutherland indulged in some sweeping and eloquent dicta on the plight of uncounseled criminal defendants, thereby influencing the course of decision in our time. He declared:

> The right to be heard would be, in many cases, of little avail if it did not comprehend the right to be heard by counsel. Even the intelligent and educated layman has small and sometimes no skill in the science of law. If charged with crime, he is incapable, generally, of determining for himself whether the indictment is good or bad. He is unfamiliar with the rules of evidence. Left without the aid of counsel he may be put on trial without a proper charge, and convicted upon incompetent evidence, or evidence irrelevant to the issue or otherwise inadmissible. He lacks both the skill and knowledge adequately to prepare his defense, even though he have a perfect one. He requires the guiding hand of counsel at every step in the proceedings against him. Without it, though he be not guilty, he faces the danger of conviction because he does not know how to establish his innocence. If that be true of men of intelligence, how much more true is it of the ignorant and illiterate, or those of feeble intellect.[5]

Notwithstanding these general remarks, the Court a decade later ruled that due process of law did not require the assignment of counsel to an indigent in a noncapital case. The Court did not think that the denial of counsel even on request violated a fundamental right, essential to a fair trial, when there were no special circumstances in defendant's favor. In the case before the Court, *Betts* v. *Brady,* the defendant had been clearly told the charges against him, was of normal intelligence, and was not without experience in criminal trials.[6] After the *Betts* decision, every right-to-counsel case was combed over for special circumstances. The Court began to find such circumstances in every capital case, but in noncapital cases its opinions were a tissue of bewildering inconsistency.[7]

Finally, in another landmark case, *Gideon* v. *Wainwright,* decided in 1963, the Warren Court ruled in effect that the Sixth Amendment, as interpreted in *Johnson* v. *Zerbst,* applied to all felony proceedings in the states.[8] The Court thus scrapped the special-circumstances rule which was the basis of its previous search for an answer to the question whether counsel was necessary for a fair trial. The right to counsel for all felony indigents became a fundamental right of due process of law. The operative principle thereafter was that there could be no due process, fair trial, or equal justice when the kind of criminal proceeding against a man varied with his bank account.

Having counsel is only the point of departure for having the effective assistance of counsel "at every step in the proceeding"[9] whether in or out of court. If the absence of counsel might derogate from the accused's capacity to oppose the state's charges against him, he need not stand alone against the state except when called before a grand jury. The constitutional principle is not limited to the presence of counsel at trial. The Warren Court extended the right to be represented at custodial interrogations,[10] preliminary hearings,[11] police lineups,[12] and arraignments.[13] These are among the various critical stages of a prosecution preceding trial, when there is a risk of severe injustice that results from confronting a layman with unfamiliar technical points of law and prosecutorial tactics.

The law, whatever its virtues, has always been a mysterious and difficult trap for the uninitiated. A layman caught in the intricate legal maze that envelopes even a deceptively simple criminal case is caught as helplessly as a bug on flypaper; he has no hope of extrication without the services of professional legal counsel. Even a skilled and experienced lawyer who gets in legal trouble knows that he should not defend himself. The maxim is that a lawyer who defends himself has a fool for a client. Even Clarence Darrow, the country's foremost criminal lawyer, when prosecuted for trying to fix a jury, engaged a lawyer.[14] The layman who is an uncounseled criminal defendant might as well save time and grief by presenting himself to the warden of the nearest jail. Anyone who is accused of crime or who is even suspected of it and is under investigation needs a lawyer. Of all his rights "the right to be represented by counsel," as an esteemed state jurist said, "is by far the most pervasive, for it affects his ability to assert any other rights he may have."[15] It also profoundly affects the odds whether he will escape the penitentiary. More important, this right also affects the odds whether justice will be done in his case, a matter that is of crucial interest to society as well as to him.

Our whole system of criminal justice, based on the adversary principle, is geared to a fair determination of guilt or innocence. When the prosecutorial forces of organized society are marshaled against a man accused of crime, "Abandon hope, all ye who enter here" best describes his chances if he is bereft of legal counsel. Even the innocent suspect not yet formally accused is in a high-risk situation if he faces the police and prosecutor alone and without an airtight alibi. The man who is championed by counsel retains the chance of insuring that his powerful adversaries who act for the state will behave according to the rules of a dangerous game. Shortcuts and errors that derive from overzealousness, mistaken judgment, prejudice, and legal improprieties may shamefully stain our system of criminal justice. Trial judges as well as police and prosecutors commit blunders that sacrifice individual rights and subvert the rules of evidence. No small part of defense counsel's task is to police the agencies of law enforcement by holding them accountable to the law. Overburdened in their work and ready to believe the worst, they too often stray into the paths of lawlessness in making out a case against the defendant.

A guilty man needs a lawyer and probably should not be permitted to plead his guilt without one. No layman has the experience and knowledge required to plea-bargain with the prosecutor's office. Plea bargaining refers to the off-the-record, out-of-court negotiations between prosecution and defense for a mutually beneficial trade: The defendant waives his rights and pleads guilty in exchange for a more lenient sentence, which the prosecutor may promise in order to avoid a trial and to dispose of the case with another conviction notched on his record. Only the experienced criminal lawyer can assess the probable case against his client, the admissibility of the evidence against him, and the court's sentencing practices. Only the lawyer can determine whether a man should waive his right to a jury trial, or his right not to incriminate himself by pleading guilty, or his right to cross-examine the witnesses against him. If the expertise of a lawyer is helpful to even the guilty man, it is indispensable to the innocent one and is above all the best safety factor built into the adversary system to guarantee that justice may be done.

Most cases do not even come to trial because they end in a plea of guilty. The most crucial decision any defendant must make, with the advice of counsel, is how to plead at his arraignment. A decision to plead guilty depends heavily on the deal that he can make through his counsel with the prosecutor's office. An overburdened and uncertain prosecutor may agree to reduce the charges or go easy in exchange for the defendant's relinquishing his constitutional right to challenge the accusation against him by demanding a public trial at which he reserves all his rights to challenge the evidence, confront and cross-examine the witnesses against him, produce his own witnesses, and remain silent, speaking only through his "mouthpiece," who masterminds his trial. Plea bargaining is one of the most important duties of a criminal lawyer. His vigorous and knowing advocacy on behalf of his client may save his life, if the death penalty is possible, or take years away from his punishment. It may also lead to the sentencing and imprisonment of the innocent, who have been persuaded that acquittal is not possible or probable.

PLEA BARGAINING

The plea-bargaining cases decided by the Supreme Court under Chief Justice Burger in 1970 make one yearn nostalgically for the good old days when the issues were clearer and the good guys could easily be separated from the bad guys. When the police beat a suspect with a rubber truncheon, forcing him to confess, his acknowledgment of his guilt was clearly unreliable and involuntary.[16] When the police broke his will by psychological coercion, interrogating him day and night under bright lights and denying him sleep until he finally confessed, his acknowledgment of his guilt was similarly unreliable and involuntary.[17] Even if the police merely held him incommunicado, denying him counsel and failing to apprise him of his constitutional right to remain silent, there was strong doubt that his confession, even if voluntary, was the product of a knowing, intelligent mind and an even stronger doubt that the confession was lawfully obtained.[18] But if a man has counsel, if he is given timely arraignment, if he freely confesses, and if by his plea he acknowledges his guilt in open court, can there be a due-process question or an argument that he has been denied constitutional rights? What if he pleads guilty, by arrangement, to a lesser charge than the one originally made, though he may have been guilty of the original charge and not guilty of the one he pleads to? What if he pleads guilty to a charge of second-degree murder in order to avoid the danger of the death penalty that might be imposed if a jury tried and found him guilty of first-degree murder? What if the case against him seems so strong that he pleads guilty to a reduced charge, in exchange for a lesser sentence, yet he continues to protest his innocence?

On such questions the Supreme Court's recent decisions are reminiscent of the old common-law doctrine of *caveat emptor:* Once the bargain has been struck—here, the entry of a counseled guilty plea—it is lawful and irrevocable. Brennan, who dissented for himself, Douglas, and Marshall in these plea-bargaining cases, complained that the Court had moved "toward the goal of insulating all guilty pleas from subsequent attack no matter what unconstitutional action of government may have induced a particular plea."[19] The Nixon Court did far more. It made a mockery of its rule in *Gideon* v. *Wainwright* in 1963 that every felony defendant is entitled to effective defense counsel even at state expense.[20] It vitiated the rule that a coerced confession violates due process of law.[21] And it left a shambles of the rule that a waiver of constitutional rights must be made knowingly, understandingly, and voluntarily.[22]

In the first of the plea-bargaining cases, *McMann* v. *Richardson,* which was really three cases from New York merged together and decided as one, the question was whether the defendants, each of whom had pleaded guilty, were entitled to a hearing on their postconviction allegations.[23] The question was not whether on the merits the prisoners should be released or retried because of constitutional error, but whether on their claims of irregularities they merited a hearing previously denied and unavailable. Each attacked his conviction in the New York courts by petitioning in the federal courts for a writ of habeas corpus. In each of the three cases the defendant eventually confessed and with benefit of counsel copped a plea to a lesser charge than originally made. In each, the defendant subsequently claimed that his confession had been coerced. In each, the defendant claimed in effect that his court-appointed counsel had incompetently represented him. Each alleged that his guilty plea was the product of a coerced confession and additional irregularities.

One of the defendants asserted that the police had beaten him, initially refused him counsel, and threatened him with false charges prior to his confession; he claimed also that the trial judge had threatened him with a sixty-year sentence if he was convicted after a plea of not guilty. Bereft of an opportunity to have his claim of irregularities judged by the state courts, he requested a federal hearing. The second defendant claimed that he had originally pleaded not guilty, had been beaten into confessing the crime to which he had pleaded guilty, had ineffective court-appointed counsel who conferred with him for only ten minutes prior to the day he pleaded guilty to a reduced charge, and that he had not wanted to plead guilty to something he had not done. The third defendant claimed that he had been handcuffed while interrogated, threatened with a pistol, and physically abused. He also declared that his court-assigned counsel ignored his alibi defense and assured him, wrongly, that his plea of guilty would be to a charge of misdemeanor rather than to felony; as a result, he did not understand the charge and the consequences of his plea when acknowledging his guilt in open court. The Court of Appeals for the Second Circuit in each case thought that the allegations justified a hearing; in each, the Supreme Court, speaking through White, reversed. In each, White, for the majority, focused only on the issue of the allegedly coerced confession, and he disingenuously ignored the supplementary claims of irregularity.

With respect to confessions the law seemed fairly well settled. White himself had previously summarized his understanding of it by stating, in 1968, that "an inadmissible confession preceding a plea of guilty would taint the plea."[24] The Court had previously ruled that a conviction on a plea of guilty "based on a confession extorted by . . . mental coercion is invalid under the Federal Due Process Clause."[25] Every federal court of appeals that had faced the issue, those of the third, fourth, fifth, sixth, and ninth circuits, as well as the second, thought the law was that a guilty plea was not voluntary if it was the result of an illegal confession—if, that is, the confession carried over to taint the plea.[26] This was particularly true in the second federal circuit, covering New York, where constitutionally acceptable procedures were unavailable to a defendant to test the validity of his confession, according to the Supreme Court's decision in the 1964 case of *Jackson* v. *Denno*.[27]

But White thought that the presence of counsel made all the difference. Giving wings to his imagination, he indulged in a lengthy, abstract discussion on how a counseled defendant might calculate that pleading guilty or not depended on whether he thought the law would allow his confession to be used against him. The purpose of this passage was to prove logically that the plea of guilty could not be blamed on the confession nor be deemed involuntary. But, since White clearly regarded the confession as the decisive factor in the defendant's calculations—decisive in the sense that without the confession he surely would have gone to trial and put the state to its proof, rather than plead guilty—we must conclude by White's own reasoning that the confession tainted or significantly influenced the plea. That is the opposite of what White sought to demonstrate.

He declared that the sensible course for a defendant who considered his confession to be involuntary would be to contest his guilt at a trial, or on appeal, "or, if necessary, in a collateral proceeding, and win acquittal, however guilty he might be."[28] The whole passage was prejudicially stacked against the defendant; moreover, the proposition was astounding in view of the fact that before 1964 (and the three defendants in *McMann* were prosecuted before then) New York did not provide a constitutionally acceptable procedure to challenge the validity of allegedly coerced confessions. Accordingly, trial and appeal, contrary to White, could hardly be an effective course. Moreover, the defendants could not win acquittal in a collateral proceeding, for *McMann* itself was such a proceeding, and White's holding for the Court was that a counseled guilty plea is binding and may not be attacked in a collateral proceeding, not even by proof that it was motivated by a coerced confession.[29]

The presence of counsel, White believed, settled the issue. As he saw it, the claim that the coerced confession induced the plea became "at most" a claim that because defendants may have been mistakenly advised about the admissibility of their confessions, their pleas were unintelligent and voidable.[30] By circular reasoning White concluded that their pleas were not unintelligent and voidable because they were counseled. He thought that a reasonably competent lawyer acting in good faith might make mistakes, and defendants were bound by them.[31]

By such reasoning we might conclude that a defendant is better off, at least before an appellate court, if he has not been represented by counsel or if he has demonstrably incompetent counsel. White himself declared that in these cases defendants could secure relief, based on the Court's 1964 decision in *Jackson* v. *Denno,* if they could prove "gross error" on the part of counsel when advising guilty pleas. But as he himself acknowledged, "Such showing cannot be made," because in 1953, eleven years before *Jackson* v. *Denno,* the Court had sustained New York's procedures for dealing with claims of coerced confessions, in a decision overruled in *Jackson.*[32] That the Court applied *Jackson* retroactively to defendants who had previously gone to trial made no difference here because these defendants had been convicted on counseled pleas of guilty in open court; therefore their prior confessions, if invalid, had not been used against them at a trial. In sum, a defendant assumes the risk of error in his attorney's assessment of the law and facts and is bound by his plea "unless he can allege and prove serious derelictions on the part of counsel sufficient to show that his plea was not, after all, a knowing and intelligent act."[33] One wonders how he could show that or anything, given the fact that the Court denied him a hearing.

Brennan wrote a strong dissent that could have been far stronger. He found the majority decision to be inconsistent with precedents which had been imprecisely distinguished away. His position was that the claim that an unconstitutional influence actually infected the pleading process justified a hearing: If the coerced confession induced the guilty plea, that plea "is the fruit of the State's prior illegal conduct and thus is vulnerable to attack,"[34] especially because defendants were unable, for all practical purposes, to contest their confessions under the 1953 decision of the Court. He objected to narrowing the retroactive effect of the 1964 decision that over-ruled the 1953 one, and he refused, he said, to attach "talismanic significance to the presence of counsel."[35] He preferred to take into account all the circumstances surrounding the entry of a guilty plea. Brennan criticized the Court's "formalism,"[36] meaning its abstract approach and its failure to make an evaluation until after a factual inquiry into the actual reasons that motivated the pleas. His reference to "formalism" applied also to White's notion that the pleas and not the confessions were the basis of the convictions. White was right in the sense that a guilty plea is always a literal basis for a conviction, but that fact did not dispose of the conten-tion that the plea was induced and therefore tainted because no constitutionally adequate procedures existed to test the validity of an allegedly coerced confession. Nor could Brennan accept the view that the guilty plea constituted a waiver to all the objections to those confessions. If the allegations concerning the confessions were proved, the pleas were legally invalid. The majority's reason-ing and misuse of precedent, Brennan declared, "hardly furthers the goal of principled decision-making."[37] He could explain the de-cision only on grounds of public policy: The Court determined, he thought, to preserve the sanctity of all judgments obtained by means of guilty pleas.

White, indeed, was fearful that contrary decisions in these cases might jeopardize the plea-bargaining system, without which the criminal courts of this nation would speedily become comatose. As White pointed out, about 90 percent, perhaps 95 percent, of all criminal convictions are by pleas of guilty; in felony cases only, be-tween 70 percent and 85 percent of all convictions are by guilty pleas, many or most of which, in White's language, are "motivated at least in part by the hope or assurance of a lesser penalty than might be imposed if there were a guilty verdict after a trial by judge or jury."[38] The criminal courts have an addictive dependence on plea bargaining, which, as White observed, conserves the state's "scarce judicial and prosecutorial resources"[39] for those cases, com-paratively few in number, in which there is a substantial issue of the defendant's guilt.

The system of criminal justice in this country is already acutely overloaded by a backlog of cases beyond its capacity to manage. If all defendants pleaded not guilty and demanded jury trial, indeed if only a substantial minority of them did so, there would be a catastrophic breakdown of the whole system. Defendants might never be tried. There simply are not enough courts, judges, juries, prosecutors, or defense counsel.[40] Consequently, while confessions made in the basement of the police station are usually scrutinized under a jeweler's glass by appellate judges, the criminal courts can function only by spewing out a mendacious torrent of unchallenged, staged confessions in the form of guilty pleas that result from haggling in a bargain-basement bazaar. Most who plead guilty are in fact guilty of some crime, if not the one to which they plead, and they are presumed guilty. Some who plead guilty are innocent, and many plead guilty who are innocent of the crime to which they acknowledge their guilt, though they may be guilty of still worse.[41] Sometimes pleading to false charges has its ludicrous side, as when a motorist, guilty of speeding, copped a plea to driving the wrong way on a one-way street in a community, it was later learned, that had no one-way streets. In another case, a defendant whose offense was grand theft pleaded guilty to statutory rape, although another man with the same name was the accused rapist. When the error was discovered and the thief was asked why he had pleaded guilty to the wrong charge, he replied, "Well, I thought maybe my attorney had made a deal for me."[42] Other cases are tragedies.

Plea bargaining holds dangers as well as benefits for society and for the accused, but White's one-sided presentation depicted only the advantages. Plea bargaining permits the criminal courts to survive, but part of the price we pay is giving bargain-justice rates to experienced and serious criminals who do not get the punishment they merit, while others who are not as adept at playing the system are victimized by the prosecution's severe bargaining. For the defendant whose possibility of acquittal may be slight, pleading guilty to limit the penalty is an obvious advantage, but the system operates with great inequities in softening the severity of the criminal code.[43] Its pressures may trap the innocent into pleading guilty or unduly burden his decision to risk a jury's verdict. The promise of a light sentence and avoidance of the expense and exposure of a public trial may seduce him into a waiver of his constitutional rights. Conversely, a man who might not be convicted if he put the state to its proof may yield to threats of excessive criminal charges and severe punishment should he choose trial and lose. Juries, to be sure, have convicted innocent men, but the danger of convicting the innocent is greater when the prosecution is not forced to produce its evidence in open court, run the risk of proving its charges, and demonstrate that its evidence has not been corrupted by unconstitutional tactics. A lawyer despite his finest efforts may lose his client's case at a trial, but appeal and collateral attack are still possible; by contrast, no counseled defendant may be convicted without his lawyer's direct participation and assent in the plea of guilty which, according to the decision in *McMann,* forecloses appeal and collateral attack.

One of the worst features of the Court's decision in the plea-bargaining cases was its unrealistic assumption that indigent defendants receive effective representation from court-assigned counsel. In White's romanticized Perrymasonland, there dwell many an F. Lee Bailey and Edward Bennett Williams. No doubt there are court-assigned counsel who are zealous and conscientious in the discharge of their duties, but many are inexperienced in the field of criminal law and lack the time, money, will, and investigative facilities to prepare a case effectively. Representing an indigent defendant for some modest, fixed fee entails financial sacrifice; counsel would rather get on with his regular practice and make a living. The pressures are on him to plead his client guilty, and the system is structured to expect that of him and to expect his cooperation. There are assigned counsel who are regulars within the system, friends of the trial judge and of the prosecutor's office; they tend to be Stakhonovites who work as if on a piece-rate basis. If they can persuade the defendant to plead guilty, they save themselves the labor of investigating and trying the case; the guilty plea permits counsel to collect his fee and turn expeditiously to the next case. Court-assigned counsel tend to be mediators between the system and their clients rather than champions and representatives. They operate on a presumption of guilt and mute the adversary features of criminal justice. They play Russian roulette with other men's lives.

Court-assigned counsel too often develop a stony indifference toward their clients, akin to the attitude of a physician toward a patient with a terminal or incurable disease. The one observes, "You have cancer, go to the hospital," the other, "You are guilty, go to jail." In *McMann*, one attorney allegedly conferred with his client "only 10 minutes prior to the day the plea of guilty was taken."[44] In that brief time the defendant told his story how he had been beaten into a confession and did not want to plead guilty to a crime he did not commit; and in that same brief time counsel made an on-the-spot decision to waive all his client's constitutional rights and cop a plea to a lesser charge. Counsel for another defendant in the same case ignored his alibi defense and supposedly misrepresented the charge. Query: How much skill, time, and care must counsel devote to an assigned case in order to fall within Justice White's range of acceptable competence? The Court in *McMann* found no violation of the right to effective counsel.

Counsel's performance in *McMann* was apparently par for the course.[45] Various studies tell us that defense counsel, especially court-assigned counsel, rather than the police or prosecution, are the ones who by far the most frequently suggest to the accused that he plead guilty. One investigator found that the suggestion to plead guilty came from defense counsel five times more often than from police and prosecution combined. Moreover, privately retained counsel suggested the guilty plea on first contact in almost 35 percent of the cases, while assigned counsel did so in almost 60 percent of the cases.[46] Another study showed that retained counsel did so on first contact in only 25 percent of the cases, compared to 71 percent for assigned counsel.[47]

When the accused agrees to cop a plea, counsel can rest easy in his conscience; the man was admittedly guilty anyway, and counsel at least got him a more lenient sentence. The system works to produce a congruence of interests among defense counsel, prosecution, and the criminal court. They all have a stake in avoiding trial, in disposing of cases swiftly, and in having any doubts relieved by seeing the defendant acknowledge his guilt in court at the perfunctory and ritualistic cop-out ceremony. He acknowledges, too, that he makes his guilty plea knowingly and freely, without yielding to any threat or promise. That public acknowledgment insulates police, prosecution, defense counsel, and court from accusations that they have infringed any rights of the accused or that they have badgered and cajoled him with promises, when in fact counsel on both sides, often with the court's knowledge, sometimes with its participation, have done just that. As one of the consultants to the President's Commission on Law Enforcement and Administration of Justice put it, "Because of doubts over the legality of the negotiated plea, prosecutors and defense counsel typically avoid all reference in court to the sentence to be imposed until after the plea has been tendered and accepted, and engage in the pious fraud of making a record that the plea was not induced by any promises."[48]

The record also puts the appellate judge in a position righteously to quote, as did White, the little colloquy between the defendant and the judge who convicts him on his plea, to show that there can be no mistake about the plea having been voluntary.[49] But a plea induced by promises is, like a confession, theoretically illegal— an "improper" act,[50] said White—yet the system of bargain justice rests on such promises. A confession can be withdrawn, denied, or explained, and should be corroborated by the prosecution. By comparison, a guilty plea, if counseled, is final. Consequently, the test to determine whether it has been improperly induced should be at least as rigorous as the test for the voluntariness of a confession; but judicial scrutiny might break down the system by exposing the "pious fraud" which is its mainstay. White's faith "that courts will satisfy themselves that pleas of guilty are voluntarily and intelligently made" seems unrealistic.[51]

The plea, openly made, gives the impression that standards of due process have been met. Yet that plea of guilty waives all defendant's rights—to silence, to a supposed presumption of innocence, to the requirement that the prosecution prove guilt beyond reasonable doubt, to be free from coercion, to take advantage of the rules on exclusionary evidence, and to have guilt determined by a jury. The plea is the ultimate detergent of the criminal law, since it sterilizes and washes away every non-Perry-Mason, nonadversary, nonpublic, non-due-process feature of the pretrial, nontrial, bargain-basement, assembly-line system of instant criminal justice. Like a doctor who buries his mistakes, defense counsel often purges his, and those of the prosecution as well, when advising the accused to waive all his rights and cop a plea. Plea bargaining undoubtedly can have advantages for a defendant, but in *McMann* the Supreme

Court lightly approved of the waiver of rights, protected ineffective, lazy, and perhaps incompetent counsel, and saw none of the risks, nor the constitutional infirmities, that may be part of the process. Does it offer due process or dupe process?

BARGAINING TO AVOID DEATH

The plea-bargaining cases decided the same day as *McMann* were aftermaths of *United States* v. *Jackson,* decided in 1968.[52] There the Court held unconstitutional the death-penalty provision of the Federal Kidnapping Act, which permitted capital punishment only on the recommendation of a jury. One who waived trial by jury or pleaded guilty could limit the penalty to life imprisonment. The act thereby made the risk of death the price of a jury trial. The Court ruled that the death-penalty provision "imposes an impermissible burden upon the exercise of a constitutional right. . . ."[53]

Two years later, in 1970, the Court had before it *Brady* v. *United States,* in which the prisoner attacked the sentence given to him after pleading guilty under the same federal act, and the companion case, *Parker* v. *North Carolina,* in which the prisoner similarly claimed that his guilty plea was involuntary because the state statute at the time of his conviction allowed an escape from the death penalty on a plea of guilty to the capital charge.[54] White, for the same six-man majority that governed in *McMann,* this time looked to the record, though in *McMann* he had ignored defendants' allegations. In Brady's case the prisoner originally pleaded not guilty; White inferred that Brady had been willing to risk a death sentence if convicted by a jury. Brady had changed his plea to guilty, on advice of counsel, after learning that his codefendant had pleaded guilty and was available to testify against him. Even Brennan, Douglas, and Marshall, separately concurring, agreed with White that Brady had not pleaded guilty out of fear that a jury trial risked death. The Court's unanimity on this point (and on this point alone) seems inconsistent with its previous finding that the death-penalty provision imposed "an impermissible burden upon the exercise of a constitutional right."[55] Brady prepared to go before a jury when he thought that the prosecution might not prove its case; he changed his mind because the testimony of his confederate would have convicted him, thus making death the price of the jury trial, the very test that was conclusive in the 1968 case.

White stressed the fact that Brady's plea was voluntary and counseled. White acknowledged that the 1968 opinion of the Court, from which incidentally he had dissented, reasoned that the "inevitable effect" of the death-penalty provision needlessly encouraged pleas of guilty, contrary to the Fifth Amendment, and waivers of jury trial, deterring a Sixth Amendment right. He then distorted the 1968 opinion. He said the Court had made it clear in 1968 that it was not holding the act "inherently coercive of guilty pleas."[56] The phrase is White's, not that of the Court in 1968. He then quoted the Court: ". . . the fact that the Federal Kidnapping Act tends to discourage defendants from insisting upon their innocence and demanding trial by jury hardly implies that every defendant who enters a guilty plea to a charge under the Act does so involuntarily."[57] This would seem to prove White's point that a voluntary plea was permissible. Brennan's reply to this passage was simply that the Court in 1968 had merely acknowledged the obvious fact that a defendant might plead guilty under the act for reasons unrelated to the death-penalty scheme; he might, for example, wish to spare himself and his family the agony and cost of a trial. However, Brennan stressed that not every defendant who pleaded guilty under the act did so voluntarily. That rejoinder, though correct, was scarcely adequate, because White had quoted a passage of the 1968 opinion out of context and in a way that radically altered its meaning.

When the Court had then held that the act, in White's phrase, was not "inherently coercive of guilty pleas," the Court was not making an exception for voluntary pleas of guilt, as White found. Rather, it was saying that even an uncoerced plea may be invalid if encouraged by the provisions of the act. The passage quoted by White in context reads:

> For the evil in the federal statute is not that it necessarily *coerces* guilty pleas and jury waivers but simply that it needlessly *encourages* them. A procedure need not be inherently coercive in order that it be held to impose an impermissible burden upon the assertion of a

constitutional right. Thus the fact that the Federal Kidnapping Act tends to discourage defendants from insisting upon their innocence and demanding trial by jury hardly implies that every defendant who enters a plea of guilty to a charge under the Act does so involuntarily.[58]

That means that even if he does so voluntarily in order to avoid a trial and a possible death sentence, he has pleaded under an unconstitutional scheme.

In the companion case, *Parker* v. *North Carolina,* the question was whether the guilty plea had been induced by a statute making trial by jury a joust with the hangman. That question was complicated by a second and related one, whether, as in *McMann,* the plea was the product of a coerced confession. In *Parker,* the Court took an unsettling position by virtually demurring to the questions. White, once again the spokesman, argued that even if the act under which Parker pleaded had been unconstitutional and even if his confession had been coerced, there was no basis for ungluing his plea. Said White: "It may be that under *United States* v. *Jackson,* it was unconstitutional to impose the death penalty under the statutory framework which existed in North Carolina at the time of Parker's plea. Even so, we determined in Brady . . . that an otherwise valid plea is not involuntary because induced by the defendant's desire to limit the possible maximum penalty to less than that authorized if there is a jury trial."[59] If the decision in *Jackson* had continuing validity, White's proposition could be stood on its head and yield an equally supportable one, namely that an otherwise valid plea is involuntary because induced by defendant's desire to waive trial in order to foreclose the possibility of a death penalty.

But as Brennan pointed out in his forceful dissent, the Court had undermined the rationale of the *Jackson* case. Since the penalty scheme of the act under which Parker had pleaded indisputably encouraged guilty pleas and waivers of constitutional rights, the Court's construction of *Jackson* meant that although a defendant who went to trial and was convicted could have relief from the penalty of the statute, by contrast one who succumbed to its unconstitutional pressures, surrendered his constitutional rights, and pleaded guilty could have no remedy. As Brennan said, "Where the penalty scheme failed to produce its unconstitutional effect, the intended victims obtain relief; where it succeeded, the real victims have none. Thus the Court puts a premium on strength of will and invulnerability to pressure at the cost of constitutional rights."[60] As for Parker's coerced confession, White reasoned that any coercion had been expunged by the defendant's subsequent guilty plea, which was counseled, uninfluenced by the confession, and affirmed by defendant's acknowledgment to be voluntary and not induced by threats or promises. Parker, incidentally, was a Southern black who at the time of his confession and plea, resulting in a mandatory sentence of life imprisonment, was fifteen years old. The Court majority found no way to distinguish his case from *McMann* or *Brady*.

At no point in his three opinions in these cases did White think it necessary to reply to the dissenters' reasoned arguments that the Court was making a "wholesale retreat" from previous principles, insulating all guilty pleas from attack, and ignoring conflicting precedents. For example, in a 1967 case the Court had held involuntary a waiver of the right against self-incrimination when an individual was threatened with the possibility of discharge from public employment if he invoked the Fifth Amendment.[61] Brennan's point in referring to this precedent was that threats or promises might unfairly burden the defendant's decision, making his plea involuntary and invalid even if reflecting a rational choice. Brennan should have added that the choice between waiving trial or losing life was far more coercive than the choice between waiving the Fifth or losing a job.

The Court had relied upon the presence of counsel to prove the voluntariness of the pleas, but the dissenters argued that counsel could not remove the coercive choice imposed upon the defendant by legislation that created differential penalties depending on the plea. Counsel can offset the inquisitional atmosphere of custodial interrogation whose purpose is to draw a confession, but counsel cannot insulate the accused from a legislative threat—death if found guilty by a jury—or from a legislative promise—life in return for a plea of guilty. White's spirited but one-sided defense of plea bargaining also ignored Brennan's criticism that these death-penalty cases were not at all like the give-and-take of ordinary plea-bargaining cases, because the penalty scheme, being inherently coercive and not subject to mitigation, limited the bargaining capacity of defense, leaving counsel little room for play, indeed, leaving the prosecution no room to bargain. White also ignored Brennan's argument that *Parker* and *Brady* were distinguishable from plea-bargaining cases like *McMann* because they were capital cases: "They involve the imposition of death—the most severe and awesome penalty known to our law. This Court has recognized that capital cases are treated differently in some respects from non-capital cases."[62] The *Jackson* case itself was proof of that proposition until the Court in these cases departed from the teaching of *Jackson*. In a less enlightened age, at a time when there were about 250 capital offenses, Blackstone said that upon a plea of guilty a court had to convict, "but it is usually very backward in receiving and recording such confession, out of tenderness to the life of the subject, and will generally advise the prisoner to retract it."[63]

Six months after *McMann, Parker,* and *Brady,* the Court, once again speaking through White, vacated a decision of a federal court of appeals which had relied on *Jackson*. The case was *North Carolina* v. *Alford,* another in which the accused pleaded guilty to avoid the death penalty. Here there was room for bargaining, however, and the prosecutor, in return for the counseled plea, reduced the charge from first-degree murder to second-degree. What gives this case compelling interest is the fact that the prisoner testified, "I pleaded guilty on second degree murder because they said there is too much evidence, but I ain't shot no man. . . . I just pleaded guilty because they said if I didn't they would gas me for it, and that is all." Questioned by his court-appointed counsel at a hearing held prior to the acceptance of the plea, Alford was asked whether he reaffirmed his decision to plead guilty. "Well," he said, "I'm still pleading that you all got me to plead guilty. I plead the other way, circumstantial evidence [there were no eyewitnesses]; that the jury will prosecute me on—on the second. You told me to plead guilty, right. I don't—I'm not guilty but I plead guilty." The judge asked whether he still desired to plead guilty despite his denial of guilt, and he replied affirmatively. In addition to Alford's statement, the judge heard a summary presentation of the state's case and information that Alford had a long, criminal record. Only then did the judge accept his plea, convict him, and sentence him to the maximum punishment for second-degree murder.[64]

The Supreme Court found that the counseled plea under the circumstances was voluntary and intelligent. White concluded, "The prohibitions against involuntary or unintelligent pleas should not be relaxed, but neither should an exercise in arid logic render those constitutional guarantees counterproductive and put in jeopardy the very human values they were meant to preserve."[65] Brennan, in his *Parker* dissent, had specifically answered the "arid logic" criticism that had been addressed to him and more fittingly described the majority's position; he had also said that he was at a loss to understand what human values were preserved by White's opinions.[66] Here, in his *Alford* dissent, Brennan ignored the replay, and, joined again by Douglas and Marshall, dissented on ground that the accused was obviously so gripped by fear of the death penalty that his decision to plead guilty was not voluntary. Brennan did not even bother to refute White's contention that the standard established by the *Jackson* decision for accepting a guilty plea depended upon whether the plea represented a voluntary and intelligent choice among the alternatives open to the defendant. Once again White distorted the case. In *Jackson* the Court had held that even if the plea is voluntary, it is invalid if encouraged by fear of the death penalty.

CONSTITUTIONALITY OF PLEA BARGAINING

White's opinions for the Court in the four plea-bargaining cases of 1970 provoke the question, Is plea bargaining per se an unconstitutional practice? That question was not properly before the Court, nor did the dissenters attempt to answer it. Brennan's disciplined opinions were narrowly confined—in *McMann* to the question whether the defendants' claims entitled them to a hearing, in *Parker* and *Brady* to the question whether the legislative schemes allowing death perniciously influenced the pleas of guilt, and in *Alford* to the question whether he had pleaded voluntarily. Dissenting in *Parker,* Brennan declared that "the principal flaw in the Court's discourse on plea bargaining . . . is that it is, at best, only marginally relevant to the precise issues before us. . . . Thus, whatever the merit, if any, of the constitutional objections to plea bargaining generally, those issues are not presently before us."[67] Yet the Court promiscuously decided the broader question, for White stated: "But we cannot hold that it is unconstitutional for the State to extend a benefit to a defendant who in turn extends a substantial benefit to the State [the waiver of trial] and who demonstrates by his plea that he is ready and willing to admit his crime. . . . A contrary holding would require the States and Federal Government to forbid guilty pleas altogether. . . . In any event, it would be necessary to forbid prosecutors and judges to accept guilty pleas to select counts, to lesser included offenses, or to reduced charges. The Fifth Amendment does not reach so far."[68] But the Court's perfunctory, formalistic acceptance of waivers of constitutional rights, its unwillingness to inquire more than superficially into the effectiveness and competence of assigned counsel, its refusal to see the relationship between coerced confessions and guilty pleas, and its blind trust in the ability of trial judges to discern voluntary from involuntary pleas do not command confidence in its conclusion as to plea bargaining generally.

Yet the repugnance of its reasoning does not necessarily contaminate the Court's conclusion. There can be no doubt that the constitutional rights of the criminally accused would be much better secured if the system of bargain justice did not exist, but the converse is not true that the practice of plea bargaining must violate those rights. The argument against the Court is that prosecutorial concessions always are conditioned on a forfeiture of the Fifth Amendment's right not to be a witness against oneself in a criminal cause and of the Sixth Amendment's right to a public trial. The editors of the *Harvard Law Review,* arguing the unconstitutionality of plea bargaining, summed up by asserting: "Only if the state is willing to forgo the criminal prosecution can it require the individual to speak or suffer a penalty. But since the very purpose of plea bargaining is to prosecute and convict the defendant by pressuring him to plead guilty, the practice will always violate the fifth amendment. The additional penalty imposed by plea bargaining on the exercise of sixth amendment rights makes the case against the practice even stronger. The conclusion that plea bargaining is unconstitutional depends on the determination that it exacts a price for the exercise of fifth and sixth amendment rights."[69] One might add too that sometimes prosecutorial concessions are also conditioned on a forfeiture of the Fourth Amendment right to have unlawfully seized evidence excluded, because the waiver of a trial would eliminate the check that exclusionary rules place on law-enforcement authorities.

The vulnerable point in this line of argument is the prerogative of any man to waive his rights, confess, and plead guilty. Under judicially defined safeguards, which are not adequately enforced, one may relinquish any right, even the right to counsel. There is little possibility that a jury could fairly determine guilt or innocence if a defendant did not have the benefit of effective counsel at a trial; an experienced criminal lawyer is equally indispensable in a plea-bargaining situation, which invariably requires an assessment of the charges, of the prosecution's case, and of the range of possible punishments. Yet one may freely surrender the right to counsel or any other precious right if he understands the nature of his waiver and its consequences. Except in jurisdictions whose statutes prevent a plea of guilty to a capital charge, one may even plead guilty. In one of White's mischievous remarks in these plea-bargaining cases, he said that a contrary holding "would require the States and Federal Government to forbid guilty pleas altogether. . . ."[70] That simply is untrue because a guilty plea need not be the result of bargaining; and even if it is, it need not be involuntary. The coercion may flow the other way: The defendant's threat to go to trial may force an overburdened prosecutor who is unsure of his case to make attractive concessions in exchange for a guilty plea. If a defendant may waive his rights unconditionally, surely he should be able to waive them in return for some benefit, if he can exact it.

One may agree with all this and say that it does not meet the argument against the constitutionality of plea bargaining, for that argument turns wholly on the existence of pressure as a means of extorting the plea. In a real bargaining situation, however, the pressure exists on both sides and each pays a price. The defendant is not always the victim, as the argument supposes. Moreover, the fact that pressure may have a chilling effect upon the exercise of some right does not automatically render that pressure unconstitutional. For example, a defendant without alibi witnesses may be forced to take the stand because of the pressure of the prosecution's case against him. That is, there are circumstances in which the Fifth may be constitutionally waived in the teeth of pressure.

If, for the sake of argument, plea bargaining was held to be unconstitutional or was prohibited by statute, the practice would probably continue shrouded in even greater secrecy than presently exists. It would be hard to down because it is based on off-the-record agreements which can be mutually beneficial. The practice might come to light only if a defendant was cheated of his bargain and could prove it. Assume, however, that plea bargaining was struck down and that Parker or Alford won his case. His sentence of life imprisonment would have been vacated, and he would have gone to trial. Assume that the jury convicted and he had been sentenced to death. Would he then appeal, claiming that he was entitled to the lesser sentence which his previous plea won for him? The problem, in other words, is still unsettled even in the absence of plea bargaining.

Differential sentencing for the same crime is the problem. Plea bargaining may be only a stalking horse or a scapegoat. If a plea of guilty wins a lesser sentence than might be imposed after conviction by a jury, the fear of the more severe sentence, not plea bargaining, deters the exercise of constitutional rights and induces their waiver. Differential sentencing helps create the causes and conditions for the bargaining. The solution might be to require equal statutory sentences for convictions, whether they result from an unbargained plea or a jury's verdict of guilty. But equal sentencing raises questions about the need for tailoring sentences to fit not only the crime but the criminal and his chances for rehabilitation. There is no easy solution, but plea bargaining does not inherently chill or deter the exercise of constitutional rights. The best way to cope with the problem of bargain justice is not to suppress it but to bring it out in the open, regulate its practice, and surround it with judicial safeguards that are calculated to protect both the offender and society. There should in every case be searching judicial examinations of the reasons for the charges in a case, for the waiver of any rights, and for the plea of guilty; there should be, also, examinations into the sufficiency of the prosecution's case and into both the appropriateness and equity of the bargain itself. There is a need for a searching examination into the ways of effectively regulating plea bargaining and an equal need to determine whether a plea of guilty, however voluntary, should ever be accepted in a capital case.

Whatever its dangers to the public and to the accused, and whatever merit there is in the contention that it should be held unconstitutional, plea bargaining is with us to stay, leaving its regulation the only future course. The Court took a short step in that direction in its 1971 opinion in *Santobello* v. *New York,* where there was unanimous agreement that the state, by breaking its undisputed bargain with the prisoner, had violated the principle of fairness guaranteed by the due-process clause. Burger, in his opinion for the Court, regarded the constitutionality of plea bargaining as having been settled by the *Brady* case. He described plea bargaining as "an essential component of the administration of justice," which, properly administered, should be "encouraged" as "highly desirable." Burger did not even consider whether the state's inducements could be coercive or in any way taint the plea of guilty. Significantly, he declared that when a plea was based on "a promise or agreement of the prosecutor, so that it can be said to be part of the inducement, or consideration, such promise must be fulfilled."[71] In effect he raised to the status of an inviolable contract any bargain leading to a plea of guilty, if the bargain was voluntary and knowing. Douglas concurred, as did Marshall, joined by Brennan and Stewart. The latter three differed from the majority only in believing that because the state reneged on its bargain, the prisoner should be permitted to withdraw his guilty plea. All the other Justices were of the opinion that the state court should determine whether the prosecution must fulfill its part of the bargain or whether the prisoner must have the opportunity to withdraw the plea. Thus, the whole Court in *Santobello,* taking for granted what it should have proved convincingly, constitutionally sanctified the system of bargain justice.

EFFECTIVE ASSISTANCE OF COUNSEL

Although the issue of plea bargaining must be taken as settled, however unsatisfactorily, the question of effective assistance of counsel still nags, to be decided on a case-to-case basis. As the plea-bargaining cases showed, a sympathetic greeting from an appellate court does not await the defendant who argues that he has not received the effective assistance of counsel. Indeed, counsel's management of the defense apparently has to be farcical or the merest semblance of representation before redress can be had. Mistaken judgments by an attorney, even if clearly affecting the outcome of a case, are absorbed by defendant's hide. Appellate courts seem to be extremely reluctant to grant a new trial on ground that defendant's counsel was seriously derelict in his duties as a lawyer. To hold that he was seriously derelict is like censuring him without giving him the benefit of due process of law and at the same time censuring the trial judge for having condoned blatant injustice to the defendant. The trial judge would be especially blamable for having appointed inept counsel for an indigent. Presumably a defendant who retains his own lawyer has no one but himself to blame for the consequences of his choice. Whether counsel is retained or assigned, a ruling that his client's conviction must be voided because he was incompetent might require trial judges to interfere on behalf of defendants whenever their lawyers seem to make a mistake. That would shift the burden of the defense to the trial judge, who cannot conduct the defense of the accused. At the same time, a layman who is a criminal defendant does not have the knowledge to determine whether his lawyer's skills meet the standard of professional competence in the conduct of his defense. The problem of determining whether effective assistance of counsel has been rendered seems nearly insurmountable.[72]

Tollett v. *Henderson,* a plea-bargaining case decided by the Supreme Court in 1973, illustrates the difficulty of securing the reversal of a conviction on ground that defense counsel was incompetent or ineffective.[73] Henderson, a young black man accused of attempted murder, had no lawyer when he signed a confession; subsequently, his family retained counsel for him. The lawyer apparently discharged his duty simply by arranging for a plea bargain:

Henderson pleaded guilty and received a sentence of ninety-nine years; had he chosen to go to trial he might have been sentenced to death if convicted. In jail and with the assistance of a new lawyer, he sought and failed to obtain a writ of habeas corpus in both the state and federal courts on ground that his confession had been coerced and that he had not received the effective assistance of counsel when he pleaded.

Henderson next claimed, in a new petition for the writ, that the proceedings against him were void because he had been indicted by a grand jury from which Negroes had been excluded. He argued that his first lawyer had not informed him of his constitutional right with respect to the composition of the grand jury; nor did the lawyer inform him that he might have challenged the indictment and that his failure to do so before a plea of guilty might prejudice his effort to do so later. His first lawyer swore that at the time of the case, in 1948, he did not know that Negroes were systematically excluded from the grand juries of the Tennessee county in which the case was tried. A United States District Court, whose judgment was affirmed by a United States Court of Appeals, granted Henderson's petition for a writ of habeas corpus on ground that the record did not show that he had made an intelligent or knowing waiver of his rights. The Supreme Court in a 6-to-3 opinion by Rehnquist reversed these lower federal courts.

The *McMann-Brady-Parker* trilogy of plea-bargaining decisions controlled the disposition of the case, according to Rehnquist. He admitted that the Court of Appeals had been "undoubtedly correct" in concluding that Henderson had not made an intelligent and knowing waiver of his constitutional rights; he admitted, too, that claims of constitutional deprivation resulting from counsel's failures might "play a part in evaluating the advice rendered by counsel." But he held that Henderson was stuck with his counseled plea of guilty. That foreclosed all but an argument that he did not know what he was doing by pleading guilty: "He may only attack the voluntary and intelligent character of the guilty plea by showing that the advice he received from counsel was not within the standards set forth in *McMann*"—that is, that the advice was not "within the range of competence demanded of attorneys in criminal cases."[74] But *McMann* pretty well made impossible such proof by the defendant, and this case closed any loophole. The Court ruled that the claim that an indicting grand jury was unconstitutionally selected must precede the guilty plea or follow a plea of not guilty.

Rehnquist's reasoning was circular, fencing Henderson in. Since his plea was counseled, Henderson could not attack it and therefore could not raise the issue whether incompetent counsel misled him. His only hope was to show that his plea was involuntary and unintelligent, and yet the fact that counsel represented him made the plea voluntary and intelligent. Henderson had to pay with his freedom for his lawyer's mistakes. Rehnquist seemed to think that the lawyer had not made any mistakes, but the Justice's statements were contradictory on that point.

A guilty plea voluntarily and intelligently made, said Rehnquist, who assumed the very fact he ought to have established, cannot be vacated merely "because the defendant was not advised of every conceivable constitutional plea in abatement he might have to the charge." The issue did not turn, of course, on whether Henderson had been advised of "every" such plea; it turned rather on whether he had been advised of just one: the unconstitutionality of the indicting grand jury. But Rehnquist declared that a guilty plea could not be set aside merely because counsel "in retrospect" may not have correctly appraised the constitutional issue. The plea could not be set aside even if counsel in pursuing the issue "would have uncovered a possible constitutional infirmity in the proceedings."[75] For these decisive propositions, Rehnquist offered only his own say-so, unburdened by any sort of proof. That counsel had not, in fact, made a mistake in assessing the indictment was evident to Rehnquist from a 1970 statement by a Tennessee judge that "no lawyer in this State would have ever thought of objecting to the fact that Negroes did not serve on the Grand Jury in Tennessee in 1948."[76] That was a screaming error for the Supreme Court to quote with approval in 1973.

Thus, though Rehnquist previously had admitted a violation of Henderson's constitutional right to be free from indictment by a grand jury selected on the basis of race,[77] and though the Justice admitted, too, that Henderson had not waived his constitutional right, at least not by the proper waiver standards, Rehnquist concluded, in effect, that Henderson had waived all his rights by a counseled plea of guilty; that plea broke "the chain of events which has preceded it in the criminal process," foreclosing any subsequent attack on the proceedings.[78]

This remarkably grotesque opinion earned the scorn heaped on it by Marshall, whose dissent Douglas and Brennan joined. The dissenters saw the majority opinion as an extension of the plea-bargaining trilogy of cases, because "even where counsel does not consider and present to his client the possibility of a challenge to the composition of the grand jury, the client is nonetheless held to have made an 'intelligent' guilty plea."[79] A plea bargain, as Marshall pointed out, is supposed to represent an exchange of a waiver of constitutional rights in return for leniency. Henderson had waived his right to trial by jury by pleading guilty, but he never waived his right to challenge the indictment because he never knew that he had that right. In his ignorance he could not have decided to relinquish it in order to gain some advantage. Marshall, in stressing that the case involved a clear claim to a constitutional right, asserted: "I would have thought that the fact that the Constitution placed limits on the prosecution would be very important in deciding whether a lawyer's professional responsibility required him to consult with his client before taking action that led to a relinquishment of the constitutional objection."[80]

Marshall dissociated himself from the Court's stunted concept of professional responsibility on the part of counsel. Henderson's counsel could not have faithfully represented his client without informing himself of the constitutional issues and without informing his client about them. Henderson, as Marshall indicated, might have obtained a lesser sentence had he threatened to force the state to defend its unconstitutional indictment.

That the indictment was unconstitutional Marshall proved without doubt, notwithstanding the remark by the Tennessee judge. Marshall demonstrated that it was "simply untrue."[81] No black man had served on a grand jury before 1948 in the county where Henderson had been indicted, although Negroes were then 25 percent of its population. Whenever Negroes turned up on the lists from which grand jurors were impaneled, an abbreviation for "colored" was marked next to their names, and they were excluded.

That practice, as Marshall showed, conflicted with several Supreme Court decisions from 1940 through 1947.[82] He concluded that the ease of proving unconstitutional racial discrimination in the selection of grand jurors in the indicting county persuaded him that Henderson's counsel had not acted within the range of competence demanded of attorneys in criminal cases. He did not offer advice that was competent in the light of the law at the time of the case. "An attorney of minimal competence would have realized that, where no Negroes had been summoned for service over many years and where racial designations were used, the Tennessee Supreme Court would very probably have held the selection system unconstitutional, in line with the decision of this Court."[83]

Chambers v. *Maroney* also presented a claim that the accused had been denied the effective assistance of counsel, although White, for the Court, summarily disposed of that claim in an opinion focusing on a different issue.[84] Chambers's first trial ended in a mistrial. He never thereafter saw the lawyer whom the trial court had appointed from the local legal-aid society. Just "a few minutes before the second trial began,"[85] a different lawyer from that society appeared to represent him. Chambers was convicted. He then sought a writ of habeas corpus on ground that the belated appearance of his counsel resulted in his being inadequately represented at the second trial.

The precedents seemed stacked in Chambers's favor. In the landmark right-to-counsel case, *Powell* v. *Alabama,* the Court had recognized that the duty to provide counsel "is not discharged by an assignment at such a time or under such circumstances as to preclude the giving of effective aid in the preparation and trial of the case."[86] Eight years later, in 1940, the Court decided that "the denial of opportunity for appointed counsel to confer, to consult with the accused and to prepare his defense, could convert the appointment of counsel into a sham and nothing more than a formal compliance with the Constitution's requirement that an accused be given the assistance of counsel."[87] Five years later, in *Hawk* v. *Olson,* a case that seemed exactly on point, the Court held that due process had been violated when counsel, without previously having met let alone consulted with the accused, appeared in the courtroom just as the trial was about to begin.[88]

Notwithstanding these precedents the lower federal courts ruled that Chambers had at worst suffered from only "harmless error" as a result of his new lawyer's conduct of his trial. The fact that the Court of Appeals had dealt at length with the question of effective legal counsel impressed White. He asserted that courts should, of course, make every effort to appoint counsel early, "But we are not disposed to fashion a *per se* rule requiring reversal of every conviction following tardy appointment of counsel. . . ."[89] White was not disposed to offer any reason for that holding or for his failure to consider or even to mention the precedents. Chambers had not requested a flat rule requiring the reversal of every conviction when counsel had been tardily appointed; he requested consideration whether the facts of his case did not show that he had not received the effective assistance of counsel to which he was entitled.

Inexplicably, Harlan was the only member of the Court who dissented from White's opinion. Harlan could not join the Court's "casual treatment of the issue that had been presented by both parties as the major issue in this case: petitioner's claim that he received ineffective assistance of counsel at his trial."[90] Harlan noted that the Court of Appeals opinion that had so impressed the other Justices acknowledged that "we do not know what preparation, if any, counsel was able to accomplish prior to the date of the trial" and that he was not "wholly familiar" with the case.[91] State rules required that motions to suppress evidence, whose admissibility was at issue in this case, must be made before the trial; as Harlan observed, counsel's "last minute" entrance into the case made it impossible for him to comply with those rules. The record, as Harlan read it, suggested that counsel was insufficiently acquainted with the case to know what arguments were worth making. He did not object to the admission of evidence that was the fruit of a search of "questionable validity under Fourth Amendment standards," nor was he prepared to cross-examine government witnesses. Harlan concluded: "Where counsel has no acquaintance with the facts of the case and no opportunity to plan a defense, the result is that the defendant is effectively denied his constitutional right to assistance of counsel."[92]

A similar conclusion may be drawn from another case, *Dukes* v. *Warden*, in which the Court held that a guilty plea was not unintelligent and involuntary even though a conflict of interest prejudiced Dukes's counsel.[93] When representing others in a different case he blamed Dukes for their involvement in crime. Brennan, deserting Marshall and Douglas, who dissented, wrote the Court's opinion, a desiccated recitation of facts that seemed not to have the slightest bearing on the principle that the accused is entitled to effective representation by counsel. Marshall threaded those facts together in relation to that principle. He pointed out that Dukes, as his lawyer admitted, had insistently protested his innocence and wanted to go to trial. Under strong and sustained pressure from his lawyer, Dukes pleaded guilty when he was in a weakened state after a suicide attempt; moreover, he believed that the plea was a temporary one, and he sought to withdraw it before sentencing. He and his lawyer had sharp differences. More significantly, the lawyer, in Marshall's phrase, had a "gross conflict of interest" between Dukes and other clients. The lawyer, when representing them, had made highly improper derogatory remarks about Dukes before the very judge who was scheduled shortly to sentence him. Because of those remarks, which reinforced Dukes's suspicion that his lawyer was not dedicated to his interests, Dukes sought to change his plea and his lawyer, and he requested a trial. These facts did not move Brennan and the majority; only Marshall and Douglas believed that Dukes was entitled to his day in court.

The case made no new rule of law. It, like the other effective-assistance cases, simply showed the Court's persistent reluctance to hand down an opinion that adversely reflected on the professional competence, effort, or ethics of a member of the bar. The facts of these cases—*McMann* v. *Richardson, North Carolina* v. *Alford, Tollett* v. *Henderson, Chambers* v. *Maroney,* and *Dukes* v. *Warden* —did discredit the lawyers involved or the trial judges who either belatedly appointed them or tolerated their conduct of the defense. These were not cases touching matters on which conscientious and competent lawyers should have disagreed. Many convicted persons doubtless scrutinize the conduct of their defense through the eyes of another lawyer for points that in retrospect could have been handled differently and perhaps more successfully. But these were not such cases; they did not involve debatable judgment by counsel, frivolous claims by the prisoners, or Monday-morning quarterbacking on legal tactics. These cases revealed intimidated men who pleaded guilty out of fear or because of counsel's pressure, or men who had meager or no opportunity to consult with counsel, or counsel who seemed to confuse their role with that of the prosecution, or who were unprepared, or who made serious blunders of constitutional law. The Court coddled the lawyers and kept their clients in jail in the workaday cases, mocking and sapping the broad principles of *Powell* v. *Alabama* and *Gideon* v. *Wainwright*. The prisoners may have been dangerous and contemptible men, guilty of the crimes charged, but if *Powell, Gideon,* and the Sixth Amendment meant what the Court had said they meant, those men had a right to the effective representation of counsel before conviction or before a plea of guilty was accepted against them.

The tradition of *Powell* and *Gideon* did persevere in two major cases decided by the Nixon Court. In one the Court extended the right to counsel to preliminary hearings[94] and in the other to all misdemeanor cases in which imprisonment was a consequence of a finding of guilt.[95] But the right to counsel is a sham if it is not the right to the effective assistance of competent counsel when needed. Still, the first step is to establish the right to counsel.

In *Coleman* v. *Alabama,*[96] a 1970 case, the Court went beyond a Warren decision holding that at a preliminary hearing, which is like an arraignment, the accused must have counsel.[97] The preliminary hearing in *Coleman* was the more traditional type in which there was no requirement that a plea must be made to the charges against the accused. Indeed, the purpose of the Alabama preliminary hearing is simply to determine whether there is adequate evidence against the accused—really, the suspect—to warrant presenting his case to a grand jury and, if so, to fix bail for a bailable offense. The hearing is therefore a safeguard against groundless prosecutions, and it avoids for the benefit of both sides the inconvenience and expense of proceeding further if no probable cause is demonstrated for believing that the suspect is guilty. In Coleman's case, counsel had not been assigned to him for the preliminary hearing; he did not receive counsel as an indigent until after he was indicted. Brennan, for a six-man majority, took the position that the principle of *Powell*—that the guiding hand of counsel must protect the accused at every step in the case against him—required a lawyer's scrutiny of any pretrial confrontation between the prisoner and the state's witnesses against him. The duty of the Court, Brennan averred, was to determine whether the presence of counsel was necessary to preserve the basic right to a fair trial as affected by his being able, through counsel, to cross-examine the witnesses against him and have effective assistance of counsel at the trial itself. Brennan found that the right to counsel was essential at the preliminary hearing to protect the indigent accused against any prejudice to his rights as a defendant and to ward off an erroneous or improper prosecution.

A trained lawyer could do what no layman might at the preliminary hearing. He could by his artful questioning of witnesses expose weaknesses in the state's case, thereby persuading the judge to dismiss the prosecution. By his cross-examination, skilled counsel might also lay the groundwork for impeaching the state's witnesses. He might discover the state's case against his client and be able more effectively to prepare a defense. He might also be influential in obtaining either a psychiatric examination, if warranted, or bail for the accused. Because of the services a lawyer might perform for the prisoner at the preliminary hearing, the Court held that it was a "critical stage" of the prosecution at which he is as much entitled to counsel as at the trial itself. Harlan and White concurred, because they felt constrained by the precedents. Blackmun, who had just been appointed, did not sit on the case.

Burger, at the time the only participating Nixon appointee, unloosed an ill-tempered dissent. He accused the majority of manufacturing new law on an ad hoc basis contrary to the command of the Sixth Amendment. The amendment, he observed, requires counsel only in a "criminal prosecution." Burger did not think that a preliminary hearing was a stage in such a prosecution, nor, as he declared, would he be bound by erroneous, recent decisions like Harlan and White. The Constitution did not, said a literal-minded Chief Justice, provide that counsel "be furnished for every 'critical event in the progress of a criminal case.' "[98] Burger was right in the sense that the Constitution does not even provide specifically that counsel be "furnished" at state cost to any defendant, not even to illiterate, ignorant, bewildered indigents on trial for their lives. The logic of Burger's position would turn the clock back to the pre-*Powell* era. "By inventing its own verbal formula the prevailing opinion," Burger insisted, "simply seeks to reshape the Constitution in accordance with its own predilections of what is deemed desirable."[99]

Burger made one point that is irrefutable, as did Stewart in his separate and moderate dissent. Counsel may not attend a grand-jury inquiry, which is surely, from the majority standpoint, a critical stage of the prosecution. Yet the grand jury may interrogate witnesses and even the person eventually charged with crime, and may do so in secret session. If the dictum of *Powell* is to be applied consistently, grand-jury indictments would have to be set aside as denial of the right to counsel. The Court, said Stewart, boggled at the logical consequences of its own reasoning. Rather, it ignored those consequences. Stewart stressed that Coleman's trial did not reveal that the absence of counsel at the preliminary hearing prejudiced him thereafter. There was, doubtless, an abstract quality to Brennan's opinion. He failed to show whether the facts of this case justified his remarks about the crucial services that counsel might render at a preliminary hearing. He handed down the opinion in *Coleman* on the same day that the Court decided *Chambers* v. *Maroney,* in which the majority, including Brennan, found no denial of the effective assistance of counsel even though the lawyer assigned to the case entered it unprepared moments before the trial began. The majority in *Coleman* was obviously establishing a rule of law that transcended the facts of defendant's trial. It was the only rule that the dictates of justice commanded despite the silence of the Constitution about preliminary hearings. Burger was quite accurate when he accused the Court of operating as a "continuing Constitutional convention."[100] It cannot operate in any other way. But if its rule in *Coleman* was an interpretation of the Sixth Amendment in order to do justice, it was also a rule that was largely a pretense because of decisions like *Chambers.*

NO IMPRISONMENT WITHOUT COUNSEL

The Nixon Court's foremost right-to-counsel case was *Argersinger* v. *Hamlin,*[101] a 1972 offspring of *Gideon.* In that precedent the holding was that the Fourteenth Amendment's due-process clause required the states to furnish counsel to indigent defendants accused of felonies. In *Argersinger* the Court held that in the absence of a knowing and intelligent waiver of the right to counsel, no person may be imprisoned for any criminal offense unless he has had a lawyer's assistance. Thus, where *Gideon* was restricted to felonies, *Argersinger* applied the rule of *Gideon* to misdemeanors or petty offenses if personal liberty was in jeopardy. The decision was unanimous, although Douglas's opinion for the Court did not command the concurrences of Powell and Rehnquist.

The Justices differed in part on whether there were enough lawyers in the country, especially in small communities, to represent persons accused of petty offenses. Douglas belittled the alleged radical impact of the decision on the available legal resources. He noted that the "run of misdemeanors will not be affected by today's ruling,"[102] because most misdemeanants are not imprisoned. But there are no reliable statistics on the number of lesser crimes committed annually, the number of convictions, or the number ending in imprisonment. The best that the Court could do was to cite a government study which estimated that in 1965, when there were 338,000 defendants charged with felonies, 4 to 5 million were charged with misdemeanors exclusive of traffic offenses, and there were 40 to 50 million more accused of traffic offenses.[103] Another study showed that of the nearly 1,300,000 persons convicted in New York City in 1970 for minor traffic offenses, only 24 were imprisoned or given suspended sentences, while imprisonment was the fate of only 404, or 2.1 percent of the 19,187 convicted of serious traffic offenses such as drunken driving or leaving the scene of an accident.[104] On the other hand, Douglas produced no figures to prove that ordinary misdemeanants charged with nontraffic offenses are rarely imprisoned.

Whatever its impact, the "step we take today," Burger observed in his concurring opinion, "should cause no surprise to the legal profession."[105] Three-fifths of the states in the decade between *Gideon* and *Argersinger* had already extended the right to counsel to defendants charged with crimes less serious than felonies. In 1966 the United States had extended that right to petty offenders tried in federal courts. The American Bar Association had specifically recommended that counsel should be provided "in all

criminal proceedings for offenses punishable by loss of liberty. . . ,"
and in *Argersinger,* the Solicitor General of the United States
appeared as a friend of the Court to argue on behalf of the same
rule, which the Court adopted.[106]

Any person of common intelligence who reads the Sixth Amendment would wonder why the Court announced that rule as recently
as 1972 instead of decades ago. The amendment says, "In all criminal prosecutions, the accused shall . . . have the assistance of
counsel for his defense." Indeed, the wonder is that it was not until
1932 in *Powell* that the Court held that the states must furnish
counsel to indigents in capital cases and not until 1963 in *Gideon*
that the rule of *Powell* applied to all felonies. A partial explanation
for the delay of such rulings is that the Sixth Amendment, like the
rest of the Bill of Rights, was intended as a restraint only upon the
national government and therefore did not reach the practices of
the states. But the Fourteenth Amendment, dating from 1868, prohibited the states from taking life, liberty, or property without due
process of law. From that date on, the Court might have held
either that the word "liberty" included the rights of the criminally
accused as guaranteed in the Bill of Rights or that they were inherent in the very concept of due process, thereby making them
applicable to the states. The Court steadfastly refused to take either
route until the breakthrough in *Powell.* After that, *Argersinger*
was inevitable, however leaden the feet on which justice moves.

The case began in Florida, where Argersinger was convicted for
carrying a concealed weapon. The trial judge was lenient, sentencing him to only ninety days in jail, though the offense was punishable by imprisonment up to six months and a $1,000 fine. Too
poor to have afforded counsel and not provided one by the state
because his crime was only a misdemeanor, Argersinger appealed
his conviction; he claimed that he had been deprived of the right
to counsel and, therefore, of the right to a fair trial. The state
supreme court held that the right of an indigent to have counsel
furnished by the state extends only to offenses punishable by more
than six months' imprisonment. The state court analogized from a
Supreme Court case of 1968 in which the ruling was that the right
to trial by jury in criminal cases, being fundamental to the American scheme of justice, is guaranteed in state proceedings at least

for offenses punishable by more than six months in prison. But the Court also held that there is a category of minor offenses carrying penalties up to six months that are not subject to the jury-trial provision of the Sixth Amendment.[107] The Florida court reasoned that if prosecutions for crimes punishable by less than six months may be tried without a jury, they may be tried without representation by counsel. That was not an unreasonable ruling, given the Supreme Court's 1968 opinion. But that 1968 opinion on jury trials and the Florida court's decision on the right to counsel were both unreasonable given the language of the Sixth Amendment.

The Florida court sought to make the same exception to the Sixth Amendment as the Supreme Court had made in relation to jury trials. The amendment states, in full:

> In all criminal prosecutions, the accused shall enjoy the right to a speedy and public trial, by an impartial jury of the State and district wherein the crime shall have been committed, which district shall have been previously ascertained by law, and to be informed of the nature and cause of the accusation; to be confronted with the witnesses against him; to have compulsory process for obtaining witnesses in his favor, and to have the assistance of counsel for his defense.

Douglas, in *Argersinger,* had the task of explaining why the exception made for jury trials when the crime was punishable by less than six months did not carry over to assistance of counsel in the same cases.

Douglas's explanation purported to be historical. Trial by jury and the assistance of counsel, he said, had different origins. There was historical support for limiting trial by jury to serious criminal cases but no such support for limiting the assistance of counsel in the same way. His proof of the latter point consisted of nothing more than a quotation from *Powell* to the effect that in England before the American Revolution persons accused of misdemeanors were entitled to the full assistance of counsel, while in America twelve of the thirteen colonies went beyond the English common law by fully recognizing the right to counsel in almost all criminal prosecutions. Sutherland, the author of *Powell,* was no historian. Neither he nor Douglas relied on historical evidence. In fact, the practice of the English common law was as liberal as that of the early states in recognizing the right to counsel which was, on both sides of the Atlantic, mainly a right to hire counsel.[108] Douglas was satisfied, however, that nothing in the history or language of the Sixth Amendment or in the opinions of the Court showed that counsel should not be furnished in prosecutions for petty offenses. The various rights assured by that amendment, excepting only trial by jury, extended to all prosecutions; independent historical considerations governed that single exception.

In an opinion that led to the absolute rule that counsel must be provided, unless waived, in every criminal case if the accused is deprived of liberty, Douglas peculiarly qualified his premises. He declared at one point that the right to counsel is "often" a prerequisite for a fair trial and at another that counsel "may well be necessary" for such a trial even in prosecutions of petty offenses. Douglas left the implication that in some cases justice might be done without the presence of counsel. Powell certainly thought that counsel was not always needed. But Douglas had three compelling reasons for pressing the need for counsel when liberty is at stake. The first was that the legal and constitutional questions involved in a case that might lead to imprisonment for a short time are no less complex than if the accused can be jailed for more than six months. Burger buttressed that point by stating that even if the issues in a petty case are simpler than those of a felony case, an uncounseled layman could not hold his own against a professional prosecutor.

Douglas's second reason was that counsel is needed in petty cases as well as in others because of the difficult problems posed by guilty pleas, which are even more frequent in petty charges than in more serious ones. His final reason was that persons accused of misdemeanors stand less chance of receiving justice than those accused of felonies. The enormous volume of misdemeanor cases clogs court calendars, creating an obsession for speedy dispositions "regardless of the fairness of the result."[109] Individuals become numbers on a docket, faceless persons to be expeditiously processed without adequate consideration of their rights, or of the facts of their cases, or their sentences. This "assembly-line justice" produced about five times as many convictions of those unrepresented by counsel, compared to those who face similar misdemeanor charges with the assistance of counsel.[110] Accordingly, the Court fashioned a principle of law that allowed for no exceptions, thereby serving notice on every trial judge in the nation that when a trial for misdemeanor starts, no imprisonment may be imposed at the end unless the accused has had benefit of counsel from the beginning.

Burger, for no discernible reason, concurred separately; he added nothing to what Douglas had said and did not differ from his statement for the Court on the new rule governing the appointment of counsel in petty cases. Powell, joined by Rehnquist, although concurring in the result, did significantly differ, so much so that his opinion reads like a dissent. It was a subtle one, vigorously reasoned, detailed, and should have been answered by Douglas, who wholly ignored Powell's main argument, though he responded to some of his subsidiary concerns.

Powell could not accept Florida's rule that an indigent misdemeanant can be afforded a fair trial in every case without the assistance of counsel. But he also regarded with dismay the "rigidity" of the Court's new rule. He would not hold that misdemeanants possess an absolute constitutional right to the benefit of assigned counsel. "There is," Powell declared, "a middle course, between the extremes of Florida's six-month rule and the Court's rule. . . . I would adhere to the principle of due process that requires fundamental fairness in criminal trials, a principle which I believe encompasses the right to counsel in petty cases whenever the assistance of counsel is necessary to assure a fair trial."[111] Powell would have held that the right to counsel in petty cases should be determined by trial courts "exercising a judicial discretion on a case-by-case basis."[112]

Although Powell believed that fixing a detailed set of guidelines for trial judges to follow was "impossible, as well as unwise," he offered three special circumstances for them to consider when determining whether the appointment of counsel is necessary to assure a fair trial. First, he thought the complexity of the offense charged ought to be considered. The factual or legal questions involved in a traffic infraction rarely are complex, but matters of criminal intent or constitutional issues like search and seizure and the admissibility of evidence would usually be beyond the capability of laymen. The infirmity of this position is that it did not explain how a judge might know in advance of a trial whether a skillful lawyer might affect the outcome by raising facts or legal issues that are not initially apparent. Nor is there any way of predicting whether a complex issue might unexpectedly arise in the course of a trial. The whole point of assuring the assistance of counsel is that the chances of an effective defense are dependent upon him. For a judge to conclude before a trial that there is no need of counsel is to prejudge the case in a sense and also to underestimate what counsel might be able to do. A case that seems simple to a judge at the outset might be a complex one if a lawyer devoted to the interests of his client has studied it with the perspective of an advocate, after marshaling the facts, gathering and evaluating the evidence, ferreting out witnesses, ascertaining the legal issues, and developing his strategy and tactics for the conduct of the defense at the trial.

Powell would have had the trial judge assume a role beyond his capacity—that of defense counsel. He even said that if a case went to trial without defense counsel, if the judge determined that none was needed, the judge "should intervene, when necessary, to insure that the defendant adequately brings out the facts in his favor and to prevent legal issues from being overlooked."[113] For centuries, however, in both England and America the legal fiction had prevailed that there was no need to permit counsel in felony cases because courts acted as counsel in behalf of defendants, and for centuries men went to the gallows or to prison having had the theoretical benefit of the court's counsel. Sutherland in *Powell* had rejected the argument that the trial judge served as counsel for the prisoner: "But how can a judge, whose functions are purely judicial, effectively discharge the obligations of counsel for the accused? He can and should see to it that in the proceedings before the court the accused shall be dealt with justly and fairly. He cannot investigate the facts, advise and direct the defense, or participate in those necessary conferences between counsel and accused which sometimes partake of the inviolable character of the confessional."[114] Powell could not have been oblivious to the weaknesses of his own point, for he covered it with an option that made eminent sense: If most defendants who can afford to retain counsel do so for certain offenses, that would be "a strong indication that the indigent also needs the assistance of counsel."[115] But not even that consideration could predict the effectiveness of counsel in any particular case, especially the one in which the assistance of counsel was denied.

Powell's second special circumstance for determining in advance whether counsel ought to be appointed was the probable sentence that would follow in the event of a conviction. "The more serious the likely consequences, the greater is the probability that a lawyer should be appointed."[116] One might have thought, though, that the probable sentence would be determined by the facts revealed by the trial, and their revelation could depend on the assistance of counsel. Powell's willingness in some cases to deny counsel was not consistent with his desire to retain the trial judge's sentencing discretion nor with his recognition that the consequences of a misdemeanor conviction, "whether they be a brief period served under the sometimes deplorable conditions found in local jails or the effect of a criminal record on employability, are frequently of sufficient magnitude not to be casually dismissed by the label 'petty.' "[117] Once an arrest is made that leads to a formal charge, there is simply no knowing whether the timely assistance of counsel might not have avoided the consequences of a conviction.

The third and last special circumstance consisted of the factors peculiar to each case, such as the community's attitude toward a particular defendant or his capacity to present his own case. The factors peculiar to each case are, as Powell recognized, "the most difficult to anticipate,"[118] and precisely for that reason must be left exclusively to counsel. Powell, to his credit, also recognized that judges must be sensitive and diligent if the rule of "fundamental fairness" on a case-by-case basis had a chance of working. What he did not recognize is that it could not work with any consistency or equal justice in its application. Fundamental fairness, fair trial, and special circumstances are concepts that leave judges hopelessly adrift in a sea of imprecision and subjectivity, as history had already and abundantly demonstrated.

Powell's opinion was an amazing retrogression to the 1940s,

the paleolithic era of the right-to-counsel principle. Although Powell claimed that he was in complete accord with the rule of *Gideon,* which overruled *Betts* v. *Brady* (1942)[119] in felony cases, he admitted that his own position was "similar in certain respects to the special circumstances rule applied . . . in Betts v. Brady. . . ."[120] He knew that the Court in *Gideon* had resorted to a flat rule requiring counsel in all felony cases because many state courts had failed to fulfill their responsibilities when determining on a case-by-case basis whether counsel should be appointed. He insisted, nevertheless, that the Supreme Court ought not to assume that some state courts would continue their insensitivity to the rights of defendants. Powell gave no reason at all for his good faith in the sensitivity of state courts. The very case before the Court in *Argersinger* was an example of the right to counsel being improperly denied by a state court, as Powell's own vote for reversal of the conviction demonstrated. Moreover, the state courts were not the only offenders of constitutional rights. The record of the Supreme Court during the 1940s, when *Betts* v. *Brady* was in the saddle, proved that.[121]

Two cases decided the same day in 1948 adequately illustrate the point. In one the Court ruled 6-to-3 that the prisoner, who had no assistance of counsel, had been denied due process because the trial judge when sentencing him had mistakenly considered prior charges on the assumption that he had been found guilty when he had not.[122] In the other the Court ruled 5-to-4 that there had been no denial of due process when the trial judge in sentencing the uncounseled prisoner mistakenly thought that life imprisonment was mandatory for a four-time offender.[123] Only a medieval scholastic, or a jurist, could find in those two cases, so differently decided, a significant variant of what the Constitution commands on behalf of the uncounseled prisoner. The cases showed that the Supreme Court itself, when applying the rule of fundamental fairness, or due process, or fair trial, or special circumstances, could not enunciate any clear standard for the guidance of lower courts, or for its own guidance, and had not done so from *Betts* to *Gideon.* That rule was demonstrably an unworkable failure, and precisely for that reason had been overruled in *Gideon.* As Black said in a 1970 case, "For one, I still prefer to trust the liberty of the citizen to the plain language of the Constitution rather than to the sense of fairness of particular judges."[124]

In *Argersinger* Powell opposed the majority's rule because he thought that the Constitution did not mandate a right to the assistance of counsel in a prosecution leading to imprisonment, though the language of the Sixth Amendment in fact applies to all prosecutions. Powell also opposed the rule because he thought it was "rigid," "absolute," "completely inflexible," and "mechanistic." It was indeed, just as his rule was functionally elastic to the point of meaninglessness, inducing the Court to formulate its new objective rule. Powell also opposed it because he thought it would inevitably lead to an ever broader "prophylactic" rule requiring the appointment of counsel to indigents in all petty cases, not just those in which the trial court reserves the option of a prison sentence on conviction by assigning a lawyer to the defense. Powell had in mind the fact that the Fourteenth Amendment does not distinguish between a taking of property and a taking of liberty: Neither may be taken without due process. Thus, if the logic of the new rule were to be pushed to its limits, counsel would have to be assigned even in a case leading to a petty fine. Powell complained that the majority opinion suggested no constitutional basis for differentiating between deprivations of property and liberty, with the result, he predicted, that a "drastic enlargement of the constitutional right to free counsel" loomed ahead.[125] Douglas's response to Powell's argument *ad horrendum* was evasive; the case before the Court, Douglas said, involved a jail sentence, making unnecessary a decision on any other point.

If there is a demand to a right to counsel in a future case involving a petty fine, the Court might at that appropriate time satisfy Powell's fears by drawing the line at deprivation of liberty. Should doing that not answer his point that property is equally deserving of protection, the Court might argue that distinctions can be made. The exception from the Sixth Amendment of the right to jury trial in cases leading to less than six months' imprisonment is an example. Powell himself distinguished between trial by jury and the right to counsel when necessary for a fair trial, finding the latter more fundamental than the former. In the case of an uncounseled indigent whose prosecution leads to a fine, his incapacity to pay might save him from the sentence. In 1970 the Court ruled that holding an indigent prisoner in jail, beyond his sentence, to work off a fine at the rate of $5 a day violated the equal-protection clause of the Fourteenth Amendment.[126] A year later the Court similarly held that imprisoning an indigent for involuntary nonpayment of his fines also violated equal protection.[127] To avoid the possibility of an inverse discrimination against those who are able to pay their fines and must, the Court in those cases suggested installment payments.

Nevertheless, Powell believed that the rule of *Argersinger* benefitted indigent defendants compared to those who might afford to retain their own counsel, however great the hardship. The point was a valid one. In the federal courts and in some local jurisdictions defendants of modest means are disadvantaged compared to indigents; the latter receive at public expense more than many nonindigents can afford—free trial counsel, free appellate counsel, free transcripts, and other benefits, whose costs might beggar a middle-class person who works for a living. Some competent criminal lawyers who represent indigents refuse to take other clients unless they pay fees many times higher than the government provides.[128] A comparable problem exists with respect to welfare, education, medical, unemployment, and other benefits for which the public pays, but as regards free counsel and legal expenses, the price is one that the public must pay for equal justice. The irony is that while the justice one gets cannot tolerably depend on what he can afford to pay for, that is the kind of justice that the nonindigent receives. Powell thought it anomalous that the Court in *Argersinger* extended the right of appointed counsel to cases in which nonindigents would rarely retain counsel, but that seems a farfetched fear. When, as in *Argersinger,* the penalty on conviction could be six months in jail and a $1,000 fine, anyone who can afford counsel will retain a lawyer. The solution, if there is one, to covering the indigent's cost of legal expenses is to treat them like a fine, repayable in time by installments when possible.

Powell's concern for the equal-protection problems that the rule of *Argersinger* precipitated was not wholly unfounded. He presented two hypothetical situations which could result in unfairness, depending on whether trial judges decided in advance to leave open the option of imprisonment. Suppose two indigents face the same charge, one with assigned counsel and the other without. "Since," as Powell said, "the services of counsel may be essential to a fair trial even in cases in which no jail sentence is imposed, the results of this type of pretrial judgment could be arbitrary and discriminatory."[129] On the other hand, Powell's second situation was not beyond easy remedy. If the sentence in a petty case is "five days in jail or $100 fine," there is little likelihood, though Powell thought otherwise, that the defendant who can pay the fine will do so, while the indigent guilty of the same offense pays no penalty and will escape punitive action even on a repetition of the offense. A trial judge will surely appoint counsel on a repetition of the offense, if not on the first occasion, to preserve the possibility of a jail sentence. Judges, as Powell predicted, will find that the rule of *Argersinger* means that in practice counsel should be appointed for indigents in all but the most minor offenses where jail sentences are rarely imposed.

To Powell such an expansion of the right to counsel, like the rule of *Argersinger* itself, would overtax the financial and legal resources of local governments. The cost of free counsel would, he feared, be more than the public can endure. There were, he thought, simply not enough lawyers to handle all the cases, nor enough courts, and in localities where lawyers are numerous enough to be assigned to indigents, the case burden on courts would be enormous. Young lawyers fresh out of law school, Powell thought, would be assigned to most petty cases with results he believed would be less than salutary. They have every incentive—the desire to make a reputation, the time, the need for experience, and even fees lucrative to a novice—to go to trial, explore every possible defense including elaborate constitutional issues, and make appeals, thereby "stretching out . . . the process with consequent increased costs to the public and added delay and congestion in the courts."[130] Delay and congestion, he declared, were the very causes of "assembly line justice." That might be true, but no indigent defendant effectively championed by a young lawyer in the ways Powell depicted would be the victim of "assembly line justice."

In view of the fact that the Supreme Court does nothing to

insure the effective assistance of counsel and is satisfied, rather, with the mere presence of counsel, Powell's fears were probably exaggerated. His own rule of fundamental fairness on a case-by-case basis would probably ease the trial-court calendars at the expense of congesting the appellate courts with appeals and collateral attacks by way of habeas corpus. If Powell proved to be right about the congestion of trial courts, one solution would be to create more of them and more trial judges. Another would be the solution mentioned by Douglas and recommended by the American Bar Association. Whole categories of petty crimes that harm only the offenders, such as public drunkenness, narcotics addiction, vagrancy, and deviant sexual behavior, should be transferred from the judicial system to public social-service agencies; and other petty offenses such as traffic violations should be transferred to special administrative agencies. Whatever the solution, the fact that legal resources and courts are overtaxed is not a good enough reason to deny the right to counsel. Powell's thoughtful analysis of the problems inherent in the rule of *Argersinger* did not justify his conclusion that the remedy lies in stunting the Sixth Amendment.

PRETRIAL IDENTIFICATION

Kirby v. *Illinois*,[131] which was decided within a week of *Argersinger,* presented the Nixon Court in its most characteristic stance in a criminal-justice case: As it took a backward step, it insisted that it was standing still because a step forward would not be justifiable. *Kirby* raised the basic question whether a suspect is entitled to the assistance of counsel when needed, immediately on being taken into custody and being confronted by his accuser. The Warren Court's most controversial criminal-justice cases had raised similar issues. In *Escobedo* (1964) the Court held that the right to counsel does not depend on whether the prosecution has lodged formal charges against a suspect who is being subjected to police interrogation. In *Miranda* (1966) the Court held that before the police may interrogate a suspect, he has a right to be advised that he is entitled to the assistance of counsel and that a lawyer will be appointed for him if he cannot afford one. In *United States* v. *Wade* (1967)[132] the Court announced the rules that *Kirby* would amend. An accused person has a constitutional right to counsel at a pretrial lineup when the police exhibit him to witnesses for identification as the criminal. To deter the police from violating this rule the Court formulated an exclusionary principle: No identification is admissible in evidence at a trial if originating in an identification before trial and in the absence of counsel.

In each of these cases the Warren Court pushed the right to counsel back to the early stages of a criminal proceeding. The theory was that custodial interrogation and confrontations by accusers are such critical steps in a prosecution that a lawyer must be on hand for the prisoner so that he may have the assistance of counsel to safeguard his constitutional rights and, by observing the development of the prosecution's case, to preserve the opportunity of making an effective defense at the trial. In 1970 in the post-Warren era, the Court's decision in *Coleman* v. *Alabama* similarly protected the right to counsel in a preliminary hearing that preceded grand-jury proceedings.[133] Burger, the only Nixon appointee who participated in the case, dissented, as did Stewart. In *Kirby,* a new majority coalesced when Stewart joined the four Nixon appointees and became their spokesman. White, dissenting apart from the "Warren" trio of Brennan, Douglas, and Marshall, said nothing beyond the terse observation that *Wade*'s rulings "govern this case and compel reversal of the judgment of the Illinois Supreme Court."[134]

The majority believed that the Illinois Supreme Court had discovered a valid distinction between *Wade* and *Kirby:* The identification of Kirby had preceded his indictment. Kirby and a confederate were arrested on suspicion of robbing a man named Shard. The two had in their possession papers bearing Shard's name, his social security card, and traveler's checks belonging to him. They explained at the time of their arrest that they had won the checks in a crap game, an inept story because it did not explain their possession of Shard's other property and the checks themselves were not negotiable unless countersigned by him at the time of their use. (At their trial the two changed their story, claiming that they had found Shard's belongings in an alley just before their arrest.) After the police officers arrested and brought them to the police station, they learned that Shard had reported the robbery the previous day. Shard, on being summoned to the station by police car, immediately identified Kirby and his confederate as the men who had robbed him.

Several crucial facts emerge from this confrontation. There was no custodial interrogation, as in *Escobedo* or *Miranda*. The police did not give the *Miranda* warnings to the suspects, who should have been advised not only of their rights to silence but of their rights to counsel. Shard identified them in a room where they were alone with police officers rather than at a lineup from which he would have had to pick them out of a number of men. There is no knowing whether he walked into the room confidently expecting to make an identification after having been told by the police something like, "We got the two guys who robbed you." They did not receive the benefit of counsel until their arraignments. Both were found guilty at a trial where the decisive evidence against them was Shard's identification testimony.

In his opinion for the Court, Stewart noted at the outset that the doctrine of *Miranda* had no applicability in Kirby's case, which did not involve custodial interrogation. That was true but did not explain the Court's glaring failure to consider that the prisoners did not receive the *Miranda* warnings which extend beyond the Fifth Amendment issue. The *Wade* exclusionary rule, said Stewart, contrasting it with the *Miranda* exclusionary rule, derived from the Sixth, not the Fifth, Amendment. The Court had "firmly established" that the Sixth Amendment right to counsel "attaches only at or after the time that adversary judicial proceedings have been initiated. . . ."[135] On behalf of this proposition Stewart cited nine precedents, from *Powell* on, including *Gideon, Wade,* and *Coleman.* In *"all"* these cases, Stewart declared in italics, "adversary judicial proceedings" of a criminal character had been the context within which the right-to-counsel issue had arisen. That proposition was accurate, but it did not prove that the right to counsel began only when adversary judicial proceedings began; indeed, none of the precedents dealt with the question when the Sixth Amendment right first becomes operative, making the assignment of counsel mandatory—none, unless it be *Escobedo*.

That, said Stewart, was the "only seeming deviation," but he distinguished that case as "not apposite" for two reasons. First, the Court "in retrospect" had allegedly perceived that the purpose of the doctrine of *Escobedo* was not to vindicate the constitutional right to counsel "as such, but, like *Miranda*, 'to guarantee full effectuation of the privilege against self-incrimination. . . .' "[136] The authority for that statement was a post-*Escobedo* case from which Stewart derived his second reason: The holding of *Escobedo* was limited to its facts.

There is much to be said for Stewart's construction of *Escobedo*. The Court had required the right to counsel in that case to secure the prisoner's right against compulsory self-incrimination. But it was a Sixth Amendment case, as Goldberg, for the Court, made clear in his very first sentence and throughout his opinion. On the question when the right to counsel attached, Goldberg pointed out that Escobedo's interrogation was conducted before he was charged with any crime, a fact that "should make no difference. . . . It would exalt form over substance to make the right to counsel, under these circumstances, depend on whether at the time of the interrogation the authorities had secured a formal indictment. Petitioner had, for all practical purposes, already been charged with murder."[137] One might similarly say that for all practical purposes, Kirby had already been charged with robbery when Shard identified him in the station house. For that reason both *Escobedo* and the *Miranda* warnings required the presence of counsel, not in this instance to protect Kirby against an involuntary confession, but to supervise the identification procedures and the circumstances surrounding them in order to cross-examine effectively at the trial. The Court's summary dismissal of *Miranda*, notwithstanding the warnings required by that case in respect to the right of counsel, and the Court's distinguishing *Escobedo* by reference to a subsequent interpretation hardly comport with the canons of proof; the Court should have turned to the sources, the particular precedents in dispute, to find out what they said, not to later opinions "in retrospect." That was a device that Stewart would use again, with the same misleading effect. But, if a later decision can be used to construe away or limit an earlier one, then a still later one can reinvigorate and expand the earlier one. Indeed, *Wade* explicitly relied on *Escobedo* and *Miranda* to show that counsel must be present at pretrial confrontations before adversary judicial proceedings have been initiated.[138]

Having disposed of the encumbering precedents, Stewart declared that the beginning of judicial proceedings in a criminal case marked "the starting point of our whole system of adversary criminal justice."[139] Only then, he reasoned, has the government committed itself to prosecute, and only then does the defendant find himself opposed by the prosecutorial forces of organized society which require him to be represented by counsel to cope with the intricate procedural and substantive issues of law. In short, the "criminal prosecutions" to which the Sixth Amendment referred began when the police concluded their investigation and the courts took over at preliminary hearings, indictments, arraignments, and trial. In *Kirby,* said Stewart, the Court was asked to import into a routine police investigation a constitutional right that became operative only "after the onset of formal prosecutorial proceedings. We decline to do so."[140] Surely, Stewart did not mean what he said nor say what he meant. The right to counsel at the very least begins *with,* not after, the onset of formal prosecutorial proceedings, and to be effective at all, the defense lawyer must have some time to familiarize himself with the case and prepare for it even *before* the onset of formal prosecutorial proceedings. As an afterthought, Stewart referred to a case decided after *Wade* to explain it.[141] In that later case the Court declared that the rationale of *Wade* was that an accused is entitled to the assistance of counsel at any critical stage of the "prosecution," which Stewart defined as the beginning of adversary proceedings, and that a postindictment lineup is such a critical stage. Wade was identified at a lineup held after his indictment, but the Court should have looked at the opinion in that case for its rationale, rather than at a case "in retrospect." Stewart had dissented from *Wade.*

Viewed broadly, *Kirby* defined the point at which the right of counsel begins. Stewart defined that point as the beginning of adversary proceedings or of a criminal prosecution as prescribed by the Sixth Amendment. But the amendment does not define when a criminal prosecution begins, although its framers probably meant the trial of the accused. When the Sixth Amendment was adopted there were no organized police forces as we know them. The confrontation by one's accusers occurred mainly at his trial, when the evidence against him was marshaled. All Sixth Amendment rights referred originally to the trial stage of a prosecution. Indeed, all but the right to counsel must refer to the trial—the right to a public trial, a speedy trial, a trial by jury, compulsory production of witnesses in one's behalf, and the right of cross-examination. Today, however, as the Court said in *Wade,* which Stewart did not bother to examine as a direct source although it was most apposite in *Kirby,* the "law enforcement machinery involves critical confrontations of the accused by the prosecution at pretrial proceedings where the results might well settle the accused's fate and reduce the trial itself to a mere formality. In recognition of these realities of modern criminal prosecution, our cases have construed the Sixth Amendment guarantee to apply to 'critical' stages of the proceedings."[142]

The Warren Court had expanded its understanding of the initiation of accusatorial or adversary proceedings to the point when a suspect is taken into custody after arrest. The mainstay of our accusatorial system, the Court had said more than once, is the Fifth Amendment right against compulsory self-incrimination.[143] It becomes operative to preserve the adversary character of our criminal law when the police, not the courts, have a person in custody, which is long before a "prosecution" begins in a technical sense. There is nothing "judicial" about the proceedings in a police station, but by the pre-*Kirby* decisions of the Court the right to counsel began in the police station, when it is needed, to preserve the adversary nature of subsequent stages of the prosecution, even though "prosecution" be defined as the initiation of charges or the point at which courts supersede the police. The *Miranda* Court had made the point directly. When the individual is in custody or otherwise deprived of his freedom of action in any significant way, "It is at this point that our adversary system of criminal proceedings commences. . . ."[144] Only a few months before *Kirby* in a case involving the right to speedy trial, White, for the Court, declared that because arrest interferes with one's liberty, it is "arrest and holding to answer a criminal charge that engages the particular protections of the speedy-trial provision of the Sixth Amendment."[145] Accordingly, to claim that the right to counsel does not begin at the same time is nonsense. Even if the Sixth Amendment's text governs the triggering of the right to counsel, the word "prosecution" does not and cannot mean trial, nor does the amendment say that the right to counsel exists only when charges are lodged. Stewart imported into that amendment a rule restricting the right to counsel to the point in time when charges are lodged. Since the letter of the amendment is of no help in construing that right, the Court had to interpret it. Stewart did so in a way that required him to manipulate the precedents with less than candor in order to shrink the right to counsel. The dissenters piled scorn on him for his uncraftsmanlike performance and for making the Sixth Amendment right a nullity at the point when it was keenly needed.

Brennan's dissent zeroed in on the "error" of admitting the evidence of Shard's testimony that he had identified Kirby in the police station. The police having failed to advise Kirby of his right to counsel, all of Shard's identification testimony should have been excluded in accordance with *Wade*'s exclusionary rule. Stewart had scarcely paid ceremonial attention to *Wade,* dismissing it on finding that an indictment had preceded the identification at the police lineup. For Brennan, *Wade* contained all the constitutional wisdom necessary to decide *Kirby.* He quoted and paraphrased column after column of the *Wade* opinion; he had written it, and he obviously cherished it. There is no doubt that it was so broad that it blanketed Kirby's case.

In *Wade* Brennan had emphasized that the Sixth Amendment's guarantee "encompasses counsel's assistance whenever necessary to assure a meaningful 'defense.' " He had also claimed that *Escobedo* and *Miranda* stood for the principle that the accused has the guarantee "that he need not stand alone against the State at any stage of the prosecution, formal or informal, in court or out, where counsel's absence might derogate from the accused's right to a fair trial." That was surely a spacious interpretation of those cases, leading, Brennan said, to the controlling rule of *Wade* that the Court must scrutinize "*any* pretrial confrontation of the accused" to determine whether the assistance of counsel might make a difference to the defense.

In view of the fact that Shard had positively identified Kirby and his confederate, one might think that counsel could not have aided his defense. Brennan, again relying on the language of *Wade* to show its applicability, explained that the confrontation of the suspect by the victim of the crime is "peculiarly riddled with innumerable dangers and variable factors which might seriously, even crucially, derogate from a fair trial."[146] Therefore, to preserve the right of a "meaningful" cross-examination at the trial, the first line of defense must be to prevent the hazards of unfairness and unreliability always possible in eyewitness identifications. The police might lead the witness to an identification by unwitting or deliberate suggestions, especially when confrontations occur in secrecy. The victim is likely to be resentful and eager to agree with the police. Consequently, the trial that for all practical purposes seals the suspect's fate might take place not in the courtroom before judge and jury but at the pretrial confrontation in the room in the police station where the victim says, "That's the man." Once a witness has made an identification, he rarely changes his mind, despite the possibility of a mistake. As an expert on eyewitness identification wrote, the "show up," which presents to the victim of a crime only the suspect for identification purposes, "constitutes the most grossly suggestive identification procedure now or ever used by the police."[147]

Even if Brennan's analysis was correct about the need for counsel's presence at the pretrial confrontation, in this case there seems to have been no way for Kirby's counsel to have preserved that "meaningful" right to cross-examination. If the police are convinced that they have the right man and send a patrol car to pick up his victim to identify him, defense counsel would have to be present from the time they meet the victim to the time of the pretrial confrontation in order to monitor any suggestiveness that might exist in the conversation between the police and the victim. Under the circumstances they will not likely be discussing only the weather and the latest baseball scores on the trip to the police station.

The disadvantage to the accused deriving from exclusive

police access to the identifying witness is peculiarly compensated for later by the leeway given to defense counsel on cross-examining witnesses. To prevent the conviction of the innocent, our system permits defense counsel to try to make even a truthful witness uncertain, confused, and contradictory. Indeed, counsel's interest in his client, rather than in ascertaining truth or aiding justice, induces him to attack the credibility of the state's case even if he knows that he is defending a guilty man. In *Kirby* the jury understandably found the defendants guilty beyond reasonable doubt. The verdict could not conceivably have changed as a result of the presence of defense counsel at the pretrial confrontation. Brennan, Douglas, and Marshall, of course, were not concerned with Kirby's guilt or innocence; that was the task of the jury. They, like the majority of the Court, were concerned with the question whether principles of constitutional law as determined by the Sixth Amendment were properly enforced in the case. Unlike the majority, the dissenters did not think that the right to counsel was a subject for their protective mantle only when a "prosecution" began in a judicial sense.

Brennan declared that the initiation of adversary judicial proceedings was "completely irrelevant" to the question whether counsel was needed at a pretrial confrontation. He thought it plain that in a confrontation for identification purposes conducted after arrest, the same hazards are present as in a confrontation held after the onset of formal prosecutorial proceedings. Stewart, he observed, did not deny that fact. Brennan differed from Stewart in believing that the arrest marked the starting point of our system of adversary criminal justice. He characterized as a "mere formalism" Stewart's view of the pretrial confrontation as simply a routine police investigation. To Brennan it was a critical stage in the prosecution, no different in substance from a postindictment confrontation at which counsel, according to *Wade,* must be present if the identifying witness's testimony is to be accepted.

Having clarified his position, Brennan assaulted the majority's. Stewart professed not to have departed from *Wade*'s rationale, yet he found it not by reading *Wade* but a later opinion that did not even involve the Sixth Amendment.[148] Brennan, in a display of one-upmanship, quoted a still later opinion that accorded with his own.[149] He took note of the facts of three cases decided after *Wade* in which no member of the Court had seen any significance in whether there had been a formal charge lodged before a pretrial confrontation, and in those cases confrontation preceded the lodging of charges.[150] In one of these cases the Court summarized *Wade* as holding "that the confrontation is a 'critical stage,' and that counsel is required at *all* confrontations."[151] Even the dissenters in *Wade* had not found in the opinion of the Court the limitation imposed by the majority in *Kirby,* namely that the right to counsel begins only with charges. White, joined by Stewart and Harlan, had at the time said of *Wade:* "The rule applies to any lineup, to any other techniques employed to produce an identification and *a fortiori* to a face-to-face encounter between the witness and the suspect alone, regardless of when the identification occurs, in time or place, and whether *before* or after indictment or information."[152]

Little wonder then that the majority's twisting and contorting of *Wade* angered the *Kirby* dissenters, and little wonder that all eight United States Courts of Appeals that faced the question had applied *Wade* to preindictment confrontations.[153] And little wonder that the *Kirby* majority felt the need of adding a curious extenuating paragraph to the conclusion of their opinion. Having denied the applicability of the Sixth Amendment to a preindictment confrontation that might be prejudicial to the suspect, Stewart concluded by saying that due process of law "forbids a lineup that is unnecessarily suggestive and conducive to irreparable mistaken identification." To that proposition Stewart added an even more curious footnote as if acknowledging the need for some principle of justice to balance that advocated by Brennan. The footnote stated: "In view of our limited grant of certiorari, we do not consider whether there might have been a deprivation of due process in the particularized circumstances of this case. That question remains open for inquiry in a federal habeas corpus proceeding."[154]

Kirby emasculated *Wade.* The Court left that precedent intact for any pretrial confrontation that follows the initiation of a prosecution as defined by Stewart. But the juridical status of *Wade* bears no relation to the far more important practical effect of

Kirby. Since the vast majority of lineups are staged prior to indictment, *Wade* is fated to remain legally controlling but virtually meaningless as an effective protection when needed. Still, nothing that *Kirby* said remotely suggested an overruling of *Wade.* Accordingly, *Kirby* can be viewed as an oblique defiance of Congress, which had expressed its hostility to *Wade* in a statute that was also aimed at *Miranda.* In the Omnibus Crime Control and Safe Streets Act of 1968, Congress had provided that the "testimony of a witness that he saw the accused commit or participate in the commission of a crime . . . shall be admissible in evidence" in all federal trial courts.[155] The legislative history of this provision shows that Congress viewed *Wade* as a "harmful blow at the nationwide effort to control crime." Accordingly, Congress designed the section of the act of 1968 "to counter this harmful effect."[156]

By limiting but not repudiating *Wade,* the Court made less likely a future decision that its constitutional rule can be superseded by a mere legislative enactment. Should the anti-*Wade* section ever be sustained, the Sixth Amendment would have a lesser scope in federal prosecutions than in state prosecutions. A dual standard for the right to counsel would be intolerable, not only because the amendment ought to have the same meaning in all prosecutions, but because federal criminal defendants should not be subjected to deprivation of rights accorded to state criminal defendants. The anomalous denial of equal protection that would flow from a decision upholding the anti-*Wade* section would require either a voiding of the statute or an overruling of *Wade* to bring about an equality of rights in the state and federal courts. The more likely possibility in the event of a test case would be for the Court to read the act, contrary to its intent, as allowing the introduction of the disputed testimony only if the rule of *Wade* has been respected. Powell, in a one-sentence concurrence in *Kirby,* said that he went along with the result reached by the Court because he would not extend *Wade*'s exclusionary rule. There is not much likelihood that any of the Justices for whom Stewart spoke would significantly restrict *Wade*'s exclusionary rule any more than they had.

The "Warren" trio of Brennan, Douglas, and Marshall would not agree, and their case in point is *United States* v. *Ash,* decided in 1973.[157] Brennan, who wrote their dissent in *Ash,* used overstatement that is more characteristic of Douglas. "In my view," said Brennan, "today's decision is wholly unsupportable in terms of such considerations as logic, consistency and, indeed, fairness. As a result, I must reluctantly conclude that today's decision marks simply another step towards the complete evisceration of the fundamental constitutional principles established by this Court, only six years ago, in *United States* v. *Wade.* . . ."[158] He added, too, that the Court's opinion was "a triumph of form over substance," represented a "crabbed view of the Sixth Amendment," and sought "to rewrite *Wade.*"[159] Blackmun's opinion for the Court in *Ash* did not merit such intramural recrimination. He weakened the effective assistance of counsel and strongly defended the use by the prosecution of photographs for identification purposes, but he did not eviscerate the principles of *Wade.* Blackmun, in fact, reaffirmed those principles, at least in the abstract, with enough vigor to entrench them beyond direct attack. *Ash* simply refused to extend those principles without taking refuge, as did *Kirby,* in a spurious definition of the point at which a criminal prosecution begins. The court below, by a vote of 5-to-4, decided as Brennan would have, but the courts of appeals in nine other circuits had sustained the prosecutorial position that Blackmun defended.

The constitutional issue in *Ash* was whether the Sixth Amendment requires that defendant's counsel be present when the prosecution, after the indictment, conducts a photographic display, containing the defendant's picture, to determine whether witnesses to the crime can identify him. The facts of the case substantiate Brennan's contention that any pretrial identification, especially from a photograph alone, presents grave dangers that an innocent defendant might be convicted. Two men wearing stocking masks robbed a bank. None of the witnesses could describe their faces. Five months later, after a tip from an informer that Ash was one of the robbers, an FBI agent included his mug shot in a photograpic display of five Negro males of the same age, height, and weight. The witnesses, according to Blackmun, "made uncertain identifications of Ash's picture"; according to Brennan, "none" made a "positive" identification. That they could make any sort of photographic identification of a masked robber, without some sort of suggestion, was amazing. Nevertheless, *Kirby* foreclosed any challenge to that preindictment identification. An indictment based on it charged Ash with the crime. Two years later, during which time the prosecutor never held a lineup, there was a trial. The day before it, he belatedly sought to determine whether his witnesses would be able to make in-court identifications; so, he and the FBI agent held another photographic display for the witnesses. Had there been a lineup, Ash's counsel would have had to be present. Three out of four witnesses selected Ash's picture, and at the trial, when they finally saw him in person, they identified him again as the robber of three years earlier. The question before the Court was not whether Ash was guilty; that was for the jury to decide. The question, rather, was whether Ash's constitutional right to the assistance of counsel had been violated by excluding his lawyer from the pretrial photographic identification.

Blackmun gave the question full-dress treatment by reviewing the purposes of the Sixth Amendment's guarantee of counsel and the cases which extended the right to counsel to critical stages of a prosecution before trial. He found that the core purpose of the guarantee was to assure the assistance of counsel when the intricacies of the law and the advocacy of the prosecutor confronted the accused. That led Blackmun to the principle that defense counsel has a right to be present at any pretrial stages that are "trial-like confrontations." At a postindictment lineup, as in *Wade,* the prosecutor has opportunities to take advantage of the accused in various ways, among them suggestive influences on the witnesses who are present for identification purposes. Defense counsel has a right to be present to monitor that critical confrontation in order to preserve the opportunity of reconstructing the event at the trial and by cross-examination to reveal to the jury any suggestiveness or unfair influences.

The government had argued in *Wade* that if counsel was required at a lineup, he would also have to be present at other steps in the preparation of the prosecution's case, as, for example, when identification is made by taking and examining fingerprints, blood, or other physical samples. The Court, in *Wade,* had disagreed on ground that the absence of defense counsel in such instances did not disadvantage the defendant; the defense could independently duplicate the same scientific identification, present its own experts at the trial, and cross-examine the prosecution's experts. Blackmun concluded that *Wade* did not require the presence of counsel if scientific identification would be verified and if a reconstruction of the pretrial identification could be accurately made at the trial. "If accurate reconstruction is possible," he said, "the risks inherent in any confrontation remain, but the opportunity to cure defects at the trial causes the confrontation to cease to be 'critical.' "[160] Incredibly, he applied that reasonable test unreasonably to pretrial photographic identification. Having arrived at what he called "the threshold analysis," Blackmun shut his eyes to the unreliability of identification from photographs and to the seriousness of the inherent risks of convicting the innocent. His opinion became a model of Justice wearing a blindfold to screen out reality.

The trial, Blackmun said, was as effective a place for challenging a photographic identification as for challenging the prosecution's other pretrial interviews. The photographs were as available to the defense as to the prosecution, and the defense could stage its own photographic identifications. Cross-examination could reconstruct the prosecution's photographic display and capitalize on the inability of a witness to select the right picture. Blackmun recognized that a display could be rigged. There might be repeated displays, for example, containing the accused's picture as the only common denominator, thus tending to promote identification of him. But cross-examination at the trial could show that a display had been rigged that way, and the defense had countervailing devices "such as the use of a sufficiently larger number of photographs to counteract this possibility." Blackmun did not explain how defense counsel would get access to the photographs and the government's witnesses in order to check the prosecution's results when he could not even get access to the display put on by the prosecution.

Blackmun acknowledged that a pretrial photographic identification offered the possibility of unfair prejudice to the defendant. He countered by observing that the prosecutor had available to him a whole bag of dirty tricks that would achieve the same result. He might conceal evidence favorable to the accused, manipulate testimony, and contrive laboratory tests. "In many ways the prosecutor, by accident or design, may improperly subvert the trial. The primary safeguard against abuses of this kind," Blackmun claimed, "is the ethical responsibility of the prosecution."[161]

The Court's analysis foundered on its explicit trust in the ethical behavior of the prosecution. That trust is the theme song of the Nixon Court, betraying the very idea of constitutional limitations on government. Neither liberty nor justice can flourish under a government whose powers are trusted to be ethically exercised; its powers must be so constitutionally restrained that they cannot otherwise be exercised. That is the point of the Bill of Rights. It, not the ethics of the prosecutor, is supposed to be the "primary safeguard" against the abuse of power. At the very least Blackmun should have ruled that the Court's obligation to protect the innocent required in a case like Ash's the simple device of insuring, if not a primary, at least a secondary safeguard: the presence of defense counsel at pretrial photographic identifications. Instead, Blackmun alleged that the risks inherent in photographic displays were not so pernicious that "an extraordinary system of safeguards is required."[162] Accordingly, the opinion closed with the holding that "the Sixth Amendment does not grant the right to counsel at photographic displays conducted by the Government for the purpose of allowing a witness to attempt an identification of the offender."[163]

Brennan's dissent, stripped of its apocalyptic attitude and its misrepresentation of Blackmun's position, was far more convincing. Brennan was right in declaring that *Wade* was broad enough to cover photographic as well as corporeal identification. Experts agree that the major problem of criminal justice, where guilt or innocence is concerned, is eyewitness identification; erroneous identification is probably "the major cause of known wrongful convictions."[164] If mistakes can be made when the witness confronts the accused in person, the risk of misidentification is greater, as Brennan pointed out, when he sees only a picture and from his memory of it then makes an in-court identification. *Wade* had sought to minimize the high incidence of miscarriages of justice that result from mistaken identification caused by the suggestiveness inherent in "the manner in which the prosecution presents the suspect to the witnesses for pretrial identification."[165] Brennan elaborately spelled out the possibilities for impermissible suggestion in the context of a photographic display—the repetition of the same picture, an arrangement calling attention to it, and comments by the prosecutor "may lead an otherwise uncertain witness to select the 'correct' photograph."[166] The prosecutor need not ask a witness whether a particular picture looks familiar. His subtle gestures, inflections of voice, facial expressions, or "other almost imperceptible means of communication might tend, intentionally or unintentionally, to compromise the witness' objectivity."[167] Accordingly, if the defense attorney is not present at the pretrial photographic display, he has as little chance of reconstructing it at the trial by cross-examination as he has of reconstructing a lineup identification from which he is absent. The rationale of *Wade,* which reposed slight trust in the prosecution's methods, lent "no support whatever to today's decision," as Brennan ruefully said.[168] Significantly, however, the Court purported to follow that rationale.

The mixed record of the Nixon Court in Sixth Amendment cases showed toward the right to counsel little of the hostility that permeated the Fifth Amendment cases on the right against self-incrimination. The two sets of cases share in common a hard disinclination to overturn convictions and reflected a sympathetic understanding of police and prosecutorial values. But the right to counsel is not in bad odor in the high court. Professional courtesy and a decent respect for the difficult tasks of criminal-trial lawyers quells any impulse either to subvert the Sixth Amendment or to brand the efforts of counsel as ineffective.

By rejecting claims that prisoners have been denied the effective assistance of counsel, the Court keeps a tight lid on the expectations of professional competence, saves trial judges from the embarrassment of being overruled for having permitted injustices, and keeps undisturbed the convictions won by the law-enforcement agencies. *Argersinger,* the most important of the Sixth Amendment cases decided by the Nixon Court, extended the assistance of counsel to any prosecution that could result in a loss of liberty; but it was a decision in accordance with a recommendation of the American Bar Association.

The plea-bargaining cases preserved the judicial system from being inundated by a docket of trials that would sink it. In those cases and others raising the issue whether defense counsel offered effective assistance, the groundwork had been thoroughly prepared for insuring that *Argersinger* will not really alter the conviction rate in any way that threatens society or the law-enforcement agencies. When a lawyer's work is done, any semblance of effort on his part, even if nothing more than a hurried conference with the prosecution to get some leniency, will guarantee that he has not breached the level of professional competence required of him. Thus, decisions like *Gideon* and *Argersinger* give employment to members of the bar and at least the appearance of justice without jeopardizing the operation of a criminal-justice system that survives on guilty pleas. The forces of law and order have no cause for complaint about the Sixth Amendment decisions of the Nixon Court.

CHAPTER FIVE

The Sixth Amendment: Trial by Jury

As a result of decisions made in 1970 and 1972, the Supreme Court has radically transformed the meaning of trial by jury in American criminal cases.[1] The Sixth Amendment begins, "In all criminal prosecutions the accused shall enjoy the right to a speedy and public trial by an impartial jury. . . ." In 1930 the Court had said

> That it means a trial by jury as understood and applied at common law, and includes all the essential elements as they were recognized in this country and England when the Constitution was adopted, is not open to question. Those elements were: (1) That the jury should consist of twelve men, neither more nor less; (2) that the trial should be in the presence and under the superintendence of a judge having power to instruct them [the jurors] as to the law and advise them in respect of the facts; and (3) that the verdict should be unanimous.[2]

Despite the unqualified Sixth Amendment right to trial by jury in "all" criminal prosecutions, the law seemed to be settled, prior to 1970, that a judge sitting without a jury could try misdemeanors or petty crimes. In 1970 the Court opened to question that which it had earlier said was unquestionable. What had been settled was changed, leaving nothing standing of the old law except that a jury trial must be supervised by a judge.

259

MISDEMEANOR CASES

The Court's new reading of the Constitution requires a trial by jury if a misdemeanor can be punished by imprisonment for more than six months, a rule by no means radical in itself, but the Court's new reading of the Sixth Amendment left its precedents in a shambles and repudiated centuries of experience. The amendment now means that a jury in a criminal trial may be smaller than the historic common-law jury of twelve—how much smaller is uncertain, but a jury of six is constitutionally valid. A jury may also return its verdicts by less than a unanimous vote—how much less is uncertain, but a vote of 9-to-3, which formerly "hung" a jury, is now adequate to convict without violating the Sixth Amendment. One person holding out against the rest could in such cases no longer be a barrier to a decision. Whether a substantial majority of a jury of only six is constitutionally valid is now an open question. In the language of Justice Harlan, that the Court could reach such results "would have been unthinkable" before 1970.[3]

The judicial revolution began with two cases decided the same day in 1970. The opinion in the first, when taken alone, was innocuously liberalizing on its face, but it left the gate open to six-man juries even in federal trial courts, and it invited the opinion two years later that approved of less-than-unanimous jury verdicts. The first case was *Baldwin* v. *New York*. It was a spinoff of a Warren Court decision of 1968 which ruled that the Fourteenth Amendment, which denied any state the power of taking life, liberty, or property without due process of law, extended to the states the Sixth Amendment right to trial by jury.[4] That would seem to mean the right to trial by jury in "all" criminal prosecutions, a guarantee that repeats a provision of the main body of the Constitution (Article III, section 2) which says that the "trial of all crimes, except in cases of impeachment, shall be by a jury."

Neither Article III nor the Sixth Amendment restricts the right to trial by jury to only major crimes, serious crimes, or felonies, nor do these provisions exclude trial by jury in cases of minor crimes, petty ones, or misdemeanors. There is no legal significance in the fact that the main body of the Constitution speaks of "all crimes" and the Sixth Amendment of "all criminal prosecutions."[5] A judicially endorsed exception to the right to trial by jury had existed before 1970, the Constitution and the Sixth Amendment notwithstanding. From the colonial period petty offenses could be tried without a jury, as the Court long ago held.[6] But the meaning of "petty offense" remained obscure.[7] Congress in 1930 defined it not in terms of the offense itself but in terms of its punishment: Any offense for which the federal penalty is imprisonment for not more than six months or $500 or both is a petty one.[8]

In extending the Sixth Amendment's trial-by-jury provision to the states in 1968, the Court had ruled that a crime whose penalty is less than six months does not require trial by jury. But the Court did not explicitly state that there must be a trial by jury if the penalty could exceed six months. Indeed, the Court flatly refused on that occasion to settle "the exact location of the line between petty offenses and serious crimes."[9] New York City, sustained by the highest court of the state, drew that line at one year. *Baldwin* v. *New York* in 1970 raised the question whether the states could deny trial by jury when the punishment is greater than for a petty offense so defined. The state court's legal reasoning was supremely unimportant compared to its avowed concern for the disastrous consequences that might result from a ruling that Baldwin, a misdemeanant, must receive a trial by jury. The New York City Criminal Court tried about 130,000 misdemeanor cases annually, a case load about thirty-nine times greater than the state's next-largest city, Buffalo, and very far out of proportion to the difference in population. "While this [fact] alone," said the New York high court, "would suffice as a reasonable basis for not providing for the more time-consuming trial by jury of misdemeanors in the Criminal Court of the City of New York," further justification existed in the "chaotic calendar conditions and delays" in that court and in the constantly increasing crime rate.[10] Harlan, who found such considerations persuasive, estimated that requiring the nation's greatest city to try its misdemeanants by jury might increase the congestion and delays in its courts "by as much as a factor of eight."[11]

The Supreme Court, dividing 5-to-3, reversed Baldwin's conviction on the ground that he had been denied his constitutional right to trial by jury. But there was no majority opinion of the Court. White delivered a plurality opinion joined only by Brennan and Marshall. Black and Douglas concurred separately in the judgment, but not in the rule of *Baldwin,* which was that "no offense can be deemed 'petty' for purposes of the right to trial by jury where imprisonment for more than six months is authorized."[12] Baldwin had received the maximum sentence of one year for the misdemeanor of pickpocketing.

White's opinion was based on practical, not constitutional, considerations. The decisive fact for White was that New York City alone in the nation denied the accused a trial by jury for an offense punishable by imprisonment for more than six months. Even New York State would have tried Baldwin by a jury if his offense had not been committed within the city's jurisdiction. "This near-uniform judgment of the Nation," White declared, furnished "the only objective criterion" for drawing a line between offenses which are, and those which are not, serious enough to be tried by a jury.[13] White acknowledged that a person who faced loss of his freedom for less than six months, as well as damage to his career and reputation, would not appreciate the Court's definition of a crime serious enough to be tried by a jury. White believed that society's interest in "speedy and inexpensive non-jury adjudications" outweighed the onerous disadvantages facing petty defendants whom the Court denied a right to trial by jury. But he also believed that speed and cost, "administrative conveniences," considered in the light of practices everywhere outside of New York City, could not justify denial of a jury trial in cases where the possible punishment exceeds six months in jail.[14]

Black, joined by Douglas, heatedly complained that White's opinion was "little more than judicial mutilation of our written Constitution."[15] Black would have ruled that the Constitution plainly required a jury trial for all accused persons without exception. Black was right from the standpoint of strict construction, but he looked at only the language of the Constitution. White had looked at only the practices of the nation's courts, but he had the support of many precedents upholding the denial of jury trial to persons not accused of serious crimes. Black regarded the precedents, which White virtually ignored, as judicial amendments to the Constitution, substituting "all serious crimes" for "all crimes" and "all criminal prosecutions." Black added sarcastically that the three members of the Court in the plurality had amended the previous amendment by substituting the phrase "all crimes in which the punishment for more than six months is authorized." They had weighed the advantages to the accused against the administrative inconvenience to the state, "magically concluding that the scale tips at six months' imprisonment." The framers of the Constitution and of the Bill of Rights had engaged in all the balancing that Black thought necessary. They had decided that "the value of a jury trial far outweighed its costs 'in all crimes' and 'in all criminal prosecutions.' "[16]

Burger's constitutional literalism was of another brand. His brief dissent found nothing in the Constitution commanding a uniform pattern of jury trials for state and federal courts. Nor did he find anything "in the 'serious' crime coverage of the Sixth or Fourteenth Amendments" that would require the Court to invalidate the trial scheme of New York City.[17] His reference to "the 'serious' crime coverage" of the amendments was, of course, a reflection of the kind of judicial amendment to the Constitution that Black had deplored. Burger, by contrast, deplored the kind of judicial amendment that the Warren Court had made in 1968 when extending the federal jury-trial provision to the states. Harlan and Stewart shared Burger's view. Harlan's dissent correctly pointed out that whenever the Court incorporated a federal right within the Fourteenth Amendment, that right was "applicable to the States with all the subtleties and refinements born of history and embodied in case experience developed in the context of federal adjudication."[18] The Court had asserted in 1969 that once it decided "that a particular Bill of Rights guarantee is 'fundamental to the American scheme of justice' . . . the same constitutional standards apply against both the State and Federal Governments."[19] That principle justified applying to the states the federal standard for a petty offense. The same principle also required the application to the states of the federal standard for a twelve-man jury that reaches its verdict unanimously in criminal trials.

As a matter of fact, when extending to the states the federal right of trial by jury, the Court in 1968 reiterated that it meant that "every" criminal charge must be "confirmed by the *unanimous* sufferage of *twelve*" jurors.[20]

JURIES OF SIX

Baldwin seemed to lay a snare for the Court. By applying the federal standard of a jury trial, it implied the need for a unanimous verdict by twelve jurors in cases where an offense could be punished by a sentence of more than six months. White gave the impression that considerations of efficiency, such as the speed and cost of jury trials, could not stand in the way of constitutional rights, at least not in "serious" cases. *Williams* v. *Florida,* decided the same day, presented another and far more significant aspect of the Court's attitude on trial by jury; it mitigated the demands that *Baldwin* placed on the criminal courts. *Williams* ruled that a jury of only six fulfills the constitutional requirement of trial by jury.[21] A six-man jury can be selected in half the time of the traditional twelve-man jury, costs only half as much, and may reach its verdict more quickly.

The opinion of the Court in *Williams,* once again delivered by White, amazingly massed a 7-to-1 majority. Blackmun had not been appointed in time to participate in the decision. Marshall was the only member of the Court from whose eyes the scales did not fall. Yet the occasion called for a stalwart champion to defend trial by jury as it had been known in Anglo-American jurisprudence since the fourteenth century. What was required in the way of a dissenting opinion was a minute, critical evaluation of the opinion of the Court, a demonstration of the values peculiar to the twelve-man jury, and a reasoned repudiation of the six-man jury as a failure to protect those values. Marshall did not accept the gauntlet. In a remarkably unreasoned and indolent dissent, amounting to a mere printed page, Marshall announced that he was standing pat with the past. His opinion brings to mind the remark of Holmes: "It is revolting to have no better reason for a rule of law than that so it was laid down in the time of Henry IV. It is still more revolting if the grounds upon which it was laid down have vanished long since, and the rule simply persists from blind imitation of the past."[22] Marshall adhered to the rule that the same standards should apply to both the state and federal governments, and also to the rule announced in an 1898 decision that the jury guaranteed by the Sixth Amendment should consist of "twelve persons, neither more nor less."[23] White, as a matter of fact, did not violate the same-standards rule. He simply diluted the federal right to a jury of twelve by reducing it to the lowest common denominator, Florida's jury of six, the rule in all noncapital trials in Florida. A six-man jury in a United States trial court would satisfy the Sixth Amendment; Congress had only to enact a statute to that effect to bring about the change.[24] Harlan, who concurred in the judgment that a jury of six was constitutionally sound for those states that wanted it, vigorously objected to the Court's diminution of the federal right under the Sixth Amendment.

The *Williams* case involved a noncapital felony. After the jury returned a verdict of guilty, the court sentenced the prisoner to life imprisonment. *Baldwin,* by contrast, involved only a misdemeanor punishable by a maximum sentence of one year. If there is a place in the American system of criminal justice for a six-man jury, it is in a case like Baldwin's, rather than Williams's.

New York's judiciary quickly got the message of *Williams* and amended the rules of the Criminal Court of the City of New York to provide for trials by six-man juries in all misdemeanor cases.[25] The results did not at all justify the earlier predictions that the system would collapse through weight of procedure. The results would not have justified those predictions even if twelve-man juries had been required. Trying a misdemeanor case by a jury, if by only a six-man jury, took considerably more time in New York City's courts than a trial by a magistrate. Indeed, a judge can try and decide an average of twenty cases in a week, but he can conduct only two six-man jury trials during that same period.[26] Yet *Baldwin,* by vesting a right to trial by jury, paradoxically resulted in very few such trials. The striking impact of *Baldwin* was that it enormously stimulated plea bargaining and, indirectly, improved the criminal-justice system of New York City.

Only about 7 percent of New York City's misdemeanants who

request trial by jury follow through to the trial itself and a final verdict. An overwhelming number, 98 percent, of those who request trial by jury plead guilty before the trial begins.[27] The reason is that their right to a trial by jury, thanks to *Baldwin,* enhances the plea-bargaining position of defendants. One city prosecutor said, "All any [defense] lawyer has to do to get a reduced charge is to demand a jury trial."[28] Thus, by giving defendants a strategic lever to use against the prosecutor's office, *Baldwin* kept the number of jury trials down to insignificance. The guilty got a break, but so did the innocent, who could plead guilty in exchange for a sentence corresponding to the time spent in jail before their pleas. The severity of sentences substantially decreased for those who struck a bargain and pleaded guilty, and most did.[29]

Baldwin also visibly enhanced the dignity of misdemeanor proceedings in the Criminal Court of New York City. There was a strong brake on the previously frenzied assembly-line system of justice. In the few cases that went to trial, the presence of a jury influenced all the participants, including judges and prosecutors, to observe procedural niceties and courtroom etiquette. Even nonjury trials before judges alone reflected an improved atmosphere of decorum.[30] Equally significant, defendants who could not afford bail and remained in jail awaiting trial by jury while the plea-bargaining process went on received preference on the jury docket, thus speeding up their trials and their pleas.[31] None of these salutary effects should have been surprising, because experience elsewhere, in California for example where all accused of misdemeanors are entitled to a jury trial, demonstrates no significant increases in delayed justice, clogged court calendars, or additional costs to the public.[32] The experience in New York City after *Baldwin* argues for an extension of the right to trial by jury even in cases where the maximum possible penalty is less than six months, validating the Black-Douglas position in that case.

New York City's experience with six-man juries in misdemeanor cases does not, however, validate the Court's *Williams* opinion. That experience proves only that six-man juries are better than none, not that they are better than twelve-man juries. Incredibly, there are no empirical studies of six-man juries in the two states, Florida and Utah, that use them in felony cases, nor of the five-man jury in Louisiana. Until such studies are the basis for comparing the operation and verdicts of juries of differing sizes, there is no factual validity for the *Williams* opinion. The statistical probability is exceedingly high that empirical comparisons of the two juries will destroy whatever plausibility there may seem to be in White's position that there is no significant difference in their functioning and their results. His opinion in any case will remain a hodgepodge of bad reasoning and guesswork. A judicial opinion that is unfounded yet reaches the right result commands obedience only by virtue of its authority, not by virtue of the soundness of its argument. Whether the Court reached the right result in *Williams* is most dubious.

The question before the Court was whether the six-man jury violates the Constitution. At no point in his opinion did White analyze how a six-man jury functions. He could not because he simply did not know how its verdicts compare with the verdicts of twelve-man juries in similar cases. Before the Court took the momentous step of constitutionally endorsing a shriveled jury that has been foreign to the experience of the federal trial courts since the founding of the republic and is not known in felony cases in forty-seven of the fifty states, the Court should have invited re-arguments on the question whether the two juries exhibit significant differences.[33] The one point that stands out from a reading of White's opinion is that nowhere did he justify a jury of six except to allege that it fulfilled the purposes of trial by jury and that "there is no discernible difference between the results reached by the two different-sized juries."[34] White's strategy, rather, was to attack the jury of twelve and, on finding that he could not justify its exact size, to validate the jury of six.

The Court should have placed the burden of proof on those advocating the reform whose constitutional validity was in question. White retrospectively placed the burden on the hapless member of the Miami bar who was representing Williams. Counsel directed his principal argument on behalf of Williams to a wholly different issue, whether Florida's notice-of-alibi rule violated his right not to be an involuntary witness against himself.[35] The lawyer's brief allotted only a bit more than a page to the constitutionality of the six-man jury and did not suggest that the size of the jury might affect its verdict. Surprisingly, the NAACP, which filed an *amicus curiae* brief in the case, did not even challenge the six-man jury. Given the emptiness of Marshall's dissent and the idiosyncratic character of Harlan's concurring opinion— he was chiefly interested in assaulting the position of the Court that the Fourteenth Amendment incorporates the Sixth Amendment—the Court simply had no exposure to any view contrary to its own. Its own view was that twelve was a chance figure and therefore should be eliminated as a constitutional requirement. That lent no validity to the figure of six which Florida used as a means of cheapening and expediting trial by jury.

Harlan's approach on this point was far more sensible. He would not overturn the Court's previous holdings sustaining the twelve-man jury as the only jury demanded by the Constitution unless the precedents proved to be "practically or jurisprudentially unworkable, or no longer suited to contemporary life. . . . Surely if the principle of *stare decisis* [standing by past decisions] means anything in the law, it means that precedent should not be jettisoned when the rule of yesterday remains viable, creates no injustice, and can reasonably be said to be no less sound than the rule sponsored by those who seek change, let alone incapable of being demonstrated wrong."[36] The state of Florida had not even attempted to make a demonstration of that kind in its brief and argument before the Court. Nor did White, for the Court, make such a showing.

White began with a historical investigation to determine why juries had been fixed at exactly twelve in their size. He responsibly examined the writings of the foremost legal historians who had studied the origins of the common-law jury and concluded that they have not been able to explain conclusively why, six centuries ago, the size of the jury emerged as twelve. From that fact White drew the utterly unsubstantiated conclusion that the traditional size of the jury "appears to have been a historical accident, unrelated to the great purposes which gave rise to the jury in the first place."[37] But our uncertain knowledge of the original reason for the size of the jury does not prove that it was an accident or that it is unrelated to the great purposes of the jury system. The jury of twelve has unquestionably fulfilled those purposes. White did not dispute that. He claimed, rather, that a jury of twelve was unnecessary to fulfill those purposes.

White then reframed the question before the Court. "The question before us," he said, "is whether this accidental feature of the jury has been immutably codified into our Constitution."[38] By way of a negative answer he first reviewed the precedents and found, accurately enough, that although they consistently endorsed the figure of twelve, they offered no rationale for it. Then he examined the historical evidence relating to the adoption of the Sixth Amendment. White conceded at once that twelve was the size of the jury as of 1789, when the Constitution was ratified, but he denied that the evidence necessarily showed that the jury referred to in either Article III of the Constitution or in the Sixth Amendment preserved twelve as the size of the jury. The records, in fact, made no reference to the size of the jury. "It may well be," White acknowledged, "that the usual expectation was that the jury would consist of 12. . . . But there is absolutely no indication in 'the intent of the Framers' of an explicit decision to equate the constitutional and common law characteristics of the jury."[39] But there is also "absolutely no indication" that the framers intended any size of the jury but twelve. They did not provide for twelve because they took for granted that particular characteristic of the jury. Twelve was the size of the jury specified in the constitutions of the states at that time, and the purpose of the Bill of Rights was to quiet the popular fear that the new national government would violate the traditional liberties of the people. Among those liberties a jury of twelve was pre-eminent. Trial by jury, commonly called at that time "the palladium of our liberties," was trial by a jury of twelve. Any suspicion that a jury fewer in number would be possible under the Sixth Amendment would surely have led to its rejection by the state legislatures that ratified it. White's discussion of the intent of the framers with respect to the size of the jury was a fruitless and unhistorical effort to cast doubt on whether the Sixth Amendment incorporated a jury of twelve. Harlan disposed of White's effort with the rejoinder that the Court on many occasions had declared that the interpretation of the Constitution "is necessarily influenced by the fact that its provisions are framed in the language of the English common law, and are to be read in the light of its history."[40]

On discovering "nothing" in history or in its own precedents explaining why a jury must be twelve and only twelve in number, the Court cut the historical anchor of trial by jury. Yet history revealed no reason for altering its size.

The Court's logic dictated the erroneous rule that the jury of twelve must be rejected if there was no reason for it. It did not find that reason, though one existed; but by the Court's own abstract logic, history showed no rationale for a jury less than twelve. Accordingly, a jury of lesser size, being devoid of a historical rationale, should also be rejected. In any case, history was not as "accidental," "fanciful," "mystical," "superstitious," or "religious" as White made it out to be. The rationale of twelve evolved not in the fourteenth century, when the figure of twelve was fixed, but in the centuries afterwards as a result of practical experience with juries of twelve. They worked effectively, which is the reason that the original accident, if it can be called that, kept recurring, as Harlan tartly observed, for six continuous centuries.

White, having found that the classical jury of twelve was no more than some sort of reflexive genuflection toward a happenstance fact of the fourteenth century, next turned to the crucial part of his opinion. It was whether the policies implicit in trial by jury bore any relationship to jury size. As White put it, "The relevant inquiry, as we see it, must be the function that the particular feature [size] performs and its relation to the purpose of the jury trial. Measured by this standard," he declared, "the 12-man requirement cannot be regarded as an indispensable component of the Sixth Amendment."[41]

In view of the fact that a verdict—at least until 1972—had to be unanimous,[42] one man who held out against conviction could thwart a verdict of guilty. Accordingly, the chances of finding that one juror would be increased if juries were larger than twelve. The larger jury would be more favorable to the accused or less likely to convict; it would also, as it grows in size, increase its chances of being more representative of the community which should share in the verdict. The jury symbolically epitomizes the community. The smaller the jury becomes, the less representative it is likely to be. The historical wisdom that inheres in the number twelve consists of its manageability as a deliberative body without too much sacrifice of its representative character and without unduly deferring to the state's interest in efficiency and convenience. Such consideration underlay the policies of trial by jury. The state has an interest in keeping juries small, cheap, and conducive to deliberate speed. But the larger juries cost more and are more unmanageable. A jury of twelve is a compromise between a jury twice as large or half as large.

The Court's functional interpretation of trial by jury was the historic one that John Adams and Thomas Jefferson would have understood: The jury is a safeguard to the accused against the oppression of the state; only a free government would let the community, acting through its representatives on the jury, decide whether a fellow citizen should be deprived of his liberty. White saw the jury as a buffer between the accused and the state, interposing the common-sense judgment of laymen whose determination of guilt or innocence speaks for the society which shares the responsibility for the verdict, but from that generalization he made the unwarranted inference that the jury's performance of its role does not depend on its size. He realized that at some point a jury might become too small to fulfill its purpose except as a mere factfinder, but he thought that the case before the Court did not require it to decide on the minimum size of a jury, though "we do not doubt that six is above that minimum."[43]

That rightly provoked Harlan to demand why six are essential if twelve are not. He also protested that the Court had provided "no standard" for determining the size of the jury.[44] White in fact advanced three standards: The size of the jury "should probably be large enough" to promote group deliberation, to keep the jury immune from intimidation, and to allow for a representative cross section of the community.[45] White should have put that proposition emphatically. His tentative phrasing of "probably" drained the point and exposed him to the criticism that he had expressed the dangerous and nonsensical view that size was unrelated to a jury's function. To state that the jury's performance "is not a function of the particular number of the body that makes up the jury," but to add that there is "little reason" to believe that a jury of six could not perform as a jury of twelve, "particularly if the requirement of unanimity is retained,"[46] is to offer a contradiction. "Little reason" for so believing was, like the use of "probably," a peculiar

way to express a major constitutional finding. If there is "little reason" for the belief that six do not achieve the results of twelve,
there is some reason for that belief, and if there is some, there is
uncertainty about the finding.

White sought to dispel that doubt; neither evidence nor theory
"suggests the 12-man jury is necessarily more advantageous to the
defendant than a jury composed of fewer members."[47] His very
phrasing of the point, by the use of "necessarily," was, like his use
of "probably" and "little reason," an implicit concession that
twelve is better than six and that the relationship between the size
of the jury and its function is significant. White's first point by way
of rebuttal was that there is really no safety in numbers for the defendant merely because a twelve-man jury doubles his chances of
finding one juror who will deadlock the jury by holding out for an
acquittal. No black defendant and no defendant in a political trial
would likely agree. The advantage, White thought, might as easily
belong to the state because it needed only one out of twelve to insist on a verdict of guilty and thus prevent an acquittal. He recognized, however, that a hung jury is an advantage, though only a
"minimal" one, to the accused, who remains unconvicted and has
the prospect of avoiding a conviction if subsequent juries are also
hung. There is, then, safety in numbers for the accused, but White
insisted that as between a jury of six and one of twelve the odds
of hanging the jury are "slight."

White was wrong on several counts. The equal chance of the
prosecution or the defense to find the one sympathetic juror on its
side exists statistically only if the jurors divide equally on the first
ballot. But juries do not split 6-to-6 on the first ballot except in
very rare cases. In the foremost empirical study on juries, which
the Court cited in its opinion, *The American Jury* by Professors
Harry Kalven Jr. and Hans Zeisel of the University of Chicago
Law School, only 4 percent of juries split down the middle on the
first ballot.[48] Furthermore, another study using sophisticated statistical analysis shows that the mathematical probabilities of finding
one juror to hold out for or against conviction change with the
size of the jury.[49] By White's logic a jury of six is unconstitutional
if it does not serve the function of a jury of twelve, and it does not
with respect to finding the juror who will deadlock the verdict.

White's simple arithmetic was not equal to the task in still another respect. He relied on Kalven and Zeisel to show his recognition of the fact that a hopelessly deadlocked jury is not simply the result of an eccentric or stubborn juror. As White put the point, decisions by a small group are "likely to be influenced by the proportional size of the majority aligned against them. . . . Thus if a defendant needs initially to persuade four jurors that the State has not met its burden of proof in order to escape ultimate conviction by a 12-man jury, he arguably escapes by initially persuading half that number in a six-man jury. . . ."[50]

White failed to understand the psychology of small-group deliberation and decision-making. Zeisel, the coauthor of *The American Jury,* pointed out that its findings "were quite different" from what White represented them to be.[51] The proportion of ten out of twelve may be the same as five out of six, and four holdouts against conviction on the initial ballot on a jury of twelve may be proportionally the same as two holdouts on a jury of six. But proportion alone is not functionally significant. What counts, rather, is a substantial number of allies to bolster one's position and psyche. Kalven and Zeisel stated, "It requires a massive minority of 4 or 5 jurors at the first vote to develop the likelihood of a hung jury."[52] The reason is that a juror will very likely change his position if most of the others oppose him. Psychologically, two initial doubters out of six is not the same as four out of twelve. The point is not merely theoretical. There is hard evidence to support the position, denied by White, that a jury of twelve is more than minimally or slightly advantageous to the defendant compared to a jury of six. Zeisel studied the frequency of hung juries in criminal trials in Miami's courts and compared the results with the national average of hung juries. He found that Miami's six-man juries deadlocked only half as often as twelve-man juries.[53]

White had cited as his strongest proof six studies which showed "that there is no discernible difference between the results reached by the two different-sized juries."[54] The citation looked impressive, but its contents were not. The six studies compare the different-sized juries in civil, not criminal, cases. The studies are also brief, impressionistic, and unreliable on the point for which White cited them. Zeisel summarized each of the six to disinter the substance buried in White's citation and laconically observed, "This is scant evidence by any standards."[55] "No" evidence would be more accurate. A law-school student was capable of revealing the Court's scandalous misuse of the studies. Of one study in which the clerk of a civil court had offered his belief that the verdicts of six-man juries were comparable to those of the traditional juries the student-author remarked:

> Of course, such a totally unscientific opinion is of no merit in a rigorous attempt to compare the behavior of the two juries. It is devoid of any records of trial results and reflects nothing more than the impressions of the court clerk. The other articles cited discuss the obvious fact that reduced juries are somewhat cheaper and more expeditious, but they provide no analysis of the verdicts that are returned.[56]

White's final claim was also groundless. "Theory" to the contrary, "in practice the difference between the 12-man and the six-man jury in terms of the cross section of the community represented seems likely to be negligible."[57] Something that "seems" likely is not a statement of fact, but of mere speculation. The same student-author who creamed White for his use of the six studies plotted an elaborate and complicated statistical model to determine representativeness. He concluded:[58]

> When the number of jurors is reduced from twelve to 6, the decreased representation makes the defendant's fate more a matter of the chance involved in selecting the petit jury. Consequently, the actual verdict is less likely to reflect the opinion of a "representative cross section of the community." . . . The role of the jury is impaired whenever the verdict becomes less representative. . . . If the purposes of the jury are fulfilled, the verdict must be a function only of the defendant's behavior and the representative opinions of the community. . . . The statistical fluctuations in the selection of the petit jury render the defendant's fate more a matter of chance—and less a product of his behavior and of the community's values—as the number of the jurors is lowered.

Zeisel came to similar conclusions using a simple arithmetical model that anyone should understand. Zeisel assumed a community in which 90 percent of the population shared identical viewpoints and the remaining 10 percent differed. He then analyzed the composition of six- and twelve-man juries drawn by lottery, and he proved that "the smaller the size of the jury, the

less frequently it even approaches community representation."[59]
Out of every 100 twelve-member juries, 72 would have at least
one representative of the minority opinion, while only 47 out of
100 six-man juries would have at least one. "It is clear, then, that
however limited a twelve-member jury is in representing the full
spectrum of the community, the six-member jury is even more
limited, and not by a 'negligible' margin."[60] The minority opinion
has even less of a chance of having two spokesmen on the six-man
jury. The probability of having a second minority representative
on the jury is three times greater on the twelve-man jury than on
the smaller one.[61] The 10 percent minority opinion in Zeisel's
hypothetical community might, with the same results, be a minority
of class, an ethnic or racial group, a political faction, an age or
occupational group, or any other cross section of the community
that might be of considerable significance in a particular trial.

Zeisel concluded that a six-man jury "provides a lesser safeguard for the defendant than a twelve-member jury."[62] Surely that
is the reason that no state provided for fewer than twelve jurors
in capital cases, a policy White himself said suggested implicit
recognition of "the value of the larger body as a means of legiti-
mating society's decision to impose the death penalty."[63] The
larger jury, by the same reasoning, is a more representative body
to legitimate society's decision to impose imprisonment.

That an accused should be judged by a jury of his peers is an
ideal that too little corresponds with reality; *Williams* simply in-
tensified this unrepresentativeness. In Florida, where the *Williams*
case arose, a defendant has less than a 50 percent chance of being
tried by a six-man jury that includes a black. As the *University
of Florida Law Review* stated, "A system that has half its juries
composed entirely of white members does not accurately reflect
the community ethnic ratio since, according to Florida population
totals, one in every six residents is black and since a disproportionate number of criminal defendants are black. Expanding the jury to
twelve members would more than double the likelihood of a black
juror, but there still would be a twenty-four percent chance of an
all-white jury."[64] The student using sophisticated math in his jury
study concluded in general, "six jurors never fulfill the purpose of
the jury as well as the 12 required at common law . . . the six-

man jury significantly changes the probability of conviction" and "convicts different persons."[65]

If the Court had correctly applied its own tests to determine whether the size of the jury alters its functions and results, the jury of six would have been held unconstitutional. Confidence in the Court is shattered when it overturns its own precedents, rejecting centuries of experience on the basis of an irresponsible use of evidence, unsupported premises, and groundless conclusions. The historical twelve-man jury deserved a better requiem. Legislatures seeking economy and ways to loosen the logjam of cases in criminal courts have only to accept the Court's invitation to pass laws providing for six-man juries. The consequent sacrifice of a constitutional right—or rather, of what used to be a constitutional right —has the Court's approval, though it is phrased in fictions that disguise the sacrifice. The tragedy is not merely that the Court was wrong about so crucial a matter but that it did not know what it was talking about.

NONUNANIMOUS VERDICTS

Under Due Process of Law

Any opponent of the Court-approved six-man jury system would recognize that it retained one virtue: the requirement of a unanimous verdict. In companion cases of 1972, the Court heaved that requirement into the judicial gutter, leaving the jury system in the states unrecognizable from a constitutional standpoint. In reality the system did not change, for the states have not yet shown an inclination to exercise their new license to shoot down the historic principle that verdicts speak for a unanimous voice. But the Court declared a permanent open season on that principle when it sustained the laws of the two aberrant states, Louisiana and Oregon, which permit majority verdicts of 9-to-3 and 10-to-2 respectively. Unlike *Williams,* which sparked only a feeble dissent from one Justice, *Johnson* v. *Louisiana* and *Apodaca* v. *Oregon* provoked strong, well-reasoned dissents and the closest possible splits on the Court.[66] Those cases were far more important even than *Williams* in altering the meaning of the Sixth Amendment.

Where the unanimous jury verdict prevails as a requirement, the juror who is the least convinced that the prosecution has proved its case must be listened to and persuaded by the other jurors, who cannot return a verdict of guilty without settling his doubts. Although the Court claimed that its novel holding on the validity of majority verdicts did not diminish the prosecution's burden of proof in criminal cases, that in fact is the consequence.

Douglas, dissenting, said "a 'law and order' judicial mood" had lowered the barricades against convicting the innocent.[67] *Johnson* and *Apodaca* are archetypal specimens of the Nixon Court in action. The majority opinions reflected policies desired by the Nixon Administration. When Rehnquist was Assistant Attorney General testifying before a Senate committee on behalf of the Department of Justice, he recommended the abolition of unanimous jury verdicts in federal trial courts.[68] Congress nonetheless retained the requirement of unanimity. A year later the Court barely left it standing for federal juries because Powell suffered from "constitutional schizophrenia."[69] Powell joined the other Nixon appointees and White to read out of the Constitution the unanimity requirement for state criminal juries that everyone previously assumed was in it because of tradition, experience, and judicial dicta. *Williams* had been an example of extreme judicial activism devoid of political coloration because Black, Douglas, and Brennan had joined in White's opinion. *Johnson* and *Apodaca* showed a rampant and irrational activism. There was nothing conservative about the way supposedly conservative Justices decided the cases, except for the narrow escape of the unanimous federal criminal jury. Douglas, lamenting the Court's "radical departure from American traditions,"[70] protested that the "vast restructuring of American law which is entailed in today's decisions is for political not for judicial action. . . . We life-time appointees, who sit here only by happenstance, are the last who should sit as a Committee of Revision on rights as basic as those involved in the present cases."[71] As the oldest practicing activist on the Court, Douglas should have known what he was talking about.

As the Chief Justice's hatchet man in the field of criminal justice White would, but for Powell, have applied the new Sixth Amendment rule to federal trial courts. Yet White himself in 1965 had referred to the "system of trial by an impartial jury of 12 men who must *unanimously* agree on a verdict, the system followed in the federal courts *by virtue of the Sixth Amendment.*"[72] In 1968 he had declared that trial by jury meant that every criminal charge must be "confirmed by the *unanimous* suffrage of twelve jurors."[73] In 1970 in *Williams* White had found little reason to believe that a jury of six functions differently from a jury of twelve, "particularly if the requirement of unanimity is retained."[74] He observed on that occasion that unanimity "may well serve an important role in the jury function, for example, as a device for insuring that the Government bear the heavier burden of proof."[75] Two years later he found nothing constitutionally defective in verdicts by a "heavy" majority vote and no constitutional basis for verdicts by a unanimous vote. White was inconsistent in announcing the Court's position, as were other members of it. Even more important is the fact that his 1972 opinions conflicted with received tradition on the principle of unanimity.

In cases of felony or serious crime juries have always operated on the basis of unanimous verdicts except in Louisiana since 1898 and in Oregon since 1934. Although other institutions, even appellate courts, function on the principle of majority rule, in a democracy no institution except a jury can lawfully find a person guilty of crime. Because of its unique and awesome responsibility, the criminal jury is the only institution that must make its decisions by a unique standard of proof: It is bound by the requirement of proof beyond reasonable doubt. An appellate court can affirm a jury's conviction but it cannot render a verdict of guilty. It decides, rather, whether that verdict was reached at a trial that conformed with the law. The burden on the prosecution of proof beyond reasonable doubt, as the yardstick to measure whether the defendant did in fact commit the crime charged against him, is founded on the policy that the presumption of innocence must be overcome by a certainty of guilt—at least the certainty that is attainable within the realm of human fallibility. Because of the exacting standard of proof beyond reasonable doubt, not despite it, some verdicts benefit the guilty. The system is stacked to protect the defendant to the extent possible. Despite that standard, some innocent people are convicted.[76] Juries make mistakes; they are sometimes prejudiced. A maxim of the Anglo-American law, dating back to time immemorial, as the English say, asserts that it is better to acquit many guilty men than to convict one innocent man.[77] That "almost heroic commitment to decency"[78] is the basis of the standard of proof beyond reasonable doubt.

The Court by way of dicta had many times over the years assumed that proof beyond reasonable doubt is constitutionally required as a reflection of a profound judgment about the way justice should be administered. Yet no holding had been made on the issue until as late as 1970, when the Court decided in the case of *In re Winship* that due process of law protects the accused against conviction except upon proof beyond reasonable doubt of every fact necessary to constitute the crime charged against him. In view of the requirement of due process of law in both the Fifth and Fourteenth Amendments, the holding applied the identical standard against both the United States and state governments. Brennan, who delivered the opinion of the Court, stated that the reasonable-doubt standard plays a crucial role in the American scheme of criminal justice because it is "a prime instrument for reducing the risk of convictions resting on factual error" and "provides concrete substance for the presumption of innocence" which "lies at the foundation of the administration of our criminal law." The standard of reasonable doubt defined the prosecution's burden of proof because it was "indispensable to command the respect and confidence of the community in applications of the criminal law" and preserved the "moral force" of that law from dilution by a lesser standard of proof that would leave people "in doubt whether innocent men are being condemned." It also secured the confidence of the citizen that the government could not judge him guilty of crime without convincing a jury "with utmost certainty."[79]

The standard of proof of guilt beyond reasonable doubt has been inextricably entwined with the principle of a unanimous verdict, making it an indispensable if not fail-safe bulwark against jury bias in times of popular passion or when the defendant is a member of an unpopular political minority, religious sect, or ethnic group. Unanimity means that a single juror may veto all others, thwarting an overwhelming jury majority. *Johnson* and *Apodaca* changed that, in effect making convictions possible by a preponderance of the evidence. The two cases were different from a technical standpoint and were therefore separately decided. Because Johnson's Louisiana trial occurred before the Court extended the Sixth Amendment trial-by-jury requirement to the states, he could not claim that the amendment by incorporating the unanimity requirement protected him against a 9-to-3 verdict. He relied instead on two arguments founded on the Fourteenth Amendment. The first was that its due-process clause, by embodying the standard of proof beyond reasonable doubt, requires unanimous verdicts; when even one member of the jury still possesses such a doubt at the end of the jury's deliberation, guilt cannot be said to have been proved beyond such a doubt.

That argument, White said for a five-member majority of the Court, was not persuasive. It asked the Court to assume that the majority of the jury, which favors a verdict of guilty, will ignore the minority and vote to convict even if deliberation has not been exhausted and the minority jurors may have reasonable doubts which, if pursued, might persuade the members of the majority to acquit. White did not believe that the majority jurors would behave that way. There were no grounds, he reiterated, for believing that the majority jurors would "simply refuse to listen to arguments presented to them in favor of an acquittal, terminate discussion and render a verdict."[80]

There was, on the contrary, a compelling reason for thinking that that was exactly what happened in Johnson's case. His jury, trying him for a felony, had "deliberated" for less than twenty minutes, yet returned a verdict that had the concurrence of only nine jurors. Inexplicably, the dissenters on the Court did not refer to this fact, although it strongly suggests that the jury made its verdict in Johnson's case with unseemly haste, a lack of deliberation, and little merit. The dissenting Justices very likely did not mention the fact that Johnson was black and that three jurors were black because the record did not reveal the identity of the jurors who voted for acquittal.[81] Regardless of their identity, allowing a conviction by a jury's vote of 9-to-3 means that the jurors on retiring to the jury room, where they are supposed to deliberate on the evidence before making up their minds, may take a poll before deliberating, and if nine vote for a guilty verdict on the first ballot, they may return the verdict without the need of having heard the minority's viewpoint. Louisiana law permits precisely what the majority of the Court could not believe, and the case before it seemed to be proof of that fact. White, however, simply insisted that there was no evidence showing that the majority jurors had ignored the reasonable doubts of the minority or otherwise had acted irresponsibly.

White was utterly unrealistic. The fact that the deliberations of a jury are secret makes it impossible for a defendant to secure the kind of proof that White demanded. In an analogous situation the Court does not demand of a defendant proof that there was deliberate racial discrimination in composing the jury lists from which his jury was selected; the Court infers the existence of that discrimination from the fact that no blacks have served on juries in a given jurisdiction over a very long period of time.[82] That kind of situation existed in Johnson's case with respect to the conduct of his jury. The nearly instant verdict delivered over the objections of three jurors was sufficient to warrant the inference of irregularity. White chose, however, to repose his unsupported faith in the abstract belief that a majority of jurors "will cease discussion and outvote a minority only after reasoned discussion has ceased to have persuasive effect or to serve any other purpose—when a minority, that is, continues to insist upon acquittal without having persuasive reasons in support of its position."[83]

Thus, White denigrated the minority members of the jury for being unreasonable because they were not convinced of guilt beyond a reasonable doubt. He ignored the fact that a jury which may render a verdict by a majority vote behaves differently from a jury that is bound by the requirement of unanimity. Where that requirement exists, deliberation can be meaningful. In about one case out of every ten, an initial minority of jurors manages to persuade an initial majority to change their minds, and these could be cases of special importance.[84] Regardless of the identity of the defendant or the issues in his case, he is entitled to the benefit of doubt when the prosecution has tried and failed to convince three jurors of his guilt. Contrary to White, every juror on a jury that has been properly selected must be presumed to be reasonable. "The juror whose dissenting voice is unheard," as Marshall said in his dissent, "may be a spokesman, not for any minority view-point, but simply for himself—and that, in my view, is enough. The doubts of a single juror are in my view evidence that the government has failed to carry its burden of proving guilt beyond a reasonable doubt."[85] Even with a requirement of unanimity the initial vote of the jury is likely to become the final verdict,[86] though there is always the possibility that the necessity of considering the minority view might lead to conversion. When a verdict represents merely a majority view, the initial vote creates a majority that cannot be checked if it meets the requisite number to be decisive.

The dissenters saw the jury as an entity incapable of rendering a verdict by the undisputed standard of proof beyond reasonable doubt if any member remained unconvinced. The majority of the Court saw the jury as twelve individuals, a majority of whom could decide the verdict if they were satisfied beyond reasonable doubt regardless of the doubts of the minority. White quoted approvingly from the so-called *Allen* charge, which trial judges sometimes use to persuade the minority to reconsider their position in the light of the fact that they are a minority and might therefore be wrong. But White did not mention that the *Allen* charge is relevant, if at all, only to a case in which the jury is deadlocked. Nor did he quote that part of the *Allen* charge which explains to deadlocked jurors that "the very object of the jury system is to secure unanimity."[87] That passage omitted by White is on the same page from which he approvingly quoted. Yet he insisted that the vote of the three minority jurors neither impeached the verdict of the nine nor demonstrated that guilt was not in fact proved beyond a reasonable doubt.

To underpin his conclusion, White claimed first that the fact that reasonable men can disagree does not show that the prosecution has failed to meet its burden of proof or that the jury is unfaithful to the reasonable-doubt standard. Yet the fact that reasonable men can disagree is itself evidence that there is reasonable doubt, not the unreasonable doubt that White previously alleged on the part of the stubborn, minority jurors. In a federal court, White also reasoned, a hung jury led not to an acquittal but to a retrial at which time the defendant might be convicted, proving that the lack of jury unanimity should not be equated with the existence of reasonable doubt. If a hung jury was proof of the existence of reasonable doubt, the defendant would be acquitted; a majority verdict, like a hung jury, did not imply reasonable doubt.

White twisted law and logic when he alleged, "If the doubt of a minority of jurors indicates the existence of a reasonable doubt it would appear that a defendant should receive a directed verdict of acquittal rather than a re-trial. We conclude, therefore, that verdicts rendered by nine out of 12 jurors are not automatically invalidated by the disagreement of the dissenting three."[88] On such reasoning the Court ruled that the 9-to-3 verdict, by following the standard of reasonable doubt, did not violate due process of law.

There are several defects in such logic. In the first place, a hung jury is a legitimate outcome of a criminal trial, not a breakdown of the trial process. A mistrial resulting from a hung jury, as a lower federal court declared, "is a safeguard to liberty. In many areas it is the sole means by which one or a few may stand out against an overwhelming contemporary public sentiment. Nothing should interfere with its exercise."[89] That was said in a unanimous opinion rejecting the *Allen* charge whose hostility to hung juries White approvingly quoted. By allowing 9-to-3 verdicts the Court very much interfered with hung juries. Considerably more than half of the juries that deadlock under the unanimity requirement would be able to return verdicts under the 9-to-3 rule.[90] In the second place, a hung jury most certainly means that the prosecution did not convince the jury beyond reasonable doubt. It does not acquit, because of the requirement that a verdict of not guilty, like a verdict of guilty, must be unanimous. Otherwise, White's logic could be stood on its head. He was using the example of a hung jury to prove that a majority verdict showed no failure of the reasonable-doubt standard. Yet, in the abstract one could argue, contrary to White, that a hung jury proves the existence of reasonable doubt: The defendant is not convicted when the jury has reasonable doubt; he is not convicted when the jury hangs; therefore, the hung jury shows reasonable doubt. Analogously, a majority jury shows the same doubt. The trouble with such reasoning and with White's is that abstract logic ignores the legitimacy of a trial ending in no verdict.

Marshall, dissenting, proved a third defect in White's logic. It led to the conclusion that a defendant can be retried after a hung jury initially results in a mistrial, and on the retrial he may be found guilty beyond reasonable doubt. To White that established that a majority verdict, like no verdict, did not show a failure of proof beyond reasonable doubt. Marshall rightly called that conclusion "a complete *non sequitur.*"[91] Moreover, a conviction on retrial, following a hung jury, proves nothing about the initial trial and thus does not establish the validity of a majority verdict. The second trial may be very different from the first for a variety of reasons. A guilty verdict at the second trial does not, therefore, impeach the doubts of the dissenting jurors at the first trial. "But that conclusion," Marshall declared, "is wholly consistent with the view that the doubts of dissenting jurors create a constitutional bar to conviction at the trial that produced those doubts. Until today, I had thought that was the law."[92] Marshall did not add the obvious fact that in a federal trial the jury that convicts, following a mistrial, must reach a unanimous verdict.

If White was right in claiming that the burden of proving guilt beyond reasonable doubt did not change when a 9-to-3 verdict is permissible, then the verdicts returned by a nine-juror majority would be the same as those returned by unanimous juries of twelve. That is, the ratio of convictions to acquittals would remain stationary. There are about two guilty verdicts in the United States for every verdict of not guilty.[93] The same ratio should prevail in Louisiana, which permits verdicts of 9-to-3. Unfortunately there is no study of the conviction ratio in Louisiana. However, an estimate can be made on the basis of statistical probabilities. Logically, winning an acquittal should be easier under the 9-to-3 system than under the system requiring a unanimous verdict of twelve. Yet the conviction ratio roughly doubles when a majority of nine decides the verdict. About 5.6 percent of all criminal cases tried by juries in the forty-eight states requiring unanimous verdicts end in hung juries.[94] The conviction ratio for a 9-to-3 system is based on the percentage of juries deadlocked under the unanimity rule but which would convict by a majority vote of nine or more. Since the last vote of deadlocked juries is known,[95] the estimate can be made. Louisiana, as Douglas proved in his dissent, would obtain a substantially higher conviction rate, because if the deadlocks under a unanimity rule became verdicts under a 9-to-3 rule, 56 percent of all deadlocks would become verdicts. Of these the prosecution would win forty-four cases for every twelve that it loses.[96] Douglas might have added that that meant there would be verdicts of guilty in 79 percent of the cases that would otherwise be deadlocked by jury splits of 9-to-3, 10-to-2, and 11-to-1 under the unanimity system (44% divided by 56% = 79%).

Another way of asking what the effect of a 9-to-3 system is on defendant's chances is to compare the percentage of jurors he must convince in order to avoid a conviction. Where the rule of unanimity prevails, he needs only one favorable juror out of twelve; under the 9-to-3 system, he must persuade four times as many jurors, or one-third of the jury rather than one-twelfth. These figures lead to the conclusion that the 9-to-3 system yields a substantially higher conviction ratio and substantially fewer hung juries by which a defendant can avoid conviction; therefore, the burden of proof in the 9-to-3 system must be substantially lower than in the unanimous-verdict system.

Johnson's second Fourteenth Amendment argument was that Louisiana's complex system of different jury sizes and different verdict sizes denied him the equal protection of the laws. The state requires unanimous verdicts of twelve in capital cases, unanimous verdicts of five-man juries for crimes that *may* be punished by hard labor, and 9-to-3 verdicts from twelve-man juries for more serious crimes that *must* be punished by hard labor. The Court could find "nothing invidious" in that scheme because it served a "rational purpose"—to "facilitate, expedite, and reduce expense in the administration of criminal justice."[97] *Williams,* White said, held that the states are free to try defendants with juries of fewer than twelve. In *Johnson* the court took for granted the constitutionality of a five-man jury on the ground that six was held constitutional in *Williams.* By the same reasoning, or lack of it, a jury fewer than five would also be constitutional.

Johnson had been tried by a jury of twelve of whom three dissented; he argued that by abolishing the requirement of unanimity, the state disadvantaged him compared with those who are tried for capital crimes or for lesser crimes than his by a five-man jury that must be unanimous. White conceded that Johnson was correct with respect to the trial of capital crimes; in such cases the state made conviction more difficult by requiring unanimity. White also admitted that the state's proof "could perhaps be regarded as more certain if it had convinced all twelve jurors instead of only nine."[98] However qualified, that proposition reads like an admission that the burden of proof is greater under the unanimity rule than under the 9-to-3 rule. Had Johnson's offense been a capital one, the jury verdict of 9-to-3 would have saved him from conviction. That fact, White asserted, did not prove a denial of the equal protection of the laws because capital crimes may be treated differently from others. But Louisiana also tried noncapital crimes differently, utilizing a majority verdict of a twelve-man jury for some and a unanimous verdict of a five-man jury for others. The state, White observed, "obviously intended to vary the difficulty of proving guilt with the gravity of the offense and the severity of the punishment."[99] That implied that a lesser crime required a lower standard for proof of guilt, yet the standard is supposed to be, in all cases, proof of guilt beyond reasonable doubt.

Johnson argued also that the variance in proving the standard of guilt was irrational because the prosecution's task of convincing nine jurors out of twelve in a case of serious crime was easier than convincing a unanimous jury of five in a case involving a lesser crime. White refused to reply to that argument on the incredible ground that Johnson was "simply challenging the judgment of the Louisiana Legislature."[100] Indeed, he was making such a challenge on constitutional grounds, relying on the equal-protection clause of the Fourteenth Amendment. The Court simply dodged a resolution of the issue by asserting that the Louisiana scheme was rational, because the scheme saved time and money. The definitive reply to such a judgment was once made by Black when he said:

Trifling economies . . . have not generally been thought sufficient reason for abandoning our great constitutional safeguards aimed at protecting freedom and other basic human rights of incalculable value. Cheap, easy convictions were not the primary concern of those who adopted the Constitution and the Bill of Rights. Every procedural safeguard they established purposely made it more difficult for the Government to convict those it accused of crimes. On their scale of values justice occupied at least as high a position as economy.[101]

The rational-basis test used by the Court to decide an equal-protection question was appropriate for regulatory legislation of a social or economic character. In such a case the Court presumes the constitutionality of the legislation and requires its attackers to demonstrate that because it serves no rational basis it is unconstitutional. However, the appropriate test for determining the validity of a statute that directly affects fundamental personal rights should be stricter than the rational-basis test. When a state creates special classifications that grade rights like trial by jury, as Louisiana did by its triple jury system, the Court should acutely scrutinize those classifications and demand of the state proof that it has a compelling need for them that can be satisfied in no other way; at the very least the Court should demand proof from the state that its interest in the system of classifying juries outweighs the claim of a constitutional right. All states but two use the unanimity rule for felony trials; consequently, if the Court had held that the equal-protection clause can be satisfied only by the unanimity rule, it would not have imposed a heavy or unusual burden on Louisiana and Oregon, which try felonies by majority verdicts.[102] Use of the rational-basis test in *Johnson* bucked the trend of decision, suggesting that the Nixon Court might no longer use the strict-scrutiny test which imposed on the states the burden of constitutionally justifying legislation that adversely affected the rights of the criminally accused.

That Louisiana's jury scheme adversely affected Johnson was indisputable. To escape conviction by hanging the jury he needed four jurors out of twelve on his side. A defendant tried for a lesser offense by a five-man jury operating on the principle of unanimous verdict needed to persuade only one juror. Furthermore, the burden on the prosecution is twice as heavy when it has to convince five jurors out of five than when it must convince only nine out of twelve.[103] The prosecution has still another advantage when confronting a jury of twelve that decides by a majority of nine: There is less chance of having to cope with jurors who represent a minority viewpoint which, if sympathetic to the defendant, has the highest standard of proof. If, for example, that minority constitutes 10 percent of the population, of every 100 jurors selected at random, 44 of every 100 five-man juries will have a minority representative compared to 72 of every 100 twelve-man juries.[104]

But the prosecution can virtually ignore three members of the twelve-man jury and still win. Only 11 of every 100 twelve-man juries will have as many as three minority representatives, and they can be ignored, but 44 of every 100 five-man juries will have a minority representative who cannot be ignored.[105]

From any standpoint there is nothing rational in a complex jury scheme that makes the prosecution's burden of proof easier in cases where the defendant is subject to heavier punishment. The Court's unreasoned *ipse dixit* that Louisiana's scheme did not violate the equal-protection clause was, in White's language, not persuasive.

Under the Sixth Amendment

Nor was White's opinion in the companion case, *Apodaca* v. *Oregon,*[106] any more persuasive. Oregon tries felonies by a twelve-man jury which decides verdicts by a majority of not less than ten. Apodaca was convicted under the ten-man majority system after the Court in 1968 had extended the Sixth Amendment's guarantee of trial by jury to the states. That decision meant that the federal standard of trial by jury became the standard for the states. Since federal juries must return unanimous verdicts, the question in *Apodaca* was whether Oregon's majority-jury verdicts violated the Sixth Amendment.

Apodaca was the case in which the Court nearly ruled that the Sixth Amendment does not require unanimous verdicts even in federal trials. White, Burger, Blackmun, and Rehnquist would have so ruled. In their view the requirement of unanimity "was not of constitutional stature,"[107] and on the settled principle that the same standard applies to both United States and state courts, they supported the constitutionality of Oregon's majority-verdict system. The four dissenters in *Johnson*—Douglas, Stewart, Brennan, and Marshall—also followed the same-standard principle, but they believed that because the Sixth Amendment embodies the requirement of unanimous jury verdicts, no state can permit a majority verdict. Thus, eight members of the Court supported the same-standard principle, but they divided 4-to-4 on whether a majority or a unanimous verdict should constitute the standard.

Powell was the decisive man, and his opinion was odd as well as decisive. He believed that, on the basis of history and precedent, the Sixth Amendment requires a unanimous jury verdict to convict in a federal criminal trial, and he alone believed that the Fourteenth Amendment's incorporation of the Sixth Amendment's right to trial by jury did not mean that the states must provide jury trials that are the same in all respects as federal jury trials. In the 1968 opinion extending the Sixth Amendment to the states, Powell found nothing that required the same standard for the size of the jury or for the unanimity of the verdict. Thus, Powell concurred separately with the Douglas wing to save the unanimous verdict in federal criminal trials, and he concurred separately with the White wing to allow majority verdicts for states wanting them.

White's opinion for a four-man plurality was similar to his opinion in *Williams*. He said that the requirement of unanimity, like the twelve-man jury, dated back to the Middle Ages and had become an accepted rule at the time of the adoption of the Constitution, but that did not mean that the Constitution preserved the unanimity rule. The Sixth Amendment as originally proposed referred to "the requisite of unanimity," but the final draft omitted this reference, proving either that the framers thought it to be superfluous, because unanimity was implicit in the very concept of a jury, or that the deletion had "some substantive effect," as White said.[108] He chose to believe the latter interpretation and claimed that the framers explicitly rejected unanimity, preferring instead to leave such specification to the future. That conclusion was unhistorical. The purpose of the Sixth Amendment was to bind the federal government to the system of trial by jury that was traditional and familiar. Majority verdicts were unknown in criminal trials when the Sixth Amendment was adopted. The states would never have ratified it if there had been a suspicion that it did not mean a jury trial by a jury which decided its verdicts unanimously.

White then turned to a functional interpretation of trial by jury to decide whether the jury in contemporary society must be bound by the rule of unanimity. He found that the jury served a single function: It interposed the common-sense judgment of a group of laymen between the accused and the state which accused him.

"A requirement of unanimity, however, does not materially contribute to the exercise of this commonsense judgment."[109] Relying
on *Williams,* White reasoned that a jury will come to its judgment,
thus fulfilling its function, as long as it "consists of a group of
laymen representative of a cross section of the community who
have the duty and the opportunity to deliberate, free from outside
attempts at intimidation, on the question of a defendant's guilt."[110]
Thus, from a functional viewpoint, there was "no difference" between juries that decided by verdicts of 10-to-2 or 12-to-0. In
either case the defendant is "equally well served" in having the
judgment of his peers interpose between him and the state.

When stating that unanimity is unnecessary for obtaining a jury
verdict, White acknowledged that unanimity would cause juries
to hang in "some" cases where majority verdicts will convict or
acquit. *The American Jury* by Kalven and Zeisel was White's authority for believing that the effect on the defendant would be the
same. Kalven and Zeisel state that when verdicts must be unanimous, "the probability that an acquittal minority will hang the
jury is about as great as that a guilty minority will hang it."[111]
That leaves the impression, on which White capitalized, that
dumping the unanimity rule would not affect the conviction ratio.
Clearly, however, the data in *The American Jury* proves the in-
validity of that impression, because the conviction ratio does significantly change. Kalven and Zeisel meant only that the chances
that a minority favoring acquittal will finally agree with a majority
favoring conviction are about the same as the chances that a minority favoring conviction will finally agree with a majority favoring acquittal. Kalven and Zeisel did not mean that minorities
favoring acquittal hang juries as often as minorities favoring conviction. Their data establishes the opposite, as Douglas so effectively demonstrated in a dissent that makes one wonder whether
the four-member plurality cared at all for the integrity of their
argument. Analyzing the statistics on juries that deadlock under
the unanimity requirement, Douglas proved that in Oregon, where
the 10-to-2 verdict prevailed, the conviction rate would more than
double the national average.

The disadvantage to defendants and the benefits to the prosecution in Oregon may be stated in another way. Of the cases that

would be deadlocked by jury votes of 11-to-1 and 10-to-2 under the unanimity rule, 42 percent would be decided in Oregon. Of these, 81 percent would be verdicts of guilty and only 19 percent verdicts of acquittal.[112] These figures vividly indicate that the burden of proof diminishes when the unanimity rule is abandoned. The fact that the defendant needs to convince three jurors instead of just one to escape conviction is an additional indication. A verdict of 10-to-2 may acquit as well as convict, and winning ten jurors should be easier than winning all twelve. But, as Douglas said, although a statute authorizing a majority verdict appears to be deceptively neutral, "the use of the nonunanimous jury stacks the truth-determining process against the accused."[113]

The deliberation by the jury changes character, too. Douglas stated, "Human experience teaches that polite and academic conversation is no substitute for the earnest and robust argument necessary to reach unanimity. As mentioned earlier, in Apodaca's case, whatever courtesy dialogue transpired could not have lasted more than 41 minutes."[114] Where the unanimity rule prevails, only about 2 percent of all cases are deadlocked by votes of 10-to-2 and 11-to-1. In fact, 25 percent are decided in Oregon by such votes.[115] That does not mean that if Oregon switched to the unanimity rule juries would be deadlocked in 25 percent of the cases. Deliberations would take longer to arrive at unanimously, and if the national average prevailed, only 5.6 percent of juries would deadlock.

Even if White had been correct in the careless assumption on which he founded his opinion, that majority verdicts benefit the prosecution and the defense equally, Apodaca was entitled to individual consideration. White seems to have believed that the statistics showed generally that the number of acquittals and convictions by nonunanimous juries had the same ratio as in the verdicts of unanimous juries. Apodaca sought, however, to prove that Oregon's system disadvantaged him personally.

Apodaca's chief argument was that the Sixth Amendment's guarantee of trial by jury, which extended to the states "by virtue of the Due Process Clause of the Fourteenth Amendment," required a unanimous jury verdict in order to give substance to the reasonable-doubt standard. White curtly dismissed that argument as groundless, because "the Sixth Amendment itself has never been held to require proof beyond a reasonable doubt in criminal cases."[116] The standard of reasonable doubt, he observed, developed separately from both the concept of a jury and the rule of unanimity. "The reasonable doubt argument is rooted, in effect, in due process and has been rejected in Johnson v. Louisiana. . . ."[117] That *Johnson* rejected the reasonable-doubt standard was an extraordinary admission. A critic of that opinion would argue that by permitting majority verdicts, the Court had indeed rejected the standard of reasonable doubt which can subsist only under the unanimous verdict system. In *Johnson* White had insisted that a nine-man verdict did not violate the standard of reasonable doubt required by due process of law. Moreover, in *Apodaca* he acknowledged that the Fourteenth Amendment's due-process clause extended that standard to the states, and the Court had so held in a 1970 opinion that remained unquestioned.[118] Thus White, like Humpty Dumpty, made words mean what he wanted them to mean, transforming the meaning of thoughts. True enough, the Sixth Amendment does not refer to the size of a jury, or to the unanimity rule, or to the standard of reasonable doubt. Nor does it refer to much else that the Court has held it to mean, such as the indigent's right to counsel or to free transcripts. In *Apodaca* the Court saw only the letter of the amendment, not its spirit or its traditional meaning. White's strict construction of the amendment radically transformed it, as Douglas protested. This was a case of strict construction resulting in judicial activism nearly gone berserk. Marshall declared that strict construction here had left only a "skeleton" of the concept of a jury; it was just a cross section of laymen interposed between the accused and his accuser. The same strict construction, Marshall said, "cuts the heart out" of the requirements of reasonable doubt and unanimity.[119]

If literalism must be the rule of the day, and if due process of law is the constitutional buttress for the standard of reasonable doubt, the Fifth Amendment's due-process clause, which is identical to the Fourteenth's, embodies that standard. But there is no need for a case that would require the Court to recognize that the standard applies equally to federal and state criminal trials. White was careless in stating that *Johnson* rejected the reasonable-doubt standard and in leaving the impression that *Apodaca* rejected it too, as he was careless in much else that he said in those opinions. In fact, the Fourteenth Amendment's due-process clause, as *Johnson* confirmed, requires the states to prove guilt beyond a reasonable doubt. The real issue, rather, was whether the standard of reasonable doubt can be enforced only by faithful enforcement of the requirement of unanimous jury verdicts. That issue seemed settled by historical experience with the unanimity rule and the fact that forty-eight states out of the fifty, as well as the United States, require unanimous verdicts in felony trials. Unanimity and proof of guilt beyond reasonable doubt had become locked together by traditional practices; the one was the key to the other. Yet both *Johnson* and *Apodaca* decided otherwise at least for state criminal trials.

White had two other strings to his bow. One was that despite a long line of decisions requiring juries to reflect a cross section of the community, the unanimous verdict is not a necessary precondition for the effective enforcement of the cross-section requirement. The other was that though majority verdicts eliminate many juries that would deadlock under the unanimity rule, there is no dilution of the protection that defendants receive merely because of the disappearance of many hung juries under the majority verdict system. White seemed to stand on firmer ground on the first point. The Constitution forbids the deliberate exclusion of identifiable segments of the community from the lists that provide the names of jurors, but the Constitution does not guarantee to a defendant a right to be tried by a jury which represents some distinctive minority or minority viewpoint. White added with much less validity that the Court could not assume that when a minority happens to be represented on a jury, its viewpoint will not be heard simply because it can be outvoted. "They will be present during all deliberations, and their views will be heard."[120] As in *Johnson,* White refused to believe that a jury would decide its verdict based on prejudice rather than on the evidence, or that a jury would in its deliberations ignore a minority viewpoint that presents a reasonable argument for acquittal. White mistook the appearance for the reality. In Oregon, as in Louisiana, a jury on retiring to the jury room may immediately take a first ballot, and on finding the requisite majority to decide the verdict, may return that verdict without deliberation. Nothing in the laws of either state prevents that from happening.

Notwithstanding the validity of White's argument that no one has a constitutional right to be tried by a jury on which a particular minority is represented, one does have a right to be tried by a jury whose representative character has not been diminished in practice as well as in appearance. A twelve-man jury is as externally representative when it decides by a verdict of nine or ten as by a verdict of twelve. But reducing the number required for a verdict is, as Zeisel said, "reduction with a vengeance, for a majority verdict is far more effective in nullifying the potency of minority viewpoints than is the outright reduction of the jury to a size equivalent to the majority that is allowed to agree on a verdict."[121] When ten can decide the verdict, the prosecution can disregard a hypothetical minority of 10 percent of the population in all but 11 percent of the cases, and if nine can decide the verdict, as in Louisiana, the prosecution must cope with that minority in only 2.6 percent of the cases, the number in which four minority representatives will turn up every 100 times.[122] White's representative cross section of the community is only cosmetically representative where majority verdicts supplant unanimous ones.

The representative character of the jury is one of the three features that White claimed a jury must possess in order to fulfill its function as the fact-finder interposed between the accuser and the accused. Another feature was freedom from intimidation. But that speaks to an unreal problem. A juror who is bribed or frightened cannot sway the verdict; he can only deadlock the jury. None of the hung juries studied by Kalven and Zeisel suggested that juries deadlocked for suspicious reasons.[123] The remaining indispensable feature of the jury by White's standards is deliberativeness. Douglas effectively revealed the unsubstantiality of White's faith in the majority-verdict jury. The views of a minority can be overridden by the majority if there is no need to consider them. No safeguard like the rule of unanimity guarantees the duty of deliberating when the majority may summarily disregard a minority to reach its verdict.

Stewart, who like Douglas was joined by the other dissenters, reinforced Douglas's points. Supporting the requirement of unanimity, Stewart contended that it provided the one rule that can insure "a constitutionally valid verdict," because unanimity alone insured that a jury must deliberate and consider the views of dissenters before a verdict can be reached. Under the 9-to-3 or 10-to-2 systems, such deliberation would be necessary only in the very few cases where the division of the jury threatens to hang it. "Under today's judgment, nine [or ten, in Oregon] can simply ignore the views of their fellow panel members of a different race or class."[124] They can also ignore the views of a juror with a different viewpoint, as Marshall pointed out. Unlike White, Stewart believed that the vital functions of a jury cannot be discharged except by adherence to the unanimity rule which served to "minimize the potential bigotry of those who might convict on inadequate evidence, or acquit when evidence of guilt was clear."[125] The Court, Stewart said with accuracy that was devastating— though White did not see the need of a rejoinder—"has never before been so impervious to reality" about the possibility of jury irregularity or misconduct.[126]

Many cases showed that juries can act improperly. That is why, said Stewart, the Constitution requires a change of venue—relocating a trial—when a local jury may be inflamed by bias. That is why the Constitution demands protection against press coverage or influence by court officers that might prejudice a jury. That juries cannot always be trusted is also the reason for excluding certain evidence, like involuntary confessions, which might prejudice the jury despite cautionary warnings of the trial judge.

In sum, Stewart's opinion reflected the wisdom of traditional learning about jury behavior. More than a century ago an authority on juries commented:

> One advantage resulting from the rule [of unanimity] no doubt is that if any one juror dissents from the rest, his opinion and reasons must be heard and considered by them. They can not treat these with contempt or indifference, for he has an absolute veto upon their verdict, and they must convince him or yield themselves, unless they are prepared to be discharged without delivering any verdict at all. This furnishes a safeguard against precipitancy, and insures a full

and adequate discussion of every question which can fairly admit of doubt.[127]

Another old authority declared:

> If it be said that the majority should be allowed to rule . . . because their superior numbers furnish a *probability* that they are in the right, one answer is, that the lives, liberties, and properties of men are too valuable . . . to justify the destruction of them by their fellow-men on a mere balancing of probabilities, *or on any ground whatever short of certainty beyond a reasonable doubt.*[128]

Before *Williams,* the six-man jury case, the Court had explicitly and repeatedly rejected the concept that the Fourteenth Amendment applies to the states only a "watered-down" version of the guarantees of the Bill of Rights. In 1968, when White delivered the opinion of the Court extending the Sixth Amendment to the states, he summarized the then prevailing view:

> I am not bothered by the argument that applying the Bill of Rights to the States "according to the same standards that protect those personal rights against federal encroachment," interferes with our concept of federalism in that it may prevent States from trying novel social and economic experiments. I have never believed that under the guise of federalism the States should be able to experiment with the protections afforded our citizens through the Bill of Rights.[129]

In his concurring opinion in *Johnson-Apodaca,* Powell explicitly adopted the discredited view when he said that nonunanimous jury verdicts "reflect a legitimate basis for experimentation and deviation from the federal blueprint."[130] The result reached by the wing of the Court for which White was the spokesman reversed the trend of decision by the Warren Court during the 1960s by applying a watered-down version of the Sixth Amendment to the states. Douglas emphasized that point in his dissent. Moreover, nonunanimous jury verdicts particularly damage public confidence in the moral force of the criminal law and in the verdicts themselves. Several years before *Apodaca,* the *Oregon Law Review* evaluated the 10-to-2 verdict system and concluded that it led to the conviction of defendants, "some of them undoubtedly innocent," who would not have been convicted under a requirement of unanimity.[131] That concisely summarized the matter.

Williams, Johnson, and *Apodaca* are pro-prosecution decisions. Trial by a jury of fewer than twelve or by a jury that reaches majority verdicts increases the chances of conviction and reduces the burden of the prosecution. By strengthening the prosecution's chances at the trial stage of a case, these decisions also put the prosecution into a position to ride booted and spurred on accused persons during the pretrial plea-bargaining stage. The pressures on the innocent to plead guilty are therefore greater than in twelve-man, unanimous jury systems.

Given the Court's stripped-down functional approach to what constitutes a jury, there is a possibility, though an unlikely one, that the Court may in the future approve of verdicts reached by lesser majorities and smaller juries than were given "constitutional stature" in these cases. Approval of the six-man jury in *Williams* yielded easily to approval of a five-man jury in *Johnson.* The Court did not find any significance in a jury of five or six other than that it would be large enough to discharge its function. There was no rationale that defined the irreducible size of the jury. Similarly, the Court did not find any special significance in a verdict by a nine-man majority other than that it showed that a "heavy" or "substantial" majority of the jury had been convinced of guilt. The Court did not even say that such a majority was constitutionally required, nor did it define such a majority. That was the reason why Blackmun added a very brief opinion of his own in *Johnson,* saying that while he approved of the 9-to-3 system, a 7-to-5 one "would afford me great difficulty."[132] Blackmun phrased his point in a way that suggested that he would accept a verdict of 8-to-4, and there is nothing in the White or Powell opinions to indicate their disagreement. Neither *Johnson* nor *Apodaca* established a rational standard for the irreducible size of a majority verdict. When the twelve-man unanimous jury verdict is abandoned, where is the stopping point? A 2-to-1 majority on a jury of three represents the same ratio as an 8-to-4 majority on a jury of twelve. No state is likely to establish three-man juries that decide by majority verdicts, but the nearly standardless opinions of the Court do not pose any constitutional barriers to such a development. The title of Zeisel's article, ". . . And Then There Were None,"[133] suggests that the jury-enfeebling measures sustained by the Court point criminal juries in the direction followed by the ten little Indians. If the Court's opinions were not so badly reasoned, its results might be more acceptable on constitutional grounds. The opinions are not acceptable on intellectual, statistical, or any other grounds. Douglas best explained *Johnson* and *Apodaca* when he said they reflected a law-and-order judicial mood.

JUVENILE PROCEEDINGS

In 1971 in *McKeiver* v. *Pennsylvania*, the Court held that due process of law does not mandate trial by jury in state juvenile proceedings.[134] Until 1967 juvenile offenders had been subject to a special species of law, as if the writ of the Constitution did not penetrate the doors of the juvenile courts. In the *Gault* case of 1967 the Warren Court began the "constitutional domestication" of that special species of law,[135] perhaps the Warren Court's most commendable accomplishment in the field of criminal justice. In 1970 the Court augmented that reform.[136] The sweeping revision of state criminal-justice systems which the Court instituted on a case-by-case basis during the decade of the 1960s seemed scheduled for application to juvenile-delinquency proceedings. But, in 1971 *McKeiver* aborted that movement. The problem of coping with juvenile offenders thus reverted back to the states.

Until the beginning of this century the criminal law treated minors who broke the law as adults. Then, the states dazzled the imagination by establishing a radical new field of juvenile law and procedure. Humanitarian advocates of change backed the passage of legislation in state after state which created separate juvenile courts unencumbered by traditional criminal procedures and rules of evidence. The new theory was that the state, as the benevolent parent-custodion of wayward youth, should be free to administer justice for the purpose of individual rehabilitation rather than deterrence and punishment. With the salvation of the child as their foremost objective, the new juvenile courts became a substitute for the criminal courts, now reserved for adults. Because the juvenile proceeding was not intended to be an adversary criminal prosecution, the states exempted juvenile courts from the rigors and severities of the criminal-justice system and from all constitutional requirements that attached to criminal prosecutions. The judge of the juvenile court, like Andy Hardy's father, was supposed to be the wise and firm but friendly parental figure who doffed his forbidding black robe and came off his bench to sit at a table next to the youngster in trouble, ready if necessary to place a comforting arm around him. These reformers of three-quarters of a century ago understood that environmental problems beyond their immediate control caused delinquency. They eliminated trial by jury, representation by counsel, public trials, the stigma of a guilty verdict, the strict rules of evidence, and the other trappings of a criminal case. Informality, speedy action, flexibility, and judicial discretion characterized the new proceedings. Psychology and social work supplemented law. Probation and paternalistic corrective institutions replaced prisons—all to serve the child's needs and re-educate him as a useful citizen of society.[137] The "highest motives and most enlightened impulses led to a peculiar system for juveniles, unknown to our law in any comparable context."[138] The system probably worked well enough for a time, but by the third quarter of the twentieth century it had become a tragic failure.

In the *Gault* case of 1967, for the first time the Supreme Court confronted an issue arising from juvenile-delinquency proceedings and decided it on constitutional grounds. The treatment of juvenile offenders had so greatly degenerated that the Court felt compelled to say, "Under our Constitution, the condition of being a boy does not justify a kangaroo court."[139] Juveniles who were pronounced "delinquents" received neither the protections constitutionally guaranteed to adults nor the special solicitous care intended for children. Juvenile justice had come to mean in far too many cases a hasty trial before an arbitrary or untrained juvenile court judge who spent on the average about fifteen minutes for a hearing that could result in incarceration until the offender was twenty-one, stigmatizing him as a criminal in virtually the same way as if he had been an adult.[140] Discretionary procedure turned out to be no adequate substitute for due process of law and no guarantor of fairness or accuracy in findings of fact. In *Gault,* the Court quoted Roscoe Pound's remark that the "powers of the Star Chamber were a trifle in comparison with those of our juvenile courts."[141]

Gault was fifteen at the time of his appearance before a juvenile court for having made a lewd phone call. For the same offense an adult in his state faced a maximum sentence of a $50 fine or imprisonment for two months. Gault's sentence was six years. On finding that a juvenile proceeding is comparable in seriousness to a felony prosecution, the Court required that juvenile proceedings must guarantee the specific due-process rights that the juvenile court had denied to Gault: The delinquent who faces deprivation of liberty must have adequate and timely notice of the charges against him, the right to be represented by counsel with the assurance that counsel will be appointed for indigents, the right against compulsory self-incrimination, and the right to confront and cross-examine prosecution witnesses.

The Court decided *Gault* in the same year in which the President's Commission on Law Enforcement and the Administration of Justice published a Task Force Report on *Juvenile Delinquency and Youth Crime,* a devastating commentary on the failures of the juvenile system. Many juvenile judges had proved to be unfit for their demanding roles as beneficent father figures familiar with sociology and psychiatry as well as law. One-fifth were not members of the legal profession; one-fifth had no college education at all; and one-half had never completed their undergraduate education.[142] The Task Force Report said:

> What emerges, then, is this: In theory the juvenile court was to be helpful and rehabilitative rather than punitive. In fact the distinction often disappears, not only because of the absence of facilities and personnel but also because of the limits of knowledge and technique. In theory the court's action was to affix no stigmatizing label. In fact a delinquent is generally viewed by employers, schools, the armed services—by society generally—as a criminal. In theory the court was to treat children guilty of criminal acts in noncriminal ways. In fact it labels truants and runaways as junior criminals.
>
> In theory the court's operations could justifiably be informal, its findings and decisions made without observing ordinary procedural safeguards, because it would act only in the best interest of the child. In fact it frequently does nothing more nor less than deprive a child of liberty without due process of law—knowing not what else to do and needing, whether admittedly or not, to act in the community's interest even more imperatively than the child's. In theory it was to exercise its protective powers to bring an errant child back into the

fold. In fact there is increasing reason to believe that its intervention reinforces the juvenile's unlawful impulses. In theory it was to concentrate on each case the best of current social science learning. In fact it has often become a vested interest in its turn, loathe to cooperate with innovative programs or avail itself of forward-looking methods.[143]

Although juvenile delinquents who were sentenced to corrective institutions were supposed to be sent to special juvenile institutions, more than 100,000 were confined in adult institutions—probably because there are not enough separate facilities for juveniles.[144] The juvenile institutions are too often overcrowded, understaffed, high-security jails for young criminals, providing little education, vocational training, counseling, or job placement.[145] *Gault* did not address itself to most of these matters; it dealt only with some of the requirements of due process of law that are necessary from arrest through trial to insure fairness.

Winship, which the Court decided in 1970, was the case of a twelve-year-old thief who had been tried for violation of the criminal law and after a finding of guilt on the basis of a preponderance of the evidence had been confined for a period of not less than eighteen months nor more than six years. The Court held that due process of law demands proof of guilt beyond a reasonable doubt even in delinquency proceedings. As in *Gault,* the Court asserted that respect for the due-process rights of minors would not impair the fact-finding process or derogate from the express policies of juvenile courts to act informally, speedily, and flexibly, or to differentiate a finding of delinquency from a criminal conviction that would result in a loss of civil rights, or to dispose of cases with a view toward rehabilitation rather than punishment, or to confine the offender if necessary in an appropriate institution.[146]

Three members of the Court, including the new Chief Justice, dissented in *Winship.* Burger's opinion reflected an animosity toward *Gault* and an unrealistic attitude toward juvenile justice that was incredible in view of the Task Force Report of three years earlier. He clung to the chimerical ideals of the juvenile system which experience had shown to have resulted in failure. The original concept of the system, Burger said, was "to provide a benevolent and less formal means" than the criminal courts for treating the "often sensitive problems of youthful offenders." Burger believed that there was nothing inherently wrong with the system. Its failures, he believed, resulted from inadequate staffing and facilities. He found nothing wrong with the procedure of convicting a juvenile on proof of guilt short of proof beyond reasonable doubt. He opposed "further strait-jacketing of an already overly-restricted system." What it needed, he said was fewer, not more, of "the trappings of legal procedure and judicial formalism." Burger concluded:

> My hope is that today's decision will not spell the end of a generously conceived program of compassionate treatment intended to mitigate the rigors and trauma of exposing youthful offenders to a traditional criminal court; each step we take turns the clock back to the pre-juvenile court era. I cannot regard it as a manifestation of progress to transform juvenile courts into criminal courts, which is what we are well on the way to accomplishing.[147]

Burger's view triumphed a year later when the Court decided two cases which it consolidated as one. They were *McKeiver* v. *Pennsylvania* and *In re Burrus*.[148] McKeiver was a member of a gang of teen-agers who stole twenty-five cents from some other teen-agers; he was convicted for robbery, larceny, and receiving stolen goods. Burrus was a black girl with a group of others engaged in a peaceable demonstration on a public road to protest against discriminatory school assignments. She was convicted for willfully impeding traffic. Both McKeiver and Burrus had been tried by juvenile courts which denied their requests for trial by jury. Although each was placed on probation, each had faced a possible incarceration for five years.

In 1968 the Court had incorporated the Sixth Amendment's right to trial by jury within the Fourteenth Amendment's due-process clause, and in 1970 the Court held that the right to trial by jury applies to any offense punishable by imprisonment for over six months.[149] But those cases dealt with criminal prosecutions of adult offenders. By votes of 6-to-3 in McKeiver's case and 5-to-4 in Burrus's, the Court sustained their convictions, holding that due process of law does not extend to juvenile proceedings the right to a jury trial.

The opinion of the Court spoke for only a plurality of four—Blackmun, the spokesman, Burger, Stewart, and White. Harlan delivered a terse concurring opinion. Like Douglas, Black, and Marshall, who dissented, Harlan believed that juvenile-delinquency proceedings had become in many crucial respects like criminal trials. Given the fact that adults accused of crime must be tried by a jury, except in petty cases, Harlan declared that juveniles should be entitled to the same right "so long as juvenile delinquency systems are not restructured to fit their original purpose."[150] Yet he concurred with the plurality judgment on the perverse ground that he could not accept the precedent, from which he had dissented, that extended the right to trial by jury to the states.[151] Harlan had the right reason for voting in favor of trial by jury, yet refused to do so on the uncharacteristic ground that he could not accept the controlling precedent.

Brennan believed that trial by a juvenile-court judge sitting without a jury was potentially dangerous in the absence of some check on the judge's conduct that served the same purpose of a jury trial. He found that check in the element of publicity. In Pennsylvania, where McKeiver was tried, there was no bar to the presence of the public or the press at a delinquency proceeding. That fact satisfied Brennan's demand for a means of focusing public attention upon the facts of the case and exposing improper judicial behavior. Accordingly, he voted to affirm McKeiver's conviction. In Burrus's case, however, he voted to reverse because North Carolina banned the general public from the hearing, thus allowing no adequate substitute for the checking effect of trial by jury. In the absence of publicity there might be a misuse of judicial authority, especially, as Brennan pointed out, in a case involving racial protests. The trouble with Brennan's position was that most delinquency proceedings are conducted in near secrecy, as far as the general public is concerned, in order to protect the child from public condemnation. Furthermore, publicity would be an effective deterrent against judicial misconduct, if at all, only in the few sensational cases that attracted the public and the press. The routine juvenile case, like a mugging or a car theft, would attract no one. Brennan had fastened upon the wrong device to insure the fairness required by due process of law.

Blackmun, speaking for the plurality, distinguished the precedent because he could not accept the evidence. Like Burger's dissent in *Winship,* Blackmun's opinion was founded on the premise that the juvenile system is fundamentally sound as well as enlightened; consequently, the Court should not abandon hope for its improvement or alter its character. Although the Task Force Report of 1967 found that the system was inherently defective, Blackmun hoped that money spent the right way might be the remedy. The Task Force Report explicitly declared that greater resources for additional staffing and facilities could not cure its defects because, "There are problems that go much deeper. The failure of the juvenile court to fulfill its rehabilitative and preventative promise stems in important measure from a grossly overoptimistic view of what is known about the phenomenon of juvenile criminality and of what even a fully equipped juvenile court could do about it."[152] Blackmun fully acknowledged the failures of the juvenile system but could not bring himself to believe that they are inherent. He noted that the Task Force Report did not recommend trial by jury for juvenile offenders or abandonment of the system. He spoke of it as offering "the idealistic prospect of an intimate, informal protective proceeding."[153] Stressing its "high promise," he alleged that its defects were merely the result of inadequate resources. "We are reluctant," Blackmun declared, "to disallow the States to experiment further and to seek in new and different ways the elusive answers to the problems of the young, and we feel that we would be impeding that experimentation by imposing the jury trial."[154]

That was the voice of goodwill, not of reason. Blackmun ignored Harlan's contention, echoed by the dissenters, that juvenile-court proceedings are substantially criminal in character and, if principles are consistent, should provide trial by jury until sufficiently reformed to serve the original purposes of the system. Blackmun observed that the precedent extending the Sixth Amendment to the states had not held juvenile proceedings to be criminal prosecutions within the meaning and reach of that amendment, but he failed to explain how fundamental fairness, which due process of law requires, is assured by the juvenile system.

Blackmun found significant differences between the juvenile

system and the regular criminal courts. They do in fact differ both in theory and in practice, but the practice is checkered. When the ideal is approached, informality and discretion lead to paternal understanding, yet there is no proof that understanding in turn leads to rehabilitation. Trials by juvenile-court judges also show summary hearings tinged by judicial bias, mistake, or caprice. At the least the proceedings create a strong disposition to prejudgment. The judge has pretrial access to files showing the juvenile's prior record; there are repeated reappearances of the same probation officers, police, and social workers as witnesses; the judge becomes hardened by exposure to hundreds of similar cases. Blackmun regarded this view of the matter as ignoring "every aspect of fairness, of concern, of sympathy, and of paternal attention that the juvenile court system contemplates."[155] He offered not a bit of proof that contemplation matched reality in most cases, if in any. He ignored the teaching of *Gault* that the benefits of the system should be "candidly appraised," and the warning of the Court on that occasion, "Neither sentiment nor folklore should cause us to shut our eyes. . . ."[156]

Blackmun opened his eyes to look at the Task Force Report, then shut them as if in disbelief of the facts that spoiled the theory. He refused to confront the rationale of *Gault* that juvenile proceedings are essentially criminal, not warranting a difference in treatment. Blackmun emphasized that they ought not to be. He used idealism like a broom to sweep away the defects of the system. If too many juvenile judges lack the time, the resources, and the training to fulfill the objectives of the system, and if the extension of due-process rights to accused juveniles need not result in stigmatizing delinquents as criminals, there is no realistic foundation for the holding that the Constitution does not mandate trial by jury in delinquency proceedings. If such proceedings are significantly different from criminal trials, justification for a different trial procedure exists. Whether the significant differences exist depends on whether one sees the glass half empty or half full. If the Court focused on the seriousness of the punishment that can result from an adjudication of guilt, theory and practice require trial by jury in juvenile proceedings. As the dissenters stressed, when the state uses its juvenile courts to prosecute a criminal act, when the issue at the trial is whether the child committed that act, and when the child faces the prospect of confinement for several years until he reaches the age of twenty-one, he should be entitled to the same procedural protections as adults. The delinquency proceeding is itself permeated with characteristics of a criminal prosecution. The due-process clause guarantees trial by jury and prohibits state denial of rights "to any person," not to "any adult person." Douglas noted that juvenile records showing a finding of delinquency, which for all practical purposes is equated by society as a finding of criminality, are available to the police, the armed forces, the FBI, other government agencies, and even to schools and private employers. In practice, juvenile proceedings are scarcely secret even when the press and public are excluded. Aside from the fact that witnesses, social workers, probation officers, lawyers, and police officers are present, there is no confidentiality in the adjudications.

Blackmun himself summarized this argument made by Mc-Keiver's counsel: The delinquency proceeding begins with a document that is like an indictment; the accused is detained in a prison prior to trial; the lawyers engage in plea bargaining and make the usual motions routinely seen in a criminal prosecution; the court in practice follows the usual rules of evidence; the customary defenses are made; the press and public are admitted to the hearing; the delinquent, on a finding of guilt, may be incarcerated in what amounts to a prison until his majority; and, the stigma attached to a verdict of guilt approximates that of an adult criminal proceeding. Having summarized the argument, Blackmun promptly forgot it.

To fasten trial by jury to the juvenile system, he claimed, would tend to "remake the juvenile proceeding into a fully adversary process" and "to place the juvenile squarely in the routine of the criminal process."[157] The traditional delays, formalities, and clamor of the criminal prosecution, said Blackmun, would impair the character of the system and inhibit needed reforms. He failed to substantiate that crucial claim. Instead he said that trial by jury "would not remedy the defects of the system" which "relate to the lack of resources and of dedication rather than to inherent unfairness."[158] Trial by jury, Blackmun insisted, is not even necessary, because a jury is not needed for accurate fact-finding. Juries are not usually used in military trials or in equity cases, or in workmen's compensation, in probate, or in deportation cases, or in cases that may result in punishment for less than six months. Moreover, the Court would not assert that a trial before a judge alone is necessarily unfair. Blackmun's argument still did not explain how a juvenile-delinquency proceeding guaranteed fairness when the basic question is whether the accused has violated a criminal law and the possible punishment is very serious. He did not deny that due process guaranteed fundamental fairness, but claimed that a jury trial is not constitutionally required to insure fundamental fairness because a jury is not necessary for accurate fact-finding. Yet it may be necessary to thwart judicial misconduct.

Blackmun had a severely constricted view of the function of a jury. It exists to do more than determine whether the accused committed the crime charged. Indeed, if a jury is not necessary for accurate fact-finding, then the Court had other reasons in mind when requiring the Sixth Amendment's right to trial by jury in state cases involving serious punishment. Fundamental fairness, however elastic a standard, necessitated a trial by jury as a body of laymen interposed between the accused and his accuser in order to curb judicial prejudice, error, arbitrariness, or other misbehavior. The very presence of a jury helps to preserve impartiality even in fact-finding. A jury is not toughened by exposure to countless similar cases. It is more likely to give serious consideration to the case than the judge, especially when fifteen minutes is about the average time he can devote to a delinquency proceeding. By interposing a neutral force between the judge and the accused, a jury helps to prevent possible discrimination, as was probably inherent in Burrus's case, and the likelihood of a too speedy and perhaps erroneous adjudication. In McKeiver's case, for example, as Blackmun acknowledged, the evidence showed that he was convicted despite the juvenile court's admission that the testimony of two of the witnesses against him was inconsistent and weak.

Contrary to Blackmun, there is at most only slight evidence that a jury trial would impair the unique qualities of a juvenile proceeding. Trial by jury would intensify its already existing adversary nature, but that would be no barrier to achieving the fundamental objectives of the juvenile proceeding. A minority of states permit trial by jury for juveniles without the disastrous consequences predicted by Blackmun. Douglas, dissenting, did what Blackmun failed to do: He evaluated the experience of those ten states and concluded that trial by jury did not derogate from the ideals of the system. The vast majority of juvenile cases, like criminal prosecutions of adults, never go to trial; they are settled at the pretrial stage. Even in large metropolitan areas in the states which permit jury trials for juveniles, the number of juveniles who request and go through with trial by jury is insignificant. There were no more than fifteen jury trials over a period of five and a half years in most jurisdictions, and in the few where there were more than that, there was no suggestion or evidence that juries impeded the system of juvenile justice. Blackmun's fears that granting the right to trial by jury would injure the juvenile system were groundless. If there are delays in the system, the rising incidence of juvenile crime rather than trial by jury is the cause.

As Douglas also showed, jury trials affect only the adjudicatory or fact-finding stage of a juvenile proceeding. From the standpoint of the ideals of the system, the jury could not affect the judge's disposition of a case. A jury at the trial stage would take from the judge the power to sift from the evidence the probable causes of the delinquent's behavior. Nevertheless, the jury has little or no concern for the social, economic, and psychiatric factors per se. All such matters remain within the judge's ken and competence at the point where they determine a sentence that suits the rehabilitative needs of the delinquent. The judge, after a trial by jury, would retain exclusive authority to determine sentence and remedial treatment. The best judge probably knows that his disposition, however well-considered, is only a trained guess. As an expert in the juvenile field has said:

> . . . the failure of the juvenile courts to deliver on their own promises goes back to causes that lie deeper than faulty institutional forms, incompetent and unqualified personnel, and meager resources. It goes back to the fact that, despite the material progress of our knowledge about juvenile delinquency, we simply do not know enough to diagnose, predict, and prescribe for a very large proportion of offenders.

If all our courts and correctional agencies were staffed by Ph.D.'s in clinical psychology and sociology and provided with unlimited resources, we would still not know in many cases—and some would say in most cases—whether the needs of "treatment" would be better served by letting the offender go free or by incarcerating him for two or three years.[159]

In his *Winship* dissent, Burger expressed a desire to mitigate the "trauma of exposing youthful offenders to a traditional criminal court. . . ."[160] Blackmun echoed that view in *McKeiver*. The dissenters saw the matter very differently. Douglas spoke of the trauma that results from exposing minors to the expeditious, informal procedures of the juvenile court. "The fact is," said one juvenile-court judge whom Douglas quoted approvingly, "that the procedures which are now followed in juvenile cases are far more traumatic than the potential experience of a jury trial. . . . To agree that a jury trial would expose a juvenile to a traumatic experience is to lose sight of the real traumatic experience of incarceration without due process. The real traumatic experience is the feeling of being deprived of basic rights."[161] Denying the offender's right to trial by jury also vitiates his plea-bargaining strength.

Blackmun did not trouble to respond to Douglas's argument, which in 1967 in *Gault* had represented a majority view of the Court. *McKeiver* stood for the proposition that "despite disappointments of grave dimensions," as Blackmun said, the juvenile-delinquency proceeding will continue to operate on minimal due-process standards. *McKeiver* short-circuited the expectation that the Court would demand the rights of the accused for juveniles who face the prospect of serious punishment. The Court did not set back the clock to the pre-*Gault* era; it stopped the clock. Model legislative proposals and recommendations of government commissions, to which Blackmun referred, have not been implemented by the states. As a result of *McKeiver,* the states are free to do nothing or to "experiment"—not that jury trial would prevent experimentation. The states can do nothing and perpetuate the failures of the system, safe in the knowledge that the Court will no longer impose the obligation of respecting constitutional rights beyond the requirements of *Gault* and *Winship*.

CHAPTER SIX

The Sixth Amendment: Fair Trial

PROBLEMS OF EVIDENCE

Fair trial, a near synonym for due process of law, is constitutional shorthand for a whole cluster of rights, many of which are enumerated in the Sixth Amendment. Like justice itself, fair trial is a principle of such abstraction, complexity, and subjectivity that a judge can play on it as if it were an accordion to be squeezed and stretched to render whatever meaning he seeks to express. Ultrasophisticated judges have intoxicated themselves into believing that fairness, the core of the principle, lays down an objective standard for their guidance. More literal-minded judges, who claim to eschew any allowance for judicial preference, convince themselves that they are obeying the clear dictates of words on parchment, however nebulous or qualified those words may be.

Whether fairness derives from the text of the Constitution or the conscience of the judge, it nourishes the moral strength of our system of criminal justice. Without fairness, whatever that may mean in a particular case, the sense of injustice is outraged and the system loses the respect which it must have to endure. On behalf of fairness the greater part of the Bill of Rights imposes restraints upon government; the Bill of Rights speaks in the main about the procedural guarantees of the criminally accused. The

310

reason is not that our fundamental law seeks to pamper criminals by breeding technical niceties for their advantage or by multiplying loopholes through which they can escape the consequences of their guilt. The reason, rather, is that because a free society tries to decide questions of guilt or innocence fairly, it requires that those who protect us by bringing criminals to justice must not themselves set an example of lawlessness or commit any act that contaminates the system.

Thus, fair trial embraces numerous rights, some of which, like fair trial itself, are not referred to by name in the Constitution. They are customary rights that represent civilized glosses spun by judges from the principle of fairness. The presumption of innocence and the requirement of proof of guilt beyond reasonable doubt are examples of extraconstitutional principles of fair trial. Each of the rights that the Constitution explicitly recognizes is itself no more than a brief epitome of a principled generality that allows, indeed requires, judicial explication. For example, one of the essential ingredients of fair trial is that no man should be compelled to be a witness against himself in a criminal case. The Supreme Court interprets that principle as applicable to any proceeding, even a civil one, and as applicable in the absence of a criminal accusation. The Constitution states only the epitome. The task of the Court is to say whether it means not only that the police may not beat a confession out of a suspect, but that the prosecution may not even use in evidence a confession that he makes in response to quiet interrogation if he is ignorant of the fact that the law did not require him to answer. The same constitutional principle is the touchstone for holding that the prosecution may not call the jury's attention to the fact that a defendant did not dare take the stand in his own behalf, nor may the prosecution suggest to the jury that his desire to avoid cross-examination permits an inference of guilt. So, too, the right to be assisted by counsel means, by judicial interpretation, that the state must provide counsel for an indigent and that the right extends to an identification at a pretrial lineup if held after formal accusation, but not before then, though even after then the right does not extend to pretrial identification made from photographs.

The Supreme Court carves exquisite distinctions from the principle of fair trial and from the bare bones of principles that are constitutionally explicit but not self-explanatory. Thus, the right of all persons to a jury trial in a criminal prosecution does not exist for juveniles or for adult offenders who are subject to imprisonment for not more than six months. The Court reads into or out of the text pretty much as it wills, guided, of course, by history, precedent, the policies presumably expressed by particular constitutional guarantees, and by society's needs and values as they are understood by the Justices. The Court has acknowledged that it may settle for less than the best. The Constitution, as the Court said, "does not guarantee trial procedures that are the best of all worlds, or that accord with the most enlightened ideas. . . ."[1] "A defendant," the Court has reiterated, "is entitled to a fair trial but not a perfect one."[2] Whatever he gets is mandated by the Court as the oracle of the Constitution, and whatever the Court mandates is determined by the composition of its membership at the moment. Its imprimatur, or denial of it, becomes by the process of judicial exclusion and inclusion on a case-by-case basis another facet of the meaning of fair trial.

The broad issue in a case may be fair trial or due process of law, but its resolution, almost invariably, turns on reference to specific guarantees. If an accused does wish to testify on his own behalf, has he been denied fair trial by a requirement that he must take the stand as the first witness for the defense? If a defendant's cellmate turns out to be a policeman whose undercover task was to solicit incriminating admissions, does that policeman's testimony at the trial rob the proceeding of its essential quality of fairness? Questions such as these, the workaday issues that come before the Court for decision, hinge on the meaning of particular constitutional protections that are facets of fair trial. Two cases of 1972 involving these questions, *Brooks* v. *Tennessee* and *Milton* v. *Wainwright,* are illustrative. In *Brooks,* which seemed to involve a comparatively innocuous practice, a judgment resulted requiring the reversal of a conviction.[3] The spirit of the Warren Court prevailed over the votes of three of the Nixon appointees. In *Milton,* which seemed to involve a deceitful practice, a judgment resulted that the Constitution had not been sullied.[4] White and Powell, who sided with the majority in *Brooks,* switched over to

Burger, Blackmun, and Rehnquist in *Milton* to form a new majority.

Regulating the Accused's Right to Testify

Brooks presented for the Court's review an archaic Tennessee requirement that a defendant wishing to testify "shall do so before any other testimony for the defense is heard. . . ."[5] Brennan, for the Court, ruled that Tennessee had unconstitutionally abridged the Fifth Amendment's right against self-incrimination and the Sixth Amendment's right to counsel. The state's avowed purpose was to promote the cause of truthful testimony. Its theory was that the defendant, who has a right to be present throughout his trial, may otherwise wait till all his witnesses have testified and then tailor his own testimony to accord with theirs. To prevent his perjury the state demanded that if he wished to take the stand, he must do so before any other witnesses on his behalf. The trial court prevented Brooks from testifying because he failed to take his turn first.

Brennan saw in the state's requirement an impermissible burden on the exercise of one's right to remain silent unless he chooses to speak. The choice, Brennan explained, is always a hazardous one, for an individual exposes himself to impeachment and cross-examination if he testifies. He cannot know how effective his witnesses will be until they have actually testified, and therefore he may not know at the very beginning of his defense whether his own testimony will be necessary or even helpful to his cause. The state exacted "a price for his silence by keeping him off the stand entirely unless he chooses to testify first. This, we think, casts a heavy burden on a defendant's otherwise unconditional right not to take the stand."[6] Whether he should testify or whether his case is strong enough without his risking the stand are tactical questions that require the guiding hand of counsel. Tennessee deprived the defendant of that guiding hand by preventing counsel from planning the defense. Stewart joined the holding on the right to counsel only.

Burger and Rehnquist both wrote dissenting opinions, each joining in the other's opinion with the support of Blackmun.

Burger, focusing on the Fifth Amendment issue, claimed that the only burden cast on the defendant was his decision whether to testify at a given point of time. "That the choice might in some cases be easier if made later," said Burger, "is hardly a matter of constitutional dimension."[7] Since Brooks had not taken the stand, Burger noted that he had not been compelled to incriminate himself. No one argued that he had. The argument, rather, was whether the state law chilled his Fifth Amendment right. Burger ignored the fact that the trial court, relying on the state law, denied Brooks's motion, made at the close of the state's case, that he be permitted to testify after other defense witnesses.

Rehnquist, addressing himself to the Sixth Amendment question, also was insensitive to the constitutional claim. He alleged that the Court had elevated defense counsel "to the role of impresario with respect to decisions as to the order in which witnesses shall testify at the trial."[8] Rehnquist sounded as if he were speaking of some other case. Only the testimony of one witness was at issue: the defendant's. "The notion," said Rehnquist, "that the Sixth Amendment allows defense counsel to overrule the trial judge as to the order in which witnesses shall be called stands on its head the traditional understanding of the defendant's right to counsel."[9] That grotesque proposition ignored the fact that state law regulated the timing of defendant's own testimony. Rehnquist could not perceive that the statute raised a constitutional issue with respect to the right to counsel.

The Deceitfully Obtained Confession

Two weeks after *Brooks, Milton v. Wainwright* presented a classic question of criminal law: Can the state use dirty methods to trap a criminal into a confession of guilt? The police arrested Milton on suspicion of murdering his wife. Holding him incommunicado for eighteen days without charging him, they questioned him incessantly until he confessed under the pressure. After he was indicted, he retained a lawyer who advised him not to discuss his case with anyone. On the possibility that his confession could be questioned as involuntary or unreliable, because of the circumstances under which it had been obtained, the police sought to obtain another confession. They planted an officer in Milton's cell, who posed as a fellow prisoner under investigation for murder. The officer ingratiated himself with Milton, "confessed" his own fictitious crime, and got Milton to boast how he had committed his.

At Milton's trial the officer was the state's star witness. His "devastating" testimony about Milton's incriminating story made in the secrecy of the prison cell was repeatedly referred to by the prosecutor. The state also relied on Milton's first confession. After the jury found him guilty, the judge sentenced him to life imprisonment.

Fourteen years later Milton's case came before the Supreme Court for review on habeas corpus. By that time he had lost his appeals challenging his preindictment confession. The constitutional issue before the Supreme Court was whether the use of his unsuspecting postindictment confession violated his right to the assistance of counsel. Burger, for a bare majority of the Court, ruled against Milton. The Chief Justice elaborately described the crime and the trial, though he neglected to mention the circumstances surrounding the first confession. Stewart, dissenting, said that it was "tainted by the indicia of unreliability,"[10] but neither its probative value nor its involuntary character was before the Court. The only confession at issue was the one made by Milton out of the presence of his counsel to the police officer posing as his confidential cellmate. Burger professed that the reasons for assigning that officer to his undercover duty were "not altogether clear."

The descriptive character of Burger's opinion far exceeded his analysis of the constitutional issue. Burger noted in closing that the writ of habeas corpus had limited scope; the federal courts, he said, do not sit to retry state cases "but rather to review for violation of federal constitutional standards."[11] In doing so, he added, the Court could not close its eyes to the "overwhelming evidence of guilt" which he had vividly described. He used one sentence to dispose of those federal constitutional standards which raised the question of fair trial: "Assuming *arguendo* [for the sake of argument] that the challenged testimony should have been excluded, the record clearly reveals that any error in its admission was harmless beyond a reasonable doubt."[12] The reason for this astounding assertion was that the state had presented other proof of guilt that was "overwhelming"—the initial confession plus some corroboration in the form of circumstantial evidence. At no point did Burger discuss Milton's claim that he had been denied a fair trial because he had been tricked into a confession out of the presence of counsel in violation of his Sixth Amendment right. Burger's opinion was not badly reasoned; it was simply not reasoned. The reference to "harmless error" concluded judgment, and all the remaining verbiage summarized the facts.

Stewart, joined by Douglas, Brennan, and Marshall, dissented. In 1964 Stewart had written the opinion of the Court in *Massiah* v. *United States*.[13] In that case the police, with the cooperation of a codefendant who turned state's evidence, bugged his car, listened to his conversations with Massiah, and testified to Massiah's incriminating statements. The Court held that after a defendant has been indicted, the use of his incriminating statements that have been obtained without the protection afforded by the presence of counsel contravenes the basic dictates of fairness in the conduct of a criminal prosecution and violates the right to counsel. *Massiah* rested on *Powell* v. *Alabama,* a 1932 case which Stewart in *Massiah* called "one of the truly landmark constitutional decisions of this Court."[14] Under the guise of finding "harmless error," said Stewart in *Milton,* the Court now turned its back on the great precedent and on *Massiah. Powell* v. *Alabama* guaranteed the right to the assistance of counsel at every critical stage of a prosecution. In *Milton* the surreptitious interrogation of the defendant in the absence of his counsel, said Stewart, violated the most rudimentary constitutional principles requiring that he be afforded the "full and effective assistance of counsel." The police tactic employed here destroyed that assistance. Elemental concepts of due process of law contemplated that an indictment be followed by a public trial protected by all procedural safeguards. A Constitution guaranteeing the aid of counsel at such a trial, Stewart insisted, "could surely vouchsafe no less to an indicted defendant interrogated by the police in a completely extrajudicial proceeding."[15]

Stewart could find no basis for the Court's holding that the evidence given by the officer who testified to Milton's in-cell confession was "harmless error." An error in admitting relevant evidence which can adversely influence a jury cannot be harmless, Stewart observed; he added that on the question whether a jury might have been adversely influenced, the state must "prove beyond a reasonable doubt that the error complained of did not contribute to the verdict obtained."[16] Surely, there was at least a reasonable doubt whether the introduction of the testimony in question did not contribute to the verdict. He concluded, accurately, that the Court had refused to rule on the constitutional question presented by the case. "That question," he declared, was "whether the great constitutional lesson of *Powell* v. *Alabama* is to be ignored."[17] Burger had not even alluded to *Powell,* nor had he bothered to distinguish *Massiah.* His opinion for the Court, having evaded the Sixth Amendment fair-trial issue, read like a judgment that an obviously guilty man must not benefit from his constitutional rights if the result would question whether he had received a fair trial.

Brooks dealt with the exclusion of evidence—the testimony of the defendant who could not take the stand when he pleased; *Milton* dealt with the admissibility of evidence—the testimony of the officer who covertly obtained the confession. A large percentage of the criminal-justice cases decided by the Supreme Court deal in one way or another with the admissibility or exclusion of evidence. Such cases may be classified as falling within the province of the Fourth Amendment if the question relates to evidence obtained by an allegedly unreasonable search and seizure, or within the province of the Fifth Amendment if the question relates to evidence allegedly obtained by compulsion of self-incriminatory testimony, or within the province of the Sixth Amendment if the question relates to evidence obtained against an accused who allegedly has not received the benefit of counsel. All such cases involve the principle of fair trial. The rules governing the admission and exclusion of evidence are basic to that principle. Many fair-trial cases turn on the law of evidence without reference to a specific constitutional guarantee other than the one that is the most comprehensive and vague of them all—due process of law. *Moore* v. *Illinois,* which the Court decided at the same time as *Brooks* and *Milton,* is an example.[18]

Prosecutorial Disclosure

Moore, which grew out of a prosecution for murder, put the question whether the state denied the accused a fair trial by failing to disclose to him certain evidence that could have been of assistance to his case. A just cause is not furthered by corrupting the adversary process. If, for example, the state rigs the evidence against the accused by presenting testimony known to be perjured, there is obviously a denial of fair trial. Our system of criminal justice suffers whenever a court is deceived and a defendant, even a guilty one, is unfairly convicted. The suppression of evidence by the state can have the same result. In criminal cases society marshals its investigative and prosecutorial forces against the defendant. With rare exceptions, even defendants of unlimited means cannot match the state's capacity to investigate a crime and assemble the evidence concerning it. Because the adversary process depends on the ability of each side to present its own evidence and rebut the other's, and, more important, because justice is the objective of a criminal prosecution, fair trial requires that the accused have access to information in the possession of the state that helps his cause. The leading precedent is *Brady* v. *Maryland,* in which the Warren Court held, in 1963, that "the suppression by the prosecution of evidence favorable to an accused upon request violates due process where the evidence is material either to guilt or to punishment, irrespective of the good faith or bad faith of the prosecution."[19]

In Moore's case the prosecution, in response to a pretrial motion by the defense, agreed to disclose all statements made to the police or the prosecutor by persons called to testify at the trial. After his conviction, Moore learned that several items of evidence unknown to him at the time of his trial had not been produced. He claimed that the state's suppression of the evidence that aided his cause deprived him of a fair trial. One piece of undisclosed evidence was a diagram of the scene of the crime, showing the locations of the victim, his killer, and the other persons present. A police officer had drawn the diagram on the back of a statement given by a man who was there. According to the diagram, one of the witnesses who identified Moore as the murderer was seated in a direction opposite to that indicated by him in his trial testimony, and therefore, according to Moore, made his being an eyewitness impossible. The other undisclosed evidence concerned the testimony of a man who claimed that two days after the murder he overheard Moore make an incriminating remark. Moore learned after his trial that the police had convincing proof that the witness misidentified him.

The evidence in the case was so complicated that Blackmun for a five-man majority and Marshall for the four dissenters sharply disagreed about what the facts in the case were as well as about what they proved. Accordingly, Blackmun's cock-certain assertion that the undisclosed evidence could not have helped Moore's case is not persuasive. Indeed, it is disturbing.

Blackmun's opinion purported to follow the precedent of *Brady v. Maryland*, as did Marshall's dissent. "The heart of the holding in *Brady*," said Blackmun, "is the prosecution's suppression of evidence, in the face of a defense production request, where the evidence is favorable to the accused and is material either to guilt or to punishment."[20] In a gratuitous aside, Blackmun added that there is no constitutional requirement that the state must make a complete and detailed account to the defense of all its investigatory work on a case. Such a requirement might be burdensome, but it might aid the cause of justice, a consideration that Blackmun did not evaluate. Nevertheless, Moore had not requested the prosecution to put at his disposal the entire file on his case. Marshall replied to Blackmun, "When the State possesses information that might well exonerate a defendant in a criminal case, it has an affirmative duty to disclose that information. . . . [i]f evidence is clearly relevant and helpful to the defense, it must be disclosed. . . . It is the State that tries a man, and it is the State that must insure that the trial is fair."[21] Blackmun did not contradict those propositions; that he disagreed with them is inconceivable.

His tactic was to claim that the undisclosed evidence was not "material" to Moore's case and therefore would not have affected the outcome. Yet there is no knowing how the jury would have decided if Moore had had the means of impeaching the testimony of an eyewitness as well as the testimony of the witness who misidentified him. Marshall, as cock-certainly as Blackmun, concluded the opposite—that the diagram and identification evidence were not only material to the defense; "they were absolutely critical." "The materiality of the undisclosed evidence in this case," Marshall added, "cannot be seriously doubted."[22] Yet five members of the Court seriously doubted it. The majority saw no denial of fair trial. The dissenters declared, "There can be no doubt that there was suppression of evidence by the State and that the evidence that the State relied on was 'false' in the sense that it was incomplete and misleading."[23]

If Blackmun's opinion is not satisfying, the reason is not that he was wrong—if he was wrong—on the facts and their implication; the reason, rather, is that he did not adequately explain why the undisclosed evidence was immaterial. It seemed relevant, important, and likely to influence the capacity of the defense to rebut the state's evidence at least with respect to the misidentification. As to the diagram that supposedly contradicted the testimony of a self-claimed eyewitness, Blackmun declared that he was not persuaded that the diagram showed that the eyewitness's testimony was false, because the diagram did not prove that from where he was sitting he could not have turned to face in the direction of the shooting. The fact remains, however, that the diagram contradicted his testimony that he sat facing in the direction of the shooting. The state's failure to disclose the diagram deprived the defense of its chance of discrediting his testimony. The missing evidence necessarily altered the effectiveness of the case which the defense based on an attack upon the identifications made by prosecution witnesses. That the Court divided narrowly even as to the facts of the case suggests that the jury could conceivably have returned a different verdict had the undisclosed evidence been available to the defense. That the trial judge in a murder case would have ruled out that evidence as immaterial passes belief.

The Burden of Proof

Moore v. *Illinois* made no new law. It went off, rather, on differing judicial conceptions of the materiality of undisclosed evidence. *Brady,* which was the Warren Court's measure for insuring fair trial in such a case, remained intact. Brennan, who was a member of the *Brady* majority, sided with Blackmun, a fact suggesting that the opinion in *Moore* did not abuse *Brady*. Nor did the dissenters —Marshall, Douglas, Stewart, and Powell—allege that the majority had impaired the effectiveness of the precedent. Accordingly, *Moore* cannot be characterized as injuring an essential guarantee of fair trial, but it did nothing to help it either. Even so, the case did not mirror an undue sympathy by the Court for a prosecutorial position.

That cannot be said of *Barnes* v. *United States*,[24] at least not in the view of Douglas, who dissented. Brennan and Marshall also dissented, but did so in an opinion apart from Douglas's. *Barnes* reunited the four Nixon appointees, whom White and Stewart joined. *Barnes* did not focus on the admissibility or exclusion of evidence. The issue was on the sufficiency of the evidence. The trial judge, in addressing the jury, had approved of an inference of guilt on a point essential to proving the crime charged. In 1970, however, the Court had held that due process of law requires "proof beyond a reasonable doubt of every fact necessary to constitute the crime."[25] The question in *Barnes* was whether the prisoner had been denied a fair trial by proof of guilt that fell short of proof beyond a reasonable doubt.

The evidence established that Barnes possessed recently stolen United States Treasury checks payable to people whom he did not know, and there was no explanation consistent with his innocence for his possession of them. But neither was there evidence proving his knowledge of the fact that they had been stolen from the mails, and without proof of such knowledge, Barnes, however guilty of some crime, was not guilty of the federal crime with which he was charged. The trial judge had instructed the jury that they would be justified in inferring from Barnes's unexplained possession of the checks that he knew they had been stolen from the mails. Powell's opinion for the Court sustained the trial judge's instruction to the jury. Powell noted that for centuries courts have instructed juries that an inference of guilty knowledge may be drawn from the fact of unexplained possession of stolen property. The evidence "was clearly sufficient to enable the jury to find beyond a reasonable doubt that petitioner knew the checks were stolen. Since the inference thus satisfies the reasonable doubt standard . . . we conclude that it satisfies the requirement of due process."[26]

Douglas condemned as "treacherous" the Court's sanction of presumptions and inferences to prove an element of crime, "for it allows men to go to jail without any evidence on one essential ingredient of the offense. It thus implicates the integrity of the judicial system."[27] To Douglas, allowing the inference that the accused possessed the checks with the knowledge that they were stolen was equivalent to dispensing with the requirement of the presumption of innocence. There was no way, he contended, of determining the likelihood that Barnes knew that the checks were stolen from the mails as charged. Checks can be stolen from various sources—homes, offices, or purses, for example—that would make their unlawful possession a local rather than a federal crime. Convinced that the trial judge's instruction denied the accused a fair trial, Douglas declared that the Court's opinion "will be applauded by prosecutors, as it makes their way easy. But the Bill of Rights was designed to make the job of the prosecutor difficult. . . . What we do today is, I think, extremely disrespectful of the constitutional regime that controls the dispensation of criminal justice."[28]

Brennan, joined by Marshall, restricted his dissenting opinion to a discussion of the prosecution's burden of proving guilt beyond reasonable doubt of every essential element of the crime. He thought that the trial judge's instruction denied due process of law, "because it permitted the jury to convict even though the actual evidence bearing on 'knowledge' may have been insufficient to establish guilt beyond a reasonable doubt."[29] By way of answering Powell's emphasis on the fact that Barnes's possession of the checks was unexplained, Brennan in effect took the view that the burden of proof rested on the prosecution. From the fact that Barnes had checks not belonging to him it did not inevitably follow, as Powell contended, that he knew that they had been stolen from the mails. Douglas had pointed out that they might have been stolen from some other source; Brennan agreed, observing that people often used such checks to pay for goods and services. His main point was correct: By authorizing the jury to rely exclusively on inference in determining the element of knowledge, the trial judge's instruction "relieved the Government of the burden of proving that element beyond a reasonable doubt."[30]

THE ENTRAPMENT DEFENSE

Barnes was similar to *Moore* in the sense that the Court in each case relied on an important precedent which safeguarded the right of fair trial and in each case found that there had been no violation of fair trial. In *Moore* the precedent required disclosure of material evidence favorable to the accused, but the Court found that the undisclosed evidence was not material. In *Barnes* the precedent required proof beyond reasonable doubt of every element of the crime, but the Court found that inference of one crucial element did not change the burden of proof. The Nixon Court has been adept at artfully applying a precedent favorable to the accused and yet sustaining his conviction. That pattern is discernible in the controversial "entrapment" case, *United States v. Russell* of 1973.[31]

Douglas had thought that *Barnes* implicated the integrity of the judicial system. The same judgment may be made of *Milton v. Wainwright,* where the Court accepted in evidence a confession obtained by the deceit of an undercover police officer out of the presence of the prisoner's counsel. In that case government deceit compromised or circumvented a constitutional right, though the Court decided to the contrary. The entrapment case implicated the integrity of the judicial system, as did *Barnes,* and unquestionably involved government deceit, as did *Milton,* for the usual worthy objective of bringing a criminal to justice, but this time there was no serious question whether a constitutional right had been breached and no specter of lawless law enforcement. Entrapment is a means of securing enough evidence to convict by using undercover officers to lure a person into the commission of the crime of which he is suspected.

Ordinarily the duty of an officer of the law is to deter crime and apprehend those who commit it, not to incite or instigate it. However, there are certain offenses of a clandestine character or of a consensual character that are difficult to expose and punish except by some degree of covert government participation. Official deceit may be immoral or shocking, but it is not necessarily illegal or unconstitutional. Society's war against organized crime would win far fewer battles if fraud, stealth, and ruses were not weapons in the armory of law-enforcement agencies. Infiltration and entrapment are particularly effective in uncovering crimes that involve gambling, narcotics, and prostitution. Nevertheless, the government cannot fight crime with crime. The problem for the courts is to determine the standards of permissible conduct by government agents.

If a government agent secretly gains the confidence of a radical organization and encourages its members (who have done no more than "bad-mouth" the Establishment and advocate its overthrow) to engage in terrorist activities and if he provides them with the weapons and bombs to do so, he has become an agent-provocateur who has conceived and procured the commission of crimes that would not have occurred but for him. If, to give an extreme example, an officer posing as an importer approaches a law-abiding person with no criminal record and induces him to smuggle certain contraband, the officer has passed the law's tolerance and the smuggler's guilty conduct may be legally excusable. When entrapment goes too far, it creates a legal defense which, like insanity or killing to save one's own life, merits a verdict of not guilty. The question, and a very delicate one, for the law to determine is whether the evidence proves that entrapment is a sufficient defense by a person who has in fact committed the crime charged against him.

Russell was a member of a small drug ring that illegally produced and sold methamphetamine, popularly known as "speed." The Federal Bureau of Narcotics and Dangerous Drugs assigned an agent to locate the secret laboratory and arrest those who operated it. Passing himself off as a representative of an organization that sought to control the manufacturing and distribution of "speed," the agent made contact with Russell's drug ring and made them an offer: In return for one half of their production and being shown their laboratory facilities, he would supply them with a certain chemical that was difficult to obtain yet was essential to the manufacture of "speed." Russell agreed. The agent supplied the chemical, witnessed its conversion into "speed," received his

share, and bought more. Having obtained evidence of illegal manufacture and sale, he returned to the laboratory with a search warrant, seized additional evidence, and made arrests. At the trial
the judge gave the standard entrapment instruction to the jury: The
mere fact that a government agent provides a favorable opportunity to one willing and ready to break the law is not entrapment;
but, if the defendant had no previous intent to commit the offense
and did so only because the government agent induced him, the
jury should acquit. The jury convicted, and Russell appealed on the
ground that the facts showed entrapment as a matter of law. The
Court of Appeals agreed on the ground that the government agent
had participated in a criminal enterprise to an intolerable degree
by providing a scarce ingredient for "speed," thus making the
prosecution repugnant to the American criminal-justice system.
The Supreme Court reversed.

In *United States* v. *Russell* the Court divided 5-to-4 in sustaining a conviction against a defense of entrapment. Rehnquist delivered the opinion of the Court. Brennan joined the separate
dissents of Douglas and Stewart, while Marshall joined Stewart.
Rehnquist's opinion was judicious, well-reasoned, and fairly con-
siderate of opposing views, which he critically evaluated. He did
not represent new law nor turn his back on settled law by engaging in questionable distinctions. Rehnquist rested squarely on
the two entrapment cases which the Court had previously decided,
the first in 1932 in an opinion by Chief Justice Hughes and the
second in 1958 in an opinion by Chief Justice Warren.[32] Like
them, Rehnquist wrote a principled opinion that was sensitive to
the claims that the government must not break the law nor engage
in reprehensible conduct that undermines the integrity of the
courts. Not that the government activity challenged in *Russell* by
the defense of entrapment was ethically commendable. It involved
deception, solicited a crime, and provided the means for its
commission, yet not at the expense of any constitutional rights.
The dissenters in *Russell* also wrote highly principled opinions
meriting respect. They voiced the views held in 1932 by Justices
Roberts, Brandeis, and Stone and in 1958 by Justices Frankfurter, Douglas, Harlan, and Brennan. *Russell* was a replay of
the two earlier cases with one significant difference: When the

Court split in 1932 and again in 1958, the Justices who disagreed with the opinion of the Court reached the same result by a different route. They did not dissent; they concurred in the reversal of the convictions that were before the Court for review. In 1973 Rehnquist spoke for a majority that upheld a conviction, while the four dissenters voted to affirm a Court of Appeals decision that ordered reversal of that conviction.

Rehnquist observed that in the two precedents, when the Court recognized and sustained entrapment defenses, the defendants had initially refused to make illegal sales but finally capitulated to repeated and persistent importunings of undercover agents posing as friends. In 1932, when Hughes for the Court first defined entrapment, he focused on the intent or predisposition of the defendant to commit the crime, as Rehnquist pointed out. The entrapment defense, Hughes said, is not simply that law-enforcement officers instigated the crime but that they instigated its commission by luring an innocent person with no previous disposition to commit it. Entrapment occurs, according to Hughes, "when the criminal design originates with the officials of the government, and they implant in the mind of an innocent person the disposition to commit the alleged offense and induce its commission in order that they may prosecute."[33] "The predisposition and criminal design of the defendant are relevant," Hughes ruled, but "the controlling question" was "whether the defendant is a person otherwise innocent whom the government is seeking to punish for an alleged offense which is the product of the creative activity of its own officials."[34]

In his concurring opinion in the 1932 precedent, Roberts did not basically differ from Hughes on the definition of entrapment. He called it "the conception and planning of an offense by an officer, and his procurement of its commission by one who would not have perpetrated it except for the trickery, persuasion, or fraud of the officer."[35] But unlike Hughes, Roberts did not believe that the question of entrapment should be submitted to a jury for decision. Entrapment in his view was so outrageous that public policy required the trial court to preserve "the purity of its own temple" and to protect itself as well as the government "from such prostitution of the criminal law."[36] Proof of entrapment at any point in a case required a court to stop the prosecution, quash the indictment, and set the defendant free. Roberts also disagreed on the question whether the government might rebut a defense of entrapment by showing that the officer had reasonable cause to believe that the defendant was a person predisposed to commit the offense. Such proof, said Roberts, usually amounted to no more than that the person had a bad reputation or a prior criminal record. When entrapment is proved, Roberts concluded, the "courts must be closed to the trial of a crime instigated by the government's own agents."[37] As Rehnquist said in *Russell,* the difference between the opinions by Hughes and Roberts is that the former focused on the predisposition of the defendant and the latter on the question whether the government instigated the crime. In 1958, when the issue again came before the Court, Frankfurter reflected Roberts's view by stressing that dirty methods by the government cannot be countenanced nor can the courts permit any undermining of public confidence in the fair and honorable administration of justice which depends on the rule of law. Chief Justice Warren, for the majority in 1958, followed Hughes by drawing a line between "the trap for the unwary innocent and the trap for the unwary criminal."[38]

Having reviewed the precedents, Rehnquist confronted Russell's argument that the government's instigation of the crime violated due process of law. Comparing entrapment with coerced confessions and illegal searches and seizures, he argued that his prosecution should be barred in order to deter the kind of official conduct that led to it. Rehnquist found the analogy imperfect because the reason behind exclusionary rules was the government's failure to observe its own laws; in this case, however, the government infringed no constitutional right, violated no law, and committed no crime. Although the Court might one day have a case showing official conduct "so outrageous that due process principles would absolutely bar the government from invoking judicial processes to obtain a conviction," said Rehnquist, this was hardly such a case. The government agent's contribution of an essential chemical for the manufacture of "speed" was unobjectionable, because the criminal enterprise was already under way and the chemical itself was a harmless substance whose possession was illegal.

Accordingly, the law-enforcement conduct in this case stopped considerably short of violating the fundamental fairness mandated by due process of law. Gathering evidence to prove illegal manufacturing of drugs in the past is nearly impossible, Rehnquist observed. Agents must therefore resort to one of the few practical means of detection, "the infiltration of drug rings and a limited participation in their unlawful present practices." In order to gain acceptance by the criminals, the agent must be able to offer something of value. Such conduct is permissible and does not shock the sense of justice.[39]

Russell had supplemented his due-process argument by claiming that the Court should adopt the views stated in the concurring opinions of Roberts in 1932 and Frankfurter in 1958, thus broadening the defense of entrapment. Having conceded on his appeal that he may have been disposed to commit the crime, Russell's only hope for a reversal of his conviction was an abandonment by the Court of its rule that a predisposition to commit the crime vitiated the defense. Mere proof of government instigation of the crime would then be sufficient to establish a valid defense of entrapment. Rehnquist refused, however, to repudiate the opinions of the Court expressed previously by Hughes and Warren. Repudiation would mean that the government could not show predisposition to answer proof that it instigated the crime. If the government lost its opportunity to rebut the charge of instigation, there would be no way of obtaining convictions of offenses consisting of secret activities. The defense of entrapment, Rehnquist declared, should not be available to one who planned to commit a crime and then committed it at an opportunity presented by a government agent. The precedents established that affording such an opportunity and using deceit did not defeat the prosecution. There are circumstances, Rehnquist concluded, "when the use of deceit is the only practicable law enforcement technique available. It is only when the Government's deception actually implants the criminal design in the mind of the defendant that the defense of entrapment comes into play."[40]

Douglas delivered an impassioned dissent in which Brennan joined. They concluded their judgment on the mere fact that the government instigated the crime by supplying a chemical ingredient to make the particular batch of "speed" for which Russell was prosecuted. After quoting Brandeis's condemnation of the use of foul or revolting means to accomplish desired ends, Roberts's condemnation of the prostitution of the criminal law, and Frankfurter's condemnation of intolerable police conduct, Douglas closed his ill-considered and epithetical opinion with an oversimplification: "Federal agents," he said, "play a debased role when they become the instigators of the crime, or partners in its commission, or the creative brain behind the illegal scheme."[41] That, Douglas thought, was what the undercover agent had done in this case when he supplied the accused with an ingredient for the illegal manufacture of the drug.

Stewart, supported by Marshall and Brennan, was judicious, analytical, and detailed. His dissent had far greater clarity and force than its precursors by Roberts and Frankfurter. Stewart described two theories of the defense of entrapment. The one used by Rehnquist, which was based on the precedents set by Hughes and Warren, was "subjective" in character. It focused on the question whether the accused was "otherwise innocent" or not disposed to commit the crime but for the government's inducements. Under this theory, the nature and extent of the government's participation does not matter if the criminal design originated with the accused or if he had a "predisposition" to commit the crime. The subjective approach allows the jury to decide whether the defense of entrapment is valid.

Stewart preferred an "objective" approach to entrapment, which he found in the concurring opinions of Roberts and Frankfurter. His descriptions of the objective approach, based on quotations from Frankfurter, made it sound several leagues away from objectivity. The entrapment defense, Frankfurter had said, was grounded on the belief that "the methods employed by the Government to bring about the conviction cannot be countenanced."[42] Thus, the focus should be on whether the government's conduct falls below the standards "to which common feelings respond, for the proper use of governmental power."[43] Stewart rephrased Frankfurter's test for entrapment in a way that seemed to lend it objectivity: The question is "whether—regardless of the predisposition to the crime of the particular defendant involved—the government agents have acted in a way likely to instigate or create a criminal offense."[44] That question, like any other on the lawfulness of government conduct, Stewart declared, should be decided by a court, not a jury. Even the subjective test focused on the conduct of the government by assuming that the defendant should be exempt from punishment if he would not have violated the law but for the government's inducements.

Criticizing the subjective test, Stewart argued that to describe a defendant as "otherwise innocent" or not predisposed to commit the crime is "misleading" and "irrelevant." The fact that he actually committed the crime demonstrated that he was not innocent. He may not have conceived the crime, but he was predisposed to it because he proved to be capable of committing it. That a government agent induced him to commit it does not make him more innocent or lacking in predisposition than he would be if a private person induced him to commit it. The defense of entrapment does not apply in the latter instance. "Since the only difference between these situations is the identity of the temptor, it follows," said Stewart, "that the significant focus must be on the conduct of the government agents, and not on the predisposition of the defendant."[45] That led Stewart to conclude that the purpose of the entrapment defense was not to protect otherwise innocent persons; it was, rather, to "prohibit unlawful government activity in instigating crime." Rehnquist had not ignored this argument. In effect he agreed that government instigation of crime triggered the entrapment defense, but only if the government had implanted the criminal intent in the mind of the defendant and then lured him to commit the crime in order to punish him. When, however, the evidence showed an ongoing criminal activity, government instigation is not by itself sufficient to prove entrapment.

Stewart, nevertheless, hammered away at what he believed to be the error of focusing on the accused's predisposition to commit the crime. It carried the danger, he contended, of allowing the introduction of otherwise inadmissible evidence—hearsay, suspicion, and rumor—to prove predisposition. The prosecution might also prove predisposition by relying on the defendant's bad reputation or past criminal behavior and by relying too on the prejudicial account of the agent. His suspicions of the defendant, when presented to a jury as the reason for luring him into the commission of the crime, became a self-fulfilling prophecy. The agent believed him to be guilty and proved him to be so by enticing him to the crime. A jury would likely believe the predisposition from the unquestioned proof of guilt.

The dangers of which Stewart spoke were imaginary in this case, and they were by no means inherent in the majority's conception of entrapment. The evidence here did not raise questions concerning the defendant's reputation or previous record or the use of hearsay and rumor. Nor did the evidence show that at the instigation of the government agent, Russell had established his laboratory to manufacture "speed" or had converted for criminal purposes an already existing facility previously used for innocent purposes. Stewart acknowledged that the government may lawfully employ undercover deceptions. "Indeed," he declared, "many crimes, especially so-called victimless crimes, could not otherwise be detected. Thus, government agents may engage in conduct that is likely, when objectively considered, to afford a person ready and willing to commit the crime an opportunity to do so." Stewart followed that proposition with another that he stated as if it presented a significant difference: "But when the agents' involvement in criminal activities goes beyond the mere offering of such an opportunity, and when their conduct is of a kind that could induce or instigate the commission of a crime by one not ready and willing to commit it, then—regardless of the character or propensities of the particular person induced—I think entrapment has occurred."[46]

Stewart's formulations were not convincing. The person "not ready and willing" is "otherwise innocent." If a person "objectively considered" is in fact "ready and willing" to commit a crime, he has the propensity or predisposition to do it. The question, contrary to Stewart, is not whether the government instigates the crime but whether the government has done more than offer to such a person an opportunity to commit it. To say, as Stewart did, that the government should not engage in the "impermissible manufacturing of crime" was not to state a difference from the position of the majority of the Court. Nor did they disagree with Stewart's belief that the federal courts should bar the prosecution when necessary "to preserve the institutional integrity of the system of federal criminal justice."⁴⁷ But they also believed, in Rehnquist's words, that the government does not manufacture crime when it is confronted by a "criminal enterprise already in process. . . ." Its existence shows that the accused was "ready and willing" or predisposed to commit the crime. Stewart, however, claimed that "it does not matter whether the respondent [Russell] was predisposed to commit the offense of which he was convicted,"⁴⁸ because the issue, he believed, turned on the conduct of the undercover agent. In this case the agent supplied the chemical to manufacture the batch of "speed" for which Russell was convicted. That, for Stewart, was "objective" proof that the government instigated a crime for which the entrapment defense as a matter of law should have barred the prosecution.

The best that can be said for Stewart's "objective" explanation of the entrapment defense is that it would shut the Court's eyes to one side of the evidence and was no more objective than the Hughes-Warren-Rehnquist "subjective" test. All that Stewart proved was that the defense of entrapment cannot arise unless the government instigates a crime. But that fact is merely the beginning of an analysis to determine whether the evidence proves impermissible entrapment. Predisposition to commit the offense is relevant to proving criminal intent, which is necessary for proving guilt. The only convincing feature of Stewart's view was his proposition that when unlawful government conduct is the question, the courts should as a matter of law decide it. An anti-prosecutorial position, like that revealed by the dissenters, lays no greater claim to objectivity than a pro-prosecutorial position. The majority of the Court favored the prosecution's position. Nevertheless, Rehnquist had the better argument because the test of entrapment which he applied was a more balanced one than Stewart's. Nothing in Rehnquist's opinion impaired the entrapment defense as a device of insuring fair trial. The Court left that defense as secure a protection for the unwary innocent as it had been. The entrapment defense, which had resulted in reversals of convictions in the precedents, failed in this case. The reason is not that the Court misused that defense, but that the evidence in this case showed it to be inapplicable. Russell was, in Warren's words, in speaking of another defendant, an "unwary criminal" and not an "unwary innocent." Had the Court affirmed the judgment of the court below on the theory of entrapment embodied in the Roberts-Frankfurter-Stewart position, the result would have really handcuffed the cops and coddled criminals to a far greater degree than the worst nightmares of the critics of *Miranda*.

THE CONFRONTATION CLAUSE AND THE HEARSAY PROBLEM

The Hearsay Rule and Its Exceptions

The confrontation clause of the Sixth Amendment expresses, in the words of the Warren Court, "an essential and fundamental requirement for the kind of fair trial which is this country's constitutional goal."[49] Where there is no respect for the right of confrontation, individuals are often condemned on the charges of faceless informers who testify in absentia by depositions. Every word of the Sixth Amendment militates against that kind of proceeding. Its confrontation clause states that the accused in all criminal prosecutions "shall enjoy the right . . . to be confronted by the witnesses against him." In a broad sense its meaning is transparent, yet it is pregnant with obscurities and paradox.

Like the self-incrimination clause, the confrontation clause cannot literally mean what it says, nor does it say what it means. Taken literally, the right of the accused to confront the prosecution's witnesses might mean merely the right to meet them face-to-face in court as they testify against him. The clause means both more than that and less. It means less because there are circumstances in which the accused cannot confront the witnesses against him and because the evidence against him may not consist of only the testimony of witnesses. It means more because when a witness is available or the evidence is mute, the prosecution must produce the witness in open court for cross-examination and exhibit the evidence for critical scrutiny.

The accused cannot confront the opposing witness whenever a court admits evidence against him that is an exception to the rule against hearsay. A familiar illustration of such an exception is the dying declaration. With his dying breath a murder victim may name his assailant. The victim may be mistaken or a liar, but witnesses to his dying declaration who did not see the assailant commit the crime may testify against the alleged assailant by stating under oath that they heard the dying man identify the defendant as his killer. The legal theory is that a dying declaration is trustworthy; given that and the unavailability of the deceased, justice demands the admission of hearsay evidence. Its value derives not from the first-hand knowledge of the declarant (who in this instance is dead), but from the truthfulness and competency of the witness who repeats what he heard someone else say.[50]

The declarant or original source may be unavailable for a variety of other reasons. He may be physically ill or mentally incompetent; his whereabouts may be unknown or he may be beyond the reach of the state's subpoena powers; he may be physically available yet unwilling to testify on Fifth Amendment grounds or no longer be able to recollect accurately. In all such cases of unavailability, as of death, witnesses may testify to certain kinds of statements made by the absent declarant; the condition is that the state has a need to introduce the evidence by hearsay because it cannot be produced in any other way and there are circumstantial guarantees of the reliability of the evidence. The unavailable declarant may, for example, have given former testimony that is material to the state's case.

Even if he is available, the state need not produce him as a witness when indicia of need and trustworthiness supposedly support the hearsay evidence that the state offers to prove the truth of the matter asserted. The prosecution, for example, may offer business records to prove the guilt of a person charged with fraud without having to produce the record-keeper. The exceptions to the "hearsay rule," which is really the rule against hearsay, allow for the use of a wide variety of written and printed evidence including business, government, family, medical, and church records. Thus, marriage certificates can prove bigamy without there being a requirement of producing the persons who conducted the marriage ceremonies. The availability of the declarant or original source is immaterial as to most exceptions to the hearsay rule. Another illustration is the category of "excited" or "spontaneous" utterances. A person who witnesses a crime may, under the stress of excitement, make a spontaneous statement incriminating the accused, and others may testify that they overheard the declarant's statement. Although emotional stress often impairs the accuracy of observation, the theory of the law is that a statement produced by a startling event is more likely to be true than the declarant's subsequent testimony on the witness stand. Thus, others may testify to what they heard him say, though they did not see the crime first-hand.

There are numerous exceptions to the hearsay rule, twenty or thirty depending on the system of classifying them.[51] All deprive the accused of his normal opportunity to test by cross-examination the veracity and memory of the person who is the source of the evidence against him.

If the accused had an absolute right to cross-examine that source, there could be no hearsay evidence—that is, no exceptions to the hearsay rule—and all evidence would have to consist of testimony by live witnesses present in court. Our courts could not conduct their business, nor would the ends of justice be served, without the benefit of evidence that constitutes exceptions to the hearsay rule. If the purpose of trial is to reveal the truth, a hearsay rule that allowed no exceptions would deprive the trier of fact—the jury or a judge sitting without a jury—of much relevant evidence and in many cases would make the prosecution impossible. Yet the need to keep exceptions bitted and bridled is obvious. Hearsay is usually suspect and is not the best evidence. Testimony should be subject to cross-examination under oath and before the trier of fact, who can watch the witness's conduct on the stand. Allowing exceptions presents the real possibility of shriveling the rule against hearsay to the point that only its shadowy principle remains. Moreover, every exception that is allowed becomes paramount to the right of confrontation, a part of the supreme and fundamental law of the land. To subordinate any constitutional safeguard to a mere common-law rule of evidence would reverse the order of legal values and jeopardize the fairness that is the object of that safeguard. Nevertheless, there is ever increasing pressure within the legal profession to widen existing exceptions to the hearsay rule and to increase their number, thus raising the fear that the exceptions might swallow the rule and with it the constitutional right.

That right has its origins in the hearsay rule which predated the Constitution by about a century.[52] The objective of the confrontation clause was to guarantee to an accused person the protections that the hearsay rule affords, chiefly the right to cross-examination. The rule also requires testimony to be given under oath and in open court so that the trier of fact, while scrutinizing the witness's demeanor when he is testifying, may evaluate his credibility. But the central value that the hearsay rule and the confrontation clause protect is the right to cross-examination, which Dean Wigmore, the master of evidence, called "the greatest legal engine ever invented for the discovery of truth."[53] By no means do all authorities agree with Wigmore. Recent reformers of the Federal Rules of Evidence say that "common sense" tells that much evidence not given under "the three ideal conditions"—cross-examination, oath, and scrutiny of demeanor—"may be inherently superior to much that is."[54]

Still, the hearsay rule and the right to confrontation are so closely related that there is a constitutional question of crucial importance whether any or all of the exceptions to the rule come within the interpretations of the clause. The exceptions are not fixed; they tend to swell in reach and number. Did the framers of the Sixth Amendment mean to allow evidence admissible only under the exceptions known to them? If so, the result would be to freeze hearsay exceptions in a point of time long outdated by changes in the law of evidence. Did the framers mean to allow any exceptions that might become part of the law of evidence as it evolved in the future? If so, the constitutional right would be at the mercy of statutory amendments to the law of evidence and of judicial opinions that shape the rules of evidence supposedly in consonance with the supreme law of the land. History is silent or inconclusive on the intentions of the framers of the Sixth Amendment, and if the amendment itself seems clear, it is not. The framers knew about the exception for dying declarations, yet their language makes no allowance for it or for other exceptions. The confrontation clause, once again, declares that in "all" criminal prosecutions the accused "shall" enjoy the right of confrontation. The word "all" is absolute and the word "shall" seems mandatory or imperative. Therefore, the clause appears to constitutionalize the rule against hearsay evidence without any of its exceptions. Yet, criminal courts in the United States have always admitted evidence that comes within the exceptions to the rule on the ground that necessity and reliability provide adequate substitutes for the values ordinarily safeguarded by confrontation and cross-examination. The Supreme Court has sustained the admission of evidence under hearsay exceptions, making them exceptions to the right to confrontation.

The problem of admitting evidence under exceptions to the hearsay rule was not, until the time of the Warren Court, a serious or controversial one. In 1953, just before Warren became Chief Justice, the Court observed that the Fourteenth Amendment's due-process clause does not protect the "privilege of confrontation."[55] The Sixth Amendment's confrontation clause applied only to trials in federal courts, and the overwhelming number of criminal cases came within the jurisdiction of the states. There were few Supreme Court cases on the confrontation clause growing out of trials in federal courts until about a decade ago. Significantly, in its first major case on that clause, the Court in 1895 took the position that evidence admitted under a recognized exception to the hearsay rule did not conflict with the Sixth Amendment.[56] In 1927 the Court suggested that the confrontation clause did not remodel the law of evidence: "The right of confrontation did not originate with the provision in the Sixth Amendment, but was a common-law right having recognized exceptions. The purpose of that provision, this Court has often said, is to continue and preserve that right, and *not* to broaden it or disturb the exceptions."[57] A few years later the Court remarked in an aside that exceptions to the right to confrontation "are not even static, but may be enlarged from time to time if there is no material departure from the reason of the general rule."[58]

So matters stood until 1965 when the Court initiated a series of decisions that seemed to constitutionalize the hearsay rule under very tight restrictions against exceptions. *Pointer* v. *Texas* was the path-breaking case.[59] The Court there held that "the Sixth Amendment's right of an accused to confront the witnesses against him is a fundamental right and is made obligatory on the States by the Fourteenth Amendment." The Court also held that the right of confrontation "must be determined by the *same standards* whether the right is denied in a federal or state proceeding."[60] A state court had allowed the introduction in evidence, over the defendant's objection, of the transcript of an absent witness's testimony given at a preliminary hearing when the defendant was not represented by counsel. At the trial the witness was unavailable, having moved out of the state. The Supreme Court disallowed the exception, recognized by the state, for hearsay evidence based on prior recorded testimony; but, the opinion of the Court, given by Black, narrowly focused on the fact that because counsel had not represented the accused at the preliminary hearing, he had no effective right to cross-examine the witness against him. Black observed that the Court had previously recognized "the admissibility against an accused of dying declarations and of testimony of a deceased witness who has testified at a former trial. Nothing we hold here is to the contrary."[61] Black's reference to those two exceptions to the hearsay rule and the Court's nationalization of the right to confrontation under the same-standards principle seemed to place a definite limit on the admissibility of hearsay evidence.

In *Barber* v. *Page,* decided three years later, the Court went further in holding that evidence admitted under a recognized hearsay exception violated the accused's confrontation right.[62] In *Pointer* the Court had conceded that if the accused had counsel at the preliminary hearing and an adequate opportunity for him to cross-examine, the case would have been different. *Barber* dissipated that concession to the hearsay exception for prior recorded testimony. Although the defendant had counsel at the preliminary hearing, he in effect waived the right to cross-examine the testimony of a key witness. At the trial that witness was absent because he was in a federal prison in an adjoining state. The Court ruled out the admission at the trial of the witness's preliminary-hearing testimony against the defendant, saying, "we would reach the same result . . . had petitioner's counsel actually cross-examined Woods [the absent declarant] at the preliminary hearing."[63] The reasoning was that the right to confrontation "is basically a trial right," allowing the jury to weigh the demeanor of the witness. The function of the preliminary hearing, by contrast, was simply to determine whether probable cause existed to hold the accused for trial. The Court ruled that the absent witness was not really unavailable because the state had made no effort to get him there. Because there was no failure of a good-faith attempt to produce him, his pretrial testimony did not come within the unavailability exception to the hearsay rule; accordingly, to introduce his hearsay testimony at the trial violated the accused's right of confrontation. *Pointer* and *Barber* illustrated a new willingness on the part of the Court to examine critically the admission of hearsay testimony in order to decide whether it afforded sufficient safeguards to warrant sidestepping the confrontation right. The simple fact that the prior recorded testimony in each of these cases had come within a traditional exception to the rule against hearsay, as construed by a state court, was not sufficient, as it used to be, to conclude judgment.

In other cases the Warren Court also searched beyond technicalities that satisfied lower courts and found other violations of the confrontation clause. In *Douglas* v. *Alabama*[64] and *Bruton* v. *United States*[65] the disputed statements, not having been admitted in evidence against the defendants, were not hearsay as to them. Nevertheless, the Court ruled that those statements were in effect hearsay, because they created situations prejudicial to the right of confrontation. In *Douglas,* the state called as a witness the defendant's convicted accomplice, but he refused to testify on Fifth Amendment grounds. The prosecutor, under the guise of refreshing his memory, read the testimony that he had given at his own trial. That testimony implicated Douglas. Technically, the prosecutor had not offered it to prove the truth of the accomplice's previous statements and, therefore, it was not hearsay as to Douglas. The Court held that the jury might infer that the disputed testimony was evidence against the defendant, despite the fact that he had no opportunity to cross-examine.

In *Bruton* there was an analogous situation. The trial court admitted in evidence the testimony of an officer who had received the oral confession of Bruton's codefendant who did not take the stand. Therefore, Bruton could not cross-examine him, although his confession incriminated both. Because that confession was hearsay as to Bruton, the judge instructed the jury to consider it as evidence against the codefendant only. The Court reversed Bruton's conviction, ruling that there was a substantial risk that the jury had not been able to separate the evidence between Bruton and his codefendant. The judge's instructions violated Bruton's consti-

tutional right of cross-examination, even though the disputed testimony was not received in evidence as proof of the truth against
him. In several other cases, the Court sustained a variety of other
claims based on the confrontation clause.[66]

The legacy of these cases which the Warren Court passed on to
the Court under Chief Justice Burger was an extremely sympathetic attitude toward the right of confrontation. Before the 1960s
the Court's opinions favored the admission of hearsay exceptions.
The Warren Court guardedly subordinated such exceptions to the
fast-paced expansion of the confrontation clause. It looked beyond
hearsay versus nonhearsay distinctions in order to serve the interests that the clause safeguards. It required confrontation and cross-
examination regardless of technical distinctions, when there was a
risk of prejudice to the defendant's case. Unavailability, the source
of a variety of hearsay exceptions, appeared no longer to be a sure
basis for introducing out-of-court or previous testimony. The
Court gave the impression, which alarmed exponents of exceptions
to the hearsay rule, that their continued use might lead to a consti-
tutionalization of the rule itself with a minimum of constitutionally
sanctioned exceptions. The trend of decision provoked an apprehension that the confrontation clause even exceeded the scope of
the hearsay rule without its train of exceptions. The admission of
confessions other than the defendant's seemed, on the basis of recent decisions, to deny the rights of confrontation and cross-examination. Testimony once thought to be intrinsically reliable and
necessary to serve the search for the truth failed to meet the higher
standard authorized by the Sixth Amendment clause.

The Court, under the principle of sustaining old constitutional
rights long denied, excluded evidence that much modern authority
would validate. The trend outside the Court was in the direction of
allowing greater flexibility in the use of hearsay evidence, or exceptions to it, and in finding technical distinctions that permitted
evidence to fall within the realm of admissibility. When experts on
evidence and lower courts would have left to the jury, as the
trier of fact, the task of evaluating the probative value of evidence,
the Court found higher values in the confrontation clause on grounds
that it embodied rights so basic that exceptions had to run the
judicial gauntlet. At the least, there was considerable uncertainty

as to the meaning of the newly rediscovered confrontation clause in relation to recognized exceptions to the hearsay rule and, particularly, to new exceptions that recent state legislation and lower courts had been advocating. The Warren Court, if it did nothing more, reversed a long-standing trend toward cribbing and confining the confrontation clause. The Court, it seemed, was unshackling the clause.

After Warren's resignation, however, the Court began braking and reversing the trend of decision by reinstating old hearsay exceptions to their accustomed recognition and undamming the obstacles to experimenting with new exceptions. Beginning in 1970, the new view became that of the pre-Warren one, resulting in a validation of "reforms" of the law of evidence and denials of claims based on the confrontation clause. The Court began to upset assumptions that the new-modeled confrontation clause was a burgeoning source for inhibitions on old and evolving rules that thwarted cross-examination. With *California* v. *Green*[67] and *Dutton* v. *Evans*,[68] both decided in 1970, the Court began a full-scale retreat; it would not bar the path to innovations that promised to build a new order of criminal justice founded on revitalized and dynamic hearsay exceptions.

Prior Inconsistent Testimony

California v. *Green* presented an innovation for the Court's consideration. California's recent revision of its code of evidence provided that the hearsay rule did not make inadmissible the evidence of a prior statement made by a witness who gave inconsistent testimony at a trial. For the first time the Court had to decide whether the confrontation clause excludes the substantive use of prior inconsistent testimony by a witness who is available and present for cross-examination at a trial. An old exception to the hearsay rule permitted the use of prior inconsistent testimony only for the purpose of impeaching the veracity of a witness who changes his testimony at a trial. There was a hearsay ban on the use of his earlier testimony as substantive evidence, that is, as evidence to prove the truth of his previous assertions. Only testimony subject to cross-examination at the trial itself was not hearsay under the old rule. The introduction at the trial of his former testimony to prove his earlier assertions was hearsay, because the defendant could not cross-examine the record showing the prior testimony and, second, the trier of fact had not watched the witness's demeanor when he offered it. California's reform of its code of evidence changed the law, on the theory that the usual dangers of hearsay evidence are nonexistent when the witness is present at the trial and subject to cross-examination at that time.

California prosecuted and convicted Green for furnishing marijuana to a minor. Earlier, an undercover policeman had arrested the minor for selling that drug. The minor named Green as his supplier and testified against him at his preliminary hearing. Green had counsel who cross-examined "extensively," according to White in his opinion for the Supreme Court. Brennan, the lone dissenter, stated that counsel did not conduct a "searching" examination; he did not, for example, ask the vital question whether the minor was under the influence of drugs. At Green's trial, the prosecution called the minor as a witness, but on that occasion he was evasive and uncooperative. He claimed that he could not remember how he got the marijuana, because at the time of the event he was under the influence of LSD, a hallucinogenic drug that prevented him from distinguishing between fact and fantasy. The prosecutor read from his testimony at the preliminary hearing, and the trial court, acting under the state's new code of evidence, admitted the previous testimony as evidence of the assertions made by the minor against Green on that earlier occasion. The witness said he still could not remember the actual events. On appeal of Green's conviction, the state supreme court declared that recent decisions of the Supreme Court "impelled" a finding that the revised code of evidence was unconstitutional insofar as it permitted the substantive use of prior inconsistent statements of a witness, even if defense counsel had cross-examined him at the earlier hearing. The state supreme court held that the confrontation clause excluded evidence that did not originate before the trier of the fact and was not subject to cross-examination at that time.

The Supreme Court disagreed. Blackmun, who had just been appointed, took no part in the case. Burger, who joined White's opinion for the Court, added brief remarks of his own which surprisingly suggested that in his view rules of evidence established "nonconstitutional standards." In effect he saw no constitutional issue in the case. The purpose of his comment, he said, was "only to emphasize the importance of allowing the States to experiment and innovate, especially in the area of criminal justice." The Constitution did not require "that we must have absolute uniformity in the criminal law in all the States. Federal authority was never intended to be a 'ramrod' to compel conformity to nonconstitutional standards."[69]

Speaking for most members of the Court who had joined its recent opinions expanding the confrontation clause, White was considerably more circumspect. Harlan, concurring separately, summed up White's opinion by saying: "The precise holding of the Court today is that the Confrontation Clause of the Sixth Amendment does not preclude the introduction of an out-of-court declaration, taken under oath and subject to cross-examination, to prove the truth of the matters asserted therein, when the declarant is available as a witness at trial."[70] That was the holding on the question whether a state may change its hearsay rules, consistent with the confrontation clause, to allow the substantive use at the trial of prior inconsistent statements. White conceded that the rule against hearsay and the confrontation clause "are generally designed to protect similar values," but he denied that "the overlap is complete and that the Confrontation Clause is nothing more or less than a codification of the rules of hearsay and their exceptions as they existed historically at common law."[71] Recent decisions proving that there was no "congruence" had held that recognized hearsay exceptions violated the clause. This case, White contended, proved that the opposite proposition was equally true: The admission of evidence in violation of the hearsay rule "does not lead to the automatic conclusion that confrontation rights have been denied."[72]

White presented two unrelated arguments to prove that the state's revised code of evidence was constitutional. He based the first on the fact that there was a provision for the examination of the witness at the trial; he based the second on the more extreme and dubious proposition that the availability of the witness for cross-examination at the trial was immaterial. The second propo-

sition robbed the first of its meaning. The first was that prior inconsistent assertions become valid evidence against the defendant if
the declarant is available as a witness at the trial. If he is, there is
no abridgment of the core values protected by the confrontation
clause, because he can testify under oath and subject to cross-examination before the trier of fact, who observes his demeanor.
White claimed that even if none of these circumstances surrounded
the prior statement, the fact that the witness was present and testified at the trial under the proper circumstances cured potential
defects in that statement. Belated cross-examination, according to
White, provided a constitutionally adequate substitute for cross-
examination that is contemporaneous with the original assertion,
especially when the witness repudiates the charge he had made
against the defendant.

White's argument did not meet the fact that the witness's earlier
charge against the defendant became evidence of his guilt at the
trial, despite the fact that the witness repudiated the charge at that
time. Surely, the reliability of the earlier testimony is questionable
if the subsequent testimony by the witness is significantly different.
When a witness is present at the trial and testifies subject to cross-
examination, there seems to be no compelling need to make substantive use of his previous testimony nor need to use it to determine his knowledge of the event. If he cannot remember it at the
trial, cross-examination at that time cannot prove the veracity of
his earlier statement. Verification that he made it is not verification
of its credibility.

White conceded that "some demeanor evidence that would have
been relevant in resolving this credibility issue is forever lost"[73] by
the admission of the prior testimony. He found sufficient compensation in the fact that the jury had a chance to observe and evaluate the witness's demeanor as he disavowed or qualified his earlier
statement. White did not consider that the witness's demeanor at
the trial merely provided an opportunity to determine the truthfulness of his claim that he could not remember the event to which
he had earlier testified; his trial demeanor was no measure of the
truthfulness of what he said at the hearing. Apparently, what he
said and how he conducted himself at the trial did not matter in
view of the fact that the Court favored the admission of his prior

testimony under any circumstances. The opportunity for effective cross-examination at the trial did not really matter, as White acknowledged. What mattered was that the witness testified at the preliminary hearing "under circumstances closely approximating those that surround the typical trial."[74] Thus, had he been unavailable at the trial, his prior testimony was admissible. The rule that emerged from *Green* was that the defendant's right of cross-examination at the preliminary hearing "provides substantial compliance with the purposes behind the confrontation requirement, as long as the declarant's inability to give live testimony [at the trial] is in no way the fault of the State."[75] In the end, then, the Court let the state have its cake after eating it. The state could make substantive use of the prior testimony if it was given under cross-examination, and cross-examination at the trial cured any previous defects.

In his solo dissent, Brennan addressed himself to the issue presented by the facts. He tried to map out a theory of the confrontation clause that would assess the validity of the exception to the hearsay rule for prior inconsistent statements, but he did not argue that the clause embodied the hearsay rule or was broader than it. In a footnote he buried the concession that if the witness was willing and able to testify at the trial about the event, "the demands of the Confrontation Clause may be met, even though the witness contradicts his pretrial assertions."[76] The basic fact of the case for Brennan was that the witness was unable to remember the event because of his admission that he had been under the influence of LSD at the time. That, for Brennan, justified disregarding any pretrial account by the witness.

White had found nothing in the Court's recent precedents to show that a confrontation problem existed when a trial court admitted prior inconsistent testimony as substantive evidence. Brennan relied on *Douglas* v. *Alabama* to support his contention that the confrontation clause banned the substantive use of a prior statement when the declarant was present at the trial but unwilling to testify. There was no significant difference, in Brennan's view, between a witness's failure to testify at the trial because of unwillingness and his failure to do so because of inability to remember. In either situation, the introduction of a pretrial statement simply made the witness "a conduit for the admission of stale evidence, whose reliability can never be tested before the trial factfinder by cross-examination of the declarant. . . ."[77]

In Green's case, the witness gave his pretrial statement under oath and subject to cross-examination before the jury. Brennan found slight significance in that fact, because, as the Court had said in *Barber* v. *Page,* the nature and objectives of a preliminary hearing and of a trial are substantially different. The preliminary hearing, at which the witness in *Green* had given his prior testimony, was, in the words of the state court, "a rather perfunctory uncontested proceeding" whose object was to decide whether to hold the defendant for trial. Brennan's point was that the witness's failure of memory at Green's trial denied the defendant an operative opportunity to cross-examine at any time, let alone at the crucial time, which was at the trial itself. Given the premise, which the Court accepted in *Barber,* that the "right to confrontation is basically a trial right," and given the limited purpose of a preliminary hearing, Brennan concluded that cross-examination on the earlier occasion could not satisfy the trial right. Cross-examination at the hearing, he said, "pales beside that which takes place at the trial," if the witness can recollect the event. The hearing merely determines probable cause for a trial, the trial guilt or innocence. If the prosecution can make substantive use at the trial of testimony at the hearing, Brennan argued, then hearings would become full-scale imitations of trials, attended by requests for delays that would give counsel time to prepare for extensive cross-examination. Wholly apart from the "unsettling effects" of the Court's opinion on preliminary hearings, Brennan believed that the rule of *Green* undermined the confrontation clause. In addition to the lack of a searching cross-examination at the hearing and at the trial, where the witness's memory failed him, "observation by the trial factfinder of the witness' demeanor as he gives his prior testimony is virtually nonexistent." Summing up, Brennan declared:

> In short, it ignores reality to assume that the purposes of the Confrontation Clause are met during a preliminary hearing. Accordingly, to introduce preliminary hearing testimony for the truth of the facts asserted, when the witness is in court and either unwilling or unable to testify regarding the pertinent events, denies the accused his Sixth Amendment right to grapple effectively with incriminating evidence.[78]

As a result of *Green,* the confrontation clause excluded the substantive use of prior statements if the defendant had no opportunity to cross-examine at the hearing and if the declarant is unavailable at the trial. In exceptional but rare circumstances, such as the dying declaration, even prior statements never subject to cross-examination meet the demands of the Sixth Amendment.

Extrajudicial Declarations

Six months after *Green,* the decision of the Court in *Dutton* v. *Evans*[79] questioned the validity of the view that cross-examination is the central value of the confrontation clause. However limited was the cross-examination of the witness in *Green,* at both the preliminary hearing and the trial, he was in fact subjected to some cross-examination, and the state produced him as its witness at the trial. *Dutton* was a much tougher case that the Warren Court would have decided differently, in all probability. A 5-to-4 vote decided *Dutton,* but the Court did not simply divide into two wings. "Not surprisingly," said Harlan in his concurrence, "the difficult constitutional issue presented by this case has produced multiple opinions."[80] No opinion mustered a majority. Stewart wrote an opinion for a plurality of four. Harlan cast the decisive vote, agreeing with the result of the plurality opinion but on utterly different grounds. Blackmun and Burger, who were members of the plurality (White also joined Stewart), added an additional reason for reaching the same result. Marshall spoke for the pre-1970 view, now represented by the minority: himself, Black, Douglas, and Brennan.

The case came to the Court on appeal from a decision of the United States Court of Appeals for the Fifth Circuit, holding unconstitutional, as a denial of the confrontation clause, a Georgia statute relied upon by the state to introduce hearsay evidence at a murder trial. Georgia tried and convicted Evans for the brutal murder of three policemen who chanced upon a trio of thieves in the act of stealing a car. One turned state's evidence and testified as the only eyewitness against the other two, Evans and Williams, at their separate trials. Georgia law required that the testimony of an accomplice be corroborated. The trial judge admitted as corroborating evidence a remark attributed to Williams, Evans's other accomplice. A man named Shaw, one of many prosecution witnesses at Evans's trial, testified that he heard Williams make the remark. Shaw, an inmate of the prison to which Williams had returned after his arraignment, claimed that he asked Williams, "How did you make out in court?" and Williams allegedly replied, "If it hadn't been for that dirty son-of-a-bitch Alex Evans, we wouldn't be in this now."[81]

As Stewart said of Shaw's testimony, "The confrontation issue arises because the jury was being invited to infer that Williams had implicitly identified Evans as the perpetrator of the murder when he blamed Evans for his predicament."[82] Actually, the confrontation issue arose because the state never produced Williams at any time to testify, subject to cross-examination, whether he made the remark, what he meant by it, and whether it was true. Shaw, a criminal, testified to what he said Williams told him about Evans. Williams's remark was purely extrajudicial, that is, not made in the course of a judicial proceeding. Williams made it, if he made it, out of court, when in prison. Evans never got a chance to cross-examine Williams. The trial judge's instructions to the jury indicated that the remark attributed to Williams could provide corroboration for the eyewitness account by the other accomplice, who testified for the state. "Slight evidence from an extraneous source identifying the accused as a participator in the criminal act," the trial judge said, "will be sufficient corroboration of an accomplice to support a verdict."[83] Thus, the case involved damaging hearsay evidence against the defendant based on an extrajudicial declaration by an accomplice whom the state did not make available for cross-examination.

The prosecution relied on an unusual exception to the hearsay rule in order to introduce Shaw's testimony of Williams's declaration as substantive evidence of Evans's guilt. Georgia law permits the use of a co-conspirator's declaration made during the pending stage of a criminal enterprise. But Georgia had not charged Evans with the crime of conspiracy; the charge was first-degree murder. Ordinarily the declaration of a co-conspirator is admissible only if made during the conspiracy, not after law-enforcement authorities have apprehended and charged the conspirators. The conspiracy can hardly be said to be pending when the conspirators are in prison awaiting trial. There is a federal exception to the hearsay rule used in federal conspiracy trials that is much narrower than the Georgia rule. In a federal court, the exception to the hearsay rule allows the introduction in evidence of an extrajudicial declaration by one of the conspirators only when he makes it in the course of and in the furtherance of the conspiracy, "and not," said Stewart, "during a subsequent period when the conspirators were engaged in nothing more than concealment of the criminal enterprise."[84] Stewart did not, however, question the relevance to this case of Georgia's broader rule allowing the use of out-of-court declarations by a co-conspirator during the concealment stage. Marshall, dissenting, questioned its relevance and its constitutionality. Stewart accepted its relevance on the basis of its application by the Georgia courts.

The plurality focused on two questions. Was the Georgia rule unconstitutional because it did not conform to the hearsay exception applicable to conspiracy trials in federal courts? If not, was the Georgia rule unconstitutional because it conflicted with the confrontation clause? Stewart's answer to the first question was that the federal hearsay exception was not a product of the confrontation clause, but of the Court's power to make rules governing the federal law of evidence. Accordingly, the state was under no obligation to follow the federal standard and could apply its own "long-established and well-recognized" exception to the hearsay rule.

That exception, Stewart argued in response to the second question, did not deny the constitutional right of confrontation. The Sixth Amendment's clause and the hearsay rule, though stemming "from the same roots," were not equivalents. Thus, an exception to the hearsay rule did not necessarily violate the confrontation clause. Describing the precedents on the clause, Stewart concluded that whenever in the past the Court had excluded evidence on confrontation grounds, the evidence was "crucial" or "devastating," while in this case it was merely "of peripheral significance at most."[85] Stewart failed to explain the meaning of his terms. Perhaps he meant that the disputed hearsay testimony offered by Shaw, unlike the testimony of the eyewitness accomplice, was not necessary to convince the jury that Evans was guilty beyond a reasonable doubt. The hearsay was hardly of peripheral significance, however, if it was necessary for corroboration.

Shaw was only one of nineteen witnesses, in addition to the eyewitness, a fact that Stewart stressed, but he did not even imply that the testimony of any of the others furnished the necessary corroboration. There is nothing in the various opinions suggesting that any testimony but Shaw's connected Evans with the crime of murder. The other witnesses seemed to testify about the auto theft whose discovery by the three police officers led to their murders. Evans's counsel cross-examined Shaw thoroughly and effectively, to be sure, but Stewart did not explain why the state had not clinched its case by producing Williams, the source of the disputed evidence, for cross-examination. The defense could have subpoenaed Williams, but by calling him as its own witness could not have cross-examined him. At one point Stewart asserted that "the possibility that cross-examination of Williams could conceivably have shown the jury that the statement, though made, might have been unreliable was wholly unreal."[86] If that was true, there would have been no harm to the state's case had it produced Williams; in any event, both the test of reliability and the confrontation clause, which Georgia's hearsay exception balked, demanded that he be produced to determine the truthfulness of his testimony. If Shaw's testimony was merely peripheral, the prosecution had no compelling need to introduce it. Need and reliability are the tests for the admission of hearsay. Peripheral evidence does not meet the test of need, especially when the prosecution does not produce the declarant who was its source. Shaw's evidence certainly failed the test of reliability.

The astonishing fact is that Stewart himself acknowledged in a footnote that the cross-examination of Shaw "was such as to cast serious doubt on Shaw's credibility and, more particularly, on whether the conversation which Shaw related ever took place."[87] Blackmun, joined by Burger, regarded the admission of Shaw's testimony as merely "harmless error if it was error at all," a position not accepted by the other seven members of the Court. The evidence of the unreliability of Shaw's testimony was so strong that Blackmun and Burger seemed to fall back on the "harmless error" doctrine to explain away that testimony as if it had never been given. Blackmun referred to detailed proof, which no member of the Court contested, that the conversation to which Shaw testified was fictitious, because he and Williams were in different rooms separated by a door through which sound did not carry. Blackmun was "at a loss" to understand how the jury could have believed "this astonishing account by Shaw of his conversation with Williams in a normal voice through a closed hospital room door. "I note also," said Blackmun, "the Fifth Circuit's description of Shaw's testimony as 'somewhat incredible' and as possessing 'basic incredibility.' "[88] The four dissenters agreed on this point. Marshall lampooned Stewart's statement that cross-examination of Williams would make "wholly unreal" the possibility that Shaw's account was unreliable. "A trial lawyer might well doubt, as an article of the skeptical faith of that profession, such a categorical prophecy about the likely results of careful cross-examination," Marshall declared.[89] Stewart's acknowledgment that the disputed testimony was founded on a conversation that may never have occurred destroyed his effort to find "indicia of reliability" for Shaw's testimony.

Williams made his alleged remark implicating Evans (if he made the remark) under circumstances which in Stewart's opinion "gave reason to suppose that Williams did not misrepresent Evans's involvement in the crime."[90] One might think that more than supposition ought to be required to validate hearsay evidence that corroborated the crime of murder, especially when the veracity of the witness was questionable. Stewart based his supposition mainly on the fact that Williams's alleged statement was spontaneous and against his own interest, thus establishing the indicia of reliability. A spontaneous statement against one's own interest is a good basis for an exception to the hearsay rule, though Georgia's wholly different exception, relating to the testimony of co-conspirators, was the only basis for introducing Shaw's evidence.

Harlan, concurring in the judgment but in none of Stewart's reasoning, declared that Marshall's dissent, which led to a position that Harlan could not accept, satisfactorily answered Stewart. Harlan referred to the "failure of Mr. Justice Stewart's opinion to explain the standard by which it tests Shaw's statement, or how this standard can be squared with the seemingly absolute command of the [confrontation] clause. . . ."[91] Marshall too criticized the opaqueness of Stewart's standard. Stressing that Shaw's testimony, under Georgia law and the trial judge's instructions, constituted the necessary corroborative evidence, Marshall showed that there was a very real possibility that the hearsay was prejudicial to Evans. Harlan apparently endorsed Marshall's confession that he did not understand Stewart's inquiry whether Shaw's testimony was "crucial" or "devastating." Marshall found "impossible . . . to believe" that the introduction of Williams's declaration via Shaw's incredible testimony did not contribute to the jury's verdict.[92]

Had Williams been unavailable for any reason, the state might have justified the introduction of his extrajudicial declaration. Stewart did not consider the question of availability; Williams, who was in state custody, was readily available. The state offered no reason for not producing him. By ignoring the question of availability and focusing on supposed indicia of reliability, Stewart made almost impossible any proof that a hearsay exception violates the confrontation clause. His opinion for the plurality reads as if the Court had to dilute the meaning of the Sixth Amendment's clause and distinguish away all the precedents from *Pointer* v. *Texas*,[93] the landmark case of 1965, through *California* v. *Green,* in order to reach a result sustaining Evans's conviction. His guilt seemed abundantly clear, and the crime was monstrous. The plurality and Harlan apparently recoiled from a judgment that would unglue the jury's verdict of guilty. Accordingly, the five who concurred in the judgment reversing the Fifth Circuit found necessary a reading of the confrontation clause and of the precedents that allowed the states to admit previously excluded hearsay, thereby increasing the chances of guilty verdicts. Stewart's opinion, like Harlan's, had an ad hoc tone.

Harlan's opinion reads as if it were principled, but he advanced a newly discovered theory in this case after admitting that he had changed his mind about the validity of his views in *Green* only six months earlier. In that case he believed that an availability rule should confine the meaning of the confrontation clause. The witness in *Green* was available and testified under cross-examination. Therefore, Harlan's availability rule enabled him to join the Court's judgment in that case, sustaining the conviction. The same rule, if applied in Evans's case, would have confirmed the Fifth Circuit's finding that Georgia had denied the defendant's confrontation rights. Harlan then advanced his new theory that the state's law of evidence determined what testimony was admissible under due-process standards that posed no bar to the hearsay. The testimony having been admitted, the witness must be cross-examined; the fact that Shaw was cross-examined was enough for Harlan. He would have subordinated the confrontation clause to the due-process clause as the measure whether evidence should be admitted. Harlan was alone in his newfound view.

The plurality purported to rely on the confrontation clause, but construed it in a way that permitted a judgment sustaining conviction. The "mission" of the clause, according to Stewart, "is to advance a *practical* concern for the accuracy of the truth-determining process in criminal trials by assuring that 'the trier of fact [has] a satisfactory basis for evaluating the truth of the prior statement.' "[94] The inner quotation derived from *California* v. *Green,* but Stewart followed little else of that case. His interpretation of the confrontation clause converted the requirement of the Constitution that the accused in "all" criminal prosecutions "shall" be confronted with the witnesses against him into a mere "practical concern" that the jury has a "satisfactory" basis for an extrajudicial declaration. Stewart's opinion neglected to fulfill the policies that the Court in *Green* had recently asserted that the clause served. *Green* literally confronted the witness against him; Evans did not. The witness against Green was sworn; Williams's alleged statment was unsworn, though Shaw, of course, testified under oath. In *Green,* the jury could observe the demeanor of the witness whom the defense cross-examined; in *Evans* there was no cross-examination of Williams and no demeanor evidence because the state did not produce him. Had the Court applied the tests of *Green,* and, of course, of *Pointer* and its progeny, the judgment in *Evans* would have had to be different. *Green* required testimony given "under circumstances closely approximating those that surround the typical trial."[95] Notwithstanding Stewart's imprecise and dubious "indicia of reliability," eight members of the Court, including the four in the plurality, explicitly questioned the credibility of Shaw's testimony based on an alleged statement by Williams made in prison, not under judicial supervision—and, Harlan, the ninth Justice, indicated his belief that cross-examination of Williams might have impeached Shaw's testimony.

In his closing remarks, Stewart revealingly quoted a 1934 statement by the Court:

> There is danger that the criminal law will be brought into contempt —that discredit will even touch the great immunities assured by the Fourteenth Amendment—if gossamer possibilities of prejudice to a defendant are to nullify a sentence pronounced by a court of competent jurisdiction in obedience to local law, and set the guilty free.[96]

Stewart's reliance on that assertion suggests that the plurality felt impelled to tailor its opinion to reach a result that kept Evans in prison. Harlan's switch to a new theory suggests the same. The Blackmun-Burger reliance on "harmless error" to explain away the admission of Shaw's "incredible remark" had the same effect. The rest of the Court disagreed that the hearsay was harmless error. Under the Blackmun-Burger test for harmlessness as applied in this case, no exception to the hearsay rule would ever be likely to fall victim to the confrontation clause.

Marshall wrote a stunning opinion that exploited every weakness in Stewart's. Analyzing the line of cases that began with *Pointer,* Marshall argued effectively that "the majority reaches a result completely inconsistent with recent opinions of this Court, . . . In my view, those cases fully apply here and establish a clear violation of Evans' constitutional rights."[97] To Marshall, Stewart's opinion was devoid of authority and unreasoned. That an old and recognized hearsay exception was the basis for admitting Williams's extrajudicial declaration was not enough for Marshall. He refused to believe that state rules of evidence governed constitutional interpretation or justified "the wholesale avoidance" of recent precedents. Stewart sought to avoid equating the confrontation clause with the rule against hearsay, but his opinion came very close, Marshall claimed, to establishing a reverse equation "that would give any exception to a state hearsay rule a 'permanent niche in the Constitution' in the form of an exception to the Confrontation Clause as well."[98] To the dissenters, *Pointer* and its progeny had not constitutionalized the rule against hearsay; that, said Marshall, was "a prospect more frightening than real"; it was a specter that "is only a specter." But he did not sound convincing when he insisted that the position that he championed permitted "flexibility and innovation in a state's law of evidence."[99]

The inquiry, according to Marshall, should have been limited to the question whether Evans had an opportunity to confront and cross-examine Williams. Stewart, by contrast, had looked for "whatever 'indicia of reliability' may cling to Williams' remark, as told by Shaw." Cross-examination, Marshall replied, was the only way to determine whether Williams in fact made a spontaneous declaration against his own interest:

> If "indicia of reliability" are so easy to come by, and prove so much, then it is only reasonable to ask whether the Confrontation Clause has any independent vitality at all in protecting a criminal defendant against the use of extrajudicial statements not subject to cross-examination and not exposed to a jury assessment of the declarant's demeanor at trial. I believe the Confrontation Clause has been sunk if any out-of-court statement bearing an indicium of a probative likelihood can come in, no matter how damaging the statement may be or how great the need for the truth-discovering test of cross-examination. . . . The incriminatory extrajudicial statement of an alleged accomplice is so inherently prejudicial that it cannot be introduced unless there is an opportunity to cross-examine the declarant, whether or not his statement falls within a genuine exception to the hearsay rule.[100]

Hearsay for the Defense

By the end of 1973 the Court had decided four more confrontation-clause cases of significance. In the 1971 and 1972 cases, the Court continued on its course of mapping withdrawals from broad interpretations of the Warren era.[101] The precedents remained the law of the land, but the new opinions blunted their force and reach. However, in *Chambers* v. *Mississippi,* a 1973 case, the Court's persistently generous attitude toward exceptions to the hearsay rule benefitted a defendant for the first time.[102] The Court was consistent in its doctrine, though the prosecution and defense exchanged their customary stances toward the admission of hearsay. Moreover, Marshall, Brennan, and Douglas, who had dissented in the confrontation-clause cases of 1970–72, joined the opinion of the Court in *Chambers*. That opinion, by Powell, reads as if it is a vintage of the late 1960s. Only Rehnquist dissented, but on the jurisdictional point that the Court should not have decided the constitutional issue on which he did not give an opinion.

Mississippi convicted Chambers for the murder of a police officer. The murderer may have been a man named McDonald, who on three separate occasions spontaneously admitted the killing to different friends. McDonald also gave a sworn confession of his guilt, but at the preliminary hearing, a month later, repudiated it. The police thereafter dropped interest in him. At Chambers's trial, after the state failed to call McDonald, Chambers called him and managed to get his sworn confession admitted as evidence before the jury; but, the state on cross-examination showed McDonald's repudiation and let him tell his own story of his actions on the evening of the murder. On the ground that McDonald was not an "adverse" witness, the trial judge prevented Chambers from challenging either McDonald's story or his repudiation of his confession. In Mississippi, courts follow the old rule that a party may not impeach his own witness. Thwarted in his attempt to present his defense by cross-examining McDonald, Chambers then sought to introduce the testimony of the three men to whom McDonald had admitted the killing. The trial judge sustained the state's objection against the admission of hearsay evidence. Thus, the trial judge, applying local law, frustrated Chambers's defense, and he lost his appeal in the highest court of the state.

Powell, for the Supreme Court, agreed with Chambers that the strict application of the state's rules of evidence "rendered his trial fundamentally unfair and deprived him of due process of law."[103] Observing that a criminal defendant must have a fair opportunity to defend himself against the state's accusation, Powell stated, "The rights to confront and cross-examine witnesses and to call witnesses in one's own behalf have long been recognized as essential to due process."[104] The availability of confrontation rights do not depend, Powell said, on whether the accused or the state initially put on the stand the witness who gave damaging evidence against the accused. As applied in this case, the state's "adverse" witness rule denied the right to cross-examination.

The Court also found that the state's exclusion of the hearsay testimony crippled Chambers's chances for a fair trial. Powell conceded that out-of-court statements "lack the conventional indicia of reliability" and, therefore, ordinarily are excluded; but, he noted the development of numerous exceptions to the hearsay rule that allowed the admission of hearsay statements under circumstances that "provided considerable assurance of their reliability," as in this case. McDonald had made his various oral confessions spontaneously, against his own interest, to friends soon after the murder. Ample evidence corroborated those confessions. Moreover, if there was any question of their truthfulness, McDonald had been in the courtroom, under oath, and could have been cross-examined so that the jury could evaluate his responses and demeanor. Thus, the trial court had excluded testimony that "bore persuasive assurances of trustworthiness" and that was subject to cross-examination. "In these circumstances," Powell concluded, "where constitutional rights directly affecting the ascertainment of guilt are implicated, the hearsay rule may not be applied mechanistically to defeat the ends of justice."[105]

In *Chambers,* the Court evenhandedly held that defendants may introduce hearsay exceptions from which they benefit, as long as the usual indicia of need and reliability obtain. The case produced an ironic twist of the rules that the Court developed initially on behalf of prosecutors. Innovation and flexibility, which were usually code words for reforms in the law of evidence that eased the prosecution's burden of proof, became allies of an accused's right to defend himself. The rationale for innovation and flexibility has unchangingly been that they serve the ends of justice by aiding the truth-determining process. But the confrontation clause, fair trial, and due process of law very rarely required the admission of exceptions to the hearsay rule that favored the defendant. *Chambers* v. *Mississippi* was an interesting freak.

Continuing Retreats

The more representative confrontation-clause cases were those of 1971 and 1972, when the Court held against claims that the states denied Sixth Amendment rights. *Nelson* v. *O'Neil*[106] was the first of three such cases after *Dutton* v. *Evans*. The broad question in *Nelson* was whether there were any circumstances in which a codefendant's out-of-court, oral confession, which was hearsay against the defendant, could be used in evidence against the defendant at their joint trial. In the leading precedent, *Bruton* v. *United States* (1968), the Court held that to place before the jury the codefendant's confession violates the confrontation clause if the confession implicates the defendant and he cannot cross-examine the codefendant who does not take the stand.[107] In *Nelson*, however, the codefendant took the stand, denied making the confession to which a police officer testified, and denied the crime. His trial testimony was favorable to the defendant. The trial judge instructed the jury not to consider the confession, which was hearsay as to the defendant, when reaching a verdict. The jury found both men guilty. O'Neil, the defendant, appealed on the ground that telling the jury to disregard the evidence inadmissible against him did not protect his confrontation rights under *Bruton*. On appeal, a federal district court set aside O'Neil's conviction, and the Ninth Circuit agreed. Those courts relied heavily upon a dictum in *Bruton* to the effect that if the witness who allegedly made the extrajudicial confession failed to affirm it at his joint trial with the defendant, the latter cannot cross-examine him. The Supreme Court, disagreeing with the lower federal courts, circumvented the dictum.

Stewart, who had written *Bruton*, properly distinguished it from the case before the Court. *Bruton*, he said, excluded out-of-court hearsay only when there cannot be cross-examination of the declarant at the trial. In *California* v. *Green*,[108] decided the year before *Nelson* v. *O'Neil*, the Court held that the admission of a prior statement creates no confrontation problem if the accused cross-examines the declarant of the statement at the trial. Stewart relied on *Green* as a limitation on *Bruton*, but he misused *Green*. In that case the prior statement was not a confession by a codefendant, and it was testimony given in the course of a regular judicial proceeding, rather than a mere out-of-court assertion. Stewart, however, assumed that the rule of *Green*, which related to prior recorded testimony, applied to an extrajudicial, oral confession. The fact that the codefendant in *Nelson* did not affirm his alleged confession—indeed, he denied it—did not constitutionally matter, according to Stewart. What mattered was that the codefendant testified favorably to O'Neil by denying that they committed the crime. Had the codefendant affirmed the confession, O'Neil could have cross-examined him, but under no circumstances could cross-examination have served O'Neil better than the codefendant's denial of the confession. Stewart concluded that there is no violation of confrontation rights when a codefendant takes the stand to deny an alleged confession implicating the defendant and proceeds to testify in his favor. To hold otherwise, Stewart said, "would be unrealistic in the extreme."

Brennan, joined by Douglas and Marshall, dissented in an opinion of slight merit, and Marshall added brief remarks of his own. To admit the confession against its alleged declarant and yet to instruct the jury to ignore the confession as evidence against the defendant, because it was hearsay, risked the danger that the hearsay might prejudicially influence the jury against him. That was the reasoning in *Bruton* on which the dissenters relied, as if there were no difference between the cases. They failed to consider that in *Bruton,* the codefendant, who allegedly made the out-of-court confession, did not testify at the trial, while in this case he did. The jury heard him tell his story, subject to cross-examination, and witnesed his demeanor. On the other hand, justice demands a solution to the problem which derives from joint trials that involve hearsay confessions. Perhaps, as the dissenters suggested, the state should try the defendants separately in such cases.

In the first of the two 1972 cases on the confrontation clause, *Bruton* was again in controversy. This time, however, the Court did not merely distinguish it. The tactic, rather, was to treat it as if, under the circumstances, it did not matter. The case, *Schneble* v. *Florida,* involved a joint trial of two men accused of murder.[109] Police officers testified that each had orally confessed, incriminating the other. The testimony concerning each confession constituted hearsay as to the other defendant, neither of whom could cross-examine the other, because neither took the stand. The jury convicted both. Schneble appealed on ground that the admission of his codefendant's confession, via the police officer's testimony, violated *Bruton.* Even though the trial judge instructed the jury to disregard that confession when weighing the evidence against Schneble, the danger was too great that the confession would prejudice the jury against him—according to *Bruton*.

By a vote of 6-to-3, the Court held that the violation of *Bruton* did not automatically necessitate a reversal of conviction. In this case, said Rehnquist for the Court, "the properly admitted evidence of guilt is so overwhelming, and the prejudicial effect of the codefendant's admission is so insignificant by comparison, that it is clear beyond a reasonable doubt that the improper use of the admission was harmless error."[110]

The Court really decided the case on the question whether there was "overwhelming" evidence that made the constitutional error harmless. The evidence was overwhelming only because of Schneble's own confession. He claimed that it was the direct result of police coercion, and it probably was. The dissenters, speaking through Marshall, asserted, "it is impossible to read the record and to conclude that the evidence so 'overwhelmingly' establishes petitioner's guilt that the admission of the codefendant's statement made no difference to the outcome."[111] Marshall was obviously wrong, since the majority found no such impossibility.

Despite Rehnquist's rhetoric about "overwhelming" evidence, he and Marshall agreed that without Schneble's confession and the evidence deriving from it, "the State's case against Schneble," as Rehnquist said, "was virtually non-existent."[112] The dissenters pointed out that the accused initially denied his guilt and denied being present when his codefendant committed the murder. "Only after he was subjected to a series of bizarre acts by the police designed to frighten him into making incriminating statements did petitioner 'confess,' " said Marshall.[113] But the trial judge, after satisfying himself that Schneble's confession was voluntary, admitted it in evidence, and later he instructed the jury to disregard it if they believed that it was involuntary. The Court agreed to hear the case on the confrontation-clause issue only, and therefore it was not free to rule on whether the controversial confession was involuntary. But the Court was free to speculate whether the jury had weighed the confession against the accused. Rehnquist thought that the jury must have believed that the confession was voluntary and used it as the basis for conviction; otherwise, he reasoned, the jury lacked evidence to convict. Marshall made the farfetched assumption, which he could not prove, that the jury completely disregarded the confession and all the evidence derived from it. He then reasoned that the jury convicted Schneble because it did not disregard the codefendant's confession implicating him. Marshall's reasoning was unsound, although Rehnquist did not even trouble to show that. If the jury was capable of ignoring the defendant's confession, because it was involuntary, the jury was equally capable of ignoring the codefendant's confession as hearsay against Schneble. It probably believed the confessions of both defendants.

"There remains," as Marshall said, "a deep and haunting doubt as to whether a constitutional violation contributed to the conviction."[114] The dissenters found "impossible" to believe that the constitutional error was harmless, and they implied that the Court intended to "emasculate" *Bruton*. Significantly, however, the dissenters attacked not the doctrine of harmless error but its application in this case. The evidence seemed to be more tainted than overwhelming, yet evidence obtained or admitted improperly may be true. *Schneble* does not read like a miscarriage of justice. It does read like a subordination of constitutional principles to sustain a conviction. It also stands for the proposition that if there is some evidence against the accused other than the confession of his codefendant, courts and prosecutors can introduce that confession in violation of *Bruton* because they are engaging in "harmless error."

The only other confrontation-clause case that is worth noting was *Mancusi* v. *Stubbs,* decided by a 7-to-2 vote.[115] Brennan deserted Marshall and Douglas to join the majority. The doctrine of harmless error, which the Court did not mention, seems to have provided the basis of the decision. Tennessee convicted Stubbs for murder and kidnaping. He killed a woman and shot her husband, who survived to testify against him. On appeal, a state court reversed the conviction because the belated appointment of counsel for Stubbs denied him the effective assistance of counsel. At the retrial, the chief prosecution witness was no longer available to testify; he had permanently returned, after the tragedy, to Sweden, the country of his origin. The trial court admitted in evidence the record of his prior recorded testimony at the first trial. The constitutional issue was whether, in the light of *Barber* v. *Page* (1968), the admission of the absent witness's testimony deprived Stubbs of his confrontation rights. In *Barber* the Court had ruled that the admission of the preliminary hearing testimony of an absent witness violated the Sixth Amendment given the fact that the state had not made a good-faith effort to secure the attendance of the witness who was in prison in the next state. In Stubbs's case, the state had made no effort whatever to secure the attendance of the absent witness; the state assumed his unavailability from the fact that he had permanently left the United States. Rehnquist, for the Court, observed that there was no legal authority or machinery that would enable a state to produce a foreigner, while Marshall complained that the state had not even requested him to return. The dissenters would have rigidly applied the rule of the precedent. The Court ruled, however, that the indicia of reliability surrounding the testimony made it good evidence. Even the dissenters did not contest the fact that Stubbs had ample opportunity at the first trial to confront and cross-examine the witness who subsequently left the country. The decision was not unreasonable, but the casual way the Court skirted the precedent was an additional sign that the Warren Court's confrontation-clause decisions were losing vigor. The good-faith effort that the Court no longer required seemed to be an effort that the Court itself was no longer making.

SPEEDY TRIAL

One of the components of fair trial and the first one mentioned in the Sixth Amendment is the right to a "speedy" trial. Not until 1967 did the Court describe that right as "fundamental" and apply it to the states through the due-process clause of the Fourteenth Amendment.[116] On that occasion Warren traced the origins of the speedy-trial clause to the Assize of Clarendon (1166), Magna Carta (1215), and the Habeas Corpus Act (1679). Sensitive to these great antecedents, the framers of the Sixth Amendment sought the same objective, to prevent prolonged detention prior to trial, but they left no clues as to the meaning of speedy trial.

The Court, which has had to interpret its meaning in only a few cases, has never specifically defined it; indeed, it has carefully avoided doing so. In 1905, when first construing the clause, the Court severely weakened it by holding that the right to a speedy trial "is necessarily relative. It is consistent with delays and depends upon circumstances."[117]

Fifty-two years later the Court was no more specific and once again relied on the circumstances to decide a case. There had been a two-year delay before the sentencing that was necessary to complete a trial, but the Court ruled that in the absence of proof by the prisoner that the delay was "purposeful or oppressive," there was no denial of speedy trial when the prosecution promptly remedied the delay upon discovering its fault.[118] This was the first of five decisions by the Warren Court on speedy trial. In 1959 the Court said that the "essential" meaning of speedy trial was "orderly disposition, and not mere speed."[119] In 1966 the Court held that a delay caused by a retrial after the reversal of a conviction does not ordinarily violate the right to a speedy trial. This case, however, marked the glimmerings of a breakthrough in the interpretation of that right by stating three basic reasons for it from the standpoint of the accused. Speedy trial was "an important safeguard," said the Court, "to prevent undue and oppressive incarceration prior to trial, to minimize anxiety and concern accompanying public accusation and to limit the possibilities that long delay will impair the ability of an accused to defend himself."[120] The Court did not explain what it meant by "long delay," but a year later when the facts showed an indefinite postponement of the trial, the right won its first victory; however, the Court felt no need to state the criteria by which to determine whether the right had been violated.[121] In the only other speedy-trial case decided by the Warren Court it ruled that a state has a constitutional duty, on demand of a prisoner, to make a good-faith effort to bring him to trial on a pending state charge even when he is in a prison in another jurisdiction.[122]

This judicial history of the speedy-trial guarantee demonstrates that the Nixon Court inherited a legacy of narrow decisions that did very little to illuminate what Warren had called "one of the most basic rights preserved by our Constitution."[123] It spoke to the problem of delayed justice that reached staggering proportions when Burger became Chief Justice. The crime rate had zoomed phenomenally in the decade of the 1960s, congesting the dockets of the criminal courts beyond anything known in past experience. An article in *Life* magazine vividly highlighted the plight of tens of thousands of accused men by telling the story of José Santiago, who had spent ten months in New York City's "Tombs" waiting for his case to come to trial. His claim that he was innocent, which was probably not true, was unshakable until his lawyer counseled him that if he persisted in demanding a trial, he would have to wait several more months in jail and then face the risk of a fifteen-year sentence if the jury found him guilty, while if he pleaded guilty he would be released immediately.[124] The plea bargain was arranged, but at the last moment Santiago refused to plead guilty and returned to jail. Accused persons who cannot afford bail are held in jail until they come to trial. Over half the population of local and county jails consists of persons who have not been convicted of the crimes of which they are accused.[125] In New York City, where severe riots broke out in the Tombs in 1970, 40 percent of the inmates had been awaiting trial for over a year in the terribly overcrowded conditions characteristic of urban jails.[126] In the federal trial courts, 30 percent of all pending cases in 1970 awaited trial for more than a year, a situation officially described as an "emergency."[127]

The costs of such a situation to society and to the parties involved are massive and severe. Society foots the financial bill and suffers more crime. Public taxes pay for welfare assistance to the families of those who cannot afford bail and for the expenses of confining the accused, while they undergo disruption of all normal relationships, lose their jobs, and suffer the dehumanizing experience of jail. Most are found to be guilty in the end, but many are innocent, and even the guilty are entitled to their day in court if they plead innocent. Those who are finally acquitted can never regain what they have lost as a result of pretrial detention. Even the innocent who are free on bail are victimized, at the very least, by anxieties caused by prolonged delay before trial. And the longer they wait for trial, the greater the chances that they may not be able to establish their innocence. A speedy trial is the best insurance against a miscarriage of justice because extended delays tend to blot out memories and alibis; witnesses and other evidence may be lost.

Those who are ultimately convicted but can afford bail while awaiting trial also exact a high price from society. The longer a man awaits trial, the greater his temptation to jump bail, become a fugitive from justice, and commit new crimes. Half of the federal cases awaiting trial for a year or more involve fugitive defendants.[128] The guilty who are out on bail are also in a stronger position to take advantage of harassed, overworked prosecutors who find themselves forced to agree to plea bargains that are favorable to criminals; when a prosecutor cannot cope with his case load, he tends to permit pleas of guilty to lesser offenses in order to dispose of cases and yet maintain the appearance of a record of convictions. Many criminals who are out on the streets while awaiting trial resume their life of crime. Rearrest rates for defendants on bail vary with the nature of the offense and the locality. Narcotics offenders and robbers who make bail have an extremely high rearrest rate, ranging to 70 percent in the District of Columbia.[129] Significantly, the longer a bailed defendant must await trial, the greater are the chances that he will be rearrested for another crime. Most serious crimes committed by such persons occur after the first two months following release. A study of the recidivism rate in the District of Columbia showed that 68 percent of crime committed by persons on bail occurs more than thirty days after release, that a man out on bail for four months is twice as likely to be rearrested as one who has been awaiting trial half that time, and that the peak period for recidivism corresponds with the lengthiest delay following bail for a first arrest.[130] Speedy trial leading to speedy conviction and punishment of the guilty is about as effective a deterrent as there is against recidivism and, by example, deters crimes by others.

Former Attorney General Ramsey Clark, in his book *Crime in America*, wrote:

> Ironically for all the hue and cry about judicial decisions that have reversed convictions, delay in trials is responsible for failures and dismissals in a much greater number of cases. A survey of the rea-

sons cases could not be prosecuted in the District of Columbia estimated that lapse of time was the cause seven times more frequently than the failure to promptly arraign an accused as required by the *Mallory* decision, the failure to give warnings required by *Miranda*, and violations of other decisions invoking exclusionary rules. With the passage of time, witnesses die and disappear, memories fade, evidence is misplaced and the sense of urgency is transferred to more recent crimes. Inefficiency, not fair rules, reduced convictions.[131]

An expeditious resolution of cases by fair trial is the foremost safeguard of individual liberty and of public safety. If the criminal-justice system is breaking down, one of the major reasons is that the courts fail to work expeditiously. There are many reasons for the fact that criminal justice travels on leaden feet strewing injustice among accused persons and causing injustice to society. Insufficient funds for enough courts, supporting personnel, prosecutors, and juries is one reason. The annual budget for the entire federal judicial system, as Burger pointed out, amounts to considerably less than the cost of the C-5A military transport plane.[132] Many local criminal courts are incredibly mismanaged, operating as if the era of the quill pen and horse-drawn buggy was still with us. Despite the congestion of his criminal docket a judge may take off the entire summer for a vacation without a replacement. Rarely is there a procedure for staggering vacations or for shifting judges around when pressures build up in one court or a judge becomes ill in another. The President's Commission on Law Enforcement and Administration of Justice referred in a Task Force Report on courts to the "widespread consciousness of the archaic and inefficient methods used in many courts to process, schedule, and dispose of their business."[133]

The increase in the sheer volume of cases, caused mainly by the increase of the population and in the crime rate, is probably the foremost cause of delayed justice. The increase in procedural safeguards for the criminally accused, resulting from judicial decisions that seek to insure fairness, also exacts a price in slowing down the system. Lengthy trials delay the beginnings of others. Burger stated in 1970 that the length of a trial of a criminal case in a federal court doubled in ten years because of the closer scrutiny demanded of confessions, identification witnesses, and evidence seized by the police. "These changes," he declared, "represent a deliberate commitment on our part . . . to values higher than pure efficiency when we are dealing with human liberty."[134] But exclusionary rules requiring special hearings on the admissibility of evidence are by no means the only cause or the major cause of trials proceeding at a snail's pace. In the federal courts, where the judge may conduct the examination of prospective jurors, it seldom takes more than a day to select a jury to try a criminal case. In the overwhelming majority of local criminal courts, the lawyers control the examination of prospective jurors, and they jockey for juries that will be most favorable to their respective sides, taking an inordinate amount of time in the process. The law guarantees only an impartial and qualified jury, not a favorable one, yet the impaneling of the jury too often becomes a ridiculous waste of the court's valuable time at considerable expense to the public and inconvenience to hundreds of prospective jurors and witnesses too.[135] Delayed justice, whether caused by inefficient methods or insufficient funds to cope with overburdened dockets, discredits the criminal-justice system. The Sixth Amendment right to a speedy trial has become almost a farce, yet it offers the best hope for justice when speed is deliberate enough to allow fairness.

Trials are rarely so speedy that they dispense with justice rather than dispense justice, though there are cases in which the defense has had inadequate time to prepare itself or to argue that certain evidence is unconstitutional and should be excluded from the trial. In complex cases the prosecution too must have adequate time to mass its evidence and be shielded from defense efforts to make too much haste. Summary justice can be as bad as delayed justice. In 1947 there was a case before the Supreme Court in which the defendant had been arraigned, tried, convicted, and sentenced to life imprisonment for first-degree murder in just one day. He was not even represented by counsel. The Court held that he had been denied fair trial.[136] In 1967 there was an Oklahoma case in which a migrant worker who could not understand English did not know that his counsel, who had no time to prepare his defense, had pleaded him guilty. As the state appellate court declared, "He was arraigned on one day, and found himself in the penitentiary the next day, doing a life sentence for murder."[137] Too swift a resolution of a criminal case can be as injurious to justice as too slow a resolution. In 1966 the Supreme Court said, "A requirement of unreasonable speed would have a deleterious effect both upon the rights of the accused and upon the ability of society to protect itself."[138] It is better that justice should travel on leaden foot than walk roughshod over constitutional rights, but it is better by far that justice travel swiftly with fairness.

The fact that delayed justice is unfair to all and has become a massive problem kindles renewed interest in the Supreme Court's interpretation of the long-neglected Sixth Amendment clause on the right to a speedy trial. Burger, in an off-the-court statement, offered the opinion in 1970 that if ever the law "is to have genuine deterrent effect on criminal conduct . . . we must make some drastic changes. The most simple and obvious remedy is to give the courts the manpower and tools—including the prosecutors and defense lawyers—to try criminal cases within 60 days after indictment and let us see what happens. I predict it would sharply reduce the crime rate."[139]

Distinguishing Delays

Unfortunately Burger's performance as a member of the Court bears no correspondence to the boldness of his recommendation for a flat sixty-day time limit to implement the speedy-trial guarantee. Two months earlier he was the author of the Court's opinion in *Dickey* v. *Florida* in which he sustained a claim that there had been a denial of the right to speedy trial.[140] Burger chose narrow grounds that turned on the circumstances of the case. For the Court to have decreed a time limit defining speedy trial would have been overbold and even foolish, given the vital need for resources that would enable the courts and prosecutors to meet the time limit. Ordinarily, the denial of some right of an accused person results in a reversal of conviction, but the state may prosecute again if the denial has been remedied. However, the denial of the right to a speedy trial is unique, for the only remedy is a drastic one: dismissal of the charges. *Dickey* v. *Florida* had provided the opportunity for a modicum of judicial statesmanship; Burger and the Court failed to meet the challenge.

Dickey, a federal prisoner, made repeated efforts to obtain a trial to resolve state charges of armed robbery pending against him. No valid reason existed for Florida's failure to try him for seven years after issuing a warrant for his arrest. When he was tried at last over his protests that he had been denied a speedy trial, he was convicted. But during the seven-year period, two defense witnesses had died, others disappeared, and so had police records pertaining to his case. The circumstances showed intolerable prejudice to Dickey resulting from the state's inexcusable failure to try him on his demand. That is, the loss of evidence impaired his capacity to mount a defense. The Supreme Court held that the state had denied him a speedy trial.

The decision was unanimous, but Brennan, joined by Marshall, concurred separately in an opinion that was easily the best analysis that had been made of the right to a speedy trial. For Brennan the case could not be decided simply because Dickey had protested delays and demanded a trial, or because the state could not justify the delays, or because the delays caused actual prejudice. Brennan believed that the right involved in the case was important enough to merit fuller consideration than the Court had given to it in this case or in its precedents. The "basic questions about the scope and context of the speedy-trial guarantee remain to be resolved," he said, and he meant to consider them.[141]

Brennan first identified two issues concerning the right to a speedy trial: the point during the criminal process when it becomes operative and the criteria to judge the constitutionality of delays. Each issue had to be examined in the light of the purposes served by the right. It protected both the accused and society by penalizing official abuse of the criminal process. A speedy trial spares the accused the disabilities, incompatible with fairness, that spring from delay; such disabilities include oppressive incarceration, undue anxiety, and impairment of one's ability to defend himself. With the passage of time, witnesses and evidence might be lost and memories fade. Time could diminish the defendant's capacity to counter the charges and, equally, the prosecution's capacity to prove its case. The public stake in the effective prosecution of criminal cases militated against delays that deferred punishment. Deliberate government delays for the purpose of obtaining an advantage over the accused abuse the criminal process and lessen the deterrent value of a conviction. Deliberate delay might also injure the accused even when the delay precedes arrest or indictment. Unlike the government, the party who will be the object of the prosecution does not know that charges are pending; he may therefore fail to take steps necessary for his defense. Tentatively, Brennan concluded that the right to a speedy trial applies "to any delay in the criminal process that occurs after the government decides to prosecute and has sufficient evidence for arrest or indictment."[142]

The main part of Brennan's analysis considered three criteria that should be used to determine the constitutionality of delays. These were the source of the delay, the reasons for it, and the question whether it is prejudicial. The length of the delay—a factor most directly relevant to a fixed time limit for trial, such as the sixty-day period recommended by Burger—was in Brennan's mind a consideration related to the reasons for delay and the likelihood that it had prejudicial effects. In passing, Brennan mentioned that "one temporal standard could very likely govern most prosecutions,"[143] but he did not recommend one.

Brennan distinguished delays caused by the government and those by the defense.[144] If, for example, the defendant makes dilatory motions, presumably because delay serves his interest, he in effect waives the right to a speedy trial. On the other hand, Brennan explicitly and elaborately rejected the so-called demand-waiver rule that dominated judicial theory about the right to a speedy trial. According to this rule, a defendant who does not affirmatively demand a speedy trial waives his right to it. Even if the government is responsible for a deliberate and prolonged delay, the failure of the defense to object to it will be taken as an acquiescence that defeats a subsequent claim that there has been a denial of speedy trial. Brennan favored rejection of the demand-waiver rule for several reasons.

First, it conflicted with a realistic understanding of the effect of delay. The rationale for the rule is that defendants welcome delays as favorable to them. That is not necessarily true, Brennan argued, because delay does not inherently benefit the accused any more than the prosecution. The passage of time threatens the ability of both sides to present their positions. Second, to imply a waiver by the defendant of his right to speedy trial when he does not protest against delay by the government is to equate his silence or inaction with waiver. That, Brennan said, "is a fiction that has been categorically rejected by this Court when other fundamental rights are at stake. Over 30 years ago . . . we defined 'waiver' as 'an intentional relinquishment or abandonment of a known right or privilege.' We have made clear that courts should 'indulge every reasonable presumption against waiver' and that they should 'not presume acquiescence in the loss of fundamental rights.' "[145] Thus, no affirmative action by an accused should be necessary to preserve his right to a speedy trial. Affirmative action is necessary only to waive that right. Finally, to imply from defendant's silence or inaction a waiver of the right places on him the burden of insuring a speedy trial. That burden belonged on the government, which has the responsibility of prosecuting "out of fairness to the accused and to protect the community interest in a speedy trial." Thus, the accused does not waive his right because of the government's failure to prosecute him. Brennan might have added that the demand-waiver rule conflicted with the presumption of innocence because an accused should not have to demand the opportunity to establish his innocence.

Obviously, if an accused is not the source of the delay, the government is. Brennan believed that government delay is unreasonable if its purpose is to harm the accused, or if it is unnecessary whether intentionally or as a result of negligence. The tests for the legitimacy of government delay should be whether it is avoidable, prejudicial, overlengthy, or the result of insufficient resources and personnel to carry forward the prosecution. Brennan suggested that the absence of means to prosecute logjammed cases might require turning loose some accused persons. In his mind practical considerations, such as case loads, if resulting in prolonged delays, could not justify encroachments on the accused's right to a speedy trial.

The final consideration that Brennan evaluated was prejudice. In Dickey's case a loss of witnesses and evidence abundantly proved prejudice to his chances for a fair trial. Brennan, however, advanced a bold argument on the issue of prejudice, as he had on the demand-waiver rule. He would not have required the defendant to prove actual prejudice, as Dickey did. Brennan would have assumed the existence of prejudice as a means of preventing the denial of constitutional rights without a remedy. Because the government has the burden of proof in a criminal case, Brennan believed that the defendant cannot always show prejudice to his right to a fair trial. There is no sure way of proving that a witness or some evidence, once present, would have benefitted the accused, nor is there a way to prove that memories have faded because of the passage of time. The extent to which delay prejudices an accused is, ironically, proved by his difficulty in establishing that prejudice. Similarly, delays that defeat the public interest in speedy trial as a means of bringing criminals to justice and deterring others may be prejudicial to society. The defendant does not have to prove prejudice resulting from denial of other Sixth Amendment rights such as the right to counsel, confrontation, public trial, or an impartial jury. Courts assume prejudice in such instances. Thus, when the right to a speedy trial is at stake, "it may be equally realistic and necessary to assume prejudice once the accused shows that he was denied a rapid prosecution."[146]

Brennan conceded the difficulty of determining how long a delay must be to justify an assumption of prejudice. Standards for making that determination would have to be developed, he said. Until the delay reaches the critical point, the accused would have to prove that it actually harmed his case. Most courts required the accused to provide such proof; but, if there were appropriate standards for measuring a necessary delay on the part of the prosecution, as, for example, the need to locate a crucial witness, the government ought to bear the burden of proof because it is more likely to know the reasons for the delay.

In his closing remarks, Brennan observed that his analysis provided "no definitive answers." He was prompted to point out some of the major problems that courts must confront when defining the speedy-trial guarantee, because he thought it should receive "a more hospitable treatment than it has yet been accorded."[147] His concurring opinion, despite its failure at a number of points to define standards, was a tour de force and a most commendable achievement compared to Burger's opinion for the Court and the precedents that had done so little to illuminate the right at issue. Burger had taken for granted the validity of the demand-waiver rule and the need of the accused to prove actual prejudice. Brennan made his best contribution on those two issues.

The Flexible Test

In the next case, *United States* v. *Marion*, decided a year later, the Court again reached a unanimous result.[148] This time it ruled that the facts showed no denial of speedy trial, but again the Court divided on its reasoning. The question was one that Brennan had discussed in his *Dickey* opinion, whether there could be a violation of the right to speedy trial prior to arrest or indictment. In *Marion*, three years had elapsed between the alleged criminal acts—complicated business frauds—and the bringing of charges. White as the spokesman for a six-man majority ruled that a criminal prosecution within the meaning of the Sixth Amendment's right to a speedy trial begins only with arrest or accusation. In this case accusation had preceded arrest. According to White, the amendment afforded no protection to those not yet accused or arrested. Statutes of limitation provided a protection against unduly delayed accusations, White said. In the absence of proof that a delay in bringing accusation "caused substantial prejudice to appellees' rights to a fair trial and that the delay was a purposeful device to gain a tactical advantage" for the government, the Court could not honor a claim that there had been a denial of speedy trial before the commencement of a criminal prosecution.[149] In this case there was no showing of actual prejudice or any government intention to gain an unfair tactical advantage.

Douglas, who seemed to have slept through the *Dickey* case, now championed Brennan's position that in some circumstances a delay in initiating a prosecution can impair the right to a speedy trial. Brennan and Marshall joined Douglas's concurring opinion. There was a consensus that the case presented complex crimes involving interstate activities, difficulties on the part of the government in locating witnesses who were victims of fraudulent business schemes, and a need to reconstruct those schemes. Accordingly, all members of the Court agreed that the government required more than the usual time to mass its case before bringing charges. The case did nothing to advance the cause of judicial definition of speedy trial other than to exclude from its ambit most delays occurring before accusation or arrest. *Marion* showed the Court dealing on an ad hoc or piecemeal basis with only that aspect of the right to speedy trial which the facts presented. All preceding speedy-trial cases showed the same piecemeal approach, making Brennan's concurring opinion in *Dickey* stand out even after the Court attempted an overall analysis in *Barker* v. *Wingo* in 1972.[150]

Powell's opinion for the Court in that case was the most important ever handed down on the right to a speedy trial. For the first time the Court treated the right comprehensively and sought to establish criteria to judge a claim of its denial. Moreover, Powell spoke for a unanimous Court. White, joined by Brennan, wrote a concurring opinion, but concurred in the opinion of the Court as well as in the result that it reached. That Brennan, and Marshall, who was with him in *Dickey,* could have joined Powell's opinion is inexplicable, because Powell swerved away from Brennan's previous rejection, without qualifications, of the demand-waiver rule and from his qualified rejection of the rule that the accused has the burden of proving prejudice. Indeed, *Barker* represented a Pyrrhic victory for the right to a speedy trial. Powell elaborately explained its values to society as well as to accused persons, yet he denigrated it in various ways. He refused to define the right in terms of a fixed time limit, while acknowledging that appellate courts in the exercise of their supervisory powers might establish a fixed time limit. He categorically rejected the demand-waiver rule, yet he undermined his own rejection of it. He analyzed the criteria for establishing guidelines for lower courts, yet adopted a complicated and nebulous balancing test that allows lower courts to do merely as they please. He sought to explain the meaning of a speedy trial, yet indecisively abandoned the task as hopelessly difficult. In the end, notwithstanding Powell's labors, the Court had identified the problems and did nothing to settle them, leaving the law for practical purposes substantially as it was before the case—no further advanced than the Court's 1905 opinion which said that the right to a speedy trial was necessarily relative, consistent with delays, and dependent on the circumstances of each case.[151] Significantly, Powell quoted that statement with approval.

He began his opinion by saying that the right to a speedy trial is "generically different" from all other constitutional rights of accused persons because society's interest in providing for a speedy trial "exists separate from and at times in opposition to the interests of the accused."[152] The same, contrary to Powell, may be said of any other right of accused persons. In a broad view, everyone has an interest in seeing that the criminal law is fairly enforced without staining the system. Every right of the accused exists to prevent a miscarriage of justice. Yet the system is an adversarial one that pits society against the accused. Society has a right to evidence, for example; yet, if the law-enforcement agencies seize evidence unreasonably or coerce it from the mouth of the accused, it cannot be used against him, however good or real that evidence may be. Every right of the accused can and does benefit guilty persons as well as the innocent. Any Sixth Amendment right may defeat justice, even though it exists to serve justice. To predicate an analysis of the right to speedy trial on the mistaken ground that it uniquely serves antagonistic social and individual interests opens an easy passage to downgrading what is supposed to be a fundamental right. *Barker* did not downgrade the right to a speedy trial because the Court had never really upgraded it to the status of a fundamental right except rhetorically. *Barker* kept the right downgraded—and kept the empty rhetoric.

The inconsistency between the Court's preachment and its practice was reflected in Powell's remaining introductory remarks on the point that the right to a speedy trial is unlike any other right of the accused. A second difference, he said, was that deprivation of speedy trial may work to the accused's advantage, because delay may weaken the prosecution's case. From that undeniable possibility Powell drew the extraordinary conclusion that unlike denials of other rights, "deprivation of the right to speedy trial does not *per se* prejudice the accused's ability to defend himself."[153] The proper formulation would have been that delay does not necessarily prejudice his ability to defend himself if the delay promotes fairness or is caused by the accused. That some delays seriously weaken the prosecution is true, but no more so than that others equally impair the defense. Powell chose at that point in his opinion to see only one side of the issue; Brennan's treatment in *Dickey* of the problem of prejudice resulting from prosecutorial delay was fairer. Moreover, the flat assertion that denial of the right to speedy trial "does not *per se* prejudice the accused's ability to defend himself" conflicted with the Court's discussion of the factor of prejudice in a 1966 opinion,[154] and with Powell's discussion of that case and of prejudice in his opinion in this case.

He ended his introductory remarks on the uniqueness of the right to a speedy trial by calling it the most vague of procedural rights. The Court confessed that it could not say "how long is too long" or "do more than generalize" about the circumstances that imperil the values which the "relative," "amorphous," and "slippery" right protects.[155] The rights against "unreasonable" searches and seizures, "cruel and unusual" punishments, "excessive" bail, or denial of life, liberty, or property without "due process of law" seem scarcely more self-explanatory. Even rights that seem to be definite, like the right not to be compelled to be a witness against oneself or the right to the assistance of counsel, have proved to be perplexing and uncertain, as the teeming number of Supreme Court decisions on them would suggest.

Powell was not wrong about the uniqueness of the right to speedy trial. He was misleading. One could argue that every right of the accused is exercised in opposition to society or is in some respects unique. Powell accurately observed that other rights could be waived at some fixed point in the criminal process, unlike this right. That became a tactical point for presuming a waiver of this right under some circumstances, even in the absence of a knowing and intentional waiver. Powell also observed that the denial of no other right "leads to the unsatisfactorily severe remedy of dismissal of the indictment when the right has been deprived," permitting the possibility that a guilty defendant may get off free.[156] A year later, in 1973, the Court unanimously held that dismissal is indeed the "only possible remedy" for the denial of the right to a speedy trial and reversed a decision of a lower court to the effect that a reduction of sentence can compensate for denial.[157] In *Barker* the distinction based on the severity of the remedy became an extenuating circumstance that led to a failure by the Court to define the right in a way that allows proof of its denial to be objectively demonstrated. The whole introductory section of Powell's opinion, which was unsympathetic to the right, seemed calculated to rationalize a test for evaluating claims of its denial that was as relative, amorphous, and slippery as the right itself is supposed to be.

Two "rigid" or "inflexible" approaches, said Powell, might eliminate "some of the uncertainty which courts experience in protecting the right." One was a fixed time limit for trial, the other the demand-waiver rule. The latter, of course, did not aid in "protecting" the right at all; rather, it helped to eliminate it. A constitutional rule requiring the government to provide a trial within a specified time from arrest or accusation would certainly define the right, but would not protect it unless the time specified was no longer than necessary for both sides to prepare adequately for trial.

Powell pointed out that the United States Court of Appeals for the Second Circuit had "promulgated rules for the district courts in that circuit establishing that the government must be ready for trial within six months of the date of arrest, except in unusual circumstances, or the charge will be dismissed."[158] He noted too that the American Bar Association recommended the same type of rule.[159] He did not note that Congress at that time was considering a speedy-trial bill that set a sixty-day limit between accusation and trial,[160] nor that the Court would soon be promulgating its own recommendation. Two months before *Barker,* the Court itself had amended rule 50(b) of the Federal Rules of Criminal Procedure, requiring that six months later all federal district courts must "prepare a plan for the prompt disposition of criminal cases which shall include rules relating to time limits within which procedures prior to trial, the trial itself, and sentencing must take place. . . ."[161] The Court promulgated this rule under supervisory powers delegated to it by Congress. In *Barker,* however, Powell asserted that for "this Court to engage in legislative or rule making activity" would be inappropriate. "We do not establish procedural rules for the States, except when mandated by the Constitution. We find no constitutional basis for holding that the speedy trial right can be quantified into a specified number of days or months."[162] The Court recognized that the states might make such a quantification, and many had, though with slight consistency. State statutes fix time limits for trial that range from seventy-five days to three years.

Powell declared that nothing in the Court's opinion indicated disapproval of judicial rules, adopted by a court in its supervisory capacity, that set fixed time limits for the normal disposition of cases. The chairman of the American Bar Association Section on Criminal Law, who is a member of the Colorado Supreme Court, remarked that "*Barker* will not provide much guidance for the lower courts. The Court in *Barker* did not attempt the type of leadership in the criminal justice field that was supplied by the Warren Court. The opinion does not set the guidelines or establish procedures to implement the right to a speedy trial."[163]

Having rejected a Court-imposed fixed-time rule, Powell proceeded to reject the equally rigid demand-waiver rule, which the court below, in this case, had applied against Barker. After repeating the arguments that Brennan had made in *Dickey* against the demand-waiver rule, Powell concluded, "We reject, therefore, the rule that a defendant who fails to demand a speedy trial forever waives his right."[164] Then he blunted rejection of the demand-waiver rule by replacing it with another that has a similar effect. Rejection, said Powell, "does not mean, however, that the defendant has no responsibility to assert his right. We think the better rule is that the defendant's assertion of or failure to assert his right to a speedy trial is one of the factors to be considered in an inquiry into the deprivation of the right."[165] Powell explained that the new rule permitted a trial court to exercise its "discretion based on the circumstances," so that a greater weight can be given to a knowing failure to object to a delay than is given to delay that has the acquiescence of defense counsel without the accused's knowledge. The new, flexible rule, declared Powell, "would also allow a court to weigh the frequency and force of the objections as opposed to attaching significant weight to a purely *pro forma* objection."[166] That meant that if defense counsel is not alert to a growing delay and does not object, vehemently and often, at every point of delay, he can in effect waive his client's right to a speedy trial, because a court need not attach much significance to a belated objection against delay. The impact of the new rule was like that of the demand-waiver rule, notwithstanding its rejection. That fact emerged more clearly as Powell developed for the Court "a balancing test, in which the conduct of both the prosecution and the defendant are weighed." That test, which was presented as if it were new—"the rule we announce today"—compelled courts "to approach speedy-trial cases on an *ad hoc* basis."[167] That was the bankrupt basis of the test that had always prevailed, if it could be called a test. Unlimited judicial discretion hardly qualifies as a test. Powell did no more, as he admitted, than to "identify some of the factors which courts should assess" to determine whether there has been a denial of speedy trial.

He named four factors, the first being the length of delay. In keeping with the indecisiveness and elasticity of his opinion, he said that whether a delay is too long "is necessarily dependent upon the peculiar circumstances of the case." The government's reason for the delay was the second factor. "Here, too, different weights should be assigned to different reasons."[168] A deliberate delay to hamper the defense would weigh more heavily against the government than a valid delay caused by a missing witness, while a delay caused by negligence or overcrowded dockets would weigh less heavily than a deliberate delay and more than a valid delay. On this weighty point White and Brennan, concurring, declared that the government could not justify delay in ordinary criminal cases simply by asserting that because its resources are limited each case must wait its turn. Consideration of overcrowded dockets or prosecutorial case loads could not in their opinion prevail against a defendant's desire for a speedy trial. The delay, White and Brennan believed, should relate only to the facts of the case itself. They were right. The Court unfairly made the accused carry the burden of delay beyond his own control which the government, his adversary, had caused.

Powell's third factor was "the defendant's responsibility to assert his right. . . . We emphasize that failure to assert the right will make it difficult for a defendant to prove that he was denied a speedy trial."[169] Squaring the practical effect of that proposition with the supposed rejection of the demand-waiver rule and with the Court's reaffirmation that waiver must be knowing and intentional is a task for Sisyphus. If a defendant has not demanded speedy trial, or if he has not demanded it with "frequency and force," and if he has not waived his right to a speedy trial, how does he prove that the prosecution has deprived him of the right?

Is the burden of proof on him? Why should it be on him if the prosecution has the obligation of bringing him to trial and if the defense is not at fault for causing the delay? Powell identified the factors involved in weighing a claim that the right has been deprived, but he did not identify the practical questions, let alone avert the difficulties that they present.

How can a defendant prove prejudice? That was the fourth factor that Powell discussed. "Prejudice," he said, "of course, should be assessed in the light of the interests of defendants which the speedy trial right was designed to protect."[170] Those interests are clear enough. A defendant who cannot make bail is subjected to "oppressive pretrial incarceration," and cannot gather evidence, contact witnesses, or otherwise prepare his defense, Powell explained. A bailed defendant is "disadvantaged by restraints on his liberty and by living under a cloud of anxiety, suspicion, and often hostility." Most important, speedy trial protects the accused's ability to mount his defense. Delay that impairs his ability to defend himself "skews the fairness of the entire system." When witnesses die or disappear, "the prejudice is obvious," although Powell did not explain how a court could evaluate the materiality of testimony never given. If out of fairness prejudice should be assumed when the prosecution is to blame for the delay, Powell should have said so. He recognized that time erodes memories of witnesses who do testify and that loss of memory "is not always reflected in the record because what has been forgotten can rarely be shown."[171] Yet he dropped the point, having made it, without following, as Brennan had in *Dickey,* with the principle that a prolonged delay which is not the fault of the defense warrants a presumption of prejudice unless rebutted by the prosecution.

Having identified length of delay, reason for delay, failure of the accused to demand trial, and prejudice as four factors to be weighed, Powell concluded by virtually approving of any speedy-trial test that a court might apply. He declared: "We regard *none* of the four factors identified above as either a *necessary* or *sufficient* condition to the finding of a deprivation of the right of speedy trial." The four were related and "must be considered together with such other circumstances as may be relevant," though none of the four has "talismanic qualities."[172] Thus, the Court would not or could not lay down anything more than nebulous and unworkable considerations. Its opinion mandated a judicial flexibility that has proved to be a failure. Moreover, for all of Powell's rhetorical concern about the interest of society in having persons accused of crime brought to swift justice, his ad hoc or case-by-case balancing test ignored that interest.

To protect society's interest the Court should have taken an affirmative stand against prosecutorial delay caused by crowded dockets and workloads. The Court did nothing to compel the government to bring to trial persons rotting in jail untried or indefinitely out on the streets on bail. Many accused persons, as Powell emphasized, want delays that stave off the inevitable day of judgment and erode the state's case against them. He should have emphasized that the state has an obligation to society to prosecute actively regardless of the wishes of the accused. Its obligation to prosecute actively is far greater than the obligation of the accused to object with "frequency and force" to prosecutorial delays. If the accused has had time to prepare for trial, he has had time enough. The Court should have done something to prevent trial courts from routinely approving of motions for continuance or delay. Defense counsel frequently obtain delays of trial simply because their clients have not paid them.[173] The rule of the Second Circuit allowing a maximum of six months' delay immediately produced an increase in guilty pleas and in convictions in cases decided by trial, by forcing prosecutors to prepare cases earlier than was their habit.[174]

In *Barker* the facts of the case showed that delayed justice undermines the public safety. A man accused of beating two elderly people to death with an iron tool was freed on bail after ten months of confinement and remained at large in the community for more than four years thereafter awaiting the trial at which the state finally convicted him. The length of the delay in bringing him to trial was so unusual that the Court called Barker's case "close." Because the Court found no significant prejudice resulting from the delay and Barker himself had sought to avoid trial, there was a unanimous decision that the state had not deprived him of his due-process right to a speedy trial. The ad hoc or case-by-case balancing test permitted that decision, as it permitted an opposite decision. Sustaining the conviction was the just result because its only alternative was to set free a man guilty of what Powell called "a vicious and brutal murder." The opinion of the Court, however, should have protected society from letting a man like Barker go untried for so long. Most of the delay in his case derived from the state's difficulty in first convicting his accomplice. The strategy of the state was to convict the accomplice first so that his testimony could be used to help convict Barker. After conviction, the accomplice could not plead the Fifth Amendment, because the problem of self-incrimination disappeared on a verdict of guilty. Yet the state had no guarantee that a convicted murderer would trade a life term for a lengthy term by cooperating as a witness against Barker.

The Court developed no rule that would bring Barker to speedy trial or protect innocent men from prolonged delays caused by the government. The Court's opinion really settled nothing—except Barker's belated claim of deprivation of speedy trial—when it settled on the case-by-case balancing test that depended on specified and unspecified variable considerations that courts may weigh in speedy-trial cases. The Court failed to use its "adjudicatory process" to determine the meaning of the Constitution's requirement of speedy trial in a way that either protected the public and the accused, or in a way that gave meaningful guidance to lower courts. *Barker* simply produced a watered-down version of the right to speedy trial that can mean all things to all lower courts. Powell's opinion subordinated the Court's powers as the final interpreter of the Constitution to its little-known supervisory powers to legislate rules of procedure for federal courts. Fairness should depend on the Court's opinions on the Constitution, rather than on its congressionally delegated authority to make bylaws. *Barker* cheapened the constitutional process. The Court gave an obfuscatory opinion while obliquely, by administrative means, it initiated a search by the district courts for a solution to one of the major problems in the criminal-justice field. Rule 50(b), which called for plans "for achieving prompt disposition of criminal cases," affected only the federal trial courts.[175] *Barker* remains the final word for the state trial courts.

CHAPTER SEVEN

The Eighth Amendment:
The Death Penalty

The Constitution, Jefferson once lamented, is "a mere thing of wax in the hands of the judiciary, which they may twist and shape into any form they please."[1] In cases decided in 1971[2] and 1972[3] the Supreme Court misshaped the constitutional law on death by opinions that were contradictory, uncraftsmanlike, and inconclusive. The Court disposed of the cases, but the issues, substantially unsettled, hauntingly remain.

CAPITAL-SENTENCING PROCEDURES

In *McGautha* v. *California* and *Crampton* v. *Ohio,* decided together in 1971, the defendants, charged with first-degree murder, had pleaded not guilty.[4] Their juries tried, convicted, and sentenced them to death. Their cases called into question the capital-sentencing procedures of every state in the Union. There was not the slightest suggestion that innocent men had been convicted or that the juries had not discharged their duties in the routine manner according to state law. The juries had absolute discretion to decide whether the defendants should live or die, raising the basic issue of the cases: Is due process of law violated by capital-sentencing procedures that are untrammeled by any standards to govern the jury? The Court by a 6-to-3 vote sustained prevailing practices.

383

Though its decision was not unreasonable, its opinion was—it was an intellectual disgrace that invites comparison with the explanation offered by the judge in W. H. Auden's poem who declared, "Law is the Law." The Court's opinion, given by Harlan, provoked the wrathful dissenting Justices to caricature. Douglas, joined by Brennan and Marshall, observed: "We need not read procedural due process as designed to satisfy man's deep-seated sadistic instincts. We need not in deference to those sadistic instincts say we are bound by history from defining procedural due process so as to deny men fair trials. Yet that is what the Court does today."[5] Brennan, joined by Douglas and Marshall, declared that the Court "is led to conclude that the rule of law and the power of the States to kill are in irreconcilable conflict. This conflict the Court resolves in favor of the States' power to kill. . . . Not once in the history of this Court, until today, have we sustained against a due process challenge such an unguided, unbridled, unreviewable exercise of naked power."[6]

In McGautha's case the California jury, as did juries in five other states, held a bifurcated or two-stage trial, first deciding the issue of guilt; in a subsequent proceeding or penalty trial, the jury heard arguments and evidence from both sides on the issue whether the sentence should be aggravated or mitigated. It then fixed the sentence. Crampton's Ohio trial was the more common unitary type in which the jury decides simultaneously on the verdict and the penalty. Both McGautha and Crampton claimed that the unfettered and unreviewable power of the jury to return a death sentence in the absence of any governing standards was fundamentally lawless, a violation of the Fourteenth Amendment's command that no person shall be deprived of life without due process of law.

Juries fix the death penalty in probably no more than one-fifth of the cases in which defendants are found guilty of capital crimes, raising the question whether there is a rational or constitutionally tolerable basis for the exceptional verdicts that do call for execution. Harlan, for the Court, acknowledged that the argument against standardless jury discretion had an "undeniable surface appeal,"[7] but he rejected it curtly on the sole ground that the formulation of standards which capital juries can understand and apply is "beyond present human ability."[8] Harlan did not analyze and explain this crucial proposition; he asserted it as if it were self-evident. Harlan offered instead an authority, a British study of capital punishment. Brennan, in his dissent, said that that official study reached conclusions substantially like those urged in 1785 by Archdeacon William Paley in justification of England's "Bloody Code" of 250 capital crimes, and, Brennan added, Harlan neglected to mention that the Report of the Royal Commission was not accepted.[9]

The majority opinion was extraordinary not just because it was unreasoned. In a case dealing mainly with the meaning of the due-process clause, Harlan passingly mentioned the clause only once after stating the prisoners' contention. It was also unconvincing; it made no effort to respond to or acknowledge Douglas's disquisition on the continuing evolution of the meaning of due process of law. Nor did Harlan respond to or acknowledge Brennan's exposition on the reasons for believing that some standards for the guidance of a death jury were both possible and, in consonance with the due-process clause, indispensable. He simply ignored the almost ninety pages of dissenting opinions. Douglas was discursive and at points irrelevant and Brennan was repetitive; each was hyperbolic and apoplectic, and each misrepresented Harlan's opinion. Yet, both made powerful points that deserved to be answered with candor and professional expertise. Brennan systematically gutted the majority opinion. Harlan did not answer by his transcendant remark that the Court's function was "not to impose on the States, *ex cathedra,* what might seem to us a better system for dealing with capital cases,"[10] and that the Constitution "does not guarantee trial procedures that are the best of all worlds."[11] As the dissenters replied to this, the Court's concern was not with the wisdom of state policies, but "with the constitutional barriers to state action. Procedural due process is one of those barriers. . . ."[12]

Following the speedy dispatch of the California case, Harlan turned to the case from Ohio. Crampton claimed a due-process right to plead to the jury for his life, free from any adverse consequences on the issue of guilt. His contention was that the determination of his guilt and punishment in a single stage created a constitutionally intolerable tension between his Fifth Amendment right not to be a witness against himself in a criminal case and his right to be heard, without jeopardy, on the issue of punishment. In effect, he claimed a right to the kind of bifurcated trial offered in the California case, in order to be able to address the jury on the issue of punishment without having waived his right to silence on the issue of guilt. Thus, the unitary trial unconstitutionally forced him to waive one right in order to exercise the other.

Harlan, rejecting the argument as meritless, declared that it could not be supported by anything in the history, policies, or precedents relating to the Fifth Amendment. On the history of the matter he offered a brief paragraph. He invoked two authorities, Wigmore on *Evidence* and my book, *Origins of the Fifth Amendment* (which shows Wigmore to be untrustworthy on the history of the subject). Harlan also observed that at the time of the framing of the Fifth Amendment an accused person was not allowed to testify in his own behalf; thus, said Harlan, nothing like Crampton's dilemma could have arisen, historically.

Harlan was a careless reader, for my book supports Crampton's position. True enough, Crampton's dilemma would not have occurred in the eighteenth century, but only because he would have been heard in a unitary trial without jeopardy of his right not to be a witness against himself. Referring to the English practice, I point out that changes in procedure made it possible for a defendant to present his defense through witnesses and by counsel. "As a result, though he always retained his right to address the court unsworn at the close of his trial, and to range freely over any matters of his choice, he was no longer obliged to speak out personally in order to get his story before the jury, to rebut incriminating evidence, or to answer accusations by the prosecution."[13] Discussing the felony defendant in colonial America, I say, "He was, to be sure, excluded from the stand in the sense that he was not permitted to give testimony even if he wanted to. His interest in the case disqualified him on the theory that his evidence was unreliable. He was, nevertheless, permitted to tell his story unsworn at least in a final statement to the court."[14] I also state, "His incompetency, which was established at about the time when the right against self-incrimination became firmly secured, blended with the idea that he should be safe-guarded against cross-examination that might elicit his self-incrimination. The two principles, however diverse in origin and purpose, worked to the same end: the protection of the accused from exposure to questions whose answers might tend to put him in criminal jeopardy."[15]

I must add, in passing, a point that I develop in great detail throughout that thick book, that the right against self-incrimination constantly expanded in its meanings and applications; it was a dynamic and imperialistic concept at the time of the framing of the Fifth, and was closely linked to the evolving concept of due process of law and to the whole cluster of criminal procedures whose object was to insure fair play to the criminally accused. Harlan misread the principles and policies implicit in the Fifth, as well as its history. The framers of the Fifth saw it as the central feature of the accusatory system of criminal justice. They wanted more than minimizing the possibilities of convicting the innocent; they were not less concerned about the humanity that the fundamental law should show even to the offender. The Fifth reflected their judgment that just procedures in which the accused made no unwilling contribution to his conviction were more important than punishing the guilty. I find it hard to believe that the framers of the Fifth, which includes both the due-process clause and the right against self-incrimination, would agree that there was no constitutional requirement to provide an accused with the opportunity to speak to the jury free from any adverse consequences on the issue of guilt. The right to be heard on the question of one's ultimate fate seems elementary. The effectiveness of the criminal process in protecting society would not be diminished if the Court in *Crampton* had construed due process of law as requiring at a unitary trial the old practice of permitting the accused to make a statement, if he wished, before the conclusion of the trial. For Douglas, of all people, to speak about "the evolving gloss of civilized standards"[16] was ironic, but he was right in saying that the Court's opinion "stops the growth and evolution of procedural due process at a wholly arbitrary line. . . ."[17]

Brennan, too, was right in stating that the Court erred "from its premises to its conclusions."[18] He was strongest on the point that standardless capital sentencing violated due process. He repudiated the idea that the question before the Court was whether juries are obligated to follow standards so precise as to be capable of mechanical application. Disclaiming that the function of the Court is to legislate a code of standards for the jury's guidance, he sought to prove that a state's capital-sentencing policies could be rationally defined. The impossibility of perfect mechanical standards did not for him justify the failure of the Court to control lawless action by failing to require the states to impose some minimal standards. He conceded the necessity for discretionary judgment on the part of a capital jury but insisted that its judgment be bounded by state guidance on penological policy. A state might, for example, decide that only first-degree murderers who cannot be rehabilitated should be executed. Absent any standards, a jury's decision for death is inevitably made in a legal vacuum. Capital sentencing devoid of the protections ordinarily available to prevent arbitrary, inconsistent, and unreviewable action strikes at due process of law.

Brennan carefully analyzed the capital-sentencing practices of both Ohio and California. He found, as the Court did not deny, that state law deliberately left juries to their own absolute discretion with no responsibility for explaining their verdicts, making it impossible to know how or why one jury might decide against death and another for it. A state, Brennan reminded, may not take one life for reasons it would not apply to another. He said, in a proposition that Harlan summarily denied, that where life is at stake, it is "an interest of such transcendent importance" that the decision to execute requires "procedural regularity far beyond a decision simply to set a sentence at one or another term of years."[19] In a different case Harlan himself had expressed the point quite strongly when he said: "I do not concede that whatever process is 'due' an offender faced with a fine or a prison sentence necessarily satisfies the requirements of the Constitution in a capital case. The distinction is by no means novel, . . . nor is it negligible, being literally that between life and death."[20] Although the right to liberty may not be to some as precious as the right to life, the logic of Brennan's position on standards for jury guidance also justifies the proposition that where liberty is at stake, it is an interest of such transcendent importance that the decision to imprison, especially for a long time, similarly requires a high degree of procedural regularity. Still, life or death is a unique question, just as death is a unique punishment, for it repudiates all possibility of rehabilitation and exacts the final retribution. Accordingly, Brennan's conclusion is convincing: The Court's decision rested on "nothing more solid than its inability to imagine any regime of capital sentencing other than that which presently exists."[21]

DEATH AS A CRUEL AND UNUSUAL PUNISHMENT

In 1972, one year after the *McGautha-Crampton* decision, the Court handed down its sensational opinions in *Furman* v. *Georgia* and companion cases, collectively called the "death-penalty" cases.[22] *McGautha* and *Furman* are incompatible. There is no way to reconcile them. If the Court had correctly decided *McGautha*, *Furman* was bad law. However, it was *McGautha* that was wrongly decided and made bad law; Brennan's opinion should have been the opinion of the *McGautha* Court. Not that *Furman* was much better; perhaps Powell's dissent in *Furman* should have been the majority opinion in that case.

The *Furman* Court was so fragmented that it split at least four different ways, perhaps six, and every member of the Court delivered an opinion, altogether 243 pages. No opinion mustered a majority. Although a five-man majority concurred in the disposition of the cases, there was not even a plurality opinion because the five divided into three groups—Brennan and Marshall, Douglas alone, and Stewart and White. Not one of the five actually joined in the opinion of any other, despite the similarities between Brennan and Marshall and between Stewart and White.

The ostensible issue in *Furman* was whether the death penalty as such violated the Eighth Amendment's ban on "cruel and unusual punishments," enforceable against the states through the Fourteenth Amendment.[23] Although the death penalty for first-degree murder and for forcible rape was held unconstitutional in the cases before the Court, only Brennan and Marshall were of the opinion that the death penalty was absolutely unconstitutional for all crimes and under all circumstances. Despite headlines that the Court had banned the death penalty, it did not. Even after ample time to read all the opinions, some leading members of the bar still misconstrued them as "outlawing capital punishment."[24] A brief *per curiam* opinion preceding the nine signed opinions stated,

"The Court holds that the imposition and carrying out of the death penalty in these cases constitute cruel and unusual punishment in violation of the Eighth and Fourteenth Amendments."[25] The key words were "in these cases." In some other cases, particularly in those where death is the mandatory penalty, capital punishment may be, and probably is, still constitutionally valid.

McGautha had involved capital-sentencing procedures, not capital punishment itself. *McGautha* was a due-process-of-law case while *Furman* was a cruel-and-unusual-punishment case, a distinction that a specialist could find meaningful. Much of the reasoning in *Furman*, though by no means all of it, made the two cases indistinguishable in any realistic sense. The conflict between the two cases as well as the chaos of judicial interpretations in *Furman* derived from the fact that White and Stewart joined the three *McGautha* dissenters to make a new and bare majority. The most recent members of the Court, Powell and Rehnquist, joined the remnants of the *McGautha* majority, Burger and Blackmun. Although each of the four Nixon appointees wrote a separate opinion, each concurred in each other's dissents, thus constituting a solid bloc of four, unlike the fragmented majority. The position of the dissenters, in brief, was that the constitutional prohibition against cruel and unusual punishments did not on any ground preclude a sentence of death not barbaric in nature. The lack of a plurality opinion among the majority makes the cement that held them together especially vulnerable to erosion. There was a wide breach between the White-Stewart position and the positions of the others in the majority. Even Douglas's position theoretically allows for the death penalty in some cases. If the objections of White and Stewart can be met by new state laws, a rehearing of the question before the Court as presently constituted could result in a different disposition. One additional Nixon appointment could convert the dissenting four into a new majority.

The swing men in the death-penalty cases were White and Stewart. Their votes determined not only the outcome but the ambiguity of the holding or, rather, holdings in the cases. White's opinion, though similar to Stewart's had a peculiar flavor of its own, displaying an insensitivity to the claim that capital punishment cannot be justified by a rationale based on retribution. Indeed, White almost glorified the theme of society's righteous vengeance for crimes punishable by death. The issue before the Court, he declared, is not whether the death penalty is unconstitutional per se, nor was the issue whether statutes were unconstitutional on their face if requiring death for first-degree murder or rape. White made clear that he did not mean that no system of capital punishment could comport with the Eighth Amendment. As he saw the issue, the Court was confronted by cases in which state laws had permitted the death penalty but had not required it. The problem was that too few received society's ultimate revenge. When death is not imposed as a sentence with sufficient frequency, it is no longer an effective deterrent to capital crimes and satisfies neither a general need for retribution nor any other end of punishment. The death penalty is not cruel and unusual in a constitutional sense if it serves social ends. "It is perhaps true," White declared, contradicting the rationale of his opinion, "that *no matter how infrequently* those convicted of rape or murder are executed, the penalty so imposed is not disproportionate to the crime and those executed may deserve exactly what they received."[26] Death is exacted "with great infrequency even for the most atrocious of crimes." If society's ends are not served by capital punishment, it becomes "pointless and needless." The fault lies not with the extreme penalty but with its rare imposition. Juries have become so merciful that the threat of execution "is too attenuated to be of substantial service to criminal justice."[27] Under White's view, frequent executions as a deterrent to capital crimes would be both salutary and constitutional.

White did not bother to mention *McGautha* by name nor to distinguish it, yet his reasoning was inconsistent with his concurrence in *McGautha*. There, White had agreed, as had Stewart, that giving juries an untrammeled discretion to find for life or death "is inoffensive to anything in the Constitution."[28] The Court refused in that case to admit that there could be any standards to guide a capital jury's discretion. Now, in *Furman,* White altered his position. As if following Brennan's *McGautha* dissent, White complained that "there is no meaningful basis for distinguishing the few cases in which it [death] is imposed from the many cases in which it is not," despite like circumstances. Capital punishment was not inherently defective under the Constitution; the defect was in the policy of vesting such discretionary sentencing authority in juries, so that the imposition of death "as it is presently administered" in cases like those before the Court, became cruel and unusual, contrary to the Eighth Amendment.[29]

Stewart's opinion had a different tone, yet it also conflicted with his *McGautha* position. Like White, he refused to hold that death, however unique as a punishment, is constitutionally impermissible in all circumstances. He did not agree with Brennan and Marshall that retribution is a "constitutionally impermissible ingredient in the imposition of punishment."[30] In the cases before the Court the state laws had not expressed a determination that forcible rape or murder could be deterred only by death sentences imposed upon all who commit those offenses. The fact that these were not cases in which death was mandatory in the event of conviction made all the difference to Stewart. Juries were left free to mitigate sentences by merciful verdicts. Accordingly, the death sentences in the cases before the Court were "cruel" because they passed the threshold of a punishment, such as life imprisonment, that would satisfy state laws. Moreover, execution was an "unusual" punishment because of its infrequent imposition. These death sentences were cruel and unusual, said Stewart in a striking though misleading phrase, "in the same way that being struck by lightning is cruel and unusual."[31] But cruel in the constitutional sense means barbaric, highly excessive, or greatly disproportionate to the crime.[32] Moreover, the metaphor drawn from a natural catastrophe was scarcely comparable to a jury's verdict in favor of death, however erratic or infrequent it might be, nor are the odds against being sentenced to death for a capital crime remotely like those against being struck by lightning. Stewart insisted that the prisoners under sentence of death in the *Furman* cases were "among a capriciously selected random handful" of those convicted for the same crimes.[33] He declared, "I simply conclude that the Eighth and Fourteenth Amendments cannot tolerate the infliction of a sentence of death so wantonly and so freakishly imposed."[34] Thus, Stewart, though distinguishing *McGautha* as a due-process rather than an Eighth Amendment case, in effect decided on due-process grounds that were consonant with those advanced by Brennan's *McGautha* dissent.

Burger, unable to conceal his irritation at the defection of White and Stewart, assailed them for their disrespect toward the principle of *stare decisis* (standing by precedent) and for their inconsistency. Although they purported to rest on Eighth Amendment grounds, their positions, Burger said, were founded on the prevailing application of capital-sentencing procedures—precisely the issued settled in *McGautha.* The critical factor in their opinions was that the sentencing discretion of juries had not been exercised in an acceptable fashion. Burger found "ironical" their view that the flexible sentencing system had "yielded more mercy than the Eighth Amendment can stand."[35] White and Stewart both professed to interpret that amendment, yet their view of it was unprecedented. More important, their concurrences constituted "essentially and exclusively a procedural due-process argument," for its burden was that "discretionary sentencing in capital cases has failed to produce evenhanded justice."[36] Burger could not fathom such views because they contradicted the *McGautha* decision, which had been made after much deliberation documented in 130 pages of opinions. "All of the arguments and factual contentions accepted in the concurring opinions today were considered and rejected by the Court one year ago." Burger thought "it would be disingenuous to suggest that today's ruling has done anything less than overrule *McGautha* in the guise of an Eighth Amendment adjudication."[37] Powell made a similar assault on Stewart and White, his unpredictably wayward brethren, and also concluded that *"McGautha* simply cannot be distinguished." The various opinions on the majority side, Powell said, "would, in fact, overrule that recent precedent."[38]

Stewart had indeed found a technical distinction between *McGautha* and *Furman,* though White never mentioned the precedent. Brennan, the author of the principal *McGautha* dissent, referred to that case only in passing, saying that the Court had held in favor of the right of juries to decide, as they do, on the death penalty wholly unguided by any standards, thus making capital-sentencing procedures no guard against the capricious selection of criminals for execution.

Marshall, like Brennan, delivered a long opinion in the death-penalty cases but skipped over *McGautha* and any encumbrances that it might impose upon the Court. Only Douglas among the

Furman majority faced *McGautha* with some candor. The Court, he said, had already refused to hold that the discretion of juries to send a person to death should be governed by any standards. Thus, "we are now imprisoned in the *McGautha* holding,"[39] for it prevented an argument that the vice of capital punishment lay in the process by which the death penalty is inflicted rather than in the penalty itself.

One suspects that Douglas found himself a prisoner of *McGautha* for tactical reasons. He apparently wanted to relieve his feelings in some feisty rhetoric on the question of the death penalty itself. He acknowledged that between *McGautha* and *Furman* there was a "tension" that highlighted the correctness of Brennan's *McGautha* dissent, in which he had joined. But instead of voting to overrule *McGautha,* Douglas leaped over it as if it foreclosed the right decision in *Furman*. The right decision was the one he relegated to a footnote in which he made his own rapier thrusts at White and Stewart, whose *Furman* opinions he exploited:

> I should think that if the Eighth and Fourteenth Amendments prohibit the imposition of the death penalty on petitioners, because they are "among a capriciously selected random handful upon whom the sentence of death has in fact been imposed," opinion of Mr. Justice Stewart, or because "there is no meaningful basis for distinguishing the few cases in which [the death penalty] is imposed from the many cases in which it is not," opinion of Mr. Justice White, statements with which I am in complete agreement—then the Due Process Clause of the Fourteenth Amendment would render unconstitutional "capital sentencing procedures that are purposely constructed to allow the maximum possible variation from one case to the next, and [which] provide no mechanism to prevent that consciously maximized variation from reflecting merely random or arbitrary choice." McGautha v. California, 402 U.S. 183, 248.[40]

Such a decision would have been quite different from the one reached by any of the five in the *Furman* majority. Douglas's own opinion, however earnest, reads as if an enemy of Brennan and Marshall had sought to parody them. What he wrote was an intellectual atrocity, filled with non sequiturs and irrelevant or distorted historical examples that meandered through the clauses of the Fourteenth Amendment. "Whether the Privileges and Immunities route is followed or the due process route, the result is the same," Douglas announced.[41] That sentence mangled historical evidence, assumed the fungibility, or interchangeability, of distinctive constitutional provisions, and made hash out of a century of precedents differentiating them. Douglas cast his opinion from the clause guaranteeing the equal protection of the laws. "There is increasing recognition," he declared, offering no proof, "of the fact that the basic theme of equal protection is implicit in 'cruel and unusual' punishments."[42] The rarely imposed death penalty was applied, for the most part, in a discriminatory fashion against the poor, the young, the ignorant, and the downtrodden. In short, it was reserved for Negroes and whites who are "niggers" in their own society, though he did not use the term.

Taken as a whole, there has rarely been so garbled, illogical, and frenetic an opinion on behalf of a position that can be persuasive though not convincing. Douglas did not go as far as Brennan and Marshall, for Douglas did not absolutely reject the death penalty. He allowed for it under the Eighth Amendment if legislatures would enact "penal laws that are evenhanded, nonselective, and nonarbitrary, and . . . require judges to see to it that general laws are not applied sparsely, selectively, and spottily to unpopular groups."[43] This seemed to mean that Douglas would find no violation of the Eighth Amendment, nor of any clause of the Fourteenth, if capital juries are no more merciful when the defendant on trial for his life is a well-to-do white man without radical connections. The "Leopolds and Loebs, the Harry Thaws, the Dr. Sheppards and the Dr. Finchs of our society are never executed," Douglas said, "only those in the lower strata, only those who are members of an unpopular minority or the poor and despised."[44] Douglas's sensitivity to society's unfortunates was not matched by a corresponding sensitivity to their victims. When, for example, he recounted the facts of the various cases before the Court, he told how Elmer Branch, "a Black, entered the rural home of a 65-year-old widow, a White, while she slept and raped her, holding his arm against her throat." He then robbed her and when leaving warned that if she told anyone what happened, he would return to kill her. "The record is barren," Douglas asserted, "of any medical or psychiatric evidence showing injury to her as a result of Branch's attack."[45]

Summing up, Douglas reverted to the grounds of the *McGautha* dissent. He stated that "these discretionary statutes" permitting death or a lesser penalty "are unconstitutional in their operation," not on their face.[46] If the "elite" suffered the same penalties for the same crimes or if "the minorities or members of the lower castes" did not suffer harsher penalties, the case might be different. "Whether a mandatory death penalty would otherwise be constitutional," Douglas ended, "is a question I do not reach."[47] A mandatory death penalty was not before the Court and thus required no judgment.

Brennan and Marshall assumed the task of finding constitutional validity in the abolitionist position that the Eighth Amendment prohibited any capital punishment.[48] To argue as a matter of public morality or policy that the state should not take a life as a penalty for crime is an appropriate task for legislation. The responsible jurist who must contend with constitutional law has a different task. In this case the text of the Constitution itself seemed confining, indeed, seemed to erect an insuperable barricade against acceptance of the abolitionist position. The prohibition of the Eighth Amendment against cruel and unusual punishments appears in the same Bill of Rights that clearly sanctions the death penalty. The Fifth Amendment begins with a guarantee that the death penalty shall not be a threat to anyone who, at least in a federal case, has not had the benefit of grand jury proceedings: "No person shall be held to answer for a *capital,* or otherwise infamous crime, unless on a presentment or indictment of a Grand Jury. . . ." The same amendment in two other clauses shows that the death sentence is constitutionally permissible under conditions that do not violate certain rights of accused persons: "nor shall any person be subject for the same offense to be twice put in jeopardy of *life* or limb; . . . nor be deprived of *life,* liberty, or property, without due process of `law." In 1868 the Fourteenth Amendment made an identical due-process clause applicable to the states, allowing them to take life as a penalty after providing due process of law. Thus, the Constitution itself in four places recognizes and permits capital punishment, a penalty that was common when the Fifth, Eighth, and Fourteenth Amendments were adopted. Even if the cruel-and-unusual-punishments clause "is not susceptible to precise definition," as Brennan admitted, the death penalty per se did not fall within the ban of that clause, nor did its framers think so.[49] Yet, what seemed like an impregnable constitutional fortress against the abolitionist position was, to Brennan and Marshall, merely a triumphal archway along its path. Blackmun, in his dissenting opinion, concluded, "although personally I may rejoice at the Court's result, I find it difficult to accept or to justify as a matter of history, of law, or of constitutional pronouncement." The Court had gone too far: "It has sought and has achieved an end."[50]

Blackmun's words fit Brennan and Marshall more than the others in the majority. The two abolitionists would have dramatically rewritten the supreme law of the land by judicial interpretations, but they believed that their standards of judgment were judicial and objective. Their elaborate disquisitions may be reduced to the proposition that death is a cruel and unusual punishment in the constitutional sense because it does not "comport with human dignity."[51] That phrase was Brennan's, and he used it as if it had talismanic properties that would transform the language of the Constitution, judicial precedents, and history. He condemned the death penalty as not comporting with human dignity, as offensive to it, or as degrading to it.[52] Brennan, and Marshall, who agreed, were right: Death is dehumanizing. But death as a penalty for crime is not a cruel and unusual punishment in the constitutional sense—at least not before this case. To rule that the death penalty violated the Eighth Amendment because it does not comport with human dignity was to rest on a rhetorical device devoid of legal or constitutional content, a highly subjective and nonjudicial test, as were such companion tests as "abhorred by popular sentiment," "unnecessary and excessive," and "uncivilized and inhuman."[53]

Brennan agreed that his determination should be "as objective as possible."[54] Acknowledging that the "danger of subjective judgment" is acute when the question before the Court is whether a particular punishment is cruel and unusual, he gave examples from a 1947 opinion by Frankfurter of subjective standards or tests to be avoided: calling a punishment one that "shocks the most fundamental instincts of civilized man," or "offends a principle of justice 'Rooted in the traditions and conscience of our people,' " or "repugnant to the conscience of mankind."[55] Brennan criticized

Frankfurter because nowhere in the latter's opinion was there any explanation how he arrived at his standards. Brennan's standards were no less imprecise, overarching, and subjective; his criticism of Frankfurter substantially applies to his own opinion.

Marshall's opinion was an even greater failure in this regard. He declared that the average citizen knowing all the facts concerning capital punishment would, "in my opinion," said Marshall, invoking Frankfurter's test, "find it shocking to his conscience and sense of justice."[56] To arrive at his conclusion that the death penalty violated the Eighth Amendment, "we have had to engage in a long and tedious journey," he said. "Yet, I firmly believe that we have not deviated in the slightest from the principles with which we began."[57] Marshall was right; he began with subjective principles that by definition held the death penalty void. Like Brennan he sought and achieved an end.

Both Brennan and Marshall gave full explanations of their position, but their explanations were like judicial Band-Aids covering their very personal and very humanitarian reading of present-day values. Burger and Blackmun professed sympathy for their abolitionist arguments but were wholly unconvinced, as were the other members of the Court. Yet Brennan and Marshall must also be credited for their review of those precedents in which the Court had construed the cruel-and-unusual-punishments clause. They were equally candid in expressing their belief that the past, far from confining them, freed them to express new law.

The precedents on the Eighth Amendment's clause help explain the vehemence of the dissenting opinions. That clause had not been the subject of numerous decisions. Among the precedents were three cases in which the Court had held that the punishments at issue were unconstitutionally cruel and unusual. In one a man who had falsified an official document had received a sentence that included twelve years at hard and painful labor with his ankles in chains day and night.[58] In the second, a wartime deserter who was a native-born citizen had been deprived of his citizenship.[59] In the last, a narcotics addict had been sentenced to jail simply because of his illness.[60] The death penalty was not involved in any of these cases, the only ones in which the Court previously found a violation of the Eighth Amendment, although the opinions in all three contained illuminating discussions of the meaning of the cruel-and-unusual-punishments clause.

In significant contrast the Court sustained sentences of death in two major capital cases as not conflicting with the clause. In its first opinion construing it, in 1879, the Court unanimously upheld a sentence of public execution by a firing squad.[61] In 1890 the Court unanimously sustained electrocution as a permissible mode of inflicting the death penalty.[62] Judicial explanation of the cruel-and-unusual-punishments clause in these and related cases accurately concluded that a punishment falling within the prohibition of the Eighth Amendment would be unnecessarily cruel either because it inflicts lingering and deliberate pain or is grossly unsuited to the crime. Crucifixion, breaking the body on the wheel, burning at the stake, boiling in oil, disemboweling alive, and other forms of torture were common examples advanced by the Court of punishments that were calculated to produce human suffering. The electric chair when first introduced was unusual in the sense of being novel, but not unusual in the constitutional sense because its purpose was to inflict the death penalty in a speedy and humane manner. The Court said in its 1890 opinion, "the *punishment of death* is *not cruel* within the meaning of that word as used in the Constitution. It [cruelty] implies there was something inhuman and barbarous,—something more than the mere extinguishment of life."[63] In neither the firing-squad case nor the electric-chair case could the means of execution have been sustained if the death penalty itself, however mercifully inflicted, was cruel and unusual.

Both Brennan and Marshall had insisted that the cases before them in 1972 were cases of first impression. Brennan conceded that the precedents revealed that the Court, when ruling on various methods of execution, "has assumed in the past that death was a constitutionally permissible punishment. Past assumptions, however, are not sufficient to limit the scope of our examination of this punishment *today*. The constitutionality of death itself under the Cruel and Unusual Punishments Clause is before this Court for the first time. . . ."[64] Marshall said that the fact that the Court had in the past expressed opinions on the constitutionality of the death penalty "is not now binding on us." He declared, "There is no holding directly on point," and took the position that the Eighth

Amendment by its nature requires that in the absence of "a very recent decision" precedent must "bow to changing values, and the question of the constitutionality of capital punishment at a given moment in history would remain open."[65]

In *Trop* v. *Dulles,* a recent opinion (1958), but not a "very recent" one, a plurality of the Court, speaking through Warren, declared:

> Whatever the arguments may be against capital punishment, both on moral grounds and in terms of accomplishing the purposes of punishment—and they are forceful—the death penalty has been employed throughout our history, and, in a day when it is still widely accepted, it cannot be said to violate the constitutional concept of cruelty.[66]

Both Brennan and Marshall circumvented this statement in footnotes. It was a dictum not necessary to the decision of a noncapital case and referred to a time when execution was "still widely accepted."[67] To Brennan, that left open the future constitutionality of capital punishment, and to Marshall the dictum recognized "that as public opinion changed, the validity of the penalty would have to be re-examined."[68] Anyway, Marshall added, *Trop* "is 15 years old now" and time changes many minds. But the two abolitionists did not consistently treat *Trop.* They relied on it for points that fit their argument, and they found in it an invaluable principle for guiding their judgment, namely Warren's statement, which both quoted, that the cruel-and-unusual-punishments clause "must draw its meaning from the evolving standards of decency that mark the progress of a maturing society."[69] Thus a penalty once constitutionally permissible was not necessarily permissible "today." Both Brennan and Marshall openly rejected the Constitution's sanction of the death penalty, the history surrounding the framing of the Eighth Amendment, the history of capital punishment in this country, and the Court's own precedents; both stressed the here and now, the values of "today" as each perceived them.

At one point Marshall virtually dismissed as irrelevant his own detailed discussion of the precedents and the history of capital punishment in America, for he concluded that his "historical foray" led to the question "now to be faced whether American society has reached a point where abolition is not dependent on a successful grass roots movement in particular jurisdictions, but is demanded by the Eighth Amendment."[70] In effect, the question he asked was this: In view of the fact that the democratic process had failed to achieve abolition, should the Court impose a new public policy upon the country by a novel construction of the cruel-and-unusual-punishments clause? His inconsistency as well as some of his arrogance lay in the fact that he believed that though public opinion did not demand an end to the death penalty, the people of the United States today find it "morally unacceptable."[71] Earlier in his opinion Marshall alleged that an excessive punishment would be cruel and unusual regardless of public sentiment to the contrary. Then he declared that even if a punishment was not excessive and if it still served a legislative purpose, "it still may be invalid if popular sentiment abhors it."[72] Marshall believed that the death penalty was invalid because popular sentiment did abhor it, but he offered no proof of that. He claimed that public-opinion polls on the death penalty were not reliable because the people were not "fully informed" about it; if they were, they would find it "shocking, unjust, and unacceptable."[73] Marshall flatly declared that they do "at this time" believe it to be morally unacceptable.[74] In support of this he asked a question that was not only stacked, but unjudicial and nonconstitutional in character. For Marshall it was determinative: "In other words, the question with which we must deal is not whether a substantial proportion of American citizens would today, if polled, opine that capital punishment is barbarously cruel, but whether they would find it to be so in the light of all information presently available. . . . With respect to this judgment, a violation of the Eighth Amendment is totally dependent on the predictable, subjective, emotional reactions of informed citizens."[75] Marshall sounded as if he had mastered the ancient art of reading entrails. In a footnote he added that the fact that the constitutionality of capital punishment depends on the opinion of informed citizens "undercuts the argument that since the legislature is the voice of the people, its retention of capital punishment must represent the will of the people."[76] Like Brennan, Marshall had his own standards, tests, and formulae to demonstrate his case.

Brennan, too, cut himself off from history. He took comfort in

Warren's flexible interpretation of the cruel-and-unusual-punishments clause in *Trop*. Brennan also found that the Court had made a similar statement in a 1910 case when it said that because time works changes and brings about fresh purposes, a principle, like that of the Eighth Amendment, to be "vital, must be capable of wider application than the mischief which gave it birth."[77] That, Brennan declared, showed that the Court had "decisively repudiated the 'historical' interpretation of the Clause."[78] On the contrary, the statement in context proved only that specific punishments not known to the framers of the clause may or may not be constitutional. Nevertheless, Brennan had a strong point, and he did not sever himself from prior language of the Court, nor even of the Constitution itself, if his purpose could be served. He relegated to one of his footnotes a stunning retort to the dissenters who so heavily stressed the fact that the language of the Fifth Amendment authorized the death penalty. One of its clauses prohibited placing any person in double jeopardy of life "or limb." By way of proving that time, changing standards, and a progressive civilization can alter or abort even the text of the Constitution, Brennan asserted correctly that no one now contends that the reference to jeopardy of limb "provides a perpetual constitutional sanction for such corporal punishments as branding and earcropping, which were common punishments when the Bill of Rights was adopted."[79] Not one of the four dissenters took note of the point; it was irrefutable. If mutilation as a punishment has become unquestionably cruel and unusual, despite its constitutional sanction, why not the death penalty?

Brennan developed point by point a complicated test for determining whether capital punishment had become unconstitutional. It was a test that incorporated four principles which he found "inherent" in the ban against cruel and unusual punishments. He summed up the test as follows:

> If a punishment is unusually severe, if there is a strong probability that it is inflicted arbitrarily, if it is substantially rejected by contemporary society, and if there is no reason to believe that it serves any penal purpose more effectively than some less severe punishment, then the continued infliction of that punishment violates the

command of the Clause that the State may not inflict inhuman and uncivilized punishments upon those convicted of crimes.[80]

Brennan then asked the question whether the death penalty "is today consistent with the command of the Clause that the State may not inflict punishments that do not comport with human dignity."[81] That, of course, was *his* reading of the clause against cruel and unusual punishments. Applying his test of four principles, he reached the inevitable inference that death today is a violation of the Eighth Amendment. Death, he reasoned, is a unique punishment, the ultimate sanction reserved only for the most heinous crimes. Death "is today an unusually severe punishment, unusual in its pain, in its finality, and in its enormity."[82] In every respect it was in a class by itself, "uniquely degrading to human dignity."[83]

The infrequency with which it is inflicted proves, Brennan claimed, that the death penalty is an arbitrary punishment. Like Marshall, he provided statistical data to demonstrate a steady decline in the actual infliction of the supreme penalty. During the 1930s, the average number of executions annually was 167, in the 1940s 128, in the 1950s 72, and in the 1960s still fewer. Yet, over the same four decades, the population increased dramatically while the number of capital crimes committed far outstripped the population growth. The last execution in the United States occurred in 1967 when a de facto moratorium began as a result of pending cases that challenged both capital-sentencing procedures and the death penalty itself.[84] Powell suggested that, even before the moratorium began, judicial decisions expanding the scope of the constitutional guarantees of the criminally accused had the effect of further diminishing the number of executions.[85] Nevertheless, Brennan showed that before such decisions could have much impact, the number of executions continued to fall, averaging 48 annually for the years 1960–62. The figures show such a progressive dwindling in the infliction of the death penalty that it became, Brennan correctly said, a "contemporary rarity."[86] For the decade of the 1960s there was a fairly steady average of 106 death sentences imposed annually, and 127 in 1970, yet not nearly that number of sentences were carried out, because an average of 44 a year were commuted to imprisonment, or resulted in transfers to mental institutions, or ended in judicial stays of execution or grants of retrial or other orders stopping the original sentences of death. From his examination of the data, Brennan observed that when a nation of more than 200 million people inflicts the death penalty "no more than 50 times a year, the inference is strong that the punishment is not being regularly and fairly applied. To dispel it would indeed require a clear showing of nonarbitrary infliction."[87] That brought him back to his *McGautha* dissent and the point that capital-sentencing procedures as well as the actual incidence of execution proved that in capital cases the infliction of death "smacks of little more than a lottery system."[88] Nowhere in his opinion was Brennan stronger, but the issue in *Furman* was not on capital-sentencing procedures; nor did the infrequency of executions prove that death was a cruel punishment.

Applying another principle of his test, he said that capital punishment "has been almost totally rejected by contemporary society."[89] His proofs did not substantiate that allegation. The first was that the methods of execution had changed during our history; the gallows and firing squad had given way to electrocution and lethal gas, while public executions, once thought to be a deterrent to criminal behavior, had long been rejected as debasing and brutalizing. Contrary to Brennan, the changing circumstances that surrounded infliction of the death penalty did not establish the cruelty of today's methods of execution or the penalty itself, nor its unacceptability to society. Nor did the fact that there has been a "drastic decrease" in the number of capital crimes on the books. Nor did the fact that mandatory death sentences had yielded to a discretionary power in juries to recommend imprisonment for those found guilty of capital crimes. Brennan was replaying his *McGautha* theme. But proving that "virtually all death sentences today are discretionarily imposed"[90] scarcely established that capital punishment is either cruel or rejected by contemporary society. Brennan did show that nine states had abolished the death penalty outright by statute, that a tenth, California, had done so by a recent judicial decision,[91] that five more states have restricted the death penalty to extremely rare crimes, and that six other states, while retaining the penalty on the books, have made "virtually no use of it." But the reverse side of the data shows that the remaining 29 states inflicted the death penalty with enough regularity to show that contemporary society had not yet rejected it.

Undaunted, Brennan concluded that the statutes authorizing death, the cases resulting in execution, as well as the opinion polls and referenda approving of the death penalty, simply "underscored the extent to which our society has in fact rejected this punishment." His conclusion was circular: The refusal of society to inflict death "save in a few instances" compelled the "inference" on his part that "there is a deep-seated reluctance to inflict it. Indeed, the likelihood is great that the punishment is tolerated only because of its disuse."[92] There were, Brennan noted, 608 men on death row as of December 31, 1970, awaiting the outcome of the Court's decision, and before the moratorium there was almost one execution a week in the United States—"no more than 50 times a year."[93]

Applying the final principle of his test, Brennan sought to demonstrate that death is an excessive punishment because it did not serve penal purposes any more effectively than less severe punishments. The states had presented to the Court two arguments to the contrary—deterrence and retribution. The first was that the death penalty more effectively than life imprisonment deterred potential criminals from committing capital crimes. Brennan, rejecting that argument as unsupported by the evidence, deferred by and large to Marshall's proofs that the threat of death has no greater deterrence than the threat of imprisonment. Marshall very carefully and responsibly evaluated the evidence, which he himself characterized as inadequate, inaccurate, and tricky to use. His honest summary was that although "abolitionists have not proved non-deterrence beyond a reasonable doubt," they have demonstrated convincingly that capital punishment "is not necessary as a deterrent to crime in our society." He added, "This is all that they must do."[94] Needless to say, the dissenters thought otherwise. But no one made the point that the death penalty operates most effectively as a deterrence upon those who are executed: They never again commit crime. On the other hand, Marshall was correct in concluding that no one has ever proved that executing some people will deter others. Some, yes; most, no.

Both Brennan and Marshall observed that the validity of the

deterrence argument depended on swift and sure execution for the commission of a capital crime, and both almost conceded that our system of administering criminal justice, with its complicated protections of the accused, is largely responsible for robbing the death penalty of its deterrent force.[95] The logic of this proposition would seem to imply that the fault lay at least in part with the courts rather than in the failure of capital punishment as a deterrent, and the remedy lay in judicial reforms rather than in throwing out the death penalty. Brennan and Marshall claimed that, at best, death as a deterrence operates most effectively on people who can think rationally about the commission of capital crimes and the consequences that follow.[96] Such people probably expect to escape detection or if caught know that they are not confronted by the probability of swift and sure execution; the risk of death, Brennan said, is "remote and improbable," so that there is "no reason to believe that as currently administered the punishment of death is necessary to deter the commission of capital crimes."[97] That, too, was a proposition implying that our system is administered ineffectively rather than that the death penalty is an ineffective deterrence. Indeed, our criminal courts are so clogged and the wheels of justice turn so slowly that even imprisonment as a deterrence has lost much of its effectiveness.

The same weakness appeared in Brennan's rebuttal of the states' argument that executions serve to manifest the community's outrage at the commission of capital crimes. "If capital crimes require the punishment of death in order to provide moral reinforcement for the basic values of the community," Brennan declared, "those values can only be undermined when death is so rarely inflicted upon the criminals who commit the crimes."[98] That proposition, too, spoke to the breakdown of our system of criminal justice, but Brennan reinforced his rebuttal with an ethical point. Doubting whether executions strengthened the moral code of the community, he claimed that their more likely effect was to "lower our respect for life and brutalize our values."[99] This response failed to recognize the obligation of society to the victims of atrocious crimes and to their families. Some crimes, such as the rape of a child or the deliberate murder of an innocent victim, possess a dimension of enormity that demand a response by the state beyond imprisonment. Our respect for life may be lowered and our values brutalized when rapists and murderers are not executed. Capital punishment is less brutal than some crimes that invoke it.

Such an assertion, of course, raises the argument of retribution which, Brennan said, "in this context means that criminals are put to death because they deserve it."[100] Brennan's statement, which he advanced with obvious scorn, would be true in the same sense that any punishment, as Marshall recognized, is based in part on retribution.[101] The most important element of retribution, however, is not vengeance; it is a consideration of the need to protect society against those who commit crimes that violate the most fundamental social tenets. That does not mean that death rather than life imprisonment is the only appropriate answer, but it could mean that the state might decide that in some cases death is an appropriate retributive answer.

Brennan and Marshall insisted that if death is not the mandatory sentence and if a lesser sentence such as life imprisonment is possible, then the maximum sentence is excessive in the constitutional sense of being cruel and therefore impermissible. But, as Brennan noted, "life" imprisonment is a "misnomer," because rarely, "if ever," does a sentence mandate life imprisonment without possibility of parole.[102] For him the possibility of such a sentence meant that a criminal could not reach the point where further crimes are not punishable.[103] Brennan also expressed the belief that "techniques of isolation" could eliminate or minimize the danger that a capital prisoner posed to society. Surely one with Brennan's compassion should recognize that solitary confinement for an extended period is a punishment "degrading" or "offensive" to human dignity. Nor does life imprisonment without hope of parole necessarily "comport" with human dignity or the possibility of rehabilitation. Anyone who reads newspapers or watches television knows also that lifers can and do kill fellow inmates and prison guards, or sometimes escape to resume their vengeance on society.

When rehabilitation is farfetched and the crime is atrocious, and yet death is not exacted as a penalty, the protective as well as retaliatory purpose of the criminal law is not served. Brennan was right in saying that concepts of criminal justice change, since many crimes once capital have become noncapital. He was right too in saying "no immutable moral order requires death for murderers and rapists."[104] Moral orders are not immutable, but in a stable representative system of government, legislatures acting for society, rather than appellate judges, should determine which crimes deserve the extreme penalty whether for reasons of insurance to protect society or to express its outrage and revulsion. Yet Brennan cannot be countered in the final point he made before summing up his long opinion. He reverted to his *McGautha* theme: As administered today, the death penalty is unjustifiable. It probably does not deter nor can it be justified as a necessary means of retribution when "the overwhelming number of criminals who commit capital crimes go to prison. . . ."[105] That was an irrefutable argument against the present administration of the death penalty, not against the penalty itself.

Marshall's opinion was similar in substance to Brennan's. Despite his heavy reliance on criminological and sociological studies, his opinion was like an intellectual landscape pitted by overgeneralizations, unsubstantiated speculations, and standards more suited to ethical philosophy and to legislative policy considerations than to constitutional law. Like Douglas, Marshall said capital punishment had a discriminatory impact on the poor and minority groups. Douglas used the point about discrimination in the context of an equal-protection contention that could make constitutional sense in a case not dealing with the Eighth Amendment. Marshall used the point in support of his guess that the public would oppose capital punishment if only the facts about it as he understood them were known. He was scoring a propaganda point, not a constitutional one, because he sought to "convince even the most hesitant of citizens to condemn death as a sanction. . . ."[106] His statistics showed that since 1930 almost as many Negroes had been executed for murder as whites and that nine times as many had been executed for rape, proving that the number of Negroes executed was greatly disproportionate to their percentage of the population. Marshall explained that the higher rate of execution among Negroes was "partially due to a higher rate of crime," but he concluded that "there is evidence of racial discrimination."[107] His surmise was very probably accurate as to the existence of discrimination in the use of the death penalty in rape cases and possibly inaccurate in murder cases. Marshall offered no statistical data in support of his generalizations for the 1930–70 period.

Recent government figures show that Negroes, who constitute only about 12 percent of the population, are accused of half the rapes and over 60 percent of the murders—an astounding disproportionate criminal rate.[108] Burger's list of the sixteen states that still permitted the death penalty for rape, at the time of this case, shows that every one was a Southern or border state except for Nevada.[109] Burger claimed that the data showing racial discrimination in the impact of the death penalty covered periods when Negroes were systematically excluded from juries and when many states still maintained an official policy of racial segregation.[110] What Burger implied was that the situation had changed, and indeed it has. Juries have acquitted a number of Negroes, including Black Panther leaders like Huey Newton and Bobby Seale, who had been accused of capital crimes, including the murder of policemen. As Powell said, racial bias in the trial-and-sentencing process has diminished, and the day when juries did not represent minorities has passed. Never before in our history has there been a greater assurance of a fair trial for all citizens. Discriminatory imposition of the death penalty is far less likely today because standards of criminal justice, Powell asserted, have become "favorable to the accused."[111] That assertion doubtlessly reflected his personal belief that the pendulum had swung too far in the direction of the rights of criminal defendants, but he was correct in implying that Marshall and Douglas's views on the discrimination issue lacked convincing evidence. Reliable and up-to-date evidence showing the continued imposition of the death penalty in a racially discriminatory manner might well raise an equal-protection issue. That was not the issue in this case. As Burger pointed out, the Court had agreed to hear and decide on the Eighth Amendment question only.

Powell most effectively responded to Marshall's point about discrimination. Conceding that the death penalty "falls more heavily on the relatively impoverished and underprivileged elements of society," Powell took note of the obvious fact that they have been subject in every society to greater pressures to commit crimes. That they constitute a disproportionate share of capital criminals was a "tragic byproduct of social and economic deprivation, but it is not an argument of constitutional proportions. . . ." Powell accurately observed that the same discriminatory argument could be made with respect to those sentenced to prison. From a constitutional standpoint, the due-process clause makes no distinction between the deprivation of life or of liberty. If its discriminatory use made the death penalty cruel and unusual, discrimination similarly rendered invalid other punishments for crimes of violence. Yet, abolition of criminal sanctions would neither attack the causes of the higher incidence of punishments imposed on minorities and the poor, nor leave society with any viable system of criminal justice. "The basic problem results not from the penalties imposed for criminal conduct," Powell correctly declared, "but from social and economic factors that have plagued humanity since the beginning of recorded history. . . ." The constitutional issue before the Court did not relate to the problem of the causes of crime nor the incidence of punishment.[112]

Marshall's supposition that society would condemn capital punishment if only it knew that "innocent people have been executed"[113] is possibly the strongest argument against the death penalty, because death being final the execution of an innocent man would be the supreme and tragic miscarriage of justice. Whether innocent men are in fact executed under our system is speculative. Marshall was imprecise in his allegations in this respect. Having opened the subject by flatly declaring that "there is evidence that innocent people have been executed before their innocence can be proved,"[114] he ended by saying, "we have no way of judging how many innocent persons have been executed but we can be certain that there were some."[115] He cited several studies showing that although innocent people had been sentenced to death, none had been actually executed; he also cited one study by an author, who later modified his position, contending that eight innocent persons were actually executed.[116] The risk, however horrifying, appears slight, as the same author concedes. It is a risk that inheres in any system of criminal justice, in ours probably least of all. There is also the risk, far more substantial, that innocent men are imprisoned for noncapital as well as capital crimes. Penalties are not abolished because miscarriages of justice occur. The irrevocability of execution makes it a very special case, but if we must speculate, as Marshall did, the failure to execute raises the possibility that those who are sentenced to prison instead of death may commit other capital crimes. Recidivists who leave prison by the escape route or by pardon or parole may kill or rape far more innocent people than the state kills by execution. To argue against the death penalty on the ground that innocent persons have been executed is an argument from policy not suited for judicial consideration in a case whose question is whether the death penalty is cruel and unusual. To guess that we can be certain that some innocent persons have been executed, though we do not know how many, is to invite a retort to Marshall's confident assertion that there is "no alternative but to conclude that capital punishment cannot be justified on the basis of its deterrent effect."[117] We do not know how many would-be capital felons have been deterred by the thought of execution, "but we can be certain," in Marshall's words, "that there were some." Yet, apart from speculation about executing the innocent, we do not know as a fact that the death penalty is an effective deterrence generally.

Another highly questionable feature of Marshall's opinion, and of Brennan's, was his statement that according to the precedents the death penalty is excessive, unnecessary, and without a legislative purpose. Marshall declared that Burger and Powell had sought "to ignore or to minimize" that aspect of the Court's precedents.[118] On the contrary, they demolished Marshall's allegation. Burger's review of the precedents revealed that Marshall had taken the word "unnecessary" out of context, altering the meaning it had in the precedents. The Court had used "unnecessary" in its first Eighth Amendment opinion in 1879 when it said that punishments of torture and "all others in the same line of unnecessary cruelty" are forbidden. "Unnecessary" in an Eighth Amendment case had, until 1972, been associated with extreme cruelty akin to torture.[119] Powell showed that the word had also been used in connection with the concept of disproportionality; particular sentences may be cruelly excessive or disproportionate for particular crimes, but, as the precedents showed, only if "grossly" excessive or "greatly" disproportionate, indicating that the Court might strike down a penalty only in extraordinary cases.[120] Burger and Powell found nothing in the precedents, and there was nothing, to show that the death penalty itself had ever been regarded as excessive, unnecessary, or without a legislative purpose.

All four Nixon appointees dissented, but Powell and Rehnquist voted as their predecessors, Black and Harlan, would have. In *McGautha,* Black had pointlessly gone out of his way to include in his brief concurrence a dictum that the ban on cruel and unusual punishments could not be read to outlaw capital punishment.[121] Harlan had been the author of the Court's opinion in *McGautha;* he could not have voted to sabotage it, as the majority Justices did in *Furman.* Powell's dissent in *Furman* had the intellectual candor and power usually associated with Harlan, but Powell did not have Harlan's influence with Stewart and White. If Harlan had lived, one or both of those apostates from *McGautha* might have been convinced otherwise. In any event, Powell, like Burger, acquitted himself well.

Since the four dissenting justices in *Furman* presented their opinions in order of seniority, Rehnquist, the junior member, was left with very little to say. He said it briefly in a simplistic essay on the virtues of judicial self-restraint.[122] Despite his brief service on the Court at the time, his preachment came from one without clean hands. The same may be said of the disquisitions on judicial self-restraint by Burger and Blackmun, both of whom had demonstrated in many cases a contempt for precedents of the Warren Court. That fact, however, did not sap the validity of what they had to say about the proper role of the judiciary in *Furman.* One suspects that self-restraint is too often a convenient instrumentality to be invoked whenever they happen to agree with the precedents or the legislation before the Court. In this case, however, there is a ring of sincerity in their devotion to judicial deference to legislative judgment, for both Burger and Blackmun expressly went on record as stating that if they were free to vote on the death penalty as legislators, policy as well as ethical considerations would enlist their deep-seated abolitionist sympathies.[123] Burger, if not buying the abolitionist position wholesale, would at least restrict the death penalty to a few of the most heinous crimes, while Blackmun expressed his opposition to the penalty without qualifications. Their point, however, was that as judges they were not at liberty, in Burger's words, to "enact our personal predilections into law."[124]

Burger and Powell wrote the main dissenting opinions. To a far greater degree than Brennan and Marshall, they directly faced most of the arguments advanced by their opposition and explained why they could not accept them. Douglas had written a soliloquy that was oblivious to the dissents; Brennan, however elaborately explaining his own position, tended for the most part to avoid conflicting contentions. Marshall met them on a few points. Both Burger and Powell wrote opinions that merit greater respect for their intellectual force and openness as well as for taking into consideration the majority opinions. They engaged in a debate, emerging with opinions that will probably prevail in the long run as more convincing on balance. Both Burger and Powell, while showing respect for the precedents took neither an antediluvian nor a rigid stance. They accepted the positions that the Eighth Amendment embodies moral standards with respect to the meaning of cruelty, that it could not be restricted only to those punishments regarded as cruel and unusual in the past, and that it changed in meaning with the evolution of democratic and civilized values.[125] In effect, they agreed that the question whether capital punishment violated the Eighth Amendment was appropriate for judicial review. Nevertheless, they found that the case for abolishing the death penalty fell far short of being conclusive. Accordingly, they deferred to legislative judgment, which in a democracy reflected the prevailing standards of decency or morality.

The facts about public opinion on the death penalty, as revealed by the dissenters, showed no new consensus validating any confident assertions that contemporary society rejected it as abhorrent. The death penalty, at the time of this case, was still authorized by forty states, the District of Columbia, and the United States for a variety of crimes. Four times in the preceding eleven years, and as recently as January of 1971, Congress added to the crimes for which the death penalty was possible. Nor had anything new happened in the states that made the situation today different from what it had been in the past.[126] During recent years in more than half the states retaining the death penalty, bills had been introduced to repeal or modify it. In only a few instances did those bills get out of committee for a vote on the floor, and then, with a few exceptions, the votes were not even close.[127] New York in 1965 restricted the use of capital punishment to cases involving the murder of a policeman and murder by a prisoner serving a life sentence. Oregon a year earlier had abolished the death penalty. But elsewhere, both public-opinion polls and referenda, as well as legislative actions, revealed continued majority support for the death penalty.[128] As Powell summed up the facts, recent history "abundantly refutes the abolitionist position."[129] Burger required "obvious indications that capital punishment offends the conscience of society to such a degree that our traditional deference to the legislative judgment must be abandoned"[130]—a fair enough test. Finding no such indication, he thought it proper to ask in effect, but not without some bewilderment, why does the situation today suddenly demand a judicial decision that capital punishment is cruel and unusual? There was nothing to show that legislatures had lost touch with current social values.[131]

Unlike the majority Justices, Burger did not equate "unusual" with "infrequent." "Unusual," as Marshall conceded at one point, meant a new and inhuman punishment.[132] The rarity of the infliction of the death penalty did not make it unusual in the constitutional sense. Burger acknowledged that juries were inconsistent; there were prisoners on death row who would not be there if tried by a different jury or in a different state. In that sense, said Burger, virtually justifying the *McGautha* dissents, the fate of capital defendants is controlled by "fortuitous circumstance."[133] But he refused to admit that unevenhanded justice infringed the Eighth Amendment.[134] Nor would he or Powell admit that the imposition of the death penalty was in fact "freakishly rare," a characterization that Burger described as hyperbole.[135] During the 1960s, juries returned 1,057 sentences of death, a rate of about two a week. There were no reliable facts comparing the number of cases in which death sentences were imposed and the total number in which death was statutorily permissible, but various estimates showed that death was the verdict in about 20 percent of the cases.[136] Brennan and Marshall focused mainly on the actual infliction of death, but the dissenters' data on the frequency of verdicts for death was pointed at the majority's contention that the death sentence was unusual and repugnant to the community's moral sentiment.

Burger exposed the double standard employed by Brennan and Marshall. They found in jury verdicts recommending mercy an expression of civilized standards renouncing legislative authorization of capital punishment, but when juries recommended death, Burger noted, the majority members of the Court saw arbitrary and capricious decisions that conflicted with prevailing standards of decency.[137] If the selective imposition of death was proof of a rejection of capital punishment in cases where it was not imposed, the cases showing its imposition just as surely proved its acceptance.[138]

Powell and Burger did not find anything in the abolitionist position that convinced them that capital punishment was unjustifiable from the standpoint of deterrence or retribution. Both served valid legislative purposes until proved otherwise. The evidence provided an "empirical stalemate"[139] which could not be resolved simply by imposing upon the states the burden of demonstrating the effectiveness of the death penalty as a deterrence or its morality as retributory justice. The alarming increase in the rate of violent crimes could suggest that no criminal punishment deterred crime; to argue that life imprisonment was as effective a deterrent as death was to raise the question whether a briefer imprisonment was as effective as life.[140] Powell quoted a 1968 opinion by Marshall stating that the old and still raging debate on the validity of "the deterrence justification for penal sanctions has not reached any sufficiently clear conclusions to permit it to be said that such sanctions are ineffective" for all people.[141] The evidence, Powell thought, as Marshall apparently once did, was too inconclusive to warrant a judicial conclusion that a legislature had acted irrationally when grounding a death statute in part on its deterrent value.

Powell agreed that retribution alone might seem an unworthy justification for capital punishment in a moral sense; he recognized a utility in a system of criminal justice that required public support. Despite a conflict in the jurisprudential literature on retribution as a factor in punishment, there was a consensus, Powell concluded, "that, not infrequently, cases arise that are so shocking or offensive that the public demands the ultimate penalty for the transgressor."[142] As Marshall had noted in his 1968 opinion—in a nondeath case—the Court "has never held that anything in the Constitution requires that penal sanctions be designed solely to achieve therapeutic or rehabilitative effects."[143] The remark was comparable to that of Burger's in *Furman,* that the Eighth Amendment "is not addressed to social utility and does not command that enlightened principles of penology always be followed."[144] Powell concluded persuasively that as a matter of policy and precedent "this is a classic case for the exercise of our oft-announced allegiance to judicial restraint."[145] He deplored the Court's decision as an "enormity" in the sense that it invalidated hundreds of state and federal laws.[146]

The decision left the future of capital punishment in the United States "in an uncertain limbo," to use Burger's phrase. The immediate effect of the decision was clear; it emptied the death rows in prisons throughout the nation, both state and federal. The decision of the California Supreme Court four months earlier had reprieved 107 convicts awaiting execution, including the depraved mass-murderer Charles Manson and the assassin of Robert Kennedy, Sirhan Sirhan;[147] the decision in *Furman* reprieved more than 600 more, many of whom, to paraphrase White's tough phrase, deserved death for their crimes. A great many doubtless fell into the category of the luckless who had been capriciously sentenced to die when others in like cases had been sentenced to prison. The sentences of all were set aside not because the death penalty itself is cruel and unusual, as Burger pointed out, but because "juries and judges have failed to exercise their sentencing discretion in acceptable fashion."[148]

The Court did not rule that capital punishment is per se a violation of the Eighth Amendment, nor that the punishment is impermissible for particular classes of crimes, nor that mandatory death sentences for such crimes are cruel and unusual. The Court did prevent Congress and all of the states from legislating on capital punishment "except," as Powell stated, "in a manner consistent with the cloudily outlined views of those Justices who do not purport to undertake total abolition."[149] Burger made a similar point when he declared that until legislation could be passed that satisfied Stewart and White, juries and judges "can no longer be permitted to make the sentencing determination in the same manner they have in the past."[150] In effect, there was a majority only in the silent overruling of *McGautha:* Unfettered sentencing discretion, if not a violation of the due-process clause, in some way violates the cruel-and-unusual-punishments clause. In 1967 the President's Commission on Law Enforcement and Administration of Justice concluded unanimously that "the present situation in the administration of the death penalty in many states is intolerable."[151] Powell had been a member of that Commission. In his *Furman* dissent, he quoted from its report and said that he still subscribed to its views. *Furman* made the administration of the death penalty in all states unconstitutional. Powell thought that nothing short of a constitutional amendment could reverse the Court's judgment— surely an overstatement. He believed that in the absence of such an amendment, "all flexibility is foreclosed. The normal democratic process, as well as the opportunities for the several States to respond to the will of their people expressed through ballot referenda . . . is now shut off."[152]

Burger more accurately and with considerable wisdom summed up the situation. Statutory action rather than constitutional amendment will suffice to remedy the "limbo"[153] into which *Furman* had cast capital punishment, but "significant statutory changes" would have to be made to satisfy the pivotal concurring opinions.[154] Since the Court assumed that the death sentence was randomly and unpredictably meted out, legislatures will have to find ways to provide "standards for juries and judges to follow in determining the sentence in capital cases or by more narrowly defining the crimes for which the penalty is to be imposed."[155] That was as much as admitting that if Brennan's *McGautha* dissent can be satisfied by appropriate standards to fetter the discretionary element in sentencing, the death penalty will be constitutional. Burger conceded that "if such standards can be devised or the crimes more meticulously defined"—and he was skeptical about that possibility—"the result cannot be detrimental."[156] Clearly a statute fixing a mandatory penalty of execution for anyone convicted of a given crime would be constitutional if administered with consistency, if, that is, juries did not acquit well-to-do Wasps and convict poor or minority defendants who were charged with the same crime. Burger, however, strongly believed that a mandatory death sentence for conviction, denying juries the flexibility of bringing in a guilty verdict on a lesser charge, would be so regressive and contrary to enlightened practice that he "would have preferred that the Court opt for total abolition."[157]

Whatever the solution, the decision in *Furman* necessarily forces legislatures, state and national, to re-evaluate with considerable care the crimes for which death might be justified and to determine standards for the guidance of juries and trial judges in capital cases. Burger was not at all displeased that legislatures have been given this "unavoidable responsibility"[158] as well as the opportunity to prove that capital punishment is a subject on which they can act more effectively than courts. *Furman*, however wrong as a matter of law or history, and however wrong in reversing irrevocably the sentences of death for many who were justly convicted without caprice or unfairness, did indeed have the salutary effect attributed to it by Burger. Whether the legislatures of this country will seize the responsibility and opportunity forced upon them by the Court is a problem that only time will answer—time and the Court when it passes upon the results in the various cases that will undoubtedly emerge out of the new legislation.

In a federal system that legislation on capital punishment will surely be varied. Some states may, as Burger said, abolish it completely or reinstate it on a selective basis. But *Furman* implicitly raised a question that could have arisen long ago when death as a punishment was abolished for a particular crime or crimes in one state but continued in others: No matter how constitutionally permissible are the standards for guiding juries in capital cases, no matter how restricted are the crimes for which death may be inflicted, no matter whether death is mandatory on a finding of guilt, if the same crime in one state is punishable by execution but by a lesser sentence in another, has the equal protection of the laws been provided? *Furman* also leaves unsolved, *inter alia,* the whole problem of unequal punishments even short of death for the same crimes in a given state or in different states all of which are subject to the same supreme law of the land. Notwithstanding the advantages that are supposed to inhere in the experimentation allowable within a federal system, liberty, like life, has a constitutional value that should not be impaired by unevenhanded systems of criminal justice. If the question of capital punishment is ever constitutionally resolved, the question of standardization of punishments will probably arise under the equal-protection clause if not the due-process clause. Within a framework allowing for flexibility of sentencing that takes rehabilitative possibilities into account, there should be similar punishments for the same crimes in all of the states. But, whether the punishment should fit the crime or fit the criminal is a problem that society has never satisfactorily resolved. To impose the same punishment on persons committing a similar crime can be as unjust as imposing unlike punishments for a similar crime. In the sense that no two people are alike, no two cases are the same—a fact that necessitates some discretion in the imposition of the death penalty. Not all discretion is necessarily arbitrary or capricious.

The unpopularity of the Court's decision in *Furman* is attested by the fact that several months later, according to a Gallup Poll, 57 percent of the nation favored capital punishment, an increase of 7 percent from the figure at about the time of the decision, and 67 percent favored death for drug sellers.[159] Moreover, in half a year after *Furman,* more than half the states were considering reinstatement of capital punishment for selected crimes. By the end of 1973, twenty-one states had passed new statutes making death virtually mandatory for first-degree murders and felony murders devoid of mitigating circumstances.[160] In a radio speech to the nation, supplemented by a message to Congress, President Nixon in March of 1973 recommended that "harsh measures" be imposed "without pity." He exploited popular sentiment with characteristic oversimplifications, condemning "soft-headed judges" and a "permissive philosophy," and he scorned the idea that social injustice breeds crime.[161] Claiming that capital punishment for specific crimes had an "effective deterrent effect"—a fact never proved and quite probably wrong—Nixon nevertheless advocated a policy whose merits deserved the serious attention of Congress.

To meet the Court's objections to capricious and arbitrary capital-sentencing procedures, Nixon recommended novel and meticulous procedures for a new federal law restoring the death penalty. Many of the new state acts have adopted the same procedures, which, ironically, are substantially like California's as sustained by the Court in *McGautha.* Nixon proposed that capital punishment should be meted out only for a few federal crimes: wartime treason, espionage, and sabotage; assassination of government officials; the murder of law-enforcement officers and prison guards; and skyjacking, the bombing of public buildings, and kidnaping that results in death. The trial of an accused would be in two stages: the first to determine guilt or innocence, and the second, after a verdict of guilty, to determine the penalty. At the penalty trial, the jury would be required to take into consideration aggravating and mitigating factors. Death would be mandatory in the absence of mitigating factors such as mental impairment, youth, or acting under duress, while the finding of any aggravating factors, such as creating a risk to life, killing for hire, or a heinous crime like skyjacking, bombing, or kidnaping resulting in death, would require a mandatory sentence of death.[162]

Most of the new state statutes imposing death for specified categories of murder follow a similar two-stage trial, including a separate penalty trial that weighs aggravating and mitigating factors. Such statutes retain a desirable but confined element of jury discretion. In late 1973 the Court refused to reconsider its decision in a companion case to *Furman* or to consider the validity of a 1965 New York statute that imposed mandatory capital punishment on those who murder police officers or prison guards, or who commit any murder while already under sentence for life.[163] Several important new state statutes took effect during 1973 and others were scheduled to go into operation at the beginning of 1974, including those of California and Ohio. Congress has not yet responded with a new federal death-penalty law. In view of the fact that *Furman* did not overrule *McGautha,* despite the views of the *Furman* dissenters, the spread of the two-stage trial with its separate penalty hearing will require the Court, sooner or later, to consider its constitutionality under the Eighth Amendment. Death-sentence cases will inevitably crop up and increase in number, requiring ultimate decision. By the close of 1973 there were already forty-four prison inmates living in new "Death Rows," half of them in North Carolina.[164] New rulings by the Supreme Court will necessarily turn on what White and Stewart believe to be arbitrary and capricious impositions of death.

CHAPTER EIGHT

Conclusions

In a figurative sense, Richard M. Nixon now and for an indefinite period in the future casts four votes in criminal-justice cases decided by the Supreme Court. The Court under Burger has not veered dramatically away from the Court under Warren in other areas of constitutional law. Criminal justice is the one field that Nixon expressly desired to influence by appointing men who shared his law-and-order philosophy. Cases that deal with the rights of the criminally accused under the Fourth, Fifth, and Sixth Amendments are the largest category of cases on constitutional law decided by the Court. The trend of decision in such cases by mid-1972 was abundantly clear. By then the four Nixon appointees had been together for six months. When the term of the Court closed, in June 1972, a reporter at a press conference, referring to the President's objective of balancing the Court to strengthen the "peace forces" against the "criminal forces," asked him whether the Court was balanced yet or needed "another dose of strict constructionism if that occasion should arise." Nixon replied, ". . . I feel at the present time that the Court is as balanced as I have had an opportunity to make it." But for the death-penalty decisions—and he clearly hoped Congress would remedy these—he seemed satisfied for the time being with the criminal-justice work of the Court.[1]

Evaluating the Court for the term ending June of 1972, Professor Philip B. Kurland of the Law School of the University of Chicago, one of the nation's foremost experts on constitutional law, observed that many of the prevailing attitudes of the Warren Court were no longer dominant. Although Kurland had written an unsympathetic critique of the Warren Court, the fact that the Nixon Court reached a "watershed in constitutional law" simply as a result of changes in personnel disturbed him. "For, if the meaning of the Constitution is as fluid as the personal whims of the Court's membership would make it, it is really no constitution at all."[2] Kurland's real complaint was that the Nixon Court has not given convincing reasons for departing from settled meanings of the provisions of the Constitution. He understood that judicial decisions, as Max Lerner once quipped, are not babies brought by constitutional storks, even though members of the Court sometimes pretend that the facts of judicial life are not fit knowledge for the public. Occasionally, when a new majority mauls a precedent to which a Justice is attached, he will denounce a decision made possible by a simple change in the membership of the Court. As Black angrily declared in 1971, the "precious rights of citizenship should not be blown about by every passing political wind that changes the composition of this Court."[3] Douglas, always more iconoclastic and skeptical of illusions, acknowledged that, "changes in membership do change decisions; and those changes are expected at the level of constitutional law."[4] The reason is that constitutional law is public policy writ large in the fundamental law. It is the least technical branch of law, the most akin to statecraft, and the one in which precedent is of the slightest influence.

That the Nixon Court favored law-enforcement values is no surprise. Burger, Blackmun, Powell, and Rehnquist got their seats on the bench because of their supposed or known lack of sympathy for the rights of the criminally accused. In one respect they have been remarkably forbearing to date—and shrewd. They have avoided dramatic overrulings of precedents in the area of criminal justice. Precipitous repudiations of established doctrines would appear too much as an act of arbitrary will; decisions should not look like the obvious result of subjective choices. In the art of judging, a proper regard for appearances counts. One must seem to appreciate the values of coherence, stability, and continuity with the past. Judges, especially judges who are reputedly conservative, ought to avoid sudden, radical shifts in constitutional doctrine. Any man who reaches the highest court is sophisticated enough to appreciate the strategic and political values of achieving desired objectives by indirection. Overruling is a device of last resort, employed when other alternatives have failed. The Nixon Court has raised the use of alternative routes to a high art by relying on more subtle means than overruling in order to alter the course of the law. It reinterprets precedents, distinguishes them away, blunts them, obliterates them, ignores them, and makes new law without the need of overruling or being bound by the past. It nourishes the impression that it is a standpat Court, which merely refuses to endorse further expansions of the rights of the criminally accused. It cultivates the illusion, suitable to the image of a conservative court, of having some respect for precedents; at the same time, it narrows them until they become meaningless and moribund. When new cases arise it finds factual distinctions, always available, that allegedly warrant watering down the constitutional right at issue. New decisions have a corrosive effect on previous ones. While the Nixon Court goes about its quiet business of creating its own regressive "revolution" in the criminal law, striking a pose of doing no more than refusing to open new frontiers, it has systematically closed old frontiers and made daring incursions that cripple many rights of the criminally accused.

A recent illustration is *United States* v. *Calandra,* decided early in 1974, a case that should depress anyone who cares about the Court, or the Constitution.[5] The heading of the front-page story of *The New York Times* accurately summarized the holding of the case: "Court Says Grand Juries May Use Illegal Evidence."[6] The grand jury subpoenaed Calandra to ask him questions based on evidence seized during an unconstitutional search of his place of business. A federal district court granted Calandra's motion to suppress the evidence and ordered that he need not answer any of the grand jury's questions based on that evidence. The Court of Appeals for the Sixth Circuit affirmed, holding that the Fourth Amendment's exclusionary rule bars questioning based on evidence obtained in an unlawful search and seizure. The Supreme Court, voting 6-to-3, reversed both lower federal courts.

Five times during the course of his opinion for the Court, Powell claimed that to apply the exclusionary rule of the Fourth Amendment to grand-jury proceedings would be *extending* it, and on two of those occasions he said the Court merely declined to make "an unprecedented extension" of the rule.[7] The effort to seem prudent by avoiding rash departures was labored and deceptive. Seeking to show how broad are the investigatory powers of grand juries, Powell declared that they may even return indictments based on evidence "obtained in violation of a defendant's Fifth Amendment privilege against self-incrimination, Lawn v. United States, 355 U.S. 399 (1958)."[8] The case cited proved no such thing, for the defendant's counsel explicitly waived a right to object to the evidence in question; indeed, he welcomed its introduction as proof of his client's innocence, and the opinion of the Court made no reference to a request for the exclusion of evidence obtained in violation of the right against compulsory self-incrimination.

There was, however, a precedent of 1920 in which the Court clearly decided that the exclusionary rule applies to grand-jury proceedings. Holmes, for the Court, stated that the "essence of a provision forbidding the acquisition of evidence in a certain way is that not merely evidence so acquired shall not be used before the Court but that it shall *not* be used *at all*."[9] In a footnote to his *Calandra* opinion, Powell explained why the 1920 precedent was distinguishable. The dissenters—predictably, they were Brennan, Douglas, and Marshall—believed that the precedent "controls this case" and rebutted Powell's contrived distinctions, none of which altered the crucial fact that for over half a century the exclusionary rule barred grand juries from using evidence derived from illegal searches and seizures. To talk about an "unprecedented" or a "proposed" *extension* of the exclusionary rule, as if its application to grand-jury proceedings was novel, broached judicial perjury.

Powell also described the exclusionary rule as merely "a judicially-created remedy designed to safeguard Fourth-Amendment rights generally through its deterrent effect, rather than a personal constitutional right of the party aggrieved."[10] That the Fourth Amendment does not expressly provide for the exclusionary rule is literally true, but most "personal constitutional rights" are judicially created in the sense that they are interpretations of the text of the Bill of Rights. Powell himself, for example, referring to the Fifth Amendment, stated that a grand jury "may not force a witness to answer questions in violation of that constitutional guarantee"; he added that a grand jury may not compel the production of incriminating books and papers. The self-incrimination clause of the Fifth Amendment does not refer to grand juries or to books and papers, yet Powell described them as "personal constitutional rights."[11] The Fourth Amendment, which was at issue in *Calandra,* does not stipulate that warrants must be issued by detached and neutral magistrates, or that a police officer seeking to establish probable cause for a warrant must offer some corroborative evidence if he is acting on a tip, or that words captured by electronic eavesdropping come within the ambit of the amendment. Yet not even the *Calandra* majority would deny the constitutional status of these established readings of the amendment. As Brennan pointed out in his dissent, when extending the exclusionary rule to the states in 1961, the Court described it as "part and parcel of the Fourth Amendment's limitation" upon government and as "an essential part of both the Fourth and Fourteenth Amendments. . . ."[12] Brennan also dwelled on a major rationale of the exclusionary rule that the Court neglected. Powell referred to it only as a deterrence against police misconduct. Brennan, who spoke more broadly of government misconduct, quoted Holmes, Brandeis, Warren, and others to prove that the Court had always taken the position that the purpose of the rule was also to maintain the integrity of the judicial system by preventing the use of tainted or illegal evidence at any stage of a criminal proceeding. Otherwise, the government would profit from the fruits of its lawlessness with the cooperation of the judiciary.

In 1961 the Court sought "to close the only courtroom door remaining open to evidence secured by official lawlessness" in violation of Fourth Amendment rights. The Court held that "all" evidence illegally obtained came under the ban of the exclusionary rule.[13] In *Calandra* Brennan feared that the Court had left the door ajar, signaling that the majority had "positioned themselves to reopen the door still further and abandon altogether the exclusionary rule in search and seizure cases."[14] Given the opinion of the Court in *Calandra,* with its downgrading of the rule to a "judicially-created remedy" rather than a constitutional right, and with its wretched distinctions that shriveled various precedents, Brennan's fears may yet come true. That seems unlikely, however. A trademark of the Nixon Court is its reluctance to overrule precedents outright, and it would have to overrule a whole line of cases going back to 1914 if it sought to abandon the exclusionary rule of the Fourth Amendment. Furthermore, Powell's opinion seems to have the effect of permitting an indictment on the basis of evidence that would not be admissible to prove guilt at a trial. More than once Powell spoke of "the inadmissibility of the illegally-seized evidence in a subsequent criminal prosecution of the search victim." He even declared that in a trial the defendant is entitled to suppress the derivative use as well as the fruits of a violation of the Fourth Amendment. "The prohibition of the exclusionary rule," he declared, "must reach such derivative use if it is to fulfill its function of deterring police misconduct."[15]

Of course, as long as words mean whatever the Court wants them to mean, the future may disclose that *Calandra'*s endorsement of the exclusionary rule at least in criminal trials had an escape hatch. If the rule's rationale is merely that it deters police misconduct rather than official or governmental misconduct, proof already exists to demonstrate that the rationale is unfounded. By permitting grand juries to use evidence admittedly obtained from an unlawful search and seizure, the Nixon Court showed a lack of concern for the integrity of the administration of criminal justice.

Calandra is a characteristic illustration of the Nixon Court in action in a criminal-justice case. A comparison of some of its other holdings with Warren Court precedents reveals the new trend of decision. The Warren Court held that a police officer seeking a search warrant from a magistrate must prove that his informant is trustworthy and his tip reliable. The Nixon Court allowed the magistrate to credit unverified hearsay by issuing a warrant without proof of the truth of an anonymous tip.[16] The Warren Court ruled that judges must indulge every presumption against implied waivers of constitutional rights and reaffirmed the old doctrine that a person may not make a valid waiver unless he intentionally and understandingly gave up a known right. Accordingly, the Warren Court would not agree that acquiescence to a claim of lawful authority constituted a consent to a search, waiving Fourth Amendment rights. Almost beyond belief, the Nixon Court held that the established standard for a waiver of rights does not apply to Fourth Amendment rights, thereby downgrading them. Accordingly, a consent to a search made without knowledge that one has a right to refuse is a voluntary choice, even if an unknowing one, that allows the police to capitalize on a person's ignorance of his rights; the police are under no constitutional obligation to inform anyone that he can say no to a request for a search.[17] The Nixon Court also held that a counseled plea of guilty forecloses all scrutiny of the question whether the defendant understood the various rights sacrificed by his plea. Unless a lawyer is stupefyingly incompetent, the Court presumes that the defendant has had the effective assistance of counsel; the defendant takes the risk of his lawyer's mistakes.[18]

The Warren Court ruled that electronic eavesdropping is subject to the warrant requirement of the Fourth Amendment; it held against warrantless government intrusions into conversations that have a justifiable expectation of privacy. The Nixon Court, seeing no relevance in an expectation of privacy, held that no warrant is required when one party to a conversation wears a secret bugging device.[19] The Warren Court agreed that a policeman who has a reasonable suspicion, based on his own observations or on authenticated information, may stop and frisk a person. The frisk is a safety precaution, and if it leads to a search the evidence seized must relate to the cause of arrest. The Nixon Court gave the police a free hand by finding that an unauthenticated tip from an informer of questionable reliability justifies a stop and frisk. The discovery of a weapon validates an arrest and a search for any evidence of crime. Moreover, if there is probable cause for an arrest, even if for only a traffic violation, the officer may conduct a full search and seize any evidence of crime, however unrelated to the cause of arrest.[20]

The contrasts between the Warren and Nixon Courts in Fifth Amendment questions are equally stark. The former ruled that a failure of the police to advise a suspect of his right to silence tainted a confession, making it inadmissible as evidence of guilt. The Nixon Court undermined that holding by deciding that the confession can be introduced as evidence to impeach the witness's credibility. A jury is not likely to distinguish between evidence that proves guilt and evidence that impeaches credibility. Moreover, the Nixon Court condoned illegal conduct by the police by accepting an admittedly illegal confession.[21] The Warren Court held unconstitutional statutes that compelled gamblers and Communists to provide a link in a chain of evidence that might incriminate them by compulsory registration. But the Nixon Court could not even detect a Fifth Amendment issue in a statute that required automobile drivers to identify themselves when involved in an accident.[22] The Warren Court held that a grant of transactional or absolute immunity against future prosecution requires a person to answer all questions without fear of incriminating himself. The Nixon Court held that the Fifth Amendment requires only a grant of use and derivative-use immunity, which exposes a person to prosecution for the offense to which the questions relate if the police find evidence supposedly independent of his testimony.[23]

The Warren Court had construed Sixth Amendment rights far more generously than the Nixon Court. The former applied to the states the same standards for trial by jury as exist for federal trials. The latter held that the Sixth Amendment does not require the states to provide for the traditional criminal jury of twelve members who decide verdicts unanimously; nonunanimous verdicts and juries of less than twelve meet the requirements of the Constitution.[24] The Warren Court held that a guilty plea induced by promises that deprive it of its voluntary character is void, as is a state act that permitted the defendant to escape a possible death penalty, if convicted by a jury, by pleading guilty. Such a statute, according to the Warren Court, impermissibly burdened the right to trial by jury and needlessly encouraged its waiver. The Nixon Court found that once a defendant enters a plea of guilty on the advice of counsel, he has voluntarily waived all his rights and cannot raise the question whether his plea was the result of an inducement to avoid the more severe penalty.[25] The Warren Court extended various rights of the criminally accused to defendants in juvenile-delinquency proceedings, including the right to counsel, to notice of charges, to cross-examination, and to exemption from compulsory self-incrimination. The Nixon Court refused to extend the guarantee of trial by jury to juvenile defendants.[26] The Warren Court found that the use of a self-incriminatory statement obtained without the protection afforded by the assistance of counsel violated due process of law. The Nixon Court saw only a harmless error when a state tricked a prisoner into a confession by planting a police officer in his cell to pose as a cellmate, out of the presence of the prisoner's counsel.[27]

The Warren Court consistently upheld the right of confrontation by insisting that the right to cross-examine prosecution witnesses is basically a trial right. Accordingly, testimony at a preliminary hearing that had not been subjected to cross-examination was inadmissible at a trial, unless the state could not produce the witness. The prior confession of a defendant implicating his codefendant, according to the testimony of a police officer, was also inadmissible if by reason of the Fifth Amendment the person who allegedly confessed refused to take the witness stand and be cross-examined. The Nixon Court held that statements made at a preliminary hearing are admissible at a trial even though the witness, who was present in court, could not be cross-examined because he could not remember. The Nixon Court also accepted a codefendant's out-of-court confession, though the defendant, whom the testimony incriminated, had no opportunity to cross-examine. Moreover, the Nixon Court accepted in evidence against a defendant incriminatory hearsay remarks by a person whom the state might have produced in court but did not.[28]

The Warren Court regarded the suppression of evidence favorable to an accused person as a violation of due process; the Nixon Court ruled that such evidence was immaterial, even though it concerned the identification of the defendant by the prosecution's alleged eyewitness.[29] The Warren Court required the presence of counsel at a police lineup conducted for the purpose of identifying an alleged criminal. The Nixon Court emasculated that ruling by limiting it to lineups held after indictment, thereby denying the right to have counsel present at the vast majority of lineups, which are held before indictment. The Nixon Court also held that even after indictment, when eyewitnesses make an identification of the defendant from photographs, he has no right to have counsel present to monitor police suggestions or preserve the right to effective cross-examination at the trial.[30]

In all these cases where the Nixon Court stepped backward while claiming that it was standing still in order to avoid a forward step, the prosecution won. In the case sustaining six-member juries, Marshall dissented alone. Brennan dissented alone when the Court approved of the use of testimony from a preliminary hearing not subject to cross-examination at trial. Had Brennan participated in the transactional-immunity case, he would have joined Douglas and Marshall in dissent. A remarkable feature of the alignment of the Justices is that Brennan, Douglas, and Marshall dissented in all the other illustrative cases, which are only a representative sampling of the pro-prosecutorial decisions.

The Court did not, of course, always decide in favor of the prosecution, nor did it always avoid new doctrines extending the constitutional rights of the criminally accused. There are fewer than a dozen of such criminal-justice decisions since Burger became Chief Justice, and in all of them Brennan, Douglas, and Marshall were the core of the majority. There were three rare unanimous decisions in favor of the criminally accused. In one the Court extended the guarantee of the right to counsel to any prosecution that could result in imprisonment.[31] In the second the ruling was that the President has no inherent power to tap and bug domestic subversives without a warrant issued by a court.[32] In the third the Court held that the only remedy for a denial of the right to speedy trial is freeing the defendant.[33] Except for Rehnquist's dissent on a jurisdictional point, the Court was also united in a fair-trial case when it extended to a defendant the benefit of a hearsay exception that had the usual indicia of reliability.[34]

In other decisions favorable to the accused, the Court divided closely. The most important was the death-penalty decision. The four Nixon appointees, dissenting, supported the constitutionality of the death penalty. Each of the five Justices in the majority wrote his own opinion, in which no one else concurred. Moreover, the majority did not overrule the decision of the preceding year holding that a jury's standardless discretion to return a verdict for death does not violate due process of law.[35] The Court also ruled, 5-to-3, that there can be no conviction except on proof of guilt beyond a reasonable doubt even in juvenile-delinquency proceedings.[36] The Chief Justice, who was the only Nixon appointee at the time, was among the dissenters. In another case, however, the Court approved of a trial judge's instructions to a jury that proof of guilt of an essential element of a crime can be inferred rather than proved beyond reasonable doubt.[37] Brennan, Douglas, and Marshall dissented, and did so again when the Court ruled that proof by a preponderance of evidence, rather than proof beyond reasonable doubt, is sufficient to establish the voluntariness of a confession.[38] When Burger was the only Nixon appointee, he also dissented from a 5-to-3 holding that the right to trial by jury extends to any defendant whose punishment might exceed imprisonment for six months.[39] In a major case on warrantless searches and seizures, the Court by a 5-to-4 vote narrowed the scope of search incident to arrest and of seizure of evidence in plain view.[40] Burger again was with the dissenters. In a later Fourth Amendment case, Powell deserted the other Nixon appointees by joining the decision, in a narrow concurrence, that reversed a conviction based on evidence seized in a warrantless search by roving border patrolmen.[41] Powell also sided with the majority, leaving the other Nixon appointees in dissent, when the Court ruled that to require a defendant to give his testimony as the first witness for the defense, if he means to testify at all, violated Fifth and Sixth Amendment rights.[42] None of the other Nixon appointees has disagreed with the others when his vote affected the result of a criminal-justice case, and Powell has done so only in the two cases mentioned.

Statistics on how members of the Court vote in criminal-justice cases confirm the impression that one derives from reading the opinions. In Burger's first year on the Court, 1969–70, he and Douglas had the lowest incidence of agreement between any two members. They voted together in 46 percent of all cases. Burger agreed most often with Stewart, voting with him in 76 percent of all cases. The highest incidence of agreement existed between Brennan and Marshall, who joined together in 90.5 percent of the cases. That year the Court was not badly polarized. White voted more often with Marshall and Brennan than with anyone else; moreover, every pair of Justices, except Burger and Douglas, voted together in over one-half the cases.[43] The departure of Warren and Fortas and the arrival of Burger did perceptibly alter the trend of decision. In the preceding year, the Court had voted in favor of a civil-liberties or civil-rights claim in 81 percent of the cases. In Burger's first year that figure fell to less than 56 percent, while the Chief Justice himself voted in favor of the right claimed and against the government in less than 31 percent of the cases.[44]

Blackmun added to Burger's influence during his second year on the Court, 1970–71. The two men rarely differed. That fact, plus the fact that they came from the same state and are old friends, gave rise to the gibe that they were the "Minnesota Twins." They voted together 107 times in 119 cases, or 90 percent of the time, and in 100 cases they were voting in the majority. Burger's incidence of agreement with Douglas fell to 37.4 percent that term, and White began to drift toward Burger and Blackmun, voting with them more often than with any other member of the Court.[45] During Burger's third year, 1971–72, Powell and Rehnquist entered the scene in time to write as many opinions of the Court as Burger and Blackmun. The division of the Court into two wings became apparent. A year earlier, Black and Harlan tended to form a centrist faction toward which Stewart gravitated and, less frequently, White. The Justices who replaced Black and Harlan joined the right wing at the expense of the center, and White headed in the same direction. The four Nixon appointees voted with each other more than with any other member of the Court. The highest correlation of agreement was between Burger and Rehnquist, who agreed in 86 percent of the cases; the lowest was between Douglas and Rehnquist, who voted together only 27 percent of the time. The Nixon four frequently coalesced as a solid voting bloc. They all joined the same opinion in over 64 percent of the cases in which they participated, and voted for the same result even more frequently.[46]

When the Court divided sharply by votes of 5-to-4 or 6-to-3, the Nixon four flocked together in almost 71 percent of the cases, while on the left, the trio of Brennan, Douglas, and Marshall joined together 64 percent of the time. To win, the trio needed the votes of both Stewart and White, a combination that occurred in 22 percent of the cases. More than twice as often, White swung over to the Nixon four, and in 29 percent of the cases Stewart did so too. In 5-to-4 decisions, White provided the fifth vote eight times as often as Stewart. Stewart, who had been on the right wing of the Warren Court, became the centrist Justice of the Nixon Court; the views of the Nixon four pushed him over to join the trio on the left with increasing frequency. Both in closely divided cases and in all cases, Stewart voted most often with Marshall, least often with Rehnquist. Although Stewart's degree of variance from any member of the Court was not striking, for the first time he voted more frequently with Brennan than with White or Burger. In closely divided cases, White voted twice as often with Burger and Blackmun than with Douglas. In 82 percent of all closely divided cases, White was with the majority; no one else was on the winning side as often. Counting all cases, not just closely divided ones, White had no sharp degree of variance with any member of the Court except Douglas. Rehnquist and Douglas were at opposite extremes of the Court. When Rehnquist wrote its opinion, Burger and White joined him on every occasion, Blackmun and Powell most of the time, but the members of the trio on the left joined him only from one-fourth to one-third of the time.[47]

In 1972–73, when all four Nixon appointees were together for the first time for a full term of the Court, they continued to act in close formation. They voted together in 107 cases out of 153, and in 101 of those 107 occasions, White gave them a fifth vote. The highest incidence of agreement on the Court, counting all cases, was between Burger and Blackmun, who voted together 85.7 percent of the time. Rehnquist, on the far right, voted least often with other Nixon appointees, ranging from a low of 74.4 percent with Blackmun to a high of 84.7 percent with Burger. The lowest correlation on the Court was the 30.7 percent figure for Rehnquist and Douglas. Powell, the most moderate of the Nixon appointees, had correlations ranging from 45.5 percent to 57.3 with the three Justices on the left. Agreement among members of that trio reached a high of 83 percent for Brennan and Marshall and a low of 64.8 percent for Brennan and Douglas. The trio voted as a bloc as often as the Nixon appointees did. At the center, Stewart voted least often with Douglas, 48 percent of the time, and most often with Powell, 69.5 percent of the time. But Stewart agreed with Brennan and Marshall about as often as he did with Burger, Blackmun, Rehnquist, and White. White paired with each of the Nixon appointees at least 75 percent of the time. His incidence of agreement with the trio on the left ranged from a low of 41.4 percent with Douglas to a high of 55.4 with Brennan. That White and Stewart had shifted their alignments, White to the right and Stewart to left-center, is evident from the fact that in Burger's first year White had voted most frequently with Brennan and Marshall, while Stewart had voted most frequently with Burger.[48]

The figures given above relate to all cases, regardless of the issue, decided by the Court in written opinions. That includes all aspects of constitutional law. An analysis of just criminal-justice cases is far more appropriate to the subject of this book. Eliminating those criminal-justice cases in which there was broad agreement on the Court accentuates the alignments of its members. Powell and Rehnquist took their seats in January of 1972; by June they had participated in fourteen closely divided criminal-justice cases. From October 1972 to June 1973 the Nixon four were together for the full term of the Court. There were twenty-two closely divided criminal-justice cases that term. The chart shows the percentage of agreement between every pair of Justices in the thirty-six closely divided criminal justice cases decided during the first year and a half of the Court's present membership.

Rehnquist and Marshall agreed only once in thirty-six cases, or 2.8 percent of the time. Brennan and Douglas agreed with Rehnquist only once in thirty-six cases. The highest incidence of agreement on the Court existed between Marshall and Douglas at one extreme and between Rehnquist and Burger, and Blackmun and Burger, at the other. Each pair voted together in thirty-two of the thirty-six cases, or 88.9 percent of the time. The right and left wings stand out in bold relief. Brennan, Douglas, and Marshall paired together at least 80 percent of the time, while the voting alignments of Burger, Blackmun, and Rehnquist also ranged upwards of 80 percent. The fourth member of the right wing, Powell, broke away from Blackmun in one extra case, reducing their correlation to 77.8 percent. But Powell voted with Burger and Rehnquist slightly more often than Brennan voted with Douglas and Marshall. The figures show that in closely divided criminal-

**Judicial Agreement on Decisions in
Closely Divided Criminal-Justice Cases
January 1972–June 1973
Percentages**

	Blackmun	Brennan	Burger	Douglas	Marshall	Powell	Rehnquist	Stewart	White
Blackmun		16.7	88.9	16.7	13.9	77.8	80.6	41.7	77.8
Brennan	16.7		8.3	80.6	83.3	8.3	5.6	55.6	30.6
Burger	88.9	8.3		8.3	5.6	86.1	88.9	33.3	75.0
Douglas	16.7	80.6	8.3		88.9	13.9	5.6	55.6	30.6
Marshall	13.9	83.8	5.6	88.9		11.1	2.8	58.3	27.8
Powell	77.8	8.3	86.1	13.9	11.1		83.3	47.2	75.0
Rehnquist	80.6	5.6	88.9	5.6	2.8	83.3		33.3	66.7
Stewart	41.7	55.6	33.3	55.6	58.3	47.2	33.3		52.8
White	77.8	30.6	75.0	30.6	27.8	75.0	66.7	52.8	

justice cases, Powell is no moderate. His agreement with the liberal trio ranged from a low of 8.3 percent to a high of 13.9 percent. If, however, all cases, not just criminal-justice cases are counted, and if the count includes those cases in which the Court showed broad agreement, Powell voted with the trio in from 45.5 to 57.3 percent of the cases during the 1972–73 term. In closely divided criminal-justice cases during the year and a half, the highest incidence of agreement between a Justice on the right and one on the left was 16.7 percent, indicating Blackmun's correlation with both Douglas and Brennan.

White is decidedly to the right rather than the center. He voted with Rehnquist in two-thirds of the cases and with the other Nixon appointees three-fourths of the time, but his incidence of agreement with the trio on the left was less than one-third. White is the only member of the Court for whom the figures for the fourteen closely divided criminal-justice cases decided in the spring of 1972 show a significant variation from the figures for the twenty-two cases decided in the following term of the Court. The fourteen cases include several important ones in which White was on the side of Brennan, Douglas, and Marshall with respect to the result but on wholly different grounds. Thus, the chart exaggerates White's area of agreement with the trio on the left. The figures for his pairing in the twenty-two cases of the 1972–73 term show agreements with the Nixon four ranging from 77.3 percent with Rehnquist to 90.9 percent with Burger, and his agreement with Brennan and Marshall was 22.7 percent, with Douglas 27.3 percent. White's alignment is with the right wing. He and Stewart agreed in only about half the cases. Stewart's voting record shows no startling variations, although, significantly, he agreed with the trio on the left more than half the time and with the Nixon appointees only about one-third of the time, except for Powell, with whom he voted in almost half the cases.

The chart shows, then, two polar wings of the Court, one consisting of five members on the right, another of three on the left, and Stewart in the middle tending toward the left. White's vote is the key one that creates a majority when he joins the Nixon appointees. In that sense, White is the Court's swing man. If White goes with the Nixon four in about three-fourths of the criminal-justice cases, that many get decided by at least a five-man majority. If Stewart joins White about half the time, the Court resolves an additional 50 percent of the cases by a vote of 6-to-3. Brennan, Douglas, and Marshall win the remaining few by securing the support of both White and Stewart. Significantly, the Nixon four rarely break lockstep when the defection of one might change the result of a criminal-justice case.

Examining the results reached by the Court and the voting records of the Justices tells about as much as Kinsey's quantification of orgasms tells about love. Similarly, the boxscore of a baseball game is an unreliable measure of how well the contestants played. Two or more members of the Court may cast their votes for the same decision for utterly different reasons, which no statistical analysis can reveal. In a case involving the right to counsel at a police lineup, for example, White wrote a one-sentence opinion saying that a precedent, with which he had disagreed, governed the case and compelled a reversal of conviction; Brennan, joined by Douglas and Marshall, wrote an elaborate critique of the majority opinion and an explanation of the reasons that counsel should be present at the lineup.[49] The chart on voting alignments, which measures only results, shows White and Brennan voting together. They did, but that fact tells only a small part of the story. Similarly, the chart does not reflect the fact that the five Justices who voted together against capital punishment disagreed whether the death penalty was cruel and unusual, or an arbitrary and capricious penalty because of the untrammeled behavior of juries, or a violation of the principle of equal protection because juries discriminate against the poor.

The way the Court reasons or reaches its result is as important as the result itself; in the long run, perhaps, the Court's reasoning is even more important because a decision based on an unsound rationale is not likely to survive. A rationale may be unsound because it plays fast and loose with the relevant precedents or with truth; it may be overbroad, illogical, or biased; or, it may be one-dimensional by ignoring opposing arguments. The Court's respect for the judicial process, for the need to strive for objectivity even if unattainable, and for the requirements of professional expertise, in short, its craftsmanship, is a vital aspect of its work. Assessment of the Nixon Court's craftsmanship is as subjective as the art of judging, and experts will doubtless disagree, as they have about the Warren Court's craftsmanship. Concern for the validity of the route by which the Court reached its decisions is a major theme of Archibald Cox's book *The Warren Court,* the most sympathetic account yet published. Again and again, Cox subjects the Court's opinions to the scrutiny of an analytical, questioning mind, and again and again he fretted because the Court, though having reached the just result, failed to convince its critics.[50] Nevertheless, Charles Alan Wright, a conservative constitutional lawyer, writing when criticism of the Warren Court reached a fever pitch, asked, "What Court in the past achieved a higher level of professional craftsmanship than the present Court? The great opinions of Chief Justice Marshall surely fail the test. . . . Has any later Court done better?"[51]

The Nixon Court has done a lot worse in its criminal-justice opinions. It does not confront complicated constitutional questions with appropriate disinterestedness. Its opinions do not provide intellectually convincing explanations for its results. Far too often the majority simply issues edicts. Its fiat cannot command respect when the majority abuses or ignores precedents or refuses to consider fairly and seriously the arguments advanced by dissenting opinions. The majority faces away from, instead of facing, opposing views. There is too little debate in majority opinions. They fail to weigh criticisms. In brief, they do not develop carefully reasoned judgments. The majority seems to engage in result-oriented adjudication which is a corruption of the judicial process that leaves too far behind the idea of the rule of law enforced by impersonal and impartial judges. In constitutional cases, as in any other, the judge who first chooses what the outcome should be and then reasons backwards to supply a rationalization, replete with rules and precedents, has betrayed his calling: Having decided on the basis of prejudice or prejudgment, he has made constitutional law little more than the embodiment of his own policy preferences.

The Nixon Court writes opinions that have the sound of stump speeches for the prosecution. The majority Justices stand for law and order, but there is little reason to respect their work when they do not respect their dissenting brethren or critics who ask if there is something called law and the Constitution to which decisions should conform. The decisions of the Court represent what the majority at the moment happen to think is best for the country, but they do not persuade anyone who believes that a judge who does his job faithfully will with some regularity reach judgments that conflict with his personal views as a private citizen. Blackmun's anguish in the death-penalty case is almost unique for a Nixon appointee. All four, and White too, vote for the rights of the criminally accused about as often as snarks are sighted alighting on the roof of the Supreme Court building. Worse, their opinions lack cogency, rigor, and on more occasions than are fitting, intellectual rectitude. The heirs of the Warren Court, Brennan, Douglas, and Marshall, are by no means above judicial sin, but they commit it with considerably less frequency and are no longer in a position that makes its commission count. Everyone makes mistakes. Even Frankfurter and Harlan had their lapses and gaffes. But the majority that now controls the Court in criminal-justice cases has elevated the lapse and the gaffe to familiar events on decision day. Their opinions tend to make bad law in the sense of being badly crafted, as well as in the sense of tarnishing the Bill of Rights. The Court, as Professor Kurland declared, "ought to be able to explain why it is doing what it is doing." If it changes constitutional law, "it ought to state the reasons why it thinks the change is appropriate or necessary. . . . And when it does say why, it ought to do so honestly and not disingenuously or fraudulently."[52]

Justice Holmes is supposed to have said of his Chief Justice, William Howard Taft, that he honored him as former President and respected him as Chief Justice, but thought that as a lawyer he was no damn good. The lawyers who today constitute the majority of the Court in most criminal-justice cases are no damn good as judges. They are more like advocates for law enforcement's cause. The national press oversimplifies the work of the Court by characterizing its decisions and the Justices themselves as liberal or conservative. Even the *Harvard Law Review* divides the members of the Court into liberal and conservative voting blocs.[53] If Brennan, Douglas, and Marshall are liberal activists, the Nixon four and White are conservative activists. To attribute their opinions to strict construction of the Constitution is either foolish or deceptive.

The Bill of Rights requires an ardently sympathetic if not a liberal activist Court. There is no way for the guarantees of the Bill of Rights to have real meaning if not enforced by unstinting judicial affirmations that keep restraints upon government. No one wants to hobble law enforcement, no one wants the Bill of Rights to rot, and no one has ever proved that law enforcement cannot be effective against crime and be observant of the Bill of Rights at the same time. The fundamental law is an instrument of society, existing not as art does for art's sake but as a means for the sake of society's ends. Society requires a risky degree of freedom as well as an unremitting attack on the causes of crime and on law-breakers, even when the culprit is a policeman, a prosecutor, or a President. If officials protect society by any means at hand, they trade freedom for security. Any means to a justifiable end is, in a free society, a noxious and dangerous doctrine.

The Nixon Court surrendered to that doctrine when it condoned admittedly illegal police practices, sanctioned the use of illegal evidence, allowed warrantless searches and seizures unrelated to the cause of arrest, upheld the prosecution's failure to disclose evidence of value to the accused, permitted unknowing waivers of rights, and denied the effective assistance of counsel. Regrettably, one can expand this list showing the Court's determination to find means to sanitize or legitimate law-enforcement conduct that brings shame on the administration of the criminal-justice system. Stunting the Fourth, Fifth, and Sixth Amendment rights of the criminally accused may increase the prison population but will not have any effect on crime nor help solve its causes, any more than the Nixon Administration's habitual juggling of crime statistics can prove that crime is no longer a problem.

The trouble with the Administration's reports of crime statistics is, as *Time* said, that they are "like a set of crooked corporate books—deceptive." The President himself assured the nation that "the hour of crisis has passed" because of the dip in the urban crime rate. He did not mention that the cities to which he referred declined in population or that violent crime was still on the increase, especially in the suburbs, although the rate of increase is slowing down. Only a week later, in another speech scorning "soft-headed judges," Nixon recommended extremely harsh penalties for criminals. Despite the supposed passing of the crime crisis, there has been an unprecedented government crime wave, prompting a wag to suggest that Nixon took crime off the streets and put it in the White House.[54]

There is a subtle danger that the Nixonian ethic may penetrate the chambers of the Supreme Court. After the close of the 1972–73 term, one Washington lawyer ominously remarked, "The Court has been Nixonized." He meant only that "Nixon has left his stamp on the Court, and consequently on American law. It could last for a generation."[55] But the Court's fidelity to the Bill of Rights has become dangerously attenuated. Its integrity is at issue when it winks at official lawlessness, warps precedents, or reasons woefully.

A hieromancer can read the entrails of a sacrificial chicken for portents of the future. Anyone adept at that art knows that the Nixon Court will continue to undermine many criminal-justice achievements of the Warren Court. Those not skilled at reading entrails predicted that the Nixon appointees, being conservative jurists, would respect not subvert precedents. All of us who possess perfect hindsight can now decipher the writings in the ashes of an increasing number of opinions that for all practical purposes are dead.

Notes

CHAPTER ONE: The Supreme Court

1. The best general works on the Warren Court are Archibald Cox, *The Warren Court* (Cambridge, Mass., 1968); Alexander M. Bickel, *The Supreme Court and the Idea of Progress* (New York, 1970); Alfred M. Kelly and Winfred A. Harbison, *The American Constitution*, 4th ed. (New York, 1970), chs. 33–35; Philip B. Kurland, *Politics, the Constitution, and the Warren Court* (Chicago, 1970); and, Anthony Lewis, ed., *The Warren Court: A Critical Evaluation* (New York, 1970).

2. Quotation from John D. Weaver, *Warren: The Man, the Court, the Era* (Boston, 1967), pp. 335–36, 342–43.

3. "Retirement of Mr. Chief Justice Warren," June 23, 1969, 89 S. Ct. 17, 18, 19.

4. Aug. 8, 1968, in *Vital Speeches of the Day*, Vol. 34 (Sept. 1, 1968), p. 676.

5. Sept. 29, 1968, quoted in Richard Harris, *Justice: The Crisis of Law, Order and Freedom in America* (New York, 1970), p. 23.

6. *New York Times,* June 15, 1969, p. 43, col. 1.

7. Strunk v. U.S., 412 U.S. 434 (1973).

8. McNabb v. U.S., 318 U.S. 332, 347 (1943). See also Malinski v. N.Y., 324 U.S. 401, 414 (1945).

9. Shaughnessy v. U.S., 345 U.S. 206, 224.

10. *Crime in the United States: 1972.* Uniform Crime Reports (Washington, 1973), pp. 1–4. For a discussion of crime statistics, see below, last chapter.

11. Charles Nott, "Coddling the Criminal," *Atlantic Monthly* (1911), discussed in Yale Kamisar, "When the Police Were Not 'Handcuffed,'" *New York Times Magazine,* Nov. 7, 1965, reprinted in Donald R. Cressy, ed., *Crime and Criminal Justice* (Chicago, 1971), pp. 46–57.

12. Escobedo v. Ill., 378 U.S. 478, 490 (1964).

13. Miranda v. Ariz., 384 U.S. 436, 483 note 54 (1966), quoting Hoover, "Civil Liberties and Law Enforcement: The Role of the F.B.I.," *Iowa Law Rev.*, Vol. 37 (Winter 1952), 175, 177–82.

14. See generally, Leonard Downey, *Justice Denied: The Case for the Reform of the Courts* (New York, 1971), and James Mills, "I Have Nothing to Do With Justice," *Life*, Vol. 70 (March 12, 1971), 57–68.

15. David Fellman, *The Defendant's Rights* (New York, 1958) is the best summary of the constitutional law of criminal justice for the pre-Warren Court. The only book on the Warren Court and criminal justice is Fred P. Graham, *The Self-Inflicted Wound* (New York, 1970).

16. Rochin v. Cal., 342 U.S. 165, 172–73 (1952).

17. Powell v. Ala., 287 U.S. 45 (1932). See also Palko v. Conn., 302 U.S. 319 (1937).

18. Rochin v. Cal., 342 U.S. 165.

19. Brown v. Allen, 344 U.S. 443 (1953).

20. Mapp v. Ohio, 367 U.S. 643.

21. Robinson v. Cal., 370 U.S. 660 (1962).

22. Gideon v. Wainwright, 372 U.S. 335.

23. Malloy v. Hogan, 378 U.S. 1 (1964).

24. Pointer v. Tex., 380 U.S. 400 (1965), Klopfer v. N. Car., 386 U.S. 213 (1967), Washington v. Tex., 388 U.S. 14 (1967).

25. Duncan v. La., 391 U.S. 145, and Benton v. Md., 395 U.S. 784 (1969).

26. Griffin v. Ill., 351 U.S. 12, 19.

27. Smith v. Bennett, 365 U.S. 708 (1961) and Douglas v. Cal., 372 U.S. 353 (1963).

28. Townsend v. Sain, 372 U.S. 293 (1963) and Fay v. Noia, 372 U.S. 391 (1963).

29. In re Gault, 387 U.S. 1 (1967).

30. Hamilton v. Ala., 368 U.S. 52 (1961); White v. Md., 373 U.S. 59 (1963); Massiah v. U.S., 377 U.S. 201 (1964); Escobedo v. Ill., 378 U.S. 478 (1964); U.S. v. Wade, 388 U.S. 218 (1967).

31. Miranda v. Ariz., 383 U.S. 436 (1966).

32. See Earl Warren, "The Law and the Future," pamphlet reprint from *Fortune* (Nov. 1955), p. 11.

33. Ullmann v. U.S., 350 U.S. 422 (1956).

34. Belan v. Bd. of Ed., 357 U.S. 399 (1958); Lerner v. Casey, 357 U.S. 468 (1958); Nelson v. County of Los Angeles, 362 U.S. 1 (1960). The Court also upheld against First Amendment claims the

denial of membership in a state bar association to a person who refused answer to questions concerning Communist affiliations. Konigsberg v. State Bar of Cal., 366 U.S. 36 (1961). The Warren Court sustained the government in numerous internal-security cases involving the First Amendment.

35. Breithaupt v. Abram, 352 U.S. 432 (1957) and Schmerber v. Cal., 384 U.S. 757 (1966).

36. U.S. v. Wade, 388 U.S. 218 (1967) and Gilbert v. Cal., 388 U.S. 263 (1967).

37. Hoffa v. U.S., 385 U.S. 293 (1966).

38. Lewis v. U.S., 385 U.S. 206 (1966).

39. Osborn v. U.S., 385 U.S. 323 (1966).

40. McCray v. Ill., 386 U.S. 300 (1967).

41. Warden v. Hayden, 387 U.S. 294 (1967), overruling Gouled v. U.S., 255 U.S. 298 (1921).

42. Katz v. U.S., 389 U.S. 347 (1967), overruling Olmstead v. U.S., 277 U.S. 438 (1928).

43. Terry v. Ohio, 392 U.S. 1 (1968).

44. The material on Warren's resignation, Fortas's nomination, and Fortas's resignation derives from Robert Shogan, *A Question of Judgment: The Fortas Case and the Struggle for the Supreme Court* (Indianapolis, 1972), chs. 5–8 *passim*.

45. "Remarks Announcing the Nomination of Judge Warren Earl Burger to Be Chief Justice of the United States," May 21, 1969, in *Public Papers of the Presidents of the United States. Richard Nixon: 1969* (Washington, 1971), p. 388.

46. "Conversation with Newsmen on the Nomination of the Chief Justice of the United States," May 22, 1969, in *ibid.*, pp. 392–98.

47. Sidney Zion, "Nixon's Nominee for the Post of Chief Justice," *New York Times,* May 22, 1969, p. 36, col. 2.

48. Work v. U.S., 243 F 2d 660, 665 (1957).

49. Edwards v. U.S., 256 F 2d 707 (1958).

50. Williams v. U.S., 345 F 2d 733, 736 (1965). In U.S. v. Wade, 388 U.S. 218 (1967), the Supreme Court upheld the constitutional right to have counsel present at a police lineup.

51. Goldsmith v. U.S., 277 F 2d 335 (1960). Rule 5A of the Federal Rules of Criminal Procedure originated in McNabb v. U.S., 318 U.S. 332 (1943), reconfirmed in Mallory v. U.S., 354 U.S. 449 (1957). Goldsmith was an exception to Mallory.

52. Killough v. U.S., 315 F 2d 241 (1962).

53. *Ibid.,* 245.

54. *Ibid.,* 258–60 *passim*.

55. Levin v. Katzenbach, 363 F 2d 287 (1966).

56. Borum v. U.S., 380 F 2d 595, 602 (1967).

57. Frazier v. U.S., 419 F 2d 1161, 1176 (1969).

58. U.S. v. Jackson, 417 F 2d 1154, 1157 (1969).

59. Burger, "The Courts on Trial," *American Bar Association J.,* Vol. 44 (Aug. 1958), 738–41, 798–99.

60. "Remarks on Trial Advocacy: A Proposition," *Washburn Law J.,* Vol. 7 (Fall 1967), 15–24.

61. "Who Will Watch the Watchman?" *American U. Law Rev.,* Vol. 14 (Dec. 1964), 1–23.

62. "Paradoxes in the Administration of Criminal Justice," *Journal of Criminal Law, Criminology and Police Science,* Vol. 58 (Dec. 1967), 428–32, reprinting commencement address at Ripon College, 1967.

63. Donald McDonald, "A Center Report: Criminal Justice," *The Center Magazine,* Vol. 1 (Nov. 1968), 69–77 *passim.*

64. Burger, "Rulemaking by Judicial Decision: A Critical Review," Sept. 4, 1968, reprinted in *Nomination of Warren E. Burger.* Hearing before the Committee of the Judiciary. United States Senate, 91st Cong., 1st Sess., June 3, 1969, pp. 39–40.

65. *Ibid.,* pp. 40–44.

66. *Ibid.,* pp. 44–46.

67. *New York Times,* Feb. 1, 1973, p. 9, col. 1 and Feb. 4, 1973, E, p. 10, col. 1.

68. *Nomination of Warren E. Burger,* p. 5, cited above, note 64.

69. *Ibid.,* p. 7.

70. *Ibid.,* p. 13.

71. *Cong. Rec.,* 91st Cong., 1st Sess., Vol. 115, p. 15176 (June 9, 1969).

72. "Retirement of Mr. Chief Justice Warren," June 23, 1969, 89 S. Ct. 17, 18.

73. *Ibid.,* 19–20, for Warren's response.

74. Wilson, *Constitutional Government in the United States* (New York, 1908), p. 157.

75. Warren, "The Law and the Future," pamphlet reprint from *Fortune* (Nov. 1955), pp. 6–11 *passim.*

76. *New York Times,* July 4, 1971, p. 1, col. 5, and p. 24.

77. McCollum v. Bd. of Ed., 333 U.S. 203, 237–38 (1948).

78. Coleman v. Ala., 399 U.S. 1 (1970).

79. Powell v. Ala., 287 U.S. 45, 69 (1932).

80. 399 U.S. 1, 9.

81. *Ibid.,* 12.

82. *Ibid.*, 14.

83. *Ibid.*, 19.

84. *Ibid.*, 22–23.

85. *Ibid.*, 23.

86. "Fundamental Constitutions of Carolina," 1669, sections 80 and 120, in Francis N. Thorpe, ed., *The Federal and State Constitutions, Colonial Charters, and Other Organic Laws* (Washington, 1909), Vol. 6, pp. 2782, 2786.

87. James M. Beck, *The Constitution of the United States* (New York, 1922), p. 221.

88. To Spencer Roane, Sept. 6, 1819, in *The Writings of Thomas Jefferson,* Andrew A. Lipscomb and Albert Ellery Burgh, eds. (Washington, 1904–07), Vol. 15, p. 278.

89. Irving Dilliard, ed., *The Spirit of Liberty: Papers and Addresses of Learned Hand* (New York, 1953), p. 81.

90. Frankfurter, "Supreme Court, United States," *Encyclopaedia of Social Sciences* (New York, 1934), Vol. 14, p. 480.

91. Oct. 21, 1971, *Public Papers of the Presidents of the United States. Richard Nixon: 1971* (Washington, 1972), p. 1055.

92. McKeiver v. Pa., 403 U.S. 528 (1971).

93. Baldwin v. N.Y., 399 U.S. 66 (1970).

94. Oct. 21, 1971, *Public Papers . . . Nixon,* pp. 1054–1055.

95. Edward S. Corwin, *Twilight of the Supreme Court* (New Haven, 1934), p. 117.

96. "The Nature of the Judicial Process," (1921), in *Selected Writings of Benjamin Nathan Cardozo,* Margaret E. Hall, ed. (New York, 1947), p. 110.

97. Holmes, *The Common Law* (Boston, 1881), p. 35.

98. Albert P. Blaustein and Roy M. Mersky, "Rating Supreme Court Justices," *American Bar Association J.,* Vol. 58 (Nov. 1972), 1183–89.

99. On Black, see Stephen P. Strickland, ed., *Hugo Black and the Supreme Court* (Indianapolis, 1967); Wallace Mendelson, *Justices Frankfurter and Black* (Chicago, 1961); John P. Frank, "Hugo L. Black," in Leon Friedman and Fred L. Israel, eds., *The Justices of the United States Supreme Court, 1789–1969* (New York, 1969), Vol. 3, pp. 2321–46, hereinafter cited as *The Justices.*

100. John P. Frank, "William O. Douglas," in *The Justices,* Vol. 4, pp. 2447–69; "Justice William O. Douglas: A Symposium," *Yale Law J.,* Vol. 73 (May 1964), 915–998; Vern Countryman, *William O. Douglas of the Supreme Court* (New York, 1959).

101. David L. Shapiro, ed., *The Evolution of a Judicial Philosophy:*

Selected Opinions and Papers of Justice John M. Harlan (Cambridge, 1969), and Norman Dorsen, "John Marshall Harlan," in *The Justices,* Vol. 4, pp. 2803–20.

102. Stephen J. Friedman, ed., *An Affair with Freedom: Justice William J. Brennan* (New York, 1967); Friedman, "William J. Brennan," in *The Justices,* Vol. 4, pp. 2849–65; John P. Frank, *The Warren Court* (New York, 1964), pp. 113–32.

103. Frank, *The Warren Court,* pp. 133–48, and Jerold H. Israel, "Potter Stewart," in *The Justices,* Vol. 4, pp. 2921–37.

104. Frank, *The Warren Court,* pp. 149–64; Lance Liebman, "Swing Man on the Supreme Court," *New York Times Magazine,* Oct. 8, 1972, pp. 16–17, 94–95, 98, 100; Robert Zelnick, "Whizzer White and the Fearsome Foursome," *Washington Monthly,* Vol. 4 (Dec. 1972), pp. 46–54; and, Fred Israel, "Byron R. White," in *The Justices,* Vol. 4, pp. 2951–61.

105. Escobedo v. Ill., 378 U.S. 478, 499 (1964).

106. Miranda v. Ariz., 384 U.S. 436, 542, 543 (1966).

107. John P. McKenzie, "Thurgood Marshall," in *The Justices,* Vol. 4, pp. 3063–89.

108. J. Dudley McClain, "The Supreme Court Controversies of Presidents Roosevelt and Nixon," *Ga. State Bar J.,* Vol. 8 (Nov. 1971), 145, 165–68.

109. *Ibid.,* 171.

110. *New York Times,* March 17, 1970, p. 21, col. 1.

111. TRB's column, *New Republic,* Vol. 163 (Oct. 3, 1970), p. 4. For a vivid account of the Carswell affair, see Richard Harris, *Decision* (New York, 1971).

112. "Remarks to Reporters about Nominations to the Supreme Court," April 9, 1970, *Public Papers of . . . Nixon, 1970,* p. 344.

113. Quoted in Joseph Foote, "Mr. Justice Blackmun," *Harvard Law School Bulletin,* Vol. 21 (June 1970), 18, 19.

114. Dep. Att. Gen. R. G. Kleindienst to Sen. J. Eastland, April 15, 1970, in *Nomination of Harry A. Blackmun.* Hearing before the Committee on the Judiciary. U.S. Senate, 91st Cong., 2d Sess. . . . April 29, 1970, pp. 12–15.

115. Jones v. Alfred H. Meyer Co., 392 U.S. 409 (1968).

116. Mitchell v. Stephens, 353 F 2d 129 (1965).

117. Maxwell v. Bishop, 398 F 2d 138, 147 (1968). The third capital-punishment case was Pope v. U.S., 372 F 2d 710 (1967).

118. *Nomination of Harry A. Blackmun,* p. 59.

119. Jackson v. Bishop, 404 F 2d 571 (1968).

120. Ashe v. Swenson, 399 F 2d 40 (1968).

121. Ashe v. Swenson, 397 U.S. 436 (1970).

122. *Nomination of Harry A. Blackmun,* p. 33.

123. *Ibid.,* p. 35.

124. *Ibid.,* p. 43.

125. See Memorial Proceedings for Black, 92 S. Ct. 5–83, Oct. 4, 1971, and for Harlan, 92–A S. Ct. 5–47, Jan. 10, 1972.

126. *New York Times,* Sept. 24, 1972, p. 20, col. 3.

127. *Time,* Nov. 1, 1971, pp. 14–20.

128. *New York Times,* Oct. 12, 1971, p. 42, col. 1.

129. *Ibid.,* Oct. 14, 1971, p. 1, col. 8.

130. *Time,* Nov. 1, 1971, p. 14.

131. See note 94 above, p. 1053, and *New York Times,* Oct. 12, 1971, p. 1, col. 8 and p. 25.

132. *Time,* Nov. 1, 1971, p. 18.

133. On Powell, see A. E. Dick Howard, "Justice Powell and the Emerging Nixon Majority," *Michigan Law Rev.,* Vol. 70 (Jan. 1972), 445–68.

134. *New York Times,* Oct. 22, 1971, p. 25, col. 6.

135. *Nominations of William H. Rehnquist and Lewis F. Powell, Jr.,* Hearings before the Committee on the Judiciary. U.S. Senate, 92d Cong., 1st Sess., Nov. 3, 4, 8, 9, and 10, 1971, p. 259.

136. *New York Times,* Oct. 22, 1971, p. 25, col. 6.

137. See notes 105–06 above.

138. *The Challenge of Crime in a Free Society* (Washington, 1967), pp. 303–08, reprinted in *Nominations of Rehnquist and Powell,* pp. 238–44. The case on comment is Griffin v. Cal., 380 U.S. 609 (1965).

139. *Nominations of Rehnquist and Powell,* p. 230.

140. *Ibid.,* p. 263.

141. *Ibid.,* p. 246.

142. Aug. 1, 1971, in *ibid.,* pp. 213–17 and reprinted in *New York Times,* Nov. 3, 1971, p. 45.

143. *Nominations of Rehnquist and Powell,* p. 263.

144. See note 142 above.

145. *Nominations of Rehnquist and Powell,* pp. 127, 231–32, on Miranda.

146. *Ibid.,* p. 220.

147. *Ibid.,* pp. 231–32, 257, on Escobedo.

148. *Ibid.,* p. 227.

149. *Ibid.,* p. 232.

150. *Ibid.,* p. 258.

151. *Ibid.,* p. 219.

152. *Nomination of Lewis F. Powell, Jr.,* 92d Cong., 1st Sess. Sen. Executive Report No. 92–17, Nov. 30, 1971, pp. 5–8.

153. U.S. v. U.S. District Court, 407 U.S. 297 (1972).

154. *Time,* Nov. 1, 1971, p. 18.

155. *Ibid.; Nominations of Rehnquist and Powell,* pp. 2, 42–48, 154, 313–14; *Nomination of William H. Rehnquist,* 92d Cong., 1st Sess. Sen. Executive Report No. 92–16, Nov. 30, 1971, pp. 1–2, 13–19, 44–53.

156. Oct. 23, 1971, editorial.

157. *Nominations of Rehnquist and Powell,* p. 304.

158. *Time,* Nov. 1, 1971, p. 19.

159. *Nominations of Rehnquist and Powell,* p. 11.

160. *Ibid.,* p. 4.

161. Rehnquist, "The Making of a Supreme Court Justice," *Harvard Law Record,* Oct. 8, 1959, reprinted in *New York Times,* Nov. 11, 1971, p. 47. The editorial quoted in the article is in the *New York World,* April 23, 1930.

162. *Ibid.*

163. *Nominations of Rehnquist and Powell,* pp. 28 and 311, quoting Rehnquist, "Who Writes Opinions of the Supreme Court?" *United States News and World Report,* Dec. 13, 1957, p. 75. See also *Nomination of Rehnquist,* Sen. Exec. Rpt. No. 92–16, Nov. 30, 1971, p. 44.

164. *Nominations of Rehnquist and Powell,* p. 312, quoting Rehnquist, "The Bar Admission Cases: A Strange Judicial Aberration," *American Bar Association J.,* Vol. 44 (March 1958), 229.

165. Yates v. U.S., 354 U.S. 298.

166. Service v. Dulles, 354 U.S. 363.

167. Watkins v. U.S., 354 U.S. 178.

168. Sweezy v. N.H., 354 U.S. 234.

169. *Nominations of Rehnquist and Powell,* p. 54, reprinting letter to editor, *Washington Post,* Feb. 14, 1970.

170. *Ibid.,* pp. 19–20, 24, 26–27, 31, 32.

171. *Nomination of Rehnquist,* Sen. Exec. Rpt. No. 92–16, p. 5.

172. *Ibid.,* pp. 24–25.

173. *Ibid.,* pp. 32, 46, 49, 52.

174. *Ibid.,* pp. 54–55.

CHAPTER TWO: *The Fourth Amendment: Search and Seizure*

1. *New York Times,* July 1, 1973, sec. E, p. 6, col. 1.

2. *Ibid.,* June 25, 1973, p. 1, col. 4, and p. 22.

3. U.S. v. Rabinowitz, 339 U.S. 56, 63 (1950).

4. On probable cause, see Rex D. Davis, *Federal Searches and Seizures* (Springfield, Ill., 1964), pp. 268–309.

5. Johnson v. U.S., 333 U.S. 10, 13–14 (1948).

6. Donald M. McIntyre, Jr., "Search and Seizure," in Lawrence P. Tiffany *et al., Detection of Crime* (Boston, 1967), p. 100.

7. *Ibid.,* p. 122; see also pp. 100–04. Additionally, see Fred P. Graham, *The Self-Inflicted Wound* (New York, 1970), p. 204.

8. Davis, *Federal Searches,* ch. 3, on searches incident to arrest, also covers emergency situations, and ch. 4 on consent searches. See also McIntyre, "Search and Seizure," in *Detection of Crime*, chs. 9–11.

9. See the data in Mapp v. Ohio, 367 U.S. 643, 652 note 7.

10. 18 U.S. Code, sect. 2236. On the subject of this paragraph, see, generally, Richard A. Edwards, "Criminal Liability for Unreasonable Searches and Seizures," *Virginia Law Rev.,* Vol. 41 (June 1955), pp. 621–632.

11. 18 U.S. Code, sect. 2234.

12. 18 U.S. Code, sect. 242.

13. *New York Times,* June 25, 1973, p. 22, col. 1, and Aug. 25, 1973, p. 1, col. 2. See also *Los Angeles Times,* Oct. 30, 1973, p. 1, col. 1.

14. Caleb Foote, "Tort Remedies for Police Violation of Individual Rights," *Minnesota Law Rev.,* Vol. 39 (April 1955), 493, 498–99. See also Comment, "Federal Agents Conducting Unreasonable Search and Seizures Are Liable for Damages under the Fourth Amendment," *Texas Law Rev.,* Vol. 50 (April 1972), 798, 799–801. On the difficulties in suing the police, see generally the symposium of articles on "Police Tort Liability," *Cleveland-Marshall Law Rev.,* Vol. 16 (Sept. 1967), 397–454.

15. 42 U.S. Code sect. 1983.

16. Monroe v. Pape, 365 U.S. 167 (1961). See also Lucero v. Donovan, 354 F 2d 16 (1965).

17. Bivens v. Six Unknown Named Agents of Federal Bureau of Narcotics, 403 U.S. 388, 391 note 4 (1971).

18. *Ibid.* For comment on the circuit decision, see *Harvard Law Rev.,* Vol. 83 (Jan. 1970), 684–90.

19. See Comment, "Federal Agents Conducting Unreasonable Search and Seizures Are Liable for Damages Under the Fourth Amendment," *Texas Law Rev.,* Vol. 50 (April 1972), 798–806.

20. 232 U.S. 383 (1914).

21. Mapp v. Ohio, 367 U.S. 643. See also Ker v. Cal., 374 U.S. 23 (1963). For the evolution of the exclusionary rule in Supreme Court decisions, see Jacob W. Landynski, *Search and Seizure and the Su-*

preme Court (Baltimore, 1966), ch. 3. Landynski has, in effect, updated his excellent book in a series of three articles on "The Supreme Court's Search for Fourth Amendment Standards," *Connecticut Bar J.*, Vol. 45 (March 1971), 2–39; (June 1971), 146–86; (Dec. 1971), 330–71. The articles deal with the problems of warrantless searches, stop and frisk, and searches incident to arrest and the search of automobiles.

22. The best study of the origin and framing of the search-and-seizure clause is Nelson B. Lasson, *The History and Development of the Fourth Amendment to the United States Constitution* (Baltimore, 1937).

23. Elkins v. U.S., 364 U.S. 206, 217 (1960).

24. Mapp v. Ohio, 367 U.S. 643, 660 (1961).

25. *Ibid.*, 659–60.

26. Miranda v. Ariz., 384 U.S. 436 (1966).

27. U.S. v. Wade, 388 U.S. 218 (1967).

28. Pointer v. Texas, 380 U.S. 400 (1965).

29. Elkins v. U.S., 364 U.S. 206, 217, 222 (1960).

30. Mapp v. Ohio, 367 U.S. 643, 659 (1961), quoting Cardozo in People v. Defore, 242 N.Y. 13, 21 (1926), and Brandeis in Olmstead v. U.S., 277 U.S. 438, 485 (1928). The remark about judicial integrity is from Elkins v. U.S., 364 U.S. 206, 222 (1960).

31. Bivens v. Six Unknown Named Agents, 403 U.S. 388, 418 (1971).

32. Donald J. Newman, *Conviction: The Determination of Guilt or Innocence Without Trial* (Boston, 1966), p. 3 note 1. See also Brady v. U.S., 397 U.S. 742, 752 (1970).

33. Terry v. Ohio, 392 U.S. 1, 14 (1968).

34. McIntyre, "Search and Seizure," in Tiffany *et al.*, *Detection of Crime*, pp. 183–99, and Dallin H. Oaks, "Studying the Exclusionary Rule in Search and Seizure," *Univ. of Chicago Law Rev.*, Vol. 37 (Summer 1970), 665, 683, 701, 720–24.

35. 403 U.S. 388, 418 (1971).

36. *Ibid.*, 417. See also, Oaks, "Studying the Exclusionary Rule," cited above, note 34, pp. 724–31.

37. Oaks, "Studying the Exclusionary Rule," pp. 699, 700, 708, 739, 741–42. See also Graham, *Self-Inflicted Wound*, pp. 136, 137, 138, and 212.

38. 403 U.S. 388, 417 (1971). See also Oaks, "Studying the Exclusionary Rule," pp. 726–27.

39. Oaks, "Studying the Exclusionary Rule," p. 755.

40. 403 U.S. 388, 422.

41. *Ibid.*, 424.
42. 399 U.S. 30 (1970). For comment, see "Supreme Court Review (1970)," *J. of Criminal Law, Criminology and Police Science,* Vol. 61 (Dec. 1970), 484, 504–06.
43. See Chimel v. Cal., 395 U.S. 752 (1969). Vale was tried before the Court decided Chimel. The Court decided his case before deciding whether Chimel was retroactive, so that the rule of Chimel played no part in Vale. Shortly after, the Court held that Chimel is not retroactive. See Williams v. U.S., 401 U.S. 646 (1971) and Hill v. Cal., 401 U.S. 797 (1971). On Chimel, see note 70, below, and related text.
44. 399 U.S. 30, 41.
45. See cases cited in "Supreme Court Review (1970)," *J. of Criminal Law, Criminology and Police Science,* Vol. 61 (Dec. 1970), 484, 506 note 28.
46. 399 U.S. 42 (1970). For comment, see "Supreme Court Review (1970)," cited in preceding note, pp. 507–508; "Warrantless Search of Automobile Held in Police Custody Does Not Violate the Fourth Amendment," *Vanderbilt Law Rev.,* Vol. 23 (Nov. 1970), 1370–76; "Warrantless Automobile Searches: The Meaning of Chambers v. Maroney," *American Trial Lawyers J.,* Vol. 34 (1972), 174–201; and, Wayne R. LaFave, "Warrantless Searches and the Supreme Court: Further Ventures into the 'Quagmire'," *Criminal Law Bulletin,* Vol. 8 (Jan.-Feb. 1972), 9–30. LaFave, one of the nation's experts on search and seizure, disagreed with the results in both Vale and Chambers.
47. The leading case is Carroll v. U.S., 267 U.S. 132 (1925). See article in preceding note on "Warrantless Automobile Searches" for a discussion of the cases. See also McIntyre, "Search and Seizure," cited above in note 6, pp. 148–53, 171–75.
48. 399 U.S. 42, 51.
49. *Ibid.*, 52.
50. *Ibid.*
51. *Ibid.*, 63 note 8.
52. *Ibid.*, 65.
53. See cases cited in "Supreme Court Review (1970)," *J. of Criminal Law, Criminology and Police Science,* Vol. 61 (Dec. 1970), 484, 508 note 45.
54. 401 U.S. 560 (1971).
55. *Ibid.*, 566 note 11.
56. *Ibid.*, 566.
57. *Ibid.*, 570.
58. *Ibid.*, 574.

59. *Ibid.,* 565 note 8.

60. Spinelli v. U.S., 393 U.S. 410, 415 (1969), referring to Aguilar v. Texas, 378 U.S. 108 (1964).

61. Brinegar v. U.S., 338 U.S. 160, 175–76 (1949). See also, Davis, *Federal Searches and Seizures,* pp. 270–79.

62. See U.S. v. Ventresca, 380 U.S. 102, 108 (1965).

63. 378 U.S. 108.

64. 393 U.S. 410, 429.

65. 403 U.S. 573 (1971).

66. *Ibid.,* 578, quoting Nathanson v. U.S., 290 U.S. 41, 46 (1933).

67. The complete affidavit is in 403 U.S. 573, 575–76.

68. *Ibid.,* 583.

69. *Ibid.,* 600.

70. 403 U.S. 443 (1971). For comment, see "The Supreme Court, 1970 Term," *Harvard Law Rev.,* Vol. 85 (Nov. 1971), 237–50; Jacob W. Landynski, "The Supreme Court's Search for Fourth Amendment Standards: The Extraordinary Case of *Coolidge* v. *New Hampshire,*" *Conn. Bar J.,* Vol. 45 (Dec. 1971), 330–71; John G. Miles, Jr., and John B. Wefing, "The Automobile Search and the Fourth Amendment," *Seton Hall Law Rev.,* Vol. 4 (Fall-Winter 1972), 105–144; Philip S. Mortensen, "*Coolidge* v. *New Hampshire,*" *Suffolk U. Law Rev.,* Vol. 6 (Spring 1972), 695–704.

71. Boyd v. U.S., 116 U.S. 616, 635 (1886), quoted in 403 U.S. 443, 454.

72. 403 U.S. 443, 490. White's remark is in *ibid.,* 513.

73. *Ibid.,* 483–84.

74. 395 U.S. 752 (1969). For comment, see "The Supreme Court, 1968 Term," *Harvard Law Rev.,* Vol. 83 (Nov. 1969), 161–67; La-Fave, "Warrantless Searches," cited in note 46 above; "Searches Incident to a Lawful Arrest Limited to the Area within Reach of the Arrestee," *Duke Law J.,* Vol. 1969 (Oct.), 1084–90; "The Scope of Search When Incident to a Lawful Arrest," *Southwestern Law J.,* Vol. 23 (Dec. 1969), 959–64; and, "Search and Seizure Since Chimel v. California," *Minn. Law Rev.,* Vol. 55 (April 1971), 1011–30.

75. See Harris v. U.S., 331 U.S. 145 (1947) and U.S. v. Rabinowitz, 339 U.S. 56 (1950). Chimel overruled both cases.

76. 395 U.S. 752, 763.

77. 403 U.S. 443, 493. See also Burger's remarks about the Coolidge case in his Bivens dissent, on the same day, 403 U.S. 388, 418–19 (1971).

78. 403 U.S. 443, 457.

79. 399 U.S. 42 (1970).

80. 403 U.S. 443, 463 note 20.

81. *Ibid.,* 462.

82. *Ibid.,* 466.

83. *Ibid.,* 468.

84. 413 U.S. 433 (1973).

85. 413 U.S. 266 (1973).

86. 413 U.S. 433, 454.

87. *Ibid.,* 454, quoting Camara v. Municipal Court, 387 U.S. 523, 539 (1967).

88. 413 U.S. 266 (1973).

89. 412 U.S. 291 (1973).

90. 395 U.S. 752 (1969).

91. 412 U.S. 291, 304.

92. 412 U.S. 218 (1973).

93. Davis, *Federal Searches and Seizures,* p. 171.

94. 412 U.S. 218, 231.

95. Johnson v. Zerbst, 304 U.S. 458, 464 (1938), quoted in *ibid.,* 235.

96. 412 U.S. 218, 242.

97. *Ibid.,* 243.

98. *Ibid.,* 243, 245.

99. *Ibid.,* 288.

100. *Ibid.,* 277.

101. Terry v. Ohio, 392 U.S. 1 (1968).

102. Adams v. Williams, 407 U.S. 143 (1972).

103. 392 U.S. 1, 16.

104. On stop and frisk, see Lawrence P. Tiffany, "Stopping and Questioning," in Tiffany *et al., Detection of Crime,* pp. 6–98.

105. *Ibid.,* 24 note 21.

106. Adams v. Williams, 407 U.S. 143, 148 note 3.

107. Sibron v. N.Y., 392 U.S. 40 (1968).

108. Tiffany, "Stopping and Questioning," p. 85.

109. Terry v. Ohio, 392 U.S. 1, 14–15.

110. 392 U.S. 1, 38.

111. Peters v. N.Y., 392 U.S. 40 (1968).

112. 407 U.S. 143, 147.

113. *Ibid.,* 159, 162. For comment on Adams v. Williams, see "The Supreme Court, 1971 Term," *Harvard Law Rev.,* Vol. 86 (Nov. 1972), 171–81, and "Supreme Court Review (1972)," *J. of Criminal Law, Criminology and Police Science,* Vol. 63 (Dec. 1972), 469–70, 525–28.

114. 94 S. Ct. 467 (1973).

115. Quoted in McIntyre, "Search and Seizure," cited in note 6 above, p. 131.

116. *Ibid.,* pp. 132 and 134.

117. Quoted in 94 S. Ct. 467, 470 note 2.

118. *Ibid.,* 477.

119. *Ibid.,* 472, quoting Weeks v. U.S., 232 U.S. 383, 392.

120. *Ibid.,* quoting Agnello v. U.S., 269 U.S. 20, 30. Italics added.

121. *Ibid.* Italics added.

122. Chimel v. Cal., 395 U.S. 752, 762–63 (1969).

123. 392 U.S. 1 (1968).

124. Peters v. N.Y., 392 U.S. 40, 77 (1968).

125. 94 S. Ct. 467, 475, citing Closson v. Morrison, 47 N.H. 484 (1867) and quoting Holker v. Hennessey, 141 Mo. 527, 539 (1897). Italics added.

126. *Ibid.,* quoting People v. Chiagles, 237 N.Y. 193, 197 (1923). Italics added.

127. *Ibid.,* 478–79.

128. *Ibid.,* 480–81.

129. *Ibid.,* 482, quoting U.S. v. Humphrey, 409 F 2d 1055, 1056 (1969).

130. *Ibid.*

131. Coolidge v. N.H., 403 U.S. 443 (1971).

132. On the subject generally, see Samuel Dash *et al., The Eavesdroppers* (New Brunswick, N.J., 1959); Alan F. Westin, *Privacy and Freedom* (New York, 1967); Edward Long, *The Intruders* (New York, 1966).

133. Arthur R. Miller, *The Assault on Privacy: Computers, Data Banks, and Dossiers* (Ann Arbor, Mich., 1971), p. 161.

134. Title III, Omnibus Crime Control and Safe Streets Act of 1968, which became Title 18 U.S. Code, sections 2510–20.

135. Westin, *Privacy and Freedom,* p. 131, relying on Dash *et al., passim.*

136. See Dash *et al.,* chs. 3–4 on "Prohibition Jurisdictions" and "Virgin Jurisdictions."

137. *Annual Report of the Director of the Administrative Office of the United States Courts, 1972* (Washington, 1973), Appendix III, Report on Applications for Orders Authorizing or Approving the Interception of Wire or Oral Communications, for the Period January 1, 1971, to December 31, 1971, pp. 527, 535. The *Annual Reports* are the official source for all statistics on wiretapping and eavesdropping.

138. *Privacy and Freedom,* p. 127.

139. For figures summarizing the *Annual Reports* from 1969

through 1971, see Herman Schwartz, *American Civil Liberties Union Report on the Costs and Benefits of Electronic Surveillance—1972*, reprinted in *Warrantless Wiretapping*. Hearings before the Subcommittee on Administrative Practice and Procedure of the Committee on the Judiciary, United States Congress, 92d Cong., 2d Sess., June 29, 1972, pp. 203–12, hereinafter cited as Schwartz, *ACLU Report—1972*. The official *Annual Reports* do not give the total number of different persons whose conversations were intercepted or the total number of intercepted conversations, but these totals are easily computed from the figures given for the number of installations authorized, state and federal, and the average number of persons and of conversations intercepted per installation. Preliminary figures for 1972 show 841 installations of which 206 were federal and the remainder were state, 81% of the latter being in New York and New Jersey. *New York Times,* May 6, 1973.

140. Schwartz, *ACLU Report—1972*, pp. 210–11, in *Warrantless Wiretapping*, which also includes the exchange between Sen. Kennedy and the Dept. of Justice, pp. 70–76. The satistics are also available in the Appendix to Douglas's opinion in U.S. v. U.S. District Court, 407 U.S. 297, 334 (1972).

141. Same citations as in note 140 above.

142. Quoted in U.S. v. U.S. District Court, 407 U.S. 297, 330–31 (1972).

143. Schwartz, *ACLU Report—1971*, quoted in Livingston Hall *et al., January 1973 Supplement* to *Modern Criminal Procedure*, 3rd ed. (St. Paul, 1973), p. 147.

144. Clark, *Crime in America* (New York, 1970), p. 290.

145. Schwartz, *ACLU Report—1972*, p. 207.

146. On the number of arrests and convictions during the years 1969–71, see *Annual Report . . . 1972*, cited above, note 137, p. 546, and Schwartz, *ACLU Report—1972*, p. 207. Preliminary figures show that the number of convictions in 1972 was 402. *New York Times,* May 6, 1973.

147. *Annual Report . . . 1972*, pp. 532–34.

148. Schwartz, *ACLU Report—1972*, p. 207.

149. *Crime in America,* p. 294.

150. Berger v. N.Y., 388 U.S. 41 (1967) and Katz v. U.S., 389 U.S. 347 (1967).

151. Title 18 U.S. Code, sect. 2512 (2) (c) (d).

152. 401 U.S. 745 (1971).

153. See cases cited above, note 150.

154. 343 U.S. 747 (1952).

155. For a history of the Supreme Court's decisions on wiretapping and electronic eavesdropping, see Landynski, *Search and Seizure and the Supreme Court*, pp. 198–244, covering through 1963. See also Walter F. Murphy, *Wiretapping on Trial* (New York, 1965) for a case study of Olmstead v. U.S., 277 U.S. 438 (1928), the first wiretap decision in which the physical trespass rule originated.

156. Silverman v. U.S., 365 U.S. 505 (1961).

157. Wong Sun v. U.S., 371 U.S. 471, 485 (1963).

158. Berger v. N.Y., 388 U.S. 41, 59, 60 (1967).

159. Lopez v. U.S., 373 U.S. 427, 438–39 (1963).

160. U.S. v. White, 401 U.S. 745, 748 (1971).

161. Katz v. U.S., 389 U.S. 347, 351 (1967).

162. *Ibid.*, 353.

163. Schwartz, *ACLU Report—1972*, pp. 204, 205.

164. U.S. v. Harris, 403 U.S. 573 (1971).

165. Katz v. U.S., 389 U.S. 347.

166. See "The Supreme Court, 1970 Term," *Harvard Law Rev.*, Vol. 85 (Nov. 1971), 257, citing Brief for Petitioner [U.S.] at 22–23.

167. On the question of retroactivity, see Desist v. U.S., 394 U.S. 244 (1969).

168. Lopez v. U.S., 373 U.S. 427 (1963).

169. Hoffa v. U.S., 385 U.S. 293 (1966).

170. Lewis v. U.S., 385 U.S. 206 (1966).

171. 401 U.S. 745, 751.

172. *Ibid.*, 752.

173. On the issue of consent in third-party bugging, see R. Kent Greenawalt, "The Consent Problem in Wiretapping and Eavesdropping: Surreptitious Monitoring with the Consent of a Participant in a Conversation," *Columbia Law Rev.*, Vol. 68 (Feb. 1968), 189–240. See also Edmund W. Kitch, "Katz v. United States: The Limits of the Fourth Amendment," in Philip B. Kurland, ed., *Supreme Court Review 1968* (Chicago, 1968), 133–152.

174. 389 U.S. 347, 352.

175. 401 U.S. 745, 759, quoting Brennan's dissent in Lopez v. U.S., 373 U.S. 427, 465–66 (1963).

176. 401 U.S. 745, 770, quoting Westin, *Privacy and Freedom*, p. 131.

177. 401 U.S. 745, 789, 790. For comment on U.S. v. White, see Joseph Bisceglia, "Electronic Surveillance and the Supreme Court: A Move Pack?" *De Paul Law Rev.*, Vol. 21 (Spring 1972), 806–21; Eric T. Saunders, "Electronic Eavesdropping and the Right to Privacy," *Boston U. Law Rev.*, Vol. 52 (Fall 1972), 831–47; "The Su-

preme Court Review (1971)," *J. of Criminal Law, Criminology and Police Science*, Vol. 62 (Dec. 1971), 463, 489–93; "The Supreme Court, 1970 Term," *Harvard Law Rev.*, Vol. 85 (Nov. 1971), 40, 250–58.

178. 407 U.S. 297 (1972). For comment, see "The Court and Electronic Surveillance: To Bug or Not to Bug—What Is the Exception?" *St. John's Law Rev.*, Vol. 47 (Oct. 1972), 76–106; "Fourth Amendment Held to Require Search Warrant for Wiretapping in Domestic National Security Cases," *Indiana Law Rev.*, Vol. 6 (1972), 314–30; "The President of the United States Has No Authority to Conduct Wiretaps against Domestic Threats to the National Security without a Judicial Warrant," *George Washington Law Rev.*, Vol. 41 (Oct. 1972), 119–34; Kevin J. Caplis, "Electronic Surveillance and the Fourth Amendment: Warrant Required for Wiretapping of Domestic Subversives," *De Paul Law Rev.*, Vol. 22 (Winter 1972), 430–50. For background, see "Wiretapping and Electronic Surveillance—Title III of the Crime Control Act of 1968," *Rutgers Law Rev.*, Vol. 23 (Winter 1969), 319–88; Herman Schwartz, "The Legitimation of Electronic Eavesdropping: The Politics of 'Law and Order,' " *Michigan Law Rev.*, Vol. 67 (Jan. 1969), 455–510; Athan G. Theoharis and Elizabeth Meyer, "The 'National Security' Justification for Electronic Eavesdropping: an Elusive Exception," *Wayne Law Rev.*, Vol. 14 (1968), 749–71; Gerard J. Kenny, "The 'National Security Wiretap': Presidential Prerogative and Judicial Responsibility," *Southern California Law Rev.*, Vol. 45 (Summer 1972), 888–913; "Developments in the Law—The National Security Interest and Civil Liberties," *Harvard Law Rev.*, Vol. 85 (April 1972), 1130, 1244–83.

179. See Lewis F. Powell Jr., "Civil Liberties Repression: Fact or Fiction?" *Richmond Times-Dispatch*, Aug. 1, 1971, reprinted in *Nominations of William H. Rehnquist and Lewis F. Powell, Jr.*, Hearings before the Committee on the Judiciary, United States Senate, 92d Cong., 1st Sess. . . . . Nov. 3–10, 1971, pp. 213, 214–15.

180. 407 U.S. 297, 316, 317.

181. Alderman v. U.S., 394 U.S. 165 (1969).

182. *Time,* June 4, 1973, p. 25.

183. 407 U.S. 297, 300 note 2.

184. *Ibid.,* 310 note 10.

185. *Ibid.,* 299. Italics added.

186. *Ibid.,* 314.

187. Quoted in 407 U.S. 297, 302, quoting 18 U.S. Code, sect. 2511 (3).

188. 407 U.S. 297, 316, quoting 403 U.S. 443, 481 (1972).

189. 407 U.S. 297, 313, citing 389 U.S. 347 (1967).
190. 407 U.S. 297, 318.
191. *Ibid.*, 319.
192. *Ibid.*, 320.
193. *Ibid.*
194. *Ibid.*, 321.
195. *New York Times,* June 22, 1972, quoted in *Warrantless Wiretapping,* cited in note 139 above, p. 148.
196. Laird v. Tatum, 408 U.S. 1 (1972).
197. The figure of 25 million is from *Time,* June 4, 1973, p. 23. The quotation is from Justice Douglas, in 408 U.S. 1, 24.
198. 408 U.S. 1, 28.
199. Gelbard v. U.S., 408 U.S. 41 (1972).

CHAPTER THREE: The Fifth Amendment: The Right Against Self-Incrimination

1. Malloy v. Hogan, 378 U.S. 1 (1964).
2. Griffin v. Cal., 380 U.S. 609 (1965).
3. Miranda v. Ariz., 384 U.S. 436 (1966).
4. Garrity v. N.J., 385 U.S. 493 (1967).
5. Spevack v. Klein, 385 U.S. 511 (1967).
6. In re Gault, 387 U.S. 1 (1967).
7. Albertson v. S.A.C.B., 382 U.S. 70 (1965); Marchetti v. U.S., 390 U.S. 39 (1968); Grosso v. U.S., 390 U.S. 62 (1968); Haynes v. U.S., 390 U.S. 85 (1968).
8. Murphy v. Waterfront Comm., 378 U.S. 52 (1964).
9. Schmerber v. Cal., 384 U.S. 757 (1966); Gilbert v. Cal., 388 U.S. 263 (1967); U.S. v. Wade, 388 U.S. 218 (1967).
10. Tehan v. U.S., 382 U.S. 406 (1966); Johnson v. N.J., 384 U.S. 719 (1966).
11. Williams v. Fla., 399 U.S. 78 (1970).
12. 353 U.S. 657. See also Gordon v. U.S., 344 U.S. 414 (1953).
13. The Jencks Act, 18 U.S. Code, sect. 3500. See Walter F. Murphy, *Congress and the Court* (Chicago, 1962), ch. 3.
14. 373 U.S. 83.
15. Michael Moore, "Criminal Discovery," *Hastings Law J.,* Vol. 19 (March 1968), 865, 912. See also, Jerry E. Norton, "Discovery in the Criminal Process," *J. of Criminal Law, Criminology and Police Science,* Vol. 61 (March 1970), 11–38; John W. Katz, "Pretrial Discovery in Criminal Cases," *Criminal Law Bulletin,* Vol. 5 (Oct. 1969), 441–462; and, Barry Nakell, "Criminal Discovery for the Defense and

the Prosecution," *North Carolina Law Rev.*, Vol. 50 (April 1972), 437–516; "Prosecutor's Duty to Disclose," *U. of Chicago Law Rev.*, Vol. 40 (Fall 1972), 112–140; Lewis Katz *et al., Justice Is the Crime* (Cleveland, 1972), pp. 181–93.

16. 399 U.S. 78, 82.

17. *Ibid.*, 82, 83.

18. *Ibid.*, 85.

19. *Ibid.*, 86.

20. *Ibid.*, 105, 106.

21. See, *e.g.*, Frankfurter's comment in Ullmann v. U.S., 350 U.S. 422, 438 where he declared that the "sole concern [of the privilege against self-incrimination] is, as its name indicates, [!] with the danger to a witness forced to give testimony leading to the infliction" of criminal penalties. The Fifth Amendment vests a right not to be a witness against oneself criminally.

22. See Leonard W. Levy, *Origins of the Fifth Amendment: the Right Against Self-Incrimination* (New York, 1968), chs. 11–13.

23. 399 U.S. 78, 114.

24. *Ibid.*, 107–08.

25. *Ibid.*, 115.

26. Levy, *Origins of the Fifth*, pp. 101–02, 107, 182–84, 274.

27. 399 U.S. 78, 105.

28. *Ibid.*, 112.

29. Wardius v. Oregon, 412 U.S. 470 (1973). On the subject generally, see note, *Harvard Law Rev.*, Vol. 76 (Feb. 1963), 838–42; Moore, "Criminal Discovery," *Hastings Law J.*, Vol. 19 (March 1968), 865–917; and Kendall Bishop, "The Self-Incrimination Privilege: Barrier to Criminal Discovery?" *California Law Rev.*, Vol. 51 (March 1963), 135–45.

30. 401 U.S. 222. An indispensable article on the Harris case, to which I am greatly indebted, is Alan M. Dershowitz and John H. Ely, *"Harris* v. *New York:* Some Anxious Observations on the Candor and Logic of the Emerging Nixon Majority," *Yale Law J.*, Vol. 80 (May 1971), 1198–1227. For other comments on the case, see Erwin Davis, "Statements Obtained in Violation of Miranda May Be Used for Impeachment," *Arkansas Law Rev.*, Vol. 25 (Summer 1971), 190–200; Stanley B. Kent, "Harris v. New York: The Death Knell of Miranda and Walder?" *Brooklyn Law Rev.*, Vol. 38 (Fall 1971), 357–70.

31. Miranda v. Ariz., 384 U.S. 436 (1966).

32. Escobedo v. Ill., 378 U.S. 478 (1964).

33. Quoted in Dershowitz and Ely, p. 1203, citing Transcript of Oral Argument, p. 12.

34. *Ibid.*, p. 1203 note 31, citing Transcript, p. 19.
35. *Ibid.*, p. 1206, citing Transcript, p. 25.
36. *Ibid.*, p. 1206 note 42, citing Transcript, pp. 25–26.
37. *Ibid.*, p. 1222, citing Brief of the D.A. of N.Y. County, p. 12.
38. 401 U.S. 222, 224.
39. Dershowitz and Ely, p. 1199, speak of "the intolerability, of what is, at best, gross negligence concerning the state of the record and the controlling precedents."
40. 401 U.S. 222, 229 note 2.
41. *Ibid.*, 224.
42. 384 U.S. 436, 476–77.
43. 401 U.S. 222, 230.
44. *Ibid.*, 224.
45. *Ibid.*, 225.
46. *Ibid.*, 226.
47. *Ibid.*, 226 note 2.
48. 347 U.S. 62 (1954).
49. Weeks v. U.S., 232 U.S. 383 (1914). Mapp v. Ohio, 367 U.S. 643 (1961) applied the rule to the states.
50. 401 U.S. 222, 224.
51. 347 U.S. 62, 64.
52. *Ibid.*, 65. Italics added.
53. Agnello v. U.S., 269 U.S. 20 (1925).
54. *Ibid.*, 35.
55. 401 U.S. 222, 225.
56. Charles T. McCormick, *Handbook of the Law of Evidence* (St. Paul, 1954), sect. 39, p. 77.
57. Bruton v. U.S., 391 U.S. 123, 135.
58. 401 U.S. 222, 225.
59. *Ibid.*, 232.
60. Olmstead v. U.S., 277 U.S. 438, 485 (1928).
61. See Riddell v. Rhay, 404 U.S. 974 (1971), for a case similar to Harris v. N.Y. in which the Court denied a petition for a writ of certiorari, over the dissenting opinion of Douglas, joined by Brennan, who declared: "Yet, after *Harris*, there is no longer any real incentive for police to obey *Miranda*." *Ibid.*, 976.
62. Olmstead v. U.S., 277 U.S. 438, 479 (1927).
63. Title 18 U.S. Code, sect. 3501 (1969 Supp.). See "Recent Statute: Title II of the Omnibus Crime Control and Safe Streets Act of 1968," *Harvard Law Rev.*, Vol. 82 (April 1969), 1392–1403; "Title II of the Omnibus Crime Control Act: A Study in Constitutional Conflict," *Georgetown Law J.*, Vol. 57 (Nov. 1968), 438–60; Michael A.

La Fond, "Survey of Title II: Omnibus Crime Control and Safe Streets Act of 1968," *American Univ. Law Rev.*, Vol. 18 (1968), 157–77; Thornton Robison, "Police Interrogation of Suspects: The Court versus the Congress," *California Law Rev.*, Vol. 57 (May 1969), 740–77.

64. See Yale Kamisar, "A Dissent from the *Miranda* Dissents: Some Comments on the 'New' Fifth Amendment and the 'Old' Voluntariness Test," *Michigan Law Rev.*, Vol. 65 (Nov. 1966), 59, 62, 94–104; "Developments in the Law of Confessions," *Harvard Law Rev.*, Vol. 79 (March 1966), 935, 963–84.

65. Malloy v. Hogan, 378 U.S. 1 (1964).

66. 404 U.S. 477, 486 note 14.

67. *Ibid.*, 488–89.

68. Compare "Recent Statute: Title II of the Omnibus Crime Control and Safe Streets Act of 1968," *Harvard Law Rev.*, Vol. 82 (April 1969), 1392–1403, which suggests alternative courses for the Court to follow when construing the statute; and, John Henry Wigmore, *A Treatise on Evidence in Trials at Common Law* (10 vols.), Vol. 3, rev. ed., John A. Chadbourn, pp. 938–41, describing Title II of the Act of 1968 as a "patchwork provision which attempts to provide a substitute for *Miranda* in federal prosecutions. It would seem to fall short of the requirement for a valid substitute. . . . It should be emphasized that the legislation is limited in scope to federal prosecutions, but, even as so limited, its constitutionality is most dubious, so long as *Miranda* remains without modification. On the point, the minority statement [of members of the Senate Judiciary Committee who opposed the statute] . . . compels assent."

69. 402 U.S. 424 (1971). See Bernard D. Meltzer, "Privilege Against Self-Incrimination: The Hit-and-Run Opinion," *The Supreme Court Review: 1971*, ed. Philip Kurland (Chicago, 1972), pp. 1–30; "The Supreme Court, 1970 Term," *Harvard Law Rev.*, Vol. 85 (Nov. 1971), 269–82; Jesse S. Waldinger, "California v. Byers: Hit-and-Run Statutes and the Privilege Against Self-Incrimination," *Brooklyn Law Rev.*, Vol. 38 (Winter 1972), 728–47.

70. Shapiro v. U.S., 335 U.S. 1, 55 (1948).

71. 402 U.S. 424, 453.

72. *Ibid.*, 453–54.

73. *Ibid.*, 459.

74. *Ibid.*, 434.

75. Malloy v. Hogan, 378 U.S. 1, 11–12 (1964), quoting Hoffman v. U.S., 341 U.S. 479, 486–88 (1951). See also U.S. v. Burr, 25 Fed. Cases 38, 40 (No. 14692e), (C.C. Va. 1807).

76. 402 U.S. 424, 429.

77. U.S. v. Sullivan, 274 U.S. 259, 263 (1927).

78. Shapiro v. U.S., 335 U.S. 1 (1948).

79. See cases cited in note 7, above.

80. 402 U.S. 424, 462–63.

81. *Ibid.*, 473.

82. *Ibid.*, 442.

83. *Ibid.*, 439.

84. *Ibid.*, 449.

85. See cases cited in note 7, above.

86. 402 U.S. 424, 447. Italics added.

87. *Ibid.*, 445–46.

88. *Ibid.*, 448.

89. Murphy v. Waterfront Comm., 378 U.S. 52, 55 (1964).

90. Levy, *Origins of the Fifth.*

91. See "The Scope of Testimonial Immunity Under the Fifth Amendment," *Northwestern Univ. Law Rev.*, Vol 67 (March-April 1972), 106–17; Ilene J. Lashinsky, "Freedom from Self-Incrimination: Transactional Immunity as the Only Fair Standard," *Law and Social Order*, Vol. 1971, pp. 811–21.

92. 406 U.S. 441. For comments, see "The Supreme Court, 1971 Term," *Harvard Law Rev.*, Vol. 86 (Nov. 1972), 181–89; Sally A. Treweek, "The Unconstitutionality of Use Immunity: Half a Loaf Is Not Enough," *Southern California Law Rev.*, Vol. 46 (Dec. 1972), 202–20; "Kastigar v. U.S.: the Required Scope of Immunity," *Virginia Law Rev.*, Vol. 58 (Sept. 1972), 1099–1117; Lawrence Rubenstein, "Immunity and the Self-Incrimination Clause," *American J. of Criminal Law*, Vol. 2 (Feb. 1973), 29–46; "Self-Incrimination: Choosing a Constitutional Immunity Standard," *Maryland Law Rev.*, Vol. 32 (1972), 289–304; "Testimonial Immunity," *Loyola U. Law J.*, Vol. 4 (Winter 1973), 193–211; "Statute Granting Use and Derivative Use Immunity Sufficiently Broad," *Fordham Law Rev.*, Vol. 41 (March 1973), 712–22; "Standards for Exclusion in Immunity Cases after Kastigar and Zicarelli," *Yale Law J.*, Vol. 82 (Nov. 1973), 171–88.

93. Levy, *Origins of the Fifth,* pp. 328, 359, 365–66, 384–85, 389, 402–03, 495.

94. *Ibid.*, 427–29, 515–16 note 35.

95. Ernest Eberling, *Congressional Investigations* (New York, 1928), pp. 150–60; Telford Taylor, *Grand Inquest* (New York, 1955), pp. 35, 215–17; Comment, "The Federal Witness Immunity Act in Theory and Practice," *Yale Law J.*, Vol. 72 (Summer 1963), 1568–1612.

96. 142 U.S. 547 (1892).

97. *Ibid.*, 585–86. Italics added.
98. 161 U.S. 591 (1896).
99. *Ibid.*, 595.
100. Hale v. Henkel, 201 U.S. 43, 67 (1906).
101. Murphy v. Waterfront Comm., 378 U.S. 52 (1964).
102. 350 U.S. 422.
103. *Ibid.*, 437–38; also, 429–30, 434–35.
104. 378 U.S. 52 (1964).
105. Malloy v. Hogan, 378 U.S. 1 (1964).
106. U.S. v. Murdock, 284 U.S. 141 (1931). See also, Fellman v. U.S., 322 U.S. 487 (1944).
107. For historical background, see J. A. C. Grant "Federalism and Self-Incrimination," *U.C.L.A. Law Rev.*, Vol. 4 (June 1957), 549–82 and Vol. 5 (Jan. 1958), 1–25, and Grant, "Immunity from Compulsory Self-Incrimination in a Federal System of Government," *Temple Law Q.*, Vol. 9 (1935), 57–78.
108. 378 U.S. 52, 54 (1964). Italics added.
109. *Ibid.*, 79.
110. 382 U.S. 70 (1965).
111. *Ibid.*, 80. See also Stevens v. Marks, 383 U.S. 234, 244–45 (1966).
112. 18 U.S. Code, sect. 6002. See "Constitutional Law—Immunity Statutes—Section 201 of Organized Crime Control Act of 1970, Which Provides Only Use and Fruits Immunity, Violates Fifth Amendment," *Vanderbilt Law Rev.*, Vol. 24 (May 1971), 815–21; "The Scope of Testimonial Immunity Under the Fifth Amendment," *Northwestern Law Rev.*, Vol. 67 (March-April 1972), 106–17; and, "Witness Immunity Statutes: the Constitutional and Functional Sufficiency of 'Use Immunity,' " *Boston Univ. Law Rev.*, Vol. 51 (Fall 1971), 616–64.
113. Organized Crime Control. Hearings before Subcommittee No. 5 of the Committee on the Judiciary, House of Representatives, 91st Cong., 2d Sess. on S. 30, and related proposals . . . 1970. Serial No. 27, pp. 293, 294, and qv. at p. 296.
114. 378 U.S. 478, 490 (1964).
115. Organized Crime Control. Hearings, p. 117.
116. Quoted in Kastigar v. U.S. 406 441, 452 note 36.
117. Federal Immunity of Witnesses Act. 91st Cong., 2d Sess. Report No. 91-1188, June 15, 1970. Report of Committee on the Judiciary, re H.R. 11157, p. 8. *Congressional Record,* Vol. 116, 91st Cong., 1st Sess. H. 9708.
118. *Cong. Rec.,* Vol. 116, 91st Cong., 1st Sess., H. 9708, Oct. 7, 1970.

119. Organized Crime Control. Hearings, pp. 527, 552–59.
120. Piccarillo v. N.Y., 400 U.S. 548 (1971).
121. 406 U.S. 441, 444.
122. *Ibid.*, 453.
123. *Cong. Rec.*, Vol. 116, 91st Cong., 1st Sess., H. 9708, 9720; Organized Crime Control Act of 1969, Report of the Committee on the Judiciary, United States Senate, 91st Cong., 1st Sess., Report No. 91-617, Dec. 18, 1969, pp. 53–55, 145; Federal Immunity Witnesses Act, p. 11; Organized Crime Control Act of 1970, House of R., 91st Cong., 2d Sess., Report No. 91-1549, Sept. 30, 1970, pp. 32, 42.
124. 406 U.S. 441, 455.
125. *Ibid.*, 457.
126. Piccarillo v. N.Y., 400 U.S. 548, 567.
127. 378 U.S. 52, 55.
128. 406 U.S. 441, 469.
129. *Ibid.*, 469–71.
130. Couch vs. U.S., 409 U.S. 322.
131. U.S. v. Dionisio, 410 U.S. 1 (1973).
132. Boyd v. U.S., 116 U.S. 616.
133. 409 U.S. 322, 338, 344.
134. *Ibid.*, 351.
135. *Ibid.*, 342.
136. *Ibid.*, 336.
137. Schmerber v. Cal., 384 U.S. 757 (1966).
138. U.S. v. Wade, 388 U.S. 216 (1967).
139. Gilbert v. Cal., 388 U.S. 263 (1967).
140. Wigmore, *Evidence* (2d ed., 1923), sect. 2251, p. 830; sect. 2263, p. 864.
141. Holt v. U.S., 218 U.S. 245, 252–53 (1910).
142. Counselman v. Hitchcock, 142 U.S. 547, 562.
143. Boyd v. U.S., 116 U.S. 616, 635 (1886).
144. 410 U.S. 19, 33.
145. 142 U.S. 547, 562.
146. Ullmann v. U.S., 350 U.S. 422, 438.
147. 410 U.S. 19, 38.
148. *Ibid.*, 37.

CHAPTER FOUR: The Sixth Amendment: The Right to Counsel

1. William M. Beaney, *The Right to Counsel in American Courts* (Ann Arbor, 1955), pp. 21, 28, 30.
2. Johnson v. Zerbst, 304 U.S. 458, 463 (1938).

3. Gideon v. Wainwright, 373 U.S. 335 (1963).

4. 287 U.S. 45 (1932).

5. *Ibid.,* 68–69.

6. Betts v. Brady, 316 U.S. 455 (1942).

7. Beaney, *Right to Counsel,* pp. 164–98.

8. Gideon v. Wainwright, 373 U.S. 335 (1963).

9. Powell v. Alabama, 287 U.S. 45, 69 (1932).

10. Escobedo v. Ill., 378 U.S. 479 (1964), Miranda v. Ariz., 384 U.S. 436 (1966), and Orozco v. Texas, 394 U.S. 324 (1969).

11. White v. Md., 373 U.S. 59 (1963).

12. U.S. v. Wade, 388 U.S. 218 (1967), and Gilbert v. Cal., 388 U.S. 263 (1967).

13. Hamilton v. Ala., 368 U.S. 52 (1961).

14. Anthony Lewis, *Gideon's Trumpet* (New York, 1964), p. 171.

15. Walter V. Schaefer, "Federalism and State Criminal Procedure," *Harvard Law Rev.,* Vol. 70 (Nov. 1956), 1, 8.

16. Brown v. Miss., 297 U.S. 278 (1936).

17. Chambers v. Fla., 309 U.S. 227 (1940).

18. Escobedo v. Ill., 378 U.S. 478 (1965); Miranda v. Ariz., 384 U.S. 436 (1967).

19. McMann v. Richardson, 397 U.S. 759, 775 (1970).

20. Gideon v. Wainwright, 372 U.S. 335 (1963).

21. Rochin v. Cal., 342 U.S. 165 (1951); Rogers v. Richmond, 365 U.S. 534, 540–41 (1961). In the latter case the Court said that involuntary confessions violate the due-process clause "not because such confessions are unlikely to be true but because the methods used to extract them offend an underlying principle in the enforcement of our criminal law: that ours is an accusatorial and not an inquisitorial system—a system in which the state must establish guilt by evidence independently and freely secured and may not by coercion prove its charges against an accused out of his own mouth."

22. Miranda v. Ariz., 384 U.S. 436, 475.

23. McMann v. Richardson, 397 U.S. 759 (1970).

24. Harrison v. U.S., 392 U.S. 219, 234 (1968).

25. Penn. ex rel. Herman v. Claudy, 350 U.S. 116, 118 (1956).

26. The cases are cited in White's majority opinion at 397 U.S. 765 note 10 and in Brennan's dissent, *ibid.,* 776 note 2.

27. 378 U.S. 368 (1964).

28. 397 U.S. 759, 768.

29. *Ibid.,* 767–68.

30. *Ibid.,* 769.

31. *Ibid.,* 770.

32. Stein v. N.Y., 346 U.S. 156 (1953); McMann v. Richardson, 397 U.S. 759, 772.

33. 397 U.S. 759, 773.

34. Ibid., 779–80.

35. Ibid., 778.

36. Ibid., 784.

37. Ibid., 786.

38. Brady v. U.S., 397 U.S. 742, 752 (1970). White's statistics derived from Donald J. Newman, *Conviction: The Determination of Guilt or Innocence without Trial* (Boston, 1966), p. 3, by far the fullest account of plea bargaining and the point of departure for all subsequent discussions.

39. 397 U.S. 742, 752.

40. Albert W. Alschuler quotes a Manhattan prosecutor as saying, "our office keeps eight court-rooms extremely busy trying five per cent of the cases. If even ten per cent of the cases ended in a trial, the system would break down. We can't afford to think very much about anything else." Alschuler, "The Prosecutor's Role in Plea Bargaining," *Univ. of Chicago Law Rev.*, Vol. 36 (Fall 1968), 50, 55. See also Arnold Enker, "Perspectives on Plea Bargaining," in The Task Force on the Administration of Justice, The President's Commission on Law Enforcement and Administration of Justice, *Task Force Report: The Courts* (Washington, 1967), p. 112; and in the main body of the report, p. 10, hereinafter cited as *Task Force Report: the Courts*.

41. On the dangers of plea bargaining to the innocent, see Alschuler, "The Prosecutor's Role," *Univ. of Chicago Law Rev.*, pp. 60–61, 64; *Task Force Report: the Courts*, pp. 11–12, and Enker, "Perspectives on Plea Bargaining," in *ibid.*, pp. 110, 112–15. On acquitting the guilty or reducing their charges, see Newman, *Conviction*, pp. 166–87. See also, Dominick R. Vetri, "Guilty Plea Bargaining: Compromises by Prosecutors to Secure Guilty Pleas," *Univ. of Pennsylvania Law Rev.*, Vol. 112 (April 1964), 865–95; Gregory J. Hobbs, Jr., "Judicial Supervision over California Plea Bargaining," *California Law Rev.*, Vol. 59 (June 1971), 962–96; "Restructuring the Plea Bargain," *Yale Law J.*, Vol. 82 (Dec. 1972), 286–312; and, Welsh S. White, "A Proposal for Reform of the Plea Bargaining Process," *Univ. of Pennsylvania Law Rev.*, Vol. 119 (Jan. 1971), 439–65. At p. 451, White refers to the pressure on the innocent to plead guilty. For a comparative analysis, see Anthony Davis, "Sentences for Sale: A New Look at Plea Bargaining in England and America," *Criminal Law Rev.*, Vol. 1971 (March-April), 150–61 and 218–28.

42. Newman, *Conviction*, p. 101.

43. See generally Alschuler, "The Prosecutor's Role," pp. 55–112; Alschuler speaks of "the horrors" of plea bargaining and thinks it should be abolished, *ibid.*, pp. 52, 64. See also, *Task Force Report: The Courts,* p. 11, and note 72 below.

44. 397 U.S. 759, 763.

45. Edward Barrett, describing the criminal courts in action, says, "Defense lawyers appear having had no more than time for hasty conversations with their clients," quoted in *The Challenge of Crime in a Free Society: A Report by the President's Commission on Law Enforcement and Administration of Justice* (Washington, 1967), p. 128. On the importance of defense counsel, see Newman, *Conviction,* pp. 197–230, 240–42; Vetri, "Guilty Plea Bargaining," *Univ. of Pennsylvania Law Rev.,* Vol. 112, pp. 887–91; *Task Force Report: The Courts,* pp. 52–60; Abraham S. Blumberg, *Criminal Justice* (Chicago, 1967), pp. 95–115.

46. Blumberg, *Criminal Justice,* pp. 92–93.

47. Arnold S. Trebach, *The Rationing of Justice: Constitutional Rights and the Criminal Process* (New Brunswick, N.J., 1964), p. 260. In using Trebach's figures, I have eliminated the "Did not answer" category and recomputed the percentages.

48. Enker, "Perspectives on Plea Bargaining," p. 111.

49. See Parker v. N. Car., 397 U.S. 790, 793 note 3, and Brady v. U.S., 397 U.S. 742, 743 note 2. In Brady's case, White said that there was no claim that the trial judge threatened Brady with a harsher sentence if convicted after trial in order to induce him to plead guilty, *ibid.*, 751 note 8; in McMann, 397 U.S. 759, 762, one of the petitioner's made precisely such a claim and White ignored it.

50. 397 U.S. 790, 796. The Court has said that "a guilty plea, if induced by promises or threats which deprive it of the character of a voluntary act, is void," Machibroda v. U.S., 368 U.S. 487, 493 (1962).

51. 397 U.S. 742, 758.

52. U.S. v. Jackson, 390 U.S. 570 (1968).

53. *Ibid.*, 572.

54. Cases cited above, note 49.

55. U.S. v. Jackson, 390 U.S. 570, 572 and 583.

56. 397 U.S. 742, 746.

57. *Ibid.*, 746–47.

58. U.S. v. Jackson, 390 U.S. 570, 583.

59. 397 U.S. 790, 794–95.

60. *Ibid.*, 808; see also 811 note 15.

61. Garrity v. N.J., 385 U.S. 493.

62. 397 U.S. 790, 809.

63. 4 Blackstone's *Commentaries* *329.
64. 400 U.S. 25, 28 note 2, and 29.
65. *Ibid.,* 39.
66. 397 U.S. 790, 811 note 15.
67. *Ibid.,* 808.
68. 397 U.S. 742, 753.
69. "The Unconstitutionality of Plea Bargaining," *Harvard Law Rev.,* Vol. 83 (April 1970), 1387, 1400. For an even more hostile analysis of plea bargaining by an able and conservative government study-group which flatly recommends its abolition, see National Advisory Commission on Criminal Justice Standards and Goals. Task Force on Courts, *Courts* (Washington, 1973), pp. 42–65.
70. 397 U.S. 742, 753.
71. Santobello v. New York, 404 U.S. 257, 260, 261, 262 (1971).
72. See Jon R. Waltz, "Inadequacy of Trial Defense Representation as a Ground for Post-Conviction Relief in Criminal Cases," *Northwestern Law Rev.,* Vol. 59 (July-Aug. 1964), 289–342, and Joseph D. Grano, "The Right to Counsel: Collateral Issues Affecting Due Process," *Minnesota Law Rev.,* Vol. 54 (June 1970), 1175, 1239–63. See also, Craig Bowman, "The Indigent's Right to an Adequate Defense: Expert and Investigational Assistance in Criminal Proceedings," *Cornell Law Rev.,* Vol. 55 (April 1970), 632–45; "Effective Assistance of Counsel for the Indigent Defendant," *Harvard Law Rev.,* Vol. 78 (May 1965), 1434–51; and, Terrell Simpson, "The Right to Effective Assistance of Counsel," *Mississippi Law J.,* Vol. 42 (Spring 1971), 213–25. On the general problem of legal aid for the accused indigent, see Lee Silverstein, *Defense of the Poor in Criminal Cases in American State Courts* (Chicago, 1965), 3 vols.
73. 411 U.S. 258 (1973).
74. *Ibid.,* 267, quoting McMann v. Richardson, 397 U.S. 759, 771 (1970).
75. *Ibid.,* 267.
76. *Ibid.,* 269.
77. *Ibid.,* 261.
78. *Ibid.,* 267.
79. *Ibid.,* 270.
80. *Ibid.,* 272.
81. *Ibid.,* 276.
82. Cases cited in *ibid.,* 275.
83. *Ibid.,* 277.
84. 399 U.S. 42 (1970).
85. *Ibid.,* 53.

86. 287 U.S. 45, 71 (1932).
87. Avery v. Ala., 308 U.S. 444, 446 (1940).
88. 326 U.S. 271 (1945).
89. 399 U.S. 42, 53, 54.
90. *Ibid.*, 55.
91. Quoted by Harlan in *ibid.*, 56 note 1.
92. *Ibid.*, 59.
93. 406 U.S. 250 (1972).
94. Coleman v. Ala., 399 U.S. 1 (1970).
95. Argersinger v. Hamlin, 407 U.S. 25 (1972).
96. 399 U.S. 1.
97. White v. Md., 373 U.S. 52 (1963).
98. 399 U.S. 1, 23.
99. *Ibid.*, 23.
100. *Ibid.*
101. 407 U.S. 25.
102. *Ibid.*, 40.
103. *Ibid.*, 34 note 4.
104. *Ibid.*, 38 note 10.
105. *Ibid.*, 43.
106. *Ibid.*, 27 note 1, 36 note 5, 38, 39, 43, and 54.
107. Duncan v. La., 391 U.S. 145, 159.
108. Beaney, *Right to Counsel,* ch. 2.
109. 407 U.S. 25, 34.
110. *Ibid.*, 36.
111. *Ibid.*, 47.
112. *Ibid.*, 63.
113. *Ibid.*
114. 287 U.S. 45, 61.
115. 407 U.S. 25, 64.
116. *Ibid.*
117. *Ibid.*, 47–48.
118. *Ibid.*, 64.
119. 316 U.S. 455.
120. 407 U.S. 25, 65.
121. Beaney, *Right to Counsel,* pp. 164–98.
122. Townsend v. Burke, 334 U.S. 736 (1948).
123. Gryger v. Burke, 334 U.S. 728 (1948).
124. Coleman v. Ala., 399 U.S. 1, 13 (1970).
125. 407 U.S. 25, 52.
126. Williams v. Ill., 399 U.S. 235 (1970).
127. Tate v. Short, 401 U.S. 395 (1971).

128. See Dallin Oaks and Warren Lehman, *A Criminal Justice System and the Indigent* (Chicago, 1968), pp. 150–51.

129. 407 U.S. 25, 54, 55.

130. *Ibid.,* 58–59.

131. 406 U.S. 682 (1972). For comments on this case, see *North Carolina Law Rev.,* Vol. 51 (Jan. 1973), 630–39; *American J. Criminal Law,* Vol. 2 (Feb. 1973), 98–107; *Iowa Law Rev.,* Vol. 58 (Dec. 1972), 404–20; *Loyola Univ. Law J.,* Vol. 4 (Winter 1973), 212–26; *Tulane Law Rev.,* Vol. 47 (April 1973), 899–906; *Indiana Law Rev.,* Vol. 6 (1972), 365–75; *Catholic Univ. Law Rev.,* Vol. 22 (Winter 1973), 467–74.

132. 388 U.S. 218 (1967). See also the companion cases, Gilbert v. Cal., 388 U.S. 273 and Stovall v. Denno, 388 U.S. 293. See Otis H. Stephens, Jr., "The Asssitance of Counsel and the Warren Court: Post-Gideon Developments in Perspective," *Dickinson Law Rev.,* Vol. 74 (Winter 1970), 193–217; "Pretrial Identification Procedures—Wade to Gilbert to Stovall," *Minnesota Law Rev.,* Vol. 55 (March 1971), 779–824; and, "Protection of the Accused at Police Lineups," *Columbia J. of Law and Social Problems,* Vol. 6 (Sept. 1970), 345–73.

133. 399 U.S. 1 (1970).

134. 406 U.S. 682, 705.

135. *Ibid.,* 688.

136. *Ibid.,* 689, quoting Johnson v. N.J., 384 U.S. 719, 729 (1966).

137. Escobedo v. Ill., 378 U.S. 478, 485, 486 (1964).

138. 388 U.S. 218, 225–27.

139. 406 U.S. 682, 689.

140. *Ibid.,* 690. Italics added.

141. Simmons v. U.S., 390 U.S. 377, 382–83 (1968).

142. U.S. v. Wade, 388 U.S. 218, 224.

143. Malloy v. Hogan, 378 U.S. 1, 8 (1964).

144. 384 U.S. 436, 477.

145. U.S. v. Marion, 404 U.S. 307, 320 (1971).

146. 406 U.S. 682, 695 quoting 388 U.S. 218, 225–28 *passim.*

147. Patrick M. Wall, *Eye-Witness Identification in Criminal Cases* (Springfield, Ill., 1965), p. 28.

148. Simmons v. U.S., 390 U.S. 377, 382–83 (1968).

149. Foster v. Cal., 394 U.S. 440 (1969).

150. *Ibid.,* Stovall v. Denno, 388 U.S. 293 (1967), and Coleman v. Ala., 399 U.S. 1 (1970).

151. Stovall v. Denno, 388 U.S. 293, 298. Italics added.

152. 388 U.S. 218, 251. Italics added.

153. For citations, see 406 U.S. 682, 704 note 14.

154. *Ibid.*, 691 and note 8 therein.
155. 18 U.S. Code sect. 3502.
156. "Omnibus Crime Control and Safe Streets Act," Senate Report No. 1097, 90th Cong., 2d Sess. (Washington, 1968), p. 53 (Calendar No. 1080).
157. 413 U.S. 300.
158. *Ibid.*, 326.
159. *Ibid.*, 338, 341.
160. *Ibid.*, 316.
161. *Ibid.*, 320.
162. *Ibid.*, 321.
163. *Ibid.*
164. Jerome Frank and Barbara Frank, *Not Guilty* (Garden City, N.Y., 1957), p. 61. See also Edwin M. Borchard, *Convicting the Innocent* (New Haven, 1932), p. xiii, and Wall, *Eye-Witness Identification*, p. 5.
165. U.S. v. Wade, 388 U.S. 218, 228 (1967), quoted in 413 U.S. 329.
166. *Ibid.*, 333–34.
167. *Ibid.*, 334. See also Wall, *Eye-Witness Identification*, pp. 73–85.
168. 413 U.S. 300, 341.

CHAPTER FIVE: The Sixth Amendment: Trial by Jury

1. Baldwin v. New York, 399 U.S. 66 (1970), Williams v. Fla., 399 U.S. 78 (1970), Johnson v. La., 406 U.S. 356 (1972), and Apodaca v. Ore., 406 U.S. 404 (1972).
2. Patton v. U.S., 281 U.S. 276, 288 (1930).
3. Baldwin v. N.Y., 399 U.S. 66, 122.
4. Duncan v. La., 391 U.S. 145 (1968).
5. Felix Frankfurter and Thomas G. Corcoran, "Petty Federal Offenses and the Constitutional Guarantee of a Trial by Jury," *Harvard Law Rev.*, Vol. 39 (June 1926), 917, 968ff.
6. Schick v. U.S., 195 U.S. 65 (1904).
7. D.C. v. Colts, 282 U.S. 63 (1930).
8. D.C. v. Clawans, 300 U.S. 617 (1937). See also, Francis H. Heller, *The Sixth Amendment to the Constitution of the United States* (Lawrence, Kan., 1951), pp. 57–59.
9. Duncan v. La., 391 U.S. 145, 162 (1968).
10. Baldwin v. N.Y., 399 U.S. 66, 135 (1970). See also "Jury Trials for Misdemeanants in New York City: The Effects of Baldwin," *Co-*

lumbia J. of Law and Social Problems, Vol. 7 (Spring 1971), 173, 177, quoting 24 N.Y. 2d. 207, 217 (1969).

11. *Baldwin* v. *N.Y.,* 399 U.S. 66, 135.

12. *Ibid.,* 69. On Baldwin, see Paul A. Battaglia, "Due Process and the Right to Trial by Jury in State Criminal Procedure," *Buffalo Law Rev.,* Vol. 20 (Fall 1970), 286–96.

13. Baldwin v. N.Y., 399 U.S. 66, 72–73.

14. *Ibid.,* 73–74.

15. *Ibid.,* 75.

16. *Ibid.*

17. *Ibid.,* 77

18. *Ibid.,* 130–31.

19. Benton v. Md., 395 U.S. 784, 795.

20. Duncan v. La., 391 U.S. 145, 151.

21. Williams v. Fla., 399 U.S. 78, 86 (1970).

22. "The Path of the Law," in Max Lerner, ed., *The Mind and Faith of Justice Holmes* (Boston, 1943), p. 83.

23. Thompson v. Utah, 170 U.S. 343, 349 (1898).

24. 399 U.S. 78, 100, 103.

25. "Jury Trials for Misdemeanants," p. 181, cited note 10, above.

26. *Ibid.,* p. 183.

27. *Ibid.,* pp. 185–86.

28. *Ibid.,* p. 187.

29. *Ibid.,* p. 189.

30. *Ibid.,* p. 191.

31. *Ibid.,* p. 192.

32. *Ibid.,* p. 197.

33. The Court "invited reargument addressed to specific questions" on the history of treason in Cramer v. U.S., 325 U.S. 1, 7 (1945), and in the School Desegregation Cases the Court also required counsel on both sides to address themselves to explicit questions framed by the Court on the original meaning of the Fourteenth Amendment, Brown v. Bd. of Ed., 345 U.S. 972 (1953).

34. Williams v. Fla., 399 U.S. 78, 101.

35. See the discussion of the case, above, in the chapter on the Fifth Amendment.

36. 399 U.S. 78, 128–29.

37. *Ibid.,* 89–90.

38. *Ibid.,* 90.

39. *Ibid.,* 98–99.

40. *Ibid.,* 124, quoting Smith v. Ala., 124 U.S. 465, 478 (1888).

41. *Ibid.,* 99–100.

42. See Johnson v. La., 406 U.S. 356 (1972) and Apodaca v. Ore., 406 U.S. 404 (1972).

43. 399 U.S. 78, 91 note 28.

44. *Ibid.*, 126.

45. *Ibid.*, 100.

46. *Ibid.*

47. *Ibid.*, 101–02.

48. (Boston, 1966), p. 487.

49. David F. Walbert, "The Effect of Size on the Probability of Conviction: an Evaluation of Williams v. Florida," *Case Western Reserve Law Rev.,* Vol. 22 (April 1971), 529, 535, 536, 539–48.

50. 399 U.S. 78, 101 note 49.

51. ". . . And Then There Were None: the Diminution of the Federal Jury," *Univ. of Chicago Law Rev.,* Vol. 38 (Summer 1971), 710, 719.

52. *The American Jury,* p. 462.

53. ". . . And Then There Were None," p. 720.

54. 399 U.S. 78, 101 note 48 cites the six studies.

55. ". . . And Then There Were None," p. 715.

56. Walbert, cited above, note 49, p. 536. For additional studies, see also, William L. Stevens, "Defendant's Right to a Trial by Jury—Is Six Enough?" *Kentucky Law J.,* Vol. 59 (Summer 1971), 996–1010; Ronald R. McMillan, "Right to Trial by Jury: A Line Is Drawn," *Missouri Law Rev.,* Vol. 36 (Spring 1971), 279–87; O. John Rogge, *"Williams v. Florida:* End of a Theory," *Villanova Law Rev.,* Vol. 16 (March 1971), 411–66 and (April 1971) 607–709. See also William R. Pabst, Jr., "Statistical Studies of the Costs of Six-Man versus Twelve-Man Juries," *William and Mary Law Rev.,* Vol. 14 (Winter 1972), 326–36; David M. Powell, "Reducing the Size of Juries," *Journal of Law Reform,* Vol. 5 (Fall 1971), 87–108.

57. 399 U.S. 78, 102.

58. Walbert, pp. 547–51 *passim.*

59. ". . . And Then There Were None," p. 716.

60. *Ibid.*

61. *Ibid.*, 720.

62. *Ibid.*, 721.

63. 399 U.S. 78, 103.

64. Thomas E. Morris, "Florida's Six-Member Criminal Juries: Constitutional, but Are They Fair?" *Univ. of Florida Law Rev.,* Vol. 23 (Winter 1971), 402, 408.

65. Walbert, pp. 551, 554.

66. 406 U.S. 356 and 406 U.S. 404 (1972).

67. 406 U.S. 356, 393.

68. Speedy Trial. Hearings before the Subcommittee on Constitutional Rights of the Committee on the Judiciary, U.S. Sen., 92d Cong., 1st Sess. on S. 895 (July 13, 1971), pp. 97, 108.

69. The phrase is Harlan's in Williams v. Fla., 399 U.S. 78, 136.

70. 406 U.S. 356, 381.

71. *Ibid.*, 394.

72. Swain v. Ala., 380 U.S. 202, 211. Italics added.

73. Duncan v. La., 391 U.S. 145, 151 (1968).

74. 399 U.S. 78, 100.

75. *Ibid.*, note 46.

76. See Edwin M. Borchard, *Convicting the Innocent: Errors of Criminal Justice* (New Haven, 1932), and Jerome Frank and Barbara Frank, *Not Guilty* (New York, 1957).

77. Levy, *Origins of the Fifth Amendment*, p. 33.

78. Kalven and Zeisel, *The American Jury*, p. 189.

79. In re Winship, 397 U.S. 358, 363–64 (1970).

80. 406 U.S. 356, 361.

81. "Non-Unanimous Jury Verdicts," *Georgetown Law J.*, Vol. 61 (Oct. 1972), 223, 228 note 25, citing Oral Argument for Petitioner, 11–12, in Johnson v. La.

82. See cases cited by Justice Stewart, 406 U.S. 356, 397.

83. *Ibid.*, 361.

84. Kalven and Zeisel, *The American Jury*, pp. 488, 490.

85. 406 U.S. 356, 402–03.

86. Kalven and Zeisel, *The American Jury*, pp. 488–89.

87. Allen v. U.S., 164 U.S. 492, 501 (1896).

88. 406 U.S. 356, 363.

89. Green v. U.S., 309 F. 2d 852, 854 note 3 (1962).

90. Kalven and Zeisel, *The American Jury*, p. 460.

91. 406 U.S. 356, 401.

92. *Ibid.*, 402.

93. Kalven and Zeisel, *The American Jury*, p. 56.

94. *Ibid.*, p. 461.

95. *Ibid.*, p. 460.

96. 406 U.S. 356, 391.

97. *Ibid.*, 363–64.

98. *Ibid.*, 362.

99. *Ibid.*, 365.

100. *Ibid.*

101. Green v. U.S., 356 U.S. 165, 216 (1958).

102. Duncan v. La., 391 U.S. 145, 158–59 note 30 (1968).

103. Paul Crowley, "Sixth Amendment Right to Jury Trial Does Not Mandate Unanimous Verdict," *Villanova Law Rev.*, Vol. 18 (Dec. 1972), 302, 318.

104. Zeisel, ". . . And Then There Were None," p. 722.

105. Jane Kober, "Trial by Jury—Unanimity in Criminal Trials," *Case Western Reserve Law Rev.*, Vol. 24 (Fall 1972), 227, 236 note 54.

106. 406 U.S. 404 (1972).

107. *Ibid.*, 406.

108. *Ibid.*, 409–10.

109. *Ibid.*, 410.

110. *Ibid.*, 410–11.

111. *The American Jury*, p. 460, quoted by White in *ibid.*, 411 note 5.

112. *The American Jury*, p. 460, table for "Last Vote of Deadlocked Jurors."

113. 406 U.S. 356, 391.

114. *Ibid.*, 389.

115. Kalven and Zeisel, "The American Jury: Notes for an English Controversy," *Chicago Bar Record*, Vol. 48 (May-June 1967), 195, 201.

116. 406 U.S. 404, 411.

117. *Ibid.*, 412.

118. In re Winship, 397 U.S. 358 (1970).

119. 406 U.S. 356, 399–400.

120. *Ibid.*, 413.

121. ". . . And Then There Were None," p. 722.

122. *Ibid.*, pp. 722–23, and Michael Masinter, "The Non-Unanimous Jury," *American Criminal Law Rev.*, Vol. 11 (Winter 1973), 537, 547.

123. "The American Jury: Notes for an English Controversy," p. 200.

124. 406 U.S. 356, 397.

125. *Ibid.*, 398.

126. *Ibid.*

127. William Forsyth, *History of Trial by Jury* (London, 1852), p. 204.

128. Lysander Spooner, *An Essay on the Trial by Jury* (Boston, 1852), p. 208.

129. Duncan v. La., 391 U.S. 145, 170 (1968).

130. 406 U.S. 356, 377.

131. Laird C. Kirkpatrick, "Should Jury Verdicts Be Unanimous in

Criminal Cases?" *Oregon Law Rev.*, Vol. 47 (June 1968), 417, 423.
132. 406 U.S. 356, 366.
133. *Univ. of Chicago Law Rev.*, Vol. 38 (Summer 1971), 710–24.
See also James L. Carroll, "Unanimous Verdict No Longer Required,"
Tulane Law Rev., Vol. 47 (Feb. 1973), 459–66; Thomas A. Lemly,
"Jury Unanimity No Longer Required in State Criminal Trials," *North
Carolina Law Rev.*, Vol. 51 (Nov. 1972), 134–45; "Comment. A
Constitutional Renvoi: Unanimous Verdicts in State Criminal Trials,"
Fordham Law Rev., Vol. 41 (Oct. 1972), 115–39.
134. 403 U.S. 528.
135. In re Gault, 387 U.S. 1. On the Gault case, see Monrad G.
Paulsen, "The Constitutional Domestication of the Juvenile Court," in
P. Kurland, ed., *The Supreme Court Review: 1967* (Chicago, 1967),
pp. 233–66, and Dan Hopson, Jr., *et al., The Juvenile Offender and
the Law* (New York, 1971), a Da Capo Press reprint of "Symposium
on Juvenile Problems," *Indiana Law Rev.*, Vol. 43 (1968), 523–676.
136. In re Winship, 397 U.S. 358.
137. On the origins and purposes of juvenile courts, see Monrad G.
Paulsen, "Kent v. U.S.: The Constitutional Context of Juvenile Cases,"
in P. Kurland, ed., *The Supreme Court Review: 1966* (Chicago, 1966),
167–75.
138. In re Gault, 387 U.S. 1, 17.
139. *Ibid.*, 28.
140. President's Commission on Law Enforcement and Administration of Justice. *Task Force Report: Juvenile Delinquency and Youth
Crime* (Washington, 1967), p. 7.
141. 387 U.S. 1 ,18.
142. *Task Force Report: Juvenile Delinquency and Youth Crime,*
p. 7, quoted in 403 U.S. 528, 544 note 4.
143. *Task Force Report,* p. 9, quoted in 403 U.S. 528, 544 note 5.
144. 403 U.S. 528, 560.
145. *Task Force Report,* p. 8.
146. In re Winship, 397 U.S. 358 (1970).
147. *Ibid.*, 376.
148. 403 U.S. 528 (1971).
149. Duncan v. La., 391 U.S. 145 (1968); Baldwin v. N.Y., 399
U.S. 66 (1970).
150. 403 U.S. 528, 557.
151. Duncan v. La., 391 U.S. 145 (1968).
152. *Task Force Report,* p. 8.
153. 403 U.S. 528, 545.
154. *Ibid.*, 547.

155. *Ibid.*, 550.
156. 387 U.S. 1, 21.
157. 403 U.S. 528, 545 and 547.
158. *Ibid.*, 547–48.
159. Albert K. Cohen, "An Evaluation of Gault by a Sociologist," in Hopson *et al., The Juvenile Offender and the Law,* p. 95.
160. 397 U.S. 358, 376.
161. 403 U.S. 528, 564.

CHAPTER SIX: The Sixth Amendment: Fair Trial

1. McGautha v. Cal., 402 U.S. 183, 221 (1971).
2. Lutwak v. U.S., 344 U.S. 604, 619 (1953), and Bruton v. U.S., 391 U.S. 123, 135 (1968).
3. Brooks v. Tenn., 406 U.S. 605 (1972).
4. Milton v. Wainwright, 407 U.S. 371 (1972).
5. Tenn. Code Annotated, sect. 40-2403, quoted in Brooks v. Tenn., 406 U.S. 605, 606 note 1.
6. 406 U.S. 610, 611.
7. *Ibid.*, 615.
8. *Ibid.*, 617.
9. *Ibid.*, 618.
10. Milton v. Wainwright, 407 U.S. 371, 383 (1972).
11. *Ibid.*, 377.
12. *Ibid.*, 372.
13. 377 U.S. 201 (1964).
14. 407 U.S. 371, 380.
15. *Ibid.*, 381.
16. *Ibid.*, 383, quoting Chapman v. Cal., 386 U.S. 18, 23–24 (1967), the leading case on the "harmless error" doctrine.
17. 407 U.S. 371, 384.
18. 408 U.S. 786 (1972).
19. 373 U.S. 83, 87 (1963).
20. 408 U.S. 786, 794.
21. *Ibid.*, 809–10.
22. *Ibid.*, 806.
23. *Ibid.*, 808–09.
24. 412 U.S. 837 (1973).
25. In re Winship, 397 U.S. 358, 364 (1970).
26. 412 U.S. 837, 845–46.
27. *Ibid.*, 850.
28. *Ibid.*, 852.

29. *Ibid.*, 853.
30. *Ibid.*, 854.
31. 411 U.S. 423. On entrapment, see William E. Mikell, "The Doctrine of Entrapment in the Federal Courts," *Univ. of Pennsylvania Law Rev.*, Vol. 90 (Jan. 1942), 245–65; Richard C. Donnelly, "Judicial Control of Informants, Spies, Stool Pigeons, and Agents Provocatuers," *Yale Law J.*, Vol. 60 (Nov. 1951), 1091–1131; Richard A. Cowen, "The Entrapment Doctrine in the Federal Courts, and Some State Comparisons," *J. of Criminal Law, Criminology, and Police Science,* Vol. 49 (Jan.-Feb. 1959), 447–55; Paul W. Williams, "The Defense of Entrapment and Related Problems in Criminal Prosecutions," *Fordham Law Rev.*, Vol. 28 (Spring 1960), 399–418; and, Michael Senneff, "Entrapment in the Federal Courts," *Univ. of San Francisco Law Rev.*, Vol. 1 (Oct. 1966), 177–87.
32. Sorrells v. U.S., 287 U.S. 435 (1932) and Sherman v. U.S., 356 U.S. 369 (1958).
33. 287 U.S. 435, 442.
34. *Ibid.*, 451.
35. *Ibid.*, 454.
36. *Ibid.*, 457.
37. *Ibid.*, 459.
38. Sherman v. U.S., 356 U.S. 369, 372.
39. U.S. v. Russell, 411 U.S. 423, 431, 432.
40. *Ibid.*, 436.
41. *Ibid.*, 439.
42. Sherman v. U.S., 356 U.S. 369, 380 (1958).
43. *Ibid.*, 382.
44. 411 U.S. 423, 441.
45. *Ibid.*, 442.
46. *Ibid.*, 445.
47. *Ibid.*
48. *Ibid.*, 446.
49. Pointer v. Texas, 380 U.S. 400, 405 (1965).
50. For the most respected and extended discussion of the hearsay rule and its exceptions, see John Henry Wigmore, *A Treatise on the Anglo-American System of Evidence in Trials at Common Law* (Boston, 1940, 3rd. ed., 10 vols.), Vol. 5 and Vol. 6, pp. 1–281. For a briefer but equally authoritative treatment, see Charles T. McCormick, *Handbook of the Law of Evidence* (St. Paul, 1954), pp. 455–634. Wigmore covers dying declarations in Vol. 5, ch. XLIX, pp. 218–58, McCormick in pp. 555–60. I have used both Wigmore and McCormick throughout the remainder of this chapter on various exceptions to the

hearsay rule; but, in order to avoid cluttering and multiplying my citations, I have not again referred to them but for a few exceptions. Both Wigmore and McCormick have detailed, analytical tables of contents, enabling the reader quickly to find their discussions on any point involving the hearsay rule and its exceptions, making my constant references to their books unnecessary.

51. The recently proposed Federal Rules of Evidence, promul gated by the Supreme Court, contain twenty-three exceptions when the availability of the declarant is immaterial (Rule 803) and five exceptions when the declarant is unavailable (Rule 804); and, following each of these two broad categories, there is an extraordinary omnibus clause which says, "A statement not specifically covered by any of the foregoing exceptions but having comparable circumstantial guarantees of trustworthiness," may be admitted in evidence. Federal Rules of Evidence, Rules 803 (24) and 804 (b)(6), in *Supreme Court Reporter,* Jan. 1, 1973, Vol. 93, paginating the section on the rules separately from the usual section of the Court's opinions. The section on the rules contains, interspersed throughout, valuable commentary in "Notes" by the advisory commission that recommended the rules. The new Federal Rules of Evidence were scheduled to go into effect on July 1, 1973, but Congress postponed that date for at least two years. *New York Times,* Feb. 1, 1973, p. 9, col. 1.

52. Francis H. Heller, *The Sixth Amendment to the Constitution* (Lawrence, Kan., 1951), pp. 104–06; McCormick, *Evidence,* pp. 483–84; Wigmore, *Evidence,* Vol. 5, pp. 9–27, 127–31.

53. Wigmore, *Evidence,* Vol. 5, p. 29.

54. Federal Rules of Evidence, p. 100, in *Supreme Court Reporter,* Jan. 1, 1973.

55. Stein v. N.Y., 346 U.S. 156, 195 (1953).

56. Mattox v. U.S., 156 U.S. 237, 243 (1895).

57. Salinger v. U.S., 272 U.S. 542, 548 (1926). Italics added.

58. Snyder v. Mass., 291 U.S. 97, 107 (1934).

59. 380 U.S. 400 (1965).

60. *Ibid.,* 403 and 407. Italics added.

61. *Ibid.,* 407.

62. 390 U.S. 719 (1968).

63. *Ibid.,* 725.

64. 380 U.S. 415 (1965).

65. 391 U.S. 123 (1968).

66. Brookhart v. Janis, 384 U.S. 1 (1966), held that where defendant had not pleaded guilty, his counsel could not agree to a truncated trial that virtually waived his right to cross-examine. Parker v. Glad-

den, 385 U.S. 363 (1966), held that a bailiff's statements to the jury against the accused and out of his hearing violated his confrontation rights. Smith v. Ill., 390 U.S. 129 (1968), held that a trial court's refusal to permit cross-examination as to an informer's real name and address emasculated the right of cross-examination. Roberts v. Russell, 392 U.S. 293 (1968), applied the rule of the Bruton case retroactively to an out-of-court confession by a codefendant. Berger v. Cal., 393 U.S. 314 (1969), applied the rule of the Barber case retroactively to the use of prior recorded testimony at a preliminary hearing when the declarant was absent from the trial. In Harrington v. Cal., 395 U.S. 250 (1969), where there were three dissenters—more than in any other Warren Court confrontation-clause case, the Court held that the facts showed "harmless error" despite the admission of out-of-court confessions by nontestifying codefendants. Ill. v. Allen, 397 U.S. 337 (1970), was a wholly different kind of confrontation case in which the Court held that the disruptive conduct of a defendant constituted a waiver of his right to be present at his own trial. For a discussion of leading cases prior to 1970, see J. Broocks Greer, "Hearsay, the Confrontation Guarantee and Related Problems," *Louisiana Law Rev.,* Vol. 30 (1970), pp. 651–72.

67. 399 U.S. 149 (1970). For comments, see "The Supreme Court, 1969 Term," *Harvard Law Rev.,* Vol. 84 (Nov. 1970), pp. 108–17; "Hearsay and the Right of Confrontation Clarified," *Utah Law Rev.,* Vol. 1970 (Sept. 1970), pp. 668–78; David A. Gradwohl, "Evidence —Confrontation Clause," *Ohio State Law J.,* Vol. 32 (Winter 1971), pp. 188–98; Erwin N. Griswold, "The Due Process Revolution and Confrontation," *Univ. of Pennsylvania Law Rev.,* Vol. 119 (April 1971), pp. 711–29.

68. 400 U.S. 74 (1970). For comments, see "The Supreme Court, 1970 Term," *Harvard Law Rev.,* Vol. 85 (Nov. 1971), pp. 188–99; "Criminal Law: Supreme Court Review (1971)," *J. of Criminal Law, Criminology and Police Science,* Vol. 62 (Dec. 1971), pp. 516–20. For articles of a more general nature, covering both California v. Green and Dutton v. Evans, see Comment, "The Hearsay Rule and the Right to Confrontation: States' Leeway in Formulating Evidentiary Rules," *Fordham Law Rev.,* Vol. 40 (March 1972), pp. 595–616; Frank T. Read, "The New Confrontation-Hearsay Dilemma," *Southern California Law Rev.,* Vol. 45 (Winter 1972), pp. 1–50; David E. Seidelson, "Hearsay Exceptions and the Sixth Amendment," *George Washington Law Rev.,* Vol. 40 (Oct. 1971), pp. 76–96; Paul J. Liacos, "The Right of Confrontation and the Hearsay Rule: Another Look," *American Trial Lawyers J.,* Vol. 34 (1972), pp. 153–73.

69. Cal. v. Green, 399 U.S. 149, 171, 172 (1970).
70. *Ibid.*, 172.
71. *Ibid.*, 155.
72. *Ibid.*, 156.
73. *Ibid.*, 160.
74. *Ibid.*, 165.
75. *Ibid.*, 166.
76. *Ibid.*, 192 note 5.
77. *Ibid.*, 194.
78. *Ibid.*, 199.
79. 400 U.S. 74 (1970).
80. *Ibid.*, 93.
81. *Ibid.*, 77.
82. *Ibid.*, 88.
83. Quoted by Marshall, J., in *ibid.*, 108 note 10.
84. *Ibid.*, 81.
85. *Ibid.*, 87.
86. *Ibid.*, 89.
87. *Ibid.*, 87 note 18.
88. *Ibid.*, 91.
89. *Ibid.*, 103.
90. *Ibid.*, 89.
91. *Ibid.*, 96.
92. *Ibid.*, 108 note 10.
93. 380 U.S. 400 (1965).
94. 400 U.S. 74, 89. Italics added.
95. 399 U.S. 149, 165 (1970).
96. 400 U.S. 74, 89–90, quoting Snyder v. Mass., 291 U.S. 97, 122 (1934).
97. 400 U.S. 74, 100.
98. *Ibid.*, 107.
99. *Ibid.*, 105 note 7, and 110.
100. *Ibid.*, 110–11.
101. Nelson v. O'Neil, 402 U.S. 622 (1971); Schneble v. Fla., 405 U.S. 427 (1972); Mancusi v. Stubbs, 408 U.S. 204 (1972).
102. 410 U.S. 284 (1973).
103. *Ibid.*, 289–90. See also 302.
104. *Ibid.*, 294.
105. *Ibid.*, 302.
106. 402 U.S. 622 (1971).
107. 391 U.S. 123 (1968).
108. 399 U.S. 149 (1970).

109. 405 U.S. 427 (1972).

110. *Ibid.*, 430.

111. *Ibid.*, 433.

112. *Ibid.*, 431.

113. *Ibid.*, 434.

114. *Ibid.*, 437.

115. 408 U.S. 204 (1972).

116. Klopfer v. N. Car., 386 U.S. 213 (1967).

117. Beavers v. Haubert, 198 U.S. 77, 87 (1905).

118. Pollard v. U.S., 352 U.S. 354, 361 (1957).

119. Smith v. U.S., 360 U.S. 1, 10 (1959).

120. U.S. v. Ewell, 383 U.S. 116, 120 (1966).

121. Klopfer v. N. Car., 386 U.S. 213 (1967).

122. Smith v. Hooey, 393 U.S. 374 (1969).

123. Klopfer v. N. Car., 386 U.S. 213, 226 (1967).

124. James Mills, "I Have Nothing to Do with Justice," *Life,* Vol. 70 (March 12, 1971), 57, 61–62.

125. "Speedy Trial: A Constitutional Right in Search of Definition," *Georgetown Law J.,* Vol. 61 (Feb. 1973), 657, 658 note 9.

126. Allen P. Rubine, "Speedy Trial Schemes and Criminal Justice Delays," *Cornell Law Rev.,* Vol. 57 (May 1972), 794 note 4.

127. *Ibid.* See also "Speedy Trial," cited in note 125 above, p. 657, and Lewis Katz *et al., Justice Is the Crime: Pretrial Delay in Felony Cases* (Cleveland, 1972), pp. 39–41.

128. Rubine, cited in note 126 above, p. 794 note 4.

129. "Speedy Trial," cited in note 125 above, pp. 657–58 note 7.

130. *Ibid.*, 660 and 670. See also Katz *et al., Justice Is the Crime,* p. 67 note 77.

131. Clark, *Crime in America* (New York, 1970), p. 204.

132. "Remarks of Warren E. Burger . . . on the State of the Federal Judiciary," Aug. 10, 1970, in 90 S. Ct. 2381, 2382.

133. President's Commission on Law Enforcement and the Administration of Justice. Task Force Report. *The Courts* (Washington, 1967), p. 80.

134. "Remarks of Warren E. Burger," 90 S. Ct. 2381, 2384.

135. J. Edward Lumbard (Chief Judge, U.S. Court of Appeals, 2d Circuit), "Trial by Jury and Speedy Justice," *Washington and Lee Law Rev.,* Vol. 28 (Fall 1971), 309, 317–18.

136. DeMeerleer v. Mich., 329 U.S. 663 (1947).

137. J. Anthony Foster, Jr., "The Right to a Slow Trial: Insuring Effective Counsel," *American J. of Criminal Law,* Vol. 2 (Feb. 1973),

67, 73, quoting Parra v. Page, 430 P. 2d 834, 837 (Okla. Crim. App. 1967).

138. U.S. v. Ewell, 383 U.S. 116, 120 (1966).

139. "Remarks of Warren E. Burger," 90 S. Ct. 2381, 2386.

140. 398 U.S. 30 (1970).

141. *Ibid.*, 56.

142. *Ibid.*, 46.

143. *Ibid.*, 55.

144. Katz *et al.*, *Justice Is the Crime*, pp. 69–81, is excellent on the causes and sources of delay.

145. 398 U.S. 30, 49.

146. *Ibid.*, 55.

147. *Ibid.*, 56–57.

148. 404 U.S. 307 (1971).

149. *Ibid.*, 324.

150. 407 U.S. 514. For comments on Barker v. Wingo, see Charles P. Schropp, "Sixth Amendment—Right to Speedy Trial—A Balancing Test," *Cornell Law Rev.*, Vol. 58 (Jan. 1973), 399–415; William H. Erickson, "The Right to a Speedy Trial: Standards for Its Implementation," *Houston Law Rev.*, Vol. 10 (Jan. 1973), 237–50; Fred C. Thompson, Jr., "Standards for the Right to Speedy Trial," *North Car. Law Rev.*, Vol. 51 (Dec. 1972), 310–16; Comment in *Vanderbilt Law Rev.*, Vol. 26 (Jan. 1973), 171–77; and, "The Supreme Court, 1971 Term," *Harvard Law Rev.*, Vol. 86 (Nov. 1972), 164–71.

151. Beavers v. Haubert, 198 U.S. 77, 87 (1905).

152. Barker v. Wingo, 407 U.S. 514, 519 (1972).

153. *Ibid.*, 521.

154. U.S. v. Ewell, 383 U.S. 116, 120, and see text, above, for note 120.

155. 407 U.S. 514, 521 and 522.

156. *Ibid.*, 522.

157. Strunk v. U.S., 412 U.S. 434, 440 (1973).

158. 407 U.S. 514, 523. On the 2d Circuit rules, see John C. Godbold (Circuit Judge, U.S. Court of Appeals, 5th Circuit), "Speedy Trial—Major Surgery for a National Ill," *Alabama Law Rev.*, Vol. 24 (Spring 1972), 265, 291–92.

159. On the A.B.A. proposals, see Rubine, cited in note 126 above, pp. 803–815; "Speedy Trial," cited in note 125 above, pp. 662–688 *passim;* Godbold, cited in note 158 above, pp. 289–291; and, Erickson, cited in note 150 above, pp. 245–250.

160. On the proposed legislation, see "Speedy Trial," cited in note 125 above, pp. 663, 670, 676, 681, 685, 694, 702.

161. On rule 50 (b), see Godbold, cited in note 158 above, p. 292. The Supreme Court promulgates rules of criminal procedure for the district courts pursuant to Title 18, U.S. Code, sections 3771–72. Rule 50 (b) is reprinted in full in Rules of Criminal Procedure for the United States District Courts . . . As Amended to October 1, 1972. Printed for the use of the Committee on the Judiciary, House of Representatives, p. 28. Rule 50 (b) provides that the plan proposed by each district court shall be submitted for approval to a reviewing panel of members of the judicial council for each circuit. Approved plans shall be forwarded to the Administrative Office of the United States Courts. The Administrative office shall report annually on the operation of such plans to the Judicial Conference of the United States.

162. 92 S. Ct. 2182, 2188. On time limits, see "Speedy Trial," cited in note 125 above, pp. 665–688, and Katz *et al.*, *Justice Is the Crime*, pp. 81–87.

163. Erickson, cited in note 150 above, p. 241.

164. 407 U.S. 514, 528.

165. *Ibid.*

166. *Ibid.*, 529.

167. *Ibid.*, 529–30.

168. *Ibid.*, 530–31.

169. *Ibid.*, 531–32.

170. *Ibid.*, 532.

171. *Ibid.*, 532–33.

172. *Ibid.*, 533. Italics added.

173. Katz *et al.*, *Justice Is the Crime*, pp. 71–72, 80.

174. "Speedy Trial," cited in note 125 above, p. 669.

175. On rule 50 (b), see note 161 above and related text.

CHAPTER SEVEN: The Eighth Amendment: The Death Penalty

1. To Spencer Roane, Sept. 6, 1819, in *The Writings of Thomas Jefferson,* Andrew A. Lipscomb and Albert Ellery Burgh, eds. (Washington, D.C., 1904–07, 20 vols.), Vol. 15, p. 278.

2. McGautha v. Cal. and Crampton v. Ohio, 402 U.S. 183 (1971).

3. Furman v. Georgia, Jackson v. Georgia, and Branch v. Texas, 408 U.S. 238 (1972). See Malcolm E. Wheeler, "Toward a Theory of Limited Punishment," Part One, "An Examination of the Eighth Amendment," *Stanford Law Rev.,* Vol. 24 (May 1972), 838–73, and Part Two, "The Eighth Amendment after *Furman v. Georgia,*" *ibid.,* Vol. 25 (Nov. 1972), 62–83. See also, Daniel D. Polsby, "The Death of Capital Punishment? *Furman v. Georgia,*" in *The Supreme*

Court Review 1972, ed. Philip B. Kurland (Chicago, 1973), pp. 1–40.

4. 402 U.S. 183 (1971).

5. *Ibid.*, 242.

6. *Ibid.*, 249, 252. See also 257, 308, and 309 for statements by Brennan misrepresenting the Court's opinion. Cf. Frank v. Mangum, 237 U.S. 309 (1915) for a classic miscarriage of justice in which the Court sustained state power against a due-process challenge.

7. 402 U.S. 183, 196.

8. *Ibid.*, 204.

9. *Ibid.*, 280–82.

10. *Ibid.*, 195.

11. *Ibid.*, 221.

12. *Ibid.*, 235.

13. *Origins of the Fifth Amendment: The Right Against Self-Incrimination* (New York, 1968), p. 323.

14. *Ibid.*, 375.

15. *Ibid.*, 324.

16. 402 U.S. 183, 241.

17. *Ibid.*, 245.

18. *Ibid.*, 249.

19. *Ibid.*, 311.

20. Reid v. Covert, 354 U.S. 1, 77 (1957).

21. 402 U.S. 183, 312.

22. 408 U.S. 238 (1972).

23. Robinson v. Cal., 370 U.S. 660 (1962).

24. Letter to Editor, *New York Times,* July 31, 1972, signed, among others, by Francis Plimpton and Simon Rifkind. The Court delivered its opinions in Furman's case on June 29, 1972.

25. 408 U.S. 238, 239–40.

26. *Ibid.*, 311. Italics added.

27. *Ibid.*, 312–13.

28. 402 U.S. 183, 207.

29. 408 U.S. 238, 311–13.

30. *Ibid.*, 308.

31. *Ibid.*, 309.

32. For historical background, see Anthony F. Granucci, "Nor Cruel and Unusual Punishments Inflicted: The Original Meaning," *California Law Rev.,* Vol. 57 (October 1969), 839–65.

33. 408 U.S. 238, 309–10.

34. *Ibid.*, 310.

35. *Ibid.*, 398.

36. *Ibid.*, 398–99.

37. *Ibid.*, 399–400.

38. *Ibid.*, 415–16, 426–27; the quotation is at 427, note 11.

39. *Ibid.*, 248.

40. *Ibid.*, note 11.

41. *Ibid.*, 241.

42. *Ibid.*, 249; see also Douglas at 255–57.

43. *Ibid.*, 256.

44. *Ibid.*, 247 note 10.

45. *Ibid.*, 253.

46. *Ibid.*, 256–57.

47. *Ibid.*, 257.

48. For a precursor of their arguments, see A. J. Goldberg and A. M. Dershowitz, "Declaring the Death Penalty Unconstitutional," *Harvard Law Rev.*, Vol. 83 (June 1970), 1773–1819.

49. 408 U.S. 238, 258.

50. *Ibid.*, 414.

51. *Ibid.*, 270.

52. *Ibid.*, 270, 274, 277, 279, 282, 285, 288, 289, 291, 305.

53. *Ibid.*, 270, 279.

54. *Ibid.*, 277.

55. Louisiana ex rel. Francis v. Resweber, 329 U.S. 459 (1947), quoted by Brennan in *ibid.*, 277 note 21.

56. *Ibid.*, 369.

57. *Ibid.*, 370–71.

58. Weems v. U.S., 217 U.S. 349 (1910).

59. Trop v. Dulles, 356 U.S. 86 (1958), plurality opinion.

60. Robinson v. Cal., 370 U.S. 660 (1962).

61. Wilkerson v. Utah, 99 U.S. 130 (1879).

62. In re Kemmler, 136 U.S. 436 (1890).

63. *Ibid.*, 447. Italics added.

64. 408 U.S. 238, 285. Italics added.

65. *Ibid.*, 329–30.

66. 356 U.S. 86, 99.

67. 408 U.S. 238, 285, note 33 (Brennan, J.).

68. *Ibid.*, 329 note 37.

69. 356 U.S. 86, 101, quoted in *ibid.*, 269 (Brennan, J.) and 329 (Marshall, J.).

70. *Ibid.*, 341–42.

71. *Ibid.*, 360.

72. *Ibid.*, 330–32.

73. *Ibid.*, 361.

74. *Ibid.*, 360.

75. *Ibid.*, 362.
76. *Ibid.*, 361 note 145.
77. Weems v. U.S., 217 U.S. 349, 373 (1910).
78. 408 U.S. 238, 266.
79. *Ibid.*, 283 note 28.
80. *Ibid.*, 282.
81. *Ibid.*, 285.
82. *Ibid.*, 287.
83. *Ibid.*, 291.
84. *Ibid.*
85. *Ibid.*, 434 note 18.
86. *Ibid.*, 291. There were only 29 executions in 1963, 15 in 1964, 7 in 1965, and 1 in 1966. *Ibid.*, 293.
87. *Ibid.*, 292 and note 44; the quotation is at 293.
88. *Ibid.*, 293.
89. *Ibid.*, 295.
90. *Ibid.*, 298.
91. People v. Anderson, 100 Cal. Rptr. 152 (1972).
92. 408 U.S. 238, 300.
93. *Ibid.*, 292, 293. For precise figures, see note 86 above.
94. *Ibid.*, 342–354; quotations at 353.
95. *Ibid.*, 302 (Brennan, J.) and 354 note 124 (Marshall, J.).
96. *Ibid.*, 301 (Brennan, J.) and 354 note 124 (Marshall, J.).
97. *Ibid.*, 302.
98. *Ibid.*, 303.
99. *Ibid.*
100. *Ibid.*, 304.
101. *Ibid.*, 344.
102. *Ibid.*, 302 note 54. The median time spent in prison by first-degree murderers who were released in California in 1971 was 12 years.
103. After the Furman decision, the Florida legislature enacted a statute requiring all death-row inmates to be given mandatory life sentences without possibility of parole. The statute affected 40 convicted killers and rapists. The Florida Supreme Court ordered that all be sentenced to "life" imprisonment but with eligibility for parole. *New York Times*, Sept. 10, 1972.
104. 408 U.S. 238, 304.
105. *Ibid.*
106. *Ibid.*, 363–64.
107. *Ibid.*, 364.
108. *Crime in the United States. Uniform Crime Reports for the*

United States—1969 (Washington, D.C., 1970), pp. 9, 12–13, 118, 127. The same source for the year 1972 shows no change in the percentages. *Crime in the United States . . . 1972* (Washington, D.C., 1973), pp. 9, 14.

109. 408 U.S. 238, 391 note 14; see also *ibid.*, 386 note 11, for data on the imposition of death for rape.

110. *Ibid.*, 389 note 12.

111. *Ibid.*, 450.

112. All quotations by Powell, J., in this paragraph are from *ibid.*, 447.

113. *Ibid.*, 364.

114. *Ibid.*

115. *Ibid.*, 367–68.

116. *Ibid.*, 366 note 156. The study contending that innocent men have been executed (eight since 1893) is H. A. Bedau, "Murder, Errors of Justice, and Capital Punishment," in *The Death Penalty in America,* ed. Bedau (Garden City, N.Y., 1967), pp. 434, 438. In 1971 Bedau declared that it is "false sentimentality to argue that the death penalty ought to be abolished because of the abstract possibility that an innocent person might be executed when the record fails to disclose that such cases occur." H. A. Bedau, "The Death Penalty in America: Review and Forecast," *Federal Probation,* Vol. 35 (June 1971), 36.

117. 408 U.S. 238, 354.

118. *Ibid.*, 331.

119. Wilkerson v. Utah, 99 U.S. 130, 136 (1879), quoted by Burger at *ibid.*, 378.

120. *Ibid.*, 457–58.

121. McGautha v. Cal., 402 U.S. 183, 226 (1971). Black joined Harlan's opinion and concurred separately in a single-paragraph opinion in which he made the gratuitous observation that the Eighth Amendment's cruel-and-unusual-punishments clause could not have been intended by its framers to end capital punishment.

122. 408 U.S. 238, 465–70.

123. *Ibid.*, 375 (Burger, C.J.) and 405–06 (Blackmun, J.).

124. *Ibid.*, 376; see also 411 (Blackmun, J.).

125. *Ibid.*, 382 (Burger, C.J.) and 419–20 (Powell, J.).

126. *Ibid.*, 385–86, 411–13, 437–38.

127. H. Bedau, *The Death Penalty in America,* p. 232, cited in *ibid.*, 439. Delaware was the exception.

128. *Ibid.*, 386, 437–39. See below, notes 159–60 and related text, for evidence of recent public opinion.

129. *Ibid.*, 439; see also 442–43.

130. *Ibid.*, 385.

131. *Ibid.*, 381–82, 385–86.

132. *Ibid.* 331.

133. *Ibid.*, 389.

134. *Ibid.*, 399.

135. *Ibid.*, 387 (Burger, C.J.) and 441 (Powell, J.).

136. *Ibid.*, 386 note 11 (Burger, C.J.) and 435 note 19 (Powell, J.).

137. *Ibid.*, 387.

138. *Ibid.*, 390.

139. *Ibid.*, 395 (Burger, C.J.).

140. *Ibid.*, 395–96.

141. Powell v. Texas, 392 U.S. 514, 531 (1968), quoted by Powell at *ibid.*, 455.

142. *Ibid.*, 454.

143. Powell v. Texas, 392 U.S. 514, 530 (1968), quoted by Powell at *ibid.*, 452.

144. *Ibid.*, 394.

145. *Ibid.*, 464.

146. *Ibid.*, 461.

147. *New York Times,* Feb. 19, 1972.

148. 408 U.S. 238, 398.

149. *Ibid.*, 461.

150. *Ibid.*, 397.

151. *The Challenge of Crime in a Free Society* (Washington, D.C., 1967), p. 143, quoted by Powell in *ibid.*, 463 note 63.

152. *Ibid.*, 462.

153. *Ibid.*, 403.

154. *Ibid.*, 400.

155. *Ibid.*

156. *Ibid.*, 400–01.

157. *Ibid.*, 401.

158. *Ibid.*, 403.

159. *New York Times,* Nov. 11, 1972, "Week in Review," p. 1, col. 7, and *ibid.*, March 11, 1973, pt. I, p. 55, col. 6.

160. *Time,* Sept. 17, 1973, p. 94; *Los Angeles Times,* Nov. 16, 1973, pt. I, p. 2; *New York Times,* March 11, 1973, pt. I, p. 1, col. 8, and *ibid.*, Dec. 25, 1973, pt. I, p. 21, col. 1.

161. *New York Times,* March 11, 1973, pt. I, p. 1, col. 8, and *ibid.*, March 15, 1973, p. 1, col. 7.

162. *New York Times,* March 11, 1973, p. 1, col. 8, and *ibid.*, March 15, 1973, pt. I, p. 24, col. 3.

163. *Los Angeles Times,* Nov. 13, 1973. See *ibid.,* Sept. 25, 1973, pt. I, p. 1, for a detailed summary of new state statutes.
164. *New York Times,* Dec. 25, 1973, pt. I, p. 21, col. 1, and *ibid.,* Dec. 30, 1973, pt. I, p. 19.

CHAPTER EIGHT: Conclusions

1. *New York Times,* July 1, 1972, p. 8, col. 8.
2. "1970 Term: Notes on the Emergence of the Burger Court," in *The Supreme Court Review: 1971,* Philip B. Kurland, ed. (Chicago, 1971), p. 265. See also Kurland's *Politics, the Constitution, and the Warren Court* (Chicago, 1971).
3. Rogers v. Belli, 401 U.S. 815 (1971).
4. Usner v. Luckenbach Overseas Corp., 400 U.S. 494, 502 (1971).
5. 94 S. Ct. 613 (1974).
6. Jan. 9, 1974, p. 1, col. 6.
7. 94 S. Ct. 613, 620, 621, 623, and 623 note 11.
8. *Ibid.,* 618.
9. Silverthorne Lumber Co. v. U.S., 251 U.S. 385, 392 (1920). Italics added.
10. 94 S. Ct. 613, 620.
11. *Ibid.,* 619.
12. *Ibid.,* 626, quoting Mapp v. Ohio, 367 U.S. 643, 651, 657 (1961).
13. Mapp v. Ohio, 654–55.
14. 94 S. Ct. 613, 628.
15. *Ibid.,* 621, 623.
16. Aguilar v. Tex., 378 U.S. 108 (1964); Spinelli v. U.S., 393 U.S. 410 (1969); U.S. v. Harris, 403 U.S. 573 (1971).
17. Johnson v. Zerbst, 304 U.S. 458 (1938); Bumper v. N. Car., 391 U.S. 543 (1968); Schneckloth v. Bustamonte, 412 U.S. 218 (1973).
18. McMann v. Richardson, 397 U.S. 759 (1970).
19. Katz v. U.S., 389 U.S. 347 (1967); U.S. v. White, 401 U.S. 745 (1971).
20. Terry v. Ohio, 392 U.S. 1 (1968); Sibron v. N.Y., 392 U.S. 40 (1968); Adams v. Williams, 407 U.S. 143 (1972); U.S. v. Robinson, 94 S. Ct. 467 (1973).
21. Miranda v. Ariz., 384 U.S. 436 (1966); Harris v. N.Y., 401 U.S. 222 (1971).
22. Marchetti v. U.S., 390 U.S. 39 (1968); Albertson v. S.A.C.B., 382 U.S. 70 (1965); Cal. v. Byers, 402 U.S. 424 (1971).

23. Ullmann v. U.S., 350 U.S. 422 (1956); Albertson v. S.A.C.B., 382 U.S. 70 (1965); Kastigar v. U.S., 406 U.S. 441 (1972).

24. Duncan v. La., 391 U.S. 145 (1968); Williams v. Fla., 399 U.S. 78 (1970); Johnson v. La., 406 U.S. 356 (1972); Apodaca v. Ore., 406 U.S. 404 (1972).

25. Machibroda v. U.S., 368 U.S. 487 (1962); U.S. v. Jackson, 390 U.S. 570 (1968); McMann v. Richardson, 397 U.S. 759 (1970); Parker v. N. Car., 397 U.S. 790 (1970); N. Car. v. Alford, 400 U.S. 25 (1970).

26. In re Gault, 387 U.S. 1 (1967); In re Burrus and McKeiver v. Pa., 403 U.S. 528 (1971).

27. Massiah v. U.S., 377 U.S. 201 (1964); Milton v. Wainwright, 407 U.S. 371 (1972).

28. Pointer v. Tex., 380 U.S. 400 (1965); Douglas v. Ala., 380 U.S. 415 (1965); Barber v. Page, 390 U.S. 719 (1968); Bruton v. U.S., 391 U.S. 123 (1968); Cal. v. Green, 399 U.S. 149 (1970); Dutton v. Evans, 400 U.S. 74 (1970); Nelson v. O'Neil, 402 U.S. 622 (1971); Schneble v. Fla., 405 U.S. 427 (1972).

29. Brady v. Md., 373 U.S. 83 (1963); Moore v. Ill., 408 U.S. 786 (1972).

30. U.S. v. Wade, 388 U.S. 218 (1967); Kirby v. Ill., 406 U.S. 682 (1972); U.S. v. Ash, 413 U.S. 300 (1973).

31. Argersinger v. Hamlin, 407 U.S. 25 (1972).

32. U.S. v. U.S. District Court, 407 U.S. 297 (1972).

33. Strunk v. U.S., 412 U.S. 434 (1973).

34. Chambers v. Miss., 410 U.S. 284 (1973).

35. McGautha v. Cal., 402 U.S. 183 (1971); Furman v. Ga., 408 U.S. 238 (1972).

36. In re Winship, 397 U.S. 358 (1970).

37. Lego v. Twomey, 404 U.S. 477 (1972).

38. Barnes v. U.S., 412 U.S. 837 (1973).

39. Baldwin v. N.Y., 399 U.S. 66 (1970).

40. Coolidge v. N.H., 403 U.S. 443 (1971).

41. Almeida-Sanchez v. U.S., 413 U.S. 266 (1973).

42. Brooks v. Tenn., 406 U.S. 605 (1972).

43. "The Supreme Court, 1969 Term," *Harvard Law Rev.*, Vol. 84 (Nov. 1970), 262.

44. (Joseph B. Robinson and Beverly Coleman) Commission on Law and Social Action of the American Jewish Congress, *The Civil Rights and Civil Liberties Decisions of the United States Supreme Court for the 1969–1970 Term* (New York, 1970), pp. 76, 80. (Mimeo.)

45. "The Supreme Court, 1970 Term," *Harvard Law Rev.*, Vol. 85 (Nov. 1971), 351. At p. 7 in the same source the figure given for the number of cases in which Burger and Blackmun agreed is 113 out of 119.

46. "The Supreme Court, 1971 Term," *Harvard Law Rev.*, Vol. 86 (Nov. 1972), pp. 297–301.

47. *Ibid.*, and Philip B. Kurland, "1971 Term: The Year of the Stewart-White Court," in Kurland, ed., *The Supreme Court Review: 1972* (Chicago, 1973), pp. 182–86.

48. *New York Times*, June 23, 1973, p. 20, col. 1, and "The Supreme Court, 1972 Term," *Harvard Law Rev.*, Vol. 87 (Nov. 1973), 304.

49. Kirby v. Ill., 406 U.S. 682 (1972).

50. Cox, *The Warren Court* (Cambridge, 1968), *passim.*

51. Wright, "The Supreme Court Today," *Trial*, Vol. 3 (April-May 1967), 1, 10–11.

52. Kurland, "1970 Term," cited in note 2, above, p. 267.

53. "The Supreme Court, 1971 Term," cited in note 46, above, pp. 298–99.

54. *Time*, Oct. 18, 1971, p. 34. See also *ibid.*, March 26, 1973, p. 69, and *New York Times*, Sept. 8, 1971, pt. 2, p. 1, col. 1, and *ibid.*, Jan. 17, 1972, editorial, "The Washington Crime Story," p. 30, col. 2. *New York Times*, March 5, 1973, p. 1, col. 3; *ibid.*, March 11, 1973, p. 1, col. 8, and *ibid.*, "News of the Week" section, Oct. 22, 1972, p. 6, col. 1. For the most recent official statistics, see *Crime in the United States, 1972*. Uniform Crime Reports (Washington, 1973).

55. *Los Angeles Times*, July 1, 1973, p. 1, col. 8.

Index

About the Author

When Leonard Levy wrote a series of articles critical of the United States Supreme Court's Jim Crow decisions, Justice Frankfurter responded, and later invited him to hear arguments presented in the great case of *Brown* v. *Board of Education*. It was the first and most memorable of Professor Levy's visits to see the Court in action. He has continued to serve as a rigorous critic of the Court, corresponding with Chief Justice Warren and Justices Black and Frankfurter, and analyzing judicial decisions and interpreting constitutional history in his books and articles. In 1969, he won the Pulitzer Prize in history for his book *Origins of the Fifth Amendment*. Now Andrew W. Mellon Professor of Humanities at the Claremont Colleges and chairman of the Graduate Faculty of History, he had earlier been Earl Warren Professor of Constitutional History at Brandeis University, where he taught from 1951 to 1970. He has received fellowships from the Guggenheim Foundation, the American Bar Foundation, the National Endowment for the Humanities, and Harvard's Center for the Study of the History of Liberty. Among his books are *Legacy of Suppression,* which won the Frank Luther Mott Prize and the Sigma Delta Chi Award; and *Jefferson and Civil Liberties: The Darker Side*. His home is in LaVerne, California.